The CIM Handbook of Export Marketing

The Chartered Institute of Marketing/Butterworth-Heinemann Mark... ...ries is the most comprehensive, widely used and ...st date stamped below. ...ting and sales currently available worldwide

As the CIM's official publisher, Butterworth-Heinemann develops, produces and publishes the complete series in association with the CIM. We aim to provide definitive marketing books for students and practitioners that promote excellence in marketing education and

...eading marketing educators for ...icate, Advanced Certificate and ...se titles provide practical study ...tioners at all levels.

...now the largest professional ...members located worldwide. Its ...areness and understanding of ...n the raising of standards of ...is key business discipline.

...URCE CENTRE
...PUS

...KS HP7 9I

Books in the series

Below-the-line Promotion
John Wilmshurst

Creating Powerful Brands
Leslie de Chernatony and Malcolm H. B. McDonald

How to Sell a Service
Malcolm H. B. McDonald

International Marketing Digest
Edited by Malcolm H. B. McDonald and
    S. Tamer Cavusgil

Managing your Marketing Career
Andrew Crofts

Market Focus
Rick Brown

Market Research for Managers
Sunny Crouch

The Marketing Book
Edited by Michael Baker

The Marketing Dictionary
Edited by Norman A. Hart and John Stapleton

The Marketing Digest
Edited by Michael J. Thomas and Norman Waite

Marketing Led, Sales Driven
Keith Steward

Marketing Plans
Malcolm H. B. McDonald

Marketing to the Retail Trade
Geoffrey Randall

The Marketing of Services
D. W. Cowell

Marketing-led Strategic Change
Nigel Piercy

The Practice of Advertising
Edited by Norman Hart

The Practice of Public Relations
Edited by Wilfred Howard

The Principles and Practice of Export Marketing
E. P. Hibbert

Professional Services Marketing
Neil Morgan

Profitable Product Management
Richard A. Collier

Relationship Marketing
Martin Christopher, Adrian Payne and
    David Ballantyne

Retail Marketing Plans
Malcolm H. B. McDonald and Chris Tideman

Sales Management
Chris Noonan

Solving the Management Case
Angela Hatton, Paul Roberts and Mike Worsam

The Strategy of Distribution Management
Martin Christopher

By the same author

Sales Management: The Complete Marketer's Guide
George Allen & Unwin

*Practical Export Management: Developing International
    Business*
George Allen & Unwin

The CIM Handbook of Export Marketing

A practical guide to opening and expanding markets overseas

Second Edition

Chris Noonan

Published on behalf of
The Chartered Institute of Marketing

OXFORD AUCKLAND BOSTON JOHANNESBURG MELBOURNE NEW DELHI

Butterworth-Heinemann
Linacre House, Jordan Hill, Oxford OX2 8DP
225 Wildwood Avenue, Woburn, MA 01801-2041
A division of Reed Educational and Professional Publishing Ltd

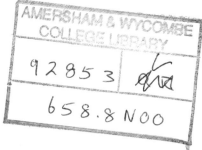 A member of the Reed Elsevier plc group

First published 1996
Second edition 1999

British Library Cataloguing in Publication Data
Noonan, Chris J.
    The CIM handbook of export marketing – 2nd ed.
    1. Export marketing
    I. Title   II. Chartered Institute of Marketing   III. Handbook of
    export marketing
    658.8'48

ISBN 0 7506 4346 3

Composition by Genesis Typesetting, Laser Quay, Rochester, Kent
Printed and bound in Great Britain

PLANT A TREE

*British Trust for
Conservation Volunteers*

FOR EVERY TITLE THAT WE PUBLISH, BUTTERWORTH-HEINEMANN
WILL PAY FOR BTCV TO PLANT AND CARE FOR A TREE.

Contents

Foreword

Never before has professional export marketing been so important for UK companies. Our 'domestic' market now encompasses 360 million of the world's most affluent consumers. Great strides are being made in the 'tiger' economies of the Asia/Pacific Rim. North America is about to flourish with the evolution of the North America Free Trade Area. South Africa is set to become the powerhouse of the African continent and a large chunk of the Southern Hemisphere.

What can UK companies do to tackle these burgeoning markets and gain a slice of the business? The answer is to become more adept at selling their goods overseas. Chris Noonan brings to this book a history of specialist overseas marketing. His recommendations and practice are founded in having been at the sharp end of promoting UK goods and services in international markets. He serves as an Accredited Trainer of the Institute of Export and regularly lectures and trains would-be exporters in the discrete skills necessary to break into new markets.

Exporting is different, but it need not be difficult – if you set about it correctly. Many of the marketing skills required are basic. 'Identify the need; satisfy the need' is the bedrock of all marketing activity. But when you are dealing with a different culture, different language, different channels of distribution and buying patterns your approach must reflect this.

I very much welcome Chris Noonan's valuable addition to the sources of reference that you can call upon. Whether you are a seasoned international trader looking to revisit your strategies and action plans or a new exporter seeking guidance before taking your first tentative steps, I commend this readable, well-researched and informative book to you.

Good luck in your international business.

Ian Campbell, Director-General, The
Institute of Export

Introduction _____

The book's scope, purpose and target audience ■■■■■■■■

This book is aimed at export marketers and international marketing practitioners. This second edition is timely as we enter a new millennium and Europe further develops as a single economic unit, with all the opportunities and threats this presents to companies, and as East Europe, China and other countries open their markets to free enterprise opportunities. Companies now face an environment of increased price competitiveness, quality improvement, greater product range innovation, expanded distribution opportunities and growth in pan-European and global brands. Barriers to trade are lowering, and aggressive marketers will steal a march on their slower and weaker competitors. Companies traditionally pursuing an opportunistic sales approach to exporting and export markets now need to become more strategic in their thinking, with a global marketing approach to developing export markets.

Exporting and international marketing require a far broader range of managerial skills and knowledge of a company's operations than do most positions in a company's management structure. Many exporters, particularly in industrial product companies, move into export sales positions from technical positions, often with little or no training in relevant skills. In addition to knowledge of company operations and products, the exporter needs developed skills in marketing, sales and negotiating techniques. Also he needs specialist export-related skills encompassing international distribution and shipping, export documentation and payments, the many legal and quasi-legal aspects of international trade, managing agents and distributors, and developing and implementing marketing strategies suited to the diverse cultures and markets for his products.

The aim of this book is to assist the export marketer to travel, trade and market internationally with increased confidence and a broader perspective of the scope of the international marketer's role, and to enable senior executives to feel competent in discussions with colleagues and subordinates who have export responsibilities. It will do that by providing, in a concise, informative and pragmatic style, a guide to the practicalities of entering and developing international markets, and an introduction to practical international marketing and export market management. The book is not about shipping practice and documentation. It is about developing international business through cross-border transfer of goods, services and technology (the latter often being neglected as a potential income earner), and about developing global marketing opportunities through improved strategic planning that leads to consistent and predictable export growth including, over time, through various expansionary routes such as branches, subsidiaries, and joint ventures.

Whilst attempting to encourage a move to a more marketing oriented approach to export market development, the order in which topics have been addressed is intended to recognize the reality that most readers already have a level of export business, probably built from pursuit of opportunistic openings for trade, or else need to pursue early opportunities to generate sales to utilize factory capacity.

Distributors in a number of international markets are often considered by their export suppliers to be particularly weak in managing the sales operations. The principles of good management vary little between markets, and applications can take account of local cultural practices. This text promotes a 'hands on' style of distributor and agent management by exporters, and can usefully be supplemented by other texts covering practical marketing and field sales management as the exporter builds his skills and experience and finds more positive ways to add value in his relationships with his market representatives.

The interested reader can also supplement the subject coverage of this book by referring to some of the additional reading material listed after each chapter, and by including discussions with specialists such as shipping forwarders, bankers, international trade lawyers, and government export agencies. The author's companion volume for the Chartered Institute of Marketing, *Sales Management*, is especially relevant reading to supplement this text and develop value-adding skill in sales management, an essential ingredient in developing agents and distributors. Participating in some of the seminars and development programmes run by various professional institutions, including the Institute of Export in London and the Chartered Institute of Marketing, is a further route to skill development.

This work is aimed primarily at export practitioners, and should be of interest to:

- chief executives, sales and marketing directors and other senior line managers who want an understanding of international marketing and export management, and the contribution it can make in their organizations
- export managers and international marketers who wish to consolidate their knowledge and experience and 'see the wood from the trees'
- other managers providing support services to an export department
- executives attending short courses in export and international marketing related subjects
- those in government service and banking who provide export support services
- students of specialist export courses or international marketing courses.

Throughout this text the use of the masculine gender should be taken to include the feminine gender, without intention to discriminate or imply anything other than that marketers of both sexes are equal in all respects as international marketers.

Chris Noonan
CJN Management Consultancy
49 Pennard Road
London W12 8DW
Tel: 020–8749–1210
noonan@cjn.co.uk

Part One

Organizing for Exports and Identifying the Opportunities

1

Why export?

This chapter will explore some of the reasons why a company should consider exporting. It will highlight:

● typical benefits a company derives from exporting
● some of the broad range of opportunities to develop an international business.

It sets the scene for the rest of the text, and will encourage the reader to adopt a flexible approach to identifying and pursuing opportunities.

The physical export of goods and services from one nation to another is at the core of international marketing activity, and as a starting point some commentary on the benefits of exporting is warranted.

One frequently hears or reads of comments, often from politicians, that the country needs to export more to improve the balance of payments. Rhetoric may imply that companies are not sufficiently aggressive in seeking international opportunities. Domestic companies, on the other hand, frequently complain that imports are killing their traditional home market for products and reducing employment opportunities and profits. Both commercial and political interests may join together in a plea for protection, including requests to impose or change import quotas, tariffs and other non-tariff barriers, or to put direct and indirect pressure on the exporting nation to reduce the trade imbalance voluntarily.

Historically, in countries and industries where protectionism has been a policy it has been to protect fledgling or stagnant industries that would otherwise not be competitive on price or quality, and might simply have to cease production, or it has been designed to give a degree of protection to assist a domestic industry that is considered essential to the industrial base of the developing country, such as defence-related industries, heavy equipment producers and possibly even automobile assembly plants. Similarly, protection may be given to other value-added projects in countries with an abundance of raw materials and labour but a shortage of technological skills. The governmental objective here may be to enable the work force to acquire industrial skills and promote diversification and a gradual shift from an agrarian economy and lifestyle.

International businessmen, and many wiser members of the political and governmental circles, realize that protectionism is generally not a satisfactory solution to trade imbalances in today's environment of increased international economic interdependence and moral commitments to developing nations. Moreover, protectionism has often been cited as a cause of inefficiencies

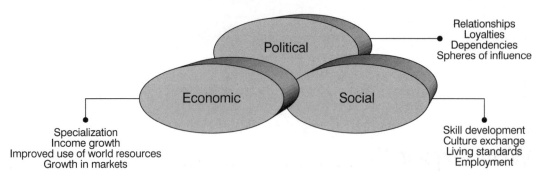

Figure 1.1 *Key benefits from trade*

in management and production practices, including poorer quality control and higher prices, and reduced rates of technological innovation.

Exports benefit the exporter and importer in the following three areas of concern: (a) political activity, (b) economic activity, and (c) social activity.

Political activity

International trade is important in building permanent relationships, loyalties, dependencies and spheres of influence. The major western industrial powers, for example, want to use trade as a medium for extending their influence and countering what they may see as subversive elements opposed to the capitalistic lifestyle. Governments are usually concerned directly with two main areas of trade: those dealing with mass feeding, health and welfare of the people (often through aid programmes) in developing nations, and those dealing with technology, training and equipment related to defence or the ongoing supply of essential resources such as energy.

Economic activity

Trade results in specialization and a cross-flow of goods and services from the country with the greatest economic advantage in production to the country with needs that

cannot as efficiently be satisfied domestically. This is clearly evident in the case of commodities such as coffee, wine or oil, where specific climates or environments are needed to produce the products yet the taste or industrial needs for these goods have resulted in enormous markets in the non-producing world. Levels of work force skills and technology also vary to such an extent world-wide that, in general, traditional agrarian and non-industrial economies need an ever-increasing range of industrial products in exchange for their raw materials and commodity-oriented exports.

Social activity

Trade brings about change and progress by transferring skills, services and products from more advanced to less advanced economies. There are those who take the position that the less developed countries are better off and would be happier in the long term without the social change, pressures and problems considered to be associated with industrialization and consumer societies. In general, this is a minority view. The population of less advanced (developing) nations is more usually considered in contemporary thinking to have the right to develop and improve living standards, including health and education facilities. International trade has its role in contributing to the development of both peoples and nations.

Generally, therefore, if freer trade encourages better use of the world's resources, and if improvements in technology, product range, and quality help advance the less developed nations by opening new opportunities and creating a greater international interdependence, perhaps reducing the belligerent threats to world peace, surely it should be encouraged?

Exporting benefits an individual country because it helps improve its own balance of payments and trade through increased foreign exchange earnings, employment, living standards, tax revenues, and utilization of industrial resources, and promotes the stature and image of the exporting nation in the world community.

Exports need not just be physical goods; they can equally beneficially include services such as banking, insurance, consultancy, technology transfer and training. Perhaps the greatest pressure on world trade since World War II has been the phenomenal rise in demand for energy resources – mainly oil – and the economic pressure this has placed on nations without domestic oil reserves to produce other goods and services needed in export markets in order to acquire the requisite foreign currency to pay for energy needs.

How the company benefits from exporting

An individual company benefits from exports through:

- increased plant utilization
- spreading operating costs over a larger output
- reduced input costs through volume purchases
- additional profit contribution
- new markets for domestic product range
- diversification opportunities into new market sectors using domestic technology
- increased volume opportunities through modifications to existing products

- developing international brands and/or company image
- improved rate of technological progress through exposure to world markets
- opportunities to sell support services, consultancy, training, technology licensing.

Increased plant utilization, in turn, gives more secure employment opportunities, better labour force morale and training, a better profit base to reward shareholders and employees, and the generation of more funds for investment. Increased production and productivity add to the gross national product. Higher profits and employee earnings increase the tax base, enabling the local and central government to generate additional funds for those programmes it sees as politically, economically and socially desirable.

The individual company can often benefit by exporting at less than full cost, particularly where spare production capacity exists, because overheads can be spread over a greater volume of output; indeed, these overheads may already have been costed in to be recovered from the planned level of domestic sales. There is a positive benefit in marginally costing exports as long as the variable production costs associated with the export orders can be recovered, along with costs of distribution. If there is spare capacity in the plant, and the domestic market cannot for any reason be encouraged or manipulated to take more products, then seek export markets, either of standard home market products or of such export-modified products as can conveniently be produced on the home production line.

There will always be individuals in any organization who can see only the problems associated with handling export orders, such as:

- payment
- credit and currency problems
- special packaging and labelling requirements
- additional quality control

- small production runs involving time-consuming changes and product modifications, and so on.

The professional export marketer has to liaise and mediate between all the departments involved in ensuring that the order is filled correctly and on time, and must motivate the less enthusiastic individuals involved in the project to contribute positively to the required effort. The export marketer is responsible for finding the profitable export markets for his company's goods and services, for identifying other products his company could be producing to meet existing or new markets, and for increasing plant utilization with the least disruption to current business activity. The keys to success in exporting are **flexibility** and **perseverance**.

As the markets for exports grow, and domestic capacity is exhausted or individual markets develop special needs, then opportunities may open up for foreign manufacturing and ventures, branches, subsidiaries, joint ventures, etc., which may form the basis of new cross-border trade relations. And the export marketer may become a fully fledged international marketer, working via multinational company networks to promote global inter-country trade and marketing opportunities.

The broader international opportunities

Whilst most companies start their international business activities by direct exports of goods or services to foreign markets, as the volume of business develops often other opportunities develop. Depending on the nature of your products and markets some of the typical range of opportunities might include the following.

- Exporting existing products and services. This is where you can export product designed for the domestic market without any further modification. Whilst this may seem an ideal situation for the exporter

(particularly for the managers involved in design and production), where an exporter can customize a product for a foreign customer then it may enable special relationships to develop.
- Exporting modified products to suit end market requirements (customer preferences or regulatory requirements) or opportunities.
  - A manufacturer of chairs was failing to find Far Eastern export markets until it lowered the height of the chair legs a few centimetres, and presented new samples to prospective buyers.
  - Scotch whisky manufacturers have developed special gift packaged formats of leading brands for export particularly to those markets where gift giving is a significant activity (such as Japan).
  - A dairy company secured a long term supply contract for a basic commodity, skimmed milk powder, to a Singaporean ice cream manufacturer by studying the customer's manufacturing processes and problems, and developing a product with modified viscosity in use, reducing the customer's wastage and down time resulting from plant breakdowns.
  - Industrial equipment manufacturers frequently find it necessary to customize products to suit end user requirements.
- Developing new products or services specifically for export markets, using existing skills and technology, and research and development expertise.
- Providing consultancy expertise (solo or in consortia), for example where you are an industry leader in technology or distribution relating to certain markets.
  Companies normally only offer consultancy services where they are unlikely to enter a market themselves directly, as it would not be logical to assist future competitors.
  - Manufacturers of plant and machinery often have a consultancy activity covering the design and operation of end product production facilities supporting

their export marketing activities, where the consultancy is intended to develop export opportunities.

- Licensing products, patents, trade marks or brand names, technology, and other know-how into markets where it is not practical to profitably develop the market through direct exports.
  - Soft drinks (Coca Cola, Pepsi Cola, etc.) are examples of consumer goods where local production and bottling and distribution are licensed, enabling a global brand to be developed where the direct shipment of soft drinks might not be economically viable (with their large water content).
  - Many industrial and consumer product manufacturers are entering licensing arrangements in China and other developing markets where there would otherwise be limited direct export opportunities.
- Franchising trade marks, know how, business formats, etc., into markets where the franchisee acquires local distribution and marketing rights in exchange for fees and royalties. Franchising primarily, but not exclusively, operates in consumer markets.
  - The Body Shop International Group have been Britain's most successful international franchisor, exporting products direct to foreign market franchisees where practical, subsequently developing some local manufacturing facilities (company owned or licensed/partnership ventures) to meet local market needs. A strategic change more recently promoted a move out of manufacturing to focus on retailing, with product supplied from contract manufacturers.
  - Fast food distributors (such as the major pizza, burger and chicken fast food brands), working in a product category where direct exports are not practical) find great scope for market development through franchising where they can build a strong brand name within and between markets.

- Opening foreign branches or subsidiaries to control local marketing or distribution.
  - Most major multinationals (such as Mars Group, Diageo, Philips, Heinz, Anchor Foods, Unilever, ICI, etc.), have networks of foreign branches or subsidiaries to control and develop the markets, frequently handling their own distribution, but sometimes just having a marketing office to support a third party distributor.
  - Many smaller companies, in both industrial and consumer markets, open branches or subsidiaries only in their major foreign markets, such as Waterford Wedgwood Group (crystal glass and bone china), and USM Texon (shoe machinery and materials).
- Forming joint ventures with local market partners who have local strength to increase market penetration (either just for distribution, or to include local manufacture).
  - This is common in both industrial markets and consumer, particularly where two joint venture partners have different but essential strengths, e.g. one may be strong in product research and development, the other in distribution (several pharmaceutical partnerships show this characteristic, and some automotive joint ventures similarly have different partner strengths in design and distribution).
  - Customarily market penetration in the Middle East (e.g. Saudi Arabia) requires a joint venture approach, with the local partner providing local market knowledge, contacts and distribution facilities.
- Inward import to the home market of goods synergistic with domestic range or distribution, and which will increase your sales turnover, market share or penetration, or help in other strategic ways to achieve goals.
- Inward licensing of products, technology, brand names, and/or inward joint ventures that open new market opportunities to you in your home

market, such as taking you into new market sectors, enabling you to incorporate new technology, saving you time and development costs, etc.
- Foreign sourcing of inputs, where you can cost effectively have inputs required in your production or marketing operations produced in foreign markets to your quality standards.
  - A UK distributor of a major imported international brand of sports goods extended his range by having sports bags produced in the Far East to his designs and quality standards, paying a royalty to the owner of the brand name. For no investment in plant, and only for the investment in inventory, he built a major product range extension, also boosting profits and brand name exposure for the brand name owner.

- Amstrad built its early entry into personal computer markets through contracted foreign manufacture, saving its own resources for investment in the marketing and market development of the products rather than tying them up in manufacturing facilities. Later it had resources to expand into direct production and to diversify its product base.

Later in the text we will look further at aspects of exporting and marketing that address these opportunities. At this introductory stage the main aim is to open the readers' minds to the range of opportunities, to illustrate that there are many ways to build international markets, sales and profits, including but not limited to direct exports.

Checklist 1.1
Exporting – the benefits and opportunities

Action points

How would you benefit by exporting?

- Increased plant utilization
- Spreading operating costs over a larger output
- Reduced input costs through volume purchases
- Additional profit contribution
- New markets for domestic product range
- Diversification opportunities into new market sectors using domestic technology
- Increased volume opportunities through modifications to existing products
- Developing international brands and/or company image
- Improved rate of technological progress through exposure to world markets
- Opportunities to sell support services, consultancy, training, technology licensing

What are your international opportunities?

- Existing products and services
- Modify products to suit end market requirements
- New products or services using existing skills and technology
- Consultancy expertise (solo or in consortia)
- Licensing products, brand names, technology
- Develop new products for new markets using research and development expertise
- Foreign branches, subsidiaries or joint ventures
- Inward import of goods synergistic with domestic range or distribution
- Inward licensing of products, technology, brand names, and/or inward joint ventures
- Foreign sourcing of inputs (value-added opportunities to foreign sourced inputs)

2

Organizing for exports

In this chapter we will address the structural organization of an export department. We will look at:

- typical key responsibilities in export management functions
- how export organizations might develop over time to serve the markets
- factors to consider in structuring an export sales and marketing organization
- ways of measuring the export marketer's performance.

The aim is to help the export manager design an organization that can function effectively in managing and building markets.

At an early stage in exporting it is necessary to give some consideration to how the export department is, or should be, organized with the aim of developing an export department that can undertake all the appropriate marketing, sales and distribution activities. In a small company the export manager does everything from soliciting orders, to designing packaging, to shipping the goods. In a larger company there will be some support staff to undertake specific tasks and responsibilities. Here we should look to identify some of those tasks and functional responsibilities, and consider how some basic principles of organization might apply in helping design a marketing and sales organization that can function effectively rather than becoming over-stretched and focused only on processing paper.

Export department functions

As a starting point it might be useful to focus on a couple of examples of top management organization structures that are typical of what we find in a number of companies (see Figures 2.1 and 2.2). I shall illustrate lower levels of the export organization later in the chapter.

A major multinational corporation is likely to have the export function (or the broader concept of international market development) represented on the board or as an independent division of the company, with recognition of its role in global marketing. In many smaller to medium-sized companies, export is a subordinate activity often under the sales and marketing functional umbrella. Larger companies may have the resources to separate functions

Figure 2.1 *Export subordinate to the sales and marketing function*

into more specialized departments and thereby define individual responsibilities more closely. There will be many companies where the sales manager also doubles as export manager, doing a balancing act travelling the world selling personally or through agents or distributors whilst also trying to keep a home sales force managed and motivated: which usually means that neither domestic nor foreign markets reach potential because of span of control limitations (discussed later).

Functional responsibilities

Whether export activities are merged within the sales and marketing department, or separated, the functional responsibilities will normally fall into the broad categories of:

- management
- administration
- planning.

Table 2.1 illustrates the separation of some of the export functional responsibilities into these categories.

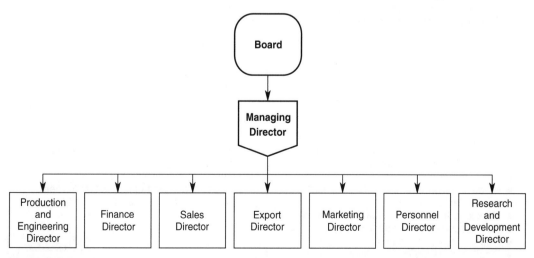

Figure 2.2 *Export as a major divisional function*

Table 2.1 *Principal export functional responsibilities*

Export sales and marketing	Shipping
MANAGEMENT	

• Brand management (including profitability)
• In-market distribution
• Market research
• Advertising and promotion
• Public relations
• Sales volume (target or budget) achievement
• Product display/merchandising
• Market outlet coverage
• Distributor sales/product knowledge training
• Provision of feedback to distributors:
  – bulletins
  – conferences
  – personal contact
  – performance feedback
• Export and market trade terms:
  – distributor margins
  – discounts and allowances
  – promotional activities
  – payment periods and discounts
  – key account performance discounts
  – warranties and sale conditions
  – order size and delivery frequencies
• Monitoring foreign market regulations
	• Shipping staff recruitment
	• Shipping staff training
	• Selecting forwarding agents
	• Negotiating freight rates
	• Optimum use of data base systems
	• Liaising with customs and excise
	• Liaising with shipping lines, etc.
	• Liaising with production departments
	• Liaising with marketing departments

ADMINISTRATION	

• Product performance and market share analysis:
  – export statistics (actual data and market share)
  – foreign market import statistics (actual data and market share)
  – foreign market sales achievements
• Regulatory compliance of product and packaging
	• Order processing (shipping):
	  – shipping space
	  – product availability
	  – production scheduling
	  – letters of credit, etc.
	• Regulatory compliance of product and packaging
	• Packaging supplies (ordering)
	• Credit control
	• Collection of payments
	• Customer service
	• Collection, collation and presentation of export department statistics

PLANNING	
• Distributor recruitment and establishing market distribution infrastructure • Sales forecasting • Product design (physical attributes, size, shape, packaging) • Marketing and sales promotional planning • Pricing policies and profit planning • New product development • Distributor management training	• Optimum shipping routes and modes of transport • Inputs to forecasting process • Forward scheduling of production to meet orders and sales forecasts

We can consider this allocation of the main functional activities in another way. The **management** category is primarily functions dealing with the current time period (the 'now'), that is, day to day operational activities that keep the business running. The **administration** category primarily consists of functions dealing with previous transactions or those currently being processed (that is 'history'). The **planning** category is primarily dealing with functions that are concerned with building the business into the future (the 'future').

Whilst there is a case that some functions might better fall in one category than another, most export marketers will probably accept the split suggested in Table 2.1. That said, the export manager should carefully monitor where time and activity is focused: is it being devoted primarily to administrative activities, or into regular export management activities? Is enough time being devoted to functional activities concerned with tomorrow's business in the planning category? All the administrative and management functional activities must be undertaken somewhere within the export department or team, but the organization can be designed so that as many of them as is practical can be handled by the shipping or export customer service team, leaving the export marketers to focus most time and effort on planning functions concerned with building future business, and those management functions that only they can perform. The export marketers are normally the most expensive resource in the department, and the best return should be obtained from that investment in skill and knowledge.

Checklist 2.1 at the end of this chapter expands more fully on Table 2.1, and can provide a basis for developing job descriptions and identifying training needs, or assessing the skills of potential export marketers against this range of functional activities.

In essence the export sales and marketing team is responsible for finding markets and achieving profitable sales of the goods, while the export shipping function provides the administrative support of getting the documentation right for the markets and getting the goods from the factory to the importer. A number of functional responsibilities could be placed under either the marketing or shipping sections, depending on what suits the internal organization better.

Export management roles

The **checklists** at the end of this chapter include some examples of the functions of several key export management positions commonly found in companies. Typically these jobs will include that of:

- the export manager
- the export market manager
- the shipping manager.

Skills and qualities in the international marketer

The range of job functions facing international marketers is far more diversified than for equivalent level of sales or marketing managers operating in the domestic market. Whilst they may not need or have the depth of expertise of their domestic marketing colleagues, in providing support to their agents and distributors they will cover skills ranging through:

- finance and accounting
- marketing and marketing research
- sales management and personal selling
- management and sales training
- forecasting and planning
- foreign legislation applicable to agency and distributor relationships and sale of goods in foreign markets
- shipping practice and regulation
- business systems, performance measurement and management controls
- human resource management.

In order to function successfully in an international environment, the export marketer will need to have **linguistic** skills in addition to being highly **numerate**, and probably to have a mix of the following personal qualities:

- being a good **organizer** and **administrator** in order to ensure market plans and programmes are developed, implemented and monitored, and to handle the wide range of administrative tasks concerned with communicating with foreign representatives
- being a good **communicator** (probably in more than one language) with internal colleagues and foreign contacts of diverse cultural backgrounds
- being demonstrably **decisive** whilst visiting foreign markets, inspiring agents and distributors with a sense of direction and confidence
- exercising good **judgement** in the decisions taken and the evaluation of information available for decision making
- having a high level of **initiative** to identify, create, and take advantage of opportunities in a diverse group of foreign markets with different needs and cultures
- having a high level of personal **stature** and **authority** to represent the company in major negotiations and contacts with senior foreign entrepreneurs, industrialists, government connections, etc.
- being **adaptable** to change and cultural variations in life-style and business practices
- having a good level of **intelligence** to assimilate wide-ranging knowledge of the skills (outlined above) concerned with export marketing and management
- demonstrating **integrity** in all business and personal dealing with foreign contacts, in business environments that often have standards of ethics and practice far different from those at home
- exhibiting **reliability** to customers and contacts, always honouring commitments and obligations
- possessing a high level of **independence** and **maturity** to cope

with the stresses and strains of operating in multi-cultural environments during long periods away from home and family.

The senior manager responsible for selecting and appointing staff to export management roles should give great thought to the matter of the skills and qualities necessary to perform effectively. Often managers who are experienced in domestic selling and marketing, or who are technical specialists, are transferred into export management positions without any special training, the assumption being that the skills and balance of personal qualities needed are the same.

Export structures and organization

In this section I want to look a little at the general principles of structuring an export organization, using pictorial organization charts, which most of us find an essential aid to understanding groupings of functional responsibilities, reporting relationships and lines of communication and instructions. Most companies group related functions into a department or division of the company as a preferred approach to organization, enabling sub-departments under more specialized managers to be formed as the company grows, and minimizing the risk of inter-departmental conflicts producing a dysfunctional effect on performance.

Activity needs analysis

The starting point for any study of the suitability of organizational structures is to identify and list the essential **activity needs** the organization must address. In the case of an export department these activity needs should be considered at the levels of:

- the company
- foreign market agents and distributors
- end users or consumers
- the products.

Table 2.2 Analysis of company, distributor, customer and product sales activity needs

Company	Distributor	Customer	Product
• utilization of spare production plant capacity • maintained or expanded levels of employment, labour utilization and skill • increase in global market share • increased international brand awareness • international distribution network • export orders • export distribution capability • product innovation • secured payment terms • profit	• diverse product range • representation of major product lines • assured product quality • reliable deliveries and supply continuity • assistance with organizing export shipment and insurance • technical support relating to usage/functionality/ maintenance • product knowledge • management and sales training • sales and marketing promotional support • compliance with local market regulations • product modifications to suit local use/needs • special packaging to suit local market regulations or preferences • assured supply continuity to meet growing market demand • security in agency or distributor agreement • extended credit • profit	• product presentations • surveys of needs • product modifications • special packaging (including own brand labels with some consumer goods) • special unit or pack sizes • promotional support • competitive prices • quality assurance and guarantees • delivery to point of use or local distribution centres • (long-term) supply contracts • technical support relating to usage/functionality/ maintenance • guaranteed (local) supply continuity of replacement products or parts • extended trade credit	• product sampling • product demonstrations • point of sale merchandising • advertising and promotional support to create awareness/ demand • special handling, storage or delivery requirements (e.g. protective packaging, refrigerated storage) • special packaging and/or usage instructions • after-sales service and maintenance support

There is more to consider in developing an organization than just the internal functional needs of the company. You must look also to the needs of your foreign representatives, their foreign market customers, and any peculiar needs of your own products. The ideal organization should then be designed to ensure that each of the needs of subordinate levels in the distribution chain (including the product) can be satisfied through its export organization. As an example, if you are manufacturing and marketing industrial plant and equipment, in addition to developing an export sales department you will need to provide an engineering and commissioning service (because the equipment needs to be installed, and the plant needs commissioning, testing and training), either directly from the internal management structure of the export department, or on secondment from another (engineering) department.

Table 2.2 illustrates a general analysis of activity needs into the four categories of company, distributors, customers and products.

This needs analysis approach to developing an organization that functions in a manner suited to the company, the channels of distribution and the products may not produce the same listing for each type of customer, trade sector or export market. You can develop an analysis list in similar format for your own particular situation.

Once the needs of each link in the distribution chain and of the products, are identified, and you have identified all the internal functions within your company that must be undertaken to produce, market and distribute the products, the next stage is to judge where in the organization structure it will be most appropriate to assign responsibility for fulfilling each of the needs and functions.

With some products a complex organization structure will result even for the selling process (which we usually think of as being undertaken by one sales person) because a range of different technical inputs is needed in the negotiation and presentation stages.

For example, negotiating a tender to design, build and commission a factory would involve engineers, architects, lawyers and other relevant specialists being available within (or on call to) the export department.

Developing the organization

In a small company the organization structure will be limited possibly to an export manager and some clerical and secretarial support (Figure 2.3). This tiny team will have to embrace all of the functions outlined earlier in this chapter until export volume enables the organization to develop with increased personnel and functional specialization.

As sales volume increases, or the product range or complexity expands, a larger organization might develop in a more traditional format, to handle increased workloads or provide additional support functions (Figure 2.4). Some of the specialist job functions may not have line management authority over other subordinates, but are essential to meet the needs of the company, distribution channels or products in a successful marketing operation.

In these charts I am less concerned with showing seniority by position than with identifying separation of functions within the export organization as it grows. Job titles will vary from company to company. It is worth bearing in mind that the job title should normally give an indication of the

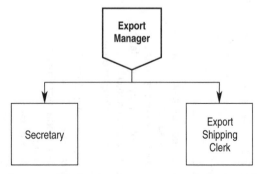

Figure *2.3 A basic export department structure*

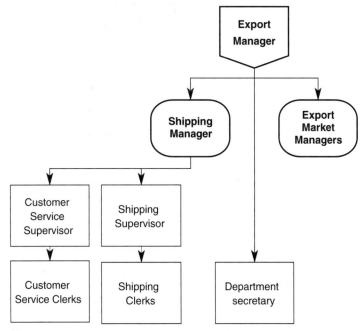

Figure 2.4 *A developing export organization structure*

job holder's primary functional responsibilities, and convey sufficient status to enable them to function appropriately and effectively with the contacts they will make in foreign markets: e.g., Export Sales Executive may convey less status than Export Regional Manager.

The growing organization will vary according to the marketing and distribution structure and service needs of an industry. Fast moving consumer goods may need a very different organization from heavy industrial equipment or service industries. The skills of job holders will also be different. Whilst consumer goods marketing may primarily need sales and marketing skills developed on the job, highly technical products may need all the requisite sales and marketing and exporting skills plus a university qualification in engineering.

Figure 2.5 shows a basic organization where the export marketing function has been separated from the export sales function, which would be quite common in many larger consumer goods companies. The numbers of persons in each job function

will be a function of workloads and management span of control limitations at each level.

Any organization function should have scope for in-built **flexibility** to take account of the changing internal and external environment within which it must function. Buying needs and practices in markets may change; new legislation in some markets may require specialist attention (as to ingredient usage and labelling); newly developing distribution outlets may put new demands on the distribution chain, e.g. the growth of speciality shops and franchised outlets in many markets.

The final organization structure should always take account of the particular skills of individuals and accountabilities of managers. In Figure 2.5 the Technical Services Manager, whilst having a functional (dotted line) relationship with the Export Director, might report directly to the Research and Development Director, the person best able to direct their specialist efforts, provide management and training, and monitor their performance.

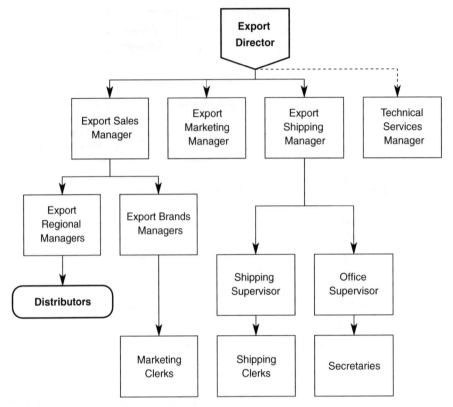

Figure 2.5 *Separating specialist functions*

Variations in specialization _____

Looking at Figure 2.5 you will notice that three factors affect the final organizational structure: **horizontal**, **vertical** and **geographical** specialization.

- **Horizontal** Functions that are mutually exclusive as a departmental sub-activity (e.g. customer service, export shipping, export marketing) but impact measurably on the performance of the department as a whole may be identified as a sub-department under a responsible manager. This functional separation may be independent of vertical tiers in the organization or geographical considerations.
- **Vertical** Within a department, as workload grows, functional responsibilities are delegated downwards to individual specialists or new

sub-departments, and tiers develop in the organizational structure.
- **Geographical** Dividing the world (by geographical proximity of markets, racial or language groupings, or other criteria relevant to your company such as product range) so that certain functions are provided within a defined area or category of markets is another factor determining the final organization.

  You may need to develop a network of sales and technical support offices, and regional distribution facilities at strategic locations to support activities in certain regions.

Span of control limitations _____

A manager's **span of control** over sub-ordinate personnel (including distributors in foreign markets) or separate functional activities is limited by:

- the nature of work being performed (skilled or unskilled)
- the knowledge or experience of the persons involved in managing or being managed (internal staff or distributors or agents)
- the physical proximity of jobs or markets
- the similarity of content of the jobs being managed
- the time available and required for training, planning, communicating, motivating, supervising and monitoring performance.

By grouping functionally related activities together in sub-departments you can limit the number of individuals and areas of responsibility reporting to each tier in the organizational structure. If you are involved in managing a shipping department, where jobs are basically similar (albeit skilled),

repetitive and performed in the same office location and you are going to be available to supervise activities daily, then it may be practical to have a large number of direct subordinates. However, if you are a travelling export regional manager, away from the office in markets for half of the year, involved in protracted negotiations, and training and planning activities in the field in diverse languages and cultural environments, then you will not be able to manage many direct subordinates back at base or control too many markets personally, but will have to build a subordinate supervisory and/or export sales network.

A common weakness in over-stretched export organizations is for the marketers to spread themselves too thinly in market management responsibilities. Many companies allocate twenty to thirty foreign

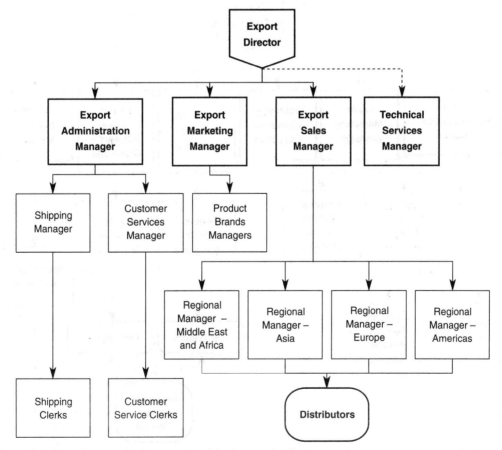

Figure 2.6 Development of a geographical organization

markets to each of the export marketers, which results in a fire fighting approach to market management rather than a planning and development approach, typically with the marketers visiting markets for two- to three-day trouble-shooting trips once or twice yearly. The style of management is discussed in later chapters. The organizational development issue is for the senior managers to clearly assess the market potential and support needs, and allocate adequate resources to develop the markets to their potential.

Other specialized structures

So far I have concentrated on a company with a single export sales structure applicable to a single synergistic product group.

But many variations to organization structures may apply if there are other product, marketing or distribution factors to consider. Some companies will find a geographical organization preferable (as in Figure 2.6) with one export marketer responsible in each market for all the company's activities, including consumer and industrial contacts and licensing. Others will choose to organize around narrower specializations, rather as in Figure 2.7. You may want to market technology in addition to selling finished product, or have one product range for consumers or retail distribution and another more suited to specialist market sectors (or for use as an ingredient or component in other manufacturing processes). The organizational structure you develop in your company should recognize

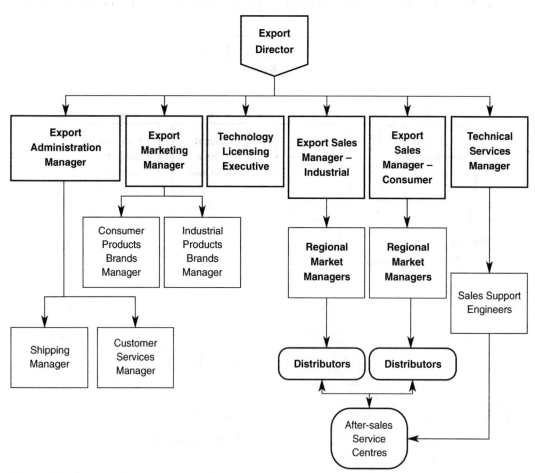

Figure 2.7 *Organization developed to serve different market sectors*

different needs and specializations in order to develop export markets to maximum sales potential.

Other organizational considerations ——

The basic principles involved in developing an organization can be applied to most types of products, markets and company situations. Whichever way you organize your company, the following are some of the other factors to consider and address in designing your organization.

Span of control
The number of managers needed within any functional department will be a factor of available time and skills to fulfil all the functional demands.

Workloads
The number of positions at any level depends on the workload capacity of individuals within each functional activity. As the workload of any individual or functional activity increases it will become necessary to sub-divide jobs or to separate some of the functions for delegation to new subordinate positions.

Functional activities
Identify the functions requiring separate management input, control and development to improve the quality and quantity of output from each person or department.

Communications
Effective communications between the various functional activities and management levels in a department are essential to provide feedback, motivation, planning, recognition, and achievement of common objectives through co-ordinated activities.

Flexibility
The organization should be flexible enough to adapt to changing market conditions. Barriers to flexibility should be recognized by senior management and avoided or removed.

Role clarification
Avoid internal conflict and dysfunctional organizations through role clarification, absence of duplication of functional responsibilities, clearly assigned responsibilities, and good communications. Where managers are unclear on their range and limits of responsibility and authority, the organization loses effectiveness and vital energies are directed to internal conflicts and politics rather than building the business.

Organizational format
The final organizational format usually has one of three emphases:

- **Geographical** – where each export marketer is responsible for sales and marketing activity in a clearly defined geographical area
- **Market sector** – where a different export sales team is developed to handle sales activity in separate market sectors with greater specialization, e.g. institutional use or domestic consumers, consumer outlets or industrial users, etc.
- **End use** – where effective penetration of an industry or a market sector or outlet type in a foreign market requires different skills or qualifications or organizational structures (including support activities).

There may be no clear-cut right or wrong organizational structure for your own company, but consideration of the guidelines covered in this chapter may help you to satisfy yourself that you are organized in the best fashion to meet the needs of your company, your distribution channels and the products, and to function effectively in a competitive marketplace where your energies are devoted to tapping potential to maximize sales and growth.

Measuring the export marketer's performance

The effectiveness of an organization can be monitored or measured by its achievement against goals and objectives. It is appropriate at this point to identify some of the key factors in the export marketer's performance and market management that can and should be measured. Later chapters expand on market planning and management of agents and distributors. Once the broad export goals and objectives are established, then for each market a range of quantitative and qualitative objectives that relate to current plans can be established. These are highlighted in the following list.

Quantitative performance measures

- Gross profit by market.
- Profit by brand or product.
- Increase in profit over base/target.
- Distributor's profit derived from company products and activities.
- Control of expenditure within budgets.
- Budgets as a percentage of turnover/profits by market/brand.
- Achievement of sales value/volume export dispatch targets.
- Achievement of market sales targets (depletions from a local distributor's stocks, where a distributor holds stocks).
- Growth/decline in market sales volumes: by export dispatches or depletions from distributor stocks.
- Changes in market share:
  - in total
  - by brand/product
  - by trade sector.
- Changes in recorded brand distribution or usage.
- Managing debtors within agreed credit limits and time spans.
- Effectiveness of promotional activity: measurable impact on sales/market shares.
- Measures of parallel trade shipments (where parallel trade – imports into the market by routes not part of the formal distribution system – is a factor in the product category or market distribution).

Qualitative performance measures

- Preparation of strategic marketing plans:
  - macro level/micro level
  - by country
  - by distributor/agent.
- Preparation of detailed sales, tactical plans by market/distributor/agent.
- Preparation of detailed advertising and promotion plans and budgets.
- Accuracy/quality of information files for each market.
- Distributor or agent relationships.
- Distributor's effective implementation of, or adherence to, marketing and sales plans.
- Distributor management skills, systems and controls.
- Distributor sales force skills, systems and controls.
- Distributor sales force effectiveness.
- Distributor compliance with company reporting requirements.

Individual companies may choose to focus on some of these more than others, according to what is relevant to their markets, distribution system and products.

Further reading

Marketing Management – Analysis, Planning, Implementation and Control. Philip Kotler (Prentice Hall). Chapter 26: Organizing and Implementing Marketing Programmes

Global Marketing Strategies. Jean-Pierre Jeannet and H. David Hennessey (Houghton Miflin 1995). Chapter 6: Organizing international and global marketing

International Marketing – A Strategic Approach to World Markets. Simon Majaro (Routledge, 3rd edition 1991). Chapter 12: Organising for International Marketing

The Marketing Book. Edited by Michael J. Baker (Butterworth-Heinemann, 4th edition 1999). Chapter 4: Organization for marketing

International Physical Distribution. Jim Sherlock (Blackwell – Institute of Export). Chapter 2: Organisation

Checklist 2.1
Effective organizational structure

Action points

Is your organization designed to:

- identify, evaluate and prioritize export markets?
- select agents and distributors?
- contract agency or distributor arrangements in compliance with applicable laws?
- train, manage and motivate agents and distributors?
- visit foreign markets at appropriate frequencies?
- have linguistic skills to communicate and to label products in prescribed foreign languages?
- prepare export quotes and/or costings?
- monitor foreign market regulations?
- set export and market terms of trade?
- prepare export forecasts, plans and budgets?
- implement export marketing plans and programmes?
- measure export and in-market performance?
- provide feedback and effective communications?
- monitor competitive activity?
- control export credit and payments?
- monitor market regulations and ensure compliance?
- provide customer service support?
- provide after-sales service and relevant technical support?
- process export orders promptly, accurately and efficiently?
- modify products or packaging as necessary to suit customer or market requirements (where feasible)?
- reflect customer needs in terms of distribution, buying practices and trade terms?
- organize and manage the physical international shipment of goods?
- prepare accurate export documentation?
- liaise with shipping lines, government agencies, etc., concerned with exporting?
- have in-built flexibility to meet changing markets and environments?

Checklist 2.1 (*Continued*)

	Action points
Are the following realistic and effective for all export department operatives:	
• reporting relationships? • spans of control? • workloads? • number/mix/range of functional activities? • internal and external communications? • organizational format? • reporting procedures, administrative systems and controls?	

If the answer to any of these questions is 'no' or a qualified 'yes', then there may be scope for organizational modifications or improvements that might increase the productivity and effectiveness of the export organization.

Checklist 2.2
Export manager functional responsibilities

	Action points

The range of functional responsibilities of the **Export Market Manager** can be split under the headings of **Management**, **Administration** and **Planning** (the MAP of activities), and will vary with:

- the nature of the products (industrial or consumer)
- the company resources supporting exporting
- the manner of sales or distribution (agents or distributors)
- the skills and experience of the export marketer.

Check the balance in use of time between activities in the **Management**, **Administration** and **Planning** categories – avoid a bias when in the office and during market visits towards administrative activities.

MANAGEMENT ACTIVITIES

Product/brand management

- Profitability by product/sector/market.
- Portfolio management.
- Market positioning (price points, selective distribution, etc.).

In-market distribution

- Outlet targeting, monitoring distribution against objectives by outlet and sector type.
- Physical distribution checks: field checks.

Market research

- Consumer/user tastes/preferences.
- Demographics.
- Product impact.
- Advertising impact and recall, perceptions.
- Consumption or use patterns/volumes.
- Consumption or use locale.
- Labelling and design factors, etc.

Checklist 2.2 (*Continued*)

	Action points

Advertising and promotion

- Designing/agreeing A & P plans.
- Setting specific promotion objectives.
- Monitoring performance against objectives.
- Controlling to plans and budgets.
- Assisting in training to implement promotion programmes.
- Field training, etc.

Public relations

- Preparing an annual plan by:
  - Journal/media
  - Product/product group
  - Trade sector/consumer type.

Sales volume achievement

- Monitoring performance against shipment targets/forecasts.
- Monitoring performance against local outlet type/sector/account targets/forecasts.
- Breaking down macro level targets to micro (account/sector/salesperson) targets.
- Receiving/monitoring local market stock returns and sales patterns.

Assisting in account development

- Assisting in making key account visits/ presentations.
- Setting up controls to monitor performance of key accounts against locally agreed objectives.
- Planning key account promotional activity.

Liaising with shipping/production departments

- Ensuring availability of goods to meet orders.
- Monitoring despatches to agreed timings.
- Monitoring shipment quantities against local stocks/depletions.

Liaising with marketing functions

- Ensuring consistency of brand strategy between markets.
- Co-operating on preparing marketing strategies by markets.
- Providing a local knowledge for planning and market positioning discussions (e.g., price, competitive activity, etc.).

Checklist 2.2 (Continued)

Product display/merchandising

- Training in aspects of product display and merchandising.
- Setting display/merchandising standards.
- Field monitoring of display/merchandising.
- Designing/establishing space management programmes at retail outlets.

Market outlet coverage

- Developing a database of market outlets (or product users), by sector, with distributors to ensure maximum coverage of worthwhile outlets (users).
- Working with distributors and field sales management to establish outlet (user) coverage policies and programmes.
- Training in, and designing, journey planning systems.
- Establishing controls to ensure scheduled journey/ outlet coverage is met.

Distributor management against agreed plans and objectives

- Formulating detailed plans, at the **macro** (country) level, and at the **micro** level of each distributor, trade sector, or product.
- Monitoring the performance of distributor against all key result areas.
- Setting standards of performance.
- Training in all relevant skills to ensure the accomplishment of plans and objectives.

Distributor periodic evaluation against agreed criteria (audit)

- Conducting periodic audits of the performance of distributors against plans, and assessing their skills, abilities, resources and their compliance with programmes and procedures.
- Audits could include distributor SWOT analysis (strengths, weaknesses, opportunities, threats).

Distributor sales/product knowledge training

- Providing detailed product knowledge training.
- Providing sales management training in 'best practices'
- Providing a source of sales skill training and field sales training to managers and salespersons.
- Designing sales management systems and controls to monitor sales team performance against key result areas and standards of performance.
- Generally working to improve the standard of professionalism towards a common international company standard.

Checklist 2.2 *(Continued)*

Management of distributor relations

- Developing good **working** relations with distributors.
- Ensuring the balance between good relationships and the inability to manage through over-closeness.
- Visiting markets regularly to promote relations, make plans, monitor performance and develop corrective action plans.
- Ensuring market visits are only made against pre-set objectives.
- Providing detailed contact reports on all aspects of in-market activity and distributor performance.

Motivation of distributor organizations

- Through relationship development.
- Through training.
- Through profit and performance enhancement, e.g. planning, control against plans.
- Through feedback on personal and inter-market performance.

Provision of feedback to distributors

- Bulletins.
- Conferences and workshops.
- Personal contact.
- Performance feedback.

Export and market trade terms

- Setting and agreeing distributor margins and trade margins.
- Discounts and allowances.
- Local A & P reserves and their use in promotional activities.
- Credit control.
- Payment periods and discounts.
- Key account performance terms within local trade discount structures (part of key account management package).
- Product warranties and sale conditions.
- Minimum order size and deliveries.

Monitoring foreign market regulations

- Obtaining all relevant data on import licensing, quotas, foreign exchange controls, ingredients/formulations labelling, packaging, advertising, etc.
- Ensuring compliance.

Checklist 2.2 *(Continued)*

	Action points

Monitoring and controlling parallel trading

- Monitoring the placement of orders which might produce parallel trade.
- Developing parallel trade where that is in the best company interest.
- Countering parallel trade through specific marketing activities where it disrupts company strategies.

Monitoring competitive activity

- Specifically reporting on activity and developments.
- Pricing policies.
- Promotional activities.
- Advertising.
- Marketing strategic issues.
- Product range.
- Imports/sales performance.
- Market shares.

ADMINISTRATION ACTIVITIES

Product performance and market share analysis

- Export statistics (actual data and market share).
- Market import statistics (actual data and market share).
- Market sales achievements.
- Performance against plans and objectives.
- Others as required by the company.

Regulatory compliance of product and packaging:

- *see above.*

Monitoring distributors' stocks and orders to optimum levels

- Receiving/monitoring local stock/sales records.
- Relating market actual sales to market sales targets objectives by product/brand/size, and key account, and trade sector.

Inter-departmental liaison

- Liaising with all other internal departments/functions involved in the marketing, production, design or engineering and research, and shipment of goods, and with the provision of support services, including sales division.

Checklist 2.2 *(Continued)*

	Action points

Credit control

- Monitoring against agreed terms.

Collection and presentation of export statistics

- Updating country files as appropriate.
- Economic data monitoring.
- Performance monitoring against plans and objectives.

Problem resolution

- Handling distributor queries.

PLANNING ACTIVITIES

Market planning in conjunction with agents/distributors

- Developing macro and micro marketing and sales strategies.
- Developing specific agreed tactics for strategy/plan implementation at macro (country) level and micro (distributor/trade sector/account) level.
- Developing training programmes to ensure plan implementation and achievement.
- Developing organization and resource studies to ensure resources available for plan implementation.

Agent/distributor recruitment

- Selection of agents/distributors against pre-agreed criteria.
- Agent/Distributor agreements.
- Monitoring compliance with agreements.
- Periodic performance audits.

Sales forecasting – inputs to forecasting process

- Macro level forecasting/targeting.
- Developing with distributor micro level forecasts/targets for each trade sector, account type, salesperson, etc.
- Establishing performance monitoring controls within the distributor organization (continuous and warning).
- Establishing a field management system to ensure field implementation and adherence to plans.

Marketing and sales promotion planning, including monitoring performance against objectives/budgets

- *see above.*

Checklist 2.2 *(Continued)*

	Action points
Pricing policies and profit enhancement planning • Market pricing studies to ensure correct positioning. • Monitoring competitive pricing and price promotional activity. • Agreeing pricing policies/points at each level of the distribution chain. • Ensuring fair (but not excessive) distributor margins. • Maximizing return to the company consistent with pursuing agreed marketing strategies. **New product development** • New products specific to market tastes/preferences/pricing requirements (regional or market specific). • Local market production (under licence, through subsidiaries, etc.). • Re-branding of established products to suit local marketing opportunities. **New business opportunities** • Company to set guidelines and objectives to encourage a proactive approach, e.g. – Licensed manufacture – Distributor acquisition – Local products. **Agent/distributor management training** • Marketing and sales management skills. • Field selling skills. • Management systems and controls (including financial and IT). • Human resource planning and management. **Monitoring the political, economic and social climates in markets** • Providing periodic reports. • Keeping abreast of current affairs and any aspects that can affect the interests of company.	

Action points

The export manager's key job functions:

- accepting responsibility for achieving objectives and export targets (volume, value, profits) by direct selling efforts and/or with the sales support of agents or distributors
- finding foreign markets for existing company products or services, or suitable products for foreign markets
- establishing an international network of agents, distributors or customers capable of importing the goods, obtaining acceptable levels of distribution, and providing after-sales service (if necessary)
- maximizing the sales effort by providing management support and advice, training, and feedback in the foreign markets
- co-ordinating the planning of international marketing efforts
- maintaining morale and motivation amongst the network of foreign agents or distributors
- interpreting and filtering company philosophies, policies and objectives to the foreign representatives
- communicating effectively with agents and/or distributors through regular market visits, sales and planning meetings, informative bulletins and performance feedback data
- becoming the company expert on business development and business practices in foreign markets, with the objective of increasing the company's global sales and market shares in foreign markets.
- identifying and prioritizing export markets
- forecasting potential sales volumes by market
- establishing company export prices that ensure competitive destination market prices
- identifying, setting and achieving market sales objectives, targets, budgets, and profit plans
- developing field programmes to implement the company's sales and marketing plans in each destination foreign market
- assisting agents and distributors develop sales organizations and management structures to achieve plans and objectives
- converting overall export plans and objectives, in liaison with the foreign importers, into specific standards of performance, sales targets, and programmes for each individual market

Checklist 2.3 (Continued)

- developing an export office sales support function, customer service function and shipping department to handle:
  credit control; invoicing and general export documentation; order processing; enquiries, invitations to quote, complaints; dispatch of sales promotional materials; market performance monitoring and feedback reporting; export costings; export distribution
- selecting and training all subordinate export marketers and shipping executives
- selecting and training all the foreign agents and distributors, and any appointed sub-distributors, dealers, service agents, etc.
- liaising with departments concerned with forecasting, domestic marketing, product development, budgeting and product costing, production planning, production, distribution, etc.
- setting export terms of trade, prices, scale discounts, promotional allowances, etc.
- communicating with subordinates, direct export customers and distributors on plans, programmes, policies, objectives, products and performance feedback
- assisting in developing and test marketing new products and seeking out new product opportunities in the foreign markets
- developing expertise in foreign market rules and regulations (including those relating to labelling, health, safety, import licensing requirements, foreign exchange regulations, product liability, agency laws) and ensuring product compliance, and limiting the exposure of the company to risk.

The export market manager's key job functions

- liaising with the export manager and other involved departments in setting foreign market targets/forecasts
- liaising with agents and distributors to agree annual sales volume forecasts and annual sales and marketing plans and programmes, assisting to whatever extent is necessary in the implementation stages
- accepting responsibility for achieving assigned objectives, targets, forecasts, budgets, etc. for their markets
- planning, with the agent or distributor, and monitoring market customer coverage to optimize effective frequency of calling in relation to potential and to maximize sales through potential outlets
- selecting, training, managing, motivating and controlling distributors

Checklist 2.3 *(Continued)*

- advising the export manager on market intelligence, competitive activity, regulations governing trade and changes in regulations, products, promotions, terms of trade
- liaising between head office departments and agents and distributors
- advising on setting terms of trade and export prices for each market, establishing local market price structures with individual distributors
- conducting negotiations with direct foreign customers on products, product modifications, quantities, prices, promotions, special offers, etc.
- negotiating special market product modification or distribution requirements
- monitoring export and foreign market import statistics to provide a measure of company performance, and providing comprehensive feedback to agents and distributors
- ensuring that the company is trading profitably in assigned export markets.

The shipping manager's key job functions:

- receiving all export orders and processing them through all stages to final arrival at the destination market, including: production scheduling, export packing, export documentation preparation, scheduling shipping or other transport mode, processing invoices and payments
- preparing all export documents required by any government agency, such as customs and excise, and liaising with any government depart. concerned with export licensing
- monitoring export statistics to markets of interest to the company, developing a database and producing comparative performance statistics
- ensuring all goods shipped comply with customer stipulations and known market regulations, in terms of both packaging and documentation
- liaising with banks
- negotiating with shipping lines and other transport suppliers for best freight rates and service, and selecting any freight forwarders to be used
- checking export customer credit, and monitoring payments
- organizing any requisite export insurance, covering both goods in transit and exposure to risks of default
- establishing all export administrative procedures
- recruiting and training all subordinate shipping staff
- assisting in the annual planning and budgeting processes
- acting as support and back-up to the marketers when they are travelling away from base.

Checklist 2.4
How can the export marketer's job be measured?

	Action points

Quantitative performance measures

- Gross profit by market.
- Profit by brand or product.
- Increase in profit over base/target.
- Distributor's profit derived from company products.
- Control of expenditure within budgets.
- Budgets as a percentage of turnover/profits by market/brand.
- Achievement of sales value/volume export dispatch targets.
- Achievement of market sales targets (depletions from a local distributor's stocks).
- Growth/decline in market sales volumes: by export dispatches or depletions from distributor stocks.
- Changes in market share:
  - in total
  - by brand/product
  - by trade sector.
- Changes in recorded brand distribution or usage.
- Managing debtors within agreed credit limits and time spans.
- Effectiveness of promotional activity: measurable impact on sales/market shares
- Measures of parallel trade shipments.

Qualitative performance measures

- Preparation of strategic marketing plans:
  - macro level/micro level
  - by country
  - by distributor/agent.
- Preparation of detailed sales, tactical plans by market/distributor/agent.
- Preparation of detailed advertising and promotion plans and budgets.
- Accuracy/quality of information files for markets.
- Distributor or agent relationships.
- Distributor's effective implementation of, or adherence to, marketing and sales plans.
- Distributor management skills, systems and controls.
- Distributor sales force skills, systems and controls.
- Distributor sales force effectiveness.
- Distributor compliance with company reporting requirements.

3

Preliminary desk research _____

In this chapter we will encourage the export marketer to take a disciplined approach to export desk research as a valuable investment of time, and will particularly look at:

- the kind of information you can normally obtain through desk research
- identify some of the key sources of useful information
- prioritizing markets to focus on those that may give the best return for the company's limited resources.

The aim is to demonstrate to the export marketer that desk research (followed, of course, by in-country market research) provides a more focused approach to marketing and market management, improves the return from the use of scarce company resources, reduces the risk of failed effort or activity, and improves overall export team productivity and export performance.

Now that you have considered that there may be opportunities for your company outside the home market, the next step is to start identifying and quantifying the opportunities through **desk research**. This can be an important planning exercise even if you are already exporting. Whilst this may seem a little unexciting, thorough basic research pays dividends in terms of time saved gaining market entry and in providing a base to more realistic plans and objectives.

Overseas travel is expensive, so as much preliminary desk research as possible should be done from the home base. Here you can consider what types of information and what sources might be available that would help you in forming a preliminary view of where to concentrate your efforts.

A common scenario in many smaller companies is to approach exporting like a blindfolded man at a duck shoot – pointing in the general direction, firing a load of buckshot, and hoping some hits a target. Just as seeing the target increases the chance of hitting the ducks, so comprehensive desk research will normally narrow your interest to a manageable number of markets where other knowledge (e.g. home market experience) suggests that you have the best chance of success in creating market demand for your products or technology. Even when you focus your efforts, making specific plans for specific markets, casual enquiries can still be processed if there is a real business opportunity, and you will quickly learn which enquiries to discount based upon your growing knowledge of markets.

Identifying current exports and potential target markets ▄▄▄▄▄

In most countries it is customary that, when an export takes place, the exporter must report to some authority (such as customs and excise) the nature of the product under appropriate **customs tariff** headings, the volume of exports, and the value.

As a starting point, the export marketer should make a study of home market **export statistics**, which will normally show:

- whether exports are taking place already
- where they are going
- the volume and value of exports
- any seasonal pattern to exports in your product categories
- who is exporting.

Home market export statistics will normally be available from government sources (e.g. customs authorities) or through trade associations, chambers of commerce, business libraries or government export promotion agencies. You will be surprised at the data uncovered by a meaningful analysis.

Chapter 15 on Export administration and performance monitoring contains an illustration in Table 15.1 of exports from one company compared with UK total exports in its relevant product categories. This example clearly shows how such a comparison can be used in focusing strategies, as in that example the exporter was missing opportunities to several major markets, illustrated by the difference in the ranking of markets as UK export destinations versus the ranking as export destinations for one single exporter.

Whilst researching export statistics you should establish if there are any onerous restrictions on exports of your goods or services to any nations. For example, any products that may be seen as providing assistance to the economic or defence development of antagonistic nations may be restricted, including defence equipment, some computer hardware and software, and some forms of consultancy. Also export restrictions may well apply to works of cultural significance, including art and antiques.

If it is known that other countries are producing similar products and are exporting them, then access to their export statistics will yield the same information on potential markets as I have noted above, and will additionally provide a basis for analysis (from FOB or CIF value/volume comparisons) of:

- comparative export prices
- competitive export quantities
- magnitude of import trade to key markets
- any seasonal trends (in the case of raw materials or commodities).

Competitive country information will normally be available through:

- the embassies of the foreign product source market
- your own government trade department or export promotion agencies (in the UK, contact the Department of Trade and Industry)
- your own embassy in the foreign producer's country
- the local offices of the European Union (for EU trade)
- or, possibly, interested trade associations at home that may like to monitor competition.

A thorough look at the export statistics available on comparable or similar products, substitute products or products where your own product would act as an input or ingredient in manufacturing or processing enables an evaluation to be made of the key countries at which you should look further – **the target markets**.

At this stage you should tabulate the information established and see what basic conclusions are apparent. It will frequently be found useful to tabulate initially in geographical regions (see Figure 3.1). From this you may be able to form summary data on the exports to listed destinations from all major sources, using this to set your priorities and objectives.

Comparative export data for widgets*									Year
Export source Importing nation	UK Vol. Val.		USA Vol. Val.		Germany Vol. Val.		Japan Vol. Val.		

North America
  USA
  Canada
  Mexico									

Latin America
  Venezuela
  Peru
  Bolivia									

Caribbean
  Jamaica
  Trinidad
  Barbados									

Africa
  Egypt
  Kenya
  Zambia
  South Africa
  Nigeria									

Middle East
  Kuwait
  Bahrain
  UAE
  Oman
  Jordan
  Saudi Arabia									

Australasia/Asia
  Japan
  Hong Kong
  Singapore
  Malaysia
  Thailand
  Indonesia
  Philippines
  Australia
  New Zealand
  India
  Sri Lanka
  Pakistan									

*Note: Values are usually in FOB terms. If possible standardize the volume units and currencies in units of comparative measurement.

Figure 3.1 *Tabulation of exports from major producers to identify potential import markets*

By this time you will have a far greater knowledge of potential markets and volumes and the prices at which recorded trade has taken place in the recent past. Since figures may often be up to three years old, you will probably be stretching your memory to recall accurately your own company's domestic or export prices at that time; in any event, it may not be too relevant a comparison if your own prices were not actually geared to quoting for exports at that time. However, your comparative analysis does give you an idea of ranking by price and volume of the competitive sources, and frequently these rankings will not have significantly changed over the short or medium term.

If you are looking for opportunities to export services or technology under a licensing agreement, then the process of desk research is fundamentally the same. Licensing is covered in much more detail later in the text. Desk research will elicit information on which markets might have industries that could use your services or technology, enabling you to identify a specific list of companies to contact.

Obtaining import data ▬▬▬

Now that you have a clear idea where the competitive sources of supply are and which are the key importing nations, the next step is to put some flesh on the bones by obtaining detailed import statistics for the product category in the markets considered sizeable enough to be of interest to you. In export, as in most other business areas, concentration of effort in specific markets with specific products is often the most rewarding strategy.

Import figures can normally be obtained through the various government departments dealing with trade (e.g. the British Overseas Trade Board in the United Kingdom, or the United States Department of Commerce offices in the United States). If these figures are not available locally for any

reason, an enquiry to the local commercial representative at the importing nation's embassy (or a chamber of commerce) may either provide the information or assist in guiding you directly to sources in the countries being studied. Alternatively, contact with your own embassy's commercial attaché in the importing country may provide the information.

Your knowledge of the trading patterns will be greatly increased by analysing data on:

● key sources of supply to the destination countries
● volume by source of supply
● CIF values by source of supply (enabling price comparisons to be made to assess competitiveness).

If there is any seasonal pattern to sales of your product, whether in supply, usage or consumer offtake, then a further breakdown of import (or export) statistics by month or quarter will probably be available through the same sources. This may have a commercial relevance, as with some seasonal products where it is necessary for customers to hold inventories for longer-than-normal periods to cover the short supply season. An exporter who can offer balanced shipments all year may be offering an indirect price advantage through reduced inventory financing. Moreover, supply availability when a competitor is in his off season may facilitate a first market entry.

You may find it useful to plot import data graphically to see if any trends are apparent (see Figure 3.2). Knowledge of the seasonal pattern of sales is important in:

● planning shipments to the market (and related production and factory stockholding of inputs and finished products)
● planning distributor stockholding (market inventories)
● planning marketing communications in phase with key selling/offtake seasons.

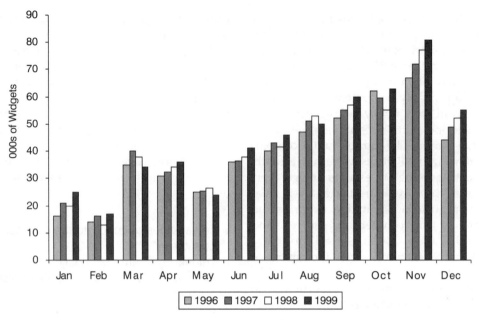

Figure 3.2 *Imports of Widgets to Spain: seasonal pattern*

Sources of desk research data ▬

Most UK exporters have a significant weakness in desk research and market knowledge compared with many exporters in other countries. It is not that data does not exist, but that we do not explore the sources. Few UK export marketers have ever visited the major commercial business libraries that stock statistical data, directories and published market research reports. The normal reasons given for this range from lack of awareness of such collections of information, lack of time, too few resources to undertake desk research, uncertainty as to what to look for or how to find data, to the belief that no data will exist which is relevant for the specific products or markets. Perhaps with some product categories data is not as readily available as we might like, in that a collection of products are grouped together in either statistical reports or market research reports, but any knowledge is better than no knowledge! Whatever the reasons for poor research, we hope amongst readers to encourage more attention to this aspect of

marketing, since the costs are usually very low in relation to the benefits.

Whilst the next section mentions some sources of information that might help produce contacts in the search for a suitable agent or distributor, there are several useful sources to be explored when undertaking desk research. These include:

● public libraries specializing in business information, e.g. in London the City Business Library, the Science Reference and Information Library, the Department of Trade and Industry library (in other cities, chambers of commerce and universities often have excellent library facilities and commercial data that may be accessed by arrangement)
● Overseas Trade Services section of the Department of Trade and Industry
● Export Market Information Centre of Department of Trade and Industry
● Statistics Office of the European Union
● British Standards Institute (for technical matters relating to product compliance, etc., particularly through their section

known as Technical Help for Exporters – THE)
- embassies of foreign countries (i.e. the London embassies of potential markets)
- chambers of commerce located in many cities
- foreign chambers of commerce located in the home market (e.g. Arab British Chamber, Anglo Taiwan Chamber, etc., located in London)
- trade associations (in the UK the major grouping being the Confederation of British Industry, but many industries have a trade association that both collects and collates market data, and also has access to a network of contacts)
- professional institutes (such as the Institute of Export in London, the Chartered Institute of Marketing, etc.)
- the Internet, a major source of data on any topic
- specialists market research companies (such as Economists Intelligence Unit, Euromonitor, Mintel, A. C. Nielsen, to mention just a few that produce detailed market research studies and/or economic studies into a number of markets).

Current addresses for a number of these sources are listed in Appendix 1, but directories available in libraries will give a greater list of possible contacts. A day trip to any of the major business libraries mentioned in London will highlight the wealth of data readily available to exporters – directories, trade statistics, other market statistics and information, market research studies, and so on. Some of these sources are discussed further in the next section.

The marketing of information has developed into a major industry in its own right. In addition to all the sources already mentioned, new sources of information in the form of computer databases that can be accessed by modem are developing rapidly to meet the information needs of businesses in the future.

Exporters are frequently amazed at the volume of market information they can collect from relevant searches on the Internet.

Readers in markets other than the UK will find similar local sources of data upon investigation.

Identification of potential importers and distributors ▪▪▪▪▪

Once you have identified your primary target markets you should extend your research enquiries to establish who are currently the main importers and to identify potential importers or distributors who may be interested in purchasing from you. A number of possible sources are commented on here.

Import data

Access to more detailed import records for individual markets may show a breakdown by both value and volume, listing each importer by name, in the same way that export records will detail the exporter's names and shipping details (except where there is a provision for non-disclosure to protect companies that might be harmed by open access to their export details in customs records). This is an excellent way to identify the dominant importers, or to cross-check other sources that purport to list importers claiming to be one of the 'biggest importers' and 'oldest established firms' in the market. Exaggerated claims tend to be the norm rather than the exception among many entrepreneurial businesses in third world countries, and it may be difficult to obtain supporting data and substantiating cross-checks.

References from other exporters

Exporters reportedly represented exclusively by an importer are an invaluable source of information on an importer's aggressiveness, performance and financial standing, and should be pursued as a matter of course. Normally, your opposite number at other companies will happily talk off the record on their experiences in a market, and give valuable commercial backgrounds on trading patterns and importers, regulations and business customs known to them.

Government export agencies

Agencies such as the British Overseas Trade Board will often have lists of potential or actual importers and distributors, or be able to obtain such lists efficiently and rapidly from their staff in the commercial sections of their embassies located around the world. Lists may be incomplete if they rely upon foreign companies to make an approach to the embassy to request a listing as an importer or distributor, or if the list issued to the exporter includes only some contacts known to the embassy. Lists may be inaccurate if companies listing with the embassy have changed address or other contact details without advising the embassy.

Chambers of commerce

There may be a foreign chamber of commerce located in the country of interest (e.g. the British or American Chamber of Commerce in Mexico City). These organizations can be identified and located through your local chamber of commerce branch and usually have a good base of knowledge and contacts with commercial enterprises. They are usually more commercially oriented than embassies and their staffs. It is nevertheless essential in drafting your enquiry to be very specific about your needs, in defining your target market sectors, and in describing your products and their uses and applications. The information you receive is a function of the quality of the enquiry you make.

Apart from foreign branches of domestic chambers of commerce, your local chamber of commerce is another useful source of data and information. They are likely both to keep a range of relevant trade directories and journals and to be able to direct to you to sources with whom they have contact, such as the local chambers of commerce operating in some foreign countries and foreign chambers of commerce operating in, say, London (for example The Arab-British Chamber of Commerce is a well-known institution providing a link throughout the Arab world). Where possible, identify the name of a specific individual to whom you can direct any written enquiry, as this invariably produces a higher rate of response and, generally, better quality information.

Banks

All too often we think of the bank only in terms of paying and receiving funds. However, if your company has a relationship with a multinational bank, or if it banks directly with overseas associates or branches in the countries of interest to you, then an enquiry from your local manager to their foreign colleague or associate will generally prove to be an excellent source of information. Data may be available on:

- potential or actual importers, or other parties suitable for co-operative ventures, banking with the foreign bank or branch;
- financial status reports on potential importers or partners;
- general knowledge on trading problems with the foreign country, including currency and exchange matters, government priorities, rules and regulations.

Telephone directories

If some of the more formal sources of information seem not to be producing adequate lists of contacts, why not try to find a 'Yellow Pages' directory for the major cities of the country of interest to you. These may be available through major libraries, chambers of commerce, government export promotion agencies, or embassies and other foreign missions, and will invariably have sections relating to your product category. If the potential contacts from this source seem scant, then try a telex or phone call to some of the listed contacts; explain your aims and objectives and ask advice on which you might contact.

Shipping lines

Another source of information often neglected in the search for contacts is the shipping lines that move the goods to the markets of interest to you. A telephone call to a forwarding agent will enable you to identify which shipping lines go where, and a call to their sales service staff may give you access to potential importers through their own records or contact with their overseas branches or representatives. The bills of lading handled by the shipping lines give them excellent access to information on who is trading in what products. There may be ethical arguments against the release of information, but my own experience has always been that they are most co-operative.

Trade directories

Most developed countries and many developing countries produce sophisticated trade directories of importers, distributors, exporters, manufacturers and service functions (e.g. Thomas's Grocery Register in the USA). These will often be available through chambers of commerce or government offices involved with international trade, or good business libraries such as the City Business Library in London. Frequently, they not only list companies but provide additional information on size, volume, products, turnover and basic financial data, and with names of known contacts.

Credit agencies

Publications by credit-checking and other commercial information services, such as Dun & Bradstreet and Kompass, contain a wealth of information enabling you to make some assessment of the strength of a company in the countries where such publications are available.

Trade associations

If there is a national trade association for your industry, then it is very possible that it has contacts with its opposite number in foreign markets. Trade associations are most co-operative in helping potential exporters and may write introductory letters on your behalf to their foreign counterparts to help in contact identification.

Published market research

The *International Directory of Published Market Research* will contain much data on existing market research studies, some of which may be useful to the exporter and save costs of commissioning special research projects. It may be found in business and commercial libraries or through agencies such as the British Overseas Trade Board.

In addition to these standard and established sources of information on markets and importers, it is always useful to make a list of all organizations, associations, companies, etc., with whom you have contact in the home market, and then consider what assistance they may be able to provide in connection with your search for export markets. A few are mentioned below.

Market research agencies

These organizations frequently commission work for clients in foreign markets, and have a network of contacts and associates. They may well have access to market information likely to be of interest and relevance to a potential or established exporter, and a meeting to discuss your objectives and needs may prove beneficial. Major business libraries may keep published summary reports of major market research work undertaken by some of the leading research publication companies, such as the Economists Intelligence Unit, Euromonitor and Mintel in the United Kingdom.

Advertising agencies

The comments under the above section apply equally here, and an early approach to any home market advertising agency may prove most fruitful. They often will be especially helpful if they are a multinational agency with subsidiaries or affiliates in markets of interest to you, as clearly their hope is to handle any resultant advertising you may eventually plan in those foreign markets.

Auditors

If your domestic auditors are part of a multinational group, then they too will have access to contacts and market data through their foreign affiliates and will generally be most co-operative. Several of the major international auditing firms produce and publish extremely useful business guides on countries in which they have a practice, and these should be obtained.

While the information-gathering process seems straightforward, and is a rather mechanical exercise, in practice it takes considerable time to elicit the information. Other people will not have your sense of priorities and urgency, and replies generally come in very slowly. You can motivate the recipients of your initial communications only by making the information requested seem interesting, available and relevant; make your contact really feel that he or she is making a significant contribution to a project that will progress.

At the conclusion of this stage of desk research, you should know:

- sources of exports of similar products
- import destinations, volumes and values
- potential importers, agents and distributors.

Further desk research ■■■■■■

Additional desk research is needed in a number of areas before you can make the first export shipment.

Health and ingredient laws and published standards _____

If you are dealing in foodstuffs, pharmaceuticals or a range of consumer products, information on health and ingredient regulations in the destination country is vital. Set standards may also be applied to certain classes of goods, particularly as regards safety and durability in use. Goods shipped that do not comply in all aspects with local laws are liable not to be allowed into the country. A mistake will be most costly if an importer finds goods not in compliance and refuses to pay a bill when due. Letters of credit may frequently specify that shipments must comply with all local rules and regulations applicable to the products being shipped. In the UK a good source of information is the **British Standards Institute** (providing support for exporters through its Technical Help for Exporters service).

Labelling and packaging _____

The foreign country is likely to have its own rules and regulations on labelling and packaging. Rules may cover:

- language of the label
- size of packages or units sold
- size of lettering
- position of labels
- colours permitted in the product
- product representations
- production and expiry codes
- product registration numbers
- ingredient statements
- safety and usage information
- names and addresses of distributors or agents, and so on.

This area of control often proves a major problem and trade barrier to producers of consumer goods, who may largely be selling to a domestic market and would find small special production runs an inconvenience. Thorough research at the outset will indicate if you can produce and be competitive while complying with all the laws.

Import licences and quotas ⎯⎯⎯⎯

Many foreign countries have forms of import licences or quotas to control imports, particularly for products seen locally as non-essential. (Limiting the availability of foreign exchange also acts as a control – see the next section.) These regulations enable the government agencies to:

- control the quantity and source of imports
- restrict imports of goods seen as 'non-essential'
- protect domestic industry
- control who is able to import
- control the allocation of foreign exchange reserves

Desk research once again will enable you to have a clear understanding of regulations relating to import control mechanisms. You need to keep yourself up to date with the latest regulations applicable to each market under your control or on your priority list and establish:

- the absolute level of permitted imports of your product
- how often and by whom licences or quotas are allocated
- whether they are allocated on a first come, first served basis or to historical importers
- whether the restrictions are imposed in monetary or volume terms
- whether licences or quotas are valid globally or for specific sources
- whether the quantities or values are fixed as part of a bilateral trade agreement or if they are variable at the whim of the government
- what is the customary period of validity of licences
- whether they are transferable from one party to another
- the availability of foreign exchange for imports
- currency control regulations (deposits on letters of credit, etc.)

Obtaining clear answers to these questions will aid you in assessing the degree of security with which you can start trading with the destination country. If you must make investments exclusively related to trade with that country, you can evaluate the risks against potential returns. There is no point investing time, effort and scarce plant manufacturing capacity (and money, particularly if advertising is involved) in small-scale orders if there is no continuity of business. A large, long-term government tender might be another matter.

If licences are necessary and are issued on a historical basis, then that limits potential importers, unless a licence is transferable and your preferred importer has assured access to a transferred licence. You have much more flexibility where licences are issued on a 'first come, first served' basis. With products that are seen as basic or essential, you may find the only importer is a government agency, which will handle all local sales and distribution. In this case, factors such as price, terms of trade and political considerations may override other commercial considerations such as quality, variety, delivery schedule, and your company's reputation. If you are dealing with a government agency, you will frequently need to spend enormous amounts of time establishing contacts in the decision-making process, which is often less clear-cut than in a private commercial enterprise.

Exchange restrictions ⎯⎯⎯⎯⎯⎯

Availability of foreign exchange in your target country for your type of product is yet another factor in obtaining export orders. Should any restrictions exist, then your research should establish the guidelines for foreign exchange being made available. One common hidden barrier to trade is where one government agency is responsible for issuing licences, and another controls the availability of foreign exchange (and tells you this must be allocated prior to shipment of an order); your representative is left going back and forth trying to get the correct allocations with parallel validity from both agencies.

In some developing nations an importer must deposit a proportion of the value of any order before any issue of licences or foreign exchange allocation. This acts as another deterrent to trade, because many importers are reliant on supplier credit to trade. Another delaying tactic inhibiting trade is where an importer pays his draft on time locally, but the central bank does not permit immediate remission of the funds overseas; instead, the bank releases remittances only according to some priority list, with the result that the supplier may wait months to receive their funds.

Internal market data ▅▅▅▅▅▅

While analyses of export and import data show volumes and values of existing trade, they do not show the potential 'hidden market', where the product (in existing or modified form) could be sold if access was obtained. Similar products may be locally produced and not imported either because of protective trade barriers or because they would just not be price competitive (as with soft drinks, which have a low ingredient cost and value).

An international marketer should look beyond pure export opportunities to other ways of entering markets, and include in their field and desk research a programme to elicit data on countries where their products could be marketed other than by export, including licensing agreements covering technology and/or brand names, or local manufacturing and distribution arrangements.

Most developed and many developing nations will have published data on production and consumption in a variety of product categories for local goods, and access to this will help seek out the additional market opportunities. Available market research, including omnibus studies, may highlight areas for consideration or further specialized research. Subsequent field visits will help identify the distribution channels and mechanisms available to organize local production if imports are not possible in competition with domestic goods.

Enquiry correspondence ▅▅▅▅▅▅

The enquiry letter you first send to an overseas embassy, chamber of commerce or other contact is the key to eliciting germane information as part of your desk research programme. It is essential that the letter clearly and concisely communicates your objectives, who you are, and what you offer for sale. You are trying to motivate a busy recipient to respond diligently to your request.

The foregoing sections of this chapter indicate that you may need data under any or all of the following information categories, depending on the nature of your products:

- recent import statistics
- lists of agents, importers and distributors
- size of local market for your products
- local economic data
- local labelling and packaging regulations
- requisite local product registrations or approvals
- health and ingredient rules and regulations
- import licence and quota regulations and administration
- foreign exchange controls
- tariffs (and any other non-tariff barriers not covered above).

The nature of your product may raise other questions to which you need answers prior to visiting the market, and it is well worth carefully listing any special circumstances before dispatching the enquiry letters. You may be supplying an item used as a component or input in another product or process, and want a list of potential users.

The letter's recipient will usually be more responsive if they see that you have done some initial research. Whenever possible try to identify the specific name and title of the individual who can help you. A professional, courteous and personally addressed letter will be more likely to produce the kind of reply you need. A letter addressed only to the commercial counsellor or chamber direc-tor is much more likely to find its way into a wastepaper basket or pending file (see Figure 3.3).

You may find that another government agency, such as the local office of the British Overseas Trade Board or US Department of

---

Mr John Smith
Commercial Section
British Embassy
PO Box 123
Riyadh
Saudi Arabia.

Dear Mr Smith,

We are producers of speciality sugar and chocolate confectionery, mainly sold in gift boxes of from one to three pounds in weight. While we do not yet export to Saudi Arabia, our initial research indicates an enormous market for imported confectionery in relation to the population, and I understand consumption is highest in the cooler months.

Our products and quality are well known, and I am enclosing a brochure to indicate our domestic product range. We can certainly consider modifications to this range if your local market requires that approach.

Specifically we would like your assistance in helping us enter your market by providing relevant information under the following categories:

- local import volume/value statistics
- local production and/or consumption statistics if available
- product registration and product approval regulations, if any
- health, ingredient and packaging and labelling regulations
- import tariffs, licensing or quota restrictions, foreign exchange regulations
- lists of potential agents, importers and distributors
- any additional information your experience indicates might be relevant

I would comment that an importer or distributor of foodstuffs would require cold storage facilities to handle and distribute our lines.

Your local knowledge will undoubtedly greatly assist our effort to commence exports to Saudi Arabia. Once we have your considered reply, I intend to visit the market shortly in order to identify a specific representative, and on that forthcoming visit I shall look forward to meeting you personally. Meantime, thank you for your assistance in helping us in these early stages to market entry.

Yours sincerely,

Bill Johnson
Export Manager

Figure 3.3 *Introductory enquiry letter to an embassy*

Factor / Market	User demand (units)	Product adaptability	Company sales potential	Distribution infra-structure	Number of potential distributors	Availability of Forex/ Licences
Singapore	80,000	Home product	10,000	Good	6	none required
Hong Kong	15,000	Home product	3,000	Fair	4	none required
Japan	300,000	Adapted product needed	25,000	Good	10	none, but some hidden trade barriers
Indonesia	45,000	Home product	6,000	Main centres only	3	licences required
S. Korea						
Malaysia						
Philippines						
Australia						
Kuwait						
UAE						
Oman						
Bahrain						
Saudi Arabia						
Jordan						
Egypt						
Algeria						

Figure 3.4 *Matrix: prioritizing markets according to relevant criteria*

Commerce (for American exporters), wishes to route all enquiries through its offices. From the exporter's perspective this is likely to reduce personal involvement and increase delays, because the recipient will have to follow prescribed procedures for a response. A direct letter to a specific individual overseas will often elicit a direct reply if that individual is aggressive and not too concerned over 'red tape', but you might consider sending a copy of correspondence to the local office of the appropriate government export agency.

Prioritizing markets

After a thorough trawl of all the available desk research data it is usually the time to set priorities in terms of which export markets to focus attention on initially. Initial visits to markets will provide a wealth of additional information that will further help you refine your list of key target markets and to establish priorities. The export marketer should list criteria relevant to his products that will help him categorize markets into priorities. Typical criteria used in prioritizing markets might include:

- existing or potential consumer or user demand in the foreign market
- suitability or adaptability of the products to meet specific needs in the foreign market
- sales volume and value potential for your company in the face of competition from other sources (e.g. competition in terms of price, availability, quality, traditional supply sources, etc.)
- existence of foreign market manufacturers with compatible production facilities or products, either to utilize your products as inputs or to compete with local products on advantageous terms
- a local distribution infrastructure suited to the product needs (i.e. refrigerated trucking for delivering frozen goods, or

dealers capable of supporting product with after-sales service)
- existence of local distributors capable of marketing the products
- current or potential protection (from imports) for locally produced products
- availability of foreign exchange for imports
- availability of import licences (if required).

A negative response to some of these factors could be a reason not to invest time and other resources into developing a market, unless you can influence positive change.

As usual, when comparative data is available, it is useful to tabulate it in some simple comparative format that enables you to see everything at a glance and helps in taking decisions. Figure 3.4 illustrates how some of the above criteria can be tabulated for a range of markets. Where possible it is better to record quantitative data, e.g. volumes or values, but against some criteria relevant to an individual export marketer's products it might only be possible to record a comment, e.g. 'suits standard product' against the criteria of product adaptability. By building up a data file on the key markets, an export marketer will come to be very knowledgeable about their demographics, market structure and characteristics, giving a more credible relationship with an agent or distributor in subsequent market planning discussions.

Further reading

International Marketing. Stanley J. Paliwoda and Michael J. Thomas (Butterworth-Heinemann, 3rd edition 1998). Chapter 4: Identifying international marketing opportunities
Principles of International Marketing Research. L. W. J. Groves (Blackwell – Institute of Export 1994)
Export Strategy: Markets and Competition. Nigel Piercy (George Allen & Unwin 1982). Chapter 2: Export in the Firm; Chapter 3: Export Marketing

International Marketing – A Strategic Approach to World Markets. Simon Majaro (Routledge, 3rd edition 1991). Chapter 5: Researching International Markets

Specific information on doing business in many of the world's markets is often available in a series of **Country Guides** available from a number of the leading **international auditors and accountancy firms**. Individual firms produce their own series of guides, often available on request. These are particularly useful where you are considering a form of market entry other than just direct exports, e.g. setting up branches and subsidiaries, joint ventures and licensing.

The **Export Market Information Centre** (see address list at the end of the book) publishes an excellent *Guide to World Wide Web Pages*, listing numerous websites useful to exporters. EMIC website: http://www.dti.gov.uk/ots/emic.

Checklist 3.1
Desk research

	Action points

Export statistics
- Identify customs tariff headings for products
- Obtain relevant export statistics from customs and excise
- Analyse historical exports by:
  - destination markets
  - volume/value
  - seasonal trends
- Identify competitive exporters, their importers, products and prices (from export FOB values)
- Obtain comparative export data for other source countries competing with similar/substitute products
- Analyse available relevant data by:
  - destination
  - volume/value
  - seasonal supply trends

Import statistics
- Supplement data in the above section by obtaining import statistics for markets significantly of interest
- Analyse the data obtained above by:
  - source
  - volume/value
  - seasonal supply trends

Importers
- Obtain lists of potential agents/distributors/importers or end users. Potential sources include:
  - BOTB/US Department of Commerce
  - chambers of commerce
  - banks and export finance bodies
  - telephone directories
  - shipping lines
  - trade directories
  - credit agencies
  - trade associations
  - advertising agencies
  - market research agencies
  - international auditors

Further desk research
- Obtain data on following subjects from sources as listed above:– health and ingredient laws
  - labelling and packaging
  - import licences and procedures
  - import quotas
  - export licences and quotas
  - exchange control restrictions
  - product registration/approval
  - import/duties/tariffs/taxes
  - import/export documentation

Supplementary checklist
- Prepare a supplementary checklist of information requirements and sources relevant to your own products

4

Market exploratory visits and distribution considerations

 In this chapter we will review some:

- aspects of initial exploratory market visits that may be helpful to the new exporter
- alternative approaches to obtaining export sales and export distribution.

The aim is to encourage and promote good trip planning, with specific trip objectives, to maximize the benefits from short market visits, and to create awareness of the distribution options that an exporter can consider, with an awareness that different markets may suit different means of distribution.

Time spent in a foreign market is costly, and, as discussed in the previous chapter, more benefit will be derived from visits where as much desk research as is practical has been undertaken from the home base. Additional research will be needed in the markets in order to:

- understand the local distribution systems and related trade customs and practice
- meet with potential local market representatives (agents or distributors)
- meet potential customers (trade channel outlets for consumer goods) or end users (for industrial products)
- further assess market sales potential
- obtain additional data that will aid market planning and market management.

Introductory letters

After the completion of all the desk research that can be done satisfactorily without visiting markets comes the planning of initial market visits. As outlined above, these are usually undertaken primarily to gain first hand knowledge of a market, its distribution channels and infrastructures, and to identify importers or agents. The desk research may have helped narrow the field, either because only a few companies have access to licences, or because the government agencies or other trade associations contacted have presented comprehensive lists and advice on agents or distributors and their relative levels of likely interest and market activity.

At this stage, and prior to making a trip, it is useful to write an introductory letter to contacts identified as potential representatives. The letter should:

- introduce your company and products clearly and concisely
- request the recipients to advise you on their:
  - interest in representing your products (or if they have a conflicting agency)
  - experience of similar products
  - market structure for import and distribution
  - import regulations and all other relevant rules and regulations pertaining to trade in your product categories
  - competitive market pricing structures
- request the recipients to provide a full presentation of their company to enable you to evaluate their ability to represent you, including details on:
  - size and turnover levels
  - ownership and management structures
  - staffing levels
  - financial data (accounts if available)
  - trade and bank references
  - facilities for product handling, storage and distribution
  - other product lines represented.

In order to motivate an early reply, you might mention that you are proposing a market visit imminently. The depth and quality of replies will greatly assist you in assessing who is hungry for business and in deciding exactly with whom to schedule appointments on your market visit. Clearly the size of potential representatives will vary in every market, and generally you will be wise to arrange meetings with several importers, distributors or agents covering the spectrum of sizes, as it will not necessarily be to your company's advantage automatically to tie in with the largest. Frequently the larger sales representatives are less hungry and less geared to market development of an unknown product line.

Planning the trip

Generally you will plan to make a trip to encompass several different but geographically related markets to economize on both time and expense. The cost of travel on export trips is invariably far greater than for a home sales effort and frequently attracts the attention of senior management. It is well worth consulting a professional business travel agent who can not only assist in optimum route planning and economy, but also obtain all requisite visas and other travel documents.

If you are visiting a country for the first time, it is usually useful to make your first appointment at the commercial section of your embassy, particularly if someone there has been especially productive in providing responses to your desk research enquiries. If they are advised well in advance of your visit and objectives, and any tentative itinerary and assistance you may need, including additional data, then much time can be saved. You can use this first appointment to obtain further advice on who you should meet and talk with. The embassy staff will often use their influence to ensure that you get an appointment with some elusive contacts at short notice: they invariably have a vast network of senior contacts both in government circles and in commercial concerns such as banks and trading companies.

Although you should pre-schedule a number of appointments, it is also very advantageous on your first trip to any market to leave one or two days free (depending on the size and importance of the market) either for additional follow-up visits with contacts scheduled in the itinerary, or for new contacts identified as having something to contribute to your market studies.

It is essential to answer all your questions while in the market. Conclusions should be formed and an action plan prepared with the co-operation and involvement of the importer you feel is most suitable as your representative. Good importers are plagued with an incessant flow of would-be exporters, and often lack the resources of the major multinational company to produce and implement sophisticated plans. You must demonstrate to your chosen representatives that you can work with them, that they were justified in giving you their time, and that together you can prepare a marketing plan that is both simple and practical to implement, monitor and control without disrupting the established business of their other principals.

It is important that you do have with you everything you might expect to require to achieve your objectives. Make a checklist well in advance, and review it prior to leaving. Some of the essential items will include:

- product samples
- product specifications, brochures and all literature and price lists
- guideline freight rates and all other production costing data to prepare market costings on special products
- production and shipping schedules and lead times
- guidelines on the production plants' ability to modify products
- list of market contacts
- summary of relevant desk research data
- itinerary and appointment schedules.

And do not forget passport, visas, currency, travellers' cheques, air tickets, credit cards, pocket calculator, and so on. It is always useful when your secretary is preparing your itinerary to have her include programme details such as flights, check-in times, hotel reservation details, appointments, including addresses and phone numbers for easy access should you need to make changes. Professionalism and efficiency at the trip-planning stage will make your life easier when you encounter the frustrations that invariably arise on the journey. Since suitcases have a tendency to go astray in transit, many business travellers make a point of carrying all papers and documents with them on the plane.

Some countries have rules on the importation of product samples, licences for commercial travellers, business visas, and other travel or visitor restrictions. Ensure that you are fully briefed by your travel agent or the appropriate government commercial agencies so that you do not arrive at the foreign airport and find that you or your samples cannot enter, or that your visit activities are frustrated by onerous regulations. Some countries may even have regulations relating to your personal tax status resulting from your visit. If entering a country or region where there is a risk to your personal safety, ensure that you give the programme of your visit to the local consulate offices of your home country.

Content and planning of meetings

Clearly, with the added cost of visiting foreign markets, time is at a premium. The people you will be meeting will expect you to know what you wish to talk about and accomplish. They will be impressed by professionalism, preparation, market and product knowledge, and a clear sense of strategy and direction.

It is generally a good idea to start the meeting with a brief but informative review of your company, its products and your objectives for the market. At your first meeting with the new contact it is better to spend less time on your own company and products and more time discussing the potential importer's company and ability to represent you. They will not be impressed by, and may react negatively to, a presentation that amounts to boasting. As language may be a barrier, prepared visual aids (e.g. videos, charts, computer presentations etc.) are especially useful in communication, and, where practical, should be translated into the language of the market.

At the commercial sections of embassies and chambers of commerce, and other institutions, you are likely to be seeking assistance and information to cover:

- potential agents, importers and distributors

- their strength in the market, including products represented, turnover, distribution capabilities, staffing, financial accounts, and credit status reports
- market import history for your product group
- competitive market activity
- import regulations (licences, foreign exchange controls, etc.)
- other relevant regulations including: packaging, labelling, safety, health, ingredients, local and imported competitive product activity
- assistance in obtaining appointments at short notice with local business contacts.

Distribution channels ▬▬▬▬

At an early stage in the evaluatory research processes the exporter needs to be considering channels of distribution and their cost, because each link in the distribution chain clearly increases the final price to the end user. The distribution chain may be very short, as in direct export to the end user (common with industrial products), or long, as in the case of a consumer product requiring handling, storage and redistribution at several wholesale and retail levels before sale to an end user or consumer. Your objective should normally be to maximize sales consistent with using the shortest possible distribution chain, minimizing the inflationary effect each link has on the final user price.

Figure 4.1 illustrates that there are several ways of developing foreign markets. Later in the text we will discuss franchising, licensing and foreign branches and subsidiaries, but at this stage we will focus only on direct exports through traditional distribution channels.

In some markets a single importer may be the most effective distributor, perhaps with their own controlled outlets through which to market your products. In another, the appointed importer may resell to a network of subordinate distributors, who in turn pass goods down the chain through sub-distributors and local dealers.

Figure 4.1 *Some alternative ways of developing markets*

Factors in studying distribution needs ___

Some of the factors that should be considered when studying the product's distribution needs in relation to the market's available tiers and channels of distribution include the following:

- The need to achieve and maintain **price competitiveness** in the foreign market if the product is not sufficiently differentiated such that price is a lesser factor in the marketing mix. A key consideration is whether the product can be priced to reach the final user at a local market price they will be willing and able to pay.
- The **physical distribution capabilities** of those distributors able and willing to

handle the products, and the effective modes of distribution within the market infrastructure, e.g. road, rail, waterways, refrigerated storage and trucking, and other limitations on handling and storage. Some potential end users may be in remote rural areas, not easily accessed, whilst major distributors may be concentrated in major cities. Also the provision of after-sales service in remote areas may be a problem for distributors. Failure to supply and service the more remote regions may lose an opportunity to develop a strong brand loyalty where competitors are also not able to tap potential markets.

- The number and geographical spread of effective and **available distribution points**, e.g. depots, industrial end users, wholesalers, retailers.
- Possible product **after-sales service needs**. If an industrial or consumer product has after-sales service or technical support needs then sale without support will result in dissatisfaction at some future time, and a distributor in a major urban or industrial centre may have to be willing to appoint local sub-distributors or service agents.
- Traditional **locally established distribution mechanisms and infrastructures**, e.g. trading houses, importers, primary, secondary and tertiary wholesaling. In some markets, such as Japan, there is a traditional distribution mechanism through trading houses down to lower tiers of wholesalers, and after-sales service needs may be satisfied either by the final distributor or by one higher in the chain.
- **Demographic characteristics of target market sectors**. You will need to study the demographic characteristics of each market or conduct a locational analysis of end user industries, and decide on the best means to ensure distribution to potential worthwhile outlets.
- **Available media for marketing communications**, including advertising and promotional support to target market

sectors; i.e. certain media may be mainly effective in cities, whereas the product may have strictly rural demand. Consumer products particularly benefit from advertising and promotional support. Urban populations in some developing nations may have access to television, cinema, magazines, etc., and have a higher literacy rate than some rural populations. In rural areas promotional support might be limited to basic point-of-sale material, posters and word of mouth communication aimed at a less literate community.

Some alternative distribution chains ___

Each stage of the distribution chain has a directly measurable cost, as does each refinement in support and service, and the export marketers have the task of evaluating the optimal balance to achieve their sales potential profitably. That may limit the length of distribution chain the exporter can effectively construct. The basic alternatives generally are:

- direct sales by the exporter through their personal representative (the export salesperson) calling on the end user during market visits
- sales on a commission basis through a locally appointed agent
- sales through a local importer/distributor who may carry stock or provide after-sales service and spare parts
- appointment of sub-distributors on a regional basis
- indirect exports such as through export agents, confirming houses, or other third parties.

The choices facing the exporter may be limited or governed by such considerations as:

- who has access to or controls import permits or foreign exchange
- who has the necessary contacts with the end users and can handle local public

relations (oiling the wheels to facilitate importation and sale of the products)
- after-sales service requirements
- the need for local stocks of product to maintain ready availability for end users.

The market requirements or best approach will possibly vary. If the product has very few potential users, as may be the case with industrial plant or ingredients, the chain may consist only of exporter and end user. However, depending on the degree of service needed by the exporter, product or importer, even that chain may benefit by being lengthened. For example, it is unlikely that it would be cost effective for an exporter of heavy plant and machinery to maintain an inventory in a region where demand might be minimal, such as dairy plant in the Middle East; but the same exporter might well feel that a market such as North America warranted local branch operations and inventories of some or all of the product range and spare parts.

In the case of branded consumer goods, the exporters are likely to find that they need a lengthier distribution chain, probably similar to that in the home market. Main and sub-distributors may be necessary to hold stock or provide spare parts and service, and to provide sales operations to distribute to the wholesale and retail trade. Direct sales by the exporter to a number of competitive wholesalers frequently results in certain of the wholesalers trying to claim sole rights on the grounds that they represent the bulk of imports and sales. However, giving sole rights to a company seen locally as only another wholesaler (as opposed to main distributor) may result in other wholesalers ceasing their sales effort. A main distributor can be involved in managing marketing plans, including media, and can offer goods on comparable terms to all local wholesalers, who will often be competing to supply the same retail outlets. Consumer demand, perhaps aided by advertising and promotional support, will often create pressure back from retailers to wholesalers to carry the product. However, a new branded consumer product frequently requires much effort and investment of time and resources to create the initial demand and distribution at consumer and retail levels in order to develop active wholesale support. A mass-market consumer item therefore needs a much greater margin between landed cost and retail price to support the frequently longer distribution chain, margins and promotional activity.

Early market investigations should ascertain the expected profit margin required by each tier in the distribution chain. Should the exporter not feel that his product can support the multi-tier margins and find an acceptable sales volume, it may be that the product will still find a limited market if aimed at a different segment from the home market. For example, a mass-market low-priced product in the home market may be aimed up-market in a foreign market, and sold at a higher price through few distribution points. Some automobiles seen as quite common vehicles (and even taxis!) in Germany are marketed as prestige status symbols into the United Kingdom and United States, where an order lead time of several months only adds to the up-market image.

As in the home market, a specialist consumer product sold into foreign markets with a narrow target market (such as designer clothes or cosmetics) may offer acceptable margins through a short and easily controllable distribution chain.

Typical tiers in the distribution chain could include any or all of the levels illustrated in Figure 4.2. The longer the chain, the more management effort will normally be required to control and manage market development.

The potential importer, agent or distributor

The previous section illustrates that it will be necessary for you as a priority to establish what kind of representation and distribution network best suits your needs and objectives in conjunction with the systems operating in the market.

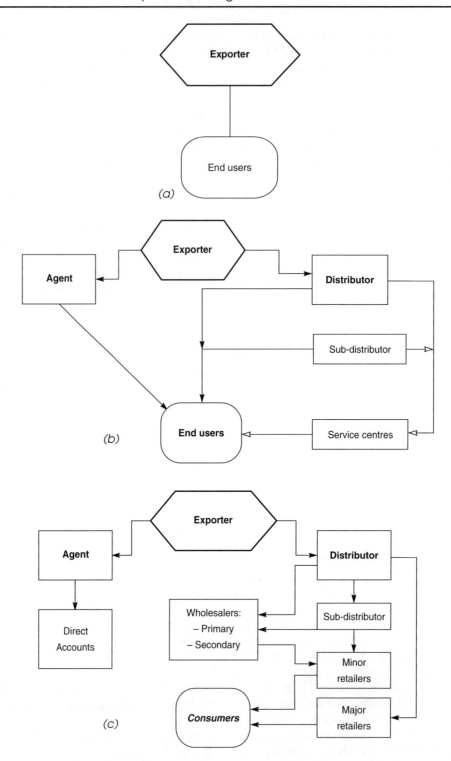

Figure 4.2 *Some alternative distribution networks. Your chain might include all those links relevant to your type of product, e.g. through either an agent or distributor. (a) Direct exports to end users. (b) Industrial exports through agents or distributors. (c) Consumer product exports through agents or distributors*

Sole importer and distributor

This is the preferred system for many companies that desire a representative to accept sole marketing responsibility, including taking possession of products and distributing and marketing those products through appropriate distribution channels to the final consumer or user.

The distributor takes his profit by adding a normal mark-up to his imported cost. They are responsible for local identification of users or retail accounts and local customer credit. In addition, he may accept full or part responsibility for any requisite advertising and promotion according to programmes arranged with the principal. Local rules and regulations may require the distributor to register with a government agency, to accept product liability as his responsibility, or to have his name and business address appear on all labelling.

One of the main areas of dispute with distributors is over the margins they may choose to take. It is usually advisable to have a formal agreement setting out guidelines for calculating or agreeing distributor margins, as overpricing may reduce competitiveness and sales volume and underpricing may devalue prestige products or result in an imbalance of price structures between neighbouring markets which is not a factor of differing import duties (possibly resulting in parallel, or 'grey', imports into a neighbouring market).

Agent

Sales agents agree only to solicit orders, normally on a fixed commission basis, and will not normally take possession or title to goods or distribute them. They more usually act as an 'indent agent' handling the sales paperwork and company contact for a network of importers and distributors that may possibly cover either different geographical regions or different trade sectors. They are responsible for motivating sales. An agent is usually chosen in a market situation where the principal feels no single importer or distributor can adequately represent his interests and ensure sales to all potential outlets. The agent should monitor stock levels and quality, solicit repeat orders, possibly help distributors make market sales to key accounts, and assist in managing local aspects of promotional and advertising programmes. A 'del credere' agent will also indemnify the principal for any loss resulting from transactions with persons introduced by the agent.

Importer with distributor

In some cases it may be found that an importer does not actually distribute to the market but resells to another distributor as soon as goods clear customs. Such a situation often arises where the importer exclusively holds certain import licences, or where other financial or quota situations dictate that the distributor needs the importer's services. Japan is a case in point, where a trading house will often provide middleman services by acting as importer but not distributor and be the banker for the transactions, while also being the sole liaison with the principal. The same trading house, while representing a principal to one or more distributors, may also represent the distributors without believing there is any actual or potential conflict of interest.

The main lesson the exporter learns by trading in many countries is to be flexible and adapt to the systems the market has already established. Trying to impose your home market conditions and systems is likely to alienate your contacts at an early stage of a relationship. Importers all round the world will tell you, 'Our market is unique ...', and you will gain no points by telling them that you know dozens of other markets that are effectively no different. Efforts to change a culture, whether business or social aspects, will invariably meet resistance and produce more negative attitudes than gently trying to modify some aspects, or trying to adapt a basically sound home product or marketing concept to meet culturally acceptable standards.

Confirming house

Confirming or export houses in the home country may often fill a middle role between seller and buyer. Such institutions basically undertake to pay the supplier for goods and to ship those goods to the foreign customer. They may extend credit to the consignee and make their margin of profit either by marking up the prices or by financing charges. They can be useful to manufacturers in the home market because they remove the payments risk from overseas transactions, frequently have a vast network of smaller customers who could not buy large initial quantities, and really can serve some companies as if they were the export division when special relationships develop.

Some export or confirming houses choose to specialize in trade with certain limited regions, and may have access to bank or other lines of credit made available for those regions. An export manager can only benefit by developing contacts with these specialist institutions, which may often accept a limited customer protection without demanding market exclusivity.

Export agent

Many smaller manufacturers, with limited people and financial resources, find great benefit from working through an export agent in the home market in the early days of their export development. These are often small companies or individuals with specialist knowledge of certain market sectors or regions, and who will travel abroad on behalf of the principal, soliciting orders, in return for a fee or commission. Many such agents do not want to be involved in taking ownership of goods or financing the transaction; they just act as the export sales arm of the manufacturer.

In Chapter 5 we will look specifically at aspects of selecting an agent or distributor, and that also relate to activities on initial market visits.

Contact reports

After completing all the in-market research and evaluation, it is essential to keep a formal record of your findings, conclusions and contact meetings: memories may be short, and, more importantly, it is crucial to avoid misunderstandings with contacts in the foreign market over interpretations of discussions. The same practice is also valuable for future market visits (which will be covered in a little more detail in Chapter 6). Once you have established a relationship with a representative, they will find it most helpful to receive a full copy or summary of your contact report, because that will summarize market visit activities and the content of meetings, record agreement on plans and programmes, and serve as a reminder of action to be taken by each party.

At the stage of initial market visits, your file contact report, which can be circulated as you feel appropriate within your own organization, should record:

- contacts made (names and addresses, titles, etc.)
- purpose and content of discussions
- observations, evaluations and conclusions
- agreements reached
- market information obtained
- marketing programme to gain market entry
- action plan and points requiring further action and follow-up.

You will rapidly develop your own way of collating data and preparing contact reports. My own preferred system generally follows one of two basic styles, depending on whether it is a first market visit and initial survey to identify data, trends and opportunities, or a repeat visit to an established representative as part of an ongoing market development programme.

Initial survey

After making a first market visit, the broad subheadings under which you might seek to develop data or evaluatory comments for inclusion in your contact report (or other trip summary report) could include:

- objective of the trip
- import statistics and data relevant to the product
- any other relevant product data, such as local production statistics
- import, health, ingredient, labelling, packaging, currency, and any other relevant regulations
- competitive activity
- store check notes (for retail products)
- notes on visits to parties providing general assistance, such as embassies, government agencies, chambers of commerce, etc.
- notes on visits to buyers or end users
- notes on visits to all potential representatives contacted
- conclusions, agreements and action plans,

Any supporting statistical data or copies of regulations can be attached to the file copy of the report since most of your colleagues are unlikely to want or need copies of such information; their interest will mainly be in seeing a positive action plan. You will want to keep clear records so that you can refresh your memory prior to making the next market visit.

Whether you are dealing in consumer goods or industrial products or services the same standards of thoroughness in research, evaluation and recording of data should be applied. Success as a professional export marketer is a function of planning and administrative thoroughness, not of miles travelled or airline meals consumed!

Repeat visit to agent

Whilst this will be covered in more depth in Chapter 6, some comments are appropriate here. Once you have an established agent, importer or distributor, your contact report will normally record information under some of the following headings:

- any changes in market regulations
- market sales achievements, inventory and forward order positions of importers
- pricing negotiations and agreements (including market pricing where goods are to be resold by a distributor)
- competitive activity
- sales, marketing, advertising and promotional strategies, plans and programmes (generally prepared in outline for, say, 12 months and updated on each interim visit)
- financial, payment and credit matters
- distribution checks (where goods are offered for sale through retailers or sub-distributors)
- staff training in product knowledge (and servicing, where necessary), management systems and sales-related matters
- other matters concerning the distributor operation, such as organizational changes, changes in facilities, etc.

Avoid the pitfall of letting the distributor or agent control your agenda during market visits, and particularly of devoting much of your very costly and valuable time to dealing with historical problems and administrative issues at the expense of planning and market development activities. Before you distribute your contact reports do re-read them to see if they read like a chronicle of problems and administrative or operational matters, or whether they make a serious contribution to market development and demonstrate that your visit added value to your business in the market.

Even with the most sophisticated distributors and agents, you will be only one of a multiplicity of principals and product lines demanding time and attention. The plans and programmes that are easiest to implement and monitor will receive greatest attention and effort from the importer, and therefore have the greatest chance of achieving your objectives. Professionalism from you will influence the importer's attitude towards you, your company and its products, and generate commitment and involvement in making a success of your marketing programme. When an agent starts telling you stories about another company's export manager who only wanted to sit by the pool during the day and tour the entertainment spots at night, read into that the message that a busy agent does not respect or need visits from any but those who want to contribute to mutual benefit.

Follow-up

The obvious is often neglected. The best time to prepare notes and contact reports is in the many hours you will spend sitting around hotels and airports, or in flight between markets. It is wise to prepare all your notes and 'thank-you' letters and whatever other correspondence the trip generates before arriving back at your home office. Once you arrive home, there will be a desk piled high with other matters needing your urgent attention. If you can just hand over your recorded notes, hand-written drafts, or a computer disk of your own report (where you travel with a portable computer that includes word processing facilities) to a secretary to finish and distribute while you attack the incoming mail, nothing will be neglected as a result of your market visits.

The contact report can usefully identify in the margin who is responsible for implementation or specific action, but do not assume it will happen without your direct follow-up with the person whose initials you have placed in the margin. As a courtesy, if you are requesting action by a colleague to assist you in implementing your full programme, such as preparing special costings or product samples or modifications, then let your colleague read a copy of your contact report so that they feel involved and committed to the success of the overall project.

To maintain goodwill and continuity of contact, you should write immediately upon your return home to all the contacts who have assisted you. Commercial contacts in embassies will be interested in knowing how you have progressed towards finding

an agent. Other institutions may just warrant a polite note thanking them for any information they were able to provide on your visit. Potential agents, importers or distributors need to be told where they stand in respect of plans to appoint one of them to represent you, and they should be thanked for the interest they have shown in representing you. Above all, the selected agent must be communicated with to confirm their appointment and to arrange any agency agreement matters in a formal manner. In the early days, occasional follow-up on the telephone will aid the building of the new business relationship and keep your company's plans higher on the agent's priority list. All too often plans and programmes made during a market visit are not implemented on schedule because the exporter fails to communicate with the agent professionally after market visits and continuously between visits.

Further reading

Principles of International Marketing. Julia Spencer (Blackwell – Institute of Export 1994). Chapter 11: Visiting Overseas Markets.

A series of useful **Country Guides** are available from DTI Export Publications, AdMail 528, London SW1 8YT. Tel: 0870 1502 500. Fax: 0870 1502 333. Website: www.dti.gov.uk/ots/publications.

There is a range of useful publications, and main titles include:

> *Hints to Exporters Visiting . . .*
> *Country Profiles*
> *New Style Country Profiles*
> *Sources of Information*
> *Doing Business With . . .*
> *Setting Up Business In . . .*

Some major banks and the main international auditors publish reports or booklets dealing with aspects of international trade and doing business in world markets. Exporters can readily check what is currently available from these sources.

Checklist 4.1
Initial market visit

Action points

Pre-visit preparation

- Introductory letter to potential importers and/or
  representatives.
  include:
  - company brochures
  - proposed visit dates
  request:
  - expression of interest
  - company description including size, turnover, facilities,
    financial data, products represented
  - trade and bank references
  - information on competitive environment
- Introductory letter to the commercial officer at your embassy
  advising:
  - proposed visit dates
  - information requirements
  - assistance required (contacts/appointments)
- Prepare agency questionnaire to give a structure to interviews
  (and possibly post ahead)

Market visit

- Make travel arrangements and confirm all appointments
- Prepare market visit kit
  include your:
  - samples
  - brochures/company accounts
  - promotional materials
  - product specifications
  - product costings
  - freight rates
  - production/shipping lead times
  - summary of collected market data
    - home export statistics
    - market import statistics
    - market production/usage data
    - labelling regulations
    - import controls

Checklist 4.1 (*Continued*)

- product registration requirements
- import duties and taxes
- exchange controls
- design, safety, use regulations
- local laws on agency/distributor agreements
- contact lists (with itinerary/appointment schedule)
- draft agency/distributor agreements
- Conduct in-market surveys on:
  - outlet types
  - competitive distribution/pricing
  - local trade price and margin structures
  - achievements of potential agents/distributors in distributing and marketing their current product ranges
  - credibility/acceptance of potential agents/distributors
- Prepare contact reports on:
  - additional market data gathered during the market visit
  - relevant discussions and meetings
  - observations, conclusions, and points of agreement
  - action plans and marketing programmes
  - other relevant information

Post visit

- Prepare and circulate a contact report
- Follow-up as required in contact report

Part Two

The Selection, Management and Motivation of Agents and Distributors

5

Identifying and selecting agents and distributors

 In this chapter we will focus on points the export marketer should be considering when identifying a potential agent or distributor. The aim is to provide a framework for a more thorough selection process and to reduce the risk that the selected agent or distributor will subsequently prove unsatisfactory.

Many companies enter exporting as an opportunistic exercise, where some enquiries come from foreign markets, and once a shipment is made the company is an exporter! Frequently before long one of the foreign customers asks for sole market agency or distribution rights, and a company that has limited resources and expertise to investigate opportunities and markets might well be tempted to make a formal appointment, on the basis that there is nothing to lose at that point in time. The problems usually come some time later, when the exporter becomes aware of greater sales opportunities than the agent or distributor seems able to develop into orders. To change an agent or distributor can be both very disruptive in the market and very costly, particularly where they can claim any compensation.

A more formal approach to selecting and appointing agents and distributors will reduce the risks of later dissatisfaction or under-performance in the market.

Considerations in selection of the agent or distributor

In this section let us assume that you are actually looking to appoint an agent or distributor in the foreign market to import or represent your products. We will look at the subsequent relationship with, and management of, the agent or distributor in Chapter 6.

When interviewing a potential representative for the role of agent, distributor or importer, you will need to establish certain basic information to assist your evaluation.

Essential topics to be addressed with your potential agent or distributor will include the following points.

- **Correct legal title and company address.** Any contract must incorporate the correct details.
- **Locations of offices, branches, subsidiaries, warehouses.** You will want to know the details of all the

agent's or distributor's operations (including branches and warehouses or service centres) and any other relevant facilities. If you are looking for national coverage of the market, then it is important that branches or service centres are strategically located near any major customer concentrations. In some countries certain industries are concentrated in particular geographic regions where they have easy access to key inputs – and these regions may not be near a capital city or port city, where many agents and distributors tend to locate themselves in order to be convenient either for goods arriving or visiting principals.

- **Ownership of the company and date of establishment.** As many agents and distributor organizations are entrepreneurially owned, the exporter will want to be clear on who the owners or shareholders are, and how actively they are involved in the management of the business. It is usually useful to check how long the company has been established and trading (and some questions of major customers in the market often will give some verification of claims).
- **Paid-up capital and reserves.** As it is more than likely that the exporting company is part of a publicly quoted company the accountants may like to satisfy themselves that a prospective agent or distributor has the resources to meet any expected financial obligations. In any event, the exporter should be concerned to check if the potential representative retains funds in his business for further growth and development, or withdraws profits for other uses.
- **Three years' accounts and financial data.** The export marketer will want assurance that the prospective agent or distributor is profitable and has the resources to meet potential commitments. It will be useful to check whether the representative has internal resources to meet an expansion such as taking on another product line, or whether he will be reliant on supplier credit for expansion. It will also be important to establish if his growth comes from acquiring new lines, or by organically building a basic product portfolio (if the former then the exporter may expect similar behaviour in the future – once sales are at a certain level, the agent/distributor might just look for expansion by acquiring further products).
- **Products represented and length of representation.** The exporter should obtain a full list of all the other products represented by an agent or distributor, with a view to ensuring their representation is compatible and that there are no conflicts of interest (such as competitive products). It is also useful to know how long each product has been represented by the agent/distributor, as this may give some indication of the satisfaction of other principals.
- **Trade and bank references.** It is essential to take up trade and bank references, to check on the satisfaction of some existing principals with the agent's/distributor's representation of their products, and to establish financial status and credit worthiness. Many exporters ask for contacts but fail to take up references.
- **Distribution capabilities.** As has been mentioned previously, the exporter should check with any prospective distributor his distribution capabilities, including warehousing and regional distribution facilities. Can he make delivery to all the potential customers in their varied geographical locations? Can he provide product support and after-sales service? Are the warehouses designed and operated to latest best practice standards, or at least sufficiently well managed to meet local market needs? Are delivery vehicles adequate in numbers, and well maintained, and suited to delivery the products in good condition?

- **Special facilities required for the distribution of your products.** Check availability of any special distribution facilities that your own products might require, either for storage in the market or for onward distribution with local transport (e.g. cold storage, air conditioned stores, secure stores, refrigerated trucks, etc.).
- **Staffing levels and company organization charts.** Obtain from the agent/distributor any organization charts for his company, and look to see if there is a workable management structure that can plan, take decisions, manage the market and marketing, and sell and distribute effectively. Are staffing levels adequate in all departments? Do employees know their role and job functions? Does the organization function smoothly or are there clear signs of disfunctioning, internal conflict, etc.? How good are communications up and down in the organization?
- **Sales and marketing organization.** It is essential to review the agent's or distributor's sales organization, to check on sales skill levels, customer relations, effectiveness of field management, sales planning activities, performance monitoring and controls. The exporter will want to establish if sales activity is carefully planned and monitored, or whether it is just a random activity where customers receive occasional calls and orders passively collected rather than product lines being proactively sold.
- **Market outlet coverage.** Every prospective agent and distributor seems to make the claim that he 'covers the whole market'. That is not borne out in the experience of most exporters. The exporter should attempt to establish how many of the assessed prospective customers are receiving sales calls, and at what frequency. The preliminary desk research or other market research may give an idea of the number of potential users (for industrial goods) or outlets (for consumer goods). This

information can be used to help establish what proportion of prospective customers are actually called on by the prospective agent/distributor, and also to clarify how well he knows his own market. Customers in parts of the market remote from the agent's/distributor's own facilities are often poorly covered, yet may be viable sales prospects.

- **Sales performance history with current agency lines, and market share data.** Another key point to establish is how the agent/distributor grows. Is it by building a core portfolio of products, or by collecting new products? A three to five year sales performance history for the main lines represented should be requested. Also, a check should be made on whether growth is coming from an expanding base of distribution for products, or purely from selling a wider product range to a static core base of customers. The exporter might reasonably conclude that the prospective representative's traditional way of operating and growing is unlikely to change for his own product line.
- **Distributor company policies and strategies.** If the agent/distributor has any particular company policies or market strategies these should be identified and clarified, to ensure they are consistent with those of the exporter.
- **Administrative systems and controls.** Establish what stock control and ordering procedures are in place in the agent/distributor organization, and what use is made of computers in managing information (of a financial, stock management and marketing nature). Are systems integrated or does each department run its own information collection and analysis (manually or by computer)? How well is information used in managing the business and forward planning?
- **Training policies and programmes.** In many markets agents/distributors do little if any formal training, generally recruiting

'experienced' staff who are assumed to be skilled or trained elsewhere. The exporter might like to research what the prospective representative's attitudes are to staff training, and what kinds of training are implemented, and whether the exporter can contribute to training relating to his products and skill areas (see Chapter 6: Managing agents and distributors).

- **Ability and commitment to implement your marketing plans.** The exporter should establish how the prospective agent/distributor approaches market planning, and to what extent he will co-operate with the exporter in making and implementing plans for the exporter's products. Is there clear evidence that the agent/distributor makes local market sales and marketing plans for his product range? If there is no evidence of proper planning, does the agent/distributor just rely on customer demand to generate sales?

- **Willingness to provide performance data.** Exporters constantly complain about the difficulty in obtaining meaningful performance data and feedback from agents/distributors (particularly from distributors). At the stage of selecting a prospective representative the exporter should clarify what performance reporting he will expect, and that the agent/distributor is both able and willing to provide it (it will be necessary to check that he can access and collate the data). If performance reporting requirements are not established at the outset (and incorporated in an agreement) the agent/distributor is unlikely to respond favourably to changing rules in the relationship subsequently. Many distributors have limited data monitoring sales by individual principal or individual products (other than stock records), since they are selling a multiplicity of lines to each customer, and tend to monitor overall sales by customer within their financial records.

- **After-sales service facilities for customers/end users.** If the products are of a technical nature, has the distributor the facilities (and willingness) to provide local after-sales servicing, and will he carry spare parts and agree to any special training in servicing and repairs (for example, will he send service engineers to the exporter's factory for training)? Check that service facilities are conveniently available to customers, as, if facilities are not available locally or at the customer's site, it can be a disincentive to purchasing.

- **Commission or gross profit margin expectations.** An agent primarily works on a commission on sales, and this will have to be discussed and agreed between exporter and agent, to ensure that it is sufficient to motivate the agent to proactive selling, but not at such a high level as to make products uncompetitive. With distributors it is essential that the exporter establishes the customary margins the distributor expects to build into local costing to cover his operations (import costs, distribution, marketing, sales activity, overheads, profits, etc.). The costing structure should be agreed between exporter and distributor, as correct positioning is the key factor in generating sales – it must reflect a competitive position in relation to the relative value in the product and other alternative products available. Many exporters fail to control distributor margins and local pricing structures, with resultant under-performance against sales potential.

Agent questionnaire

It is not uncommon to find that a prospective agent or distributor is reluctant to provide much detailed information on performance or financial aspects of his business. One way to start the information gathering process, and that adds an air of legitimacy to the request, is to develop a questionnaire form which can raise a good many of the questions in the previous section. One possible format is illustrated in Figure 5.1, and ideally it should be reasonably brief and seen by the potential agent or distributor to be asking relevant questions.

The questionnaire can either be posted ahead of your visit or used at the first meeting as a guide to discussions. Matters that might be considered more personal can be raised at the first meeting. A number of questions, particularly those concerned with performance, control systems and general management style and abilities, will be answered to your satisfaction only by visiting and working with the agent or distributor. As we will

---

Company name:

Company details

Registered office address:

Branch office locations:

Warehouse/other facilities locations:

Paid up capital:
Net asset value:

Ownership structure:

Total employees
Employees at main office:
Employees at each branch location:

Employees at each location:

Date of company registration:
Turnover for last 3 years:

Bankers:

Summary details of companies and products represented exclusively

Company: Products represented: Represented since:

Comments on handling, storage and distribution facilities

Comments on sales, marketing organization, including staffing levels

---

Note: Please complete and return this form, along with relevant supporting information such as **company accounts, organization charts,** and details of **supplier** and **bank references** to assist in considering your company's interest in representing our products.

see in the next chapter, weaknesses in any area do not preclude appointment, as long as you feel the appointee will make the effort to co-operate with you in satisfying your standards and requirements.

At this early stage of contact with potential agents or distributors you are seeking to establish whether the potential representative is well established and credible in the market; financially sound; capable of financing initial levels of imports and growing with the line.

Some of the questions likely to be on your mind include:

- Is the distributor able physically to distribute goods (and provide any requisite after sales service) either

nationally or regionally, or have they only limited geographical abilities?
- Do they grow by building on the base of existing agency lines or simply by taking on new lines to sell to a limited range of customers?
- Have they an effective management, sales and marketing organization, and management succession and training programmes?

The export manager should personally visit all the relevant facilities of the potential importer to verify their existence and suitability. Every effort should be made to establish that staffing levels are as claimed, particularly if you are dealing with smaller, less established companies.

A case example –
Mediterranean wines and spirits distributor

A United Kingdom exporter of scotch whisky appointed as his sole distributor in one Mediterranean market an old established family owned company in a major port city. The distributor had certain key strengths, in terms of financial stability, profit performance, meeting financial obligations, longevity, and representation of several well-known local brands of wines and spirits as well as imported products. The main shareholder was actively involved in the business, as managing director, and had a somewhat paternalistic style combined with autocracy.

The distributor viewed his organization as offering national coverage. He had a sales team of eight salespersons, six operating from his northern office, one in the capital city and one in the southern key tourist region). Customers were visited at least monthly, and it was common for salespersons to collect cheques for previous orders whilst making sales calls (sometimes resulting in late paying customers being 'unavailable' or unable to place new orders). The distributor's customer base was around 1600 customers, with only about 300 ordering in any typical month – with each customer ordering on average less than twice per year.

Salespersons:

- report in each morning, if based at the main office, for a briefing before leaving to make sales calls, and when practical they returned to the office late afternoon to deliver any orders, resulting in a shortened selling day

- were visiting between five and six customers per day
- had territory sales targets, set in value terms, but these were not broken down by customer nor by product, except when there were special offers or other promotional activity
- received no sales training or field management (the sales manager rarely leaving the office to work with any of the sales team).

The **distributor:**

- had no knowledge of the overall market size for the products he distributed or number of potential outlets, nor the respective share of wines and spirits going through each trade channel type
- had distribution strengths to traditional wine shops and restaurants
- covered only 1600 outlets, i.e. only 4 per cent of all outlets, yet he had a healthy and profitable growing business
- provided little coverage to outlets in the more remote country regions.

Very basic research (Nielsen data) showed at least 41,000 outlets in the whole country, in trade channels such as hypermarkets, supermarkets, self service shops, speciality bottle shops, other grocery outlets, hotels, restaurants, bars and night clubs. Depending on the product category (i.e. beers, wines, spirits) between 30 and 60 per cent (for whisky) of consumption was in the capital city region, where the distributor had only one salesperson. The region including the major port city where the office was located accounted for only 12 per cent of whisky sales, and the southern region was less than ten per cent of whisky sales. Clearly sales resources were poorly allocated geographically for the markets of our scotch whisky exporter.

The distributor did not focus sales attention on major retail accounts such as hypermarkets and supermarkets, 310 of which accounted for over 60 per cent of national retail whisky sales, because he was reluctant to offer the price discounts required by these retailers and to pay the fees involved in obtaining product listings. He did not actually monitor sales by trade channel type, and compare his own performance with national product category trends. The result was that our exporter's whisky brand was not distributed in major trade channels, but relegated to the role of speciality brand in outlets accounting for a minority of sales.

The exporter, in his ignorance of the market, had been satisfied with the level of market sales and growth, and had excellent relationships with the distributor.

The export marketer initially looking at appointing a distributor should have:

- conducted basic desk research (supplemented by in-market research) prior to appointing the distributor, which would have shown the approximate number of product outlets in the market, the trade channel structure of the market, and the split of category sales by trade channel
- conducted a thorough analysis of the distributor's sales operation, which would have shown outlet coverage in relation to the outlet universe, and in relation to the geographical split of whisky category sales
- taken a disciplined approach to distributor evaluation, which would have highlighted the lack of sales and marketing knowledge and planning, and the limited effectiveness of the sales team in driving sales proactively.

Whilst this distributor might still have been selected, as the best available, if the exporter had a thorough evaluation of both the market and the distributor he could have:

- agreed a programme with the distributor to expand outlet coverage (through a larger or re-deployed sales force) and sell into the key accounts that dominated the whisky category nationally, or
- restricted the distributor only to the northern region where he was stronger, looking for alternative distributors to cover other regions.

Without a doubt this exporter had substantially more sales potential in the market than he was achieving, but was now locked into a distributor arrangement that he would probably find difficult to change, either because of the concerns over the disruption and costs of change, or unwillingness to change from a distributor with whom they had good long term relations. In these situations excuses are often found for inaction. Thorough research into markets and agents or distributors prior to entering a representation arrangement establishes a framework for future market management in line with potential and expectations, and reduces the risk of future dissatisfaction with performance.

MARKET FIELD SURVEY Product: *Flow meters*			Market: *Mexico*		Date: *1/4/—*
User/outlet	**Type of products used**	**Current product source**	**Favoured distributors**	**Strengths/ weaknesses of favoured distributors**	**Problems with current products used**
Abel Dairies	*Volume meters on milk and yoghurt production lines*	*Swedish Controls Group*	*Spectra Imports. Habib & Co.*	*Carry stocks. Excellent after sales service.*	*Fragile in heavy use environments. Prone to jamming*
National Bottlers	*Volume measuring on soft drink bottling lines*	*Asahi Electronics*	*Habib & Co. Gomes*	*Good technical support. Local stocks.*	*Frequent servicing needs. Costs of spare parts.*

Figure 5.2 *Sample field survey form for industrial products*

Agency/distributor agreements ■

Chapter 8 deals at length with the drafting and content of agreements to cover your agency or distributor arrangements. At this point I would just mention that when a draft standard agreement is available you should take a copy of this with you on your market visits in order that you can discuss the general terms and conditions applying to the representation and distribution of your products. Having a draft agreement to discuss or leave with potential agents or distributors also helps the negotiating process by adding weight to your position that you have limited flexibility to negotiate round your standard terms and conditions.

MARKET FIELD SURVEY Product: *Men's toiletries range*												Market: *Portugal*	Date: *1/4/—*
Outlet	**In Distribution**				**Display facings**				**Pricing**				**Notes**	
	A	**B**	**C**	**D**	**A**	**B**	**C**	**D**	**A**	**B**	**C**	**D**		
Lisoboa Dept. Store	✓	✓	✓	✓	3	2	3	4	700	990	650	890	Upmarket outlet, expects promotional support, favours Chemco as a distributor	
Atlantic Store	✓	✓			3	3			750	990			Limited range of quality brands, expanded at Christmas, no preferred distributor	
Maximus Store	✓		✓	✓	2		4	2	690		625	850	Competitive pricing policy, favours Chemco & Gomes as distributors, likes merchandising support	
In Distribution: product available for sale in the outlet **Display facings**: number of product display facings on shelf fixtures **Pricing**: current displayed price of the product								Product A: Atlas Aftershave Product B: Atlas Cologne Product C: Rembrant Aftershave Product D: Rembrant Cologne						

Note to sample form: When using a field survey form note which competitor products you are monitoring by product name (and pack size if relevant).

Figure 5.3 *Sample field survey form for consumer goods*

Customer contact ▬▬▬▬▬

At some point in the selection process it will be essential to visit potential customers and end users (for industrial products) to satisfy yourself that the potential agent or distributor has market acceptance and credibility, and to get a feel for how aggressive the potential agent may be in pushing your products. One useful approach is to visit some end users or (for consumer products) store buyers on your own and tell them you are seeking a market representative and would welcome their advice. Generally you will be pleased with the helpful responses. If you also visit some potential customers with a salesperson from your potential representative, you can then form initial views on his acceptance, trade relationships and professionalism in the market.

Should you be marketing consumer products, then there is no substitute for your own random store check to establish:

- strength of competitive products (e.g. distribution, display, use)
- which distributors are most effective in obtaining displayed distribution (retail products)
- which distributors are known and respected by store managers or product end users: strength of agent/distributor relationships (e.g. reputation and goodwill) with customers

- local methods of merchandising and packaging products
- market pricing practices (e.g. product price levels, key local price points, trade margins)
- sales achievements of your potential agent with products already represented
- your potential representative's ability to implement your marketing plans and programmes
- your potential agent/distributor selling skills.

It is helpful to design simple forms or checklists to assist you in collecting and collating data on market visits, as when conducting field checks concerned with distribution. Some sample formats are illustrated in Figures 5.2. and 5.3, and another sample format, more suited to monitoring the activity of an appointed consumer goods distributor, is illustrated in Figure 6.1.

Further reading ▬▬▬▬▬

International Marketing. Stanley J. Paliwoda and Michael J. Thomas (Butterworth-Heinemann, 3rd edition 1998). Chapter 6: Marketing strategy decisions 1: direct vs indirect involvement

International Marketing – A Strategic Approach to World Markets. Simon Majaro (Routledge, 3rd edition 1991). Chapter 8: Distribution Decisions in International Marketing

Checklist 5.1
Selecting agents/distributors

	Action points

Essential topics to be addressed with your potential agent or distributor will include:

The distributor's organization

- Size of the organization
- Office, branch, warehouse and other locations
- Access to necessary levels of capital resources for investment expansion (taking new distributorships)
- Corporate history (how long established, etc.)
- Ownership and corporate structure
- Correct legal titles and address
- Compatibility of existing distribution facilities

Financial resources and performance

- Financial performance history
- Paid up capital and reserves
- Three years' accounts and financial data
- Trade and bank references
- Profit margin expectations

Marketing and sales performance

- Marketing performance history and capabilities
- Products currently represented
- Current product range compatibility
- Sales performance with other agency lines
- Commitment to your marketing plans
- Willingness to provide performance data
- Market sector shares and trends
- Market outlet coverage (of users/consumers)

Management resources

- Shareholder management involvement
- Details of key officers and managers
- Company organization and staffing
- Marketing organization

Checklist 5.1 (Continued)

	Action points
• Management skills and experience • Management training and succession • Distributor management style **Physical distribution capabilities** • After-sales service capabilities • Distribution capabilities • Availability of special distribution facilities • Administrative systems and controls	

6

Managing agents and distributors

 In this chapter we will clarify the typical role of the export marketer in managing agents and distributors, and what we normally expect from them. We will identify the main problems commonly encountered in managing market representatives. Then we will use this base to review how we can manage and motivate our agents and distributors by adding value to our relationships through:

- developing in-market activities that the agent/distributor will come to value, as well as greatly increasing our knowledge and understanding of the market
- providing useful training and other forms of support

The aim is to develop a motivational value-adding model that will promote a more **'hands-on'** style of proactive market management.

In previous chapters I discussed exploratory market visits and some of the aspects to consider in selecting agents and distributors. In this chapter we will concentrate on the management and motivation of your representative, often a difficult task.

The export marketer's role with distributors

The role of an export marketer or export manager in his own organization was reviewed in Chapter 2, Organizing for exports, but it is worth taking a moment here to consider the role of an export marketer in relation to his agents and distributors.

Your agents and distributors will look to you mainly as a provider of support and assistance, particularly in respect of:

- resolving all problems that arise in connection with orders (often concerning: product availability, packaging, labelling, quality, dispatch and shipping documents)
- providing a two-way link between your company and the distributor, exchanging information relevant to the distributor–principal relationship (such as knowledge of developments outside the distributor's market that might benefit the distributor)
- imparting product knowledge to the distributor and their sales team, who will look to you for a level of expertise they

cannot expect to acquire as a multi-product marketing organization
- training in selling skills to enhance the performance of the distributor's sales team (particularly for your products, but with spin-off benefits for other products represented)
- assisting in developing management systems that can be adapted for use by the distributor in their own company, with benefits for all parties through improved control
- planning marketing and sales activities designed to increase sales and profits, in conjunction with the distributor, using your more specialized knowledge and multi-market experience
- providing direct sales support by presenting products to key accounts in the foreign market alongside the distributor's sales team.

Your distributor's expectations of the functions you should be able to fulfil, and your own organization's dictates as to your job function (usually stated in a job description), will help you develop an activity programme for market visits.

The role of the distributor

If the export marketer is going to manage his business proactively through the distributor he needs to be clear on what he sees as the distributor's role, and have some means of measuring the distributor against these expectations. Typically, when asked to list what he expects from his distributor, an export marketer's expectations will include most of the following points. The distributor should be able to:

- import, finance and carry stocks of the exporter's products
- obtain market distribution at prices and margins competitive with alternative products within agreed distribution parameters by:
  - trade channel
  - outlet type (user type)

- provide sales force coverage geared to:
  - achieving distribution objectives
  - covering all suitable outlets or users to promote the products
  - providing display and merchandising support (retail consumer products)
  - providing product demonstrations (industrial products)
- distribute efficiently, meeting the needs of the trade channels
- extend trade credit according to local custom and practice
- work to achieve agreed objectives in respect of:
  - sales volumes
  - distribution by trade channel/outlet type
  - market share
- promote the products or brands through local advertising and promotional activity, working within agreed guidelines or to agreed strategy plans and budgets
- provide competitive market intelligence reports to the exporter
- provide period performance and data reports, to agreed formats
- manage key accounts in the best interest of the exporter's products
- set up regional distribution operations to ensure regional/national coverage
- provide after-sales service support for the products as necessary (particularly industrial products and non-consumable goods)
- support wholesalers who can expand distribution into outlets not supplied directly by the distributor
- train his staff in product knowledge and professional skills in sales, marketing and management
- participate in the annual sales and marketing planning process, providing local expertise and input, and subsequent performance reports
- provide an organization structure, both in quality and numbers, capable of achieving agreed objectives and implementing agreed plans
- provide office, warehouse and distribution premises and supporting

facilities of a suitable standard to enhance both the exporter's and the distributor's images in the market.

When listed like this it is apparent that the export marketer expects quite a lot from his distributor, and subsequent commentary will consider how the export marketer can add value to his relationship with the distributor and help the distributor develop their mutual business and perform so as to meet expectations.

In Chapter 7 we will look at auditing the performance of distributors.

The role of the sales agent

Some products are more suited to sales through a sales agent rather than a local distributor. Again, the export marketer should take a moment to clarify what he expects from his agent. Typically the role of agent is similar to that of the distributor, but might be summarized as:

- to solicit orders from all potential users or customers within the agreed geographical market and trade sectors
- to provide regular coverage (for products with repeat sales potential) through periodic sales calls on all potential users, without favour to, or neglect of, any possible users or outlets (and to provide the exporter with up to date customer lists periodically)
- to provide the exporter with all necessary information concerning negotiations, customer requirements, and such other information to enable the exporter to fulfil the contract of sale
- to represent the exporter according to the terms of the agency agreement, and:
  - not to make any claims or representations (in respect of the product, the exporter or the agent's role) outside the terms of agreement
  - not to vary terms and conditions of trade or sale outside those agreed with the exporter

  - not to take on the sale or representation of any conflicting products
- to obtain the best possible prices for the exporter's products
- to advise the exporter of competitive activity and prices
- to report on market data, imports, regulations governing trade and import of the product, etc.
- to assist with annual market and marketing planning
- to work to achieve agreed objectives in respect of:
  - sales volumes
  - distribution by channel/outlet/user type
  - market share.

Activity with distributors

Whilst visiting markets and working with your agents or distributors it is likely that your main discussions and activities will fall into the categories of:

- communicating
- planning
- motivating
- performance monitoring
- training.

Communicating

As your company's ambassador in the eyes of your foreign representative a key function will be to communicate your company's:

- philosophies
- policies
- programmes
- objectives.

Transferring factual information is relatively simple. In addition you will want to instil a little of your company's culture into the distributor's or agent's organization. That is a difficult enough task in the home market, without the added complication of cross-cultural fertilization of styles of management and doing business. Business ethics vary round the world, and your company may insist on standards alien to traders in other markets: transferring ethics contrary to existing practices will normally be a slow process.

Planning

Unless you are working through major companies in the more developed markets you are likely to find that planning assumes a lower priority amongst distributor management activities than you are used to. But even in the less developed markets the more sophisticated importers, agents and distributors are recognizing a need to make plans. It may take you a little time to instil planning disciplines, but, if the plans are realistic and results approach the levels desired, your distributor will become more positive in attitude and in allocating time to the planning process.

You are likely to want to develop plans to cover:

- marketing strategy and marketing communications
- sales strategy, trade marketing and promotional activity
- sales and promotional activity (including any advertising)
- standards of performance and objectives
- sales targets and forecasts
- shipments, depletions (sales from the distributor's local stocks), stocks and payments
- organizational development within the distributor company
- availability and use of resources (human, physical, and financial) within the distributor company.

The first four of these may relate specifically to sales and market development for your products, but the last two will also need to be addressed if the sales, marketing and distribution plans are to come to fruition. Account will also have to be taken of the local economic, political and social environments.

Motivating

The export marketer has a primary responsibility for the motivation of the agents, distributors and their sales teams in all the markets he or she is allocated responsibility for.

Motivating a sales team is an ongoing activity. A home market sales manager at least has the opportunity to keep in contact with his sales team on a day-to-day basis, since the team is a lot closer than that of the foreign distributor. The foreign distributor's sales and management team may not have English as its main language, and may also have a number of other exporters competing to be the lead line represented and promoted. So motivation is likely to be weakened by these factors.

However, the approach to motivation need be no different from operating through a home sales force. The main difference is that with foreign distributors you must gear motivational effort to the three levels of:

- owners
- managers
- field sales operatives.

Your effectiveness in motivating the team will be influenced by their internal relationships and effectiveness of internal communications.

The field sales operatives are usually at least one step further removed from your sphere of contact and communication, which adds to the pressure to concentrate your efforts on owners/managers, largely through improving their management skills (see section below on **Training**). Whilst motivation of customers, whether retail, wholesale or direct users, is always an important selling function, the export marketer is disadvantaged generally in that he has little time in any one market to develop the frequency and depth of contacts to do that personally, having to work through the local agent or distributor.

Performance monitoring

You will be greatly concerned with the sales performance of your markets, and performance feedback to your agents and distributors will, quite rightly, be an important activity function. Your foreign representative will rarely monitor performance of individual product ranges in the detail you might want. Most agents and distributors take an overall view of total commissions or profits earned, assuming that collecting more agencies and exclusive distributorships will enhance their standing in the market or will boost earnings.

The export marketer will want to establish systems, both within the foreign representative's organization and back at the home base office, to:

- measure performance against standards, targets and objectives
- provide feedback
- prompt corrective action.

In general you will want to set up a system of monthly reporting of key information from the agent or distributor, and to use this in analysis and feedback reports that can assist in monitoring progress against plans. We will look in Chapter 15 at what you may want to measure, and some basic controls that can be set up either manually or on computer databases to record performance data. At this stage suffice it to say that there is no point compiling comparative market performance statistics back at the office if your representative is not party to these (with occasional exceptions, of course, where data are seen as being of a confidential nature). So timely and comprehensive feedback is part of the communicating and performance measurement activities, and is essential if action plans are to be made to counter deviations from the market plans.

Training

This is perhaps the single most important functional activity of the international marketer, but often the most neglected. There is

no point preparing brilliant marketing plans, establishing sophisticated performance monitoring systems, and motivating through your personal example and infectious enthusiasm, if you do not support each of these with training.

As distributor training is an important topic further coverage is given later in the chapter, but, in general, areas where training is likely to be beneficial include:

- distributor management:
  - team motivation
  - sales planning
  - field sales management
  - performance measurement
  - product knowledge
- distributor salespersons:
  - selling skills
  - territory management
  - objective setting and account management by objectives
  - product knowledge.

The export marketer's visit to the distributor

Whilst in the foreign market, on what is usually a rather short visit, you will be under a great deal of pressure (much of it self-generated) to accomplish a variety of tasks and objectives. During your extended working day, time will normally be spent in meetings with your representative, customers or end users, and perhaps monitoring performance in the marketplace (field checking distribution). Whilst with the distributor or agent some of your key activities will usually include:

- reviewing sales performance
- providing feedback on company and general distributor performance (such as your export performance compared with that of other home market exporters, your share of imports to destination market, and other available data supporting estimates of performance)
- presenting new products, advertising plans and promotions

- providing appropriate sales and management training
- planning annual (or other periodic) sales and marketing programmes (or rolling forward current plans)
- reviewing achievement against current plans and programmes
- developing action programmes to counter deviations from current plans
- assisting in distributor sales team and sales management recruitment
- assisting in major sales presentations with local key accounts
- developing goodwill for the company and products.

Field work

Of course there is more to do on a foreign market visit than just hold meetings in an office. Field work with the agent or distributor's sales team, or sometimes alone conducting distribution audits, is another important market activity function. There are several aspects to field work. The main activities might include:

- making sales presentations with agents and distributors (particularly with key accounts or where the prestige of a direct visit from the manufacturer may clinch a deal)
- conducting field sales training with members of the agent's or distributor's sales team
- conducting field distribution checks (for products distributed through retail outlets) on known customers and on a random selection of outlets (to measure actual distribution versus potential distribution)
- assessing market reaction to your products, prices and promotional activities, and collecting and collating information useful in the planning (or corrective action) and performance monitoring process
- seeking and identifying new opportunities for your company to expand its range or sales activities

- problem solving (trouble shooting) where identified problems have not been handled by the agent or distributor, or where he needs your specialist assistance
- visiting distribution outlets (sub-distributors, wholesalers, specialist stockists, etc.), distribution depots, after-sales service centres
- monitoring competitive activity (pricing, distribution, product range, distributor effectiveness, promotional activity, sales performance, acceptance, etc.).

The experienced international marketer may be involved in all these activities without thinking; new representatives may want to develop a personal checklist to remind themselves of the factors relevant to their particular products and markets. Checklist 6.1 at the end of this chapter may help pull together some of the range of discussion points and activities in managing through agents and distributors.

Conducting market field audits

Conducting field audits is an important activity for export marketers when visiting their foreign markets. It is just as essential for industrial products as for consumer products that the export marketer has clear information on the effectiveness of his local distributor in stocking, selling and promoting product use or distribution. He will also need to monitor competitor activity, pricing and marketing strategies. Field audits can also highlight the strengths and weaknesses of one distributor versus another, and provide an indicator of training needs within a distributor's organization.

A typical field audit can collect information on:

- own company products and competitive product distribution, or usage, e.g.:
  - pricing
  - distribution achievements and levels, or usage levels for industrial products
  - category usage for industrial products, with company products' share of usage

- product display achievements for retail products (location, quantity and quality of display)
- promotional activities
- distributor or agent's achievements
  - with your company products
  - with other lines represented or distributed, e.g.
    - trade stock levels
    - sales growth rates
    - distribution and display
- distributor's reputation, e.g.:
  - customer service and relationships
  - sales activity
  - technical support
  - stock control
  - management.

Some of the above points that might be monitored are more relevant to consumer product markets. Usually it is best to develop a simple standard format **field audit form** (see examples in Figure 6.1(a) and (b)) to carry with you to record data and observations, including the names and addresses of any stockists visited in order that any subsequent discussions with an agent or distributor are meaningful. On some occasions you may prefer not to reveal which outlets you have visited in order that you can monitor general progress on a later visit.

Training distributors

At a number of points in this chapter I have raised the subject of training distributors. Your distributors will normally be representing quite a diverse range of companies and products, and probably working in a business environment far less sophisticated than your own. Rather than criticizing the management and sales force in the distribution company for their lack of professionalism and expertise, I would encourage taking a proactive role in training them to your standards. That will take a long time, and initially you may not have the level of co-operation you would want. However, once the distributor's owners or management see personal benefit in increased sales and profits, and reduced costs through better systems, controls and productivity, your training efforts will be appreciated and in demand.

There are two key aspects of training where you might direct attention initially. A range of topics related to your company, products and basic selling and management skills could be covered in a series of short training sessions whilst in the market (either as an intensive programme or spread over several visits if you visit a particular market with training needs regularly). This could then be supported by working with managers and sales personnel visiting contacts and customers, which provide an opportunity to practise and consolidate skills covered in training sessions.

Your main emphasis should always be directed to training the distributor management team first. Unless they develop the skills and commitment, training further down the line will not have lasting benefit (and lower-level personnel are more likely to leave to use their new-found skills to greater personal benefit elsewhere).

It is likely you will find many weaknesses in control systems. Once you have good credibility with your distributors as an exporter who really cares about *their* business, there will probably be scope to recommend alternative systems that will improve the distributors' management of your particular product range (typically, attention to stock and ordering systems, customer credit control, sales force operating procedures all pay benefits).

Training stages

Whether training in a formal training meeting or a field selling environment there are certain standard stages in the training process if the objective of changing behaviour (improving performance) is to be achieved. These stages can be identified as below.

- **Discussion.** The more a trainee understands about the background to the

FIELD AUDIT				MARKET			DATE		LOCALITY		
		Coverage		Product distribution			Product display	Point of sale material	Product pricing	Notes
Outlet		Comp-any	Comp-etitor	Prod X	Prod Y	Prod Z				

Figure 6.1(a) A model field audit form for a retail product

FIELD AUDIT	MARKET						DATE						LOCALITY		
Outlet	Coverage		Product usage			Category usage volume			Company share of category usage			Product pricing		Notes
	Comp-any	Comp-etitor	Prod X	Prod Y	Prod Z	Cat A	Cat B	Cat C	Cat A	Cat B	Cat C			

Figure 6.1(b) A model field audit form for an industrial product

proposed system of operating, what you are trying to achieve, and how the training will work and benefit him or her personally, the more easily will the actual training session progress.

- **Demonstration**. It is essential for the trainer to demonstrate his points in a sales environment. A sales trainer who does not demonstrate fails to gain credibility.
- **Explanation.** After demonstrating the practical aspects of a job, such as a stage of the selling process or an aspect of management (counselling, interviewing, appraisal, etc.), then a further analysis and explanation of what was, or should have been, happening is useful to help the pieces of the selling process integrate into one whole continuous activity.
- **Practice**. Of course the actual practice of a training point by the trainee is fundamental to modifying behaviour or acquiring a new skill. This stage is where field training is invaluable when training in selling skills. The amount of practice necessary depends on the nature of the skill and the trainee's existing level of skill.
- **Consolidation**. Practice in selling skills is not so different from learning to drive: each stage must be learnt and practised individually, and then pulled together to consolidate the total activity into a smooth flowing process.

As I mentioned earlier, with the problems of infrequency of market visits, and the limitations of time faced by a visiting export marketer, priority is best given to training distributors' management to manage and train their own teams. At the same time, many international consumer goods companies have introduced international sales trainers or sales development managers to support the work of the international marketer by spending greater time in individual key markets and providing intensive sales training.

Make use of technology in training. Company videos, product and company information on computer disks, web sites that are kept current with latest information, online Internet help lines, all offer scope internationally as well as domestically for training and customer liaison.

Basic training

If you are developing a sales training programme to increase your company and product knowledge and level of professional sales skills within your agents' and distributors' organizations you might like to include coverage of the following topics.

Company knowledge

- **History**. Often there is much of interest in the growth and development of a company, perhaps from entrepreneurial beginnings similar to those of many distributor companies.
- **Organization**. Usually the only person the agent or distributor really relates to is the export marketer who visits from time to time, with possibly a telephone familiarity with key people concerned with order processing. It is helpful to explain the details of the corporate structure and organization charts of key departments.
- **Objectives.** If your company operates to specific objectives in the domestic and international market then communicating these to your representatives (to whatever extent they are not confidential) may help to make them feel involved and committed to achieving their part of the plan.
- **Management philosophies and style.** Again, just as you are the ambassador of the company to the distributors, they are your company's ambassadors to the local consumers, users, sub-distributors, etc. The more they are indoctrinated in your corporate culture the better will they reflect the image you want in their market.

Product knowledge

- **Historical development.** The background of product development may be of interest, particularly where technical products are concerned, as distributors may like to understand the stages you have gone through in other markets getting to your present level of sophistication.

- **Production processes and techniques**. The better understanding your representative has of manufacturing matters the more he may be able to answer technical questions when marketing technical products. When the agent or distributor visits your premises then factory tours are often on the agenda. However, there are other ways of communicating your processes (where non-confidential). Videos are an excellent modern communication aid not yet utilized sufficiently by many companies in their international marketing programmes.
- **Product range features and benefits**. Without this knowledge no salesperson can properly represent your products in the market. Yet surprisingly little knowledge is trained into agents and distributors. Literature may be sent out, but formal training sessions and role-playing exercises to consolidate this vital sales knowledge are not the norm!
- **Competitors' products.** Following on from knowledge of your own products' features and benefits, it is just as important for agents and distributors to have a good level of knowledge of competitive products in order to deal with customer questions and objections.
- **Marketing programmes.** A greater awareness of how you market the products elsewhere, and the rationale behind your marketing programmes, will help motivate a distributor to greater effort.

Professional selling skills

- **Developing a sales sequence**. A distributor in a foreign market has probably never had exposure to professional sales training. As a starting point, it can be useful to develop a structured sales sequence that suits your products and trade channels.
- **Use of sales aids.** Making the best use of sales literature and samples is a skill in itself. How to carry, present to the buyer, and generally use them as a communication aid that makes a meaningful impact are all aspects of the sales process that salespeople can be trained in, and you will benefit with your agent's or distributor's growing professionalism.
- **Identifying and creating needs.** Create a need or solve a problem and you achieve the sale! Life is not quite that easy in selling, but certainly the skill to tackle a sales presentation in this fashion is not natural but the result of training. Most salespersons who have not benefited from formal training correlate *talking* with *selling*. You have a chance to show your distributors how to achieve results through planned presentations.
- **Handling objections.** Again, objection handling is a lot more than just repeating the same information but a little louder!
- **Communicating effectively.** Whether oral or written communications are the norm in the foreign market there may be scope for you to assist distributors and their staff to enhance their effective communication skills (to whatever extent language is not a barrier to you).
- **Sales administration**. In this area, you can assist by recommending entire sales force control systems designed to measure activity and results in key result areas (those that *really* make a difference to results achieved). This might include daily report systems, customer record cards, order forms, order processing paperwork, etc.
- **Journey planning.** Last but often most important is the need to introduce a formal journey planning system in order to maximize productivity. This aspect of sales management and planning is often a fundamental weakness in smaller sales

organizations, and therefore I strongly recommend that you help distributors plan their field workloads where you have a chance. They will appreciate any direct cost saving from better use of their scarcest resource (trained salespersons) and also the greater order inflow that usually results from more efficient operations.

Sales management

- **Designing and implementing promotional programmes.** If you expect a distributor to prepare and present annual marketing plans and promotional programmes, then you must assist them through advice, assistance and training.
- **Sales planning and forecasting.** Many distributors, especially in smaller or less developed markets, do very little forecasting, other than taking a view on what overall turnover level and profit they might target for. Usually, little thought is given to the forecasting of individual brands or market sectors. Assistance and training that help them refine their approaches to planning will benefit them and their other principals.
- **Territory organization and management.** All of us who have made our living by selling round the world express constant surprise at the general lack of professionalism and sophistication in planning sales territory workloads and activities, with the result that sales productivity is usually well below its potential. This is an area where your experience may help improve productivity and sales force morale and achievements.
- **Design and use of effective information systems.** Your own organization probably has a wealth of experience in systems and data processing management. If any of this is relevant and transferable to your distributors to help them control and monitor the performance of their own businesses then this will have direct

spin-off benefit to your own company. Financial and stock and order controls are often particularly weak in smaller distributor organizations. Wherever possible it will be to your advantage to link the distributors' sales reporting and performance measurement formats to your own systems for ease of comprehension and collation when market performance data are reported back to you. There may be scope for you to assist with data processing systems or recommending software compatible with your own.
- **Conducting sales meetings.** Quite apart from your occasional participation in sales meetings when in the foreign market, you might well be able to help train the local sales manager in structuring and running effective meetings that provide motivation, training and involvement of the distributor sales team. All too frequently in my own travels I have found distributor sales meetings run autocratically, with management issuing instructions without inviting participation.
- **Effective participation in exhibitions.** If your distributors are involved in local exhibitions to promote your products to the target market sectors, then you will benefit both by training them in effective exhibition participation and by providing direct support through your own attendance.
- **People management skills.** This heading includes: selection, appraisal, counselling, discipline, motivation, rewards and incentives. Management cultures differ round the world. In many developing nations in particular a wider gap is perceived between the bosses and the workers, and management styles may differ from those you are used to. You cannot change a culture in a visit, but by training, little and often, you may be able to influence styles over the longer term, resulting in a more self-reliant, motivated and productive workforce than one that is just task oriented.

Training can be fun and rewarding when you see individuals increase in self-confidence and personal performance. It may be a more lasting and valuable use of your time than sitting in meetings that focus on dealing with administrative and operational matters, such as shipping problems. You will need to balance your workload whilst visiting markets. If you are marketing industrial products or selling against major tenders then much of your personal workload will involve assisting agents and distributors actually achieve the sale. But if your products are a consumable or durable product for broader distribution through wholesale and retail outlets then your workload may benefit from placing more emphasis on training distributors than on being out doing their job for them.

Field training

As every field sales manager knows, training in the artificial environment of the office or training school is no substitute for coaching in the field sales environment. If language is not a barrier to you then you can advantageously supplement your basic training programme with field training and counselling, with the objectives of:

- imparting product knowledge
- improving personal selling skills
- improving understanding of buyer motivations
- increasing adaptability to differing sales situations
- developing administrative and organizational skills
- developing positive attitudes, to selling, to your company and to its products.

When conducting field training an essential preliminary activity is to spend some time working with managers and salespersons to assess the present levels of skills, identify any cultural practices of the foreign marketplace, and then to decide on the training priorities. You might choose to address training to any of the following key result areas.

Functional activities

Here you would identify the key functional activities of the distributor's sales team and form a view of the strengths and weaknesses, directing your attention to those that are key result areas and where you can effect improvement in performance, e.g.:

- **Use of time.** Time is our one irreplaceable resource in selling, and it is essential that the maximum amount of time in any market is spent in direct contact with customers or planning the presentations.
- **Preparation.** Sales aids, samples, literature, appointments, presentation strategies, and so on don't just happen by chance, but involve thorough preparation and planning. This activity is found by many an international marketer to be a major weakness within the sales teams of his foreign distributors.
- **Selling sequence.** Does the salesperson operate to a structured system or sequence in presenting the products? If not could a logical one be developed?
- **Call rate.** A busy salesperson is often not an effective salesperson, especially when it comes to call rate. Poor journey planning, calling back to collect money or searching for elusive buyers, or too much time visiting the office to sort out queries more efficiently processed by clerical support staff, all reduce the time available for direct customer contact. The export marketer can help the distributor analyse the use of time and improve on it.
- **Conversion rate.** The conversion rate of calls to orders is a function of effective personal selling skills and optimum use of time on a planned journey schedule. This is an area where the export marketer may make an impact through sales training.
- **Administration.** If the administrative systems are not right – either too cumbersome (asking for the recording of

irrelevant information) or not monitoring the key selling activities or providing a measurement of performance – then assistance in designing an appropriate system of control will be appreciated.

Sales techniques

To assess training needs under this category you would dissect the selling process of the distributor's sales team, retaining the good parts and rebuilding through training to overcome areas of weakness. Of course any training has spin-off benefit for all the other product lines being represented by the distributor, but your concern is to boost sales of your own products through increased sales professionalism. Some areas to look at are:

- **Pre-call planning**. Whilst this has been touched on before, it is such an important part of the selling process, particularly when calling on major accounts, that it bears repetition here. If you find your distributor's sales force weak in this area, your own expertise will greatly enhance their performance through training.
- **Preparation**. Once the basic planning is done, the call strategy decided on, and all the relevant data prepared, the final preparation stage is to book the appointment and prepare the sales literature and samples. It is always embarrassing to arrive at a call with a distributor's salesperson and find they do not have the right materials with them. So instil the discipline of checking preparation.
- **Face to face selling**. Once you are working in the field with distributor salespersons you will form views of strengths and weaknesses in the face-to-face selling situation, and be able to gear training to areas needing improvement, with a chance to make personal demonstrations and to practice.
- **Objection handling.** Objections do not go away, but just get bigger (in the eyes

of the buyer) if not answered satisfactorily. So if this is found to be a sales team weakness a basic training programme can be developed to tackle it through a school or field learning situation. Often the problem in foreign markets is that the distributor's sales team have insufficient product knowledge to answer questions fundamental to the buying process.
- **Closing techniques**. There are some cultural differences between international markets on approaches to closing the sale. Basic closing principles apply universally, and may not all be known in any formal way within your distributor's sales team. You will need to understand the culture to see which closing methods are better suited to the environment ('fear', 'positive', 'alternative', 'concession', 'assumptive', and so on).
- **Post-call follow-up**. Are the salesperson and the distributor geared to make the correct post-call follow-up, such as placing the order with your company, and ensuring that all commitments to the buyer (such as special order requirements, delivery times, modifications) are communicated to you and agreeable? Weaknesses can be addressed and perhaps some control systems developed.

Organization

How the distributor is organized, in terms both of formal organizational structure and systems and procedures, may be an area in which discussion and training could improve the effectiveness or productivity of the distributor's operations. You may be able to assist in designing and implementing improved systems.

Attitudes

If the attitudes within the distributor's management are wrong you will have an uphill task to change them, but it will become easier as you gain in credibility. If there are attitudinal problems within the distributor's sales team, you will have to communicate that to the management and work out a programme to address the issues. Negativity will affect all the product lines they represent and make it easier for competitors to penetrate the marketplace.

A framework for training _____

When it comes to any form of management or sales training it is always better to work within a structured framework that will serve to concentrate your own efforts and attention. For example, if you are planning field work with a distributor's salesperson with a view to giving some training in some of the areas previously discussed, then a framework could be:

- relax the salesperson to your presence
- observe performance in initial sales calls
- identify training needs
- assess current skill levels
- concentrate on priorities
- provide corrective training (discussion, demonstration, explanation, practice, consolidation)
- review different techniques (through example and discussion)
- obtain agreement and acceptance of the benefits of change to the new method
- encourage practical application in actual sales calls
- provide feedback (encouragement) to the trainee on their progress
- maintain contact with the trainee wherever possible to provide support and counselling
- maintain progress records if you are going to have regular contact with the trainee (or encourage the distributor's management to keep a training record).

Some of the discussion points in this review of training may propose a greater priority for training than you are used to when operating in foreign markets. But the time spent on planning, and the funds allocated to marketing and promotional activity, may prove poor investments if the people at the sharp end – the sales team – do not have sufficiently developed skills to turn opportunities into orders.

Contact reports – further pointers ▰▰▰▰▰▰▰▰

The last chapter made some reference to using a system of contact reports after market visits to summarize activities, discussions, agreements and points for further action. We can develop a discussion of the role and use of contact reports by the export marketer here.

Contact reports are basically a way of keeping a formal record of:

- your observations
- available market research and evaluations
- contacts made in the market
- discussions held (with agents, distributors, prospects, customers, and other parties)
- agreements reached
- marketing programmes agreed
- action plans and points requiring further action.

Contact report coverage _____

The style and format of your contact reports will depend in part on the activities you are expected to fulfil when on foreign market visits, and the reporting requirements within your own organization. Some of the topics you may want to consider addressing might include:

- overall summary of visit objectives, conclusions and agreements reached
- market developments:
  - changes in regulations
  - new product opportunities
  - economic trends and trading environment
- the distributor or agent:
  - organization and structure
  - management strengths and development needs

- administrative systems and controls
- order systems, stock control and levels
- distribution systems (efficiency, suitability for needs of the business and products)
- financial and sales performance
- financial resources for current and future needs
- training of salespersons, sub-distributors/dealers
- selection and evaluation of sub-distributors/dealers
- local pricing policies and profit margins
- advertising/public relations activity
- information systems
- ability to meet growth needs
- The sub-distributors/dealers:
  - locations and new location needs
  - individual site/sub-distributor performance
  - quality, commitment of resources and effort
- Competitive activity:
  - product ranges and changes
  - pricing policies
  - marketing programmes
  - distribution achievements
- Longer term market development plans:
  - overall objectives
  - resource capabilities
  - performance forecast (sales, profit, etc.)
  - supporting marketing and promotional activity
- Other contacts made:
  - purpose of meeting
  - conclusions and agreements
  - further action needed
- Other market information.

The format of a contact report need only be very simple, but it should clearly draw attention to key subject matter and points for further action, with a note of the person responsible for taking that action. Ideally the report should be presented in such a way that most of it, say the earlier pages, can be copied to the distributor for their informa-tion and action. You might keep any confidential commentary for the later pages, not to be copied to the distributor. You may prefer to draw up a standard contact report format, for word processing (see Figure 6.2), that provides a consistency in style for the recipients to recognize and adapt to, as well as some flexibility in layout.

Complex tables or copies of regulations are often better attached as appendices, so as not to distract from the body of the report and conclusions.

Problems in managing agents and distributors

Many export marketers complain about problems in managing their foreign representatives – that they are not motivated, not hungry, look for easy ways to make money rather than developing a market for good sound products, and so on. Without doubt there are problems in managing distributors and agents, but I would encourage you to develop a relationship where each of you sees the other as a partner in the market place, growing or stagnating together.

Many of the potential problems should be identified early in discussions, and addressed in an agency or distributor agreement that clearly states the rights, duties and responsibilities of each of the parties (see Chapter 8). That aside, we should just pause for a moment to note fundamental problems often not easily addressed in any formal document. The typical problems in managing agents and distributors include:

- lack of direct control
- diversity of products represented
- conflicting pressures from other principals
- limited resources (time, money and skills)
- lower levels of management and sales skills
- different motivations and objectives of the exporter and his agents or distributors

CONTACT REPORT	

To: *Export Sales Director*

Copies:
Distributor – Singapore
Technical Services Manager
Shipping Manager

Visit to: Singapore

From: *J. Adams.*

Date: *1st June 19–*

18th–25th May 19–

	Action
Visit objectives: 1 To introduce the hotel ware range of cutlery and bone china to Singapore Airlines. 2 To assist the distributor man the stand at the Asean Hotel & Catering Exhibition. 3 To re-negotiate minimum stock holding levels and ordering policies. 4 To prepare the first draft of the 199 – market plan. **Conclusions/agreements:** (i) The distributor agrees to maintain minimum stock cover of 100 place settings of each of the five main lines and to build a new key site display stand to exhibit the whole range in his new showroom on Orchard Road. (ii) Singapore Airlines have agreed to study samples of the Stratford traditional range in their flight training schools, and have requested a quote on 5000 settings. **Market development:** (a) The local economic growth is still projected through the 1990s to be in high single figures. Tourism also has experienced a boom, up 5% on last year, and is projected to continue with a new influx from Europe as a result of cheaper air fares and more airlines running cheap stop-over breaks. Five new first class hotels are on stream to open in the next twelve months, giving another 800 beds. (b) The Japanese are opening up a new hotel ware plant in Indonesia to offer cheaper products into Asean markets. **Distributor meetings:** . . . . **Other contacts made:**	

Figure 6.2 Contact report

- difficulty in accessing data and obtaining compliance with information requests
- remote control management.

Lack of direct control

The agent or distributor is an independent business, quite often owned by a local entrepreneur with a level of wealth that gives him the independence not to want, need or respond to unwelcome pressures. They will probably be representing quite a range of other principals, and will have developed their own style of operating. Interference from yourself may not be welcomed or appreciated, so you have to develop an approach to management that encourages the distributor to want and invite your input.

Their management and sales team are not under your direct control, and you will not have rights to issue instructions to them. That often puts a lot of stress on international marketers newly transferred from a domestic sales or marketing management environment where they controlled the activities of subordinate salespersons directly.

Diversity of products represented

As the principal supplying through an agent or distributor you will normally have a very narrow product range targeted to a specific market sector. Your representative, in comparison, will usually have to sell a vast range acting rather like a wholesaler in the domestic market, in order to make a comfortable living.

The diversity of products represented (often aimed at very different market sectors) strains the distributor's resources (financial, physical including storage, and human). Each product has its own merits and potential customers, yet the salespersons charged with representing the products have insufficient product knowledge and other relevant expertise to represent adequately the products to the buyers.

Where a distributor does specialize in a particular product line, they will normally represent several ranges that appear conflicting to some of the principals (although the representative will argue that they need to cater for each category of the market: high and low quality, high and low price, low technology and high technology, exclusive and non-exclusive).

The problem of your distributor or agent carrying too diverse a product range will not go away: you will probably have to tackle it by winning more sales time and attention through your personal presence, training and motivational skills, or by considering the alternatives (if sales volumes and margins warrant it) of setting up a branch sales office or other locally based exclusive representation.

Conflicting pressures from other suppliers

In addition to the diversity of the product range limiting the time and expertise available for promoting your products, when you are not in the market motivating, selling and promoting (and sometimes even when you are in the market) other principals will be there pushing their products, demanding more planning and action, providing their own product knowledge training, and generally distracting attention away from all the efforts and benefits of your own trip.

You cannot fight this problem; every manufacturer is entitled to his day in the marketplace, and to develop his own plans, programmes, systems and sales efforts with the distributor. I normally recommend the approach of *little and often*, shorter and more frequent visits to maintain momentum are often better than the once a year longer visit; but this approach must be balanced against the travel costs and importance of each market.

Limited resources

Your demands upon the distributor may require more resources than he either has, or can, make available.

You may believe that your products would prosper better if the distributor set up a special department to work on your sales full time, without the distractions of a multitude of other agency lines; but they may prefer to balance the time allocated to each line, ensuring that each of their sales team sells across the range, always bringing in an order for something, and not commit to an exclusive sales department.

Your assessment of market potential, and your proposed marketing plans, might specify certain allocations of funds to finance goods and trade credit, but the distributors might simply not be willing to commit sufficient funds to you, either because they do not have the resources, or because they have alternative uses that they think offer a better investment.

Levels of skills and motivation _____

It is likely that within your chosen agent or distributor organization you perceive a lower level of **sales** and **management skills** and **personal motivation** than you might desire. We have discussed at length how you might help through training (possibly even bringing key personnel to your own company for specific training), but even if you are willing to assist the local level of talent, formal education and business sophistication may be a limiting resource in many developing markets, possibly serving as a restriction to your market growth.

Possibly, the entrepreneur or managers running the distribution operation lack your commitment and motivation, having other sources of income perhaps, or simply being too laid back to respond to pressure.

Different motivations of the parties _____

The exporter, often a larger and more sophisticated company than his agents or distributors, usually explains his objectives for a market in such marketing jargon terms as: increased market share, greater brand awareness, broader distribution, growing sales volumes. However, the distributor may have quite a different range of objectives for his business. Because he rarely has full trust in his principals not to remove the agency or distribution rights from his company, he is often concerned with maximizing short term profit from his business, and spreading his risks. He works hard to control costs, often, in his principals' views, resisting investing in opportunities to expand sales and distribution of their products. Often he will seek new sole agency products or sole distribution rights as a way of spreading risk and increasing sales rather than building existing ranges further through aggressive proactive marketing. The differences in focus of exporter and

Table 6.1 *Typical exporter and distributor focus of objectives*

Exporter's focus of objectives	Agent/distributor's focus of objectives
• Volume • Market share • Distribution • Brand awareness	• Profit • Cost control • Security of tenure • Risk spreading

distributors' objectives might be illustrated as in Table 6.1.

We should avoid becoming cynics and look for ways to bring the objectives of exporter and his distributor closer. We will do this by adding value to the agent or distributor's business, and helping him achieve his objectives for his business, which will assist us achieve our objectives for our business in the market. A model for motivating agents and distributors is illustrated in a later section of this chapter.

Difficulty in obtaining information _____

One of the most frequent complaints from exporters is the difficulty of obtaining timely and meaningful information and reports from their agents and distributors. This ongoing problem will only be alleviated when the agent or distributor sees personal benefit to himself, rather than just a contractual compliance with a principal's agreement, from the supply of information. To the distributor, supplying information that he does not need or use in managing and monitoring his business is just a cost and a disruption of his management activities.

As a starting point, at the stage of negotiating an agency or distribution agreement all information requirements should be clarified, and their use both to the exporter and his agent or distributor explained. Thereafter, whenever reports are provided by the agent or distributor the exporter should reciprocate by returning any meaningful analysis, and showing how the data can be

A case example – changing the style of market management

A major United Kingdom exporter of consumer products, with world-wide distribution of brand name products, traditionally pursued an '**ambassadorial approach'** to foreign market management in most markets.

Marketing programmes and activities were planned, and often implemented and controlled from the corporate centre, through specialist marketers. The export marketers were charged with country management responsibilities and provided the main interface with the network of foreign market distributors. Market visit activity centred around the distributor's offices, with a focus on overall macro market planning and in building relationships with the key people.

Senior management believed that they should move towards a more '**hands-on'** style of management of market distribution. This would mean a major change in the export market managers' attitudes and skills. The starting point was to undertake a detailed audit to clarify how market management of distributors was currently being conducted by the team (of more than twenty) market managers. This was related to both their job descriptions and to 'best practice' as defined by the audit team (external consultants).

It became apparent to senior management that, whilst they had good marketing knowledge of their markets (where data could be obtained) on aspects such as market segments, consumer preferences and behaviour, market share, pricing and product positioning, etc., they had limited experience of distribution channel management and the distribution activities of most distributors. Many distributors were reluctant to provide market reports (where they had data available) showing product sales by trade channel or customer, and in most cases their distributor companies' systems and sales force operations were not open to study by the principal. Micro level activity in the markets was inadequately monitored and managed.

Apart from skill deficiencies the audit identified that the export marketers, whilst generally competent, felt at a disadvantage to many of their distributors, who were rich local entrepreneurs – they did not see what role they could fill in adding value to the distributors' businesses. They recognized that their own (company) objectives often were not in line with the objectives of individual distributors.

The key skill areas identified and included in a development programme were: developing market strategies; market planning (including breaking a macro level market plan down to micro levels for implementation); sales forecasting; setting sales objectives; key account planning; developing appropriate local market trade terms; managing distributor relations (including selecting and auditing distributors); negotiating with, and providing feedback to, distributors; distributor performance monitoring controls and performance standards; planning market outlet coverage (including building an outlet database, classifying outlets by trade sectors, prioritizing outlets, sales journey coverage planning, prospecting); organizing and structuring a distributor's local sales team; administration and control in a field sales force; field sales management and sales team training techniques; planning, organizing, implementing local sales promotion activity.

Because the audit was conducted with the full co-operation of the export marketers a positive attitude was soon developed towards a series of skill development modules that were designed and conducted over a two year period. Each participant left with a development module with several personal objectives for change-creating activity in foreign markets.

The export marketers now recognized that they had a whole new portfolio of ideas and knowledge to draw from when visiting markets, and had no trouble to identify in each market a range of value-adding opportunities where their skills and knowledge would enable them to be come involved with distributors in a more hands-on way.

- In one market a major study of the potential outlet universe was conducted, which showed weaknesses in outlet coverage, and enabled the distributor to re-deploy sales resources, expand the sales force, and increase sales across much of his product portfolio.
- In another market a study of the share of business through different sizes and types of outlets showed that inadequate resources were being allocated to key account management, and that the distributor was under-performing (relevant to the accounts' share of the product category) with several key accounts.
- A distributor stock analysis for one market showed that stocks of major brands were occasionally running so low that available stocks were effectively being rationed until the next shipment arrived. The result was that distributor sales were below potential for the products, and sales/profits were being lost to competitive products.

As distributors saw benefits from a variety of change-creating projects accruing both to the principal's business in the markets, but also across their broader portfolio of products, so they became more co-operative in sharing market information and involving the export marketers in local market planning and management. Relationships improved further as distributors saw their own objectives being addressed.

The export marketers were encouraged to plan value-adding market visit objectives (with distributors) before visits, to avoid falling into the scenario that most of a trip is spent dealing with problems rather than dealing with forward planning. They were also encouraged to network with each other to promote the transfer of experience and best practice. They, in turn, now encouraged their distributors also to network and to learn from each other's market experiences.

The entire focus of the team of export marketers moved towards a proactive hands-on style of distributor management, with the recognition that by seeking to add value to their distributors' businesses they would add value to their own business in the markets, and gain additional growth in relation to competition.

used in better managing (i.e. in planning or monitoring performance) the distributor's or agent's own business against his own objectives.

Remote control management

You are trying to manage your business through agents and distributors, over which you have no direct control and which are remote from you. No matter how close your markets are to your own centre of operations, either geographically (i.e. in Europe) or culturally (i.e. in English speaking markets) they are still at a physical or psychological distance. There is no easy solution to this. The main approaches to reducing this problem in distributor management are:

- frequency of contact, through visits, telephone contact, etc.
- closeness of involvement of the distributor or agent in the exporter's planning and decision making processes (the **partnership** approach).

The agent or distributor must **feel** that he is part of your team, and that means the export marketer must do a lot more than just pay lip service to a team partnership but demonstrate partnership at every opportunity through involvement, consul-

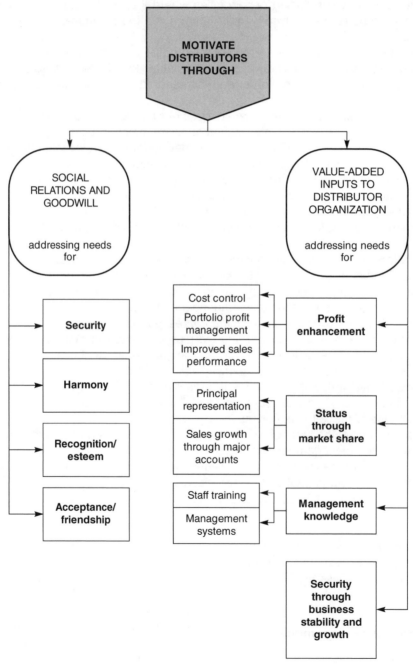

Figure 6.3 *A motivational model for distributors*

tation, frequent two-way communication and meaningful feedback.

Whichever of these problems you encounter within your distributor network, you will often be stretching your skills and experience in the effort to maintain motivation and momentum. But commitment, enthusiasm, effort and persistence will bring their rewards and respect from your agents and distributors.

The motivational model

When the issues and problems of managing agents and distributors are recognized what can we do that represents positive motivation? The traditional route to motivation was what may be termed **'ambassadorial'** representation, by which I mean that the export marketer would travel round his markets, often to fairly set schedules, and spend a few hours or days addressing problems (often the distributor would have collected a file of shipping and operational problems arising since the last visit), meeting a few selected customers, and socializing with the distributor or agent. Forward market planning would often arise on the agenda, but often just covering macro overall market planning points, mainly with the agent or distributor left to develop and implement the micro level plans, strategies and tactics that would make things happen within the local sales and marketing team. The net result of this reliance on the agent or distributor's goodwill to make things happen would often be that a disappointed export marketer would return to the market a few months later with little of what he expected to happen having been converted to reality. This situation may have arisen because the distributor failed to see the benefit to him of implementing the exporter's marketing and sales plans and strategies and did not do the things discussed, or simply that another principal arrived in the market soon after your visit and became the 'flavour of the moment', getting all the attention and activity.

To develop an approach to positive motivation we must look back at Table 6.1 highlighting the objectives of the distributor for his business. Relying on goodwill and good social relations for motivation in dealing with the agent or distributor will not satisfy all his needs or business objectives, but may make him feel more secure. Look for ways to **add value to your relationship** through activities and inputs that address his (your agent's or distributor's) focus of objectives, such as profit generation, cost control, risk spreading, and any other points particularly applicable to any distributor.

Good social relations between an export marketer and his distributors are important. But more lasting will be the appreciation for the ways you add value to the distributor's or agent's business by helping achieve his business objectives through his product portfolio in general and through your product range in particular (see Figure 6.3).

Checklist 6.1
Studies/discussions in the market

Action points

1 **Distributor's current management organization/structure to cope with business and development plans:**

- Current organization structure
- Developing organization structure
- Key personnel:
  - qualifications/experience
  - management development
- Staffing levels
- Efficiency/performance

2 **Distributor's systems and controls:**

- Inventory controls
- Sales information
  - by product
  - totals
  - sub-distributor/dealer
- Accounting/financial records
  - debtor/creditor control
  - profit and loss accounts
  - balance sheets
  - costs of operations
  - marketing
  - warehousing
  - distribution
  - administration

3 **Distributor's ordering systems and distribution facilities:**

- Optimum location
- Handling, storage, stock rotation
- Picking/packing systems
- Stock levels
- Ordering procedures
- System of distribution planning
- Capacity for growth
- General efficiency

Checklist 6.1 *(Continued)*

	Action points

4 Competitive activity

- Names
- Locations
- Ownership
- Resources
- Pricing policy/structures
- Total market size
- Company/distributor share

5 Distributor long range (5 year) plans:

- Assumptions/parameters
- Timetable of implementation
- Relationship to company plan
- Resource requirements to achieve plan
    - financial
    - physical
    - management/staffing

6 Financial performance of distributor:

- Copies of audited accounts
- Sources of expansionary funds
- Cash flow projections
- Monthly sales figures

Financial performance of sub-distributors:

- Accounts
- Profitability
- Expansion plans
- Monthly sales

7 Current and future ability to train local sub-distributors/ dealers:

- Training facilities
- Training programmes
- Technical training
- Management development

8 Local identification of sub-distributors/dealers:

- Quality control over selection
- Locations
- Identification and evaluation

Checklist 6.1 (*Continued*)

	Action points

9 Local pricing structures:
 	
● Pricing policies
● Distributor margins/costs
● Sub-distributor and dealer margins/costs
● Competitive pricing
● Import duties, local sales taxes, etc.
 	
10 Marketing/advertising activity programme:
 	
● Agencies
● Budgets
● Annual plans
● Support needs
  – materials
  – information
  – company visits
 	
11 Company information reporting requirements from distributors:
 	
● Accounts
● Sales performance (monthly)
● Stock levels (monthly)
● Forward ordering
● Annual plans
 	
12 Support provided by the company:
 	
● Training
● Technical assistance
● Market visit support
● Promotional literature
● Preparing marketing plans	

Checklist 6.2
Distributor training programme

	Action points
Training areas:	

- Product knowledge
- Company and market knowledge
- Basic selling skills
- Designing and implementing promotional programmes
- Sales planning and forecasting
- Territory organization and management
- Design and use of effective information systems
- Conducting sales meetings
- Effective participation in exhibitions
- People management skills

Link the distributors' sales reporting and perform-ance measurement formats to your own systems for ease of comprehension

Develop a sales training programme covering:

- Basic training
  - *Company knowledge*
    - History
    - Organization
    - Objectives
    - Management philosophies and style
  - *Product knowledge*
    - Historical development
    - Production
    - Product range features and benefits
    - Competitors' products
    - Marketing programmes
  - *Developing a sales sequence*
  - *Professional selling skills*
  - *Use of sales aids*
  - *Communicating effectively*
  - *Sales administration*
  - *Journey planning*

Checklist 6.2 *(Continued)*

	Action points

• **Field training**
  • *Set objectives*
    – Imparting product knowledge
    – Improving personal selling skills
    – Improving understanding of buyer motivations
    – Increasing adaptability
    – Developing administration and organizational skills
  • *Training stages*
    – Discussion
    – Demonstration
    – Explanation
    – Practice
    – Consolidation
  • *Assess training needs*
  Address training to any of the key result areas of:
    – Functional activities
    – Sales techniques
    – Organization
    – Attitudes	

Checklist 6.3
Typical contact report coverage

	Action points

Overall summary of visit objectives and agreements reached

Market developments
- Changes in regulations concerning products
- New product opportunities

The distributor
- Organization and structure
- Management strengths and development needs
- Administrative systems and controls
- Order systems, stock control and levels
- Distribution systems (efficiency, suitability for needs)
- Financial and sales performance
- Financial resources for current and future needs
- Training of sub-distributors/dealers and field support
- Selection and evaluation of sub-distributors
- Local pricing and margins
- Advertising/public relations activity
- Information systems
- Ability to meet growth needs and handle local production

The sub-distributors
- Locations and new location needs
- Individual site/sub-distributor performance
- Quality
- Commitment of personal resources and personal effort

Planning
- Review of performance against longer term plan
- Overall objectives
- Resource capabilities
- Performance forecast (sales, profit, etc.).
- (The detailed plan would comprise a separate document)

Competitive activity
- Updating on their plans, products, activities, etc.

Other contacts made:
- Purpose of meeting
- Conclusions and agreements
- Further action needed

Other market information

7

Auditing agents and distributors _____

 In this chapter we will:

- look at the main reasons why we should develop a more formalized approach to conducting a marketing audit of the performance of agents and distributors in major or worthwhile markets
- develop a model audit format.

The aim is to promote a more thorough approach to making inter-market comparisons between the performances of varied agents and distributors.

Many an exporter is heard to complain about his agents or distributors. In essence what he is saying is that they are not doing the job as he sees it, or that they are not achieving the performance results he thinks can be obtained in the market. At the other extreme is the export marketer who is perfectly satisfied with his agent or distributor, and claims he has 'the best representation in the market', often without any rational evidence but an emotional attachment built through strong social relations with his representative. Many of us have been in the position of not being too sure how good our agent or distributor is, either in terms of obtaining the best results with our products or versus other agents or distributors in the market.

One approach is to develop a system of **auditing** agents and distributors, rather as we would appraise our subordinates in the company, or in the way major marketing companies (both in consumer and industrial product categories) review their advertising agents – where they periodically put the brands up for competitive advertising strategy submissions from invited agencies in order to see who best turns the marketing strategy into a supporting communication strategy. I am not suggesting that we have a hire-or-fire approach with agents and distributors; that is neither practical nor desirable – terminating an agreement can be very costly and disruptive. But good management practice would suggest we should define what we expect from an agent or distributor and monitor performance in a disciplined and thorough way.

Why conduct an audit?

The main reasons why an export marketer might want to audit his agent's or distributor's performance on an ongoing basis are:

- to ensure that you are clear on your key result areas for the market and the distributor's achievement against these and related goals and objectives
- to measure performance in both the short and longer term against agreed standards relating to the distribution of your company products in the market

- to assess the distributor's ability to represent you in the required manner to the trade, in terms of physical distribution and trade relations, and market coverage
- to assess the distributor's ability to commit and provide the requisite human, physical and financial resources needed

Case examples – distributor audits

1. Major international soft drink licensors conduct forms of periodic marketing audits of their licensed bottlers.

2. Most major international franchisors (such as in fast foods, printing, and personal care products) have market audit systems whereby they will attempt to quantify and qualify a franchisee's performance against their assessment of his potential.

3. International licensors of industrial products will frequently have systems of auditing their licensees (again, not just financial audits to check that royalties are being calculated correctly and paid according to agreed terms). They may develop a marketing audit system to see if the licensee is developing the market in line with its potential (a normal clause within a licence agreement). Their concern is to ensure that sales are developed to increase their revenues and market penetration or share. They will want to avoid a situation where a licensee fails to develop a licensed product or service to its potential because he has other (possibly conflicting) interests (for example, he may have developed an alternative own product that he prefers to develop).

4. A few major companies with international networks of distributors (both in industrial products and consumer goods) have developed formal systems of making inter-market comparisons of distributor effectiveness. The objective is normally to ensure that action is taken to improve a weaker distributor to acceptable standards or to take decisions to change market representations (where that is a practical alternative). Whilst some companies will treat the audit as an independent activity as part of periodic distribution reviews, others incorporate it into the annual market planning process, and expect the export marketers to include in market planning documents a detailed distributor SWOT (strengths, weaknesses, opportunities, threats) analysis for each distributor. Action plans can then be made to address deficiencies.

to support your company products and market plans

- to compare the performance of your company distributor versus distributors of competitive products.
- to establish if the distributor is anticipating and adapting to changing market needs of both users/consumers and trade channels.

Ideally some external benchmarks should be identified when developing an audit so that meaningful comparative performance measures can be made over time. For example, a distributor's performance against any published market data (such as Nielsen data in many consumer goods markets, or share of imports for the product category for both consumer goods and industrial goods) may be assessed. Where any data is available on competitor product distribution or usage this may be useful as a benchmark over time.

Distributor audit measures ■■■■

An audit format can be either formalized using a standard form designed to suit your own products and markets, or it can be individually structured for each market. Whichever approach you prefer you are likely to want to include a range of **quantitative** measures and **qualitative** measures.

Quantitative measures _____

The main quantitative measures to cover in an audit of an agent or distributor are:

- agent's or distributor's turnover and share of market for your products
- your company turnover and performance against budget
  - overall
  - by brand/product
- product or brand distribution by trade channel
- key account share of trade
- coverage of the outlet or user base in the market

- stock management
  - management of own stocks for a distributor
  - management of users'/customers' stocks for an agent
- comparative performance versus competitors
  - respective turnovers, where known
  - respective market shares
  - respective distribution through the outlet or user base.

Qualitative measures _____

The main qualitative factors that should be included in an audit are:

- human resource factors
- trade relations
- marketing and sales planning
- sales activity
- communications
- facilities and systems.

These are expanded on in the **model audit form** following.

A model audit format ■■■■

A simple **audit format** can be designed (see Figure 7.1) to suit the key criteria relevant to the needs of each company. The following example illustrates a typical layout for a multi-products company, selling through several trade channels with a handful of major key accounts in the market.

How the form is used or its design modified will depend on whether the products are consumer or industrial products. If we look at the section to monitor performance through various trade channels, then, for example:

- consumer food products' trade channels might include hypermarkets/ supermarkets, convenience stores, small (neighbourhood) grocery outlets, restaurants, etc.

DISTRIBUTOR AUDIT		Market: Distributor: Date:				
QUANTITATIVE MEASURES ╲ Year	200–	200–	200–	Rating	Comment
Distributor's turnover Company budget Company actual turnover Company percentage of budget Company share of distributor's turnover					
Distributor's share of market (or share of category imports)					

Product performance
 	
Product 1
  Budget
  Actual turnover
  % budget
Product 2
  Budget
  Actual turnover
  % budget
Product 3
  Budget
  Actual turnover
  % budget
Product 4
  Budget
  Actual turnover
  % budget
Product 5
  Budget
  Actual turnover
  % budget					

Figure 7.1 A model distributor audit format

DISTRIBUTOR AUDIT		Market: Distributor: Date:				
QUANTITATIVE MEASURES	Year	200–	200–	200–	Rating	Comment
Product distribution						
Trade channel 1 =						
Product 1						
Product 2						
Product 3						
Product 4						
Trade channel 2 =						
Product 1						
Product 2						
Product 3						
Product 4						
Trade channel 3 =						
Product 1						
Product 2						
Product 3						
Product 4						
Key account share of product category trade						
Account 1						
Account 2						
Account 3						
Account 4						
Account 5						
Outlet coverage						
Estimated total customer base						
Overall % coverage						
% Trade channel 1						
% Trade channel 2						
% Trade channel 3						
% Trade channel 4						
% Trade channel 5						
Stock management						

Figure 7.1 (Continued)

DISTRIBUTOR AUDIT	Market: Distributor: Date:	
QUALITATIVE MEASURES		

Strengths	Weaknesses	

	Rating	Comment
Human resource factors ● Management style ● Management and staff attitudes (to distributor, and each other) ● Management and staff receptivity and response to training and counselling ● Current management quality and skill levels in relation to the positions they fill, the local market levels and international levels ● Management and sales training, quality and quantity ● Succession planning ● Organization structure: its functioning and adaptability in relation to the needs of products, trade channels		
Trade relations ● Negotiating ● Key account relations ● Support to trade (e.g. wholesalers) ● Management control to trade credit terms ● Relations with competitors		

Figure 7.1 (Continued)

DISTRIBUTOR AUDIT	Market: Distributor: Date:	
QUALITATIVE MEASURES		
	Rating	**Comment**
Marketing and sales planning ● Sales planning and forecasting ● Controlling to plans ● Implementing plans ● Advertising and promotion planning ● PR and sponsorship development ● Use of information technology in performance monitoring and planning ● Sales records and data base		
Sales activity ● Key account management ● Outlet stock control ● Outlet coverage: 　– quality 　– frequency in relation to turnover ● Sales development ● Product merchandising ● Use of point of sales material ● Record keeping ● Use of data in planning ● Call management to objectives		
Communications ● Distributor internal communications: 　– formal 　– informal 　– written 　– meetings ● Reports to company: 　– quality/accuracy 　– timeliness in submission ● Trade communications		
Facilities ● Office premises ● Distribution premises and transport 　– main warehouse 　– branch warehouses ● Suitability and efficiency of systems		

Figure 7.1 (Continued)

- educational products' trade channels might include general stationery stores, bookstores, educational establishments (schools themselves as direct customers), education authorities with central purchasing departments
- electric switches trade channels might include electrical trade distributors, consumer do-it-yourself retailers, construction companies (buying direct and in bulk for projects)
- for production process control equipment or other industrial inputs, 'trade channels' as a heading might be altered to 'industry type', and include those industries where the control equipment or other industrial inputs could have a use, such as in the food industry, toiletries and cosmetics industry, household detergents and cleaners industry, and so on.

Coverage of customers might be measured either by trade channel or geographical sector, and should note the actual coverage measured against potential coverage (i.e. calling regularly on 500 customers out of a universe in the sector of 1000 gives a 50 per cent coverage factor). Measuring coverage of the potential universe is critical in most markets as experience shows most agents and distributors do not call on all potential outlets/users, and often do not have complete lists of the potential customer base.

The model form illustrated in Figure 7.1 only focuses attention on five products or brands from the exporter's portfolio, on the assumption that in most cases few products account for the majority of sales, turnover and profits. Similarly we would want to measure the agent's or distributor's performance through his top five to ten key accounts, who also are likely to represent much of our business through the agent or distributor.

Ideally the findings of your audit should be discussed with an agent or distributor, in order to promote open relations and develop an understanding of your expectations and judgements of achievements. Even if you are reluctant to communicate audit feedback it is still a useful internal exercise for the export marketer, and serves to focus attention objectively on the suitability and performance of foreign market representatives.

Further reading

Marketing – An Introductory Text. Martin Christopher and Malcolm McDonald (Macmillan 1995). Chapter 8: The Marketing Audit

8

Agency and distributor agreements _____

 In this chapter we will look at:

- typical alternative routes to obtaining market sales and distribution
- the coverage and range of clauses typically included in an export market agency or distribution agreement
- some guidelines for structuring agreements.

The aim is to encourage the export marketer to develop comprehensive commercial agreements for market representation as a better protection than having no agreement or a weak agreement, and to provide a framework for a proactive approach to management of the markets.

Alternative approaches to representation in foreign markets ▬▬▬

When it comes to getting products into distribution and use in foreign markets the main alternatives facing the exporter are:

- an exclusive sales and distribution agreement with an importer or distributor in the foreign market (who takes ownership and possession of goods for resale locally)
- representation by an independent agent in the foreign market, who will normally not accept the *del credere* (customer credit) risk for customers (and does not assume ownership or possession of the goods at any time) but will solicit orders

on behalf of the principal in exchange for an agreed agency commission, usually fixed on the basis of FOB or CIF prices
- encouraging potential overseas customers to place their orders through a confirming house or independent export company
- generating sales through a specialist export agent based in the home market, but who will travel to the foreign market soliciting orders in exchange for fees or commissions
- a network of branch offices to manage the exporter's own sales operations in each country, which may include working with other distributors
- a subsidiary company in the foreign market to handle total distribution operations

- entering a licensing arrangement whereby a foreign company (or possibly a joint venture) based in the market will undertake local manufacturing and distribution.

In each of these approaches to market entry and product distribution the agent or representative will need a good level of support from the supplier's own export department.

Some of these approaches to export marketing will be examined in more detail elsewhere in the text, and in this chapter we will concentrate on the matter more frequently of concern to export marketers – agreements with foreign representatives.

It is customary in export marketing to formalize marketing and distribution arrangements with a written agency or distributor agreement. This is often essential to establish the parameters within which the foreign representative will work. When having initial discussions with potential representatives in foreign markets, it is advisable to have a standard format of an agreement prepared, since this adds legitimacy to discussions surrounding terms of agreement. It is at this stage that international marketers become amateur lawyers, having to familiarise themselves with the guidelines of agency law in the countries under their control to ensure that each agreement will be enforceable and without illegitimate clauses.

Potential agents customarily request total market exclusivity, indicating that they only put their full efforts and abilities behind those products that they alone can represent. That may be a reasonable starting point for both parties. Intensive export marketing effort can often only be planned and achieved where there is a responsible and controlled agent or distributor who will competently manage promotional activities and provide full reports on marketing matters to the principal. Nowadays, however, most companies considered medium or large develop a structured export department to handle marketing, sales, shipping, production and financial planning, and they have a network of overseas distributors

managed from the home base or overseas branch offices.

A common practice for smaller exporters just getting started is simply to have a 'gentleman's agreement' with an agent or distributor giving them trial exclusivity for a period of, say, six or twelve months while they demonstrate their ability to develop sales. This approach, which can avoid you legal costs and possibly limit your legal commitment and obligations to the importer, is useful where it is acceptable within local agency laws or regulations (see later commentary on regulations within the European Union), and where it will not prejudice your rights in any way. Lawyers will normally advise against the 'gentleman's agreement' approach: it is normally advisable to tie up your points of agreement formally to minimize subsequent disputes or to provide a reference in seeking their solution. Even where there is no formal appointment there are occasions where agency may be implied by conduct or necessity. The agent or importer will expect you to honour your arrangement and produce a formal agreement at the appropriate time if he has performed satisfactorily.

Exclusive market distribution and sales agreements

This form of agreement will normally require that the seller grant the **distributor** a territorial sales exclusivity (possibly with other limitations) in respect of specific goods or services in return for an agreement from the buyer to use the seller as the sole source of supply of those goods and services. The contract may go beyond just representation, and have very specific performance clauses concerning minimum quantities of goods to be purchased and delivered over a specified time period.

Care must be taken that restrictive practice laws in the foreign market are not infringed by any terms and conditions in an exclusive agreement.

In an exclusive distribution agreement the seller is not concerned with the credit risk for a multiplicity of small customers in the foreign market, but in an exclusive agency agreement the exporter may still have this credit risk for customers indenting through the agent where the agent does not accept the credit risk.

Export distribution agreement ─────

Some smaller manufacturers may consider the best approach to their export ambitions is to appoint a domestic company specializing in export sales (an **export agent**) as their exclusive exporter. They may have an agreement that does not specify minimum sales requirements and, in fact, find it administratively easier to pass any export enquiries received directly to their export agent.

Export agents will usually pass on orders only to match firm sales, and do not carry stock. However, they will normally accept the credit risk for their own shipments and prepare all necessary export documentation. In that respect, export agents almost act like a division of the manufacturer, and they may make their profit either by receiving a commission on sales or by buying the goods on advantageous terms and adding their profit margin before billing the foreign customer at the marked-up price.

An export agent is unlikely to have any long-term expectation of security in his arrangement to represent a manufacturer, because the manufacturer will normally want to set up his own export department to administer exports once the volume justifies that expansion in resources.

Representation to regions and market sectors ─────────────────────────

It may sometimes be necessary to divide market representation either geographically or by market sector – for example, if no one distributor can successfully cover the whole country, or a distributor does not adequately cover certain market sectors such as governmental, military or institutional sales.

Although your contacts may request national distribution rights (or agency) for all market sectors you must evaluate their ability to perform satisfactorily in all regions of the country and to all the identifiable discrete trade or market sectors. Few distributors in foreign markets have the resources and sales network to supply, sell and provide any necessary after-sales service on a national level. Most have regional strengths or may only supply to some of the potential trade channels. Where you have doubts about this there are various options, as listed below.

- Appoint a main national distributor in the foreign market, but establish a network of local sub-distributors with proven strength in their locality of operation. There may be problems establishing territorial demarcation lines if they are given regional exclusivity, but it may not be necessary to confer territorial exclusivity. The main distributor would normally import the goods initially for redistribution onward through the distribution chain (see Figure 8.1(a)).
- Appoint a network of local distributors, each importing on their own account. Territorial demarcation lines are a potential problem to be overcome (see Figure 8.1(b)).
- Appoint a main national distributor or regional distributors but reserve certain types of outlet (such as government departments, multinational corporations with buying or distribution points outside the market) for coverage by your own direct export sales operation (see Figure 8.1(c), where reserved accounts are referred to as 'house accounts').
- Appoint a single agent or distributor, or a network to cover all geographical points of the market, but allocate clearly identifiable market sectors (see Figure 8.1(d)).

Clauses in exclusive agreements ▰▰▰▰▰

Before entering into any exclusive agency representation or distribution agreement, check the local laws that may be applicable to such agreements in the foreign market. The final agreement will identify the duties and responsibilities of the two parties – seller (the exporter, who is commonly referred to in export parlance as 'the principal') and agent or distributor – and also have clauses dealing with such matters as disputes and termination of the contract.

Some countries have agency laws that will give protection to agents, after termination of a contract, in respect of future commissions on business from customers introduced by them (see commentary in the later section of this chapter on European Union regulations). They may also protect an importer who has been required by a sole distribution agreement to make special investments in order to comply with aspects of the handling and distribution of the exporter's product. It is important to know what legal rights will attach to your appointment of an agent or distributor and subsequent agreement, and in some cases it may be acceptable for you to insert a clause limiting your liability to compensation.

At the end of this chapter Checklist 8.1 covers typical subjects and issues often requiring coverage in an agency or distribution agreement. There are probably as many different forms of agreement as there are lawyers, or so it seems to the lay person, but the key points essentially cover:

- product exclusivity and product range or extensions
- territorial exclusivity
- rights to supply other parties
- limitations to export to other territories
- method of quoting prices
- duties of the principal
- duties of agent/distributor
  - performance clauses
  - special storage, handling and packaging
- principal's right to accept or refuse orders
- market pricing and costing guidelines
- marketing programmes and planning
- promotional responsibilities and materials
- payment terms

- commission arrangements
- reporting/marketing information reports
- training of agent or distributor's personnel
- warranties
- indemnities
- limits of authority
- confidentiality clauses
- trade mark/patent protection
- dispute handling
- duration of the agreement
- assignability
- termination
- non-waiver clauses
- entire agreement clause
- force majeure clause
- applicable country for legal enforcement and interpretation.

A little thought to the special commercial requirements of your own products and markets will help you prepare a list of key points to incorporate in an agreement, and these can then provide the basis for discussion with a lawyer. The more thorough your own preparation, the lower you can expect accompanying legal charges to be. More importantly, preparing your own draft of commercial terms and conditions will help structure negotiations with prospective agents or distributors.

Since there can be such a range of clauses, both parties must have the intention of producing an equitable agreement in order to progress, and the agreement must be adapted to the trade practices and conditions in the foreign market.

Major issues to be covered in an agreement

Product exclusivity and product range or extensions

The contract should define the goods or specific range of products or brands that the buyer will have exclusive sales rights to represent in the territory. Sometimes this is included in an appendix to the agreement rather than in the body.

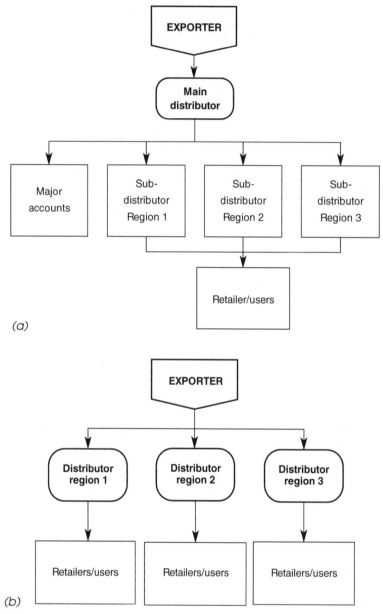

(a)

(b)

Figure 8.1 *Typical distribution chains. (a) Exporting through a main distributor. (b) Exporting through a network of regional distributors*

New product lines should be able to be added to the agreement under a 'range extension' clause.

The contract should give the manufacturer or exporter a 'get out' clause for any products he ceases to produce or offer in export markets so that the seller cannot be obligated to the buyer to produce small and unprofitable production runs. Also, you may prefer not to include any other brands manufactured and exported by your company (i.e. limit the agreement to products listed in an appendix), as you may expand with new product ranges (possible through acquisitions) that are more suited to different distribution arrangements.

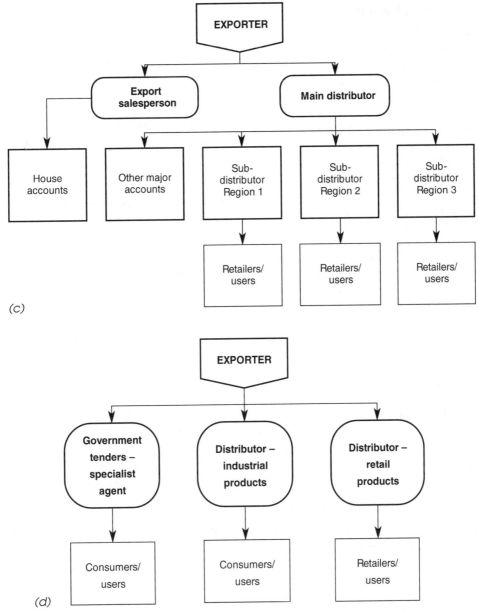

Figure 8.1 *(c) Exporting through a main distributor with house accounts serviced directly. (d) Exporting through different channels to different market sectors*

Territorial exclusivity

The geographical definition of the territory may consist of a region of the country (e.g. north-east United States), one entire country (e.g. Japan), or a collection of political units (e.g. the United Arab Emirates).

Future territorial extensions may be covered in the agreement if that is necessary or appropriate.

A mutual exclusivity binds the two parties to work together actively to build a mutually profitable business in the assigned market.

Rights to supply other parties

The seller's obligation not to by-pass the distributor and sell directly to any customers should be covered. The seller may wish to retain sales rights to certain accounts or institutions (e.g. government agencies or military establishments), but may still agree to pay a nominal commission on such 'house accounts'.

Any exclusions (e.g. NATO bases, or transnational corporations buying globally for units around the world) should be clearly identified (possibly listed in an appendix to the agreement) and understood.

In cases when the distributor cannot supply the market for any reason, which might include that he is in default of meeting payment terms to the principal or that a catastrophe affected his ability to physically distribute goods, the exporter might insert a clause retaining the right to make alternative supply arrangements. Typically it would reserve the right to make alternative arrangements, either by direct shipment or through other importers in the event the distributor fails to maintain supplies for more than thirty days. Certain reasons for a failure to maintain supplies might give cause to terminate an agreement.

Limitations to export to other territories

Any export rights from the defined territory can be addressed, as the buyer may wish to know if he can re-export to other markets or customers where he feels that he has an advantageous relationship. It may not be permissible under competition laws to restrict re-exports; on the other hand, if you have entered exclusive distribution rights in neighbouring territories you may not want parallel imports disrupting marketing programmes there.

Method of quoting prices

The agreement should clarify how the exporter will normally quote goods for sale, i.e. in ex-factory, FOB, CIF or other terms, and whether prices will be quoted in sterling or foreign currency. At some point the agreement might identify who bears bank charges, currency exchange costs, and any sundry charges occurred in exporting to a market, unless the exporter's terms of trade clarify this (in which case the agreement might note that orders are accepted and shipped under the current company standard export terms of trade).

Duties of the principal and the agent/distributor

Much of the agreement will be about this matter, and I will cover the subject in more detail later in this chapter.

Performance clauses

In return for exclusivity the distributor or other buyer may be required to accept certain performance clauses to distribute and actively promote the products, or to achieve sales targets or purchase certain minimum quantities in agreed time periods, such as each quarter or year. This clause is designed to stop a distributor or agent just collecting agencies that he then fails to develop and promote.

Special storage, handling and packaging

Any special packaging requirements (normally the exporter's responsibility) can be mentioned in the body of the agreement or a reference made to appendices to the agreement or subsequent exchanges of correspondence that will cover such matters. A general clause may often contain a phrase such as 'suitably packaged for export and to comply with all local laws and regulations dealing with the packaging and presentation of such products'.

If the products require any special storage or handling by the distributor (for example: refrigerated storage for chilled or frozen goods; stacking limits in warehouses, humidity control, etc.) then it is essential that the distributor is contractually committed to comply.

Principal's right to accept or refuse orders

Most exporters will want to retain the right to accept or refuse an order, even from an established distributor or when placed through an established agent. The reasons to retain this right can be numerous, e.g.: in case products are in short supply and the company wants to control stock allocation between markets; payment for earlier shipments may be overdue; an importer might be trying to increase orders to beat forthcoming price increases; an importer may not be managing stock control adequately; an agent may solicit orders from customers not seen as credit worthy or not considered suitable outlets for the product.

Market pricing and costing guidelines

Your prices are likely to change from time to time, and the agreement might state that 'Prices will be as agreed from time to time by the issue of an export price list by the company to the distributor'. However, if you are dealing through a distributor you may want to negotiate a local market pricing structure to control margins, where this is permissible within local laws, to reasonable levels consistent with local practice, as excessive margins will harm sales growth and possibly your reputation in the market.

The agreement may state a costing/pricing formula, that fixes distributor margins, or make a more general statement that margins will be agreed from time to time at levels that are consistent with local trade practice and ensure market competitiveness.

Marketing programmes and planning

Within the strategic plan of most companies is a section on export markets. In some companies the export marketers make their plans with minimal reference to the market agents or distributors, but that is not good practice, because if the representatives are not involved in the planning process they will not be committed to implementing and achieving plans. Within the agreement should be a clause that identifies how and at what frequency the agent or distributor should contribute to planning, and clarify the responsibilities for plan implementation.

Promotional responsibilities and materials

The seller wants to see the market grow and frequently clauses can bind distributor and exporter individually or jointly to finance advertising and promotional activity, particularly if the product is an internationally known consumer product, but also in the case of some industrial products.

It may be that both parties contribute equally to an advertising fund, or that only either exporter or distributor contributes. I have personally always favoured a joint approach to optimize the commitment to the success of promotional activities. Possibly the distributor will agree to spend a certain fixed level of funds in one year or to provide an agreed percentage, say 3 per cent of sales revenues; or perhaps the arrangement will simply be that the buyer will pay for an agreed number of advertisements in the local newspaper. Where representation is through a commission agent then it is customary that the principal bears all marketing costs such as advertising and promotional activity supporting the products.

State clearly where responsibility for planning and controlling the marketing programme lies and possibly include a reference to the supply of any promotional aids from the principal. You may wish to mention that you will work together to prepare an annual promotion plan.

Whatever your own preferred formula, the contract can set the tone for co-operation in this area.

Payment terms

General sales conditions and payment terms are commonly referred to in an agreement.

Sometimes a general clause will simply say something to the effect: 'The payment for goods shipped will be by irrevocable letter of credit confirmed by a United Kingdom bank except where subsequently agreed in an exchange of letters between the parties'. Where other payment terms are contractually agreed (such as thirty, sixty or ninety day terms, letters of credit, sight drafts, open account, etc.) these are often referred to in an agreement. In practice, even where specific terms are agreed with distributors, such as sixty days, payment is often delayed either by the distributor being slow to effect payment, or delays in bank transfers. Many an exporter is virtually acting as an interest-free banker to his distributor, extending credit beyond that needed to finance goods held in stock, either because the exporter is simply lax on credit control, or because the export marketers fail to understand the extension of credit at the various tiers in the supply chain.

You may be advised to append your current terms and conditions of sale to the agreement. These might include a provision that ownership of goods does not transfer until the goods are paid for in full, and that the distributor who resells any goods before they are paid for will hold any moneys in trust for the principal.

Commission arrangements

Commission normally applies where orders are solicited by an agent acting on behalf of an exporter and where the agent is not involved in taking possession or ownership of the goods. A distributor normally buys goods for his own account and adds his profit margin before resale. There are situations where distributors in some developing nations demand a 'commission' be paid offshore on their purchases, but this is not a sales commission in the true agency sense, but rather a way of taking some of their profits outside their market (and it inflates the price to the final user or consumer).

It is important that you make clear within the agreement on exactly which shipments commission is due to an agent. For example:

- is commission due on the first shipment only, or on all subsequent shipments until termination of the agreement?
- are commissions due on orders shipped to destinations outside the territory but generated by the agent's activity in his market?
- are commissions due on orders submitted by the agent but not shipped?
- will commissions continue on any business after termination of the agreement (there may be local laws on this), and for how long?

In addition, the agent and exporter should be clear on who is responsible for expenses incurred in generating business and the scale of commissions applicable to any level of business or transaction. Within the European Union directives regulate the agent's right to remuneration and commission, and local regulations in any foreign market should be checked before entering an agreement.

Reporting/marketing information reports

The distributor is often requested within a contract to provide certain reports such as monthly or quarterly information covering:

- sales by product or account/user
- competitive prices and products
- competitive promotional activity
- new products in the market
- distributor stock levels and forward order positions
- measurable promotional activity results
- local import and production data for comparable goods
- agent or distributor financial accounts or other disclosures of relevant financial transactions.

The information you request should be seen by the agent or distributor as relevant to the conduct of business and your mutual relationship, otherwise it simply will not be forthcoming. In general it is best to concentrate on information that impacts on marketing plans and programmes, performance measurement and forward planning.

Training of agent or distributor personnel

If the principal wishes to have the right of access to train the sales or other personnel of the agent or distributor, then this should be identified and accepted by inclusion of a suitable clause within the initial agreement. Distributors are often reluctant to take a sales force off the road for training by an individual principal, especially if that training concentrates on product knowledge rather than relating to the general sales activities.

I have already given coverage to the subject of training, and will just reiterate here that, for training to be welcome, it must be seen to enhance the performance of the distributor's sales team and extend beyond just knowledge of your company's products.

Warranties

The agent or distributor should be restricted within the agreement from providing any warranty other than that provided directly to the goods or services by the principal. Exporters have often encountered situations where an agent or distributor makes unofficial promises so as to obtain sales orders and those promises may effectively amount to an extension of a warranty.

Indemnities

The agent or distributor might be required to indemnify the principal for any losses, costs and expenses incurred by the principal and resulting from any breach of terms of the agreement and any actions or activities of the agent or distributor that breached any laws in force in the assigned territory. The distributor's facilities might be closed up for failure to comply with some local health, hygiene or safety regulations, for example, or sanctions imposed on him for non-payment of local taxes.

Limits of authority

You will not want your representative to have the rights to bind you locally except to matters agreed within the agreement (i.e. the sale of goods within agreed price parameters). You may wish to impose contractual restrictions in respect of contracting or committing you in any unauthorized way, or to limit your representative not to give any warranty (in respect of the supply or performance of products) other than those provided directly by you.

It may be wise clearly to identify that the importer acts as buyer and not agent of the manufacturer so that the buyer clearly understands that he is not empowered to bind the manufacturer in any matters of local contracts or prices and cannot create any obligation or liability for the exporter or manufacturer.

Confidentiality clauses

It would be normal to include a confidentiality clause in an agreement that restricts the agent or distributor from disclosing to any unauthorized third parties any information concerning the principal's business or products. This can be of particular importance in the case of hi-tech products, and access to confidential data might be restricted by agreement to key named personnel. Within this clause it might be appropriate in some cases to prohibit the making or taking of copies of confidential information, and to clarify that all documents provided are loan documents only, to be returned (along with any copies) on demand or termination of the agreement.

Trade mark/patent and intellectual property protection

In order to protect your patents and trade marks, you will want a clause binding the agent or distributor not to seek pre-emptive registrations in their own name, and to advise of any threats to trade mark protection that they may become aware of in the form of competitive registration applications or apparent infringements in the marketplace. The agent or distributor may be obligated to assist in any legal activity necessary to register or protect patents, trade marks and other intellectual property belonging to the principal or to help defend them locally.

Additionally, you may want to give some coverage to the treatment of confidential information, and restrict disclosure of your business secrets (and return of all documents on termination of the agreement).

Dispute handling

The method of handling disputes should be clarified in the body of the agreement. If arbitration is acceptable, then state where and how it should take place (possibly in the country of either the principal or his agent or distributor, or in a neutral third country, under the auspices of the International Chamber of Commerce).

Duration of the agreement

The time period of exclusivity should be agreed upon and defined, and the conditions to be fulfilled prior to enactment of the contract should be stated.

The agreement may be for an indefinite period until terminated on agreed notice periods, subject to neither party defaulting on any of the key agreement clauses. Or it may be for a finite period or for a particular business transaction (such as the duration of a tender). Or it may be for an initial period and automatically renewed indefinitely until a notice of termination is served.

Assignability

Any rights by either party to assign the agreement to another party not included in the original contract should be covered. For example, a principal will normally reserve

the right to terminate the agreement if the distributor sells his company or it effectively changes ownership, because it has been known for a distributor to come under control of competing interests. At the same time, the exporter probably wants to reserve the right to assign the agreement to any associate, subsidiary or holding company, or on change of ownership of the exporter.

Termination

The coverage of termination needs to be specific, including:

- notice periods and the manner of serving notice (normally in writing to an address stated within the agreement)
- transfer of residual stocks held by a distributor
- causes of premature termination, and
- other rights and duties of the parties on termination.

Termination is never a happy occasion, and in some countries local agents and distributors have residual rights after termination. You should identify these and know your exposure at the stage of first contracting. In some cases it may be practical (and wise) to insert a clause limiting the level of compensation that may be due on termination where that is permissible under local regulations. Within the European Union regulations cover minimum periods of notice due to an agent, and these may not be reduced by agreement between the parties.

Non-waiver clauses

For practical reasons not every clause in an agency or distributor agreement is always enforced strictly at all times. A clause should state that any non-enforcement of any provision at any time should not constitute a waiver of the rights of either party.

Entire agreement clause

In order to avoid subsequent disputes or claims that other considerations were assumed to apply to the agreement, such as where either party claims verbal promises were made, a clause should clarify that the written agreement constitutes the entire understanding of the agreement between both parties, and that neither has relied on any other oral or written provisions or promises not included within the written agreement.

Force majeure clause

The principal may wish to include a 'force majeure' clause to cover him against an inability to ship for reasons outside his control (such as strikes, shortage of raw materials, or anything else disrupting the normal course of business).

Applicable country for legal enforcement and interpretation

It is a common practice to include a clause stating that the agreement will be interpreted under English law and that the English courts should have jurisdiction in the event of a dispute resulting in legal action. This is a questionable practice for many markets or situations. There is no point deciding to have the agreement enforceable in the United Kingdom if you could not enforce a judgement in the agent's or distributor's own country. Also, a number of countries require agreements to be constructed, interpreted, litigated and enforced according to their own local laws in order to protect their own nationals operating in international trade. A clause should clarify which country's courts should have jurisdiction over the agreement.

Other clauses

Local agency laws. This subject has been mentioned, but cannot be over-emphasized. Any laws governing agency or distributor agreements or restrictive practices in the foreign market must be considered. Information on this may be available from your embassy or from the Department of Trade and Industry in the United Kingdom. For example, some countries will not accept a clause stating that judicial jurisdiction in disputes can be in the seller's country.

After-sales service. If the products require any after-sales servicing, then the agreement will need to give coverage to the distributor's responsibilities, and include a contractual commitment to keep spares and provide a comprehensive service (possibly at multiple locations).

Licensing rights or direct market entry. If there is any likelihood you might want to enter the market directly with your own branches, subsidiaries or local licensed manufacturing arrangements, then perhaps the agreement should clearly reserve these rights to you, and give you the option to terminate the agreement in such an eventuality, or to modify the agent or distributor's role.

Principal's credit. Customarily an agreement clause should restrict the agent or distributor from taking any action to pledge the principal's credit without prior written approval, and also to restrict the agent or distributor from incurring any unapproved liabilities on behalf of the principal.

Access to premises. A clause will normally make the point that the principal should be allowed access to any of the agent's or distributor's premises or facilities during normal working hours and with reasonable notice.

Consignment stocks. It is common in many industries for a local agent or distributor to hold some consignment stocks, particularly of spare parts, that are not paid for by the agent or distributor unless or until they are sold or used in the market. Consignment goods are normally shipped and held in store at the exporter's expense. A clause should protect the exporter's right of ownership in the goods in case the agent or distributor went bankrupt or disposed of the goods in an unauthorized fashion. The agreement should clarify that consignment goods are held in trust by the agent or distributor on behalf of the principal, and state how the principal is to be reimbursed when consignment stocks are sold or otherwise disposed of, and how stocks should be accounted for. Stock records and books of account should be kept.

Insurance of goods. Customarily a clause will require the distributor (or agent, if one is holding any consignment stocks) to maintain adequate insurance cover, at his cost, against all known and likely risks for all stocks of the principal's products. Optionally consignment goods might be insured at the principal's expense.

Non-competition. An agency or distribution agreement frequently binds the agent or distributor not to take any competing line without the prior approval of the principal, and to prohibit the agent or distributor from offering a competing product to the principal's customers in the market for an agreed period after termination of the agreement for any reasons (usually from one to two years). It will be necessary to establish for each market the extent to which any such restraint of trade clause will be acceptable and enforceable.

Notices. The addresses of both parties for the sending of any formal notices under the agreement should be identified in the agreement.

Limits of the agreement. The agreement should clarify that the agreement only applies to the specific agency or distribution arrangements as described within the agreement, and that it does not constitute any form of joint venture or partnership between the parties.

Unenforceable clauses. A clause or subclause should state that any clause that proves now or subsequently to be illegal or unenforceable shall be treated as if it is removed from the agreement and that the rest of the agreement shall stand.

Agency versus distribution arrangements

Whilst this is not intended to be a legal text, it is not possible to cover export marketing without considering matters that are primarily legal in nature. The international marketer needs a basic understanding of many legal aspects of international trade, and coverage in this text will concentrate on issues commonly encountered.

Independence of the distributor

The distributor buys the goods on his own account and is solely responsible for his customers' creditworthiness, although he has marketing responsibilities and duties to the seller or principal. Basically, the distributor is an independent company, not acting as your agent but committed by agreement to work with you in developing a market to mutual benefit.

Interdependence with the agent

The agent, whilst an independent company or individual in their own market, is empowered to act for the principal in an agreed fashion, and therefore may be like an extra finger on the hand of the company.

The agent may have a range of rights, responsibilities and duties. He may be able to bind the seller to contracts, prices, delivery schedules and performance clauses. He may also be able to agree on payment or credit terms with customers while not personally having any credit risk. Sometimes the contract will require him to take over title to goods where a buyer fails to clear these through customs or pay for them, or he may voluntarily take title in an emergency. The contract can explain the limits that the seller agrees to put on the agent's authority.

Researching potential agents

A potential agent who is going to have any authority to bind the seller in any way must be very carefully researched to establish: reputation in the market; creditworthiness; financial standing and worth (trade and bank references should be thoroughly checked); and any potential conflicting interests.

The agent or importer should satisfy you on the following criteria:

- they have high standing and reputation in the business community and are seen as experts in the products they represent
- they have no conflicting interests in respect of similar agency lines or management or financial involvement with any customer where they could limit your opportunity to sell to other parties, cause direct conflict where the agent recommends beneficial terms to their associate, or provide false credit data because of associations
- they have the organization to perform to your requirements
- they have the financial standing to pay for goods if they are required to take up distressed consignments, and they have proven records and data to support their credit recommendations for buyers.

It is always unwise to appoint any agent or sole distributor without prior personal knowledge of the organization obtained by direct market visits.

Limits to agent's authority

The contract may exclude the agent from having any power to bind the seller to specific terms and conditions, and just make the agent a negotiator between seller and buyer, leaving the buyer with all rights to conclude terms.

Disclosure of agency arrangement

An agent may or may not disclose their interest with a manufacturer when dealing with a customer. If they do not, they may be held liable or face suit as if they were the principal. Equally, a customer or confirming house may have the rights to sue a manufacturer directly if goods do not conform to specifications and standards agreed upon at the time the manufacturer accepted the order. Usually it is better to ensure that agents are obligated to tell their customers of their interests in representing the manufacturer and that they are agent for the principal.

Duties of principal and agent ▬▬

The agent

The agent must:

- act dutifully and in good faith, carrying out all lawful duties
- make proper effort to negotiate and conclude transactions on behalf of the principal
- disclose all relevant facts to customer and principal
- comply with principal's reasonable instructions
- have no undisclosed conflict of interest
- make no secret profits
- respect confidentiality
- keep records and accounts

Some of these points warrant additional comment, given in the following paragraphs.

Disclosure of facts

The agent must disclose all relevant facts, both to the principal and to the customers relating to every transaction.

Compliance with instructions

The agent should exercise diligence in carrying out duties and complying with the instructions of his principals (or notify that they cannot comply for whatever reason). They have no authority to give any warranty other than that provided by the manufacturer. Agents have a habit in some countries of stretching a point to make a sale with such comments as 'You know Alpha Beta Company will stand behind you and their products', which implies a general commitment outside the control of the supplier, and the buyer may use a product in an unapproved manner.

Conflict of interest

The agent cannot act as commission sales agent for the both seller and commission or otherwise paid agent for the buyer. Similarly, he should not act as agent for the principal and commence dealing on his own account as a principal in the same products.

Personal interest in every contract should be disclosed. Japan is an interesting case in point, where, in fact, a trading house may effectively be involved with both buyer and seller to financial benefit. Principals frequently find this frustrating yet are obliged to work within the established systems.

Secret profits

Agents should not give or accept bribes or make any other secret profits out of a transaction or their representation of the principal.

Within this guideline, one must recognize that in certain third world countries the whole purpose of having a 'connected' agent is that they can spread their largesse around to the direct benefit of their principals, and legal restriction on this covert activity imposed by a manufacturer's home authorities only leaves open additional market opportunities to competitors.

Confidentiality

The agent must keep confidential any information provided by the principal in the pursuit of mutual business, where the principal specifies that such information is not for disclosure (e.g. formulas, recipes, drawings, designs, costings, etc.).

Accounting

The agent should keep accurate records and accounts of all transactions on behalf of the principal, and submit relevant accounts to the principal as required within the terms of the agreement.

The principal

The principal must:

- act in good faith towards the agent
- pay commissions due (and provide supporting documents from the principal's records for European Union agencies)
- meet agreed expenses
- support the agent (or distributor) and provide all necessary documentation and information relating to the goods represented
- provide a written agency agreement (within the European Union)
- notify the agent of any anticipated shortfall of transactions below those the agent might reasonably expect
- advise the agent in writing within a reasonable period of time of any acceptance, refusal or non-execution of a transaction procured by the agent for the principal
- provide compensation or damages, under certain circumstances, e.g. on termination of an agency contract within the European Union.

Some of these points warrant additional commentary.

Commission

The principal must pay commissions on sales according to agreed terms. Commissions will not normally be due for payment until the buyer has remitted funds to the principal, and may not be due on bad debts (the agreement might make reference to these points). Occasionally, possibly for a higher level of commission, the agent will accept the 'del credere' (credit) risk for buyers, but most agents seek to avoid such obligations.

The principal should reserve the right to accept or reject each individual order, and the agent must understand (through the terms of the agreement) that commission will be due only on an order accepted, shipped and paid for in full. Disputes sometimes arise when an agent claims that they obtained orders and it is not their fault if the manufacturer cannot or will not ship the goods.

Commissions on external sales

The contract should specify the principal's responsibility to pay commissions on business emanating from an agent's territory but not directly procured by them. There are frequently disputes on this matter, because agents expect commission on every dispatch into their territory, and possibly on dispatches into other territories where they have a claim for motivating the purchase: for example if a foreign branch of a company located in their territory subsequently orders.

Any exclusions for house or multinational accounts should be discussed and agreed upon early on. In the case of a multinational account, with a head office in one territory and branch in another, a split commission arrangement may be acceptable to the respective agents in the two territories, since both may contribute to motivating purchases.

The agent will expect commission on all repeat orders, even if sent directly to the principal, at least for the duration of the agency agreement. It is necessary to check local agency laws to establish liability for any ongoing commissions in the event of termination of the contract. Some countries provide protection to agents for all accounts that are initially introduced by them to a principal.

Expenses

The contract should clearly state who is responsible for the agent's costs and expenses incurred in connection with obtaining orders. Generally, the agent is responsible for all normal operating expenses, but it may be agreed that the principal will reimburse costs connected with clearing samples through customs, promoting the products in the market, or pursuing outstanding payments through legal process.

Support of the agent

The principal has duties to support the agent (or distributor) with data, samples and other such sales aids as will enable the agent to represent the products effectively to potential customers. The agent or distributor is entitled to expect efficiency and promptness in the principal's handling of communications, and vice versa.

Written agreements

European Union regulations protect the right of an agent to receive a written agreement. In some markets some principals prefer to avoid written agreements. The exporter should always familiarize himself with local agency law to ensure his best interests are protected. Even where there is no formal written agreement a party who can show he represents a principal and is fulfilling the role and responsibilities of a formal agent may have certain rights and levels of protection.

Supplementary agency matters ■

Del credere risk

As has been mentioned previously, the principal may require the agent to accept the 'del credere' risk (possibly for an additional commission) and indemnify the principal for any loss resulting from failure of a consignee to clear and pay for a consignment shipped against an order obtained by the agent. The agent is often in the best position to judge the financial standing of a buyer in the foreign market, being more in touch with local conditions. Export credit insurance is no substitute for sound credit control.

Stocks

Some agents may be required to hold stocks of a product, possibly on consignment (i.e. not paid for by the agent until or unless they are sold to a customer), to meet certain market demands, such as unusual seasonal fluctuations, delays in vessels arriving with regular orders, replacement for goods damaged or lost in transit, or possibly spare parts for machinery or equipment.

In such cases it would normally be agreed that the agent could release such contingency stocks to established customers without referring back to the principal in advance, provided the customer was in good credit standing, but advise the principal of the transaction for invoicing purposes. The contract should consider the matter of responsibility in disposing of such contingency stocks, and the agent or distributor should be required to report on inventories at agreed intervals. The export representative of the principal should verify stock levels on regular visits.

It may also be that the agent would be given local responsibility for collection of payment for stocks released under their control, rather than the principal issuing invoices to the customer from the home office.

As your relationship develops with your agent, there will be many practices that will become the norm yet may not be contractually covered. In general, if your agent does not have your respect and trust, then you have the wrong agent or distributor.

Export houses

Export or **confirming houses** have a dual relationship as middlemen in a transaction between an exporter and a foreign buyer. They may be acting as agent for the foreign buyer in procuring goods to order. But in the relationship with the exporter they may be:

- acting in the role of direct buyer, taking full title for the goods and responsibility for payment

- acting as agent for the foreign importer (without liability for the payment for the goods)
- acting as agent for the foreign importer but accepting responsibility to pay for the goods (where they *confirm* the order).

If a principal is dealing with a confirming (export) house, then that institution will normally have made itself obligated to the supplier to take all goods it has ordered and to pay for such goods according to agreed terms. If the final foreign customer cancels the order or fails to pay, that does not release the confirming house or export company from its obligations to the supplier. Again, in practice, if the final overseas customer cancels an order before it is produced to special order or dispatched, the supplier may co-operate with the confirming house in not insisting that the transaction be completed, but the confirming house should understand that favour is not a foregoing of general rights to enforce contracts. A manufacturer who has made goods to special specifications or packaging requirements is likely to want to hold the confirming house or export company to its contract, or to collect any losses resulting from distressed sale of goods that possibly may not be suited to the home market.

The confirming house or export company, while responsible for all matters of payment and shipment to the customer, does not normally have responsibility for ensuring that goods comply with specifications from the customer, or for matters relating to quality or quantity of the goods. The confirming house will pass on the customer's specifications exactly as received by them, and principals dealing with confirming houses should carefully read the purchase contract applicable to each separate order to establish exactly what responsibilities the confirming house is transferring to the principal.

Freight forwarders

Freight forwarders provide a vital service to many an exporter, but particularly the smaller exporter who has not the volume of business or the resources to build a full service export department. The freight forwarder can act in effect as your shipping department, providing a range of services usually including:

- arranging transport (by road, air or sea)
- processing documentation
- arranging export packing and warehousing
- arranging insurance
- groupage and consolidation for containerization.

In some instances, freight forwarders will be acting as agents for exporters (their principal), usually charging a fee or commission; in others, they will be acting as principals themselves, providing a service for a margin included in the price.

In addition to the prices or commissions charged to the exporter, the freight forwarder may also be receiving commissions and brokerage fees customarily paid on insurance and shipping transactions (including conference rebates). United Kingdom readers would be advised to familiarize themselves with the *Standard Trading Conditions* of the **Institute of Freight Forwarders Ltd**.

Agent of necessity

On occasion, a situation may arise when an 'agent of necessity' is needed. You may have appointed an agent with limited authority who, to safeguard your interests, must take urgent action without reference to you in particular circumstances. For example, if you are shipping a highly perishable product such as fruit or frozen goods and the customer fails to clear goods through customs promptly, or the frozen container is left on the dock not plugged into electricity for an excessive period, the agent may, in your interest, have to sell these goods off the dock for best obtainable prices.

Your agent may have some protection in law for overstepping your authority if they

can demonstrate that they acted in your interest in unusual circumstances. Be careful to ascertain that the buyer of distressed goods at bargain prices was not the original consignee or their nominee, as that tactic has been used many times in places where you cannot control events. If that happens, you may have a claim against either your agent or the original consignee for losses below contract terms.

When you know your agent well, a trust relationship will develop, and you will form a comfort level in how much leeway to give. My own experience has always been that a good, reliable agent, even in the most difficult operational conditions, will seek genuinely to serve your best interests.

Country of jurisdiction

I have referred several times to the developing practice of countries giving various degrees of protection to sole agents or distributors that may entitle them to fees or commissions or other obligatory or goodwill compensations after the termination of an agreement. You should not assume that, even by including a clause, accepted by your distributor, 'that this contract shall be governed by and interpreted in all respects according to the applicable laws of England [or, say, the State of New York, USA], whose courts shall have sole jurisdiction in the event of a dispute', you are protected. The acceptability and validity of such a clause needs to be researched for each country in which you have contractual arrangements.

Style of agreement

The simpler the agreement can be, in both style and language, the easier it is for all parties to comply with its terms and conditions. If the language of the country to which the agreement applies is not English, then you should consider a professional translation to ensure that your agent is clear on all aspects of your agreed relationship. Lawyers perhaps have a tendency to use legalistic jargon or stylized prose that the layperson has trouble comprehending. Try to avoid such a presentation in contracts submitted to foreigners.

A few style guidelines for structuring a comprehensible agreement might be:

- identify subject matter with headings (in bold print)
- clearly number each clause and sub-clause
- group inter-related clauses and subject matter so that the agreement reads in a logical manner
- avoid the use of technical jargon where possible
- clearly state definitions of any technical or other terms with a particular meaning within the context of the agreement
- ensure that the agreement is comprehensive, covering all matters of agreement and setting guidelines for all issues or potential areas for future dispute
- use language that is comprehensible to the lay person (non-lawyer) charged with negotiating, implementing or enforcing the agreement
- ensure that both parties fully understand all the terms and conditions, providing a translation in the language of the agent or distributor (even if the language of the agreement is English) should the foreign party have comprehension problems (thus avoiding the 'I didn't understand' excuse).

You, the export marketer, are the best person to know the commercial aspects you wish to cover in an agency or distribution agreement, and can beneficially devote time to the first rough draft of an agreement before involving your company lawyers. Generally, an international marketer should carry sample (unsigned) standard agency or distributor agreements to the marketplace for discussion with any companies that may seriously be considered to represent the exporter.

The simpler the style and content of the agreement, the fewer arguments, and discussions will generally result on the finer points. Nevertheless, the objective of any agreement must be clearly to establish and recognize the ground rules both parties must work by; to consider duties, obligations, rights, responsibilities, disputes and terminations in return for the commissions or profits on sales.

In principle, if you end up in disputes that lead to legal action or arbitration, then it is likely that your relationship is in such jeopardy that you may be better off mutually to agree to terminate the formal arrangement and appoint a new representative.

European Union law

If your sole representation agreement involves countries within the European Union, then at the contract drafting stage you should seek legal advice to ensure that the terms of the agreement do not breach Articles 85 and 86 of the European Treaty of Rome, which are designed to prevent compartmentalization and fragmentation within the Union. European Union law disapproves of any restrictions on where a person can buy or sell within the European Union, and of market price-fixing arrangements.

With the move towards greater integration of markets within the European Union during the 1990s, and the removal or dismantling of many of the barriers to trade, more and more companies with export prospects within the European Union are setting up local operations (subsidiaries) in member countries to manage the marketing effort.

The European Union Directive 86/653 sets out the regulations to be applied to self-employed commercial agents from January 1994, and each member country within the European Union encompasses the Directive within its own national regulations applicable to agency agreements. The export marketer operating within the European Union needs to be familiar with this Directive and its application in his markets.

European Union Directive 86/653 on self-employed commercial agents ___

The key objective of the Directive is to harmonize domestic laws of member states as regards the commercial relations between agent and principal. The Directive covers mandatory rights and duties of the principal and agents and governs aspects of agent remuneration for all agency agreements covering activities within member states. Where the commercial agent is not established in any member state, and carries out all activities outside of any member state, the regulations apply only if and to the extent that both parties agree to apply the regulations. Specifically it deals with:

- termination of an agency agreement
- the agent's right to compensation payments or indemnities in certain circumstances
- the nature of restraint clauses that may be imposed on the agent.

An **agent** is defined as a 'self-employed intermediary who has continual authority to negotiate the sale or purchase of goods on behalf of and in the name of that principal'. Persons excluded from coverage under the Directive include:

- agents or distributors who purchase goods on their own account for resale
- an officer of a company empowered to enter into commitments binding on his company in his capacity as an officer
- a partner lawfully authorized to enter into commitments binding on his partners
- receivers, liquidators and trustees in bankruptcy
- commercial agents whose activities are unpaid (no form of consideration for activities)
- commercial agents operating on commodity exchanges or in the commodity market
- Crown Agents for overseas governments and administrations.

Obligations of the commercial agent and the principal

The Directive defines the main obligations of the commercial agent and the principal, and these are largely in line with what we would consider as normal for such relationships, as discussed earlier in this chapter. The commercial agent must:

- make proper efforts to negotiate and, where appropriate, conclude the transaction in respect of which he is instructed to take care
- communicate to the principal all the necessary information which is available to him
- comply with reasonable instruction given by the principal.

The principal must:

- provide the commercial agent with all necessary documentation relating to the goods concerned
- obtain for the commercial agent the information necessary for the performance of the agency contract (specifically notifying the agent if the volume of commercial transactions is likely to be significantly lower than the agent might normally expect)
- inform the commercial agent within a reasonable time period of his acceptance, refusal, or of any non-execution of a commercial transaction that the agent has procured for the principal.

Remuneration of the agent and commissions on sales

The Directive deals with rights of the agent to receive remuneration and/or commission as a reward for his sales activities on behalf of the principal. Commission is a form of remuneration that commonly varies with the value or number of business transaction. Unless a specific agreement between the commercial agent and principal defines the agent's entitlement to remuneration then the agent within the European Union shall be entitled to a customary level of remuneration, taking account of:

- the nature of the goods which form the subject matter of the agent's activities
- the place in which the agent's activities are performed.

An agent's entitlement to commission

An agent can be entitled to commission on transactions completed both during and after an agency agreement.

1 During the period covered by an agency agreement

Commission to an agent would become due:

- where the action was completed as a result of the action of the commercial agent
- where the transaction was with a third party whom the commercial agent had previously acquired as a customer for transactions of a similar kind (i.e. repeat orders from customers procured by the agent even where the customer does not place repeat orders through the agent)
- where a specific geographical area or group of customers is granted exclusively to the agent through the agreement
- where the agent has been entrusted with a geographical area or group of customers.

2 After termination of an agency agreement

Commission to a previous agent would be due:

- where a transaction was mainly the result of efforts by the previous agent made during the period of the agency contract, and the transaction was entered within a reasonable time period after the agency contract terminated

- where the customer's order reached the principal before the agency contract terminated.

Commission becomes due when:

- the principal has executed the transaction
- according to the agreement between the principal and the agent, the principal should have executed the transaction
- the third party has executed the transaction
- at the latest when the third party has performed his obligations under the transaction, provide the principal has duly performed his obligations.

This right to commission may only be extinguished where:

- the contract between principal and third party will not be executed
- and the principal is not to blame for the failure to execute the transaction.

Commission should be paid no later than the last day of the month following the quarter in which it became due.

Shared commissions and exclusions

The Directive states that:

- agency commission may be divided between a current and previous agent where it is equitable to do so, such as where the previous agent was demonstrably involved in concluding the transaction.
- agency commission shall not be due to a new agent where that commission is rightfully payable to a previous agent.

Rights to information on commission calculations

The agent has the right to:

- a statement of all commission due
- and to such information and detail on transactions and the calculation of commission as enables him to verify commission.

Contracting and terminating agency contracts within the European Union

The European Union Directive states that:

- the terms of an agency contract should be defined in a written document
- an agency contract for a fixed period that continues to be performed by both parties after that period has expired shall be deemed to be for an indefinite period.

Where an agency contract is concluded for an indefinite period the minimum periods of notice (which may not be reduced or derogated by any terms of agreement) by either party are:

- one month for the first year
- two months for the second year commenced
- three months for the third and subsequent years commenced.

Member states of the European Union have some flexibility to extend minimum periods of notice (which would normally end at the end of a calendar month, unless otherwise agreed by the parties), e.g. four months for four years, five months for five years, six months for six and subsequent years. Where the parties agree to longer periods of notice than the required minimums of a member state, the period of notice to be given by the principal should not be less than the period of notice to be observed by the agent. Immediate termination may still be permitted where:

- one party fails to perform its obligations
- exceptional circumstances arise preventing fulfilment (e.g. force majeure situations)

Indemnity and compensation of commercial agents

The agent would be entitled to a lump sum indemnity upon termination of an agency contract where:

- the commercial agent has procured new customers or has significantly increased the volume of business with existing customers and the principal continues to derive considerable benefits from the business with such customers
- payment of an indemnity is equitable having regard to all relevant circumstances, in particular commission lost by the commercial agent on the business transacted with customers.

Under the Directive the amount of the indemnity should not exceed the equivalent of one year's average annual remuneration over the preceding five years or for a shorter period if the agency contract was for a shorter period than five years. The agent should not be prevented from seeking damages in the courts through the grant of such a lump sum indemnity.

The commercial agent may, alternatively, be entitled to compensation for damage he suffers as a result of termination of an agency contract where:

- the commercial agent is deprived of commission he would have received from proper performance of the contract
- the agent had not been able to amortize the costs and expenses incurred for performance of the agency contract on the principal's advice.

Death of the agent during the period of contract shall also entitle the agent to indemnity or compensation for damages, as shall his inability to continue for reasons of age, health, etc. The agent must submit his claim for compensation in writing to the principal and within one year of the termination of the agency agreement. The principal cannot require the agent, as a condition of providing a contract, to waive his rights to compensation.

Indemnity or compensation shall not be payable where:

- the principal has terminated the agency contract because of a default attributable to the agent which would justify immediate termination of the contract under the laws of the appropriate member state

- the commercial agent has terminated the contract, unless such termination was for reasons attributable to the principal or for reasons preventing the agent continuing to perform his agency duties (e.g. age, health)
- the agent, with the principal's agreement, assigns his rights and duties under the agency agreement to another person.

Restraint of trade clauses

Restraint of trade clauses, limiting the agent's activities following termination of an agency contract, shall only be valid within the European Union where:

- it is concluded in writing
- it relates to the geographical area or group of customers covered by the agency contract
- it does not impose restrictions for longer than two years after termination of the agency contract.

National law within European Union member states may impose other restrictions on the extent or validity of restraint of trade clauses, and national courts may have powers therefore to reduce obligations on parties resulting from such agreements.

Further reading

Schmitthoff's Agency and Distribution Agreements. Stephen Kenyon-Slade with Michael Thornton (Sweet & Maxwell)

Schmitthoff's Export Trade – The Law and Practice of International Trade. Clive M. Schmitthoff (Stevens)

Principles of Law Relating to Overseas Trade. Nicholas Kouladis (Blackwell Business 1994). The entire book is relevant reading on legal aspects of international trade to the reader with a need for more knowledge, or as a reference book. Chapters 9 and 10 are particularly relevant to agency law and exemption clauses.

Checklist 8.1
Typical clauses and scope of agency and distribution agreements

Action points

- ◆ Introductory recitals
  - identification of the parties to the agreement
  - statement of the purpose of the agreement (agency or distribution arrangement or both)
- ◆ Definition of terms used
- ◆ Product range: give coverage to factors such as
  - defining the goods
  - principal to be sole source
  - packaging
  - compliance with laws in destination market
  - product deletions (right of principal to delete lines)
  - other range exclusions (some lines may be represented or distributed by another party)
  - range extensions (representation of new products)
  - other relevant considerations e.g. product liability insurance
- ◆ Agent's or distributor's territorial rights and exclusivity to geographical area or customer group (trade sector), or
  - market sector limitations
- ◆ Principal's rights to supply other agents, distributors or direct customers, i.e. where there is no exclusive agent/distributor agreement
- ◆ Limitations on exports by the distributor outside the geographical territory
- ◆ Method of quoting prices (e.g. ex-factory, FOB, CIF, etc.)

- ◆ **Duties of the principal:**
  - to act dutifully and in good faith
  - to provide all relevant information on products and to assist an agent/distributor market the products
  - to provide literature and samples
  - to inform the agent of all transactions arising from his activities
  - any agreement to reimburse an agent/distributor's expenses
  - include all rights and duties not addressed elsewhere in the agreement

Checklist 8.1 (Continued)

	Action points

◆ **Duties of the agent/distributor**
  ● to serve the principal in good faith and with due diligence, and to act in the best interest of the principal
  ● to keep the principal informed of all relevant market developments
  ● non-competition with the principal:
    – limitations on representation of competitive product lines
    – no engagement in competitive activity
  ● performance clauses
    – minimum sales performance requirements
    – annual quotas/targets
    – other performance clauses
  ● order frequency (from distributors)
  ● to permit the principal access to all premises and records concerning the distributor's business
  ● inventory levels – minimums to be held by distributor
  ● consignment stocks:
    – levels held by agent/distributor
    – ownership of consignment stocks (normally remaining with principal)
    – insurance of consignment stocks
    – pricing on sale
    – means of control/payment upon sale/books of account
  ● to provide coverage of the market with a suitably trained sales force
  ● providing after-sales service
    – spare parts/servicing
    – service centres
  ● handling market returns (damaged/ unsaleable goods)
  ● handling and storage of products
  ● physical distribution commitments
  ● to comply with all local laws governing trade in the goods and operation as an agent or distributor
  ● to keep the principal informed of all regulations governing marketing of the contract goods in the market
  ● to maintain qualitative standards, e.g., in respect of office facilities, administrative systems, etc.
  ● whether del credere risk is borne by the agent
◆ Restriction on a distributor not to alter goods or packaging
◆ Principal's right to accept or refuse orders:
  ● agent's commission only to be due and paid on orders accepted by the principal
◆ Market pricing policies
  ● prices at which goods may be offered by the agent/distributor
  ● agreed distributor margins or local pricing formulas

Checklist 8.1 *(Continued)*

- export pricing policies, and agreement that the agent/distributor will not market product at prices adversely affecting sales of the principal's goods or conflicting with marketing strategies
- ◆ Marketing programmes and plans
  - co-operation in the planning process
  - control and responsibilities
- ◆ Advertising and promotional matters
  - budgetary responsibility
  - allocation of costs and organizational responsibilities between the parties
  - control of programmes and reporting of outcomes
- ◆ Standard payment terms (for distributor)
- ◆ Processing of funds where the agent collects payments on behalf of a principal
- ◆ Commissions to agents
  - remuneration/commission levels (basis of calculation)
  - manner and frequency (and timing) of payment
  - rights to remuneration/commission after termination of agency contract
  - any excluded sales
- ◆ Reporting requirements
  - frequency and coverage of reports from agent/distributor
    - marketing and sales reports required
    - competitive activity reports
- ◆ Training of agent's personnel
  - rights to train
  - scope of training
  - allocation of training costs
- ◆ Other duties and responsibilities of parties
- ◆ Agreement on how the principal will arrange supply, or how agent/distributor may obtain alternative products, where the principal cannot supply the market from his own sources.
- ◆ Warranties provided by principal
- ◆ Indemnities to the principal provided by the agent/distributor to indemnify the principal for all costs, expenses or losses resulting from any illegal actions or breach of agreement clauses
- ◆ Limits on agent/distributor authority, e.g.:
  - not to give warranties other than those provided by the principal
  - not to hold himself out in any capacity other than as agent (or distributor) in respect of the goods
  - not to bind the principal in any contractual way without the principal's prior agreement
  - not to commence legal proceedings involving the principal without permission

Checklist 8.1 *(Continued)*

	Action points
<ul><li>not to incur unapproved liabilities in the principal's name</li><li>not to pledge the principal's credit</li></ul>♦ Secrecy/confidentiality clause<ul><li>protection of intellectual property</li><li>non-disclosure of confidential information</li><li>indemnity for loss of sales/profits through breaches of confidentiality</li><li>list of persons to be permitted access</li></ul>♦ Protection of trademarks, patents and other intellectual property<ul><li>initial registration – assisting the principal as necessary</li><li>no pre-emptive attempts at intellectual property registration by agent/distributor</li><li>no objections from agent to registrations by principal</li><li>assistance with defence of intellectual property</li></ul>♦ Rights to license production (and/or limitations) ♦ Dispute handling<ul><li>negotiation</li><li>arbitration (rules/venues)</li></ul>♦ Duration of agreement – fixed period or indefinite ♦ Renewal/extension clauses ♦ Limitations on assignability of the agreement ♦ Agreement enactment date (often subject to certain conditions being met) ♦ Termination clauses for agent/distributor<ul><li>reasonable causes for early termination</li><li>means of serving notice and addresses for notice</li><li>notice periods for each party</li><li>stock disposal (for distributors)</li><li>compensation (limits for third world markets, or within EC mandatory requirements for EC agents)</li><li>restrictions (restraint of trade clause) on agent/distributor competing with principal after termination</li></ul>♦ Non-waiver of rights clause – non-enforcement of any clause does not constitute a waiver ♦ Entire agreement clause – the agreement supersedes all previous agreements (written or verbal) and represents the entire agreement (additions or amendments to be in writing) ♦ 'Force majeure' clause:<ul><li>circumstances in which fulfilment of contractual obligations shall be deemed to be frustrated, and the agreement shall cease to be binding</li></ul>♦ Interpretation of the agreement – any clauses which assist in interpreting the contract ♦ Laws applicable to enforcement:<ul><li>jurisdiction of the courts of a specific country</li></ul>	

Part Three

Marketing and Planning Considerations in Exporting

9

Marketing principles in an international context ⎯⎯⎯⎯⎯⎯⎯⎯⎯⎯⎯⎯⎯⎯⎯⎯

 As many export marketers have not had formal training in marketing, this section of the text will develop some traditional marketing concepts from an international perspective. In this chapter we will look at some basic principles and approaches to marketing that are as relevant in the international markets as in the domestic marketing context (including factors in the marketing mix, value chain approach to marketing, SWOT analyses, and product life cycles).

The aim is to remind ourselves that it is as important and relevant in international markets as in domestic markets to have a strategic marketing approach to our exporting activities, and to develop formal marketing plans for the export product portfolio. Adopting a simplistic sales approach, where we primarily process orders and assume responsibility for the goods finishes when they are outside our immediate control, is short-sighted in that we are not in control of our markets and distribution, and are unlikely to be secure in our export trade.

In this chapter we will explore some of the strategic and marketing issues facing the international marketer. Coverage of specific aspects of marketing, such as considerations in developing export strategies, pricing, packaging, promotion and administration, comes in subsequent chapters, stimulating a greater consciousness among readers of the key roles these play in international marketing. The emphasis throughout this chapter and the other chapters of this section is for the exporter to take a strategic marketing approach to market development rather than just a sales approach. The key differences in these two approaches are highlighted in the boxed illustration.

THE SALES APPROACH TO EXPORT MARKET DEVELOPMENT	THE MARKETING APPROACH TO EXPORT MARKET DEVELOPMENT
• Tendency to export to markets that select the company (i.e. foreign importers often write to the company to enquire about purchasing, usually with a request for exclusive market sales rights).	• Company identifies those markets offering sales potential through thorough desk research, quantifies the potential, researches distribution channels, and prioritizes markets according to logical criteria.
• Opportunistic approach to exporting – sell anywhere (the 'shotgun' approach).	• Focused efforts directed to priority markets, avoiding distractions.
• Appoints agents or distributors with very little research into the markets, trade channels, or their historical performance or capabilities.	• Appoints agents or distributors only after thorough proactive research into the markets and the prospective representatives.
• Agreements tend to be basic or poorly thought through, with the exporter having minimal control over markets or marketing.	• Agreements are usually comprehensive documents providing a long-term framework for co-operation in market development.
• Export marketers are often appointed with minimal training in professional sales, marketing or exporting skills, with a heavier reliance on product knowledge.	• Devotes resources to having a professionally trained sales and marketing team, with advanced product knowledge added through training or specialist support.
• Tends to operate with a 'hands-off' approach to market management, leaving much to the local agent or distributor (often with subsequent complaints about lack of co-operation, lack of market data, conflict, etc.).	• Manages the agents or distributors with a 'hands-on' partnership style, with a sharing of market information and mutual approach to market development, helping the distributor develop his team and business.
• Pressures for achievement of export sales targets, with a focus towards shipments from the exporter's factories.	• Focuses on improved market distribution, market share, with a focus on performance at the local market level.
• The export salesperson tends to cover too many markets, with short trips geared to current sales improvement, and often with much time devoted to fire-fighting problems.	• The export marketer will manage a smaller portfolio of markets, with trips geared to longer term market development and planning, and helping the agent or distributor build his team and business.
• Export pricing tends to be based upon factory costs and achieving a margin to give an acceptable return, often with a standard export price list for all markets.	• Export pricing relates to price positioning and strategic marketing factors concerning development of the business in the foreign market.
• UK exporters usually want to price in sterling, since costs are incurred in the domestic currency.	• Exporter has a more flexible approach often pricing in whatever marketable currency will help meet his marketing objectives.

THE SALES APPROACH TO EXPORT MARKET DEVELOPMENT	THE MARKETING APPROACH TO EXPORT MARKET DEVELOPMENT
• Export planning is often very basic, focusing on factory shipments with targets based on recent performance or needs to utilize factory capacity. Frequently sales plans are heavily influenced by financial needs for profit generation from exports.	• Export planning incorporates a strategy for development in each prioritized market, as part of a global marketing strategy, with supporting market research and sales forecasts based on market potential and demand assessments.
• Product development gives little attention to export market needs or those of specific customers, with a 'sell what we make' approach, and limited flexibility to customize products.	• Product development focuses on identifying needs both in domestic and export markets, and there is a willingness to modify or customize products to meet customers' needs and develop a longer term market position.
• The export salesperson usually has minimal knowledge of trade channels, their relative shares of the product category, and the agent or distributor's coverage of trade channel outlets. Often he may have limited ideas on the number or sizes of potential users for industrial products or of target groups for consumer goods.	• The export marketer has clear knowledge of trade channel structures, a defined approach to targeting users/consumers through appropriate trade channels, and monitors the agent/distributors' coverage of trade channel outlets and performance in each trade channel versus competitors.
• Export performance monitoring tends to be done in isolation, i.e. only looking at current company performance against historical performance, with no benchmarking against external factors such as home market category exports or total product category sales in the foreign market.	• The export marketer closely monitors and benchmarks his company's export performance against domestic exports and against the best estimates of product category market sales and activity in the foreign market.
• Marketing communications (advertising and promotion) tend to be limited by a budget set as a percentage of sales turnover, and not geared to any strategic marketing decisions (such as investment strategies relating to life cycle factors, marketing objectives, etc.). Advertising and promotion activity is often left largely under the control of local agents or distributors. Effectiveness of budget use is frequently not measured or monitored.	• The marketing communications budgets are set to promote achievement of objectives derived from the marketing strategy for the export markets. Overriding control of communications strategies and planning remains in the hands of the export marketers, with performance achievement measured in relation to communications budgets to assess media or promotion format effectiveness against clear objectives.

The stages to globalization ▬

Many companies, large conglomerates and multi-nationals, refer to themselves as global marketers. Figure 9.1 illustrates some examples of the typical stages a company might progress through as it moves towards a global strategy.

Most companies start supplying local customers in their home markets, usually with a limited portfolio of products and narrow customer base. Then, at some point, an export opportunity arises, often through an approach from a foreign contact who either has a need for the products, or who spots an opportunity to import and market them in his own market. In this typical scenario, the exporter usually sees exports as a profitable by-product to domestic marketing, and develops very little foreign market knowledge, perhaps making occasional trips of very few days duration, or

relying on meeting contacts at trade fares and exhibitions. The company only seriously moves into **international marketing** when it starts to become directly involved in the marketing of its products (not just the export sale) in the foreign markets, often through marketing units established in the foreign market, subsidiaries or even joint ventures.

The move from **international marketing** to **multi-national marketing** is often a quantum leap in scale. In this transition the marketer no longer just thinks of manufacturing in domestic factories for export, but is looking at local manufacturing of product or service supply, in foreign markets, working through subsidiaries, joint ventures or other managerially controlled or influenced units that manage the business at a local level. A multi-national may be manufacturing different product ranges in different markets, or even be active in

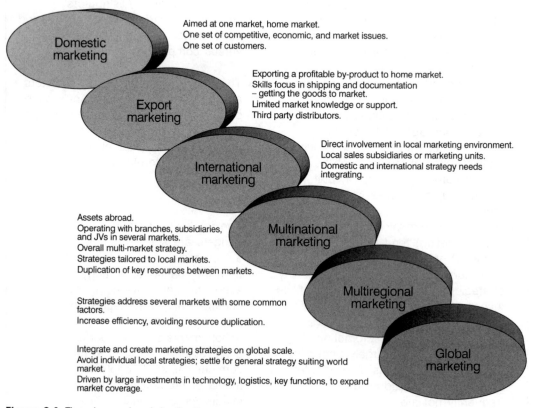

Figure 9.1 The stages to globalization

different product categories, tailoring strategies to local markets. The 1980s saw a trend to grow internationally by diversification and acquisition often in diverse product areas, as the multi-product conglomerates found favour. But in the 1990s we have witnessed a reverse trend in many multi-nationals to limit products and target market sectors as the phrase *'back to the core business'* found favour as flavour of the decade. This is part of the trend to concentration on building pan-national and global brands. At the start of the 1990s there were very few truly global brands, which I would define as brands marketed to the same target group of customers in all (open rather than state controlled) markets with the same target positioning and same core messages promoted through marketing communications. In cigarettes, historically a segment with strong local and regional brands, *Marlboro* is probably the only truly global brand. We have the soft drink giants of *Coca-Cola* and *Pepsi*, the major fast food operators such as *McDonalds*, and confectionery manufacturers such as *Mars Group*, as a few examples that we might clearly consider as global marketers. At the turn of the millennium there is a clear move to globalization of brands. More companies are focussing on core businesses, seeing the future as developing fewer products (or product categories) across more markets rather than more products across fewer markets. In tandem, more companies are developing strategic alliances with synergistic partners that give both more muscle in the market place, and greater mutual profit opportunities (for example, the close alliances between airlines, hotels, car hire companies to provide the total travel package whilst each company remains a separate business). Part of the drive to build trans-national and more global brands may be the pursuit of economies of scale, part the search for greater security through a broad spread of markets and a loyal customer base, and part the need for volume to recover product development brand building costs.

Figure 9.1 is not trying to imply that all companies should try to, or expect to, move through all these stages. There are many examples of companies that perform excellently at any of the stages. What is important is that the marketer recognizes the potential of the various opportunities available, and develops a clear strategy to pursue those opportunities.

Marketing in the global context ■

Increased international travel and international communications media make it easier to communicate product messages between markets, and help promote an environment that favours a global approach to marketing, which is both desirable and practical through **product branding, promotion**, **target market positioning** and **product pricing**.

- **Product branding.** Consumers want to use products they are familiar with, and that are produced by companies they know and trust (from personal experience or that of other persons they respect and trust). Additionally there is a status factor in using internationally known brands or products. International media carry messages round the global markets so rapidly that often a demand can exist before a product is locally available.
- **Promotion.** The range of international media available (including films, television programmes, magazines and journals, and trade marketing vehicles such as exhibitions and directories), and the speed with which product marketing messages can be communicated internationally, has greatly increased in recent years. It is now far easier to reach, and promote to, a target market group in export markets than in the past, and also substantially easier to move goods internationally. As the use of computers in home and work environments further expand this will

open additional routes for marketing communications and product promotion.

- **Target market positioning.** It is now easier to identify and target user/consumer segments in many international markets, and exporters can position products in their markets more accurately. This means that market planning can be more effective, and that promotional budgets can be used more productively.
- **Product pricing.** It is now more important that suppliers encourage a consistent approach to product pricing and price positioning (relative to competitive products and within a company's own product portfolio) between international markets, as users/consumers become more aware of differing market pricing structures in other markets, and can respond negatively. In past exporting practice it was not uncommon for an exporter to take advantage of opportunities for differential pricing, and a product that was a mass market item in the home market might be priced as a luxury in another, or vice versa in some instances. Inconsistencies in price positioning can confuse users/consumers as to how they should perceive the relative value in the product, with the risk that they then respond to the confusion by not purchasing, instead selecting product alternatives.

Global marketing is primarily about maximizing your world-wide sales, market shares, and profits through active foreign market management and a flexible approach to product sourcing, rather than the traditional approach of concentrating only on exports from UK factories (often relying on spare production capacity, disadvantageous pricing, and inflexibility in adapting/modifying products to suit local needs and cultures).

Global marketing is driven by the pursuit of economies of scale in production and distribution, and supported by a gradual convergence of consumer needs or requirements in pan-national markets as a result of global marketing strategies and promotion.

- A true global corporation is not nationalistic in its marketing strategies or location policies, but sources its materials and other product inputs world wide, manufacturing off-shore or locally if product customizing to suit market needs is necessary.
- The global corporation seeks competitive advantage by identifying its world-wide markets and then developing a manufacturing strategy that supports the marketing strategy.

Global marketing needs:

- an organized strategy
- active market management and policies, and
- a flexibility recognizing local market differences

in respect of:

- developing distribution channels (including after-sales servicing) through
  - local specialist distributors
  - foreign subsidiaries, branches, associates
  - licensing or joint ventures
- market concentration in markets where market penetration and share can be developed with security and profitably
- promoting products or services that lend themselves to international branding and promotion.

The foreign market environment ∎

Issues for the global marketer when entering foreign markets include:

- culture
- politics
- legal aspects
- commercial practices
- economic climate

Issues of culture

As illustrated in Figure 9.2, there is a range of cultural forces in any society. These cultural forces result in the cultural messages permeating the society, and the international marketer must identify the forces and messages, and be aware of how they have developed and how they affect behaviour and attitudes.

When it comes to negotiating in any foreign culture then:

- study the culture in advance – be culturally prepared
- include in your team a linguist
- be culturally sensitive
- do not try to impose your culture on the negotiations
- adopt/adapt to the other party's culture
- work at a speed suiting the other party
- do not use any behaviour that can offend the other culture.

Politics

Politics is something we must understand as export marketers, even though we should avoid positions that put ourselves at risk of alienating any political faction. The export marketer might give attention to the following political factors in assessing markets.

- Assess level of government interference in trade and commerce.
- Focus on markets with favourable political climates.
- Will your product or service attract foreign government attention because:
  - it is the subject of political debate and a populist topic?
  - other essential industries depend on the product/service?
  - the product or service is considered a local social or economic necessity?
  - the product is essential for agricultural production?
  - the product affects market national defence capabilities?
- Is competition likely to come from local manufacturers?
- Does the product need key local inputs that would otherwise be underused (labour, raw materials)?
- Does the product produce a net drain of scarce foreign exchange?

Legal environment

Legal regulations and infrastructures vary enormously, and the costs of legal involvement can be high to non-nationals in many markets. Sometimes the processes can be very slow, and may seem to favour local parties. The export marketer should

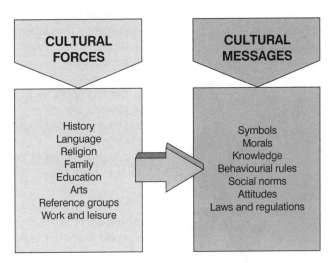

Figure 9.2 *Cultural forces and messages*

familiarize himself with the local legal environment and investigate foreign market regulations, particularly:

- rules of competition
- retail price maintenance laws
- laws applicable to agreements (e.g. agents and distributors)
- intellectual property laws (patents, copyrights, trademarks)
- product quality laws
- product liability laws and issues
- market price controls
- packaging and labelling regulations
- warranty and after-sales exposure
- taxation of local earnings (e.g. on repatriation)
- foreign management involvement in local companies (for joint ventures)

Commercial practices

It is imperative the export marketer researches local customs and practices in order to gain confidence of channel intermediaries, and partners. Look particularly at:

- business structure:
  - ownership and involvement of shareholders

- stakeholders, and attitudes of owners to stakeholders
- sources and levels of authority within organization
- systems of measurement and control
- management attitudes and behaviour:
  - personal backgrounds
  - business status
  - objectives and aspirations
  - local management style
- methods of doing business:
  - business ethics
  - negotiation emphasis and style
  - communications emphasis, style, formality
- patterns of local competition and channel structures.

Economic climate

The more you know and understand about the economy and economic and social infrastructure of a market the better you are placed in developing marketing strategies. The export marketer should research:

- the level of economic development
- the local market:
  - incomes and spread of income distribution
  - stage of industrialization or agrarianism
  - prices
  - interest rates
  - currency movements
  - employment levels
  - production
  - distribution infrastructure
  - demographic factors
  - lifestyle trends
- the investment climate and political climate
- the management of the economy and foreign exchange.

With this depth of knowledge and understanding of the workings of a foreign market the export marketer is better placed to make local plans, and to integrate these into multi-market or global strategies.

Market selection strategy ▬▬

Deciding which markets to select for development is a major concern for export marketers. As previously mentioned, all too often the markets are effectively selected by distributors or agents who offer themselves to the exporter or international market. As we are encouraging the exporter to take control of his company's destiny and marketing, Figure 9.3 illustrates some key criteria that help in assessing international markets. This figure indicates a focus on looking at:

- sales demand and future potential in the markets open for trade or development by other means (local production, licensing, joint ventures, etc.)
- considering the consumer income levels and spreads or funds available for investment
- clarifying how your products can match or be adapted to meet technical requirements suited to the foreign markets
- any benefits from trading with, or within, regional economic groups

- and if you went to stages of local manufacture, what is the availability and economic advantage in using locally available inputs?

The international marketing should collect available data and then:

- group markets according to:
  - respective stages of economic development (*developing, growth, mature*) – see Figure 9.4
  - degree of penetration of the market by the generic product category
  - criteria relevant to purchase/consumption of the product
- select target markets according to their match with key strategic criteria.

What is marketing? ▬▬▬

The export marketer may either not have a formal training or experience in marketing, or may possibly have worked in a domestic sales and marketing environment where, on transfer to international operations the mar-

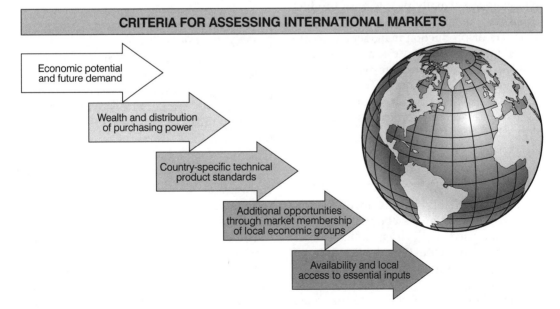

Figure 9.3 Criteria for assessing international markets

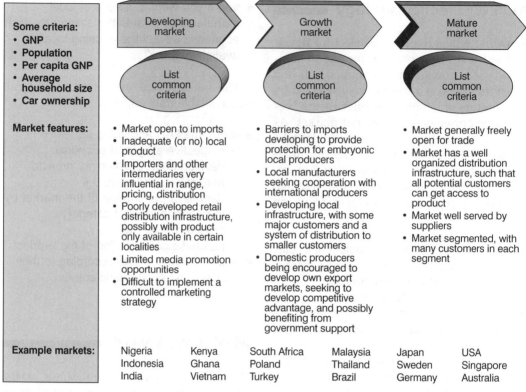

Figure 9.4 *Grouping markets according to common criteria*

keting aspect is subordinated to a drive for sales volume. In many companies the export marketers are actually people with product expertise, possibly engineers, product designers or production managers, who are moved into export because of a need to have detailed product knowledge when dealing with export market contacts. From those perspectives we will discuss and develop some key marketing principles and techniques here.

The marketing mix

Marketing probably has as many definitions as there are books about the subject. It is concerned with user or consumer satisfaction and with the identification of marketing opportunities. It is concerned with harnessing a firm's resources and focusing those resources upon the most appropriate marketing opportunities. These

two statements give us a working definition as follows:

> **MARKETING is the process of matching the resources of the business with identified user or consumer needs and creating, maintaining and then exploiting competitive advantage to satisfy those needs profitably.**

The marketing oriented company puts the customer at the centre of its business and focuses activities towards creating satisfied customers.

The demand influencing variables in the marketing mix, and that can be addressed in marketing planning, are the traditional **4 Ps** of **marketing – product, price, place** and **promotion –** and the newer additions to this 4 Ps approach of **people** and **processes.**

Consideration to these **6 Ps** in the marketing mix is every bit as relevant in international as in domestic markets, and an export marketing strategy plan should give particular coverage of each of the key points of **product**, **price**, **promotion, place, people** and **processes**. Some other recent views of the marketing mix add in additional factors, such as customer service or physical factors, but for convenience here we will consider these as falling within the 6 Ps detailed.

Figure 9.5 illustrates some of the subordinate points under each of these key factors that the export marketer has to consider in developing his marketing strategy to ensure that he has the right product in the right place at the right price and with the right promotion to suit his markets, and with the right people and processes to suit his customer needs.

Marketing mix factors can apply in different ways to the distribution trade channels and the end users or consumers, complicating the decision choices facing the international marketer. He has to take these marketing mix decisions across a range of different countries and cultures, attempting to have a consistency in marketing strategy but reflecting local environments and conditions (hence the phrase 'Think Global – Act Local').

The value chain approach in marketing

Recent thinking in marketing is focusing on the need for manufacturers to understand the '**value chain**' and the importance of adding value throughout the distribution chain or pipeline, both to suppliers and distributors (which can include foreign market importers and the various tiers in the trade channels) and on down the line to final consumers or users (Figure 9.6). This is just as relevant to international marketing as it is in the domestic context. Producers and distributors in the foreign markets must work together to improve supply chain management and product category management, sharing more information and improving the profitability of each stage in the supply chain (through increased sales volumes and lower costs) whilst also satisfying final consumer needs. This approach of

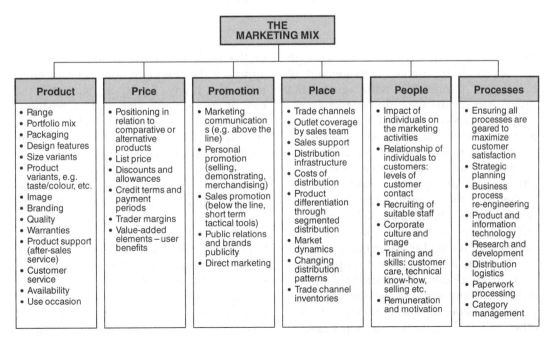

Figure 9.5 Factors in the marketing mix

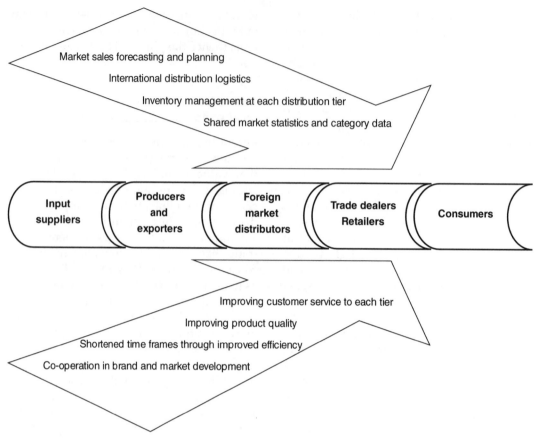

Market sales forecasting and planning

International distribution logistics

Inventory management at each distribution tier

Shared market statistics and category data

| Input suppliers | Producers and exporters | Foreign market distributors | Trade dealers Retailers | Consumers |

Improving customer service to each tier

Improving product quality

Shortened time frames through improved efficiency

Co-operation in brand and market development

Figure 9.6 *Adding value through the supply chain partnership*

the 'value chain' is very much in line with the approach to market management of building a partnership with agents and distributors, as discussed in Chapter 6.

In international markets, it is just as important that the supplier focuses his resources on that part of the chain where his company has a distinctive differential advantage. That approach would encourage a company to out-source for things it is weaker at, and build partnership relationships with other links in the chain. This differs from the traditional cut and thrust of the company, at the start of the supply chain, trying to knock down the prices its suppliers receive and imposing onerous supply terms, playing several suppliers off against each other, and at the later distribution stages of the chain also battling with the various tiers

in the trade channels. In the partnership approach the company does want to minimize what it pays for inputs, but not at the risk of driving suppliers out of business. What is more important is to help the input suppliers become more efficient and thereby reduce their cost structures, e.g. by more efficient production planning and sales forecasting from the company being passed back to input suppliers so that they can better schedule their production (minimizing their inventories and related costs). Similarly, further along the supply chain, the company should assist its international distributors increase their overall profits through the distribution and sale of company products. That will bind suppliers and distributors into a closer partnership. Information needs to be shared between links in the supply chain to ensure improved efficiency of market management with resultant cost benefits to each tier and the user/consumer.

In the case of international marketing and product distribution we can further explore the implications of this approach of adding value through the supply chain approach to marketing.

- In line with the 'hands on' approach to market management advocated in Chapter 6, the export supplier can look for positive ways to add value to the importing distributor's business. The distributor will benefit through increased sales and efficiency, in turn increasing profits (through increased sales and lowered costs), in turn increasing his strength in the market and his relationships with his local market customers.
- Feedback of better sales and marketing information to the export supplier will further improve export product and production planning, reducing export stocks and associated costs, and enable the exporter to be more price competitive when appropriate.
- Closer contact of the exporter and his distributor with the users and trade distributors (retail or wholesale) in the foreign market will also result in a two-way flow of benefits along the chain.

The overall result of a co-operative approach to managing the international supply chain will be to increase satisfaction, rewards and associated benefits at each stage of the chain, with improved product quality, customer service and overall pipeline earnings, with better pricing and costing structures for each link to and including the final user or consumer.

Key factors in developing marketing strategies

The key issues the marketer may want to address when formulating strategies,

policies and programmes include the following:

- What is the stage of development of the target destination market in respect of **political, economic, social** and **technological** factors?
- What market sectors and destination markets can the company supply efficiently and effectively?
- At what stage of their life cycle are our products?
- What specific consumer/user needs do the product(s) satisfy?
- What attributes (tangible and intangible) differentiate the company's products from competitive products (locally made in the foreign market or exported from other sources)?
- What market data or research is available on target market sectors, destination markets, and competitors?
- What are our international market share and distribution objectives?

The first of these questions can be addressed by preparing what we normally term a **PEST analysis** (see Figure 9.7). This is just a commentary in an organized fashion that identifies issues surrounding the Political environment in the market, the Economic development and related factors that might influence our decisions and activities, the Social environment and the Technical factors and their impact on trading.

Some of these questions can only be addressed by the individual export marketer who can respond in relation to his own company plans, develop an audit that covers the issues listed above, and prepare a SWOT (**Strengths, Weaknesses, Opportunities, Threats**) analysis of the company as a supplier to export markets. We can discuss a number of the issues further in this chapter, and continue looking at aspects of developing strategies and planning in the subsequent chapters of this section.

Figure 9.8 illustrates a typical grid layout for a SWOT analysis, and in the left column

PEST ANALYSIS	
The political and economic environment, and its management	**POLITICAL** **ECONOMIC**
• Structure of political parties • Structure of political institutions • Electoral system • Political risk • Regulation of trade • Government policies • Responsiveness to social attitudes and public interest groups	• Government and economic planning • Government performance against objectives • Government involvement in economic activity • Regulation of foreign investment • Growth in GNP • Employment • Inflation and exchange rate management • Taxes and duties • Distribution infrastructures	**Review of political and economic factors, and their impact on the trading environment.**
The social and technological environment	**SOCIAL** **TECHNOLOGICAL**
• Market demographics and any changing patterns • Social attitudes • Social organizations • Traditions • Languages • Religion • Family issues • Life styles • Business practices	• Stage of technological development • Impact of technology on employment • Use of technology in industry • Use of technology in the home • Agrarian/ technological mix in the economy	**Review of social and technological factors, and their impact on the trading environment.**

Figure 9.7 Typical factors considered in a PEST analysis

identifies a range of typical factors that might be considered under the relevant headings of strengths, weaknesses and opportunities or threats.

The export marketer can prepare a SWOT analysis of the company as a supplier to the markets. In annual export strategy plans there should be a SWOT analysis for the company in relation to each market, to help

focus attention on the need for a market-specific element to strategy (remember 'Think Global – Act Local'!).

Market segments and destination markets

Companies may decide to concentrate on market segments where they perceive an

SWOT ANALYSIS	
Strengths	Weaknesses
Opportunities	Threats

Historical internal factors

- Technology
- Finance
- Distributor network
- Sales resources
- Reputation
- Marketing expertise
- Market share

- Innovation
- Compatible products
- Production capabilities
- Trade relations
- Cost structures

Current and future external factors

- Economic and political environment
- New market sectors
- New product developments
- Trade channel dynamics and buying power

- Competitor activity and technology
- Legislation
- Take-overs
- Import/export controls
- Import/export trade

Figure 9.8 *Typical factors to consider in a SWOT analysis*

advantage or strength, or to concentrate on destination markets where they believe they will have or find an advantage. The international marketers may be the arbiters within the company of where the segment or destination market strengths lie. We will look more at market segmentation in Chapter 10.

Stages in the product life cycle

Traditional marketing theory postulates that all products have a finite life cycle, but the length of that cycle will vary with the nature of the products and markets. The typical product life cycle for a brand may look as in the illustration of Figure 9.9, with notations

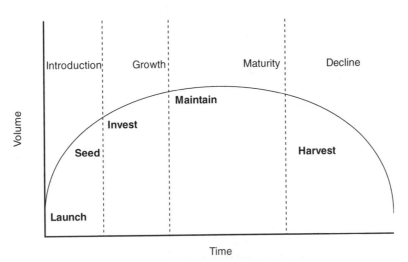

Figure 9.9 *Typical product life cycle and marketing strategies*

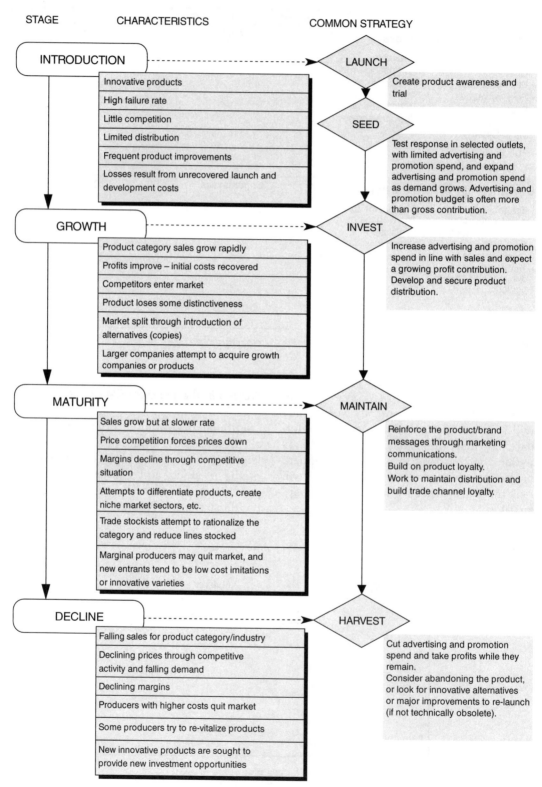

STAGE   CHARACTERISTICS   COMMON STRATEGY

INTRODUCTION ┄┄┄┄┄┄┄┄┄┄┄┄┄┄► LAUNCH

Innovative products
High failure rate
Little competition
Limited distribution
Frequent product improvements
Losses result from unrecovered launch and development costs

Create product awareness and trial

SEED

Test response in selected outlets, with limited advertising and promotion spend, and expand advertising and promotion spend as demand grows. Advertising and promotion budget is often more than gross contribution.

GROWTH ┄┄┄┄┄┄┄┄┄┄┄┄┄┄► INVEST

Product category sales grow rapidly
Profits improve – initial costs recovered
Competitors enter market
Product loses some distinctiveness
Market split through introduction of alternatives (copies)
Larger companies attempt to acquire growth companies or products

Increase advertising and promotion spend in line with sales and expect a growing profit contribution. Develop and secure product distribution.

MATURITY ┄┄┄┄┄┄┄┄┄┄┄┄┄┄► MAINTAIN

Sales grow but at slower rate
Price competition forces prices down
Margins decline through competitive situation
Attempts to differentiate products, create niche market sectors, etc.
Trade stockists attempt to rationalize the category and reduce lines stocked
Marginal producers may quit market, and new entrants tend to be low cost imitations or innovative varieties

Reinforce the product/brand messages through marketing communications.
Build on product loyalty.
Work to maintain distribution and build trade channel loyalty.

DECLINE ┄┄┄┄┄┄┄┄┄┄┄┄┄┄► HARVEST

Falling sales for product category/industry
Declining prices through competitive activity and falling demand
Declining margins
Producers with higher costs quit market
Some producers try to re-vitalize products
New innovative products are sought to provide new investment opportunities

Cut advertising and promotion spend and take profits while they remain.
Consider abandoning the product, or look for innovative alternatives or major improvements to re-launch (if not technically obsolete).

Figure 9.10 *The product life cycle – stages and strategies explained*

as to a typical brand investment and profit recovery strategy. A company may decide to pursue a different approach to investing or maintaining a brand for its own strategic reasons (possibly in export marketing including insecurity of access to foreign markets).

We can add in some comments on the likely marketing or investment strategy at the various stages of the product life cycle shown in Figure 9.9, and typically there are five main strategies, explained further in Figure 9.10 – **launch** the product, **seed** the product in outlets suited to the target market to test response prior to major investment, **invest** during the growth phase, **maintain** the product sales volume and market share during the mature phase, and **harvest** any remaining profits from the product during the decline phase. Some products will have benefited from extensive research and test marketing prior to launch, in which case fair estimates might have been made on sales potential, and heavy investment in advertising and promotion very soon after launch would be warranted to pre-empt competitive entry and activity, and to help generate a sales volume that shows a positive profit contribution and recovers pre-launch investment.

From the international marketer's perspective, the key point to recognize and take account of in developing marketing strategies is that any one product may be at very different stages in its life cycle in different markets (Figure 9.11). That will be a reflection of a range of local market factors, including the availability of competitive or substitute products, the sophistication of the foreign markets, the distribution infrastructure, local economic factors (income, employment, etc.), local market cultures, local brand awareness and loyalty, and so on.

Consumers in many less sophisticated markets are notoriously suspicious of change in their major brands, and often suspect counterfeit products. Loyalty to a brand and design might extend a product's life cycle in some markets. Exports frequently offer a way to extend the life cycle of a product, taking it into new markets where some additional sales volume and profits can be generated. That may sometimes provide breathing space to develop, test and launch new variants in the home market.

Product users or consumers tend to be different at different stages of the product life cycle, as illustrated in Figure 9.12. Five categories of user/consumer are tradition-

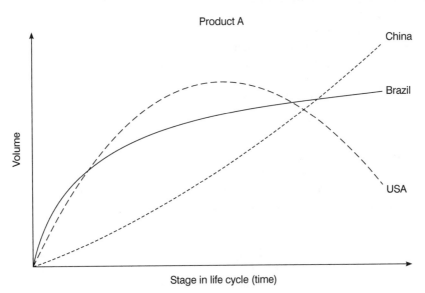

Figure 9.11 A product at different life cycle stages in different markets

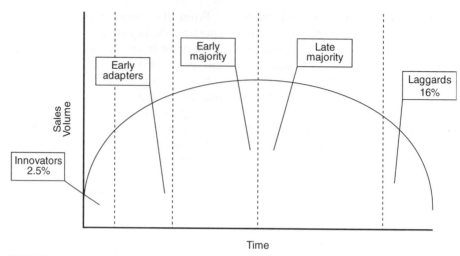

Figure 9.12 *The product life cycle in relation to consumer types*

ally identified – **innovators**, **early adopters**, **early majority**, **late majority** and **laggards** – and this has implications for both domestic and international marketing management of the product, as the marketing strategies, including aspects of the **marketing mix** such as **place**, **promotion** and **price**, may need to vary at the different life cycle stages to attract the appropriate category of user/consumer.

An example might be the 'designer' beers of recent years, often launched in a limited range of outlets frequented by **innovators** and **early adopters**, at premium prices. Distribution is initially restricted so that the mass of outlets frequented by **early majority**, **late majority** and **laggards** do not have the brand. When pressure of demand from outlets serving those customer types prompts expanded distribution, the innovators and early adopters will probably be moving on to a new brand.

New products launched into export markets will also follow a pattern of expansion through the different customer types. An established product in the home market may be directed, through distribution and marketing communications strategies, towards the innovators and early adopters in the export market, as these are the groups that respond to making personal discoveries about products. Some of our imported

'designer' beers in the United Kingdom are mass market brands in their source markets.

Products with a potentially long life cycle can often be rolled out internationally at a slower controlled pace, but hi-tech or fashion products with potentially short lives often need a rapid roll out or simultaneous launch into the major markets if obsolescence is not to occur before sales potential is achieved.

Consumer/user needs

In traditional marketing phraseology, we learn that a product should solve a problem or satisfy a need if it is to find a market. International marketers must be clear what needs their products will satisfy or what problems they can solve in order to take these factors into account in the marketing strategy. A brainstorming session will expand your thoughts from the obvious to the creative opportunities.

The user need might be for aesthetic design factors. In fact, design might create the need: the modern trend to designer kitchen implements has led to the discarding of perfectly functional models in many households in favour of a multiplicity of fancy kettles, electric toasters and so on.

In third world markets the emphasis is often on functionality, reliability and serviceability, as consumers cannot afford to discard old models when new versions appear in the stores. In some cases, even after technology has made traditional standard products obsolete at home, they can continue to find a foreign market segment where the utilitarian aspects of their design and functionality meet humbler local needs.

Product differentiation attributes

This topic is discussed in more depth in Chapter 10. Suffice it to say at this point that the more ways a product can be differentiated from competitor (or substitute) products, whether these points of differentiation are tangible (i.e. lower running costs, productivity, quality, etc.), or intangible (i.e. source, status in ownership, image, design, etc.) the greater its competitive edge and the higher price it can usually be marketed at in relation to less differentiated competitor products in any particular market.

Availability of market research data

Most exporters have limited resources, both in terms of management and funds to allocate to the pursuit of market data. That in itself perhaps limits the expertise with which markets are evaluated. In the hunt for relevant information to assist the decision-making process, the questions you face are primarily:

- What information is available?
- Where is it located or obtainable from?
- How long will it take to obtain and analyse it?
- What is the cost of obtaining it?

Chapter 3, Preliminary desk research, goes into some depth in discussing the kind of information that might be useful and available (often from government sources or published research), in terms of both market statistics and potential distribution channels, so I will not repeat all that here, but concentrate on the overall marketing approach. Suffice it to say again that there is a large amount of government-sourced data, and many very useful market research summaries on competitive activity and market shares, segment sizes, etc., available in published resources. The *Economists Intelligence Unit*, *Euromonitor* and *Mintel*, to mention just a few here, based in London, have a wealth of research, especially for European markets, that can often be tapped into. Some sources are referred to in the address list in Appendix 1.

Market share and distribution objectives

The export marketer will normally set objectives in these areas as part of the export planning process. Obviously these objectives should be realistic and achievable, and once they are established the main thrust of marketing strategy, including the marketing communications, must be put in place to promote their achievement. An agent or distributor will be highly demotivated if demands are made that he does not have the skills, power, support and means to achieve. Some markets might be treated opportunistically, with low objectives and expectations, matched by low investment and resource allocation. Other markets might be seen as strategically important for market penetration and benefit from high resource allocation.

Further reading

Marketing Planning and Strategy. Subhash C. Jain (Southwestern College Publishing (1993). Chapter 18: Global Marketing Strategies. This whole book is relevant to strategic planning.

Marketing – An Introductory Text. Martin Christopher and Malcolm McDonald (Macmillan 1995)

Marketing Management – Analysis, Planning, Implementation, and Control. Philip Kotler (Prentice Hall 1994). Chapter 4: Managing the Marketing Process and Market Planning; Chapter 14: Managing Product Life Cycles and Strategies

International Marketing. Stanley J. Paliwoda and Michael J. Thomas (Butterworth-Heinemann, 3rd edition 1998). Chapter 1: International marketing in a global economy

International Marketing – A Strategic Approach to World Markets. Simon Majaro (Routledge, 3rd edition 1991). Chapter 6: Product Policies for World Markets; Chapter 10: Marketing Planning on an International Scale; Chapter 13: Creativity and Innovation in International Marketing

Relationship Marketing. Martin Christopher, Adrian Payne and David Ballantyne (Butterworth-Heinemann). Chapter 1: Relationship Marketing

Checklist 9.1
Applying marketing principles to export markets

Action points

● Do you have a **sales** approach or a **marketing** approach to export market development?

Sales approach	**Marketing approach**
● Markets select company.	● Markets identified through research.
● Opportunistic response.	● Focused effort.
● Agents/distributors appointed with little research.	● Agents/distributors appointed after thorough research.
● Poor agreements.	● Comprehensive agreements.
● Limited training of export marketers.	● Focused training of export marketers.
● 'Hands off' market management.	● 'Hands on' market management.
● Sales target oriented.	● Market penetration oriented.
● Marketers control too many markets.	● Smaller portfolio of markets.
● Export prices based on a factory cost format.	● Export pricing based on strategic market positioning.
● Always price in sterling.	● Prices in currency to suit customers.
● Export planning focused on sales targets.	● Export planning based on strategic approach to priority markets.
● Only sells domestic products.	● Modifies products to suit market needs.
● Little trade channel knowledge.	● Good trade channel knowledge.
● Limited monitoring of export performance.	● Close monitoring of export performance with benchmarking.
● Marketing communications budgets fixed as percentage of sales.	● Marketing communications budgets geared to strategic objectives.

● Have you developed a global marketing strategy that encompasses the **6 Ps** of the **marketing mix: product**?; **pricing**?; **promotion**?; **placing**?; **people**?; **processes**?

● Have you prepared a **SWOT analysis**?

● Are you clear on the market segments you are targeting?

● Have you considered **product life cycle** factors?

● Does your export marketing strategy identify all of the potential consumer/user needs your products can address in each destination market?

● Have you identified all the points of product differentiation of your products versus competitive products available in each destination market, and taken account of these in developing an appropriate local marketing strategy?

● Have you undertaken a thorough review of all the available market research that will help the export marketing and planning processes?

10

Developing an export strategy

 This chapter will focus on issues that should concern the export marketer when developing an export market strategy. We will look at aspects of:

- marketing planning
- decision areas in strategy development
- adding value through product differentiation
- market segmentation issues
- mapping trade channels
- product profit management and investment strategies

The aim will be to provide some pointers that the export marketer may find relevant and that should be considered when developing a formal export marketing strategy plan, and to encourage a more disciplined approach to export planning from the marketing perspective and not just from the sales perspective.

The last chapter highlighted some of the key issues the international marketer should consider in developing an export marketing strategy. In this chapter, and in the other chapters of this section of the text, we will further explore the strategy development process, and we will look at the inputs normally considered in developing a practical market plan.

Why plan?

Planning is a core management function, although one that often attracts too little time within a busy export manager's schedule. The time given to planning is less critical than the quality of the planning, and with that in mind this chapter will attempt

to present a framework for the export market planning process. Planning gives a sense of purpose and direction to subsequent activities, by:

- setting objectives
- identifying priorities
- recognizing key result areas
- developing strategies and tactics
- monitoring results.

By 'key result areas' I am referring to aspects of the business which impact on the outcome of a plan, but which might not always appear in the shortlist of primary objectives. For example, in many impulse consumer products a key result area might be the effective use of point of sales material, or obtaining display siting in the most visible and accessible position in an outlet. For an industrial product a key result area might be accessing the end user of a product within an organization (usually a different person from the buyer), or the selection of key exhibitions to target specific user groups. In any form of export selling activity a key result area might be the distributor's level and use of professional selling skills, and distributor product knowledge. The export marketer should take a little time to identify and list those key result areas that demonstrably impact on his performance and ability to achieve market objectives because programmes must be put in place to address the key result areas.

The export planning must be integrated with the domestic marketing planning (illustrated in Figure 10.1) for maximum efficiency in the use of resources (human, physical and financial), and to ensure consistency of strategy and focus on company priorities (e.g. market share, penetration, profit, etc.).

Stages in the planning process ■

The full export planning process in most companies will encompass the stages of:

- developing an overall company corporate plan
- setting country objectives for each export market
- developing specific strategies to achieve objectives
- developing market sales and profit forecasts
- making specific programmes (tactics and plans) to achieve objectives (e.g. breaking down market sales forecasts by outlet or customer and setting sales targets, identifying new business opportunities such as targeting specific potential outlets or users, developing supporting promotional activity)
- developing controls to monitor results and ensure the implemented strategies and tactics produce results in line with plans

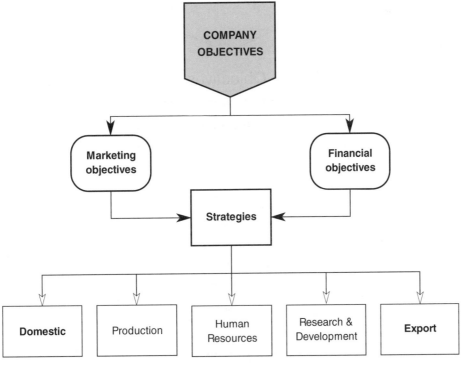

Figure 10.1 Developing strategies from company objectives

- taking corrective action where deviations from plans occur.

The export marketer must look to identify what information he needs to assist the planning process as well as considering how he can measure progress against plans and towards achieving objectives. Making a market plan means having access to **historical data** on each market (such as import and sales data) and using that historical data to project market trends, and then making reasoned **assumptions** about factors that are outside the control of the exporter and other players in his market (such as exchange rate movements and the market's economic environment). We will look in Chapter 11 at these planning inputs, and Figure 10.2 illustrates the stages in the planning process.

An alternative way of illustrating the planning process is shown in Figure 10.3. This presents planning rather like a road map, working from a starting point, with a clear destination in mind, planning the route, and having landmarks to check you remain on course.

An international strategy committee

Planning for the development of international markets is an ongoing activity. Apart from direct product exports from domestic production facilities there may be a range of other profit generating opportunities. Export market managers may not have the time or insight to broader aspects of

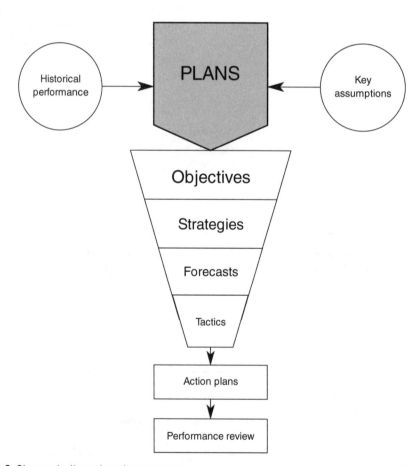

Figure 10.2 Stages in the planning process

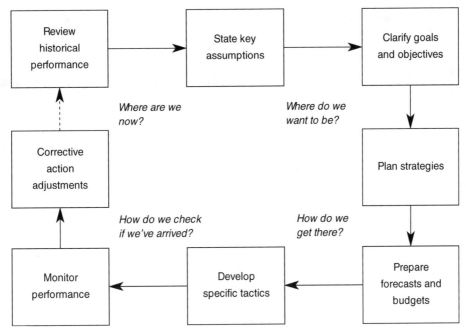

Figure 10.3 *The planning road map*

corporate strategy to plan for all the opportunities, but will have specialist knowledge to contribute to planning at the level of individual markets. In most larger organizations there will be scope for a level of international strategic planning that might involve a number of senior managers from various functional departments, under guidance from the chief executive or director designated with corporate planning responsibilities. In developing an international strategy it is valuable for the senior line manager or chief executive to give consideration to such factors as:

- the company's existing product range
- technology to develop new and modified products
- originality of know-how and technology developed within the company, particularly compared with levels of knowledge and technology considered 'public'
- other exclusive commercial expertise
- management skills within the organization

- management resources
- financial, research, technical, production and other relevant resources.

Perhaps the way to start to develop a strategy to go beyond mere physical exports is to form an **international strategy committee** internally, possibly with the role illustrated in Figure 10.4. This group might need to meet only every few months (since it need not necessarily be an operational group implementing ideas). Ideally, it should probably be chaired by someone not bound by the limitations of the current systems and practices, possibly from outside the marketing department, or even by the chief executive. Membership would probably include the senior representatives of major functional departments. Other managers with specialist knowledge or skills should be co-opted as necessary. Specific projects should perhaps be delegated to sub-committees so that they can be the subject of detailed investigations and reports.

The strategy committee could divide its attention, according to short-, medium- and longer-term priorities, to give consideration systematically to such broad areas as:

- direct product exports
- transfer of know-how and technology abroad
- foreign mergers, acquisitions and joint ventures
- import of foreign know-how and technology
- development of raw material and semi-processed material sources abroad.

Checklist 10.2 at the end of the chapter expands in more detail on aspects of these areas of business development that might be the focus of strategic study.

Marketing planning

Perhaps the most important function of the international marketer is planning. It need not be the most time consuming, but is critical in reducing the risks associated with investing in foreign market product launches, and subsequent management of a portfolio of products. At the core of planning is the consumer or user of the product,

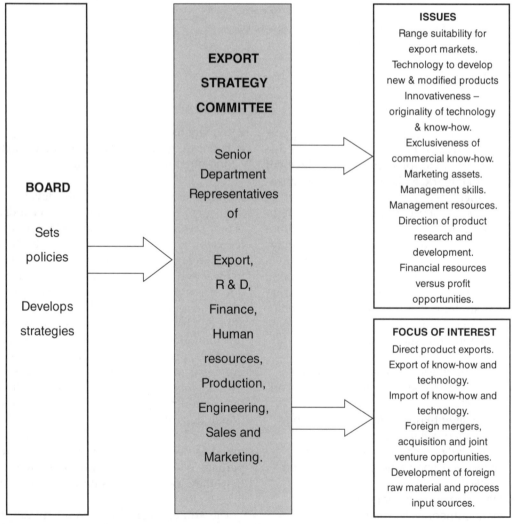

Figure 10.4 Role of the export strategy committee

the final focus of all marketing activity. Figure 10.5 illustrates the planning chain diagrammatically.

Typically basic planning would start with market research into the size and potential of the international markets, consumer/user needs, distribution channels, competitive activity, etc. The results of research will aid product planning to ensure the range offered meets market needs. In some instances special products might be developed for particular markets, in other cases the company may face production inflexibility where the choices are limited to seeking markets that can accept and develop with standard products.

Next the marketer will have to develop international distribution policies and establish a distribution network in each target foreign market, that may also include an after-sales service support operation for some type of technical products.

All this must be supported by the planning of marketing communications and promotional activity, including trade sales literature, trade and consumer advertising, as suits the particular product. This is again complicated by differing needs for different export markets, both in terms of languages and strategies.

Pricing will be a key element in international marketing, influenced by product manufacturing and distribution cost factors on the one hand, and demand factors such as the values the user/consumer will place on the product in relation to alternatives on the other. As exporters know only too well, they have much less control often over their product pricing structures in international markets. Agents and distributors can always

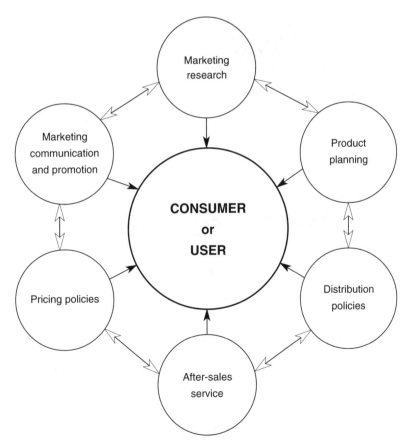

Figure 10.5 Basic planning elements in marketing

find arguments favouring lower exporter prices (have you ever found one to suggest you increase export prices!), but rarely take a sophisticated approach to managing market prices in relation to competitor products.

The marketing strategy planning process

Strategy planning essentially must include the tasks of collecting relevant data on the market, competitors, customers and the environment, as well as internal company analysis and audit, and then formulating strategy that addresses specific objectives

that take account of the analysis stage results. Implementation of a strategy results in the finer detail planning and establishing monitoring systems, as well as development of tactics for achieving the strategic objectives. Figure 10.6 illustrates the tasks the marketer must address.

In smaller organizations strategy planning and market planning will be performed by the same persons, the export marketers. In larger organizations the strategy planning will be the responsibility of a central marketing team perhaps, with the local market modification and implementation, through individual market plans, being the responsibility of the export marketers.

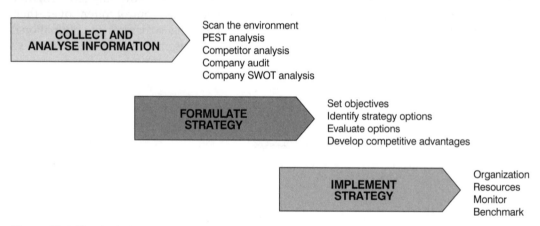

Figure 10.6 The tasks in strategy development

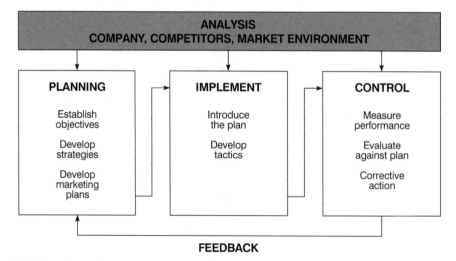

Figure 10.7 Planning – the continuous process

The planning process is continuous, as illustrated in Figure 10.7, and ongoing analysis must monitor the company, competitors, consumers and the environment, in order that any variations from planning assumptions and expected reactions and performance can be countered through corrective action programmes.

Most companies, consumer and industrial product suppliers, operate to an annual planning cycle, with set times by which central marketing and individual market plans and budgets must be prepared and submitted to dovetail into the overall company plan. Figure 10.8 illustrates typical stages in the annual planning cycle.

With the emphasis on planning and implementation, another diagrammatic model, Figure 10.9, illustrates the marketing role in market planning and programme implementation.

In this diagram, at the planning stage we would be taking a portfolio perspective, looking at the inter-relationships of all our products in the portfolio in developing strategies for investment, product pricing and product positioning within the portfolio and in relation to competition. The outcome of the planning is that we make sales and financial projections for each market and the overall export operations.

At the implementation stage, which involves both the export market manager and his local agent or distributor, action focuses on individual brands or products within the company's product portfolio, with advertising and promotional activity aimed at specific products. The outcome being achievement of sales targets and profit forecasts.

It is always useful to have a form of framework to planning. Figure 10.10

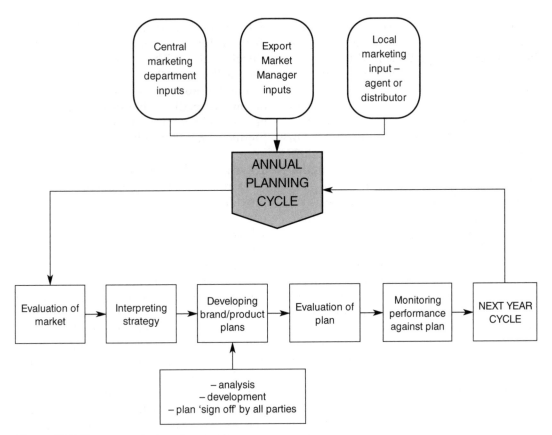

Figure 10.8 The annual planning cycle

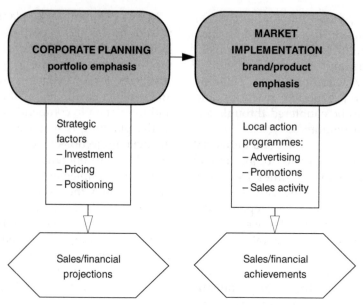

Figure 10.9 The inter-relationship between planning and implementation

illustrates a basic framework model for a market strategy plan. The **product portfolio strategy** considerations lead to the individual **brand or product strategies**. Account will then be taken of the strategic marketing mix factors, to ensure a compatibility between product factors (whether design and other physical attributes, or those related to user/consumer perceptions of the product), the pricing, the distribution channels that ensure it is in the right place both for its sale and service and consistent with the customer profiles of the distribution channels, the promotional support (above-the-line advertising and below-the-line promotions) for the product, the people involved in all aspects of providing the goods to export markets and customers, and the processes involved in producing goods and servicing markets.

Each export market will benefit from a market plan that considers this framework in relation to the individual market.

The **marketing communication strategy** for each market will develop from the strategic brand or product plans, which may be made on a global basis and adap-

ted for local markets, or might be quite different for each market where there is no global strategy. The communication strategy will normally address advertising, where the products are supported by trade or mass media advertising, supporting below-the-line promotional activity, any product brands publicity that takes the form of sponsorship or public relations activity, and the sales force. The sales force has a role in marketing communications in providing an interface between the company and the trade buyer or end user. The salesperson communicates product messages through his sales presentations, and through the use of sales literature and point of sales promotional materials.

Brand or product plans are primarily of interest to the supplier. His agent or distributor is less concerned with market shares, brand positioning and other aspects of the marketing plan, that may seem rather theoretical to him, than he is with the practicalities of achieving growing sales volume and profits through his field selling activities. The export marketer, with planning and implementation responsibility across a

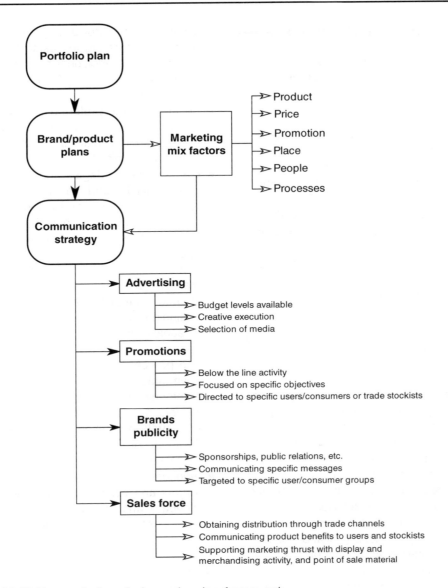

Figure 10.10 *The marketing strategy planning framework*

range of markets, has to think of planning at two levels:

- the company strategy for the for the products in the market
- a micro-level market plan, developed with the agent or distributor, that implements the marketing strategy through activities the distributor can relate to and be involved in, including detailed customer targets and specific sales distribution and promotional activities.

Now that we have highlighted some of the marketing issues in the export market planning process the other sections of this chapter contains more detailed commentary on considerations in developing strategies for export markets, and we will look further in Chapter 11 at developing the export market plan as a working document.

Developing your strategy ▄▄▄▄

To develop an effective marketing strategy to tackle the emerging international opportunities it will be essential to know:

- what your customers want from your products
- what competitive advantages you have
- your company and product strengths and weaknesses
- the strengths and weaknesses of your competitors' products and distribution activities
- external threats to your business and markets
- marketing opportunities.

The preparation of your marketing strategy should encompass the stages of:

- identifying and stating your objectives
- auditing your present product range and market position in relation to objectives, including looking at:
  - strengths, weaknesses, opportunities, and threats (SWOT analysis)
  - developments or changes in product range to meet objectives (innovation opportunities and capabilities)
  - suitability of existing distribution mechanisms and channels, or changes needed
  - organizational structure (including consideration of staff motivation, performance and commitment to the plans)
  - physical, financial and human resources
  - resource productivity (including cost advantages)
  - profitability and performance versus competitors
  - intellectual property (and protection)
- evaluating the alternative routes to achieving the objectives (which could include branches, subsidiaries, acquisitions, mergers, joint ventures, licensing, distributor arrangements or purely direct selling to customers) and identifying the additional resources and other changes needed for each alternative
- deciding on the preferred alternative route to achieving the objective, and make a specific plan to put the resources in place
- planning the strategies and tactics (in outline initially, and later in more detail) for each time span and stage of progress towards the objectives
- implementing the selected strategies for each aspect of the plan, particularly in respect of product range, priority markets, distribution modes and channels, organization
- designing the organization most likely to achieve the plans, ensuring that each person has the right mix of skills and personal qualities and the right environment (including training, communications, leadership, responsibility and accountability, measurability) to have the greatest likelihood of success in achieving objectives
- monitoring performance against plans, targets and objectives, providing feedback and taking corrective action as necessary to counter deviations.

No matter how much planning the international marketer puts in, external factors will have a bearing, and will continue to change. Instability of economic, political, legislative, social and cultural factors in some regions of the world means that marketing plans cannot be made with a high degree of certainty about external environmental factors.

It is likely that the export market plans developed by a company will contain a mixture of **maintenance** strategies for existing products and markets, and **development** strategies for new products or market sectors, and **defensive** strategies aimed to block openings for competitors.

THE TYPICAL FOCUS OF STRATEGIES

THE TYPICAL FOCUS OF STRATEGIES

Maintenance strategies:
- competitive pricing to broaden trial and penetration and block competitive activity
- expanding distribution of existing products
- higher levels of advertising and promotional activity
- efforts to extend product life cycles and to proliferate or expand variations on a product theme or to a market sector.

Product development strategies:
- innovation of new products either for existing markets or for new markets
- replacing obsolete products (or marketing concepts, for example, in retailing) with new ones aimed at the same market sectors
- trading up strategies to increase prices and profitability
- attacking competitors through innovation which makes their products undesirable through technological (or design or concept) obsolescence
- creating and exploiting new market niches.

Defensive strategies:
- making it more expensive for competitors to penetrate or enter your markets
- concentrating your activities and effort in those markets or sectors where you have most at risk or to lose
- recognizing your areas of weakness and taking countering action to avoid exposing yourself to competitive exploitation of them (e.g. tighten up on quality/service aspects to avoid user dissatisfaction).

Decision areas in strategy development

Figure 10.11 summarizes the key areas where the export marketer will be involved in taking decisions and which will impact on performance of the products in the target markets, and these points are expanded upon in the subsequent sections. In order to take decisions in these areas the export marketer needs an understanding of the subject matter of the subsequent sections of this chapter as well as an in-depth understanding of his products and markets.

These aspects listed in Figure 10.9 can be broken down further in the process of identifying what you have to offer, where

you want to sell it, and how you will promote the product in the markets, and lead towards a positive proactive export strategy and programme rather than a reactive (fill orders as they arrive), unplanned export operation.

If we consider the consumer or product user as the focus of marketing activity, and therefore the focus of decisions in the marketing mix, the export marketer, in taking his decisions, will have to progress through the stages of:

- conducting desk and/or marketing research into the markets and their needs and opportunities
- product planning to ensure the products offered meet market needs

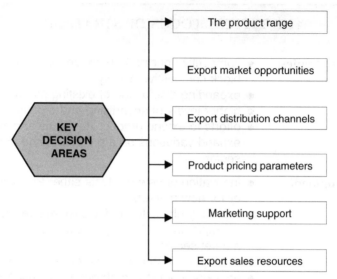

Figure 10.11 *Key considerations in developing export sales strategies*

- establishing distribution policies that meet the needs of the products, the consumers/users and the trade channel infrastructure of the markets
- establish pricing structures that take account of the marketplace, the competitive products and activity, the various levels of trade margins, local taxes, etc.
- planning product support where after-sales service is important
- developing marketing communications and promotional activity that communicate product features and benefits and the other messages associated with product positioning in the marketplace.

For the export marketer concerned with developing a more refined approach to his export strategy the following sections give additional subject coverage.

Product differentiation

Large multinational consumer goods manufacturers are used to developing market-

ing strategies that differentiate products within their product portfolios and from competition, and to segmenting markets in order to target products to specific groups of users or consumers. Many exporters do not look at aspects of market segmentation or product differentiation for export markets, adopting a 'let's just sell it' approach. This can result in products being directed to unsuitable consumers or end users, with resultant unsatisfactory sales performance as customers or an agent or distributor become disillusioned; or it can result in a value-added product being marketed like a commodity on a price basis where the differentiating features are not effectively communicated through the distribution chain.

The principles of product differentiation and market segmentation should be applied to export markets, and can apply to industrial as well as consumer goods, and to smaller producers as well as multinationals, and some discussion on aspects of adding value through product differentiation and segmenting markets as targets for specific products follows.

DECISION AREAS IN STRATEGY DEVELOPMENT

The product range	• What market segments to target product at (price, quality, use, etc.) • Branded products versus private label products • What product range to offer (taking account of: trends, preferences, traditional, fashions, technical innovations, product life cycle) • How to differentiate company products from competitors
The markets	• Customer mix, target customers or market segments • Relative importance of domestic markets versus exports • Geographical spread of markets • Cultural/linguistic factors in marketing the products
Distribution channels	• Security of access to markets • Distributor networks covering market segments • Direct end user sales (by company or an agent) • Retail/trade outlets • After-sales service support needs of products and customers
Pricing parameters	• Price positioning (in relation to competition and other products in the company product portfolio) • Trade terms of sale and customary trade margins in the markets • Discounts/performance rebates • Export distribution costs, sales taxes and import duties
Marketing support	• Marketing budgets • Advertising media and materials (suitability of company material or need to develop locally in any market) • Promotional activity supporting the products and distributors • Promotional literature • Means of promoting user/consumer trial and loyalty
Export sales resources	• Size of direct export sales force • Geographical spread of markets • Distributor or agent networks • Financial resources of the export company • Financial resources of distributors • Advertising and promotional budgets • Training resources • Rewards and incentives within distribution channels motivating achievement of sales and marketing objectives.

Adding value through product differentiation in marketing _____

At the heart of marketing is the product. This can be differentiated by value-adding factors such as:

- brand or corporate image
- after-sales service
- quality and reliability
- technical support
- user friendly manuals or instructions
- styling/design factors and other physical attributes
- customer service support and customer care
- consumer life style perceptions and aspirations, etc.

Some of these are tangible factors, but a number of them are really intangible and relate to the user or consumer's perceptions, often built through longer term marketing programmes and experience. Market research, either sophisticated through agencies or unsophisticated by face-to-face discussion with users, often gives guidance on what real or perceived attributes are seen as giving benefits, and how these benefits might be valued by consumers and users. Internal brainstorming might also produce a list of factors that add value to a company's products.

The more a product can be differentiated in the eyes of users and consumers the higher price can be attached to it in the market place and the more focused the supporting marketing programme can be in building brand awareness and loyalty.

Some companies take the policy decision to pitch their products into the mass market, with little or no attempt at product differentiation, hoping to pick off a share of the available consumers as cheaply as possible. Many companies work hard to establish formal marketing disciplines behind domestic product distribution and selling, but allow export selling to stay as a more opportunistic activity, doing little to take a focused approach to differentiating product

in each foreign market and targeting the appropriate market segments. The alternative to non-differentiation is to **differentiate** products through marketing mix factors such as:

- price
- design
- advertising and promotion
- consumer/user product perceptions
- distribution channels.

Price. Price is rarely the only basis of competition. With even the most basic commodities, other factors come into play, such as delivery times, continuity of supply, consistency of quality, etc. Providing other tangible or intangible attributes can be attached to a product, then price can be used as a differentiating factor in marketing.

In the 1950s and 1960s many Japanese products were perceived as low-quality mass market goods. Japan seemed forced to gain market entry through price, and gradually built market share. But over the last three decades there has been a switch in marketing emphasis, and product differentiation now often pitches the Japanese products at the forefront of innovative technology, commanding equivalent or premium prices to domestic products in many markets.

Design. Unique product features, designs fitting current (or desired) lifestyles or functional needs can aid product differentiation in the marketing programme. Many household goods and technological products originating from Germany and Scandinavia have built their success in international markets not on price competition, but on limiting supply and selling on quality, reliability, design, etc., (e.g. Bang & Olufsen hi-fi equipment; Bosch, Neff, AEG kitchen equipment).

Advertising and promotion. This activity immediately tackles the task of product differentiation, whether the message is simply that Wondasoap washes whiter than

Ultrawhite, or is geared to promoting awareness of where a product can be obtained. It involves a heavy commitment of funds in markets generally, but forms a larger part of the marketing strategy where market share is a dominant objective for strategic reasons (e.g. building volume to profitable levels, blocking competition, brand awareness and loyalty).

Consumer product perceptions. These perceptions are often unsupported by tangible factors. The brand loyalty factor often develops from consumers' product perceptions.

Consumers of luxury French perfumes are likely to be buying not because they have seen evidence that the product is purer, more concentrated, natural, healthy, and so on, but because of intangible lifestyle factors created through advertising. They may have a perception of what kind of person should use the product, and be putting themselves into that category. Similarly, drinkers of a premium Scotch whisky, such as *Chivas Regal*, *Dimple Haig* or *Black Label*, are purchasing the product in a bar more for intangible perceptional and lifestyle factors (perhaps making a statement of their success and affluence) than tangible benefits, since a less expensive brand will quench their thirst and meet their needs to become relaxed just as well.

Distribution channels. The channels of distribution we choose affect differential marketing. If the product is sold through every stockist of the product category (e.g. every high street supermarket or department store), then perhaps the opportunities for differential marketing are less than where certain exclusive stockists or distributors are appointed. Against this must be weighed the needs for advertising and promotional support to gain trial and market share. Some products that require specialist support, such as installation or service, will necessarily have to be distributed through a limited network of appointed dealers

If distribution channels are limited, advertising and promotional activity may be directed more cost effectively to the target users through selected media than through mass media such as television.

Frequently in export markets a product is in limited distribution not because of a conscious marketing decision or strategy, but because of an agent's or distributor's ineffectiveness to obtain broader distribution. Hence it is important that the export marketer conducts appropriate research into the market channels and agrees a specific distribution strategy, clearly identifying the trade channel outlets or users to be targeted in each plan time period.

If the aim is to maximize the market price for a product versus competition, then the company's marketing goal should be to add value, real or perceived, to its products in a way that ensures the products have perceived consumer benefits or product differentiation attributes greater than those associated with any competitive products in any particular market segment. Alternatively, specific decisions can be taken on where to position a product that gives a fair market price reflecting the differentiation attributes and consumer benefits in relation to competitive products. We will look further at this in Chapter 16, Export costing and pricing. A conscious approach to identifying what differentiates products and adds value will reduce the risk of under-pricing product, particularly where agents or distributors and customers make price their first point of attack during negotiations.

Figure 10.12 illustrates that the basic features or attributes of a product will appeal to a limited number of potential customers, primarily those treating the product as a commodity, when it comes to inter-product comparisons with several competing sources of product. As more value-added features and benefits, real or perceived, are associated with any one product in a competitive market, through effective marketing communications, the greater the number of customers that can be expected to be influenced and make favourable purchase decisions. And at higher

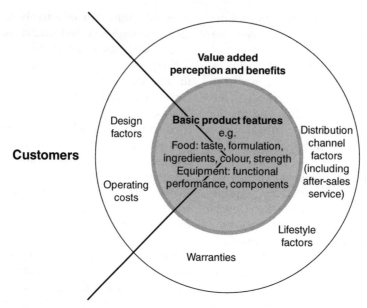

Figure 10.12 *Adding value to products in marketing*

prices than for the non-differentiated commodity oriented alternatives.

Differential advantage

The advantages to the user or consumer offered by a product that has features that differentiate it from competitive products come not so much from the features themselves, but the benefits the user or consumer derives from those features. The marketing communications must focus on communicating not just the actual feature, but the benefit. In some cases the benefit might be obvious, i.e. a computer with 10 gigabytes of memory will store more than one with half that memory. In other cases the benefit is not obvious, i.e. a single malt scotch whisky may offer the consumer a particularly pleasurable taste experience, a non-obvious (and perhaps very personal) benefit, or an industrial cleaning fluid that states a certain strength and recommended dilution level may offer a cost reduction benefit over competitors' products.

The next stage for the marketer who recognizes the importance promoting

aspects of the differential advantages of his products over competition is to identify and list all the tangible and intangible product features or attributes, and convert these to user and consumer benefits that can be promoted through the marketing communications strategy. Figure 10.13 shows some of the customer benefits derived from a few typical product features, and a similar list can be developed for any product. Whilst the features are common to all markets (unless the manufacturer makes various models to suit differing market needs), the benefits that users or consumers value the product for may vary between export markets, and local marketing communications can carry the appropriate promotional messages.

Market segmentation

It is important that the export marketing process correctly approaches the issues of market segmentation as errors mean:

● mismatching products and customer needs

SOME TYPICAL PRODUCT BENEFITS ADDRESSING CUSTOMER NEEDS

Price
- good value
- competitive
- economy in use
- payment terms (credit)
- return on investment
- depreciation

Advertising and promotion
- product familiarity
- lifestyle compatibility
- 'designer'

Consumer perceptions
- fashionableness
- pride in ownership
- packaging
- supplier's image and reputation
- scarcity value
- prestige and status

Product and design
- modern
- novelty
- functionality
- durability
- ease of use and servicing
- safety factors
- quality and reliability
- performance and efficiency
- range of options
- warranties
- labour saving
- space saving
- range of accessories
- easy instructions
- environmentally friendly

Distribution channels
- availability
- speed of delivery
- after sales service

- lost sales and profit opportunities
- leaving demand opportunities open to consumers.

In this section we will look at some of the key principles of market segmentation that should be applied to export markets within the export strategy development process.

Few companies can aim to sell their products into all market segments, either because they would not have the resources to do so, or because they would not have a competitive advantage in certain segments, or because they do not have the expertise in supplying some segments. Focusing effort on sales and distribution to certain market

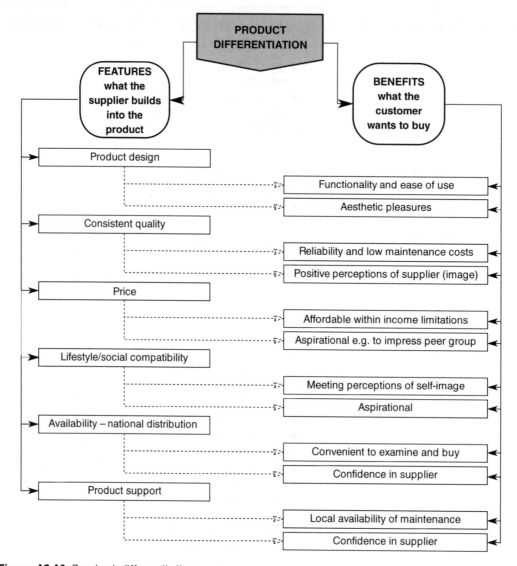

Figure 10.13 *Product differentiation*

segments generally makes a more efficient use of limited resources. When looking to identify market segments, or to target products to particular market segments already identified, there are several aspects of segmentation the marketer is likely to be concerned with, e.g.:

- the criteria for identifying and dividing the market into sub-groups of users or consumers

- factors in grouping users or consumers into specific groups, such as according to defined life styles or grouping according to the product benefits that influence choice
- developing consumer or user profile descriptions that then help in identifying and targeting current or potential users of the product
- issues that can be the subject of specific market research, such as:

- what is bought?
- who is buying?
- where is it being bought?
- why are the products being bought?
- other issues in segmenting markets and targeting segments, such as:
  - your ability to obtain distribution to supply the target market segment of users or consumers
  - your share of sales volume in a market segment
  - the responses of the trade channel outlets to your products, prices, promotions
  - the responses of consumers or users to your product, prices and promotions.

Market segments must be identifiable and separate from each other, and capable of being described in quantitative or qualitative terms that are meaningful in terms of summarizing consumer or user purchasing behaviour. Figure 10.14 illustrates these main points, and subsequent diagrams look in more detail at market segmentation.

Criteria for segmenting markets

Attempts to segment the market, or to identify likely sub-groups suitable for segmented marketing, should recognize that each segment ought to meet the following criteria.

Relevancy. The basis for segmentation must relate to the purchase or use of the product, e.g. for consumer goods, demographic or socio-economic criteria, or for industrial products relevant criteria could include the type of industrial processes used, the nature of finished product, etc.

Accessibility. Existing trade channels must exist to enable goods to be distributed to the target market segments (or the development of new trade channels must be feasible and cost effective).

Measurability. Targeted segments must be capable of being measured and monitored for planning and performance monitoring against objectives, such as sales, distribution, market share, profitability.

Potential. The segment must be sufficiently large to be cost effectively serviced and capable of producing a net profit after all costs specific to marketing and distributing product targeted to the segment, including special A & P costs and launch investment.

Segmentation factors

Markets are typically segmented by grouping consumers or users by common factors that reflect their motivational reasons to acquire and use a product. Whilst there may be several market segments, within each segment there should be clearly identifiable common profiles. Major criteria for grouping product users or consumers are:

- life styles
- product benefits.

Life style benefits are particularly applicable as a motivation to purchase consumer goods, where factors such as the target consumer's real life style, aspirations and attitudes can be important both in segmenting the market, and in subsequent marketing communications to influence trial or promote product loyalty.

Product benefits are applicable equally to consumer or industrial products, where customers are concerned with obtaining benefits standard to all products in a category (i.e. a computer that will process and store data), but additionally may derive particular personal or company benefits from a supplier (such as confidence in the supplier based on prior experience and relationships), and may also seek benefits that differentiate the product from competitors (such as the processing speed of the computer, or size of memory, or quality of components).

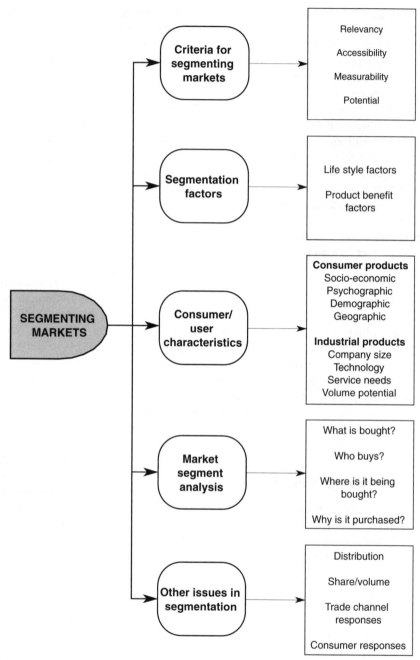

Figure 10.14 *Market segmentation*

Figure 10.15 illustrates this splitting of segmentation factors into life style and product benefits. Consumer products frequently include a mix of both life style factors and product benefits in their media communications. Industrial products can take a similar approach by featuring a major corporation using its products, encouraging smaller companies to aspire to use the same product in their operations.

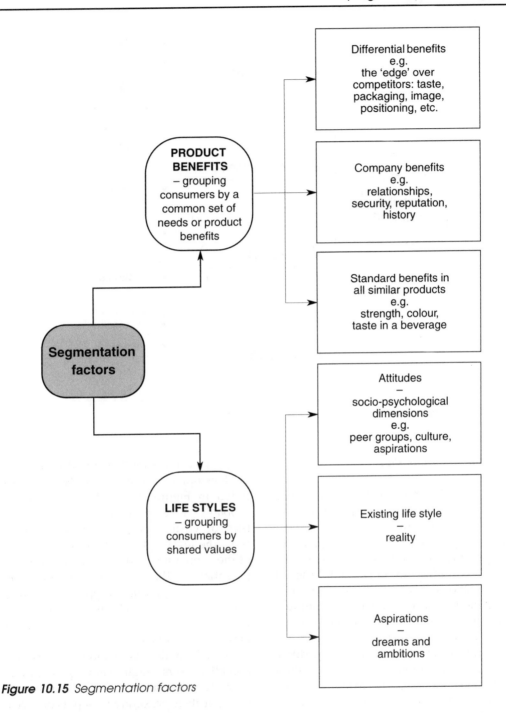

Figure 10.15 *Segmentation factors*

Characteristics for segmentation

The characteristics of the consumer or user can be very important factors in deciding how to segment markets or whom to target products to. These characteristics can be better looked at by sub-classifying them into those that apply to individual consumers, i.e. persons who purchase goods for personal use, and industrial users, i.e. those buyers who purchase goods for use in their business operations or manufacturing processes.

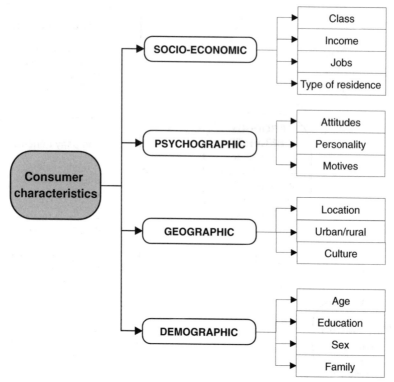

Figure 10.16 Consumer characteristics for segmentation

Consumer characteristics

Figure 10.16 illustrates that consumer characteristics for market segmentation can, typically, fall into the categories of socio-economic, psychographic, geographic and demographic characteristics, and some further sub-groupings are illustrated. Research or experience normally will provide a profile of the typical consumer for a product, or, if there is more than one motivational reason behind product purchase and use (see Figure 10.14) then there may be different consumer profiles for each of these motivational reasons. The reader may like to chart characteristics relevant to his or her own products.

Industrial characteristics

Industrial demographic characteristics will differ from consumer demographics, and some typical factors that might be relevant in developing customer profiles are illustrated in Figure 10.17. The marketer will probably develop industry segment profiles of customers covering the industry type, the level of technology used, the size of the companies in the segments, and their potential for the exporter's products, and the level of product support needed to conclude a sale (such as custom design work) or after completion of a sale (such as periodic maintenance).

Other breakdowns of industrial segment potential users might show geographical characteristics, such as the locations of the users, or their proximity to depots or service facilities. Further segmentation might also show a breakdown by buyer type – whether a professional buyer concerned primarily with financial factors, or a specialist buyer, such as an engineer or research scientist, concerned with technology and performance factors.

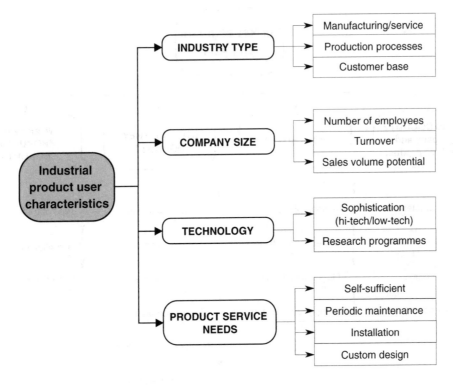

Figure 10.17 *Industrial demographic characteristics*

Other issues in segmentation ▬

A company has to look at more issues than those outlined in the preceding sections. Understanding the segmentation of markets involves acquiring a lot of knowledge of the products in a market, and the potential customers for the product, and the distribution channels. The supplier who targets a segment for his products needs to have entry to the distribution channels serving that segment, and ensure that he can meet the particular needs of the distribution channels, such as product merchandising for some consumer goods, or after-sales service for many industrial products (including, possibly, holding local consignment stocks of spares if product is sold through an agent).

The potential share or volume the supplier might expect to achieve in a market segment is likely to have a bearing on decisions as to which markets to focus effort

on. Where there is a strong market leader the costs of market entry could be too high for the smaller supplier to make an impact. Alternatively, where alternative benefits can be offered, which might include price benefits, dominant suppliers might still be vulnerable.

Figure 10.18 illustrates aspects the marketer is likely to research and analyse in deciding which market segments to target product at in each of his export markets. He will want detailed information on the range of alternative products on offer, the characteristics that differentiate one from another, and prices. As outlined previously, data may be available on consumer or user characteristics. Surveys of buyers might show why products are selected, and enable marketing communications to promote relevant messages that will encourage buyers to consider the product in relation to his needs and reasons for selecting products. Nielsen data, or similar data, might show the pattern of

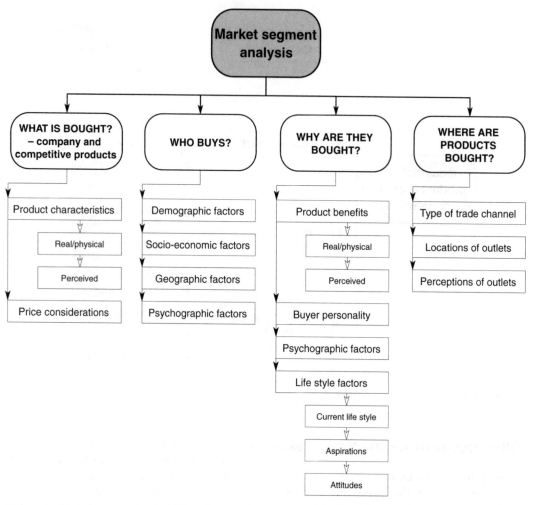

Figure 10.18 *Issues in segmentation – market segment analysis*

sales of consumer goods in sophisticated markets, but more crude survey work may be all that is practical for less developed markets or industrial products.

Mapping trade channels ▬▬▬▬

The section on segmentation deals with developing an awareness of specific market segments and prioritizing those that the exporter has the best chance of supplying and servicing profitably. Distribution to the priority segments will be obtained through the trade channels serving the network of users and consumers.

Trade channel mapping is just a term for plotting the structure of the trade channels in a market, and noting which market segments they serve and their relative importance in the marketplace. It is essential that the export marketer understands the structure of distributive trade channels in each of his markets, as this knowledge influences strategic decisions on where to target products. Understanding the structure and relationships of trade channels is essential in developing trade marketing strategies and programmes appropriate to the local market. Not every company has the resources to target either all market segments or all of the trade channels serving

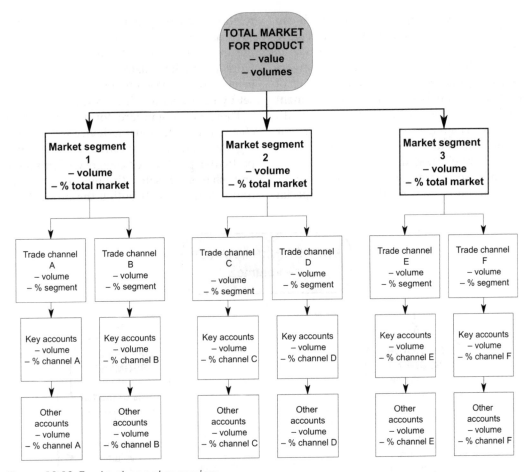

Figure 10.19 *Trade channel mapping*

the market segments, and decisions need to be taken that reflect the most profitable opportunities and the distributive strengths and expertise of the exporting company. Export marketers frequently demonstrate limited knowledge about the structure and size of trade channels, their relative importance in supplying market segments, and their sales volumes in the product category. Discussions that raise the matter of the limited extent of knowledge normally raise the responses that the agent or distributor is not forthcoming with detailed information, but the reality is often that the agent or distributor himself has limited detailed knowledge where they represent a broad product range into many trade channels.

The objectives of trade channel mapping are to:

- identify the trade channels for the exporter's products
- identify the key accounts in each trade channel
- develop a trade channel strategy.

The export marketer will want to know:

- how many trade channels are there serving each market segment?
- who are the main customers in each trade channel, the key accounts?
- where are they located?
- how many outlets have they?
- what share have they of any trade channel?

This information is essential to planning the correct allocation of sales resources, and marketing and promotional budgets. It can be illustrated diagrammatically as in Figure 10.19.

Typically, in consumer goods markets (and for some industrial products) one of the trade channels in each market segment would be wholesalers, and the other would be direct customers of the distributor. For example, if trade channel A is a wholesaler trade channel, then the wholesalers would normally service a certain range of larger (key) accounts where they have special relationships or provide a special service, such as a broader product range than just the exporter's products, and a bigger network of smaller customers who might not be able to purchase the minimum quantities set by suppliers for direct supply.

There is no standard format for a trade channel map. It is just a device for presenting data on the respective volumes of a particular product, or category of products, and shares of sales through the various trade channels distributing the product. An

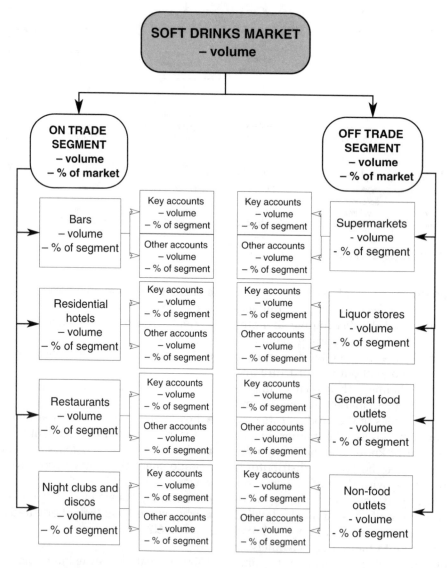

Figure 10.20 Soft drinks market – trade channel mapping

illustrative trade channel map for a supplier of soft drinks might look something like Figure 10.20.

Here the map shows two main market segments: the 'on trade', where product is served for consumption on the premises; and the 'off trade', where product is sold for later consumption at home.

Normally an export marketer will want to compare the pattern of sales into the various trade channels through his distributor. Figure 10.21 presents a schematic map that attempts to assess the respective volumes of business done by a distributor through direct customers and indirect customers (supplied through a network of wholesalers) as the starting points, and then breaking this down further by specific trade channel within each market segment. The charting can be much more detailed (and complex) if

the main segments of ON and OFF trade are further broken down to take account of specific relevant consumer characteristics purchasing through each trade channel. The export marketer would ideally want to know the customer profile of each trade channel, or be able to sub-divide each trade channel into further sub-categories that reflect segmentation characteristics of consumers.

At the very least a trade channel mapping exercise, done on a market-by-market basis, should:

- identify and highlight the trade channel structure
- give approximate shares or turnover in the product category
- identify the key accounts within each trade channel with an estimate of their

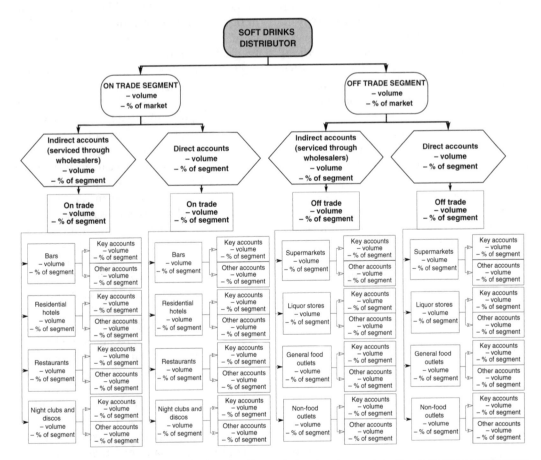

Figure 10.21 *Mapping a distributor's sales through trade channels in the soft drinks category*

product category turnover that can be compared with the exporter's sales through the respective accounts.

Figure 10.22 gives an outline trade channel structure for an industrial product, industrial cleaning fluids. Two of the trade channels served directly by suppliers are also acting as wholesalers into other trade channels, illustrated in the subordinate diagrams, and the supplier would ideally want to know their split of sales into these channels if any data are available.

Using trade channel data

A schematic diagram showing the trade channel structure needs to be supported by estimates of the values of the product category sales going through each trade channel to assist in taking decisions on where to focus sales effort, particularly in targeting key accounts.

The first stage is to recognize the various trade channels, and to separately note what share of the product segment (or total market) sales each of the key accounts that you identify has, and what share of your sales they have. If there is a difference between the account's estimated share of a market or product category and your share of your sales, then that may indicate that you have scope to further develop the account and change or improve the way you service the account to gain more of its sales. Whilst data may not always be very accurate in many markets, trade associations often serve as sources for collecting and collating data, and also key accounts in the distributive trades often make their own estimates of their market shares, which they may share with suppliers.

In most markets, whether for industrial or consumer goods, there will only be a handful of key accounts in each trade channel. It can then be useful to prepare a list that highlights the relative importance of each of these to your business over time, such as by using a simple form as shown in Figure 10.23. This is the type of data that an agent

or distributor should assist in collecting or developing, within whatever limits of accuracy available data impose on you.

Figure 10.24 illustrates how data can be tabulated in a simple format that highlights the relative importance of the various trade channels distributing to a market segment. This example presents fictional data for the Portuguese whisky market, and indicates that our fictional supplier of scotch whisky, working through his local distributor, is stronger overall in **off**-trade than **on**-trade outlets. Within the **off**-trade segment he is stronger in the major retail chains and larger grocery outlets than he is in the hypermarkets, and is very weak in smaller liquor and grocery stores, where he clearly has very little coverage of the outlets (shown by the last column that shows his outlet coverage, and that can be compared with known outlets in the trade channel listed in the first column of figures). In the on-trade channels, whilst a significant portion of his sector coverage is in hotels, he performs poorly on share, suggesting he is not calling on the major hotels, or is having problems obtaining distribution in key outlets. He does relatively well in the restaurants and clubs that he covers, less well in ordinary bars, and does nothing with the snack bar market, which, in any event, is not significant for his product category. A review of his outlet coverage pattern and choice of outlets to cover would seem advisable. In addition, another possibility is to look at the servicing of smaller accounts through sub-distributor wholesalers and cash and carry outlets, which are not serviced currently (he has chosen not to allow these outlets to carry his product, viewing them as competitors rather than an additional distribution resource to be developed).

Similar analyses can be developed for any consumer or industrial product where trade channel data is researched by the export marketer. In most cases he will find his appointed distributor will cover only a small proportion of the total outlets in the market sector, but hopefully it will be the major players. Plans can then be made to expand coverage and distribution.

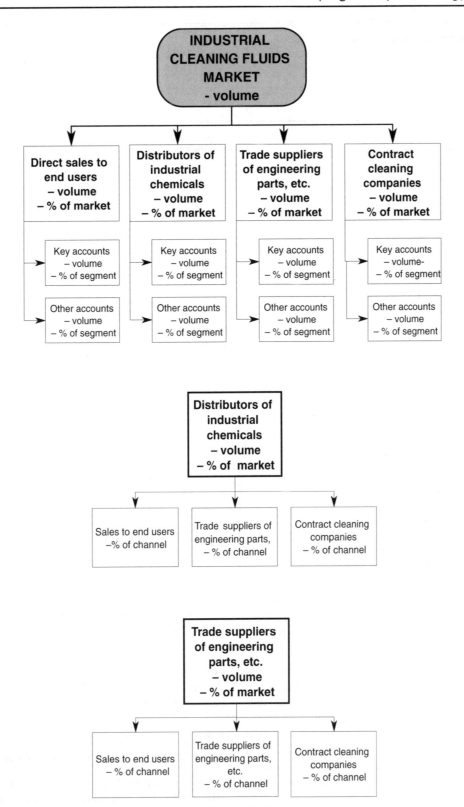

Figure 10.22 *Trade channels for an industrial product*

Top accounts' share of markets				
Market:			Turnover	
	Year	19__	19__	19__
Key accounts: Trade channel A 1 2 3 4 5 6 7 8	Number of branches			
Total trade channel A turnover. % share of total				
Key accounts Trade channel B 1 2 3 4 5 6 7 8	Number of outlets			
Total trade channel B turnover. % share of total				
Total key account turnover – all trade channels				
Total market segment turnover				
Key account % share of segment turnover				

Figure 10.23 *Tabulating key account share of market data*

Whatever products you are supplying it is important to build a picture of the trade channel structures and develop data that enables you, the export marketer, to know the pattern and relative volumes of trade through the various trade channels. Then you can compare your own distributor's performance to the overall pattern, and take informed decisions on your relative strengths and weaknesses, and ensure you are succeeding in obtaining distribution through the channels that are strong in serving your target markets.

Product profit management and investment strategies ▬▬▬

In the last chapter the concept of the **product life cycle** was discussed, along with a commentary on the normal approach to

Trade channel share of segment analysis						
Market: *Portugal* *WHISKY*	Number of outlets	Trade channel turnover 000s	Trade channel % share of segment turnover	Supplier's turnover 000s	Trade channel % share of supplier's turnover	Outlets covered directly by distributor
Off-trade segment						
Hypermarkets	20	7000	20	520	37	15
Supermarkets	310	14000	40	690	49	198
Self service stores	2520	3500	10	42	3	160
Liquor stores	9800	3850	11	48	4	187
General grocery stores	28052	6650	19	100	7	242
TOTAL OFF-TRADE	**40702**	**35000**	**100**	**1400**	**100**	**802**
Off-trade share of total soft drinks market			60		66	
On-trade segment						
Hotels	1720	4230	18	56	8	205
Restaurants	2730	940	4	141	20	240
Bars	5500	14570	62	317	45	165
Clubs	520	3055	13	120	17	110
Others – snack bars	1200	705	3	71	10	0
TOTAL ON-TRADE	**11670**	**23500**	**100**	**705**	**100**	**720**
On-trade share of total soft drinks market			40		34	
TOTAL MARKET: ON- AND OFF-TRADE	**52372**	**58500**	**100**	**2105** *3.6% of total market*	**100**	**1522** *3% outlet coverage*

Figure 10.24 *Analysing the relative importance of trade channels to a supplier*

investment in a product during the stages of its life cycle. At this point of developing the export market strategies we should consider further the matter of marketing investment in products in relation to product profit management.

The approach to investing in products will vary with the nature of the products, the market objectives, and the funds available. Typically launching and building a brand's sales require a higher level of marketing spend, as a percentage of gross sales values, than maintaining the brand once it is well established.

Active portfolio investment management ensures that the relationship between share of spend on brands and their share of market reflects the company's market investment strategy.

The general principles in allocating share of spend between portfolio products in any market are to:

- invest in a growth market with high share potential
- harvest in a declining market
- maintain the share/level of spend where the brand has reached its limit but shows no sign of decline.

A clear strategy to share of spend and brand investment should be developed for each market.

Figure 10.25 summarizes some descriptions of the stages in a product life cycle, and to the five stages illustrated in Figures 9.9 and 9.10 I have added in a category of **key brand**, to reflect the situation that many suppliers develop a product to the point that it represents a significant part of their sales, or holds a leadership position that should be defended in its product category.

The export marketer could usefully draw a similar chart, and allocate each of his products into these appropriate categories, and then use this as a reference point when looking at his marketing spend behind products in any individual market. Since a product will not always be at the same stage in its life cycle in all markets separate charts might be useful for the key markets, to

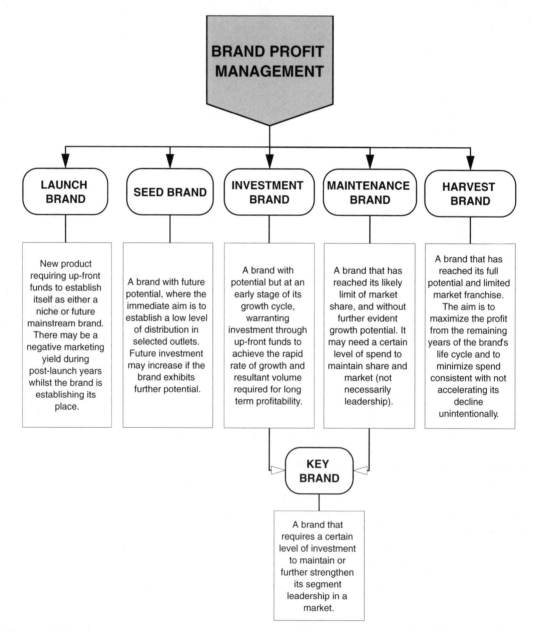

Figure 10.25 Brand profit management

compare with the overall portfolio investment strategy. This type of exercise helps to focus attention on spending advertising and promotional funds behind the right products in the right markets, rather than just allocating funds pro-rata to sales in each market. The next section, on spend in the marketing mix, comments further on this need to have an investment strategy.

Spend in the marketing mix

How much the export marketer has to spend on advertising and promotion supporting any product in any market is an important factor in developing marketing strategies, and the setting and achievement of objectives. In deciding how to spend an advertising and promotion budget consideration must be given to:

- target market/segmentation factors
- brand positioning in the portfolio (e.g. differential attributes and benefits, perceptions, price)
- weighting of budget supporting the brand
- level of spend.

Target market/segmentation factors

Once the target market segment is defined, the means of communicating with the segment can be identified. A broadly defined market segment, possibly mothers of school children, might warrant or benefit from mass media communications such as television or newspapers, or more targeted journals such as those aimed directly to mothers, or a combination. Decisions would be influenced by budget levels as well as the range of available local media. A narrow market segment, say architects, would suggest a more focused approach to media communications promoting products, such as professional journals or direct mail shots.

The alternative media can be compared on a cost per thousand basis for reaching the target segment. If television was used to reach a small group of architects, where we

might have established that only 2000 were registered with the local professional association of architects, the cost per thousand to reach these few architects is likely to be much higher using television than using a more focused media.

In other situations the target market might be quite numerous, but geographically focused. Products aimed at tourists, for example, might aim at distribution and promotion in key tourist areas, and within these areas the promotional activity might be broadly communicated through local mass media, or focused through promotional activity at tourist venues.

The export marketer needs to have a good understanding of his target market segment, its size and geographical spread, and then identify the alternative means of promoting both through media or below-the-line promotional activity, putting some estimates of the reach of the means of communicating and the cost per thousand to reach the target markets.

Brand positioning

The marketing spend behind any one product in a company's product portfolio will be influenced by how the product is being positioned in relation to other products. Each product in a portfolio needs to be considered in relation to its fellow products, and the best means of promoting and communicating identified for each product to ensure it is positioned correctly to potential users or consumers.

A mass market product, sold primarily as a basic household item, and with a broad target market, might require large budgets and mass media communications and promotional support to position it against the competition, communicate the features and benefits that differentiate it, and generate the volume needed to ensure profitability. This is a typical approach with major brands of motor vehicles. A product variant that is targeted at a more specific group of potential users will still need advertising and promotional support to communicate its positioning, but this may be more cost effectively achieved through focused activity, e.g. a sports version of a new car might have its differential attributes and benefits communicated through specialist journals favoured by readers known to match the profile of likely customers.

The export marketer with a varied product portfolio within any product category thus needs to:

- clarify the specific target segments for each of the product variants
- identify the range of media and types of promotions likely to reach and appeal to the specific target groups
- cost each of the alternatives to reach the target groups and achieve the desired level of exposure
- take decisions on the levels of budget allocated to each product variant to enable sales and marketing objectives to be achieved.

Weighting of the budget

Within any product portfolio the available budget for advertising and promotional activity can be weighted in several ways, including:

- by brand profit management priority (launch, seed, investment, maintenance, or harvest brand)

- by current sales volumes or assessed sales potential (i.e. sales targets)
- by prioritizing products under particular competitive threat
- by weighting budgets taking account of shorter term strategic or tactical problems (i.e. putting additional budgets behind a product with distribution weaknesses).

Level of spend

The level of budget will be a limiting factor in selecting media or choosing promotional formats. A small budget is unlikely to have much effect in a major media such as television advertising. Equally, a brand with a tightly defined target market and small select target group of potential consumers may waste its media budget on a mass market medium that spreads coverage thinly with a high cost per thousand at the real target audience.

Both consumer and industrial products require appropriate promotional support. Industrial products often need trade literature, trade advertising, exhibition exposure; consumer products often need media advertising, in-store promotional activity, point of sale material, etc.

Many companies allocate very limited budgetary resources to export market promotional activity compared with the

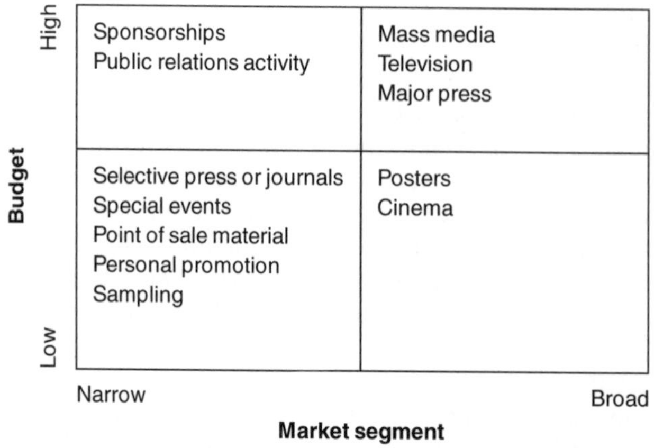

Budget	Narrow	Broad
High	Sponsorships Public relations activity	Mass media Television Major press
Low	Selective press or journals Special events Point of sale material Personal promotion Sampling	Posters Cinema

Market segment

Figure 10.26 Activity choices in relation to budgets and market segments

budgets for home market support. This is common where exports are seen as an additional or incremental sale, rather than as an independent opportunity to be developed. The export marketer has often been encouraged to focus on price as a key element of the marketing mix, in order to achieve some sales volume to utilize spare plant capacity. But that approach can be short-sighted, in that no security develops that ensures an ongoing sales level as products are not seriously marketed against competition, with clear positioning, brand identities, differential attributes and resultant benefits.

The product marketing strategy must be defined, along with market by market sales goals. The marketing cost of achieving the sales targets and implementing the strategies then needs to be assessed, and a margin built into the product costings to allow for a suitable level of advertising and promotional support. Advertising and promotional reserves should only be sacrificed to give price reductions after very careful consideration of the effect a lower level of marketing spend will have on overall achievement of strategic and sales goals. In export markets the marketers often come into conflict with agents and distributors over issues of levels of spend and marketing and promotional activity. We have all met the agent or distributor who says, 'Give me the advertising and promotion budget and I'll wheel and deal to get the sales'. He may achieve sales, but will they be achieved in a way that enhances the company and product position and reputation by meeting specific customer needs, and build product loyalty, or will he just trade the product as if it was a commodity?

Specific objectives, as well as budget levels, will have a bearing on the allocation of budgets between alternative forms of advertising and promotion support. The final budget allocation for any product will depend on which media will best reach a particular target audience in a cost effective fashion and be likely to achieve a specific objective within the overall brand plan, e.g.

a brand aimed at a younger audience may benefit more from cinema advertising than television advertising in some markets.

Figure 10.26 illustrates diagramatically a matrix to help in the decision making process of how to use available budgets. High budgets for a product with a broad target market segment open opportunities to use mass media. Low budgets for a product with a narrow target market segment favour carefully selected journals aimed to the target group and lower cost promotional activity, such as exhibitions for industrial products.

Further reading

Marketing Management – Analysis, Planning, Implementation and Control. Philip Kotler (Prentice Hall, 8th edition 1994). Chapter 11: Identifying Market Segments and Selecting Target Markets; Chapter 12: Differentiating and Positioning the Marketing Offer; Chapter 16: Designing Strategies for the Global Marketplace

Relationship Marketing. Martin Christopher, Adrian Payne and David Ballantyne (Butterworth-Heinemann 1999). This textbook is interesting reading for concerned marketers, and the principles are applicable to export markets of the late 1990s.

Marketing – An Introductory Text. Martin Christopher and Malcolm McDonald (Macmillan 1995). Chapter 5: Market Segmentation; Chapter 16: Marketing Channel Strategy. An excellent introductory text in comprehensible language for the non-specialist.

The Marketing Book. Edited by Michael J. Baker (Butterworth-Heinemann, 4th edition 1999). Chapter 12: Market Segmentation

Market Segmentation. Malcom McDonald and Ian Dunbar (Macmillan Business, 1995)

International Marketing – A Strategic Approach to World Markets. Simon Majaro (Routledge, 3rd edition 1991). Chapter 4: Segmentation on a Global Scale

Action points

Planning process

- Market evaluation
- Interpreting the strategy
- Plan design and drafting
- Evaluation of the plan: review and discussion
- Implementation
- Performance monitoring
- Outcome evaluation
- Re-start cycle

Export marketing planning responsibilities

- Market research
- Advertising and promotion
- Brands publicity
- Brand investment/profitability management
- Liaison with other central functions
- Liaison with local agencies and distributors

Available resources for planning inputs
Establish what internal resources can assist in you planning, e.g.:

Central resources:

- Marketing department
- Brands publicity
- Market research and planning
- Space planning (retail products)
- Sales promotions
- Sales administration
- Sales development

Checklist 10.1 (*Continued*)

	Action points
Local resources:	
• Company subsidiary/joint venture	
• Local advertising, promotion and PR agencies	
• Local distributor	
• Local research agencies	
Typical market planning priorities	
• Focused approach to marketing spend – promoting high profit brands with growth potential	
• Spread of price points covering all segments	
• Brand positioning through confident pricing	
• Increased emphasis on non-media promotions in markets where budgets are limited	
– merchandising	
– point of sale activity/material	
– PR and sponsorships	
– sales force development	
– added value promotions	
• Strengthen sales force knowledge of brands	
• Seek portfolio extension opportunities	

Checklist 10.2
Decision areas in strategy development

	Action points

The product range

- What product sectors to target product at: price; quality; consumption occasion
- International brand versus local market brand: company main brand; UK production of local brand; local production of local brand
- What product range to offer: trends; preferences; tradition/fashions

The markets

- Customer mix, target customers or market segments: product suitability to customer/segment
- Domestic sales versus export opportunities: relative importance and profitability of the opportunities
- Geographical spread: economic considerations in supplying all segments in all regions
- Cultural factors in marketing the products: adaptations needed to suit local cultures and languages

Distribution channels

- Distributor networks: company owned; joint venture; third party independents
- Direct user/consumer sales
- Retail outlets: criteria for supply; breadth of coverage
- Physical distribution: location of depots; delivery mode; frequency of supply
- After-sales service product support needs: location of service centres and technical skill needs

Checklist 10.2 *(Continued)*

Pricing parameters

Action points

- Exporter's quoted prices to foreign distributor or customer – taking account of distribution costs, freight, duties, taxes, etc.
- Market price positioning: target position versus competition; level versus other company brands/products
- Local market trade terms: minimum orders; payment terms – use of credit; discounts/performance rebates – parameters by channel

Marketing support

- Advertising and promotional budgets: levels; controls
- Advertising media selection: target audience; media positioning
- Promotional activity: objectives; type; frequency; performance monitoring; literature and point of sales material supporting promotional activity
- Public relations/sponsorship: what type?; how organized?; who is the target?
- Consumer trial and loyalty building: advertising; promotion; demonstration/sampling

Export sales resources

- Size of direct sales force: coverage requirements by trade channel
- Geographical spread of sales force: coverage requirements by trade channel
- Financial resources of exporter: budget limitations to sales operations
- Training resources of exporter: field sales management; skill training
- Distributor network: branches; sub-distributors
- Rewards and incentive in distribution organizations: competitive pay scales; bonus/commission criteria; non-monetary rewards/opportunities, etc.
- Key distributor sales activities: order taking/stock monitoring; presentations; merchandising/display; promotions; credit control

Checklist 10.3
Considerations in market segmentation

Action points

Criteria for segmentation:

- Relevancy to purchase/use criteria/motives
- Accessibility of segment through distribution channels
- Measurability of sales activity within the segment
- Potential of the segment to be serviced cost effectively and yield a net profit after specific marketing costs.

Segmentation factors:

- Lifestyles: grouping consumers by shared values
  - common aspirations
  - similar existing lifestyles
  - attitudes
- Product benefits: grouping consumers by common product needs/benefits
  - standard product features/benefits
  - company benefits
  - differential benefits

Consumer characteristics of customers:

- Socio-economic
  - class
  - income
  - jobs
  - residence type
- Psychographic
  - attitudes
  - personality
  - motives
- Geographic
  - location
  - urban/rural residence or lifestyles
  - cultures

Checklist 10.3 (*Continued*)

	Action points

- Demographic
  - age
  - education
  - sex
  - family

Industrial demographic characteristics

- Industry type
  - manufacturing/service
  - production processes
  - customer base
- Company size
  - number of employees
  - turnover
  - sales volume potential
- Technology
  - sophistication (hi-tech/low-tech)
  - research programmes
- Product service needs
  - self-sufficient
  - installation/periodic maintenance
  - custom design

Market segment analysis:

- Distribution – objective measures
- Share/volume – objective measures
- Trade channel responses
- Objective
  - trade price consistency
  - promotional and A & P responses
  - trade brand loyalty
- Consumer responses
- Objective
  - promotional and A & P responses
  - price responses
  - consumer brand loyalty
- Subjective
  - benefits
  - perceived
  - real
  - perceptions

Checklist 10.4
Trade channel mapping

Action points

The objectives of trade channel mapping are to:

- ◆ **Identify the trade channels serving the market segments for your products**
- ◆ **Identify the key accounts in each trade channel**
- ◆ **Develop a trade channel strategy**
  - Has a trade channel map been prepared for each market?
  - How many trade channels there are serving each market segment in each market?
    - List the trade channels for each market
  - Who are the main customers, the **key accounts**, in each trade channel?
  - Where are the key accounts located?
  - How many outlets have each of the key accounts?
  - What is the total turnover of each key account?
  - What is the market segment or product category turnover for each key account?
  - What share do you have of product category sales in each key account?
  - What share does each key account have of its trade channel (or total market)?
  - What are the sales servicing needs of each key account: e.g. consumer products
    - head office calling?
    - branch selling calls?
    - branch merchandising calls?
    - sales promoters? e.g. industrial products
    - product installation
    - product training
    - regular product servicing
  - Does the sales force organization need to be modified in any way to reflect the trade channel structure or key accounts within any trade channel, and if so, what changes are needed to provide best service and maximize sales through key accounts?

Checklist 10.5
A range of international opportunities

	Action points

Direct product exports
• direct exports
• sub-contracting manufacture
• modifying existing products
• developing new products using R & D expertise
• developing new products from new resources
• exporting raw materials or base inputs
• developing markets for part finished goods
• exporting third party non-competing products
Export of know-how and technology
• licensing manufacture
• selling know-how and technology
• supplying consultancy services
• operational management contracts
• forming consortia
 	
Foreign mergers, acquisitions, joint ventures, branches and subsidiaries
• foreign branches
• foreign distribution subsidiaries
• foreign marketing subsidiaries
• foreign wholly owned subsidiaries
• foreign joint ventures
• mergers with foreign corporations
• acquisition of foreign corporations
 	
Import of foreign know-how and technology
• obtaining foreign consultancy services:
  – to produce new products
  – to upgrade plant and equipment
• obtaining licences for complementary products
• sub-contracting manufacture for foreign concerns
 	
Import of complementary foreign products
• products synergistic with domestic products and markets
 	
Foreign raw material and input sources
• foreign buying offices
• foreign raw material processing plants
• foreign factories (subsidiaries) manufacturing inputs	

11

Inputs to export market planning

In this chapter we will be:

- developing further the market planning process, and identifying a range of local market information that should be considered relevant when preparing a plan
- considering the options of a market concentration versus market spread approach to developing export activities.

The aim is to emphasize the need to temper a strategy, particularly if it is a broader global strategy, with local market data inputs and knowledge. Researching and using this local data gives the export marketer an opportunity to involve his agent or distributor in the planning process, and particularly when breaking the macro plan down to a micro plan for implementation.

Contributions to export market planning

In the previous chapter we mentioned the need to take **historical market information** into account in planning, and then to incorporate commentary on other **assumptions** made in the planning process. We will look at these points further in this section. The key to planning is **market knowledge**. Whilst the diagrams following in this section present specific areas of planning information the export marketer should incorporate in a market plan, some general market knowledge and distributor knowledge are required in respect of the following factors:

- the economic and social environment external to the company (and distributor):
  - incomes
  - prices
  - interest rates
  - currency movements
  - employment levels
  - production
  - distribution
  - demographic factors
  - lifestyle trends
- legislative and regulatory environment
- competition (domestic and foreign)
- political considerations
- distribution channel factors
- trend and product preference patterns and changes

- user attitudes, perceptions and expectations
- distributor human resources and training
- distributor financial resources and controls

We all know the impact of the general economic and trading environment on home market sales, yet sometimes make foreign market plans without taking account of local economic cycles. There may be political considerations to factor into a plan, particularly if political changes cause market instability or if government agencies are major customers for our products. Local market regulations might impact on our strategies, perhaps simply to address matters such as labelling rules, or more complex issues such as import regulation or price controls. Competitors do not stand still whilst we make and implement a market plan, but are making their own plan concurrently, and will respond tactically to what they see us doing, and any plan should anticipate competitor response. Distribution channels in many markets are changing dynamically and for the better. As a market becomes more sophisticated alternative routes for distributing goods to users and consumers develop, e.g. hypermarkets in many westernized markets are stealing sales and market share from smaller retailers, and the growth in office technology has created new support industries for products and services. Whilst suppliers are creating change through product and service innovation, consumers and users also change in their attitudes, product preferences, perceptions and expectations: new product arrivals must be more reliable than previous models, and better suit working environments and lifestyles.

Also, critical for the export marketer making his markets' plans, account must be taken of the resources and abilities of a distributor to implement the plan. Many export marketers make great plans that appear feasible on the surface, but they are working through a distributor who has made other (perhaps conflicting) plans for

his business, or may simply not have sufficient financial resources or skilled staff to implement the exporter's market plan to best advantage.

In preparing export market plans, account must also be taken of your own company resources in respect of:

- plant production capacity (the capacity may be limited so that a good year of domestic sales would reduce the volume available for exports, or plant flexibility may be limited in that special export orders are seen as very disruptive of a continuous production process)
- limitations resulting from a need to modify products to suit certain markets
- availability of input supplies to meet expanding production
- product innovations and technology (how your own innovations and range changes will impact on the market, or how they will compare with competitor product developments)
- export marketing resources
- financial resources to fund export growth.

Many an export marketer finds that the market opportunities are greater than he can tackle within his limited resources of product, finances and staffing levels. That means assigning priorities to international opportunities, or diverting internal resources until such times as the resources allocated to international market development can be increased.

Historical market and performance data in planning

Earlier, illustrated in Figure 10.2, I referred to the importance of using available historical market and performance data in market planning. This is expanded in Figure 11.1, which shows a typical range of market data that might be available and useful in framing the market plan. Each export marketer should list available information (either within his file records or from basic desk or

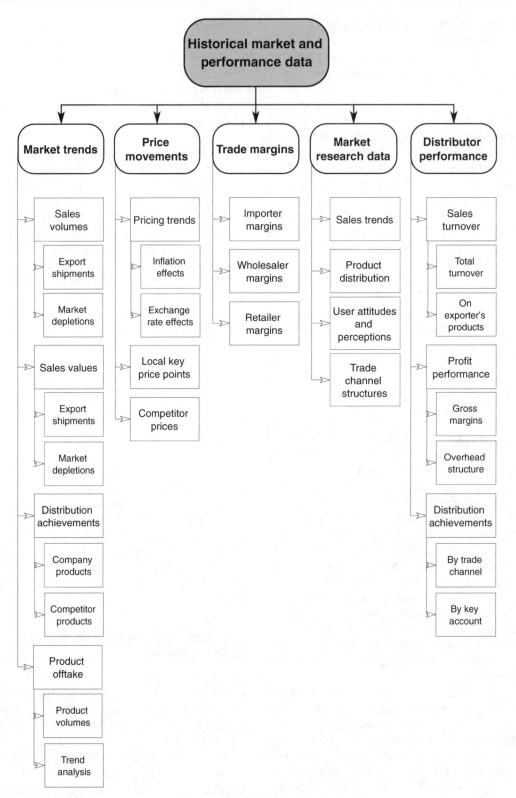

Figure 11.1 *Historical market and performance data for use in planning*

in-market research). A strategic marketing plan does a lot more than just stating a sales goal, and available information under any of the main headings of the chart might well be useful.

Export shipments should be compared with market depletions (sales from your distributor into local trade channels or to local users) to ensure there is no onerous build up of stocks. Imports into the destination market from other export sources should be monitored, as should any local production, so that you have estimates of the total market for your products, rather than looking at your own exports in isolation.

Your own distribution should be compared with that of your competitors, as a measure of the effectiveness of your distributor, and as a guide to the suitability of your products and prices to local market needs.

You will want to know about local pricing structures to ensure your competitiveness and positioning correctly in relation to competitors' products and your strategic marketing objectives. It is essential to know trade margins at each level of the distribution chain if you are to control market prices. Many exporters do not have much influence over the foreign market pricing of their products, in part because of lack of knowledge of market pricing structures and in part because of the absence of any control over their importers and distributors (where a product is re-sold rather than imported directly by end users).

Any available market research data is better than none in contributing to market knowledge and giving a historical perspective of a market. In developed markets many product categories are quite well researched and monitored either by government statistical studies or by local research agencies who make a living from selling results to interested parties. Even if data seems a little dated, it may still be better than planning in a data vacuum. Chapter 3, Preliminary desk research gave indications of data sources.

Your distributor's historical performance, such as in sales and distribution achievements both for your products and others he distributes or represents, may provide an important insight as to how he might perform in the future, and how effective he might be in implementing your marketing strategies and plans.

Key planning assumptions

There are a number of aspects of planning where we might make assumptions, as illustrated in Figure 11.2. The subsequent diagrams break each of these areas down to more specific factors where the export

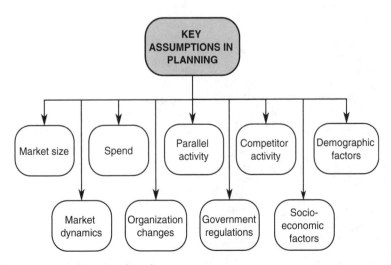

Figure 11.2 Key assumptions in planning

marketer is likely to need to make planning assumptions. Some of the sub-headings in the diagrams have planning relevance under more than one of the main headings. Also, under some of the factors the exporter might have specific data that would warrant comment under the heading of historical market and performance data, covered in the previous section.

Market size

Under this heading, when making assumptions or projections based upon assumptions, the export marketer will be looking for information relating to product volumes and values within relevant product categories or substitute products. Also he will want any information about distributors of the product category, such as how many distributors or distribution points are estimated to cover the market, and their estimated sales volumes. It will also be useful to know the numbers of users or consumers in the target market segments, and their likely level of use or demand for the product.

Whilst much data might not be specific to the product category, it can provide a base upon which reasonable planning assumptions might be made. For example, estimates of the increase in the population of working wives will help produce estimates for labour-saving kitchen devices and ready-prepared meals, etc. Estimates of population growth and growth in number of family units in a market will help suppliers of materials for building and construction products project housing needs, and therefore the potential market for their products.

Market dynamics

This is about the changes that are taking place in the product sector and distribution channels, independently from the supplier.

Figure 11.3 Assumptions about market size

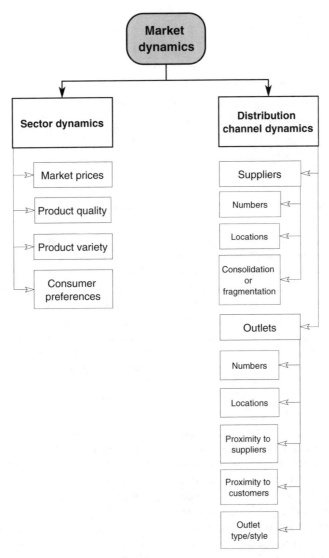

Figure 11.4 Assumptions about market dynamics

Figure 11.4 illustrates factors to consider. For example, users or consumers may be demanding higher quality products with greater reliability and lower servicing needs. Or there may be a move towards higher (value-added) or lower (basic commodity type) priced products. Consumers might be pressuring for more variety in products (such as car models with a greater range of options), or there might be movements in user or consumer product preferences, such as the move in recent years towards more environmentally friendly and natural products.

Looking at distribution channel dynamics, these are constantly changing. Suppliers merge with other suppliers, with objectives of strengthening market positions. New suppliers enter markets to service niche needs. The close proximity of a supplier to a group of end users may give a supply advantage, particularly where products require servicing support. In consumer goods the retail market is dynamic, with

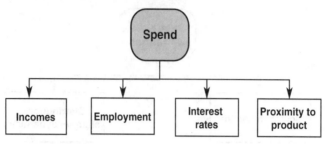

Figure 11.5 Assumptions about spend

new outlet formats servicing customer needs, e.g. the move to out of town shopping locations, the edge-of-town massive multi-product hypermarkets, countered by niche product retailers in the traditional high street environment in some markets.

The export marketer must be aware of any market dynamics that impact on his product sectors, and give consideration to these in making a market plan.

Spend

The market plan must make assumptions about the users' or consumers' spending power. Some products are essential either as industrial components or consumer necessities, and others are discretionary if funds permit purchase. The availability of disposable funds to use on the products may be a critical factor in purchase decisions. In looking at factors affecting the availability or level of funds for spending on the products the marketer may need to understand the state of the local economy, including looking at levels of employment and income trends, interest rates, and possibly even the proximity of users or consumers to distribution points where the product is available to purchase.

High interest rates may discourage investment in capital goods. High unemployment may discourage consumer spending on nonessentials. Rising incomes, low unemployment and lower interest rates might all encourage consumer and industrial spending. Knowledge of the state of the local market economy will assist in making sensible planning assumptions.

Organization changes

In some situations there may be a need to consider likely changes in either the export marketer's own company organization, or in that of his foreign market distributor. Internal company re-organizations might impact on export markets and planning. There may be changes in the product portfolios (products important in a few export markets, but unimportant in domestic markets, might be axed); corporate structures might change in a way that effects export marketing operations; companies may be bought or sold, etc. Whatever company organizational changes occur if they are likely to impact on export performance assumptions must be made at the planning stage and factored into plans.

Similarly, the distributor's organization might experience changes that might benefit or disadvantage the exporter. Employment of additional sales staff or the creation of a marketing department might work to the

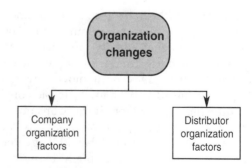

Figure 11.6 Assumptions about organizational changes

exporter's advantage. But if the distributor acquires new agencies without additional resources that might have a negative impact on an exporter's sales, as might changes in key distributor personnel. Any anticipated changes should be factored into the assumptions considered at the planning stage.

Parallel activity

In some product categories it is quite common for exporters to find a significant level of parallel trade. This is trade that is not officially sanctioned or managed by the exporter, normally by-passing official distribution channels, and possibly even including smuggling operations. Parallel trade normally develops besides (parallel to) the official exporter managed distribution operations, and often results where there are onerous duties or taxes, and corrupt officialdom, or where an exporter fails to supply (for whatever reason) sufficient goods to meet market demand, or where there are significant price differentials between markets (either as a result of taxes and duties, or higher distribution margins). Opportunistic traders will always emerge to fill market gaps where there is a possibility to develop a parallel market.

Examples of parallel trade range from scotch whisky being shipped into Japan via third countries, to branded electronic goods coming into the United Kingdom from South East Asian traders, and most goods going into West Africa through traders purchasing in Europe and by-passing official import duties and appointed distributors.

The effect of parallel trade is quite disruptive to orderly marketing, particularly of branded goods, and can often result in the same products selling at differing price levels through the alternative distribution channels. A small amount of parallel trade has a greater impact on normal trade through official distribution channels such as sole importers or agents. If 5 per cent of the total market volume enters through parallel market sources it is likely to disrupt the official imports by several times that amount, as distributors hesitate to import whilst cheaper goods are available to their customers.

When it comes to market planning, if the export marketer's products or markets attract parallel trade then this must not be ignored, but factored into plans, and estimates made both of its magnitude and effect on orderly marketing. And there may be occasions where an exporter wants to encourage the unofficial trade routes when he cannot develop an orderly market but wants to keep his products available to users and consumers in the foreign markets.

Government regulations

In some markets government regulation of trade is well established and documented, and in others it can be somewhat variable according to factors such as the availability of foreign exchange. A market plan should normally state simply the basic rules of import trade with a market, e.g. import tariff levels (relevant to market pricing and costing exercises), import licence or quota controls, sales taxes (if applicable).

Additionally, some product categories face other regulations, applicable to both local and imported goods, such as restrictions on advertising covering cigarettes and alcohol in some markets, regulations on outlets selling certain categories of products (whether for consumer or industrial use, e.g. controls often apply to wines and spirits sales, pharmaceuticals are normally limited as to outlets selling the products and subject to local prescription regulations, and hazardous goods may require special handling and storage). Labelling regulations are widespread in coverage and use in most markets.

The plan should normally summarize regulations applying to trade with and in a market and must then make assumptions as to whether these will remain consistent or change during the period of the plan.

Competitor activity

Markets are dynamic not static, and it is dangerous to plan without taking account of

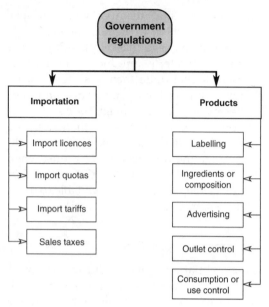

Figure 11.7 *Assumptions about government regulations*

competitors' achievements and activity, and their responses to your plan. Your own plan could pay attention to the competitors' trade distribution channels, including any relevant observations on their distributors, and

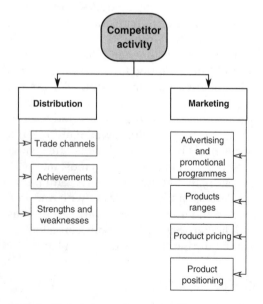

Figure 11.8 *Assumptions about competitor activity*

note their achievements in sales, product usage, distribution, and display (if a retail consumer product). The strengths and weaknesses of the competitor's distribution operation should be noted, as these can provide a benchmark against which your own distribution operation can be measured and progressed or improved.

Continuous monitoring of the competitors' advertising and marketing programmes, their product ranges (particularly noting innovations and changes), and their product pricing and target market positioning all add to the base of knowledge that help the export marketer make a better plan.

With all this knowledge the export marketer must then make assumptions about what the competitors will do in the future, during the exporter's planning period and in response to his market activities.

Socio-economic factors

The marketing of some products may be influenced by a range of socio-economic factors, and the marketer may need knowledge of these aspects and then to make planning assumptions of trends or changes.

Levels of income and employment may impact on sales of many products, but in some markets the degree of industrialization may also have an impact on sales volumes or the product mix suited to local needs. Export marketers prefer to work in a stable political environment, since political turmoil disrupts markets and trade. To the exporter it may be less important whether a market is democratic or autocratic, a free market or a centrally planned economy, as long as he can plan with some degree of predictability to the outcome. Attitudes vary between markets and cultures, and in some cases local attitudes affect the export marketer's ability to develop markets. Religious attitudes in the Muslim countries limit the scope for the sale of alcoholic products. The central planning and anti-consumerist attitudes in the former communist markets limited the scope for developing markets for western

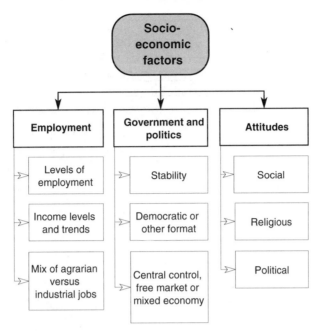

Figure 11.9 *Assumptions about socio-economic factors*

consumer goods. Antagonistic political attitudes between rival neighbours or markets of different political persuasions can force the exporter to take decisions as to which markets he wants to supply (e.g. the historical problems of supplying Israel and neighbouring Arab markets).

The export market plan should consider any socio-economic factors that will affect the implementation of the plan and present the assumptions on which the plan is developed.

Demographic factors

Planning assumptions for many products need to consider market demographics. Consumer products can be influenced by population age profiles (is the population mix getting older or younger?), the sexual balance, size of average family unit, birth rate and other factors affecting population growth (e.g., health care). Also the education of the population and resultant increase in incomes and lifestyle sophistication can impact on sales potential for many products.

The trends in population location can impact on sales planning. An urban lifestyle may open opportunities for using products different to those used in a more rural lifestyle, and physical distribution may be easier in urban areas. In many markets industrial zones are being encouraged, and the location of these zones and nature of industries being encouraged can have sales planning implications for some exporters supplying industrial products.

The export marketer needs to identify what demographic factors affect his planning process, and factor in assumptions on developments and their likely impact on sales potential.

With the wealth of market knowledge the export marketer acquires over time the planning process should become more sophisticated and accurate in its predictions about trends and sales volumes. The market plan does not need to cover every item of information or knowledge in the marketer's portfolio, but should provide commentary of those factors that affect the market planning, plan implementation and possible perform-

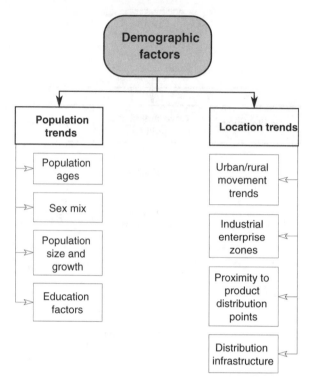

Figure 11.10 Assumptions about demographic factors

ance results. Whilst natural catastrophes cannot normally be predicted or allowed for in planning, it is a poor excuse to blame non-achievement of ambitious plans upon predictable factors or identifiable trends (e.g., if a foreign market is suffering a cyclical downturn in the economy, with resultant reduction in construction, an exporter who had experienced several buoyant years in supplying goods to the construction industry would be naive to predict ongoing growth during the recession).

Not every market warrants the same time and attention or depth of planning, and the amount of resources allocated to the market planning process should reflect the market's importance to the exporter and his ability to influence progress through planning (for most exporters there are some markets that will remain opportunistic trading markets for many years). If a manageable number of markets represent the majority of sales (remembering the Pareto rule that 80 per cent of sales nor-

mally come from around 20 per cent of markets), then the full planning process should be applied to those key markets plus the next tier down of markets seen as offering particular development potential.

Market concentration versus market spread

Much is made in export literature of the benefits of market concentration. If we look at the macro level of national export statistics we might quickly translate to the micro level (the individual company) the attitude that concentration of effort is best. Looking at United Kingdom export performance statistics, for example, will show strong concentration of exports to a limited number of key markets. One reason for the success of German companies in international markets has often been said to be concentration on few markets (in addition to marketing thrusts not depending on price competitiveness only). Earlier in the text, when discussing desk and market research, I favoured targeting key markets. For many companies that is the most suitable approach when constrained by limited resources. Some companies or product categories might, however, benefit more from spreading risk through a broader base of markets. Each export marketer should consider which approach to exporting – concentrating on few markets or spreading the risk by exporting to a broader base of markets – will make the best use of his resources, maximize his returns from exporting, and secure his exports at a level that satisfies his company's volume goals.

Market concentration

Concentrating on few key markets has the benefits of:

- enabling an increased intensity and depth of marketing support activity within available resources (including advertising and promotional activity)
- building strength through knowledge as the international marketers develop expertise in key market conditions
- building greater consumer/user brand awareness and market share (market penetration)
- blocking growth avenues to competitors (increasing their cost of market entry)
- enabling the exporter to promote other product attributes (tangible or intangible) including quality, design, innovation, product support services, image/lifestyle, distributor support, delivery, etc., rather than just selling on the basis of price
- facilitating the modification of existing products or development of new products to meet specific market needs where volumes or potential grow to the point where this is cost effective
- optimizing the use of limited management resources, minimizing the span of control limitations on managing market development and problem

solving, and minimizing the allocation of specialist resources to the export shipping and marketing activities.

Equally, market concentration puts the exporter at greater risk should any single market or group of markets collapse for any reason: for example, by the imposition of trade barriers in response to political pressures from domestic interests, or states of belligerency developing between parties to trade or third parties.

In general market concentration is likely to be a favoured approach where:

- price need not be the only basis of competition
- there is security of access to a market (a low likelihood of loss of market through the imposition of restrictive barriers to trade)
- the product requires after-sales support service (including spare part supplies and servicing)
- significant investment in establishing the product in the market, including personal selling, advertising and promotion, is needed (in some cases it is necessary to establish local representative offices to progress market development and provide technical and marketing support)
- effective distribution takes time to develop (and possibly there is limited availability of suitable distributors)
- the product is capable of achieving a significant market share
- funds are freely transferable from the market to the exporter
- special product modifications, adaptations, labelling, etc. are required for market entry.

In talking about market concentration, I am making the general assumption that companies actually *choose* their international markets. However, many smaller to medium exporters first develop exports by responding to unsolicited enquiries, and some of these early shipments bear the fruit of growth into markets that become significant to the smaller exporter. The larger exporter, on the other hand, may often have more resources at the outset to develop an active programme of market selection, including research and market visits.

Another point is that while most advocates of market concentration are thinking in terms of selling a company's products to a limited number of destination markets, another form of concentration is where a multi-product company concentrates its marketing efforts on a limited selection of its products to a wider range of destination markets. For example, a producer of toiletries and cosmetics, supplying to various price segments of the market may make a conscious decision that when it comes to exporting it will forgo competing in the potential price war in mass market segments and concentrate on building upmarket international luxury brands.

Market groupings

An extension of the market concentration strategic considerations is where a number of markets are seen as having factors that enable a common approach to marketing to be applied across the group. For example, if it is necessary to produce a special Spanish label and literature (or perhaps a Spanish version of an item of computer software), it would be logical to look a little further and see if the product could find Latin American markets open to it using the same literature and advertising and promotional campaigns.

Market groupings might be based on common language, common social and business cultures, geographical proximity, political structures, climatic similarities, trade groupings (e.g. European Community, Association of South East Asian Nations), or other factors that give the marketer reason to expect that a common marketing strategy can be applied to the exporter's products in a group of markets.

Market spread

Market concentration is not the only way to develop exports. Many a small company has

built a healthy international sales volume through spreading export activity to quite a number of markets. Whilst the concentration approach usually advocates putting the effort into around six to a dozen potentially major markets, the spread approach has enabled many a company to operate in over thirty markets.

Some of the considerations that might cause some companies not to concentrate their efforts in a handful of markets include where:

- their product is commodity oriented and not easily differentiated from competitive products, and is primarily sold on price
- the product does not require an in-market after-sales support service
- there is a risk of import restrictions (licences, currency controls, other tariff or non-tariff barriers) closing markets or limiting growth opportunities
- competitive products already have a dominant position such that the exporter may not consider the marketing entry costs (including those for advertising and promotion) to achieve a meaningful market share warranted
- the exporter does not wish to attract attention from government agencies or other international bodies lobbying to limit market dominance by foreign suppliers
- the exporter needs to spread risks between a number of markets (because of either the long lead times needed to generate orders, or the vulnerability of business to political factors)
- the exporter wishes to minimize the allocation of financial resources to international marketing and market development
- the exporter prefers to take a more passive role in export, possibly mainly responding to unsolicited enquiries and using existing human resources to process the shipments
- specialization (concentration) is by product type (rather than by market), when a broader group of destination

markets may be needed to achieve volume export sales, and the international strategy may justifiably include taking the specialist expertise to a large number of markets
- the product does not result in a regular pattern of repeat orders (such as for industrial plant and machinery or consultancy services), when a market spreading approach to exporting may be essential to maintain ongoing sales volumes.

There is a cost, often quite high, to obtaining and maintaining a large market share in most markets, and usually the exporter needs to establish specialist support services, including shipping and marketing departments. Once the costs of setting up an export department have been borne, then often there will be spare capacity within those resources that can usefully be used in fulfilling export orders to minor markets.

Further reading

Marketing – An Introductory Text. Martin Christopher and Malcolm McDonald (Macmillan 1995). Chapter 20: Marketing Planning

International Marketing. Stanley J. Paliwoda and Michael J. Thomas (Butterworth-Heinemann, 3rd edition 1998). Chapter 13: International Marketing Planning

Marketing Plans – How to Prepare Them: How to Use Them. Malcolm McDonald (Butterworth-Heinemann, 4th edition 1999)

The Marketing Plan – A pictorial guide for managers. Malcolm McDonald (Butterworth-Heinemann 1987)

The Marketing Planner. Malcolm McDonald (Butterworth-Heinemann 1993)

Export Strategy: Markets and Competition. Nigel Piercy (George Allen & Unwin 1982). Chapter 4: Market concentration; Chapter 5: Market spreading; Chapter 6: Export market choice: concentration or spreading

	Action points

Develop a formalized approach to market planning:
 	
● Establish corporate objectives
  – Marketing objectives
  – Financial objectives
● Set country objectives for export markets
● Develop specific strategies to achieve objectives
● Develop market sales and profit forecasts
● Develop specific market tactics and plans
● Develop controls to monitor performance
  – Allow for corrective actions to counter deviations
 	
Develop a portfolio of market knowledge to use in market planning, e.g.:
 	
● The market economic and social environment, e.g.
  – incomes
  – prices
  – interest rates
  – currency movements
  – employment levels
  – production
  – distribution
  – demographic factors
  – lifestyle trends
● Legislative and regulatory environment
● Competition (domestic and foreign)
● Political considerations
● Distribution channel factors
● Trend and product preference patterns and changes
● User attitudes, perceptions, expectations
● Distributor human resources and training
● Distributor financial resources
 	
In preparing export market plans take account your own company resources and limitations, e.g.:
 	
● Plant production capacity
● Flexibility to modify products to suit markets
● Availability of input supplies to meet expansion
● Product innovations and technology
● Export marketing resources
● Financial resources to fund export growth	

Checklist 11.2
Export planning – using historical market data

	Action points
In the plan note historical market and performance data, e.g.	

Market trends

- Sales volumes
- Sales values
- Distribution achievements
- Product offtake

Price movements

- Pricing trends
- Local key price points for the category
- Competitor prices

Trade margins

- Import margins
- Wholesaler margins
- Retailer margins

Market research data

- Sales trends
- Product distribution
- User attitudes and perceptions
- Trade channel structures

Distributor performance

- Sales turnover
- Profit performance
- Distribution achievements

Checklist 11.3
Export planning –
key planning assumptions

	Action points
Make planning assumptions about changes that might occur during the plan period and impact on plan implementation and performance, e.g.:	

Market size

- Volumes
  - Product availability
    - Local production
    - Imports
  - Product demand
    - Customer volume estimates
    - Values
  - Prices
    - Exchange rates
    - Import duties
    - Sales taxes
    - Inflation
  - Product mix
- Distribution outlets
  - Number of distributors
  - Distributor volume throughputs
- Users/consumers
  - Number
  - Levels of use
  - Frequency of use/purchase

Market dynamics

- Sector dynamics
  - Market price trends
  - Product quality
  - Product variety
  - Consumer preferences

Checklist 11.3 *(Continued)*

- Distribution channel dynamics
  - Suppliers
    - Numbers
    - Locations
    - Consolidation/fragmentation
  - Outlets
    - Numbers
    - Locations
    - Proximity to suppliers
    - Proximity to customers
    - Outlet type/style

Spend

- Incomes
- Interest rates
- Employment
- Proximity to product

Organizational changes

- Company organization factors
- Distributor organization factors

Parallel activity

Government regulatory actions

- Importation
  - Import licences
  - Import quotas
  - Import tariffs
  - Sales taxes
- Products
  - Labelling
  - Ingredients or composition
  - Advertising
  - Outlet control
  - Consumption or use control

Competitive activity

- Distribution
  - Trade channels
  - Achievements
  - Strengths/weaknesses

Checklist 11.3 *(Continued)*

Action points

● Marketing
  − Advertising and promotional programmes
  − Product ranges
  − Product pricing
  − Product positioning

Socio-economic factors

● Employment
  − Levels of employment
  − Income levels and trends
  − Mix of agrarian versus industrial jobs
● Government and politics
  − Stability
  − Democratic or other format
  − Central control, free market, or mixed economy
● Attitudes
  − Social
  − Religious
  − Political

Demographic factors

● Population trends
  − Population ages
  − Sex mix
  − Population size and growth
  − Education factors
● Location trends
  − Urban/rural movement trends
  − Industrial enterprise zones
  − Proximity to product distribution points
  − Distribution infrastructure

Checklist 11.4
Market concentration versus market spreading

Action points

Factors favouring concentration

- product differentiated by non-price factors
- product has attributes or branding potential to build high consumer/user awareness and loyalty
- product requires modification to meet needs of specific markets/users
- product requires in-market after-sales service
- product offers potential for high volume repeat sales
- company specialization is by market segment
- product has potential for multiple applications
- products are at a mature stage of their life cycle
- competitive products have not yet established significant market shares
- cost of market entry and development (building market share and brand loyalty) is within bounds of company resources
- company can compete on equal terms with competitors or create product differentiation
- product advertising, promotion and communication costs are high
- local authorities will not react adversely to market penetration by foreign enterprises (or product may lend itself to local manufacture at a later stage)
- key target markets offer stability without later risk of trade restrictions
- export distribution presents particular difficulties (suitability/availability of local distribution channels, special packaging, perishable products, supply limitations)
- exporter faces no unacceptable risk in concentrating marketing effort in few markets
- exporter can allocate additional (specialist) resources to developing markets as part of the market concentration strategy
- incremental costs of processing orders for any markets are high (e.g. product modifications, distribution, packaging, order processing, product training, etc.)
- exporter adopts a strategy of market penetration aimed at building market share
- exporter has in-depth knowledge upon which to base market selection decisions

Checklist 11.4 (Continued)

	Action points

Factors favouring spreading

- price is the main factor in competition
- product is commodity oriented (low buyer loyalty to brands or sources)
- product format/design is standardized and usable in unmodified form in many markets
- product does not require in-market after-sales service
- product is not of a repeat sale nature
- company specialization is by product type (rather than by market)
- limited product uses/applications of specialized nature
- product is at early stage of its life cycle
- competitive products have dominant market shares
- company cannot compete on equal terms with competitors (or build on differential product attributes)
- high cost to building product/brand awareness and loyalty
- product advertising, promotion and communication costs are low
- active market penetration strategies would draw adverse reaction from local watch-dog authorities (possibly concerned with protecting local interests from foreign competition)
- risk of imposition of tariff or non-tariff barriers
- export distribution does not present particular difficulties (special packaging, perishable products, supply limitations, etc.)
- exporter sees a strategic need to spread the risks of exporting across many markets
- exporter wishes to avoid allocating dedicated (specialist management) resources to exporting, utilizing spare capacity, or
- exporter has low incremental costs of processing and distributing additional orders
- exporter adopts an approach of responding (passively) to unsolicited orders rather than intensive active exporting
- exporter has little information to aid market selection for specialization

12

Implementing an
export strategy and
monitoring
performance _____

 In this chapter we will look at other aspects of developing the export
strategy, such as:

- tactical and strategic responses to key objectives
- implementing the plan through the distributor
- monitoring progress through competitive benchmarking.

The aim is to develop the theme that the broader macro export strategy must be broken
down to a detailed micro level market plan with the agent or distributor if it is to be
implemented effectively.

Tactical and strategic responses to typical objectives ▅▅▅▅▅▅

The export marketer in many companies sees his objectives less from a sophisticated marketing approach, and more from a pragmatic hands-on position of striving for:

- increased sales volume
- increased profit from exports.

Table 12.1 indicates some of the typical range of areas where strategic and tactical programmes can be developed that will work towards improvements in sales volumes and profits, and you will note that a number of the points concern aspects internal company operations, where change or improvement can directly impact on sales and profits, e.g. shortage of internal production capacity,

poor production planning and poor stock control will all result in customer orders not being met in full or being delayed in shipment, with a consequent loss in volume. When seeking change and improvement, look in the mirror first!

The consequences of any strategy must be assessed to see whether there is a likely net gain or loss in sales volumes, revenues and profits within a specific market, and in other markets as a result of committing resources to a strategy.

Implementing the market plan through a distributor ▅▅▅▅▅▅

Many export marketers who prepare market plans focus attention on major product

Table 12.1 *Key objectives and typical strategic/tactical responses*

Key objective	Strategic/tactical areas
Increase sales volume	• Number of export markets • Company stock control • Company production capability • Company production planning • Export shipping efficiency • Export marketing resources • Promotional activity • Adjust prices (FOB/market) • Distributor stock controls/levels • Dealer stock controls/levels • Number of distributors • Number/location of dealers/ stockists • Market sales promotional activity • Expand product range • Distributor/dealer training
Increase profits	• Increase prices • Cut costs • Focus promotional support on higher margin brands • Adjust product range focus to higher margin brands (product mix) • Increase sales

planning areas that integrate into the overall marketing mix of planning activity. Typically a macro level market plan giving coverage to a single product or a range of products or brands will focus attention on:

• shipments from the exporter and depletions from the distributor's local stocks
• product distribution (overall or through outlets serving target segments)
• product pricing
• trade marketing strategy
• consumer/user strategy
• consumer/user brand position
• advertising and promotion strategy
• market research.

The critical activity for the export marketer is to make the plan happen at the distributor level. This is made more complex where a company uses more than one distributor in a market, and has different product portfolios with each distributor. The issue for the distributor, once he has the macro level market and brand plans, is what can he tackle at the micro level to promote the achievement of the macro market plan. The overall market plan or brand plan must be broken down by the export marketer to the point where a distributor can understand what specific plans he can make, and what activities he can undertake, that address the strategies and ensure progress against macro-level goals and objectives. The export marketer can help the distributor in making his local plan, implementing it and monitoring resultant performance.

Figure 12.1 illustrates the typical topics covered in a market brand plan, as outlined above, and breaks these down to a range of sub-headings, or micro level factors, that can then be made meaningful to a distributor and turned into specific action points and local plans, strategies and tactics.

This is looked at further in Table 12.2, that illustrates a range of actions and activities where the distributor can make plans addressing the broader market or brand plan objectives, and also notes some other issues that might affect distributor planning and achievement. An export marketer should break down his own specific plans, highlighting to the distributor what areas he can address with local plans and activities to achieve the market plan objectives, and then assist in developing the implementation programme.

As a simple control discipline the export marketer might want to design a form that lists each of the major stages in the planning process for his markets. The main market plan will primarily be the work of the export marketer, but the lower level planning should, ideally, involve the local distributor or agent. A typical check list might look something like that of Figure 12.2, and this format can be modified to

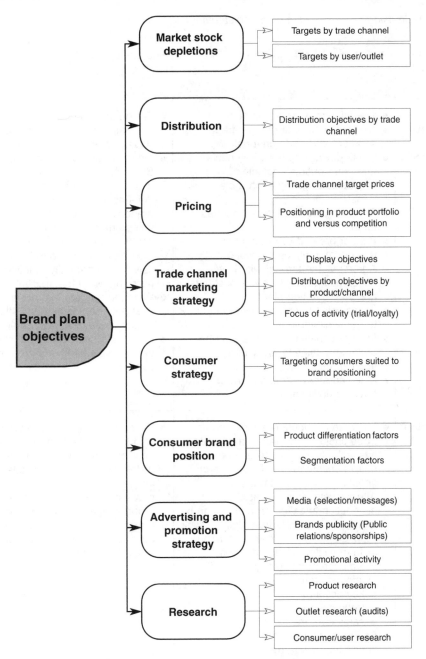

Figure 12.1 *Brand plan objectives chart*

suit industrial or consumer products. The names of the markets the export marketer is responsible for can be entered along one axis, and the dates each planning stage is completed noted in the appropriate box in the columns.

Continuous monitoring

Once a marketing plan is developed it is essential to **monitor** both its implementation and the performance outcome at every stage. The distributor normally markets a

Table 12.2 *Breaking down a market plan to distributor level activities*

Brand plan category of activity	Distributor level implementation	Factors to consider
Exporter shipments and distributor depletions	<ul><li>Place forward orders on supplier.</li><li>Allocate volume targets by trade segment and trade channel.</li><li>Break down targets by key accounts and other outlets (including wholesalers) giving each a clear target.</li><li>Communicate targets to the sales force.</li><li>Further break down targets by territory/month/journey cycle.</li><li>Agree volume targets with key accounts and link with key accounts annual promotion plan.</li><li>Agree sales force incentive plan for target achievement.</li><li>Monitor achievement of targets by outlet and sales territory (key account) monthly.</li><li>Make corrective action plans where adverse deviations occur.</li></ul>	<ul><li>Timing of mainstream media campaign: trade stock levels must be raised before media campaigns.</li><li>Timing of below the line promotions. Sales thrust on any brand must dovetail with promotional activity (i.e., don't have a volume push on one brand while operating a consumer pull promotion on another, as this confuses the trade and can result in stock imbalances, with the trade and sales force normally reacting by pursuing self interest).</li><li>Watch for targets that are evenly split over the year: sales don't follow that regular pattern in most categories.</li><li>Plan trade sales thrusts to start before implementing a promotional campaign.</li></ul>
Distribution	<ul><li>Measure distribution achievements by trade channel. Where no audit data is available develop a store check (or user) benchmark audit (sales team should not know audit base).</li><li>Alternatively, or in addition, distribution in called-on outlets can be monitored manually from daily activity reports through selective recording, or from customer record cards.</li><li>From base measures, set specific distribution targets by:<ul><li>key account</li><li>trade channel</li><li>sales territory.</li></ul></li><li>Ensure distribution targets, include specifying new target outlets/stockists/users.</li><li>Distribution measures can be value weighted, but this is usually too complex for many distributors, so basic measures against which targets can be set are:<ul><li>distribution in called on outlets</li><li>all outlets distribution from audits or random field checks</li><li>key account distribution.</li></ul></li></ul>	<ul><li>Distribution objectives must dovetail with the consumer strategy and brand position objectives. You may not want distribution in outlets unsuited to the image of the product and its positioning, as it can devalue the brand image and confuse consumers.</li><li>Trade census data is therefore essential to target distribution by brand to specific outlets.</li></ul>

Table 12.2 *(Continued)*

Brand plan category of activity	Distributor level implementation	Factors to consider
Pricing	• Price positioning within the portfolio must be clear to a distributor, to ensure trade prices provide differentials reflecting marketing strategies. • The export marketer must be aware of trade margins, and distributor discounting policies and practices through his trade terms.	• Distributor pricing policy must be consistent with brand positioning. • Promotional activity must also be consistent with price positioning (heavy discounting to obtain distribution may result in price cutting, impacting on consumer/user perceptions in relation to brands).

Trade channel marketing strategy	• For retailed products display objectives should be set for each:
	  • trade channel
	  • outlet.
	• Objectives should specify:
	  • product facings on display fixtures
	  • off-shelf features to match promotion timings.
	• Display objectives, standards and locations should be agreed with key accounts as part of annual key account negotiations and plans.
	• Trade strategies to promote trial (e.g., brand publicity activity, etc.) must be planned into an annual programme to ensure consistency with other sales/marketing activity.
	• Outlet activity to be supported by point of sale material and increased stock levels (reflected in sales targets).
	• Industrial products benefit from a trade channel strategy also, and market plans should be broken down to distributor plans, including:
	  • highlighting priority products
	  • providing product training and support to stockists/users
	  • trade marketing literature
	  • sales objectives for stockists and end users
	  • trade stock management
	  • targets for new stockists and new users (and plans for reaching them, e.g. including trade exhibitions)
		• Any display performance related bonuses should reflect brand priorities within portfolio, particularly where more than one distributor are promoting alternative brands.
		• Display achievements can be monitored (self measured) using daily activity report and from field checks.

Table 12.2 *(Continued)*

Brand plan category of activity	Distributor level implementation	Factors to consider

Consumer strategy	• Whilst consumer/user strategy is largely set by the supplying company, and a core theme developed to advertising and promotion programmes, the distributor is involved in implementation at field level, particularly through promotional and brands publicity activities, against specific objectives, e.g.:
	  • maintaining consumer loyalty
	  • increasing trial in consumer groups
	  • improving brand recall
	  • develop brand image.
		• All local advertising and promotion must be compatible with the central brand strategy, clearly supporting a key theme.
		• It is particularly important to check that the following are compatible with messages being passed to the consumer through A & P activity:
		  • local pricing
		  • distribution to appropriate trade channel outlets.

Consumer brand position	• The points of product differentiation of the brand proposition are set by the supplying company, communicated and promoted through the advertising and promotion programme.	
Advertising and promotion strategy	• This strategy is normally under the control of the supplying company. But local promotional activity must be compatible with central themes and objectives, and also timings.	

Research	• Regular audit data (such as Millwood Brown and Nielsen data for consumer products) may be available locally. If not the distributor should establish a basis for auditing distribution in relation to the target market outlets or users.
	• Local research may also be relevant to:
	  • product suitability to local needs
	  • consumer attitudes to advertising
	  • brand positioning and awareness
	  • outlet databases, etc.
	• The last two should be a particular responsibility of the distributor, who should build an outlet or user database, in terms of numbers, locations, and profiles in relation to segmentation factors and product positioning.
		• Consideration must be given to the quality and availability of local research.

Market	France	Italy	Spain			
Country plan	12 Sept.					
Brand plans	18 Sept.					
Advertising/media plan	16 Oct.					
Sales promotion plan	18 Oct.					
Brands publicity plan	18 Oct.					
Trade channel strategy plans	25 Oct.					
Key account strategy plans	5 Nov.					
Trade channel distribution objectives	5 Oct.					
Key account distribution objectives	5 Oct.					
Specific outlet/user distribution objectives	15 Oct.					
Key account sales targets	5 Nov.					
Other outlet/user sales targets	15 Nov.					
Key account display objectives	30 Nov.					
Other outlet display objectives	30 Nov.					

Figure 12.2 *Market planning control form*

range of products. Some distributors specializing in a product category, such as industrial products, have a limited product portfolio of synergistic products, perhaps with as few as half a dozen suppliers. The typical consumer products distributor in many markets has a more extensive product portfolio, frequently with thirty or more suppliers. In many developing markets the distributor has a portfolio ranging from heavy goods to fast moving short shelf-life consumer products.

The range and diversity of the distributor's product portfolio, and the pressure from a multiplicity of suppliers all demanding a share of his time and his mind, all mean that any single supplier, or principal, will have to work very hard to have his plan implemented and adhered to for its specific time period, usually a year. The risk that your plan will just be filed in a distributor's drawer, after you deliver and discuss it, is high. We have highlighted the importance of involving the distributor

Market Environment	⟺	Competitive environment	⟺	Plan performance

e.g.
- Government legislation,
  e.g.
  - product control
  - outlet control
  - import duties
  - sales taxes, etc.
- Economic data, e.g.
  - incomes
  - inflation
  - employment
  - interest rates
- Demographic factors
  - population trends
  - social trends

e.g.
- Industry data
- Distributor audits
- Usage and attitude studies
- Distribution audits (monitoring competitor performance)
- Nielsen audits
- Millwood Brown tracking studies
- Omnibus studies
- Competitor outlet coverage

e.g.
- Exporter shipments
- Market sales performance relative to targets (distributor stock depletions)
- Profit return from the export market (possibly monitored by product)
- Market shares User/consumer trial and/or product usage levels
- Advertising and promotion spend
- Distributor contacts or outlet coverage

Figure 12.3 *Monitoring the plan performance and the market environment*

Table 12.3 *Typical factors to benchmark in monitoring competition*

Some factors for benchmarking	
Consumer factors (consumer goods) • trade channel in-store service • demonstrations • merchandisers • promotional support • marketing support • media selection • media weight • advertising executions (positioning/targeting) • PR and sponsorship activity • promotions **Industrial user factors** • product tests and trials • availability from local stock • local spare parts and service facilities • product training (and installation) • product reliability in service • service costs • speed of delivery from ordering • product pricing • payment terms • product promotional support • general user friendliness	**Trade factors** • product pricing • product distribution • display • delivery system and reliability • distributor stock levels/availability • trade channel stock levels • distributor sales force structure • quality of sales representation • after sales (trade customer) service • accuracy of invoicing/paperwork • order cycle frequency and suitability to trade channel/customer needs • communications on stock/order status • co-operative A & P activities with trade outlets

in the marketing planning process, to gain his commitment to the objectives and understanding his role in implementation. You must also set in process a programme of monitoring the achievements against the plan, and the key aspects of both the market environment and competitive environment that impact on the plan, as illustrated in Figure 12.3, as both of these are dynamic and will not stand still unchanged for the duration of the planning period.

Competitive benchmarking

The export marketer should monitor continuing indicators of **competitive performance** versus other distributors/suppliers in the markets in a qualitative and quantitative sense. This serves to benchmark factors considered important to trade users and consumers in buying or promoting a company's products versus the competition.

Both for industrial and consumer products the export marketer can prepare a list of factors that are important in influencing the decision to make a purchase, at the level of the trade channel (i.e. that influence trade outlet decisions to stock a product) and at the level of the consumer or user. Table 12.3 lists a range of factors where some form of measurement of a distributor versus his competitors, or your own products versus competitive products, can be important in the trade decisions of what range to stock, and user or consumer decisions of what product to buy and use.

Once you have identified and listed the particular factors you consider it most relevant to benchmark for your own products and export markets, then you can obtain periodic qualitative or quantitative data by:

- personal observation whilst in the market and when calling on outlets and customers

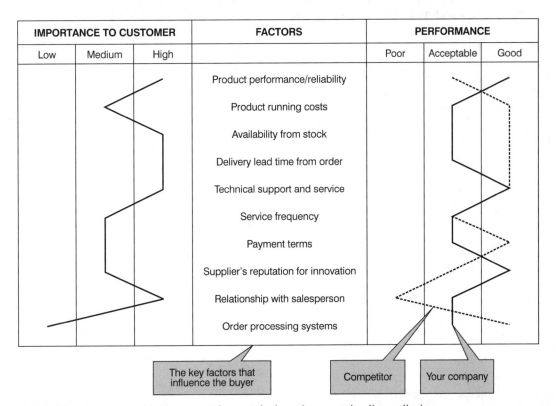

Figure 12.4 Benchmarking companies against customer selection criteria

- asking questions of trade stockists, consumers and users
- developing a system of recording key points on salesperson daily reports or customer record cards
- obtaining data from periodic market audits.

One approach to benchmarking is to develop a panel of customers (trade/consumer/user) to monitor a distributor's performance and achievements versus key competitors on a regular periodic basis. In Figure 12.4, a panel of users/consumers can be asked to identify the key factors that influence purchase decisions, or, alternatively, factors by which they judge distributors. These factors can be listed and comparisons made of your products and product offer versus key competitors. There are many ways of tabulating the identified factors, including by scoring, ranking, or showing relative importance in the mix of factors being considered. Our illustration shows the key factors in the centre column,

and then indicates in the left column whether they are of *low, medium* or *high* importance to the customer. In the right column we have invited customers to rate our own product offer versus a key competitor, using the criteria of *poor, acceptable* or *good*. We now have a tool for comparison of ourselves versus competitors, and can see illustratively our stronger and weaker points versus competition. Clearly we need to develop strength in those factors the customers most value in the purchase decision.

Further reading

Marketing Management – Analysis, Planning, Implementation, and Control. Philip Kotler (Prentice Hall). Chapter 9: Analysing Industries and Competitors

International Marketing. Stanley J. Paliwoda and Michael J. Thomas (Butterworth-Heinemann, 3rd edition 1998). Chapter 13: International Marketing Planning

Checklist 12.1
Competitive benchmarking

	Action points
Develop a survey to benchmark your own marketing and distribution expenditure and performance in relation to competitors. Agencies can assist in some of the markets, or compile a confidential outlet panel. ● **Trade factors** to be benchmarked in regular surveys include: – product pricing – product distribution – display – delivery system and reliability – distributor stock levels/availability – trade channel stock levels – distributor sales force structure – quality of sales representation – after-sales (trade customer) service – accuracy of invoicing/paperwork – order cycle frequency and suitability to trade channel/customer needs – communications on stock/order status – co-operative A & P activities ● **Consumer products marketing support factors** that can be benchmarked in regular surveys include: – trade channel in-store service – demonstrations – merchandisers – promotional support – marketing support – media selection – media weight – advertising executions (positioning/targeting) – PR and sponsorship activity – promotions ● **Industrial user factors** to be benchmarked include: – product tests and trials – availability from local stock – local spare parts and service facilities – product training (and installation) – product reliability in service – service costs – speed of delivery from ordering – product pricing – payment terms – product promotional support – general user friendliness	

13

Market research in market planning

 This chapter will:

- provide an introduction to market research
- outline areas of research that should particularly concern the export marketer, and indicate some sources of data
- discuss issues the export marketer should bear in mind when briefing a research agency
- outline the benefits of conducting periodic field audits, and give some guidelines on designing a field audit.

The aim here is to encourage the exporter to have a flexible approach to seeking and developing opportunities, maintain the export marketer's focus on research, and using the research information to improve strategic export market planning, reducing the risk factor in less planned exporting.

Market research is an essential aid to planning, and is needed to focus on longer term strategic factors and shorter term tactical decisions. It is just as much a tool in international marketing as in domestic marketing, but local market research in the export market is frequently neglected, with shortage of time or financial resources, or lack of sophistication in the market, quoted as justification. It is necessary for sophisticated planning to develop an ongoing market intelligence programme with data being collected to meet specific planning and information needs, and to monitor performance against specific objectives. The more the export marketer knows about a market the better quality decisions he will take when developing strategies and tactics, and

the less he will make decisions based on assumptions rather than knowledge. Good market research reduces the risk of pursuing unsuitable product strategies and increases the return from investment in marketing programmes.

International product development – the opportunities

Before we discuss market research in detail it is appropriate at this point to clarify the need for export marketers to have a flexible approach to international product development opportunities.

The flexible thought process

The entrepreneurial exporter should keep in the front of his mind the question: 'If I don't see a need can I create one?' As a general principle, when something new is being added to a culture that requires a cash transaction amongst a cash-poor indigenous population, market development is going to be a much longer-term project. But, as a corollary, it is often easier to add a quite new product (or service) to those available in a market than to displace an existing cultural product (or way of doing things).

Approach each market with the attitude that there will be an opportunity. It may not take the form of your preconceived ideas or plans, but an open mind will spot new opportunities that market research may confirm and give a quantified indication of size.

The key word in creating or developing markets is thus **flexibility**:

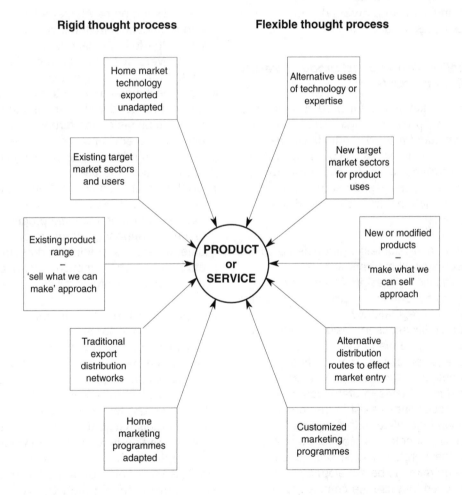

Rigid thought process

Home market technology exported unadapted

Existing target market sectors and users

Existing product range
–
'sell what we can make' approach

Traditional export distribution networks

Home marketing programmes adapted

Flexible thought process

Alternative uses of technology or expertise

New target market sectors for product uses

New or modified products
–
'make what we can sell' approach

Alternative distribution routes to effect market entry

Customized marketing programmes

PRODUCT or SERVICE

Traditional export department develops additional sales to utilize spare capacity and yield incremental profit contribution, often with limited commitment of resources.

More flexible organization structure has greater management input and greater risks and commitment of resources, aimed to produce greater long-term market shares and global profits

Figure 13.1 Alternative approaches to international market development

- flexibility of thought in seeking opportunities
- flexibility of product in taking advantage of an opportunity once you have identified or created a potential need for your goods or services.

Figure 13.1 outlines the alternative approaches to international business development. I am not trying to make value judgements as to the better approach (or whether to combine both); that will depend totally on the situation facing an individual company and the resources available to it.

Marketing standardized products versus modified products

One of the key issues for market research is often to provide data that indicates whether standardized products can be marketed or whether special modifications must be undertaken to suit local market needs. There are usually some basic questions international marketers need to put to themselves.

- Can existing domestic products be sold in some or all markets without modification in design, function or packaging, and in compliance with local rules and regulations?
- Can modifications in design, function or packaging be made that enable the domestic product concept to find acceptance in the foreign markets?
- What local tastes, preferences, cultural and social habits exist in the foreign market that relate to the exporter's industry or potential product markets?
- Can new products for specific use in foreign markets be developed and produced that use the company's existing expertise, technology and production facilities?
- Are there other ways the same inputs or ingredients could be utilized to find markets and acceptance overseas?
- If physical products cannot be exported (or, perhaps, in addition to physical

exports) are there other services (consultancy expertise, technological know-how, training, etc.) the company could export?

Once the exporter has taken the decision, based upon market research, whether to market existing products or to develop and produce modified or new products, then the next questions relate to product marketing and promotion:

- Can existing home market advertising and promotional material be adapted for use in the foreign markets, i.e. with new voice-overs or scripts, or translated for written media communications?
- Does new material need to be developed and/or produced in the foreign market to reflect local tastes, preferences, social and cultural environments or foreign regulations relating to advertising content or production and use?
- Do the distribution channel buyers and end users respond to traditional marketing and promotional programmes (such as couponing, premium offers and other incentives, product endorsements, etc.) and which promotional activities are the most successful locally?

The process of product modification and new product development for foreign markets will involve a combination of market research and process and product development research, none of which is cheap. Many manufacturers are therefore rightly reluctant to develop new products for developing markets where they have little market security and where initial development costs might not be recoverable in the short run. It is more common to prefer to market existing or modified products, even though this may be known not to maximize potential sales.

Product modification is often essential to comply with rules and regulations or conditions of use in foreign markets, or local standards applied to products. In addition, many basic items of equipment destined for use in developing markets may receive much rougher handling and less maintenance than in the home market, and users may be less concerned with appearance than with functional performance. Spare parts are often not readily available in developing nations with limited foreign exchange for imports and limited distribution and product servicing facilities. In a fashion that still amazes many of us who travel the world, local tradesmen will re-build and repair many mechanical products using locally available materials to substitute for the manufacturer's spare parts.

In considering the case for marketing standard or new/modified products, there are no really hard and fast rules, but we can develop a checklist (Table 13.1) of factors that may weigh more heavily in favour of one or other approach, and the export marketer could consider the costs and benefits of some or all of these factors in their evaluatory process.

If trade conditions dictate local manufacture under licence or local production or joint ventures as the only practical route to market entry (because of high import duties, quotas, licences, taxes, foreign exchange control, or local government policies) then the manufacturer has an opportunity to design the foreign production plant or process specifically to produce products that suit local tastes and requirements.

What is market research?

> Market research can be defined as the collection of information that will enable the marketers to take informed decisions about products and markets.

At the hub of market research and knowledge of the market environment is the aim of converting uncertainty to a measurable and

Table 13.1 *Factors in product standardization or modification*

Factor	Product standardization	Product modification
Consumer tastes[1]		✓
Cultural environment		✓
Packaging		✓
Advertising		✓
Market rules and regulations		✓
Physical use environment		✓
Production scale economies	✓	
Research and development costs	✓	
Product/packaging inventories	✓	
Target market:		
● locals		✓
● tourists	✓	
Industrial goods	✓	
High technology goods	✓	
Education/technical skills		✓
Local service facilities		✓
Consumer disposable incomes		✓

1. Note to table: This depends greatly on market sector: e.g. food tastes perhaps differ more around the world than fashion preferences (where a Paris, Rome or London label assists sales promotion) or high technology consumer goods (cameras, hi-fi equipment, etc.).

manageable risk. Chapter 3 on Preliminary desk research sets the scene for the international marketer developing a portfolio of market knowledge, and outlined how a lot of basic market information can be gleaned from domestic sources, such as good government and commercial libraries. As marketers we need information to:

- identify market opportunities
- identify actual or potential problems
- formulate programmes that exploit opportunities
- tackle problems minimizing adverse effects on the marketer's products
- monitor competitive activity, products and performance
- monitor the company's product performance in relation to competitors' products and the total category or industry
- monitor trends and the changing marketplace or market environment.

Apart from the initial market research needed to take informed decisions concerning market entry, it is also needed to focus on longer term strategic factors and shorter term tactical decisions. It is necessary for sophisticated planning to develop an ongoing market intelligence programme with data being collected to meet specific planning and information needs, and to monitor performance against specific objectives.

Market research is primarily aimed at addressing the questions:

- what is the actual or potential volume of the market?
- what volume or market share can we expect to achieve with our products?
- who buys our type of products?
- who specifies the products for use or influences buying decisions (e.g. for technical industrial products engineers, research departments, etc. might have an input to the buying process)?
- where do they buy them?
- why do they buy them?
- when are they buying/consuming them?
- what products are they buying?
- what influences the choice in purchasing?

- how do we fare against the competitors in:
  - price?
  - product distribution?
  - product/brand awareness?
  - product display (for retail consumer goods)?
  - taste/consumer preference?
  - market share?
  - promotional support and spend?
- how are our products perceived (alone and against competition)?
- what are the market dynamics of our product/trade sectors
  - consumers
    - growth/decline
    - incomes/life styles
    - demographics
  - trade channels
    - trends
    - numbers
    - locations
- what are the threats we face?
- what are the emerging opportunities?

In export markets many marketers operate in a rather blind fashion, focusing on searching out sales opportunities with very little information on how the market works and competitor activity, and often have surprisingly little knowledge of the market for their own products when they are sold through distributors rather than direct to end users. Market research, whether professionally conducted and sophisticated or based on rough data collected during market visits, is emphasized throughout this text as an essential tool in export marketing planning and market development.

The focus of market research

Typically market research is designed to answer questions concerned with our target market, their product needs, their purchasing habits and product perceptions. Some research projects are designed to address specific concerns or issues, what we might term 'ad hoc' research. Others are more of a monitoring nature, watching the market, identifying or monitoring trends and performance, commonly termed '**continuous**' research. Consumer marketers are familiar with the continuous research data provided by companies such as Nielsen.

Figure 13.2 illustrates the typical focus of ad hoc and continuous market research. Research in either of these areas might be the result of formal commissioned research through a market research agency, or be the product of the export marketer's own desk

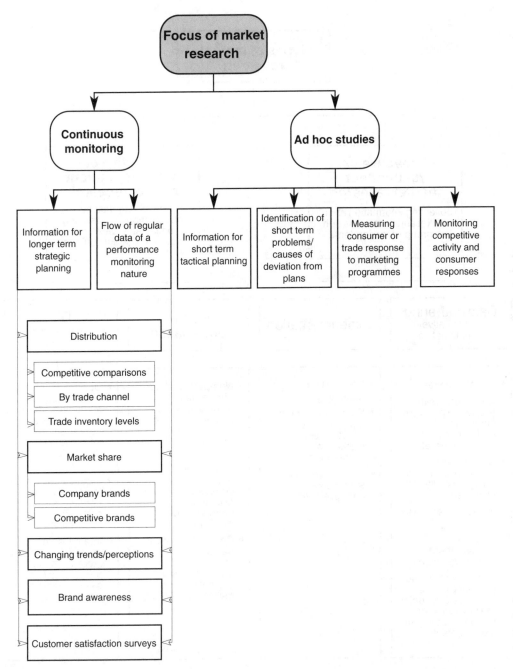

Figure 13.2 Focus of market research

research, field auditing or analysis of a distributor's field performance data. Data that can provide a source of information for analysis is frequently found from within an organization, not just externally. Much data of a macro level, such as concerning the overall performance of an economy and sectors of an economy, may be published through government statistical and information offices.

However market research is to be undertaken, at the marketing planning stage the subject of what research is needed and how it can be conducted is an important question

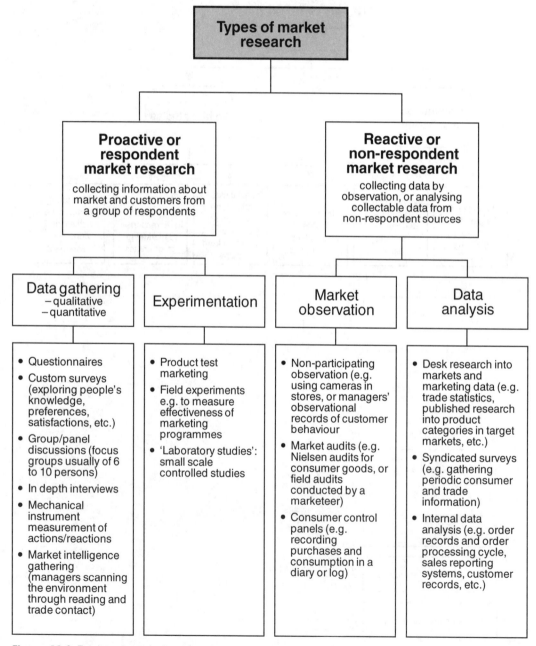

Figure 13.3 Types of market research

if the assumptions in the strategy plan are to be validated and the outcome of activity measured against the plan.

Market research, at whatever level of sophistication is practical, is an important function of the export marketer, in order that decisions are based on knowledge rather than hearsay and assumption. When we think of market research often our thoughts go first to commissioning surveys, with a team of market researchers capturing the attention of potential respondents and taking them through a questionnaire. That is only one format, and not always relevant to all information needs and product types.

Figure 13.3 illustrates that there are two main approaches to market research, proactive or **respondent research** and passive or **non-respondent research**, depending on what type of information we need to obtain. So the starting point in research is to ask:

- 'What do I need to know?'
- 'How can I obtain the information?'

Some information needs may require a broad based survey of customers or other respondents, using questionnaires, others might only require convening a small panel discussion of persons representative of the target market and with useful inputs (that might consist of a group of buyers or end users of a product). On other occasions a one-to-one in-depth interview with appropriate persons with a serious input to make might yield a wealth of information.

In Figure 13.3 we refer to gathering qualitative and quantitative data, and we can define those terms as below.

- **Quantitative research** includes anything that can produce numbers, such as data on expenditure, frequency or purchase or usage, market size, product prices, number of trade stockists, etc.,
- **Qualitative research** concerns non-quantifiable data, such as why people buy, what influences inter-product choices, customer satisfaction surveys, impact of and response to media

communication formats and messages, user/consumer behaviour and life-style factors, etc.

Considerations in deciding between internal and external research

The obvious first rule of research is to only conduct research where the likely value of the information is greater than the costs of obtaining it. Market research may not always need the services of an external specialist agency, and frequently in foreign markets, where budgets are limited, the first thoughts should be towards what research can be conducted through an agent or distributor with the help of the export marketer. Once the information needs are defined, the alternative approaches to obtaining it can be listed and evaluated on the basis of:

- **Cost.** The usual initial reaction is that internal resources are cheaper, but they are then being diverted from other productive activities. Perhaps short term staff can be hired to undertake project work where it does not require specialist research or other expertise, such as conducting telephone surveys and building outlet database information.
- **Research expertise needed.** An agency may be best suited as a resource if research expertise is needed, but otherwise internal staff or temporary staff may be trainable to fulfil basic research functions.
- **Product knowledge needed.** Internal staff are likely to have advantages where detailed product or market knowledge is required in order to conduct the market research, e.g. a special internal team might be trained to conduct follow up research on customer service, or where the research is to be of a permanent ongoing nature.
- **Speed in obtaining data.** The speed with which information is needed,

together with the required level of accuracy, may dictate either internal or external resources as best placed to conduct the research.

- **Objectivity.** Outside agencies are often more objective, in that they have no particular reason to bias data gathering or analysis. Internal resources often temper survey activity with judgements that may rule out certain research activity (e.g. missing certain outlets on the presumption they are not relevant) with resultant bias in data. Distributors tend to be prone to take very narrow views of markets, and sometimes are scathing of benefits and results of research.

- **Specialist equipment or computer programmes.** If specialist computer programmes or equipment are needed to analyse data an external agency may be better placed to supply this, e.g. for pre-testing creative material, etc.

- **Confidentiality.** If there is a risk of confidential data leaking to competitors then this may weigh against using external agencies. But data also leaks from staff employed by agents or distributors in many markets.

An overall judgement might be made as to what value-added benefit there is to using an agency (e.g. in terms of cost, expertise, time scales, etc.) versus attempting to conduct the research through internal (agent/distributor) resources. An export marketer would need to structure any internal research to reduce the risk of errors or bias, particularly through lack of objectivity. A typical example of the mistaken assumptions and lack of objectivity of a distributor to his market is where a distributor is asked questions about his coverage of the potential customer base, and automatically responds that all outlets are covered: experience shows that complete market coverage of all potential outlets is very rare. Similarly, distributors rarely monitor their service to customers in relation to either competitors or customer needs, and

are often found to be reactive rather than proactive in this area.

Export marketer activity in relation to market research ▰▰▰

The export marketer, particularly with the help of an agent or distributor, can contribute to the basic information research needs for strategic planning in several areas, especially in less sophisticated markets where there is a lack of local research agencies or where the products are of a specialist nature. Table 13.2 highlights the areas of research focus an export marketer can normally address through his own or his distributor's resources and activity, and include:

- general market research
- pricing research
- distribution research
- product research
- marketing communications.

In larger, more sophisticated companies, with specialist marketing departments, export marketers may not be involved in product and marketing communications research. But in smaller companies, the export marketer will be the instigator and analyser of all the research.

Issues for a market research agency in designing research ▰▰

The export marketer involved in commissioning market research through a specialist agency will have to satisfy himself that the agency is professional in its approach to the project, and would benefit from some understanding of the technical principles of market research. Whilst it is beyond the scope of this book to provide any extensive coverage, since we are concerned more with ensuring research is recognized as a tool in marketing, and used to benefit

Table 13.2 *Export marketer activity in relation to the focus of market research*

Category	Focus of research	Export marketer research activity and sources
General market research	Market size estimates for existing and new products.	• Distributor sales performance statistics. • Industry export figures. • Local market import statistics. • Local industry production figures. • Discussion with key accounts on sales volumes of existing brands and consumer or user purchase/consumption trends.
	Identification of market segment characteristics and consumer characteristics.	• Qualitative objective observation in outlets, and comparison with local brand mapping characteristics.
	Identification and monitoring of market trends.	• Monitoring of available statistics for distributor and competitors, as above, supported by direct impartial observations and trade discussions with a structured focus. • Active field work in trade outlets, including accompanying sales team
	Consumer and outlet data gathering.	• Gathering data in a structured format, e.g. using field check forms. • Sourced data from local trade associations or consumer/user groups. • Any appropriate published outlet data (trade directories, A. C. Nielsen data, etc.)
	Competitor research (markets, segments, prices, products, etc.).	• Trade discussions. • Field audits with structured formats, e.g. building a mini (private) audit panel to monitor during field visits. • Published audits (e.g. Nielsen)
Pricing research	Effects of price on product demand (demand elasticity).	• Monitoring distributor and trade channel sales in response to portfolio price movements. • Trade discussions about impact of general market price movements and their effect on individual products. • Consumer studies (e.g. panel studies on alternative products and prices).
	Relationship between changes in prices for all products on demand (e.g. tax increases) and on one brand only.	• As above.
	Monitoring retail price levels in outlets.	• Field audits, particularly using a panel consisting of a mix of outlets in various trade channel categories and geographical locations.

Table 13.2 *(Continued)*

Category	Focus of research	Export marketer research activity and sources
Distribution research	Outlet, consumer or user location research.	• Systematic field surveys by area, either by export marketer conducting grid type surveys, or survey projects organized in conjunction with the distributor. • Trade association data. • Local trade directories. • Independent audit data where available (e.g. A. C. Nielsen)
	Consumer/user segment locations (work/residence).	• Demographic data. • Local market knowledge of location of outlet types.
	Outlet consumer profiles.	• Field audits. • Key account profile monitoring.
	Size/volume/throughput of locations.	• Distributor sales records. • Discussions with key accounts on total product category volumes, and outlet turnovers.
	Company and competitive product distribution by trade channel/outlet type.	• Field audits by export marketer. • Sales force daily activity report control data (where requested). • Independent audits by agencies.
Product research	Researching unsatisfied user/consumer needs in relation to product categories (and company resource capabilities).	• Focus group interviews can be useful in generating new product ideas (including using brainstorming). • Interviews with users/consumers
	Product concept testing.	• Focus groups to: evaluate perceptions of products evaluate initial reactions to ideas provide a direction to product development select most promising concepts for further development evaluate commercial potential of concepts • Tests and trials (usage) with potential customers. • Panel ratings of individual or multiple concepts, making inter-panel comparisons of ratings.
	Product testing/test marketing under controlled conditions.	• Controlled field oriented testing in a limited distribution area, where users or consumers are representative of the national profile and where results can be clearly measured in relation to marketing communications, e.g. a specific television area. Results can be used to project national sales when the product is launched.

Table 13.2 *(Continued)*

Category	Focus of research	Export marketer research activity and sources
Product research *(Continued)*	Product testing/test marketing under controlled conditions. *(Continued)*	• Test marketing provides a **predictive** research tool (data can be scaled up to indicate national potential), and also provides experience in **management of the product** in the marketplace (e.g., shipping, handling, distribution problems).
	Research into packaging, pack sizes, presentation formats, price structures, etc.	• Focus groups, panel discussions, individual interviews, etc., where several alternatives are presented for comment and discussion. • Test marketing where few options need to be evaluated.
Marketing communications research	Research into media choice in relation to target markets (segments/users/consumers)	• Research the distribution or audience reach of the media (print, radio, TV, cinema). In many markets audit bureaux publish media reach data. • Location, advertisement format (e.g. colour, size, imagery, etc. in visual communications), timing, consumer perception/awareness, response, must all be assessed.
	Pre-testing: – advertising copy – content – message – brand imagery – perceptions – impact	• The marketer needs to be clear on what attributes of advertising copy he wants to test or evaluate. • Types of testing might include: – consumer juries (ranking adverts) – portfolio tests (recall tests) – physiological tests (arousal through eye movement, galvanic skin response, etc.) – theatre tests. • Advertisements (dummy or real) can include enquiry card to measure response.
	Effectiveness of marketing communications against objectives: – aided/unaided recall – consumer interpretations of brand imagery/moods – effect of advertising on buying decisions	• The marketer might measure communication effectiveness through: – sales enquiries – actual sales – recall of advertisement (message, content, etc.) in interviews.

in international markets, most basic marketing or market research textbooks will provide adequate coverage of the subject.

The export marketer, liaising with a professional market research agency, should identify any technical concerns the agency may have in designing commissioned research and be prepared to discuss methodology. Depending on the objectives of the research, a range of typical technical methodological concerns could include any of the items in the following list.

- What method should be used to collect data:
  - Personal consumer/user interviews (including visits to users or retail outlets)?
  - Telephone surveying?
  - Mail surveys?
  - Desk researching published data?
- How to maximize responses so that a meaningful analysis can be produced.
  - Non response may not bias the survey, unless non-respondents formed a particular category of the sample.
- What issues influence the design of questionnaires:
  - What information is required (optional/essential)?
  - From whom is it required?
  - Will one question on a topic generate the information, or are supplementary questions needed?
  - Will respondents answer honestly?
  - Are some questions likely to prove embarrassing or produce a negative reaction from respondents, and if so how can that be overcome?
  - Will the questions seem relevant to respondents in the framework of the survey explanation given to them?
  - Do the questions flow logically?
  - Are questions better to be direct (open or closed or multiple choice), indirect, or probing attitudes?
  - Is it practical to leave sensitive questions to the end, when a rapport is established?
  - Will the layout of the questionnaire minimize recording errors?
- What training will be needed for the survey team to collect data, analyse and interpret it?
- How should the target group sample be selected?
  - At random from the general universe?
  - According to some form of stratification (i.e. in groupings with some common characteristics) seen as relating to the products or their markets?

How errors arise in market research

Marketing research, whether at a formal structured level on an agency managed project or just at the field research level by export marketers, can produce results that are not fully accurate, and risky to base decisions on. The main causes of errors in market research are:

- sampling errors
  - the wrong specification of a target group
  - the selection of a non-representative sample
- non-response errors
  - failure to contact all the persons in a sample
  - failure of some persons contacted to provide a response (e.g. to mail enquiries)
- data collection errors
  - deliberate attempts by sources/respondents to mislead through wrong answers
  - leading questions prompting guided responses
  - failure of some of the sample to understand questions, and wrongly responding rather than admitting misunderstanding
- analytical and reporting errors
  - wrong allocation of data or responses to categories e.g. during field audits or on sales force daily reports
  - wrong tabulation of responses/data during data analysis stage
- experimental errors
  - where unforeseen factors impact on the results causing a wrong interpretation or corrupting data, e.g., such as by the launch of a competitive brand during a test market of one of your brands, or a competitive blitz

(promotion campaign) whilst you are trying to conduct a controlled test of marketing activity.

Professional agencies will normally work to minimize errors, but export marketers and distributors must work to ensure minimum errors or resultant bias in internally conducted research. Objectivity in data collection and observation is critical where any research type activity is being undertaken by an export marketer or his local representative. If questions are being asked of respondents it is important they are not loaded so as to solicit a particular response. 'What service do you expect from your widget supplier?' followed up with a supplementary question such as 'How would you rate our service against that criteria?' will normally produce a more meaningful and neutral response than 'Do you agree that our service is satisfactory?'.

Field audit data is also subject to bias if care is not taken. Outlets might be selected because they are known as customers of the distributor, rather than as product stockists of a range of competitive products only. Co-operative stockists might be favoured for inclusion in an audit and unco-operative customers neglected. As most export marketers know, there is no real substitute, when conducting a field audit, for a random survey of all stockists of a category of products in a geographical area to give a broader picture of the real levels of distribution, and make other observations on the achievements and performance of an exporter's product range versus his competitors.

The export marketer and data sources

Much data available to the export marketer is either not used or under used, perhaps because of time limitations or resource limitations to take raw data and see how it can be analysed productively. Data is usually available at three levels:

- within a company or from domestic sources, such as trade associations, or government agencies
- from a distributor organization, either as sales data or local market or economic data
- from external third party sources, as general market data (available free or for a pre-determined cost) available from government sources or agencies, or specific research commissioned for pre-agreed fees.

The export marketer should conduct his own mini-audit to check what data is available to him, other than through specific research, and what use is currently being made of available data. Table 13.3 illustrates typical data available for analysis and that can contribute to strategic planning.

Field audits as a source of market data

Vital data for market planning can be obtained by the export marketer conducting regular and thorough field audits, either on his own or with a member of the distributor's management. Data can particularly be gathered on:

- levels of product distribution in called-on and non-called-on (i.e. serviced by wholesalers) outlets
- display achievement of the company's distributor versus competitors (for consumer products)
- usage of industrial products in customer organizations
- coverage of outlets, i.e.
  - frequency of sales calls in relation to assessed potential
  - missed outlets
  - competitive coverage of the market outlets or consumers/users
- product awareness with consumer/users or trade stockists
- reaction/attitude to the distributor and the local sales team

Table 13.3 *Sources of data available to the export marketer*

Company and central research	Distributor/export marketer	Third party data

• Company market shipment records.
• Industry export data by markets and product categories.
• International data on:
  – population trends and other demographics
  – gross national products
  – per capita incomes
  – income distribution trends
  – likely exchange rate movements
  – employment levels and trends
  – competitive activity in other markets
	• Local market sales data for company products.
	• Distributor accounting records.
	• Sales force daily activity reports.
	• Customer sales records and reports.
	• Local business practices.
	• Social and cultural attitudes, social organization and structure.
	• Market dynamics.
	• Regulatory and fiscal controls affecting products.
	• Local market economic and political conditions.
		General data
		• Local publications of government monitoring data, e.g. business trend monitors
		• Import records and trade statistics.
		• Local production statistics.
		• Documents detailing regulatory and fiscal controls and proposed changes.
		• Census and demographic data.
		• Income trends and income distribution data.
		• Omnibus research published by local research agencies in markets or product sectors.
		• Audit data (Nielsen type, and brand tracking studies).
		
		Specific research
		• Panel research.
		• Audit survey data.
		• Depth interviews – consumer/trade by individual or group.
		• Controlled test/response studies.

• use of point of sales material
• implementation of local promotional activity (managed by a distributor)
• competitive activity in respect of display, pricing, distribution, promotions, product range
• customer satisfaction with products and service.

Guidelines for conducting field audits

Field audits are not a policing action, but data-gathering exercises to check the effectiveness of marketing and sales activity, and as a planning aid.

• Do not try to monitor too much on any single outlet audit visit, but focus on areas of current interest and key result areas.
• As a general rule do not just visit known stockists of your company's products, but cover all trade outlets in a geographical area on a grid basis.
• On occasions you may want to monitor only one trade channel type or only your company stockists to check a particular marketing activity.
• It is useful to have several 'panel' grids you survey on different visits to allow for the distributor's sales team having pre-visit blitz activity.

- If it is not appropriate to record data whilst in an outlet, do so immediately on leaving to ensure comprehensiveness and accuracy – don't fall into the salesman's trap of leaving recording until memory lapses dictate fictional records!
- Keep the survey record for subsequent comparison on a later visit.

It is a useful discipline for the export marketer to develop a standard format for recording field audit data relevant to his particular markets and products. For a product that is resold through sub-distributors or retailers then the audit might want to record data under headings such as those listed below.

- **Coverage**
  - Is the outlet receiving a call from the exporter's distributor?
  - Which competitors service the stockist/outlet?
  - How do the quality and frequency of coverage by competitors compare with that from the exporter's representative?
- **Distribution**
  - Which of the exporter's main products are sold through an outlet?
  - How does distribution of the exporter's products compare with distribution of competitive products?
- **Display**
  - What of the exporter's product range is on display?
  - How do the quality and quantity of display space given to the exporter's products compare with that given to competitive products?
- **Point of sale material**
  - Is the exporter's point of sale material in use in trade outlets?
  - Is competitive material in use?
  - Is material replaced regularly to ensure it is current and tidy?
- **Pricing**
  - What prices are the exporter's products resold at?
  - Are prices consistent with guidelines issued through the distributor?
  - What are the prices for competitive products?

In addition, it is likely the export marketer will want to monitor promotional activity, both supporting his own products as per his marketing plan, and of competitive products. He may also want to ask questions or note observations about the quality of the service provided by his local agent or distributor. An example of how a typical field audit form for a retail product might look is illustrated in Figure 13.4. A modified version that might suit an audit covering industrial (business-to-business) products is illustrated in Figure 13.5.

Researching the macro market environment

The commentary so far has focused on the micro levels of research, i.e. those concerned only with the exporter's products and his immediate competition in the marketplace. Strategic planning, particularly over the longer term, needs to take account of the general political, business and economic environment in a market, and particularly observe changing trends that can impact on the exporter's business opportunities. Specifically, at the macro market level the export marketer will want to build for each export market a **country file** of data covering:

- consumers or users (in relation to known relevant profile criteria for either industrial or consumer products)
- cultural trends in the markets
- the local political environment and trends (which will include fiscal, economic and legislative trends)
- technology trends (product stage in the local market life cycle, and in relation to product innovations, innovation and its impact on product life cycles, and any local aspects of regulation that impact on the development and use of technology)

FIELD AUDIT	MARKET					DATE					LOCALITY				
	Coverage		Product distribution			Product display		Point of sale material			Product pricing			Notes	
Outlet	Comp-any	Comp-etitor	Prod X	Prod Y	Prod Z										

N.B. Column headings can be varied and inserted as appropriate to each field audit.

Figure 13.4 A model field audit form: retail products

FIELD AUDIT		MARKET				DATE			LOCALITY		
	Product usage levels		Sources of supply		Prices paid for supplies		Level of customer satisfaction		Special needs or requirements	Notes	
Client/prospect	Volume	Value	Company	Competitor	Company	Competitor	Product	Service			

Figure 13.5 A model field audit form: industrial (business to business) products

- market dynamics such as changes in the distribution infrastructure (e.g. new ways of getting goods to the customers – hypermarkets, out of town shopping, direct mail supply, concentration in supply sources, mergers/acquisitions, etc.)
- the local competitive environment (from local production sources and international competitors active in the market).

Figure 13.6 illustrates these aspects of the macro market environment that the export marketer might want to research in more detail, depending on the nature of his products, and much data in the more developed markets are likely to be available through government departments and publications.

Some illustrative examples of how information might impact on strategic planning include the following scenarios:

- A manufacturer of baby products or products aimed to younger persons will be interested in the projected demographics in a market with an ageing or declining population, as this changing demographic situation might have implications for the marketing strategy, product mix, product development, advertising strategy, etc.
- Decline in inner cities and a general trend of population moves to rural areas might have implications for the distribution strategies and outlet coverage in a market.
- The economic and educational development in a less developed nation and increased westernization might have implications on traditional products sold locally, and shorten their life cycles in the market as the demand for new innovative products grows.
- Moral and religious attitudes are offended at the marketer's risk! Knowledge from research and experience in these areas might have effects on the mix of product offered for

sale, and supporting marketing communications, e.g. it would be accepted as inappropriate to use scantily clad bodies in product advertisements in many Muslim countries.
- Knowledge of the trends in cash income levels will be useful to the marketer of an international mass market product that depends on a cash transaction, but might be less useful knowledge to an exporter of industrial equipment.
- A market that has little industrial infrastructure and local manufacturing might also have limited exposure to product innovation, offering opportunities to exporters to market products otherwise at the limit of the product life cycle in developed markets. But a proactive policy by local authorities to encourage inward investment in technologically advanced industries will pressure the exporters to introduce and compete with more hi-tech or innovative products in their portfolios.
- Markets don't stand still! They are dynamic. Suppliers might be innovative in the products they develop and offer for sale; and markets have their own dynamic innovativeness in developing changing ways of distributing products. The growth of niche retail outlets in Western Europe and North America illustrates this, as does the move towards out of town shopping and warehouse-style outlets serving the public at discounted prices. The export marketer needs to watch for the dynamic trends in his export markets within the distributive trades and channels, and take account of them in marketing strategy planning.
- Competitors should not be ignored nor should it be assumed they will stand still and accept your marketing strategies. Will the market you are building be undermined by a competitor taking advantage of local investment opportunities and establishing a factory or joint venture in the market? Are local competitors of lower technology products

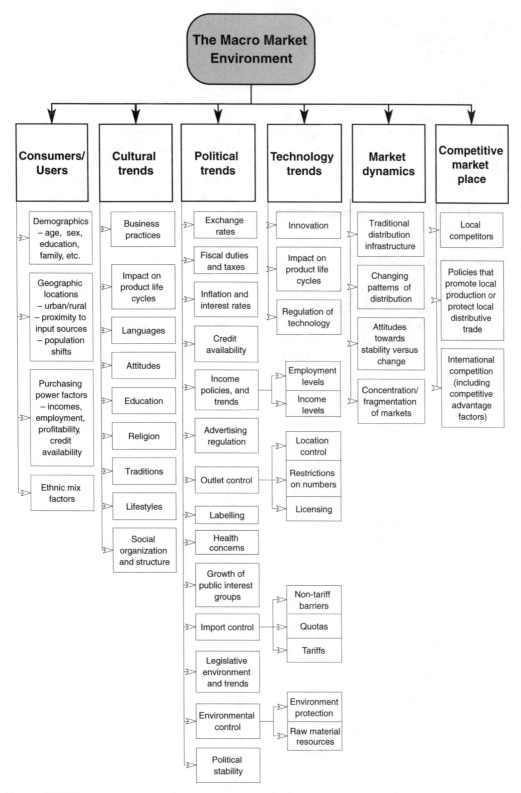

Figure 13.6 *The macro market environment*

going to buy in higher technology products on licensed manufacturing arrangements?

These are just a few of the points that might arise for some exporters, and that would encourage a thorough understanding of the market environment as well as a strategy that addresses any relevant macro level factors.

Further reading

Marketing Communications. Colin J. Coulson-Thomas (Butterworth-Heinemann). Chapter 20: Market research

Essentials Of Marketing. Geoff Lancaster and Lester Massingham (McGraw-Hill). Chapter 5: Marketing Research

Marketing Management – Analysis, Planning, Implementation, and Control. Philip Kotler (Prentice Hall, 8th edition 1994). Chapter 5: Marketing Information Systems and Marketing Research; Chapter 6: Analysing the Marketing Environment

International Marketing – A Strategic Approach to World Markets. Simon Majaro (George Allen & Unwin). Chapter 5: Research International Markets

Marketing Research – An Applied Approach. Thomas C. Kinnear and James R. Taylor (McGraw-Hill, 4th edition 1991). A detailed specialist text for the reader who wants a depth of knowledge

Marketing – An Introductory Text. Martin Christopher and Malcolm McDonald (Macmillan 1995). Chaper 6: Scanning the Environment

Marketing Research Using Forecasting in Business. Peter Clifton, Hai Nguyen and Susan Nutt (Butterworth-Heinemann 1992)

Market Research. P. M. Chisnall (McGraw-Hill, 1992)

Checklist 13.1
Opportunities for international expansion

Action points

Opportunity identification: recognize the alternative product export opportunities to foreign markets:

- for existing products
- for modified versions of current products
- for alternative market development routes

Develop a product modification or innovation programme:

- Establish the full range of goods (or services) you can produce within present limits of technology, capacity and other resources
- Consider which modifications or innovations are needed for export markets for reasons of
  - different market cultures
  - environment of product use
  - user skills
  - product handling in the market
  - manner of use
- Establish limiting parameters restricting innovation to meet or create foreign needs
  - cost
  - technology
  - resources (finance, plant, human)
  - R & D lead times
  - quality control
  - plant capacity
  - levels of market demand
  - profit potential
  - synergy
  - competitive technology/distribution, etc.
- Evaluate and conduct feasibility studies into alternative modifications or innovations in products/services. Prioritize according to:
  - costs
  - lead times
  - synergy (production, distribution)
  - sales potential

Consider the marketing implications of modification or innovation:

- compatibility with current distribution networks and availability of suitable distribution channels in foreign markets
- product after-sales support service needs
- utilization or modification of domestic marketing aids and promotional materials

Checklist 13.2
Marketing information and research

Action points

Marketing research can address the questions:

- ◆ Who buys your type of products?
- ◆ Where do they buy them?
- ◆ Why do they buy them?
- ◆ When are they buying/consuming/using them?
- ◆ What products are they buying?
- ◆ What influences the choice in purchasing?
- ◆ How do we fare against the competitors in:
  - price
  - distribution?
  - brand awareness?
  - taste/consumer preference?
  - market share?
  - promotional support and spend?
- ◆ How are your products perceived (against competition)?
- ◆ What are the market dynamics of your product/trade sectors
  - consumers
    - growth/decline?
    - incomes/life styles?
    - demographics?
- trade channels
  - trends?
  - numbers?
  - locations?
- ◆ What are the main threats you face in the market?
- ◆ What are the foreseeable new opportunities?

Have any of the following aspects of research a place in market management:

- market research?
- product research?
- pricing research?
- marketing communications research?
- distribution research?

Checklist 13.2 *(Continued)*

Action points

Factors in deciding between internal and external research:

- cost
- research expertise needed
- product knowledge needed
- speed in obtaining data
- objectivity
- specialist equipment or computer programs
- confidentiality.

Issues in designing research:

- method of collecting data
- how to maximize responses
- questionnaire design
- training surveyors
- selection of target group samples.

Field audits can be used by the export marketer to monitor:

- levels of product distribution in called-on and non-called-on outlets
- display achievement of the company distributor versus competitors
- distributor coverage of outlets
  - frequency of calling in relation to potential
  - missed outlets
- competitive coverage of market outlets
- stockist/customer product awareness
- reaction/attitude to distributor and the sales team
- use of point of sales material
- promotional activity
- competitive activity in respect of display, pricing, distribution, promotions, product range.

14

Export sales
forecasting

 In this chapter we will focus on the topic of forecasting from a practical perspective. We will look at:

- what aspects of the export operations should be subject to forecasting or budgeting
- forecasting at the macro level (i.e. at the level of the overall market for the products) and micro level (i.e. building forecasts from individual customer data)
- some basic practical approaches to using data in forecasting.

The aim is to encourage the exporter to take a more disciplined and formal approach to practical export sales forecasting using available data, either relating to company historical sales or industry data obtained from basic desk research. Whilst advanced statistical techniques (where these are appropriate) may increase the accuracy of forecasting, better use of available export data will represent significant improvement for most exporters, and encourage a move away from the common forecasting approach in many companies of simply taking last year's sales and increasing by an acceptable percentage.

Forecasting sales to export markets is often a much less sophisticated activity than forecasting domestic market sales, although many a marketer might complain that even domestic market forecasting is very hit and miss in his organization! This chapter will look at some of the issues that the export marketer might consider in developing his market forecasts. It is not intended to turn the export marketer into a statistician, and therefore the focus is on practical approaches using data that most exporters can find internally or through basic desk research. Those readers whose companies are already using more advanced statistical export forecasting

techniques, which experience shows are few, will be referred to more specialized texts.

Export forecasting is all about:

- estimating the total size of the potential market for a product or group of related products, in each of the export markets
- estimating the current level of total market demand by market (normally lower than the market potential)
- estimating the exporter's current share of the total market demand (i.e. company demand)
- forecasting forward the level of sales the company would expect to achieve in

each market based upon particular marketing strategies.

Forecasting in export markets is clearly not as easy as domestic market forecasting, in that often the export marketer works with limited data. As we will attempt to show in this chapter, simply taking last year's sales and adding a set percentage, a common export practice, is not a forecast in any sense that a marketer would find acceptable. The forecast growth of the company must be benchmarked against external data, to ensure that the company is keeping pace with the market and competition. Table 15.1 in the next chapter shows a situation where an exporter was very happy with his percentage growth year on year, until comparing his exports with the total UK product category exports, when he found he was in relative decline. Later examples in this chapter also highlight how sales can be lost through poor forecasting. The export marketer must satisfy himself that the market demand is not rising faster than the demand for his own products.

The issue of poor data availability can be addressed through:

- desk research into UK exports to the export markets
- local market research, usually in co-operation with agents and distributors, into total product category imports, and local production (where any competing products are produced locally) to estimate total local demand in each market.

Improved forecasting will, for most exporters, need far greater co-operation and sharing of data between exporter and agent or distributor, but the benefits are clearly mutual.

Terminology associated with sales forecasting

A useful starting point in looking at the subject of export forecasting is probably to develop common understanding of the standard terminology used, and an approach to developing working definitions is shown on the next page.

For simplicity and clarity here we will use the term **forecasts** to refer to any figures aimed at assessing demand for a product either at the market or company level.

In many companies the common practice with respect to sales forecasts and marketing plans and budgets is to make an estimate of sales, and then to develop marketing plans and supporting marketing expenditure budgets. This is logically erroneous, in that the subsequent sales forecast definition clearly indicates that the sales forecast is derived from the marketing strategy, which assumes a level of marketing expenditure to support the programme aimed at pursuing the strategy. To base marketing plans on sales forecasts may seem reasonable where the marketer does not expect the company's demand in the total market to be capable of expansion, but it is patently wrong where company demand is capable of expansion and influenced by marketing expenditure.

Another common scenario is that when sales run behind forecasts, the response is to cut back on the marketing budgets. If for any reason in any market the sales forecast is not being achieved then before cutting marketing expenditure the marketer should seek to establish the reason for any shortfall. If there have been changes in the marketing environment (such as imposition of import restrictions, changes in duties or taxes, etc.) then it may be reasonable to re-forecast sales and prepare new marketing expenditure budgets at the same time as making any appropriate changes to the marketing strategy. If shortfalls arise for other reasons, such as poor performance by an agent or distributor, then, on the assumption that the strategy was appropriate and the forecasts were realistic, the attention must be given to improving the performance of the agent or distributor – cutting marketing budgets will only prove a short term saving and will do nothing to help you to achieve your forecasts or potential.

Forecasting terminology

MARKET POTENTIAL

The **potential market** for a product is the total of all those persons or businesses with the means, need and opportunity to buy.

MARKET DEMAND

The **market demand** can be considered as the total volume of the product that would be purchased by a qualified customer group in a prescribed time period, in a known marketing environment. The known marketing environment is assumed to include an established political/economic/legal/social environment, an established distribution infrastructure, and predictable levels of marketing activity – advertising, promotion, etc. Changes in the marketing environment will prompt changes in the level of demand (i.e. variations in industry marketing expenditure, and stages of an economic cycle are two key variables that typically influence market demand).

COMPANY POTENTIAL

This will normally be limited by the demand that can be created as the company increases its marketing activity relative to its competitors.

FORECASTS

These can be defined as projections of **expected sales** over a particular time period based upon known parameters.

Forecasts are normally prepared for each market at the **industry** and **company** level. The **industry** forecast will make assumptions about industry marketing support for the products in the market. The **company** sales forecast should be based upon a defined marketing strategy and assumed level of marketing expenditure in pursuing that strategy.

TARGETS

These can be defined as a statement of what the exporter (or his distributor) wants to achieve in the way of market sales, and may be based mainly on data external to the company, such as competitors' known sales, market volume data, etc.

Achievement of targets is heavily dependent on developing and implementing suitable strategies and tactics, including promotional activity.

BUDGETS

These really are a projection of revenues and expenditure, and the term 'budgets' is really an accounting term that has been adopted into the language of marketers in many companies through its use in annual company plans that are largely financially based and prepared by accountants.

Budgets may or may not be based on sales performance history, and are just as likely to be a target of sales revenues, volumes and profits needed from export operations to achieve overall company financial projections.

Planning time spans ▬▬▬▬▬

Companies vary in the time spans they apply to their planning process. Forecast time spans might be defined for practical purposes as shown below.

Apart from the accuracy of forecasting depending on the stability and maturity of the overall product markets, there will be variations in the development of the market for the products between countries, and, additionally, consideration must be given to the security of access to individual markets when forecasting. A company that makes most of its export sales into Europe and North America may be able to forecast with a high degree of certainty that markets will remain open and that sales will move in a predictable direction (allowing for factors such as new product innovation). An exporter whose major markets are in the developing world, such as Africa, will have to allow for the likelihood of occasional political instability and financial crisis possibly disrupting markets significantly. The wise exporter, who knows his export sales are a critical factor in company performance, will spread his export market portfolio so that it does not just include volatile markets.

What to forecast ▬▬▬▬▬

The starting point for any forecasting is to attempt to estimate the **total market size** for the product category (or near substitutes), and then to make an estimate of the share of the total market that the company can expect to achieve, through a proactive marketing programme.

Typical considerations in forecasting ▬

Sales forecasting is primarily about predicting **sales volumes** and **sales values** (revenues). From the exporter's perspective the strategies the company plans to adopt in pursuing its marketing objectives are key considerations and must be considered when forecasting volumes and values, the product mix, and expectations of market price movements. Figure 14.1 illustrates the two sides of the forecasting equation, as seen from the perspective of the export marketer and the financial planner.

It is common for the export marketer to focus primarily on estimates of sales related figures, such as volumes and revenues. In looking at these then clearly attention must be given to the product mix expected to be sold, as variations in product mix will affect

Planning time spans	
Short term forecasts	These usually cover the period immediately ahead, such as from three to six months. Short term tactical decisions, such as promotional activity, are based on the short term forecasts.
Medium term forecasts	These usually are projecting sales volumes and values at least a year ahead, and sometimes for eighteen months to two years ahead, with a greater input of detailed marketing strategy than long term forecasts.
Long term forecasts	These typically attempt to forecast three to five years ahead, with limited accuracy, and often with coverage of the longer term diversification or expansion strategies of the company.

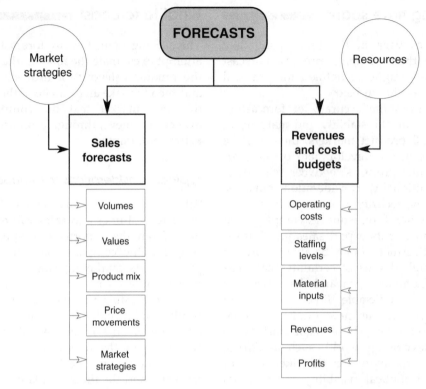

Figure 14.1 *The forecasting equation*

volumes, revenues and resultant profits. Also, since in good forecasting practice the forecast is derived from the marketing strategy (and not vice versa), account must be taken of strategies and marketing expenditure, and as these change so must the forecasts be modified to reflect the expected impact of the changes on sales volumes and values.

When the forecasts are developed from the marketing strategy for each market, then the marketers need to be involved with the accountants in preparing the budgets, taking account of any resources limitations (human, physical and financial). The values of sales should match up with the revenue budget, and estimates made of the operating costs, material inputs, and staffing levels need to achieve the forecasts. In export forecasting a common weakness is in addressing the issue of providing adequate export staffing support to enable strategies to be implemented properly and forecasts to be met. Export marketers commonly have far too large a portfolio of markets to manage effectively from a marketing perspective, and often struggle to do anything much other than a maintenance job, with a risk of resultant under performance against potential. Hence the critical need to estimate market potential and market demand and to benchmark performance and forecasts against these.

Approaches to forecasting

There are a number of approaches to forecasting, at the macro level of the total market or industry, and at the micro level of the company down to individual customers. We will look at some of these approaches, both in terms of forecasting current demand and future demand.

Macro forecasting

Macro forecasting, as the name implies, involves looking at the overall market for a product or category of products. It is about:

- studying company and/or distributor historical performance in relation to the environment (political, economic, social, legislative), industry performance, demographic factors related to company or market performance, and product demand
- relating industry demand to national levels of production, income levels, interest rates, employment, imports, demographic factors.

Trends in overall market demand for a product or category of products can be

On the sales forecasting side of the equation account must be taken of:	
VOLUMES	• by product • by customer or distributor • by market sector • by foreign market (for exports)
VALUES	• by product • by customer or distributor • by market sector • by foreign market (for exports)
PRODUCT MIX	• variations in the marketer's product portfolio and price mix may change the levels of sales volumes or values, with resultant effects on product or total profits for markets
PRICING LEVELS AND MOVEMENTS	• regionally/nationally/internationally (versus competition) • changes in product costs (inputs, etc.) • by market sector • by product type • currency movements
MARKETING STRATEGIES	• product positioning • pricing • distribution • advertising and promotional activity • product ranges • quality • presentation • consumer attitudes/preferences • changes in the market environment • regulatory controls • market dynamics/distribution channels • consumer attitudes/preferences • employment/incomes • competitive activity and marketing strategies

	Sales forecasts should be supported by resource/cost estimates, e.g.:

OPERATING COSTS	• **Sales departmental costs**
	  – wages and wage increases
	  – sales training
	  – recruitment
	  – support department costs
	  – travel and subsistence
	  – sales force expenses including vehicles
	  – bonus and incentive payments
	  – sales promotional activities (off sales budgets)
	  – customer service/shipping
	  – order processing
	  – sales planning
	  – transport and distribution of goods
	  – export distribution (where applicable)
	  – export travel and subsistence costs
	• **Marketing costs**
	  – advertising and promotion budgets
	  – promotional and display materials

STAFFING LEVELS	• sales management • sales office support staffing • marketing management • export marketing management • shipping/customer service staff levels • expansion/contraction to meet market coverage needs • natural wastage • retirement • sickness/holidays • changes in required qualifications, experience, skills

MATERIAL INPUTS	• capabilities of the company to source/produce competitively.
	  – breadth/depth of company range
	  – exchange rate movements (for imported inputs)
	  – input supply availability (labour and materials)

REVENUES	• by product • by customer or distributor • by market sector • by foreign market
PROFITS	• by product • by customer or distributor • by market sector • by foreign market

tabulated or plotted, and a company's performance against the overall market compared. Estimates of market potential, normally a higher figure than actual demand, may also be made. From this, taking account of the company marketing initiatives, some forecast estimates can be prepared showing expectations of total market demand and demand for company products within the overall market.

Micro forecasting

The typical approach to market micro forecasting is to:

- study the performance of each existing and potential account on a product by product basis over the last few years or recent sales periods and preparing forward sales estimates for the next forecast period
- build-up to territory, area and national sales forecasts for comparison with the independently prepared macro forecasts.

In many export markets the marketers do not have any useful information on the potential consumer or user universe, either because their agents or distributors do not co-operate by sharing their own knowledge, or, perhaps more serious a default, the agents or distributors actually do not have any real knowledge of the size of the market. With consumer goods some assumptions might be made from relevant demographic data, where available. But for industrial products other sources need to be researched or developed to establish the potential market, since often the agent or distributor is only servicing a small group of the total users with his limited resources.

A considered approach by the export marketer to the outcomes of macro forecasting and micro forecasting should help come to a reasoned view of realistic and achievable sales forecasts or targets. These can be looked at in relation to the overall goals and objectives for the market, and the range of marketing and sales strategies and tactics to be employed in a marketing plan to ensure their achievement.

Main methods of developing forecasts

Figure 14.2 illustrates a number of the major macro and micro forecasting techniques, split under two headings that group those dealing with **future demand** separately from those dealing with **current demand**. Some of the techniques are **quantitative**, in that there are often accessible statistical records that will form a firm basis for estimates and forecasts, and others are **qualitative**, in that they rely heavily upon the judgement of the forecasters and their market knowledge and assessments of

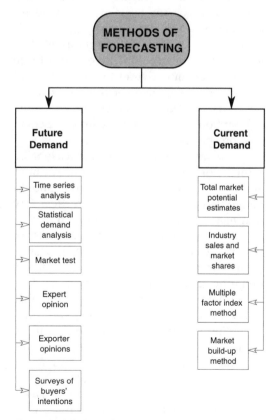

Figure 14.2 Methods of developing forecasts

trends. The quantitative techniques would mainly be compiled using appropriate computer programmes and spreadsheets.

Current demand

The starting point should be to make some estimate of market potential for each export market, and then see how this is being satisfied, i.e. current levels of demand, and the company share of the current demand can then be factored in to develop marketing strategies to develop the company's sales and market share.

Total market potential

The market potential is basically an estimate of the total sales potential for all industry suppliers in a market (a macro market forecast). As stated earlier, this will invariably be a larger number than current levels of demand. For an export market this should take account of imports as well as local production of competitive or substitute products. Quantitative techniques can lead to estimates being made of volume or value. First the forecaster must make some assumptions about what qualifies a person as a prospective buyer.

It is always difficult to make a reasonable estimate of the number of prospective buyers for a product. The target market should be profiled or qualified in any practical way that relates to product consumption or use, in order that estimates of the number of potential buyers have some rational basis.

For consumer goods, experience in the domestic market or other export markets might help develop a customer profile that could be applied to other markets, and providing groups of similar profile can be identified in the export markets then some estimate of market potential can be made.

For example, a basic profile of the scotch whisky drinker in a developed market might be a male, over thirty-five, with certain levels of income. If we have knowledge of the average consumption of the typical whisky drinker we can then add this to the equation, and find a first estimate of market potential as in the following table.

Estimating whisky market potential	
Market potential (litres volume) =	Number of males meeting the profile criteria (over age 35 years and earning at relevant income level) *times* average consumption (litres) per whisky consumer
Market potential (value) =	Number of males meeting the profile criteria (over age 35 years and earning at relevant income level) *times* average consumption (expenditure) per whisky consumer

With industrial products this kind of macro market estimate for export markets is often difficult to develop with any accuracy, although some good estimates can be built-up from micro-level data (discussed shortly).

A starting point is often to attempt to establish the number of persons employed in an industry or market sector that uses the products, and apply a ratio of usage based on experience or rational criteria.

A supplier of computers might obtain market estimates of numbers of persons employed in industrial and commercial activities (excluding agriculture) and apply a reasonable ratio (possibly based on experience in similar markets) of computers to employed persons (say one computer per twenty persons) to estimate maximum likely market potential.

A more refined approach to estimating total market potential involves taking a base number considered to represent the maximum possible level of consumers, and then applying a sequence of percentage ratios (**chain ratio approach**) that narrows down the market and to which some value or volume factors can be applied. The reader interested in this technique are referred to more specialist reading at the end of this chapter.

In many developed countries government organizations monitor industry statistics of production and consumer expenditure, and desk research to access this data (often available through UK government export agency sources) can help in developing estimates of market potential and market demand for products.

Manufacturing companies are normally classified by **standard industrial classification** (SIC) codes, and if an exporter's industrial products have applications in certain industries then accessing government statistics and lists of companies in appropriate SIC classifications will assist in estimating market potential and in subsequent sales forecasting.

Industry sales and market shares

Making quantitative estimates of industry sales and market shares is often easier for consumer goods producers than for industrial products suppliers. Whilst it may be difficult in some developed markets to build estimates, it can be a frustrating task in many less developed markets to arrive at meaningful figures that convey a sense of accuracy. There are some starting points in developing industry sales estimates, and competitor shares, including from the following sources.

- **Trade association data**. Trade associations in many countries collect and collate statistics from their members covering production and sales of relevant product categories, and these figures are frequently available to researchers.
- **Company accounts**. Company chairpersons frequently make proud

claims of success and market share in company account statements, all useful market intelligence.
- **Market research studies**. In many markets research companies such as A. C. Nielsen conduct periodic market audits of retail sales of consumer products that enables industry sales and market shares to be estimated. Other studies are made by various market researchers of particular industries or market sectors, and covering various geographic regions. Europe is well covered by published studies of quite a number of markets. Chapter 3, Preliminary desk research, outlined some additional sources of market research information.
- **Import and local production statistics**. Where physical goods move across national borders import/export records can provide some data that can help build the picture of industry size, and possibly lead to estimates of market share. Of course some products (such as computer software) may be produced in the local market, and not show in trade statistics.
- **User surveys**. With industrial products one approach to estimating industry size in export markets is to survey known product users and seek information on product usage levels. Some surveyors offer an incentive to respondents to provide information. This approach may have limited accuracy, in that there is no obligation to reply with accuracy. Also, unless all users are identified, only partial results will be known. Sometimes a ratio of usage can be developed for survey respondents that might then be applied to other non-respondent producers to build-up an industry estimate. The ratio should be for some factor that can be assessed for other non-respondent companies, i.e. a usage per employee, or usage rate relating to output (in volume or value).

  For industrial products in export markets this is the kind of survey work that can be undertaken by an agent or distributor to gain market and industry size estimates, and competitor share estimates.

Multiple factor index method

This approach to forecasting regional demand is most commonly used by consumer goods companies wanting to break down national forecasts to regional forecasts, or trying to build national forecasts from known regional data about a product category. It involves having access to a reasonable range of relevant demographic data on a population, in order to build an index relating to demand and potential for growth. The method is probably a little more complex than export marketers will normally choose to involve themselves in, unless for markets where a lot of relevant index data is readily available (often to be purchased or developed by a market research company) such as in the United States, and those readers with particular interest can refer for further reading to the list at the end of this chapter.

In some markets where government departments monitor consumer expenditure, statistics may be available to show national expenditure on a range of product categories and regional variations in expenditure, and export marketers may be able to use this data to make forecasts of regional sales as a percentage of national forecast sales.

Market build-up method

This approach to forecasting is commonly used for both industrial and consumer goods as a quantitative technique, building up from the micro level to give an overall macro assessment of sales or forecast. It does require the marketer to have access to lists identifying all the potential buyers for a product (users in the case of industrial products, and trade distribution outlets for consumer goods – unless those were sold direct to the public, when other forecasting approaches would need to be considered).

Typically trade directories would be used to identify all the potential customers in a market, or region within a market. With an industrial product, an initial profile can be developed for typical potential users, and use might be made of any listings of companies by **standard industrial classification** (SIC) codes to identify other companies matching the user profile. If there are a large number of potential customers in the product category then data obtained from a sample of users can provide broad criteria to build market demand estimates (see the earlier section on user surveys).

In a later section of this chapter we will look further at building forecasts from information for individual customers, as this is a common approach in export markets where sophisticated research is not always available.

Future demand

Predicting current potential or estimating current demand is a difficult enough task for the marketer. For foreign markets we often do not know what data is available, spend little or no time researching data, and base current and future forecasts upon our historical sales performance alone, with no comparative industry benchmark data. When forecasting the future, a much more difficult period to forecast, many more variables come into play, not least of which must be technological change and changes in consumer or user preference.

Much future forecasting activity is directed to macro market forecasts, using both quantitative and qualitative techniques.

Time series analysis

Bearing in mind the target readership for this text, practising export marketers, we will not attempt lengthy expositions of complex statistical forecasting techniques, most of which are based on analysing data over a longer time period (time series analyses) but refer the interested readers to more specialist texts. We will look briefly at some of the main macro forecasting quantitative techniques.

Time series data studies, that would normally make use of computer facilities such as spreadsheets, include the following main statistical techniques:

- **Trend fitting** is a technique where historical actual data is plotted and the trend projected.
- **Moving annual totals** or **moving annual averages** are techniques that smooth data in a time series, showing a trend that is not distorted by serious seasonal, cyclical or random fluctuations. An example of constructing a moving annual total trend follows in this chapter. A disadvantage of moving annual or moving average techniques is that they do not respond quickly to unexpected or significant changes in the pattern of sales.
- **Exponential smoothing** is where extra weighting is given either to earlier or to more recent data (depending on which data is seen as more likely to be representative of the future sales pattern), in an attempt to take account of more significant changes in the pattern of sales.
- **Forecasting from time series data using standard deviations**. Again, this quantitative technique, that can be used at the level of industry or company sales, is probably unlikely to be used by most export marketers except possibly for the most major markets. But it is a technique that can be developed quite easily using a spreadsheet computer package, and also it is a technique most suited where there is a repetitive seasonal sales pattern (i.e. monthly or quarterly). The objective is to measure the seasonal fluctuations, typically by month or quarter of the year, in terms of their deviation from the average trend, then to project the trend forward, adding back in the seasonal deviation factors for each quarter.

Statistical demand analysis

The weakness in time series forms of analysis and forecasting is that it treats sales only as a function of time, taking no account of any other demand influencing factors that affect sales, such as the effects of price and promotion, income levels, changes in population (or the mix of population where relevant, e.g. age structures, sex mix, education levels, and so on) or the introduction of new technology or product varieties. Various statistical demand techniques (often referred to as **causal analysis techniques**) are available, for those with access to computers and sufficient interest and expertise, but we will only mention them here by way of an introduction, leaving the reader to study specialist texts where appropriate.

These **causal studies**, often found in use only in the largest companies, include:

- **regression analysis**, where equations are developed that relate the volume of sales to a number of independent variables known to impact on sales performance (such as advertising, salesperson call rate, number of distribution points, promotional expenditure, display activity, etc.) and a line of regression (line of 'best fit') describes in quantitative terms the underlying correlation between any two sets of data
- **econometric models**, which look at the interdependent relationship of a number of factors that affect sales and profits
- **input/output models**, which might be very useful for ingredients or component forecasting where projections will encompass the demand for inputs in relation to outputs in user industries. This technique requires some knowledge of the expected level of output from users of the exporter's products.

Market sales tests

Normally in market sales tests for new consumer products, the products are distributed into a limited geographical sales area whose consumer profile matches closely the national pattern, and where it is judged that sales performance can be monitored closely whilst any marketing communications can also be tightly focused to the target audience.

Industrial products do not normally lend themselves to market testing in the same way, but are subjected to rigorous technical trials and tests either in laboratory test conditions or with some potential users.

National forecasts can be extrapolated from the test market results in this quantitative technique (but there may need to be a longer term discounting factor to offset any novelty value unless the test market is run for a sufficient time period).

In export markets products are not so commonly test marketed except where the brand is part of the portfolio of a major multinational corporation that is looking to seriously assess potential, possibly identify any necessary product modification to suit local market needs or preferences, and develop an appropriate marketing strategy and communications programme.

In normal export practice the marketer simply seeks sales in whatever outlets will stock the products, and attempts to build from that base. More often the export marketer does not have the budgets or resources to conduct meaningful test markets. Smaller scale market research such as panel discussion might show a local market preference for a modified product, which can be acted upon if the production environment does not dictate against product variations.

Expert opinion

In this mainly qualitative approach to macro forecasting panels of experts on the industry (both internal and external) give their reasoned opinions on trends and estimates of market volumes in this qualitative technique.

From the perspective of the export marketer his expert panel might include himself, agents or distributors, trade dealers or retail stockists, major end users (for industrial products), marketing consultants, international market researchers, trade association representatives, and possibly some government contacts where exports are influenced by political factors.

However small or large the panel is, it will have a weakness in that each participant will have limited market exposure and knowledge. That does not mean the approach should be discarded, but does suggest that it should be only one of the approaches to forecasting adopted by a company, and not the only one.

Any known historical market or company data should be shared between all the panel of experts, and each expert will add to this from his own perspective of market knowledge or insight. The experts should all state the assumptions upon which they are basing their estimates. The export marketer can then take account of panel inputs in planning marketing strategies and developing sales forecasts.

In some markets local research firms or specialist economic forecasters will develop macro market models of expected trends and demand levels for certain industries, and larger companies often avail themselves of data from these sources.

Exporters' opinions

In this approach to export forecasting the export forecaster uses his experience to make a primarily qualitative **judgement** of demand in, or sales to, each market based upon the known data and historical performance, and a considered view of the trading environment. In some instances, particularly with major branded consumer products, market research reports may indicate consumer attitudes, buying patterns, and product preferences, thereby help in observing or predicting trends. The marketer may also seek the opinion of his local agent or distributor.

The weakness in relying only on judgemental estimates in practice for export markets is that they often rely too much on the exporter's own recent sales data, taking little account of the total market and competitive activity. If an agent or distributor is under-performing against the overall market this may be missed, or even if recognized, might not be addressed through a corrective action plan. A local sales agent or distributor typically is more influenced by his distribution or sales limitations in estimating sales potential or demand than he is by independent data on the market.

Another factor that produces a weakness in basing forward forecasts on sales team opinions is that the team usually have no reasonable basis to anticipate trends that will emerge from significant technological changes.

The more data that the export marketer has available on markets and existing and potential customers, the more meaningful will be any sales estimates they produce. Later in this chapter we will look at an example of building up sales estimates from customer sales records.

Surveys of future buying plans

Surveys of future buying plans are also a key means of obtaining information that can be used in preparing future forecasts of market demand and potential. This is a qualitative technique commonly used for industrial products or larger consumer products (such as household appliances and cars), where users are asked about expected product category purchases to meet their own company needs, and the company estimates its likely share of these user estimates.

In some markets, and for some product categories, professional market research companies monitor buying intentions, and the export marketer may be able to purchase the data and use it in preparing company forecasts. In other cases no proper data is available, in which case the marketer may choose to develop his own survey of intentions.

Whilst surveying a large number of consumers about their intentions may produce data of limited meaningfulness, with a smaller target of users of industrial products surveys can be a very important planning tool, to the extent that those surveyed are willing to co-operate and that respondents are stating their intentions as honestly and accurately as they can at the time. Most industrial products have a certain life in use, and users will need to replace equipment over time, either with an identical item where it is purely a consumable product in production processes or a wearable part, or usually with more recent technology where it is equipment.

With industrial products advance knowledge of likely buying intentions and patterns can be important to plan market coverage and marketing strategies. For example, if an exporter has blitzed a market for his equipment (say industrial kitchen ovens for hotels) and obtained as many current sales as seems practical, the survey of buying intentions obtained from the other hotels in the market will allow him to plan more accurately targeted coverage of the other potential customers according to the timings of when they expect to need to replace or update equipment, and facilitate sales forecasting.

Other considerations in forecasting ▅▅▅▅▅▅▅▅

Apart from the foregoing commentaries there are other factors that may warrant consideration when preparing a forecast, such as:

- inflation
- seasonal trends
- cyclical trends
- random fluctuations
- product life cycles.

Inflation

Normally forecasts of cost factors need to allow for inflation, and if an allowance is made in costs then a similar assumption should be made about the effect of inflation on prices. In some companies they prefer to avoid taking a view about inflation in the medium to longer term plans, forecasting all values at constant costs/prices applicable at the time of forecasting, and they would then take a similar approach as they roll forward the plans to further years. However, for the short term (one year) it is normal to attempt to judge the levels of inflation and its effect on both costs and prices. Since sales plans should always include estimates of volumes (not just monetary values), these volume estimates will give a guide to the real level and trend of sales.

Export sales forecasting makes the issue of inflation more complex, since inflation will be at differing levels in most markets. Most UK exporters sell in sterling, since the accountants argue the case that because input costs are incurred in sterling, export costings and price lists should be in sterling to ensure cost recovery. The UK exporter would need to estimate the impact of inflation on export prices, and then consider how changing export prices (in sterling) will impact on sales in the various export markets when converted into the currencies of those markets, which will probably be experiencing their own inflation problems.

The equation is further complicated when account is taken of fluctuations in exchange rates. It is not uncommon for inflation to drive export prices (in ex-factory or FOB terms) in one direction (upwards), but a weakening currency may offset some or all of the impact of inflation, and can result in lower delivered market or CIF prices in the foreign currency if the exchange rate weakens by more than the inflation FOB prices over the period of the forecast. A strengthening currency in the exporting market (in this case the UK) would add another price-increasing factor to inflation in the final market. Chapter 16, Export pricing and costing, touches further on some of these issues.

If marketing strategies require control of price positioning in relation to competitive products in export markets, then the export marketer cannot ignore the possible effect on sales of inflation and exchange rates changes, as a move from a strategic price point in the currency of the export market may impact significantly on sales (particularly if sales volume is very price sensitive, as where demand is price elastic).

The alternative approach, where sales in the foreign market are price sensitive and where price positioning is an important strategic issue, is to price goods ex-UK factory (or on a FOB or CIF basis, etc.) in the currency of the foreign market. This means the exporter faces profit margin fluctuations as exchange rates vary: the accountants will be happy with increasing margins as sterling weakens, but frown on a drop in margins when sterling strengthens in relation to a particular foreign currency. The marketer will have to consider the relative importance of issues of maintaining export margins or volumes.

Seasonal trends

Many industries and their products experience seasonal sales trends, such as in holiday and leisure goods, home improvements, gardening equipment, toys, cosmetic products, etc. If the manufacturer of the finished goods experiences seasonal sales trends, then generally the suppliers of components and other inputs will face similar trends.

The seasonal sales pattern may vary between export markets, and this may complicate the issues of export sales forecasting and production planning.

Seasonality of sales affects the organization of production and the organization of the sales effort, hence it is important that export sales forecasts and other planning activities recognize the seasonal nature of business in each market and plan accordingly, rather than just spreading annual estimates evenly across twelve months.

If it is necessary to produce goods on a continuous production line throughout the year, this will result in wide variations of stock holdings, and impact on cash flow as finance is found for these stockholdings. If goods can be produced seasonally to meet demand, there may be better cash flow positions, but there may be other problems in finding suitable labour at or other input supplies at short notice.

As the reader will recognize, the export marketer faced with seasonal products will not only need to forecast market sales with a good degree of accuracy, to ensure adequate stock is produced and available for shipment (or shipped ahead of the season start as stock to a distributor), but also will need to work with his agents and distributors to ensure that seasonal coverage of all current and potential outlets or users is at a high enough level to maximize sales during key selling seasons. A multi-product distributor may have conflicting selling priorities and financing (of stock and local trade credit) with limited sales and financial resources.

Cyclical trends

Industries serving the building, construction and agricultural products markets are familiar with the cyclical nature of these markets. Sales volumes and resultant revenues and profits are often erratic, but in some instances there is a cyclical trend that can be monitored and included in planning, so that costs (and possibly investment) can be reduced in a downswing, and expansion planned early in the upswing. Where sales cycles are not of predictable length or frequency the exporter is much more exposed, but if the cycles are occurring at different times in different markets there may be a sufficient spread of markets so that the overall sales are less disruptive to the planning process and the exporter's profit performance.

Random fluctuations

Typical unpredictable events that cause random or erratic fluctuations in markets can include industrial disputes anywhere in the supply and distribution chains, natural catastrophes, conflict and political upheaval. Random fluctuations can have **positive** or **negative** effect on sales, and as they are not

normally the result of predictable events they are not normally allowed for in the market planning process.

Just as random or erratic fluctuations cannot be predicted, and therefore are not normally built into forecasts, when they have occurred the cause should be noted in the sales data records, and their impact should be assessed and adjustments made to discount their effect when monitoring sales trends and preparing forward sales forecasts.

Product life cycles

In longer term planning the marketer should consider where each of his products lies on their product life cycle for each of his export markets when developing forecasts. Traditional marketing theory teaches that all products have a life cycle (discussed in Chapter 9), where sales will rise for a period after launch, eventually reach and peak, and thereafter decline. What differs between products and markets is the length of the life cycle, the rate of growth and decline, and the levels of peak sales, in other words the shape of the life cycle graph is not identical between products and markets.

From the export marketer's perspective, not all markets move at the same rate, and many an exporter is frustrated when a product that is important in some export markets is on the domestic marketer's list of products to be discontinued. An obsolete product in sophisticated markets may have clear functional benefits, and therefore a longer life, in less developed markets. This difference in the rate of movement in product preferences between more and less sophisticated markets often arises in two situations:

- where a mechanical or technical product can be easily serviced and maintained locally in markets where access to original spare parts may be irregular
- where brand names and product variants have strong local franchises, suiting local preferences, environments or tastes.

A familiar example is where cyclists in many developing countries still prefer what we would consider 'old-fashioned' bicycles, rather than the more trendy racing or mountain bikes favoured in westernized markets, because they are seen as stronger, more suited to local roads, and easier to maintain.

Developing a practical market forecast

Having looked at the issues in export market forecasting, at this point it is worth taking time to look at developing a practical sales forecasting process based upon the available data. In this section we will develop tables and graphs using a consistent set of figures, based primarily upon real data with products and markets disguised, for Table 14.1 and Figures 14.3 to 14.13.

Information inputs for forecasting

Most historical sales performance data can play a role in forecasting. In many companies a basic problem arises over how data is recorded and presented. It is quite common for performance data to be prepared by the department responsible for financial control, and, quite naturally, that department is sometimes more interested in monitoring costs and profits than in monitoring unit sales by product and by market. The starting point in market planning is to ensure that sales performance is monitored at the level of each destination market, and that performance monitoring data records the volume and values of each product shipped on a month by month basis.

Where export market sales are through a distributor then it becomes important to receive monthly reports of the distributor's depletions (sales from his stock) in volume terms, and local values, as this provides the real measure of sales performance in the market. This local data is essential if the

final forecasts (or targets) are to be broken down to the level of targets for individual customers in the market. A macro (market level) forecast is much less likely to be achieved, or even if the forecast is achieved it might represent an under-achievement against real sales potential, where it is not broken down to the micro level on an account-by-account basis. A multi-product company will need to forecast or target separately for each product.

The basis for a simple practical forecasting process can be as follows:

- use recorded historical data to provide a base for measurement against plans and forecasting
- fit a trend line (using judgement or more sophisticated statistical techniques if practical)
- plot total industry data, and project trends similarly
- build-up forecasts by product, market sector and account, summarizing to give sales territory and national estimates (this micro-level build-up of account sales forecasts can be compared with the macro forecasts).

Forecasts should include any appropriate adjustment for any significant developments that are expected to affect sales more than a forward projection of historical sales might suggest, e.g. innovative new technology that might open the market to more consumers through price, availability, ease of use factors, etc., such as we have seen in the computer and mobile telephone industries.

Whilst the exporter will normally have access to data on his own market sales, industry data for the total product category (in volume or values) or sub categories might be available through national trade associations, market research sources, government statistical publications, or other identifiable sources. Industry estimates might not always be very accurate for any single market, but they should not be ignored as the export marketer should benchmark his performance against the total market and individual competitors (where any data is available on their sales performance).

Tabulating data and projecting trends in moving annual formats _____

The export marketer can compile a simple table of market sales data, as illustrated in Table 14.1. The illustrative graphs in Figures 14.3 to 14.6 are based upon the data in this table. This shows market sales of widgets in Hong Kong. If the exporter's local distributor provides monthly reports on his local sales from stock, then that data can be used as a more accurate reflection of the market at the local level, otherwise the exporter's monthly shipments can be used. In this example we are fortunate in having good data as it is sourced from the distributor's sales reports.

From the **actual monthly sales** reports, entered in the left hand column under each of the three years' data, the **cumulative sales data** can be tabulated (shown in the second column under each year's data) as a simple numerical summation, producing the total of the full year's sales in the last row for each year. The monthly sales data illustrated in this example shows a wide variation in local monthly sales, likely to indicate a seasonal sales pattern. But if it is not solely indicative of seasonal sales variations, highlighted in the graph in Figure 14.3(a), it might also indicate a distributor who is not supplying the market in a regular pattern because of poor stock management and control of orders from the exporter. That would be a separate issue for the export marketer to get to grips with, but here we are looking at the data in relation to observing trends and forecasting.

The cumulative sales for 1998 show an increase over 1997 of 6.5 per cent, with a further increase in 1999 compared with 1998 of 5.5 per cent. So, in this example, there is real growth in unit sales of the exporter's widgets in the Hong Kong market, albeit with a very irregular monthly sales pattern. To use this basic data to see a clearer overall

picture of sales trends we can tabulate what is termed **moving annual data.**

Moving annual data

As was referred to earlier in the chapter, when introducing some of the quantitative forecasting techniques, tabulating **moving monthly averages** of monthly sales data smoothes out wide fluctuations in actual monthly sales patterns, and tabulating **moving annual totals** (MAT) of sales smoothes out wide fluctuations in seasonal sales, showing the longer term underlying sales trend more clearly. Moving annual data is developed as follows.

Moving annual totals

This data is a useful measure of trends and performance on a year-on-year rolling basis. Once data for a full year on a monthly basis is available, the moving annual total can be developed and updated each month.

Starting from the total for the base period of twelve months, a calendar year in Table 14.1, you add the actual monthly sales figure for the next month (for volumes or values, as appropriate) to the twelve month total, and deduct the monthly sales figure for the same month in the last year, i.e. the MAT for January 1998 is 209,160 + 27,960 − 25,350 = 211,770.

This is continued for each subsequent month, so that you are always looking at a rolling year total, including all seasonal or monthly sales patterns, highlighting positive or negative sales trends.

Moving monthly averages

In the example, this figure is purely a division of the moving annual total by twelve, to show the average monthly sales on a rolling year basis. That smoothes out wide fluctuations between the sales for individual months.

In Figure 14.3 alternative ways of plotting data are illustrated, and each can be used in the forecasting process to project sales trends into the future.

Table 14.1 *Market sales data, units sold*

Market sales performance data, company sales of Widgets in Hong Kong
(including monthly sales, cumulative sales and moving annual data)

Units	1997				1998				1999			
	Actual	Cumul-ative	Moving monthly average	Moving annual total	Actual	Cumul-ative	Moving monthly average	Moving annual total	Actual	Cumul-ative	Moving monthly average	Moving annual total
Jan.	25350	25350			27960	27960	17648	211770	25560	25560	18365	220390
Feb.	30010	55360			30260	58220	17668	212020	47520	73080	19804	237650
March	13560	68920			12170	70390	17552	210630	16800	89880	20190	242280
April	13090	82010			11830	82220	17448	209370	7080	96960	19794	237530
May	18040	100050			14260	96480	17133	205590	8420	105380	19308	231690
June	13600	113650			16670	113150	17388	208660	16190	121570	19268	231210
July	8470	122120			16180	129330	18030	216370	14280	135850	19109	229310
Aug.	22890	145010			10880	140210	17030	204360	12360	148210	19232	230790
Sept.	28760	173770			25560	165770	16763	201160	29740	177950	19580	234970
Oct.	15480	189250			25130	190900	17568	210810	26390	204340	19685	236230
Nov.	8270	197520			12330	203230	17906	214870	11420	215760	19610	235320
Dec.	11640	209160	17430	209160	19560	222790	18565	222790	19240	235000	19583	235000

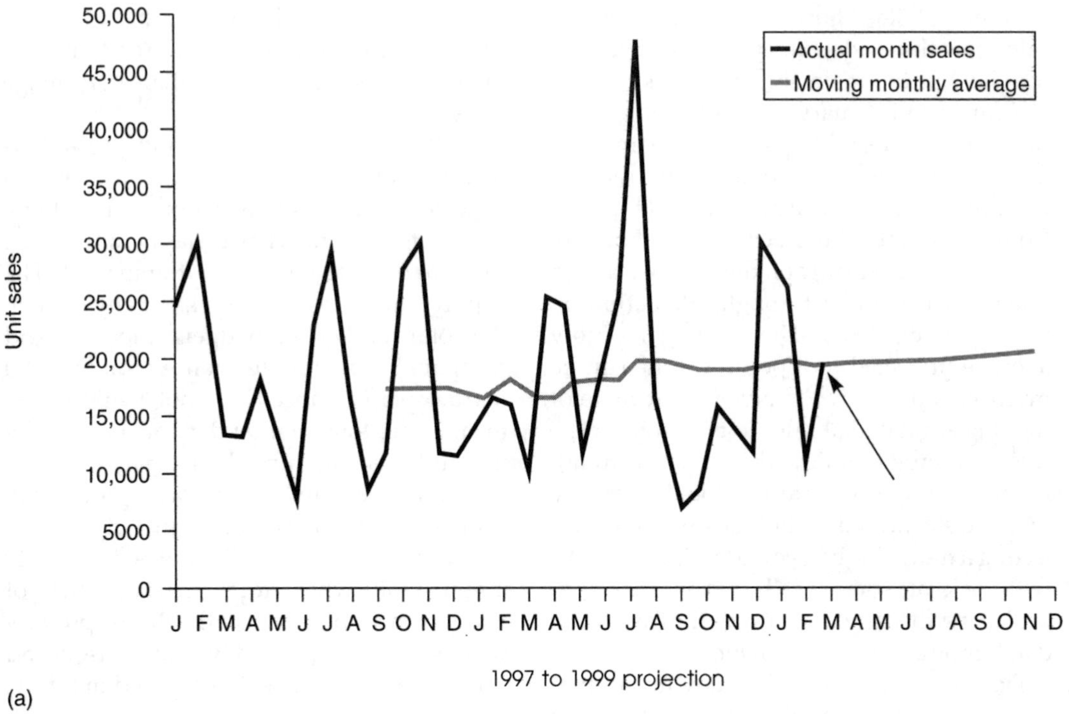

Figure 14.3 Fitting trend lines to historical performance data to aid forecasting. (a) Actual monthly widget unit sales and moving annual average of unit sales. (b) Moving annual total of widget sales and trend projection fitted by inspection

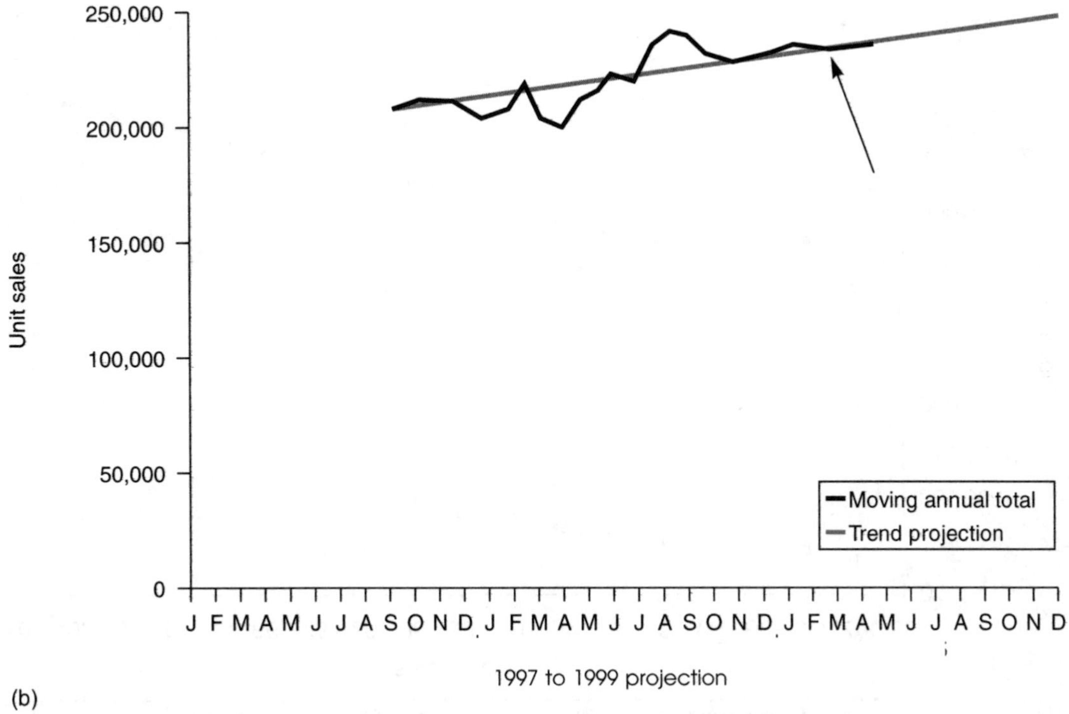

Figure 14.3(a) shows the actual monthly sales, with wide fluctuations between months but the main seasonal peak around December to February, with a lesser peak in the late summer. By plotting the moving monthly average the underlying trend is more apparent, and can be projected forward from the point where actual data finishes, indicated by the arrow on the graph, fitting a line by inspection or through calculation (in this case into 2000). The moving monthly average projected to a point in time can be multiplied by twelve to give the estimate of moving annual total sales to that point if the sales continue to follow the projected trend. In this example we are not looking at any more sophisticated techniques but just projecting a trend line by eye and judgement. We will look at some of the many ways of projecting the trend line, using the same base data, through calculation later.

Figure 14.3(b) plots the moving annual total of the data from Table 14.1, and from the point marked by the arrow this has been projected forward, fitting a trend line by inspection based on a similar percentage sales growth pattern.

So far the data recorded, and projections made, look at the market sales of the exporter's widgets in isolation, without any cross reference to what is happening in the total market for widgets in the market. The export marketer should seek out any data on the total market for widgets, plot this and compare his own performance with the total market performance. It is not usual to get meaningful total market data on a month by month basis, but annual data may be available (or calculated from local production statistics if available, plus imports, minus exports). Figure 14.4 illustrates how data might look when total market sales of widgets are plotted, with the exporter's widget sales also plotted for comparison, and some sales trend projections added in for the next five years, fitted by judgement.

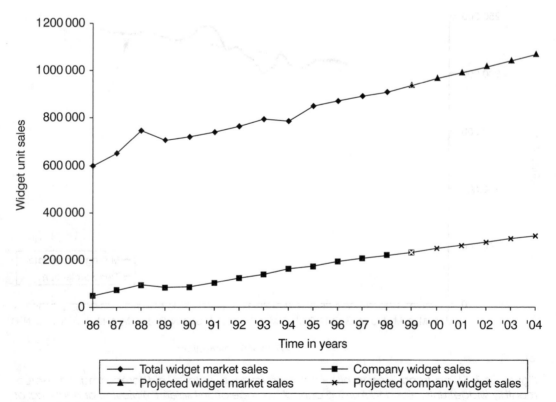

Figure 14.4 Total market widget sales and company widget sales

Plotting the total market compared with company product sales can highlight aspects of the marketing strategy that might need attention. In our example of widgets, the company widget sales have grown much faster than the market rate of growth, to the point where the exporter has approximately 25 per cent market share at the end of 1998. Whilst this may be the result of good marketing and sales activity, with product advantages communicated effectively to customers, the exporter's high share may need to be looked at in relation to potential competitors who might erode that share, and in relation to the total widget market that might be growing at a slower rate than the company's sales. The resultant considerations, taken with account to all the other information and variables, might prompt marketing strategies aimed at:

- defending the existing share, building further on customer loyalty,
- reinforcing perceptions of points of brand differentiation,
- price positioning strategies aimed at stealing a larger share through aggressive pricing, or of harvesting profit from the product possibly by confident upward pricing, or
- of diversifying the marketing effort to build other products in the portfolio.

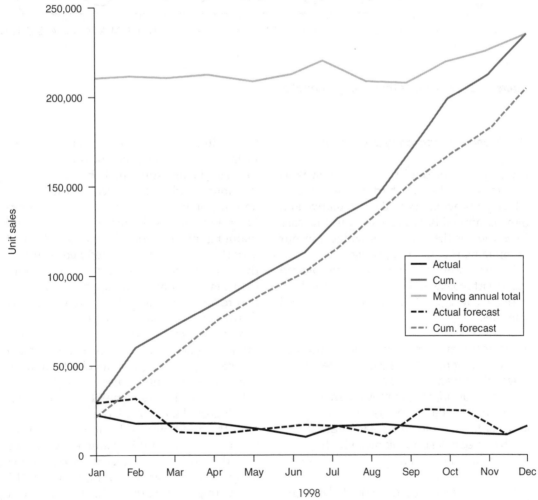

Figure 14.5 *'Z' chart – sales performance of company widgets in Hong Kong*

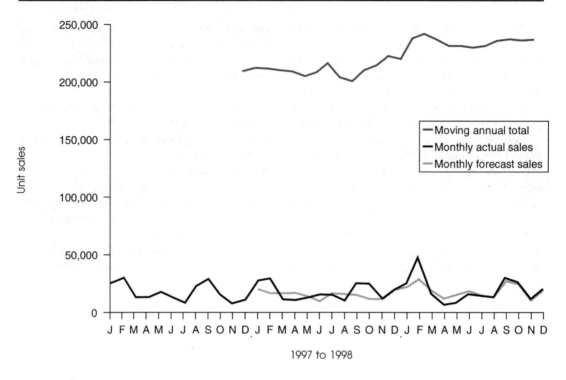

Figure 14.6 *Continuous monitoring of market sales*

The 'Z' chart in monitoring performance

Another way of depicting sales data is as illustrated in the 'Z' chart of Figure 14.5, which plots actual monthly, cumulative and moving annual data for a year, in this case 1998 sales of the exporter's widgets in our example market of Hong Kong.

In this example, where we have plotted the export marketer's forecast for 1998 along with the subsequent actual sales, we should question:

- the accuracy of the forecasting process, since the forecast cumulative sales were less than was achieved in the previous year (shown from the moving annual total at the start of the year)
- the pattern of monthly sales forecast, which bears little relationship to the actual monthly sales.

In some cases there would be valid reasons for forecasting a downturn in sales,

but with our additional data in this instance, it is suspect, possibly with a forecast being submitted by a cautious distributor rather than calculated rationally and negotiated between the export marketer and the distributor as part of a joint planning process for the market. Also, if export shipments were scheduled to match the forecast monthly sales pattern, without sufficient account of the apparent seasonal nature of sales, then it is likely that the distributor will have run out of stock at certain points in some months, or have rationed sales, and in either case actual company product sales would then have been below potential sales.

Figure 14.6 shows some of the data from our Figure 14.3 plotted over recent years with the addition of sales forecast data for the market, and in this example we can see that the export marketer has taken action in the latest year, 1999, to improve the forecasting and narrow the gap between actual and forecast sales.

In Chapter 15, Export administration and performance monitoring, we will take further this particular case, looking at what was happening with the distributor's stock and sales of widgets in Hong Kong in more detail, and see that, possibly as a result of a combination of poor forecasting and inadequate monitoring of market sales performance, there is substantial evidence of a loss of sales to the exporter through inadequate stock levels being held in the market and the shipment quantities not adequately reflecting the seasonality of sales pattern.

Developing forecasts from actual data and seasonal deviations

The previous section showed how market sales data can be tabulated and displayed graphically to show trends and give a better picture of what is happening in a market than just looking at monthly sales and cumulative data. We can go beyond a judgemental approach to forecasting and projecting trends by eye and judgement, and develop further the use of statistical techniques for forecasting, by taking the actual sales data shown in Table 14.1, and looking to see what is the seasonal pattern of sales of widgets in Hong Kong.

In this example we only have data for a short period, but it is enough to enable a seasonal pattern to be identified, and used for an improved approach to forward forecasting than just adding an arbitrary percentage figure to the previous year, particularly where, in this case, we have identified that there is a likelihood that sales have been below potential for the exporter due to poor forecasting and stock management.

The data in Table 14.1 can be used to develop forward forecasts in two ways

- forecasting from trends identified using **moving monthly averages** (or moving quarterly averages) and deviations from these
- forecasting from historical **moving annual total** data that demonstrates market sales trends.

Whichever is used by the marketer may depend on factors particular to his markets. For example, if there is a strong seasonal pattern that it is essential to recognize and plan for, in terms of shipping and stockholding, then the trend projection using moving monthly averages may be preferred. If local distributors do hold good stock levels, and it is difficult to allow for seasonal variations when planning shipments, the marketer may prefer the more simplistic approach of just developing a forecast from moving annual total trends.

Developing a forecast from moving monthly averages

In the Table 14.2 the basic data has been extracted from Table 14.1, with the inclusion of some additional monthly data for 1996 sales, and for ease of presentation the data is shown in a time sequence format. The **moving annual total** figures, **actual sales** and **moving monthly averages** are all transferred from the earlier example, extended backwards to include 1996 data. The moving annual total figures represent a rolling year, and we have divided each of these MAT (moving annual total) figures by twelve to give a moving monthly average. The moving monthly average figures are seen as representing a trend of monthly sales, and a basis from which we can estimate the seasonal pattern of the monthly sales. In some instances it is more appropriate to measure a quarterly moving total, but in this instance there does appear to be a noticeable monthly variation that might be relevant to forecasting.

Because the moving monthly average is an average of the year, the figure derived from the December 1996 moving annual total ($200660 \div 12 = 16722$) has actually been allocated in the table against the month of July (as close as we can get to half way through the year). Each subsequent moving monthly average is also allocated to a month six months before the moving annual total figure from which it is calculated.

Table 14.2 *Monthly sales of widgets in Hong Kong*

A	B	C	D	E	F	G	H
Year	Month	Actual sales	Moving annual total	Moving monthly average	Sum of pairs	2 year moving average trend	Deviation from moving monthly average
1996	Jan.	23650					
	Feb.	28500					
	March	11120					
	Apr.	11780					
	May	14800					
	June	13100					
	July	11720		16722			
	Aug.	16760		16863	33585	16793	−33
	Sept.	26400		16989	33853	16926	9474
	Oct.	19650		17193	34182	17091	2559
	Nov.	9460		17302	34494	17247	−7787
	Dec.	13720	200660	17572	34873	17437	−3717
1997	Jan.	25350	202360	17613	35185	17593	7758
	Feb.	30010	203870	17343	34956	17478	12532
	March	13560	206310	17853	35196	17598	−4038
	Apr.	13090	207620	18050	35903	17952	−4862
	May	18040	210860	17703	35753	17876	164
	June	13600	211360	17603	35306	17653	−4053
	July	8470	208110	17430	35033	17517	−9047
	Aug.	22890	214240	17648	35078	17539	5351
	Sept.	28760	216600	17668	35316	17658	11102
	Oct.	15480	212430	17553	35221	17610	−2130
	Nov.	8270	211240	17448	35000	17500	−9230
	Dec.	11640	209160	17133	34580	17290	−5650
1998	Jan.	27960	211770	17388	34521	17260	10700
	Feb.	30260	212020	18031	35419	17710	12550
	March	12170	210630	17030	35061	17530	−5360
	Apr.	11830	209370	16763	33793	16897	−5067
	May	14260	205590	17568	34331	17165	−2905
	June	16670	208660	17906	35473	17737	−1067
	July	16180	216370	18566	36472	18236	−2056
	Aug.	10880	204360	18366	36932	18466	−7586
	Sept.	25560	201160	19804	38170	19085	6475
	Oct.	25130	210810	20190	39994	19997	5133
	Nov.	12330	214870	19794	39984	19992	−7662
	Dec.	19560	222790	19308	39102	19551	9
1999	Jan.	25560	220390	19268	38575	19288	6273
	Feb.	47520	237650	19109	38377	19188	28332
	March	16800	242280	19233	38342	19171	−2371
	Apr.	7080	237530	19581	38813	19407	−12327
	May	8420	231690	19686	39267	19633	−11213
	June	16190	231210	19610	39296	19648	−3458
	July	14280	229310	19583	39193	19597	−5317
	Aug.	12360	230790	19671	39254		
	Sept.	29740	234970	19759	39430		
	Oct.	26390	236230	19847	39606		
	Nov.	11420	235320	19936	39783		
	Dec.	19240	235000	20025	39961		

In the next column, F, we have summed pairs of moving monthly average figures from column E, and divide these by two, because by doing this we are actually averaging the monthly sales over two years, thereby reducing any fluctuations from a trend.

The next column, H, is a simple calculation of the **deviation** of each individual month from the moving monthly average shown for that month. For example, for December 1997, the deviation equals 11,640 minus 17,290, which equals a negative figure of minus 5650; in other words, as is clearly seen by eye, sales in December were running well behind the monthly average for the twelve months to that point in time. Similarly, the deviations for each previous or subsequent month are calculated.

If you now refer to Table 14.3, we have tabulated these **monthly deviations** in a different format that highlights the monthly pattern. When the monthly deviations for 1996, 1997, 1998 and 1999 are totalled they are seen to sum to a positive figure of 1476 units of widgets. This sum of deviations should actually equal zero, otherwise there will be a positive bias in any forecasting.

Here we have laid out all sales for any particular month horizontally, and totalled them for each month. We only have data from a small period, in fact we are really only looking at three sample months covering the years 1996 to 1999.

To avoid any positive bias in forecasting we take the sum of deviations for the twelve months, 1476, divide that by twelve, and deduct the resultant figure of 123 from the monthly deviations to give a **corrected deviation** for each month. That figure is then divided by three to give the **average monthly deviation** from the moving monthly average (the trend).

Now we are at the point where we can start to plot data and project forward to develop sales forecasts, albeit that in this example we only have a three year time series of data to work from.

We should now plot the moving monthly averages for the three years they are available, and project the trend forward. The seasonal monthly sales forecast for each individual month can be developed by adding the appropriate average monthly deviation to the moving monthly average trend line.

Table 14.3 *Sum of monthly deviations from the trend*

	1996	1997	1998	1999	Totals	Corrected deviation	Average monthly deviation
Jan.		7758	10700	6273	24731	24606	8202
Feb.		12532	12550	28332	53414	53291	17763
March		−4038	−5360	−2371	−11769	−11892	−3964
April		−4862	−5067	−12327	−22256	−22378	−7459
May		164	−2905	−11213	−13954	−14078	−4693
June		−4053	−1067	−3458	−8578	−8701	−2900
July		−9047	−2056	−5317	−16420	−16542	−5514
Aug.	−33	5351	−7586		−2268	−2390	−797
Sept.	9474	11102	6475		27051	26928	8976
Oct.	2559	−2130	5133		5562	5439	1813
Nov.	−7787	−9230	−7662		−24679	−24802	−8267
Dec.	−3717	−5650	9		−9358	−9481	−3160
Sum	496	−2103	3164	−81	1476	0	0

From Table 14.2 we can calculate that from column D showing the moving annual totals for January 1997 to December 1999 widget sales have grown 16.1% (rounded annual rates for the three years of 4.2%, 6.5% and 5.5%). In the absence of any negative factors likely to affect this trend, a judgement approach might suggest the trend be projected forward at similar levels of growth of just over 5 per cent annually. In this example we have taken expected annual growth to continue at the approximate rate of 5.4% per annum, and projected this in the moving monthly averages by forecasting each month from August 1999 to increase by one twelfth of this percentage (i.e. 0.45% monthly growth).

In the example plotted, whilst the seasonality of sales is apparent, it is less pronounced for 2000 than for 1999, as the deviations were averaged over the previously three years (see Table 14.3). If now the export marketer ships his widget stocks into Hong Kong in a pattern to reflect the distributor's local seasonal sales, such as shipping goods to arrive in January that will be sold in February, and allowing for an additional buffer stock, then fewer sales

should be lost, and sales growth should increase. Should actual sales exceed forecast for any month, drawing from buffer stock should avoid losing sales and disappointing customers. Should sales fall short of forecast for any month then buffer stocks would increase until future shipments could be adjusted downwards sufficiently to offset sales shortfalls.

Actual sales from Table 14.2 and forecast sales from Table 14.4 can then be plotted graphically in Figure 14.7, showing the moving monthly average trend line, and we can see the resultant pattern of sales with the 2000 forecasts.

The forecast sales by the method of estimating seasonal deviations from the moving monthly average (or moving quarterly average where that is a more appropriate time period) can be built up to give a forecast of the moving annual total, by extending the data in a table such as Table 14.2. In this instance the monthly sales forecast data can be tabulated to take the moving annual total from 235,000 widgets at the end of 1999 to almost 247,000 widgets at the end of 2000, maintaining growth at slightly over 5 per cent per annum.

Table 14.4 *Developing a seasonally adjusted forecast*

	Moving monthly average 1996	Moving monthly average 1997	Moving monthly average 1998	Moving monthly average 1999	Forecast 2000 trend	Average monthly deviation	Actual monthly sales forecast
Jan.		17593	17260	19288	*20070*	8202	**28272**
Feb.		17478	17710	19188	*20160*	17763	**37923**
March		17598	17530	19171	*20250*	−3964	**16286**
April		17952	16897	19407	*20340*	−7459	**12881**
May		17876	17165	19633	*20431*	−4693	**15738**
June		17653	17737	19648	*20523*	−2900	**17623**
July		17517	18236	19597	*20615*	−5514	**15101**
Aug.	16793	17539	18466	*19627*	20707	−797	**19910**
Sept.	16926	17658	19085	*19715*	20799	8976	**29775**
Oct.	17091	17610	19997	*19803*	20892	1813	**22705**
Nov.	17247	17500	19992	*19892*	20986	−8267	**12719**
Dec.	17437	17290	19551	*19981*	21080	−3160	**17920**

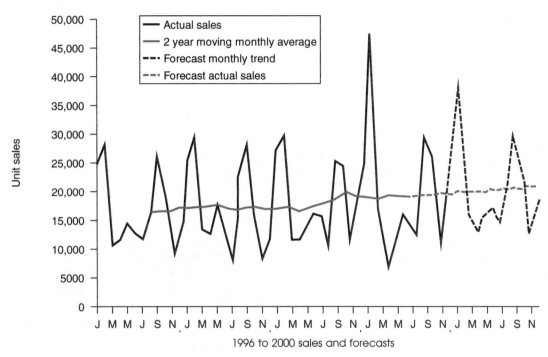

Figure 14.7 *Monthly widget sales: trends and forecasts*

All of the data developed in this example has assumed that the current growth pattern, around 5 per cent per annum, would continue. Other data suggests that the local Hong Kong distributor has lost sales through former poor forecasting and stock management. Now that forecasting is becoming more sophisticated for this market the marketer might judge that the growth rate should increase. In Table 14.4 the export marketer could exercise his judgement that sales will actually grow by 10 per cent per annum over the forecast period, due to better stock management resulting in fewer out-of-stock situations. That could be factored in either:

- by applying a consistent monthly compound multiplying factor (of $1 + \frac{10\%}{12} = 1.0083$) starting from the base month of December 1999 (moving monthly average sales of 19,597 widgets) and adding the monthly deviation for each respective month.

- or by adjusting the final forecast for individual months to reflect the expected additional sales.

When sales data is being recorded the marketer should note any particular events that cause unusual fluctuations in sales that might affect forecasting. For example, the widget sales for February 1999 in this example jumped to an extremely high figure of over 47,000 unit sales, some 50 per cent over previous February sales, even though this is a peak selling month. If this represents a serious and lasting increase in sales then it is reasonable to continue to forecast at that sort of level for future months of February. If, however, it was a freak month sales for any reason, possibly in anticipation of an expected price increase (or perhaps goods were being re-exported, unknown to the shipper), or there was an unusually heavy burst of advertising, then future forecasts should reflect the more normal level indicated using average monthly deviations in this example.

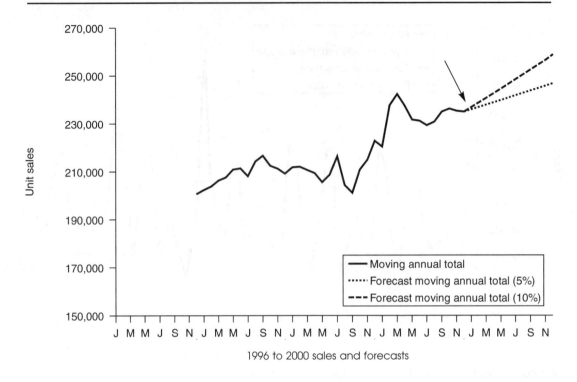

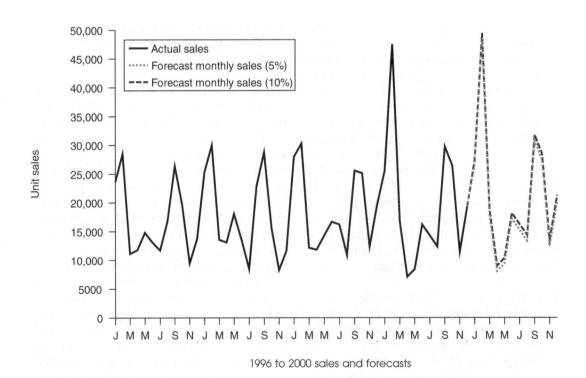

Figure 14.8 *Projecting a moving annual total to forecast sales*

Forecasting from moving annual total data

An alternative and more simple approach to forecasting is simply to take the moving annual total at a point in time, and to project it forward by a factor expected to represent the achievable growth. Normally spreadsheet packages are used in forecasting calculations that enable variations to be incorporated easily.

In the example here we have taken the actual data from Table 14.2, and made two forecasts at the level of 5 per cent and 10 per cent on the moving annual total at December 1999 (235,000 widgets). We have arbitrarily assumed straight line growth in the moving annual total for both calculations, and can use the projected moving annual totals to calculate the monthly sales that would be necessary to achieve those moving annual totals. The graphs in Figure 14.8 combine date from Tables 14.2 and 14.5.

The reader may note that one problem in forecasting by projecting a moving annual total in a straight line, and using that to calculate the monthly sales, is that it will project a pattern of sales representing the last year, which may not be fully representa-

tive of the longer run seasonal pattern. In this example we would be projecting extremely high February sales followed by low April and May figures, as per the 1999 pattern. The alternative way to build the forecast this way is to estimate the monthly sales first, and build these into the moving annual total to see what projected growth (or decline) pattern of sales is predicted.

Forecasting as in this example adds more weight to recent months and the last year than to earlier years, again producing a possible bias.

Problems in using trend data based on past sales

Whenever trends are identified and plotted they are, quite obviously, based on history, and do not allow for strong current trends, particularly when based upon averages of longer time periods. Any forecasts based on moving annual data, moving monthly averages or moving quarterly averages, or other past data must be tempered with the marketer's inputs of judgement to allow for current trends or anticipated developments. A weakness in using moving averages is that all the

Table 14.5 *Using moving annual totals in forecasting*

	Month	Forecast moving annual total (5% growth)	Forecast monthly sales (5% growth)	Forecast moving annual total (10% growth)	Forecast monthly sales (10% growth)
1999 base	Dec.	235000		235000	
2000	Jan.	235958	26518	236880	27440
	Feb.	236919	48482	238775	49415
	March	237885	17765	240685	18710
	Apr.	238854	8049	242611	9005
	May	239827	9393	244552	10361
	June	240805	17167	246508	18146
	July	241786	15261	248480	16252
	Aug.	242771	13345	250468	14348
	Sept.	243760	30729	252472	31744
	Oct.	244754	27383	254491	28410
	Nov.	245751	12417	256527	13456
	Dec.	246753	20241	258580	21292

Table 14.6 *Comparing a trends forecast with actual sales*

Year	Month	Actual sales	2 year moving average trend	Average monthly deviation from trend	Forecast based on trend
1999	Jan.	25560	19288		
	Feb.	47520	19188		
	March	16800	19171		
	Apr.	7080	19407		
	May	8420	19633		
	June	16190	19648		
	July	14280	19597		
	Aug.	12360	*forecast*		
			19627	−797	*18830*
	Sept.	29740	*19715*	8976	*28691*
	Oct.	26390	*19803*	1813	*21616*
	Nov.	11420	*19892*	−8267	*11625*
	Dec.	19240	*19981*	−3160	*16821*
		235000			*97583*

time periods being analysed are weighted equally, and information from the oldest periods are just as important in the forecasting as information from the newest periods – which is often inappropriate in real life marketing, where recent events should have more weight attached to them.

The problem is apparent in our example. If we look at the figures for 1999 only, illustrated in Table 14.6, we show a mix of the actual monthly figures, along with the forecasts that would be developed using the moving monthly average trend projection method of adding back in average deviations from trends to give a forecast.

We can see that the August 1999 forecasts would have been substantially above the actuals achieved, and that both the October and December 1999 forecasts, using the moving monthly average trend technique, were below the actual achievements. This reflects the point that the moving monthly averages are calculated from a sample of three months in this example, and in 1996 and 1997 the figures for both October and December were lower than for the more recent years, biasing figures downwards. In

the case of August, the opposite was the case: the most recent actual sales for August were below those for earlier years, biasing the trend upwards in the forecasts.

An approach to any obvious anomalies is for the export marketer to temper his forecasts and calculations with judgement, to give more weighting to recent performance patterns, although this may also present concerns about accuracy.

As a point of interest, for the figures in Table 14.6, if you total the actuals and the forecasts for the period August to December, the actual error between trend forecast and actual sales is only 1567 units of widgets over these last five months. Over the medium term of a year the forecast using this method is more likely to be more accurate than over the short term forecast for any single month, as there can be, as illustrated, significant variations in sales levels in any single month that can bias the moving monthly averages.

In essence, what we are saying is that there is no simple ideal and accurate way of producing a forecast, particularly with all the complexity of factors to be considered in export marketing. If there is additional market knowledge the export marketer might decide to apply his judgement to this knowledge, and alter the growth factor accordingly from that indicated by historical sales data. Other information might also be available suggesting the forecasts should be adjusted from the moving monthly average or moving annual total trend approaches to forecasting (including surveys, expert opinions, or panels, or through statistical quantitative techniques).

In summary of this section, the export marketer should attempt to gather and plot data on his product sales in each worthwhile market, and comparable data for the total market for his product category. Actual monthly and cumulative (year to date) sales statistics can be tabulated and graphed, along with moving annual total data and moving monthly average data that smoothes out major fluctuations and helps in identifying trends and developing more accurate forecasts. Ideally data can be prepared both for shipments to each market from the exporter as well as sales through distributors within each market, where distributors are being used as opposed to direct shipments to end users or customers. As more data becomes available and as it is used more effectively in forecasting the export marketer can expect to move from a hit and miss approach to selling into many markets towards a planned marketing approach with more predictable sales.

Building forecasts from local market sales data

Apart from using the overall data of sales to, or in, the market to monitor progress and provide a basis for market forecasting, forecasts can also be built up from the micro level by looking at the historical sales for each current customer account and potential sales to each prospective account, and comparing the two to come to a reasoned, realistic and achievable (within the forecast

period time frame) figure. To build forecasts in this way it is necessary to have sales data kept for each product to individual customers, either serviced through local market distributors, or supplied by direct shipments from the exporter.

The importance of key accounts

For most suppliers, and in most markets, a few key accounts dominate purchases (for local distribution and re-sale) or direct use of an exporter's products. The export marketer should be monitoring sales to and through these accounts. If they are being supplied by direct shipments then it is easier to access the direct shipment records. If they are being supplied through locally appointed distributors then it will be necessary to obtain data from the distributors, and that will be more forthcoming where distributors see the need for the data in forward planning, and the benefits of accuracy in forward planning to their sales throughput, cash flow and stock management.

The export marketer might design some simple form that summarizes sales history and contains an estimate (ideally based on discussions with the key account) of its likely purchases in the next planning period. A well-designed form, provided the information can be collected, can provide useful insights into the relative growth of major customers, and provide information useful to developing market sales tactics.

Table 14.7 illustrates a form, based on the earlier Figure 10.21, that can be used in key account planning. Experience of the account and judgement of its progress and prospects will play a role in forecasting its future demand for the exporter's products.

In Table 14.7 we have assumed that the export product is an industrial component sold to manufacturers of other products for incorporation in their own products. The example shows a selection of the key widget accounts in Hong Kong, showing their purchases from our widget exporter, and their estimated total widget purchase requirements for 2000. With this data the

Table 14.7 *Forecast of widget sales to key user accounts*

TOP ACCOUNTS SHARE OF MARKETS AND FORECASTS					
Market Unit sales *Hong Kong*		Company sales history			Company sales forecast	Total volume estimate
Year	1997	1998	1999	2000	2000
Key accounts	**Volume**	**Volume**	**Volume**	**Volume**	
1 Acme Toy Factory	2470	7970	8230	9000	45000
2 Car Spares Incorporated	14690	18930	16500	17500	40000
3 Wing Electronics	13780	15780	15900	16000	38000
4 Lee Mechanical Toys	7500	9560	8900	10000	36000
5 A & B Accessories	6490	9670	10350	11500	30000
6 Chan Radiophonics	–	–	–	4000	30000
7 Oriental Lighting	8240	12530	13420	15000	35000
8 Asian Electronic Industry	11420	7420	9460	10000	60000
9 Photo Accessories Ltd	6900	13600	12630	14000	50000
10 Intelligent Toys Ltd	5640	8360	10200	12000	46000
Total sales to key accounts	77130	103910	105590	119000	410000
% share of company total	36.9%	46.6%	44.9%	47.8%	
Total company sales	209160	222790	235000	249000	
Company share of market	23.4%	24.5%	25.0%	25.8%	
Total market sales	893600	910750	940000	965000	965000
Key account % share of market					42.5%

exporter can judge the importance of accounts in the market and to him in particular, and plan particular sales tactics to develop business with individual key accounts. In this example the top ten listed accounts represent 42.5% of the 2000 projected market for widgets, and the higher share of 47.8% of our exporter's projected widget sales to the market, so key account relations and development are clearly critical to him in that market.

Once the overview of the key account market is prepared, and targets or forecasts established, sales tactics must be developed and implemented to turn these targets into reality, and the exporter should then prepare and agree shipping schedules. Since not every customer may want the identical format of widget the exporter can plan production to suit shipping requirements, and minimize stock holding of product variants.

If it is helpful to the planning process the export marketer may want to summarize his sales history and forecasts or targets by category of end use, as illustrated in Table 14.8. This might be particularly useful where there are differences in the product variants needed for each industry sector or outlet type.

Table 14.8 *Sales analysis and forecasts by market sector*

Widget sales by market sector – Hong Kong				
Units Market sector	**1997**	**1998**	**1999**	**Forecast 2000**
Toys	41320	47400	48175	49800
% total	19.8%	21.3%	20.5%	20.0%
Electrical and electronics	118080	121630	133715	141930
% total	56.5%	54.6%	56.9%	57.0%
Car accessories	49760	53760	53110	57270
% total	23.8%	24.1%	22.6%	23.0%
Totals	209160	222790	235000	249000

Table 14.9 *Market sales target product summary sheet*

Market: *Portugal*														
Customer	1999 Sales	2000 Target	Jan.	Feb.	Mar.	Apr.	May	June	July	Aug.	Sept.	Oct.	Nov.	Dec.
Gomes Stores	340	355	15	15	20	20	50	70	40	30	35	25	20	15
Acme DIY	460	535	20	20	25	30	100	70	110	60	40	20	20	20
Mercados Sud	900	980	40	60	60	70	130	160	200	100	60	40	30	30
TOTALS	20960	22990	1020	1170	1340	1900	2560	2980	3100	2420	1960	1800	1540	1200

Product variant: **Wall Coverings (10 metre rolls)**

Year: *2000*

Building targets for a larger customer base

Since most exporters' products are sold to a larger number of users or outlets (i.e., retail outlets or other sub-distributors for re-sale), if forecasts or targets are being built up from the market base then a more comprehensive listing of current and prospective customers will be needed. The export marketer can design some suitable forms for data tabulation, but typically data is needed that shows the expected pattern of sales across the year, or the expected sales by product variant.

Typical example forms for developing market targets or forecasts are shown in Tables 14.9 and 14.10. Whilst the exporter is often more concerned with the volume of goods, since that reflects the real sales activity, local distributors will often want to forecast local sales values as well as volumes, since that is usually of more interest to them. In the case of goods shipped direct to end users the exporter can record both volume and the FOB or CIF value of goods, as in Table 14.10.

Whether the exporter is marketing industrial or consumer products, the same approach to building forecasts or targets can be applied, but where goods are distributed through a local network of distributors the

Table 14.10 *Market product sales targets, unit sales and FOB values*

Market: Japan	Product group: Hand cut crystal						Year: 2000	
	Royal Windsor		Buckingham		Westminster		TOTALS	
Customer	Volume	Value	Volume	Value	Volume	Value	Volume	Value
Asahi Dept Store	560	6160	380	4560	470	6110	1410	16830
Myoke Dept Store	350	3850	620	7440	720	9360	1690	20650
Shinjuku Imports	290	3190	430	5160	370	4810	1090	13160
TOTALS	21300	234300	49000	588000	47500	617500	117800	1439800

export marketer will often find it necessary to train the distributor in the planning process, as a multi-product distributor will often attach less priority to the process.

Most export marketers can improve their market sales forecasting. If the only current approach to forecasting is either taking last year's figures for shipments and aiming to better it by a certain percentage, or just developing an annual sales 'target' and dividing it into twelve equal portions, then there will be additional information available from some source that can improve upon that, and reduce the risks of a hit or miss forecasting style. As we have seen in this chapter, apart from making better use of company sales data, using local market information where distributors are selling from stock will improve forecasting accuracy. Having an external benchmark, such as industry data on market sales, will provide an additional dimension further refining forecasting. Identifying trends and incorporating them into forecasting (whether seasonal or cyclical) improves the meaningfulness.

Improving the forecasting for export markets will, like everything else the marketer involves himself in that concerns planning, take time. Benefits usually more than justify that time. Once forecasts are prepared it is not the end of the matter: when the period to which they relate commences there will be new information inputs, events, environmental changes, and so on, that will affect the sales performance and achievement of forecasts. So the medium term annual forecasts will need to be monitored frequently, at least monthly, and updated short term forecasts prepared as necessary, often quarterly, to ensure export shipments are adjusted to meet demand or potential.

Further reading

Essentials of Marketing. Geoff Lancaster and Lester Massingham (McGraw-Hill 1988). Chapter 6: Sales Forecasting

Marketing Management – Analysis, Planning, Implementation and Control. Philip Kotler (Prentice Hall 1994). Chapter 10: Measuring and Forecasting Market Demand

Practical Business Forecasting. J. A. Saunders (Gower 1987). A book for those with special interests in the subject

Forecasting Methods for Management. S. Makridakis and S. C. Wheelwright (Wiley 1987). A book for those with special interests in the subject

Market and Sales Forecasting. Gordon Bolt (Kogan Page, 3rd edition 1994)

Checklist 14.1
Forecasting and planning

Action points

Sales forecasting

- ◆ Decide on forecast period
  - One year (short term)
  - One/three years (medium term)
  - Three/five years (long term)
- ◆ Check data sources relevant to planning and forecasting
  - Internal sales records:
    - Volumes/values
    - Month by month data
    - Product data
    - Trade market sector data
    - By customer/distributor
    - (Unfulfilled order enquiries)
  - External relevant data:
    - Published data on potential markets
    - Import and local production data
    - Competitive foreign market activity
- ◆ Choose the approach to forecasting current or future demand:
  - Statistical approaches (time series analysis such as moving annual totals and moving monthly averages, demand analysis, multiple factor index method)
  - Surveys of buyers' intentions or market tests
  - Marketer's judgement, distributor's judgement, sales force opinions or expert opinions
  - Estimates of market potential
  - Industry sales and market share analysis
  - Market build-up methods
- ◆ Develop your sales forecasts at **macro** and **micro** levels:
  - Product volumes/values
  - Market/product group profitability
  - Target market share by relevant categories such as:
    - Monthly
    - Annually
    - Market sector
    - Product or product group

Checklist 14.1 *(Continued)*

<table>
<tr><td></td><td>Action points</td></tr>
</table>

◆ Consider:
  ● Market knowledge
    – Competition
    – Economic and trading environments
    – Political factors
    – Distribution channel factors
  ● Trends in market imports/sales/production
    – Regulatory factors
  ● Consumer (changing) attitudes, perceptions, etc.
  ● Product innovation
  ● Seasonal or cyclical factors
  ● Product life cycles
  ● Company resource limitations
    – Production capacity
    – Flexibility to modify products
    – Availability of inputs
    – Financial resources for exports
    – Human (marketing) resources
  ● Adaptations or specialist products for export markets
◆ Set overall company objectives for each market
  ● Market volumes/values
  ● Distribution
  ● Market shares
    Take account of:
  ● Product mix
  ● Pricing levels
  ● Marketing strategies
◆ Set objectives for each distributor/market:
  ● Trade market sector
  ● Product/product group
  ● Key account
  ● Customer
  ● Salesperson/territory

Revenue and cost budgeting

◆ Support forecasts with department budgets, taking account of costs of:
  ● Order processing and physical distribution costs
  ● Marketing communications
  ● Advertising and promotion
  ● Travel and related expenses
  ● Customer service
  ● Department salaries
  ● Export training and recruitment

Checklist 14.1 (*Continued*)

	Action points
◆ Plan staffing levels required to achieve objectives and forecasts: ● Marketing management ● Export sales personnel ● Clerical and administrative support ● Changes in the needs and mix of skills ◆ Establish availability of material inputs enabling the company to source and produce competitively, with consideration to: ● Breadth/depth of product range ● Exchange rate movements ● Input supplies availability ◆ Develop revenue forecasts by: ● Trade market sector ● Product/product group ● Key account ● Other customers ● Salesperson/territory ◆ Develop profit contribution forecasts by: ● Trade market sector ● Product/product group ● Key account ● Other customers ● Salesperson/territory	

15

Export administration and performance monitoring

 In this chapter we will look at:

- some key aspects of export administration that impact on the export marketer's job functions and market management
- monitoring export sales performance, both in terms of export shipments and local sales from distributors' stocks in order to improve market planning.

The aim is to encourage exporters to monitor export market performance in a more meaningful way, measuring performance not just in terms of shipments, but, where distributors are used, also in terms of local market sales, and then to compare the export company's performance against the industry or product category. Improved performance monitoring will enable planning and forecasting to be improved (in line with the techniques discussed in the previous chapter), reducing the risk that actual sales are below potential sales.

The preparation of timely and efficient performance monitoring data reports is essential to effective marketing management. Whether responsibility for this is assigned to individual market managers, an export shipping manager, or other specialized function, is purely an internal organizational matter. However, in addition to monitoring performance data it is also necessary (for administrative reasons as well as market development planning) to control order processing and shipping, and the controls, procedures and report systems developed within the administration section need to be accurate, detailed and timely in presentation.

The primary function of a shipping department is to be responsible for all aspects of physically fulfilling the customer's order requirements, moving the goods from the production plant to the consignee's nominated destination, and raising all documents necessary to facilitate both shipment to the destination and remission of payment back to the exporter. If mistakes occur in the mechanics of shipment or supporting documentation, these could be very costly, possibly even losing you control or possession of goods, or causing payment problems.

In this chapter I shall consider some basic procedural systems of control and performance monitoring data likely to be needed in any international marketing department. Other publications available to the exporter very competently provide pro forma export shipping documents and examples of all standard forms in use.

The controls illustrated can be adapted to computer databases and spreadsheet programmes. In particular, you will be able to computerize customer shipment records and total all transactions by market and product to provide the summary sales data needed to monitor progress and provide a basis for future budget preparations.

The following sections discuss and review some of the major areas in which the export marketer generally needs to institute control systems.

Shipping department records

Shipping log book

In essence, a **shipping log book** is a department diary, an instrument to discipline you and your shipping manager (and supporting clerical personnel) to document transactions and record the content of telephone calls related to department business. The content would generally cover, for example, telephone conversations with shipping forwarders, truckers and any other carrier, the production plant personnel and possibly any contact necessary with suppliers of materials to facilitate production, in addition to bank contacts or matters relating to documentation. Notes should specifically record the purpose of the contact, points discussed and agreements reached, with a note of any follow-up action by either party (but particularly the shipping manager) to ensure that time schedules are met.

Typical comments that the shipping log might beneficially note are illustrated in Figure 15.1.

Keeping a shorthand record is just good housekeeping and reduces the risk of problems resulting from someone forgetting to follow up on their promise to perform a specific task relating to your export transactions. The shipping log record can be adapted to a computer notebook, where all staff with a terminal can record points in a diary-like fashion. In general, on any issue of real significance, more detailed memoranda would be prepared and appropriately circulated.

Quotation book

Facsimile messages, telexes, e-mail communications, letters and telephone calls requesting quotations will rapidly accumulate, and the need for a control system to

Date	Time	Contact	Purpose/notes	Action	Signed
2 January	10.30 am	Ellie, ABC forwarders	Asked for freight rate to Dubai	Follow up 4 Jan.	Janet
2 January	12.15	Ruth XYZ Shippers	Verbally quoted £90 per metric tonne to Apapa, Nigeria	Fax confirmation requested	Wendy
2 January	15.45	Bill Jones Glasgow plant	31 December closing inventory given as 100 cases × 12 units of 'Balmoral Cream'	Re-order packaging. Schedule production run of 1000 cases.	P.J.

Figure 15.1 Example of shipping department log book

Quotation Request	Product availability	Ex-plant cost	Gross profit	Distribution costs	Quoted price	Terms	Accepted	Notes
30/11/99 Singapore Transit Auth. **Engine filters** Quantity/Product 1000 × 9364 1000 × 9366 1000 × 9365	Ex-stock	£2.80 £3.20 £4.20	£0.80 £1.10 £1.40	£0.38 £0.40 £0.45	CIF £3.18 £0.60 £4.65	CIF L/C 30 days	10/12/93	Annual bus parts tender

Quotation Request	Product availability	Cost	Gross profit	Distribution costs	Quoted price	Terms	Accepted	Notes
Star Market Dubai 5 tonnes fresh turkeys Air shipment 3rd week December	19th December	£0.50 per lb.	£0.13 per lb.	£0.18 per lb.	£0.81 per lb. CIF Dubai	Payment in advance required. Await customer response		Customer usually orders at the last moment – pressure for response

Figure 15.2 Typical quotation book layout

monitor your own handling of the enquiries will soon become apparent. If you have an export price list covering standard types of products, perhaps all you need do is send a standard response to each enquiry, including a copy of the current price list. However, if your products are commodities whose prices can vary hourly or daily, or any form of customized product, you will probably have to treat each quotation request quite separately. Using a single instrument, the **quotation book** or **quotation form**, for the whole department again reduces the risks of forgetting to act on a request.

Figure 15.2 illustrates two sample uses for different products. Some products may lend themselves better to a separate quotation sheet for each request if a significant quantity of data is involved. Remember, that whilst common courtesy demands a reply to every enquiry, avoid becoming bogged down preparing time consuming quotes for markets where you realize there is negligible potential to close a sale.

All the rough calculations, exchanges of communications, facsimile messages, telexes and relevant documentation to support the enquiry and resultant quotation should be collated together, and, if an order materializes, would normally go into the shipping file relating to that order.

Disputes often arise because the exporter was not sufficiently specific in quoting, and the buyer then makes erroneous assumptions about what is included in the quotation or the terms applied to the order. However you are responding to enquiries, your quotation must clearly answer all the points relevant to supplying the goods, detailing the full conditions applied to acceptance of the order, and include at least:

- FOB, CIF or other basis of the price quotation exactly as specified
- period of validity of quotation, and conditions applying to validity
- terms of payment acceptable (give your banker's name and details for a letter of credit – and clarify acceptable conditions for a letter of credit, such as that part

shipments be allowed, the period for which the letter of credit should be valid, and possibly who is responsible for charges incurred in opening the credit)
- pro forma invoice if requested
- potential shipping date relating to product availability
- packaging to be used, units per carton, etc.
- quantity of goods quoted for
- method of shipping, e.g. air, refrigerated container, etc.
- technical specifications guaranteed for goods to be shipped, if relevant to the product, e.g. a raw material.

Order progress record

An export order requires great attention to detail as it progresses through the many stages in the process from order acceptance to final shipment and receipt of payment. Errors may be much more difficult to rectify than with a home market transaction, partly because of the many and varied documents, and partly because goods or ownership may have passed outside the exporter's control. It is therefore sensible to keep a simple record of each and every stage.

Experience will generally show that the stages or points in time that it is critical to monitor on the **order progress record card** are as illustrated in Figure 15.3 (a computer order progress monitoring record is preferred in many companies).

Each company's circumstances or special product requirements, such as packaging, may give rise to other critical points to monitor.

Control requires only the most basic entry of key numbers and dates for each critical point from the time you receive the request for a pro forma invoice until you actually receive payment (which frequently is later than the 'payment due' date). This kind of control document reduces the risk of overlooking any key point or date relating to a consignment. You will probably find that because many dates, such as vessel sailing dates, are initially tentative it is better to make entries in pencil (if you are using a manual system), possibly in the middle column. As mentioned previously, this type of control can be set up on the computer, and monitored on an exception basis, where something has deviated from the plan (e.g. production of goods, shipping dates, payments).

A practical operational point: once you allocate a pro forma invoice number to a transaction, it will be easier to collate and follow up all subsequent internal and external documents if you use only that same reference number. Many companies who create an order progress system use a folder for each shipment or transaction and print an order progress record on the front of the folder so that a shipping manager can monitor progress at a glance.

As an aside, one area where this proves particularly useful is monitoring that letters of credit are opened with appropriate terms (e.g. allowing part shipments, or with dates of validity sufficiently long to allow for the normal order lead times), thereby saving on the costs of requesting extensions and variations. A surprising number of export marketers are unaware of the costs incurred in altering or extending letters of credit, and often do not realize that their own company

Customer name: Address:	Telephone: Telex: Facsimile:	
ORDER PROGRESS RECORD Pro forma invoice: ● Number ● Issue date Customer order number Order acceptance/acknowledgement sent Letter of credit received and checked Product availability date Product location Special export packaging requirements ● ordered ● received Goods packed Vessel name Vessel scheduled sailing date Product movement order Invoice number and date Invoice value Freight cost Consignment weight Shipping documents prepared and checked Payment documents to bank ETA of vessel at destination Payment terms Payment due date Payment received		Notes

Figure 15.3 Customer order progress record

is usually bearing these costs (often lost in with all the other corporate banking charges) because they have not specified letter of credit costs to the buyer in the terms of the quote.

Monitoring export sales performance

Whilst exporters normally do keep sales records, these are often only monitored at the level of company export shipments, usually comparing current year shipments with previous years' shipments. This is a good starting point, but the professional export marketer will want a broader range of performance monitoring data to enable him to measure his progress and benchmark performance in respect of:

- company forecasts or targets
- national exports of similar products to his foreign markets

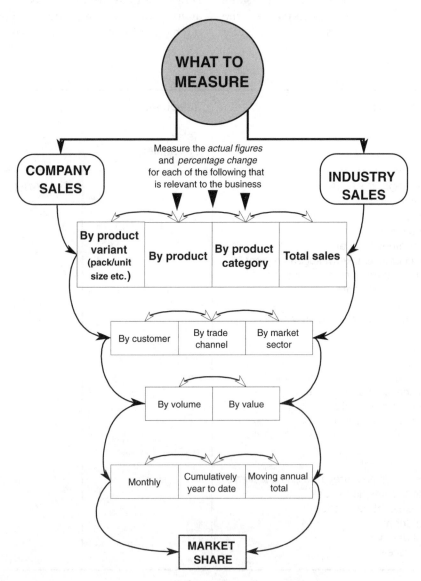

Figure 15.4 *What to measure – company and industry sales to the market*

- the activity and progress of competitors, both exporting from the domestic market and shipping into the destination markets from other foreign sources
- the overall category for his products in foreign markets (i.e. the share of category sales in each foreign market)
- the effectiveness of his agents and distributors in expanding market share, distribution and sales volumes (versus competitors).

Figure 15.4 illustrates diagramatically some of the levels of activity and information that the export marketer may want to measure and monitor on an ongoing basis, depending what is available or relevant to an individual company. The diagram emphasizes the need to monitor both company performance against itself, i.e. current performance compared with performance in previous comparable periods, and company performance in relation to an outside benchmark, such as the export performance of the industry sector.

As Figure 15.4 illustrates, measurements can be made in a number of ways to monitor performance, as listed here.

- For each foreign market a comparison of monetary performance against real performance can be obtained by comparing measurements at each level of
  - sales volumes
  - sales values.
- For each customs classification category the exporter's own performance can be compared with other industry exports on a volume and value basis for each destination market to which goods are being shipped.
- Product sales to each market can be monitored by:
  - product variant (e.g. size, design, pack, etc.)
  - product (i.e. all combinations of product variants)
  - product category (i.e. where there are several products in the same product

category, such as in power tools, soft drinks, etc.)
  - total sales for the company (all products) versus the industry or competitive companies.

Product sales can be measured both in terms of shipments to a market (and compared with total customs and excise export data to give a share of exports for each customs classification category to a market) and as sales in the local market where the exporter uses a distributor who sells from stock.

- Sales at each level of the distribution chain in each market could be measured, e.g.:
  - by customer (particularly monitoring any key accounts)
  - by trade channel (i.e. type of end users, such as building contractors and do-it-yourself outlets for electrical supplies, or supermarkets and bars for wines and spirits)
  - by market sector (i.e. electrical installation products covering all varieties of switches, cables, etc., or on-trade outlets versus off-trade outlets for wines and spirits).

To monitor performance in this detail for export markets is often difficult unless your distributors co-operate by maintaining records in a suitable format, and they are only likely to do that if they see benefits to their own businesses in having such micro level market data.

- Performance data should be monitored over various time periods in order that trends can be identified and corrective action planned where there are deviations from plan, e.g.:
  - monthly, and compared with the same month last year
  - cumulatively current year to date, versus the same period last year
  - moving annual total, showing a rolling performance and indicating longer term trends.
- Market share for each foreign market should be monitored by whatever means is most practical – information should be

collected on company sales versus the industry sales at each level, e.g.:
– by product category/total market
– customer/trade channel/market sector.
It is comparatively easy to measure a company's share of exports to each market, where customs classification numbers are known, and where goods in any particular customs classification are reasonably comparable to those of the exporter. It can also be relatively easy to obtain total import figures for each appropriate customs classification into each destination market, albeit for some developing countries the data may not be up to date and may be of limited accuracy – but a basis of measurement over time will still exist. As will be touched upon later in this chapter, it can be more difficult to obtain an estimate of total market size for many products in foreign markets where no good records are kept for local production, or where products are reproduced locally (such as software).

So many exporters only monitor their export performance against internal company historical data that it bears repetition that a company's export performance should not just be looked at in isolation, but always monitored or benchmarked against external or industry data to give a measure of comparative performance. Only by benchmarking export performance against external measures of industry or total market performance can a single company ensure it is growing versus its competitors, rather than lagging behind.

In summary of this section, an exporting company should prepare ongoing performance measurements where possible for each of the above categories:

- on a market-by-market basis
- for company sales versus national export sales (obtained from customs and excise published data) for each product type identified
- for company sales in the export market versus the total foreign market sales for

each product or category (i.e. imports to the foreign market from all sources, plus local production, minus any exports or re-exports).

In the other sub-sections of this section we will take a broader look at export performance monitoring, and examples of how performance monitoring data might be constructed.

Analyses of export shipments

Data can be monitored either using manual records or computer spreadsheets and databases. Whichever system of collating information you choose to monitor your export performance, first identify the performance criteria that can beneficially be measured. More usually you will want to establish progress and measurement against some or all of the following criteria.

- Compare the individual performance of your company against **national total exports** of the relevant product categories, as identified in customs export statistics. Figures can compare volumes, values and percentage share of each itemized customs category.
- Your company's **share of exports** in the relevant category to specific markets, monitored by volume, value and percentage share of exports to each market
- Your company's **month by month sales performance** in volume and value, recorded for total exports and by product or product type. This data can be compared with, say, the same month last year. This generally should be done both for total exports to all markets and on an individual market-by-market basis. It is also useful to measure the percentage change of this year (TY) versus last year (LY).
- **Cumulative performance** in total, and market by market, for the current year to date (updated monthly) versus last year to date, both by volume and value.

	Date	Customer	Invoice No:	Units	Value
Market dispatch record: SINGAPORE				**Year**: 2000	
Product: Electric razors					
Forecast				10,000	150,000
JAN.	01/01	Chan Ltd	0001	50	750
	15/01	Yuan Ltd	0004	25	375
	19/01	Foo Ltd	0011	100	1500
Month				175	2625
YTD				175	2625
FEB.	03/02	Wang Ltd	0019	40	600
	09/02	Chan Ltd	0023	50	750
	15/02	Foo Ltd	0027	75	1125
	26/02	Tan Ltd	0031	100	1500
Month				265	3975
YTD				440	6600
MARCH					
Month					
YTD					

Figure 15.5 *Monitoring current year dispatches*

To start an information recording process you could design a simple shipping record, as in Figure 15.5, in which the exports of electric razors to a single market are monitored for a British exporter. This example shows the individual export shipments for each month, and totals them to give a month and cumulative year to date (YTD) figure. It is always useful to note the sales forecast or target wherever you are recording performance data, as that keeps you conscious of progress against objectives.

Alternatively, the same individual data for shipments can be tabulated, but additionally we could enter the dispatch figures for the previous year, shown as last year to date (LYTD), and a comparison of the performance this year versus last year in

percentage terms (%TY/LY). Our Figure 15.6 shows that, whilst January was not a good month compared with last year, shipments picked up in February, and by the end of February dispatches for the first two months were ahead of last year by 2 per cent on units and 10 per cent on values (presumed to be FOB values).

For each separate month, say February, you can then extract the total by product and the grand total for each individual market, and place these figures on a **monthly market shipment summary** that details all active export markets and shows monthly, year to date (YTD) and a comparison with the last year to date (LYTD). Additionally, you can make a percentage comparison of this year versus last year

	Date	Customer	Invoice No:	Units	Value
Market dispatch record: SINGAPORE				**Year:** 2000	
Product: Electric razors					
Forecast				**10,000**	**150,000**
JAN.	01/01	Chan Ltd	0001	50	750
	15/01	Yuan Ltd	0004	25	375
	19/01	Foo Ltd	0011	100	1500
Month				175	2625
YTD				175	2625
LYTD				200	2800
%TY/LY				87.5%	94%
FEB.	03/02	Wang Ltd	0019	40	600
	09/02	Chan Ltd	0023	50	750
	15/02	Foo Ltd	0027	75	1125
	26/02	Tan Ltd	0031	100	1500
Month				265	3975
YTD				440	6600
LYTD				430	6020
%TY/LY				102%	110%
MARCH					
Month					
YTD					
LYTD					
%TY/LY					

Figure 15.6 *Comparison of current year dispatches with previous year*

(TY/LY). Figure 15.7 illustrates a suitable record sheet for this purpose.

Using the same format, you can transfer the month-by-month totals from the bottom of the market shipment summaries for each separate month and build these to give month-by-month comparisons (see Figure 15.8). This example shows the overall company export position to the latest month, and in the format illustrated here the export marketer can see at a glance his overall performance against the annual forecast.

This format could be re-designed to show a separate forecast for each month of the year, and subsequent performance against that monthly forecast. That might be more useful where there were strong seasonal variations to exports, and therefore it could be necessary to monitor each individual month more closely to ensure the performance in key months matches expectations.

Figure 15.7 indicates immediately that pound sterling sales values are increasing at a faster percentage rate than volume, but

Market dispatch record: ALL MARKETS							Year: 2000 Month: February		
Products	**Razors**		**Toasters**		**Hair dryers**		**Electric irons**		
Units/£000s	**Units**	**Value**	**Units**	**Value**	**Units**	**Value**	**Units**	**Value**	
Forecast	43200	648000	24000	288000	13000	135000	17000	272000	
Singapore	265	3975	140	1680	120	1248	160	2560	
YTD	440	6600	310	3720	190	1976	280	4480	
LYTD	430	6020	300	3360	180	1728	265	3975	
%TY/LY	102%	110%	103%	111%	106%	114%	106%	113%	
Dubai	330	4950	300	3600	160	1664	290	4640	
YTD	560	8400	500	6000	280	2912	410	6560	
LYTD	540	7560	480	5376	300	2880	400	6000	
%TY/LY	104%	1115	104%	1125	93%	101%	103%	109%	
Nigeria	110	1650	90	1080	20	208	150	2400	
YTD	150	2250	130	1560	40	416	250	4000	
LYTD	260	3640	140	1568	40	384	240	3600	
%TY/LY	58%	62%	93%	99%	100%	108%	104%	111%	
YTD									
LYTD									
%TY/LY									
FEBRUARY	3000	45000	2000	24000	900	9360	1050	16800	
YTD	4750	71250	3000	36000	1400	14560	1650	24600	
LYTD	4500	63000	2900	31900	1450	14210	1800	27000	
%TY/LY	106%	113%	103%	113%	97%	102%	92%	91%	
%F/cast	11%	11%	13%	13%	11%	11%	10%	9%	

Figure 15.7 Monthly market shipments summary

this basically reflects inflation, in that there was an export product price increase.

Looking at any single month usually tells us little in monitoring export performance. Year-to-date versus last-year-to-date comparisons are generally more meaningful in export analyses because there are so many distortions to affect any single month, such as delays in vessels. Figure 15.7 for February indicates a growth trend for all the individual markets and total markets. Figure 15.8 shows that whilst the year did not start off well, indicated by the January figures for all markets' exports (possibly shipments were

Market dispatch record: ALL MARKETS							Year: 2000	
Products	Razors		Toasters		Hair dryers		Electric irons	
Units/£000s	Units	Value	Units	Value	Units	Value	Units	Value
Forecast	43200	648000	24000	288000	13000	135000	17000	272000
JAN.	1750	26250	1000	12000	500	5200	600	9600
YTD	1750	26250	1000	12000	500	5200	600	9600
LYTD	1800	27000	1100	12100	530	5194	620	9300
%TY/LY	97%	97%	91%	99%	94%	100%	97%	103%
% F/cast	4%	4%	4%	4%	4%	4%	3.5%	3.5%
FEB.	3000	45000	2000	24000	900	9360	1050	16800
YTD	4750	71250	3000	36000	1400	14560	1650	24600
LYTD	4500	63000	2900	31900	1450	14210	1800	27000
%TY/LY	106%	113%	103%	113%	97%	102%	92%	91%
% F/cast	11%	11%	13%	13%	11%	11%	10%	9%
MARCH								
YTD								
LYTD								
%TY/LY								
% F/cast								
YTD = Year to date: TYTD = This year to date: TY/LY = This year/Last year comparison								

Figure 15.8 Market shipment summary – cumulative data for all markets

late), February showed an upturn, and by the end of the second month there is real growth.

At this point of recording and analysis, you have available data on:

- month-by-month and product-by-product shipments to each active market (Figures 15.5 or 15.6)
- a summary of your world-wide 'all markets' month-by-month activity (Figure 15.7)
- a cumulative 'all markets' product-by-product performance record (Figure 15.8).

This detail of analysis draws the export marketer's attention to potential problems where plans are not being met, may assist in identifying seasonal patterns not previously taken into consideration (if, say, you simply allocated the same plan volume to each month), and enables future planning and forecast preparation to be more accurate and sophisticated as you build up a historical database. If you have a relevant budget figure, this should appear at each point of measurement on each of your analysis sheets and you can show achievement by individual market month by month, total exports month by month, and percentage achievement and cumulative achievements against the budget or plan.

Clearly, many other combinations of comparisons can be prepared if you have the time and staff, but before asking a colleague to prepare data the following questions should be asked:

- who will see the data?
- who will use it?
- how will the analyses prepared contribute to monitoring performance, and improving performance and planning processes?

Your initial sales, market and dispatch analyses may not need to be very sophisticated or detailed if you start from a small base of operations. As exports grow, however, you will be pressured to produce more data to facilitate control and planning, and measure achievements in more detail. As more data become available you will benefit by preparing moving annual total analyses of dispatches and market sales (discussed in Chapter 14).

Do constantly bear in mind that there is no benefit in producing data just for the exercise of statistics. Production of statistical data is worthwhile only if:

- it measures performance against comparable relevant criteria
- it aids the planning process.

Market share of exports

Once you have built up your analyses of dispatches to each market individually and in total, in whatever fashion you find relevant and convenient, the next likely information needed to give a performance measure is your **market share** on a country-by-country basis.

In practice, for many less developed markets you will simply not obtain any meaningful or timely local data on the size of that market for many types of products. Local manufacturers may not be required to

report production data at all, or reports may be highly suspect. Even import statistics, useful if a large share of the product sales is imported, may be very late becoming available.

Therefore, the first estimate of performance that in any way relates to a share of a market is generally to **monitor your share of total exports** from your home country to the foreign market, which gives you a simple comparison of your performance against other domestic exporters to each market. This comparison is probably not worth preparing any more frequently than, say, every quarter or half year, because the leads and lags each exporter experiences will make any more frequent comparison of limited value. In this analysis, value is generally a more accurate measure than volume, unless volume is specified as kilograms, tonnes, litres or other definitive weight or volume measures that eliminate errors in comparison or resultant assumptions if, say, similar products of vastly different quality and prices are being shipped by the various exporters.

A layout is illustrated in Figure 15.9, and you may like to experiment with others that more conveniently suit your information needs. For simplicity, in this example I have assumed that the customs export data do not distinguish between different qualities and varieties of clocks (i.e. wall clocks, table clocks, mass produced or hand made, etc.), and that we can get comparisons only with total exports to each destination from the home country.

From the illustration in Figure 15.9, a comparison is drawn between the company's and the country's exports of clocks to the markets to which the company ships. In this simple example the value figures for both company and national exports have risen faster than volume exports, reflecting price increases in export product between this year and last year. However, there is a slight decline in the company's 'all countries' share of value of exports, although the volume share is maintained.

Share of UK Exports: Clocks (Units: 000s pieces, £000s FOB)							Period: Jan–June 2000
Destination	**Company**		**National**		**Company % of national**	
	Vol.	Val.	Vol.	Val.	Vol.	Val.
Saudi						
TY	9.1	38	18.8	66	48%	58%
LY	8.5	34	18.0	60	47%	57%
%TY/LY	107%	112%	105%	110%		
Singapore						
This year	4.8	20	13.3	60	36%	33%
Last year	4.7	19	13.6	59	36%	32%
%TY/LY	102%	105%	98%	102%		
Oman						
This year	2.9	12	3.1	14	94%	86%
Last year	2.5	10	3.5	15	71%	66%
%TY/LY	116%	120%	89%	93%		
This year						
Last year						
%TY/LY						
All countries						
This year	363.8	1516	760	3420	48%	44%
Last year	355	1420	736.2	3190	48%	46%
%TY/LY	102.5%	106.8%	103.2%	107.2%		

Figure 15.9 Comparison of company exports with total UK products exports

As your markets grow, and marketing becomes more sophisticated, problems will then develop in measuring only against recorded customs export figures, as these are likely to be less finely tuned into specifically relevant product categories than you would like. Also comparison with your own country's export figures in isolation gives no indication of what is happening to the total market for your product categories in the markets of the world. Fulfilling the role of a proactive export marketer rather than a reactive export shipper will mean that, as your international markets grow in importance as a part of your total business, you will need to obtain and analyse sales and marketing data for your product categories in each of your worthwhile markets. The next section discusses typical useful data for monitoring performance at the local level in foreign markets.

Table 15.1 shows a more complex, but interesting, scenario for an exporter of electrical appliances. Here we have a three year comparison of UK exports, with three main appliance product categories (referred to as a class A appliances, class B appliances and class C appliances). Added in for comparison is the actual company total figures for the three years, along with their respective percentage share of exports to the listed markets. The example has only taken the top twenty ranked markets for UK electrical appliance exports.

In this case, if the company looked at its exports in isolation the performance might seem satisfactory, as the bottom line shows it has year-on-year growth over 11 per cent and over 12 per cent for 1998 and 1999 respectively. But by looking at individual markets we see that in some it has grown in value and in share, in some it has grown in value but declined in share of UK exports, and to some major markets it does not export at all, having no local agents or distributors. The company's export market ranking in the right hand column reasonably parallels the UK export markets ranking of the left hand column, but there are some glaring differences, which would warrant investigation or commentary if this chart was part of the export strategy plan (rankings and exports to France, Italy and Portugal look as if there is a need for further investigation and action).

Whilst the company's exports have grown respectably in value terms, its total share of UK exports has declined slightly from 7.7% to 7.3%. The company's exports are less concentrated than the UK exports overall, with the company only exporting 72.7% of its goods to the top twenty markets, compared with 87% of UK total electrical appliance exports to those same twenty markets. Whilst this position has been improving slightly since 1997, perhaps the company is spreading its resources over too many smaller markets, and not developing aggressive strategies sufficiently for the larger markets.

This format of table is usually found to be highly instructive, and useful both in monitoring performance using UK export performance as a benchmark, and in prioritizing markets (previously referred to in Chapter 3), and data from customs and

excise sources or trade associations can be collated and tabulated on simple computer spreadsheets for speed and ease of production.

Monitoring profitability of export markets

Few exporters attempt to measure the profitability of export markets in what good practice would indicate was a satisfactory manner. The assumption seems to be that if there is a largish gross margin on a standard costing basis, then there will be an adequate net margin after expenses. Hence, where export profitability is measured, it is normally done at the level of all markets lumped together, i.e. for the entire export operation. The danger in this is that some markets may be very profitable, and others may be unprofitable, but marketers, not necessarily knowing which are which, may make wrong strategic and planning decisions and programmes.

It need not be wrong to export at low margins and profit levels, or even at a loss for some acceptable time periods, but clearly this should only happen where there is a long term security of market access supported by strong strategic marketing reasons, such as building market share and gaining market entry.

To sell on an opportunistic basis at reduced prices and low margins into an insecure market (as many exporters have done to their cost in dealing with developing nations) may prove very risky. If payments are not forthcoming on time and in full, a marginally profitable export order quickly becomes a loss making disaster. Even where goods are insured, such as with the Export Credit Guarantee Department, insurance normally only covers part of the order values.

Many exporting companies spread their export management and marketing resources too thinly, with marketers visiting small volume markets 'just because they were in the region'. Whilst it may be nice visiting a small, attractive island paradise for a couple

Table 15.1 *Ranked UK exports of electrical appliances 1997–1999 (£000s)*

Rank 95	Country £000s	Class A appliances			Class B appliances			Class C appliances			UK electrical appliances export totals									Rank
		97	98	99	97	98	99	97	98	99	97	Company	%	98	Company	%	99	Company	%	
1	Eire	21408	22828	25200	12870	13344	16745	2421	4786	6477	36700	2459	6.7%	40958	2867	7.0%	48421	3480	7.2%	1
2	France	13142	12321	17330	8366	7325	3918	526	1167	913	22035	115	0.5%	20815	100	0.5%	22161	110	0.5%	20
3	USA	1184	1128	2062	6937	5888	6388	4913	6424	5450	13034	1538	11.8%	13439	1626	12.1%	13900	1750	12.6%	2
4	Italy	356	1317	6084	3396	4978	4994	349	627	789	4100	–	–	6922	–	–	11868	–	–	–
5	Saudi Arabia	8621	9990	10421	459	540	743	15	44	22	9095	637	7.0%	10574	634	6.0%	11187	696	6.2%	6
6	Germany	949	630	1391	1315	1091	1340	4265	6242	6904	6529	286	4.4%	7963	320	4.0%	9634	340	3.5%	11
7	Netherlands	1520	2616	3144	813	1229	1810	3143	3611	3972	5478	696	12.7%	7456	764	10.2%	8926	896	10.0%	4
8	Spain	652	4166	5515	1894	1884	2407	203	426	518	2749	102	3.7%	6475	259	4.0%	8440	346	4.1%	10
9	Sweden	957	1122	1600	4378	6282	6059	578	504	517	5913	151	2.6%	7909	183	2.3%	8176	196	2.4%	16
10	Canada	1783	1801	2113	3941	3463	3940	1241	1536	1349	6965	620	8.9%	6800	639	9.4%	7402	720	9.7%	5
	Top 10 sub-total	50572	57919	74860	44369	46024	48344	17654	25367	26911	112598	6604	5.9%	129311	7392	5.7%	150115	8534	5.7%	5
	% UK exports	68%	68%	68%	69%	71%	67%	74%	80%	80%	69%	52.6%	–	71%	53.0%	–	70%	54.3%	–	

11	Kuwait	2362	1472	5439	216	189	392	17	15	19	2596	125	4.8%	1676	84	5.0%	5850	305	5.2%	13
12	Denmark	291	386	1459	2481	1933	3165	256	241	485	3029	60	2.0%	2560	70	2.6%	5109	80	1.6%	23
13	Portugal	1824	3441	2857	369	663	1378	186	269	358	2379	92	3.9%	4374	108	2.5%	4593	120	2.6%	18
14	Hong Kong	1332	1025	1432	2340	2264	2405	172	348	265	3849	331	8.6%	3637	331	9.1%	4102	405	9.9%	8
15	Norway	728	828	1053	1592	1754	2116	563	487	433	2884	662	31.6%	3069	994	32.4%	3602	1280	35.5%	3
16	Dubai	1754	2849	2818	274	286	261	68	54	72	2095	46	2.2%	3188	–	–	3151	–	–	–
17	Belgium/Luxem.	134	1355	1553	325	294	497	444	693	1052	902	110	12.2%	2342	138	5.9%	3103	140	4.5%	17
18	Canary Islands	627	1096	1166	783	908	1185	194	344	203	1605	–	–	2348	–	–	2554	–	–	–
19	Australia	167	49	117	1920	1387	1817	1091	701	554	3179	345	10.9%	2137	370	17.3%	2487	420	16.9%	7
20	Nigeria	131	77	141	1973	1577	1828	560	558	232	2664	47	1.8%	2211	190	8.6%	2201	150	6.8%	16
	Top 20 sub-total	59922	70497	92895	56642	57279	63388	21205	29077	30584	137780	8422	6.1%	156853	9677	6.2%	186867	11434	6.1%	
	% UK exports	80%	82%	84%	88%	88%	88%	89%	91%	91%	84%	67.1%	–	86%	69.4%	–	87%	72.7%	–	
	WORLD TOTALS	74865	85641	110026	64659	65004	72135	23766	31801	33521	163290	12551	7.7%	182447	13948	7.6%	215683	15720	7.3%	
	% Change	–	14.4%	28.5%	–	0.5%	11%	–	33.8%	5.4%	–	–	–	11.7%	11.1%	–	18.2%	12.7%	–	

of days, do the costs of the visit (management time and all expenses) warrant the investment where sales volumes and potential are small? There is an opportunity cost in visiting any market – time is often the scarcest management resource, and measures of market profitability and costs of servicing markets often bring this home to management.

Good export management practice should require that attempts are made to measure the profitability of all export operations. This can be done:

- on a market-by-market basis (suited to situations of ongoing regular supplies to the market, such as with consumer goods, industrial consumables, components and inputs)
- on a shipment-by-shipment basis (more suited to products or services that are subject to irregular orders with no regular market supply pattern, as with heavy equipment, export tenders, etc.).

At the crudest level, the export department or the finance department could produce a monthly summary of the estimated gross margin derived from all export transactions to each market on a monthly and year to date basis. Deviations from standard prices should be noted, and these in themselves would help make the export sales team or marketers aware of the consequences of price discounting.

At the next level an attempt should be made to estimate net contribution from each market (or each contract where the business is primarily concerned with occasional tenders). All too often real costs of exporting are hidden in other departments' budgets and cost structures. A couple of examples may suffice to make the point.

- If a support engineer needs to go to meet a customer, to provide training or installation assistance, has that been costed against the export market, or lost in the budget for the engineering department?

- Have the costs of financing the export transactions (goods in process or store, insurance, credit to the foreign market customers or distributors, and bank charges concerned with letters of credit, etc.) all been charged to the market or transaction, or lost in a central financing budget?
- Have the costs of providing all sales promotional materials been charged to the export market receiving them, or lost in the domestic sales and marketing budget?

To whatever extent is practical the export costs associated with developing and supporting a market should be attributed to each market, and periodic reports prepared and presented to management on the costs and market profitability. Direct costs such as travel and subsistence expenses incurred in visiting a market can be allocated against profits from the market, and can be supplemented by charging an appropriate proportion of salaries, benefits, etc., for marketers and support staff servicing the market (proportions for days spent in the market can be estimated easily, and some acceptable formula developed to attribute proportions of other personnel related costs).

Some of the typical costs incurred in exporting include:

- wages, salaries and benefits of staff directly engaged in export marketing, export sales, export shipping and customer service
- proportions of salaries and benefits of staff occasionally involved in export matters (such as technical staff, quality controllers, researchers or designers, accountants, and so on)
- foreign travel and subsistence for any personnel visiting markets (not just those identified as export marketers)
- costs of modifying products or customizing designs
- additional or special quality control costs
- special packaging requirements

- costs incurred in special production runs (if there is a serious disruption to normal production, who bears that charge?)
- special discounts or allowances to customers (users or distributors)
- sale commissions (to agents or other interested parties)
- providing special training in product use (to users or agents and distributors)
- installing and commissioning products (heavy capital plant and equipment, etc.)
- providing product promotional literature (usually to support the selling activities of agents and distributors)
- marketing communications costs (advertising and promotion costs)
- participation in exhibitions
- insuring and financing export stocks of materials and finished goods
- preparing and processing export shipping and bank documentation, etc.
- financing export credit to direct customers and distributors
- costs of export credit insurance, etc.
- costs of bank charges processing export payments and payment documentation.

The reader will probably think of some other cost factors applicable to his own products or company.

If any individual markets or customers do not show a viable level of profitable business then export management can take decisions on how to treat the market, whether as an investment market if there are strong strategic reasons to supply it, or to cease supplying the market or particular customers where there is no clear benefit.

Monitoring a distributor's local performance

The previous section discussed the export statistics that the export marketer might like to monitor. But efficient market management will only be possible where the importer or distributor is able to use statistics sourced in his local market to monitor performance within the market in compar-

ison with competitors and overall market size, trends and performance.

What to monitor

If the exporting company sells through a network of **specialist distributors**, who either sell on direct to end users/consumers, or who supply other levels of trade stockists, then there is benefit in establishing measures of **distributor performance**.

The company can measure the distributor's performance by monitoring:

- sales of company products by the distributor versus sales of competitive products in the market (a basic measure of the distributor's effectiveness)
- company sales through the distributor as a share of the distributor's total sales turnover (a measure of the importance of the principal to the distributor, and a measure of how the distributor is building the products versus the other products in the distributor's portfolio)
- distributor's share of the product category sales (providing a form of measurement of the distributor's effectiveness, but also a measure of product awareness and penetration)
- product/brand performance in the market
  - by volumes/values
  - versus competitive brands (providing a measure of the effectiveness of marketing programmes, and of the distributor's sales effectiveness)
- trade sector sales
  - by product
  - by volume/values (a measure of the effectiveness of a distributor in covering all the trade channels suited to a product, as well as a measure of the marketing communications effectiveness in communicating to trade sector buyers)
- key account sales (where the distributors have local key accounts to service)
  - by volumes/values
  - by brand

- product distribution in trade outlets or in potential user establishments (for industrial products) (a measure of the effectiveness of market coverage of the potential outlets or users by the distributor).

As a minimum, an independent distributor should have internal control systems that tabulate the following:

- actual monthly sales this year
- cumulative sales this year to date
- actual sales for same month last year
- cumulative sales for last year to date
- moving annual sales totals (volume/value)
- comparison of sales performance against sales budget
- sales by customer.

There is a strong danger that requesting too much information from agents and distributors will result in a failure to comply with information requests. Many exporters complain at the difficulty obtaining information, and this reluctance to comply is often caused by a combination of factors, including:

- too many information requests from too many principals
- distributors not collating their own information in the format required by principals
- a failure by principals to provide any feedback on what use they make of information and how the provision of information will help the distributor sell more and make more profit for his business.

Keep information requests to a minimum, and ensure you do provide feedback on the uses made of information and its relevance to building the market. It can be useful to provide any data feedback in time frames that are meaningful to the agent or distributor, rather than just the principal. For example, most exporters monitor all their data according to the time frame of their own company year, and that might be irrelevant to the time frame of the distributor's company year. Where computers are used to monitor data it is very easy to organize the printouts to cover any specified time frames, suiting the requirements of both the exporter and the distributors.

Market share

Apart from the company's share of home country exports to the various markets to which you are now shipping, your share of the market achieved by each of your distributors will be key to assessing your progress and the effectiveness of marketing programmes. If the foreign country is also a producer of goods similar to your own, then theoretically you can deduce market share by adding imports to local production and deducting exports, and dividing your own imports by this figure. However, this takes no account of changes in inventories year on year, and that figure may be particularly hard to ascertain.

The more preferred and approximate equations for assessing **market share** look like this (for either volume or value):

Preferred

Market share =

$$\frac{\text{Distributor: (Imports + Opening inventory} - \text{Closing inventory)}}{\text{Market: (Production + Opening inventory} - \text{Closing inventory + Imports} - \text{Exports)}}$$

Approximate

$$\frac{\text{Distributor total imports}}{\text{Local production + Imports} - \text{Exports}}$$

The approximate market share calculation assumes no net change in distributor or local manufacturer market inventories.

It may be especially difficult to get the degree of category analysis you want to assess your share accurately, because the local production or import figures may not identify sub-categories of main product groupings. Developing countries often have limited local reporting of production, and any reporting may be of dubious accuracy.

If the market either has no local production of the products you ship, or if local production is not reported, then you may reasonably use the difference between locally reported import figures and export figures as your market share (share of net imports) base. Consistency in using the same base of figures in comparisons at least gives you a basis for ongoing measurement, albeit with limited accuracy.

Share of net imports

Market share =

$$\frac{\textbf{Distributor total imports}}{\textbf{Market imports – Exports}}$$

Once again, this calculation has limited accuracy because it assumes that no estimate can fairly be made of inventories at either end of the period being measured.

In more sophisticated markets, it is likely that various government agencies will closely monitor all local production, imports and exports, and accurate figures would then be available to assess a market share. Manufacturers and distributors might quite possibly have to report on sales either to a government agency or on a voluntary basis to a trade association.

If you are marketing branded goods where penetration is a priority you need to work with your distributor to identify what local data are available, and where they can be accessed for the purpose of preparing your most important measure of marketing progress – **the market share**. Once you know what data are available (Nielsen data covers a range of consumer products in many developed markets) then it is a simple task to design a standard form on which to enter figures and present your share analysis for circulation to interested parties within your company.

Sales performance

In order to monitor market sales activity by the distributor, it is customary for the export marketer to seek **monthly statistical reports on stocks and sales**. A minimum report should cover:

- opening stocks (for each product/pack size)
- shipments received into stock during current month
- market sales
- closing stocks.

In addition, you may want a forward sales forecast that includes provision for forward orders to cover anticipated sales. Depending on shipping and production lead times, your distributor will probably need to plan to hold between one and three months' stocks, based upon forecast sales for each item.

Your distributor will probably be quite experienced in controlling stock levels, but in smaller markets may not have computerized systems. You may therefore find it useful at this point to review a few basic formats of simple forms that the distributor might use to control his business in your products.

Monitoring monthly sales against local sales budgets

Figure 15.10 illustrates a simplified form of a **market annual sales budget,** agreed with the agent or distributor. **Monthly totals** for actual **sales against budget** and for **percentage achievement**, as well as **comparisons with the same time last year**, can all be monitored on the same table. This example considers a manufacturer of various sundry electric items shipping to the Canary

Market depletions performance record
(Product units)

Market: Canary Isles   Year: 1999

	January	February	March	April	May	June	July	August	September	October	November	December	Year
Electric razors													
Budget	250	150	150	100	100	100	150	200	250	300	400	600	2750
Actual depletions	254	146	143	94	110	115	167	190	273	320	420	615	2847
% budget	*101.6%*	*97.3%*	*95.3%*	*94%*	*110%*	*115%*	*111.3%*	*95%*	*109.2%*	*106.7%*	*105%*	*102.5%*	*103.5%*
Last year actual	240	140	140	92	95	96	130	180	230	280	360	550	2533
% TY/LY	*105.8%*	*104.3%*	*102.1%*	*102.2%*	*115.8%*	*119.8%*	*128.5%*	*105.6%*	*118.7%*	*114.3%*	*116.7%*	*111.8%*	*112.4%*
Electric toasters													
Budget	140	100	60	60	60	60	80	100	150	200	300	460	1770
Actual depletions	130	90	83	74	50	54	76	97	152	220	366	470	1862
% budget	*92.9%*	*90%*	*138.3%*	*123.3%*	*83.3%*	*90%*	*95%*	*97%*	*101.3%*	*110%*	*122%*	*102.2%*	*105.2%*
Last year actual	140	95	55	62	55	59	75	90	135	180	276	430	1652
% TY/LY	*92.9%*	*94.7%*	*150.9%*	*119.4%*	*90.9%*	*91.5%*	*101.3%*	*107.8%*	*112.6%*	*122.2%*	*132.6%*	*109.3%*	*112.7%*
Electric irons													
Budget	160	120	80	50	50	50	80	100	130	200	300	400	1740
Actual depletions	153	147	93	41	63	72	56	103	171	210	327	480	1916
% budget	*95.6%*	*122.5%*	*116.3%*	*82%*	*126%*	*144%*	*70%*	*103%*	*114%*	*105%*	*109%*	*120%*	*110.1%*
Last year actual	146	115	75	50	46	55	72	96	120	182	269	380	1606
% TY/LY	*104.8%*	*127.8%*	*124%*	*82%*	*137%*	*130.9%*	*77.8%*	*107.3%*	*142.5%*	*115.4%*	*121.6%*	*126.3%*	*119.3%*
Budget													
Actual depletions													
% budget													
Last year actual													
% TY/LY													
Budget													
Actual depletions													
% budget													
Last year actual													
% TY/LY													

TY = This year   LY = Last year

Figure 15.10 Distributor's market sales records

Isles. The figures entered are for men's electric razors, electric toasters, and electric irons. The pattern of sales is seen here to be highly seasonal, with a Christmas peak.

The 1999 budget was closely based on the previous year's actual sales, with a budgeted growth of between 7 per cent and 9 per cent, depending on product. In this example each product actually exceeded the local sales budgets (forecasts). Whilst that would make the distributor and export marketer happy, if we look at the picture for individual months, there are some months where sales of products varied greatly from the budgeted figures. An unusually high month's sales would presumably have depleted reserve stocks, possibly contributing to a lower following month through stock shortages (e.g. electric irons in June and July).

An alternative format for monitoring the **distributor's sales performance** is illustrated in Figure 15.11, based on data in Table 14.1. This example differs from Figure 15.10 by showing the **monthly cumulative achievement against the annual forecast**, of 195,000 widgets. It also shows a **cumulative this year/last year** comparison. The particular example has some interesting points.

- The product is very seasonal, as shown by the high January and February figures.
- The year started well, but fell back on achievement against the annual forecast in May and June, possibly indicating a distributor stock shortage as earlier sales were higher than forecasts. This scenario is repeated in August and September, after high sales in July.
- The previous year's achievement was higher than the current year forecast, possibly indicating soft forecasts from the distributor, unless forecasts were submitted very early and not adjusted subsequently.
- If monthly shipments were being scheduled ahead to meet forecast sales, without regular review and adjustment to

reflect the latest sales trend, then it is likely that, even whilst sales to the market are growing, there is an under-achievement against potential as the distributor runs low on stocks at certain points, and probably rations product sales to key customers.

There is no single best way to monitor sales performance, either for export shipments (dispatches) or local market sales sales from stock. Each format may produce additional useful data and analysis of circumstances or trends. But, as mentioned before, do not try to over-monitor to the point where it disrupts selling activity.

Monitoring sales at the local market level will require the co-operation of your local distributor, who will have to supply the local market monthly sales data. Co-operation can often be gained when you, the export marketer, demonstrate the usefulness of the data in forward planning and stock control, thereby minimizing funds tied up in stock whilst maximizing sales.

Monitoring distributor stock and order positions in relation to sales

The one item of information missing from Figures 15.10 and 15.11, and which is essential to minimize the risk of out-of-stock situations, is a monthly report on stock levels held by the distributor, including a note of goods in transit.

Figure 15.12 is a very basic **stock, order and sales control** form, which can be used by a distributor to assist forward planning of orders. Firm orders are likely to be committed for about two or three months ahead, because of long shipping lead times. If a manually produced form is used, rather than a computer generated control form, tentative or budgeted figures can be entered in pencil initially, then the actual final figures can be inserted in ink when they are available. Every month you need to adjust your forward plans, altering the pencilled-in figures to take account of forecast changes in

MARKET SALES RECORD		Market: Hong Kong	Year: 1998		
Product **Units**	**Widget** **model 1**	**Widget** **model 2**			
FORECAST	**195000**				
January sales from stock Year to date Last year to date % TY/LY % Forecast	27960 27960 25350 110.3% 14.3%				
February sales from stock Year to date Last year to date % TY/LY % Forecast	30260 58220 55360 105.2% 29.9%				
March sales from stock Year to date Last year to date % TY/LY % Forecast	12170 70390 68920 102.1% 36.1%				
April sales from stock Year to date Last year to date % TY/LY % Forecast	11830 82220 82010 100.3% 42.16%				
May sales from stock Year to date Last year to date % TY/LY % Forecast	14260 96480 100050 96.4% 49.8%				
June sales from stock Year to date Last year to date % TY/LY % Forecast	16670 113150 113650 99.6% 58.0%				

Figure 15.11 An alternative format of monitoring local distributor sales

MARKET SALES RECORD		Market: Hong Kong		Year: 1998	
Product **Units**	**Widget** **model 1**	**Widget** **model 2**			
FORECAST	**195000**				
July sales from stock Year to date Last year to date % TY/LY % Forecast	16180 129330 122120 105.9% 66.3%				
August sales from stock Year to date Last year to date % TY/LY % Forecast	10880 140210 145010 97.7% 71.9%				
September sales from stock Year to date Last year to date % TY/LY % Forecast	25560 165770 173770 95.4% 85.0%				
October sales from stock Year to date Last year to date % TY/LY % Forecast	25130 190900 189250 100.9% 97.9%				
November sales from stock Year to date Last year to date % TY/LY % Forecast	12330 203230 197520 102.8% 104.2%				
December sales from stock Year to date Last year to date % TY/LY % Forecast	19560 222790 209160 106.5% 114.3%				

Figure 15.11 (Continued)

Stock and sales record
Electric Ovens

Market: Portugal   **Year:** 1999

	Jan.	Feb.	Mar.	Apr.	May	June	July	Aug.	Sept.	Oct.	Nov.	Dec.
Opening stock	300	227	275	305	290	235	165	265	265	265	565	765
Shipments received	150	150	100	100	50	100	200	100	100	400	600	200
Sales: budget	200	100	100	100	100	200	100	100	100	100	400	600
Sales: actual	220	90	70	110	105	160						
Adjustments (leakages/damages)	3	12	0	5	0	10						
Closing stock	227	275	305	290	235	165	265	265	265	565	765	365

Figure 15.12 Local market stock and order control

LOCAL MARKET DISTRIBUTOR STOCK AND SALES RECORD: HONG KONG 1998					
Product **Units**	**Widget** **model 1**	**Widget** **model 2**			
SALES FORECAST	195000				
January Opening stock – 1 Jan. Shipments (ETA: 15/1) Available for sale Sales from stock	27840 18000 45840 27960				
February Opening stock – 1 Feb. Shipments (ETA: 16/2) Available for sale Sales from stock	17880 17000 34880 30260				
March Opening stock – 1 Mar. Shipments (ETA: 21/4) Available for sale Sales from stock	4620 18000 22620 12170				
April Opening stock – 1 Apr. Shipments (ETA: 20/4) Available for sale Sales from stock	10450 14000 24485 11830				
May Opening stock – 1 May Shipments (ETA: 15/5) Available for sale Sales from stock	12620 11000 23620 14260				
June Opening stock – 1 Jun. Shipments (ETA: 12/6) Available for sale Sales from stock	9360 18000 27360 16670				

Figure 15.13 Stock and sales record for widgets in Hong Kong

LOCAL MARKET DISTRIBUTOR STOCK AND SALES RECORD: HONG KONG 1998					
Product **Units**	**Widget model 1**	**Widget model 2**			
SALES FORECAST	195000				
July Opening stock – 1 Jul. Shipments (ETA: 14/7) Available for sale Sales from stock	10690 17000 27690 16180				
August Opening stock – 1 Aug. Shipments (ETA: 25/8) Available for sale Sales from stock	11510 16000 27510 10880				
September Opening stock – 1 Sept. Shipments (ETA: 12/9) Available for sale Sales from stock	16630 15000 31630 25560				
October Opening stock – 1 Oct. Shipments (ETA: 7/10) Available for sale Sales from stock	6070 22000 28070 25130				
November Opening stock – 1 Nov. Shipments (ETA: 12/11) Available for sale Sales from stock	2940 20000 22940 12330				
December Opening stock – 1 Dec. Shipments (ETA: 8/12) Available for sale Sales from stock	10610 22000 32610 19560				

Figure 15.13 (Continued)

opening stocks and therefore orders, and of expected closing stocks.

Figure 15.12 assumes we have actual sales, adjustments, stock and shipment details, opening stock and closing stock up to May (in bold type); the light type indicates where we have pencilled in our best forward estimates to balance stock and shipments against sales budgets.

The line labelled 'adjustments' can take account of spoilage or other causes of leakage or market returns, including post-entry adjustments when an actual inventory count differs from the theoretical inventory shown in stock records. Data on market returns may help indicate if the distributor is following your guidelines on market product exchanges for limited life products.

The stock return of our widget distributor in Hong Kong, illustrated as Figure 15.13 in a different format, shows a number of points. Whilst an initial reaction to the year's opening stock suggests it is adequate, based on projected annual sales, because sales in January and February are much higher than budgeted, there appears to be a stock crisis in March (which the exporter might not be aware of without a stock report) as the scheduled shipment is not due until late in the month.

The distributor will probably have been rationing sales to key customers until the new shipment arrived. Then he has responded by advancing shipping dates by about a week for subsequent months, but still keeping quantities in line with forecast local sales. His stock levels are then inadequate to give a reserve (most exporters look to have up to two months' stock reserve held by distributors). The late arrival of the August shipment, for whatever reason, then aggravates an underlying problem of inadequate stocks, since the shipment would not have cleared until almost the end of the month, and a typical distributor would have eased up on selling whilst knowing stocks are low. Subsequent orders arrive earlier in the month, and order sizes are increased, but the end of year result would only leave

13,050 widgets to carry forward to the following year. All in all an unsatisfactory stock management position.

In Chapter 14 we developed some forward forecasts for the widget sales in Hong Kong. The approach to forecasting was primarily based on projecting a trend at approximately the current growth level of a little over 5 per cent per annum, from moving monthly averages adjusted for seasonal deviations, or based solely on projecting the moving annual total. With the additional knowledge that the distributor has been under-forecasting and carrying too little buffer stock, the export marketer could exercise his judgement and make the argument to increase forecasts and shipments by more than the projected trend over the next year, possibly projecting at least 10 per cent uplift over the twelve month forecast period.

Presenting local market sales monitoring data

As a general rule all marketing monitoring data should be shared with your distributor to help improve sales performance and market planning.

- Data should be presented in a meaningful format that highlights trends and encourages corrective action where there are deviations from plans.
- Do not assume the distributor will take time studying and analysing copious statistical reports (when he is probably receiving similar from other principals for their products), but focus on only providing performance reports that are meaningful and useful in the context of managing local distribution.
- Where statistical reports are being presented these should be accompanied by an explanation of the interpretation that the distributor should attach to them, along with suggestions for action. Some data may be presented graphically, such as moving annual data.

- Do not make the distributor produce information and tables that will neither give any measurement of progress nor marketing programme effectiveness, nor aid in future planning

The data monitoring formats illustrated in Table 14.1 and Figures 14.3 to 14.5 can all be constructed for the local distributor's sales data, and give a better understanding of the local market sales and marketing activity. The **moving annual total** (MAT) is an extremely useful performance measurement tool in marketing, having the benefit of monitoring performance on a year-on-year rolling basis, which both smoothes out unusual short-term fluctuations, such as seasonal peaks and troughs, and measures change. It can be compiled on a market-by-market or product-by-product basis, using a computer spreadsheet package, with monthly updates of new data that will prove useful in future market sales forecasting.

The discussion and examples used in this chapter outline some of the basic information controls that the export manager may develop, with the distributor, to monitor performance and improve planning for continued growth. These will give the distributor additional confidence in managing the market, and help ensure that his stock and ordering programme is in line with sales performance.

Further reading

Principles of Management In Export. James Conlan (Blackwell – Institute of Export 1994)

Checklist 15.1
Export controls and performance measurement

Controls

What administrative controls are relevant to your export operations:

- Department log book?
- Quotation book?
- Order progress record?
- Others?(identify and list)

Performance measurement

- Have you identified **key result areas**?
- Do quantitative measures exist for them?
- Is data presented meaningfully?

Do analyses measure:

- variances from your plans and forecasts?
- trends?
- promotional and advertising effectiveness?
- profitability (by destination market and product group)?
- sales performance with any market key accounts?

Specifically, is it relevant to monitor company's export performance (volume/value/share – TY/LY) versus:

- total national product sector exports, and by destination market?
- sales of the product category in each destination market?
- foreign market sales of each product or product group?

Do you monitor performance in actual volume/value terms and against forecasts:

- monthly (This year/Last year)?
- cumulatively?
- on a moving annual total and moving monthly average basis?
- other (note)?

Checklist 15.1 (*Continued*)

Action points

Do you measure change (i.e. % TY/LY):

- by market?
- by product or product group?
- by volume/value?

Are moving annual total (MAT) analyses prepared for:

- export sales volumes?
- export sales values?
- distributors' sales performance?
- export profitability?
- market shares?

Is each item of data analysis being presented in the most meaningful and easily interpreted format for action?

16

Export pricing and costing

In this chapter we will look at aspects of product pricing and product costing that the export marketer should consider in developing his approach to export pricing. We will focus on:

- factors that traditionally affect the development of an export price list by taking account of costing structures
- and factors that affect the market pricing of product in export markets.

The aim is to highlight the importance of correct price positioning within each export market as part of the export marketing mix. Price is a key factor in developing markets and sales volume, and we aim to encourage an approach in export marketing where market prices and price positioning are the focus of interest when looking at costing and pricing structures.

In considering pricing and costing a key issue is whether you just want exports to serve as an outlet for the unutilized or marginal capacity in your production facilities, or whether you are also prepared to invest in additional capacity to meet any rising export demand. The approach you take to export pricing may differ if the former is the objective rather than the latter. Here we will explore various approaches to pricing and costing that encourage profitable export market development.

Pricing considerations

Price is a critical factor in the marketing mix in international as well as domestic markets and in achieving goals and objectives. It has a key role in brand or product positioning

both in relation to other products in the company portfolio and to competitive products. Price also has a direct effect on sales volumes through:

- extending or limiting the consumer or users ability to afford the product
- suiting or not suiting the outlet profile of stockists (distributors, trade dealers, retailers).

Figure 16.1 illustrates that product price factors (including costs to the trade, trade margins, etc.) have an effect on the distribution likely to be achieved and on the levels of consumer/user demand. Product sales will normally be influenced by the breadth of distribution (both of the product and any supporting after-sales service facilities).

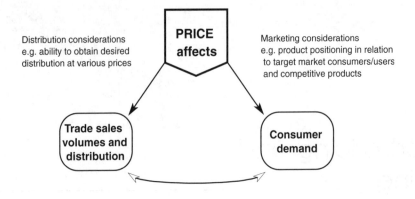

Correct pricing at trade and consumer/user levels is important in developing an equilibrium of consumer demand and trade stocks and distribution, and in achieving sales levels that match marketing objectives.

Figure 16.1 The role of price in distribution and demand

Actual sales may be below potential or planned sales (i.e. the real or forecast level of demand) if distribution is sub-optimal for the product.

The higher a company sets its product prices the narrower the likely base of consumers or users who can afford the product, either as a one-off purchase if it is an item of capital equipment, or as a regular repeatable purchase if it is a consumable product. But price is critical to marketing strategies and product positioning, as will be considered further later in this chapter, and therefore to developing demand.

Product stockists, whether retail or trade outlets, often have their own profile in the market, perhaps as value-for-money outlets, or as suppliers of quality (often associated with higher priced) merchandise, and the buyers for the various trade channel outlets will consider product prices in relation to their market profiles and marketing strategies when deciding what product ranges to carry.

Some strategy considerations in pricing

A company typically has multiple objectives is establishing its pricing policies, and

export marketing just complicates the achievement of these objectives, which are:

● profit growth
● competition (discouraging competitors from entering markets or increasing capacity to serve markets)
● building market share.

In pursuing any combination of these multiple objectives the fundamental strategic consideration for the marketer is whether to adopt an approach of:

● uniform pricing across all markets, or
● market-by-market pricing.

The strategy common for many companies in their early days of exporting is to pursue a market-by-market pricing strategy, aiming to maximize revenues, or at last to obtain the best combination of volume and revenue that yield acceptable profits while ensuring a presence in the market. Clearly this can produce an imbalance in prices between markets, and alienate agents or distributors as well as trade channel customers and users/consumers. It also leaves open profit opportunities for grey market trade by astute traders in those markets that

Some potential pricing objectives	
• Maximize long run profits • Maximize short run profits • Growth of (global) market share • Generate a prescribed return on investment • Stabilize the market • Desensitize customers to the price issue • Maintain price leadership (explicit or implicit) • Discourage new entrants to the markets • Encourage exit of marginal suppliers • Maintain loyalty of trade channels (distributors and dealers) • Give the product valued 'visibility' • Discourage 'grey market' trading	• Position products within company portfolio • Position products versus competitors' offerings in the markets • Avoid input price rise demands from suppliers • Foster image of 'fairness' with customers • Generate product interest (e.g. promotions) • Demonstrate consistency and reliability (to competitors and customers) • Discourage competitive price-cutting • Help boost sales of weaker products in portfolio, or sales in weaker markets • Avoid investigation by regulatory authorities

can buy cheaper and ship cost-effectively to the higher priced markets.

Some companies pursue a marketing strategy that will look to balance internal market prices across markets, to avoid grey market trading. This is difficult to achieve, as duties, taxes and other market distribution costs can vary significantly, and the exporter must adjust the ex-factory prices between markets in order to achieve a common market price across the destination markets. Price differences may still arise as a result of factors outside the control of the exporter, such as local trade channel margins.

Other companies will seek to establish local prices that broadly position a product similarly to a target market group, according to what they can afford. In developed markets they may be asked to pay more in local currency than in under developed markets. As previously mentioned, this tends to encourage grey trade, unless the products are very local in nature, such as a service that cannot be re-exported (e.g. developing films, professional services, fast foods).

Some multi-national companies with global or regional brands seek to vary local market pricing according to their relative strength, selling at higher prices in relation

to competition where they have strong market shares, and pricing lower in markets where they are weaker and seeking to gain market share.

There is no simple formula to arrive at a pricing policy, but many factors to consider in the pricing process. We will consider further this topic in the subsequent section on 'Marketing aspects of product pricing'.

Approaches to product pricing

There are basically seven main approaches to arriving at a market price, and the export marketer will recognize that he adopts some of these without putting labels to them, but there are strategic implications whichever approach is adopted.

- **Domestic-plus pricing.** This typically entails a price overload to the foreign market because deductions have not normally been made for domestic marketing, sales and distribution costs, or domestic trade credit. If you are to be competitive and achieve sales these exclusively domestic marketing costs should be eliminated from the export transaction.
- **Cost-plus pricing.** This involves assessing, as accurately as possible, the

costs of producing the particular units you are offering for sale, and then adding margins to give an acceptable return.

- **Target pricing.** This approach normally aims at giving a certain level of return to the company (as a percentage of cost, sales value, return on assets, etc.) or at strategically positioning the product in relation to competitors in the market place and to achieve certain defined company objectives (such as maximizing revenue or sales volume, or utilizing unused production capacity).

- **Market forces pricing.** This approach aims to assess the value (perceived or real) potential customers will put on your product and be prepared to pay for the value-added benefits they will receive (influenced by the marketing communications), and charging a price that captures this value and positions the product according to the product marketing strategy.

- **Price-taking.** This is where the export marketer accepts the going market prices set by competitors or competitive activity, and sets prices accordingly, with less attention to strategic marketing considerations or cost structures, but accepting to work with the profit margins that going-rate prices generate. In this situation the exporter is normally a price follower rather than a price leader, and the buyer often will gain the advantage in negotiations.

- **Pricing for value.** In this approach to pricing the marketer recognises the extra value benefits offered by his products, but deliberately chooses not to charge for all of them in the price, allowing users or consumers to have a recognized surplus value from high quality products over what they are paying for similar competitive goods. This approach can enable a company to break into a market, develop market share, and build customer goodwill and loyalty whilst wrong-footing some of the competitors.

It is a common approach in retailing in the 1990s, illustrated internationally by The Body Shop in developing its product offers of personal skin and hair care products, as well as Toyota with its Lexus car, and Virgin airlines with its airline travel. Many Far Eastern exporters also have used this approach to good effect, building share versus competitors.

- **Tenders or sealed bids.** Exporters in the construction and capital goods industries are usually familiar with this approach to pricing. Whilst the exporter cannot set its bid prices below its costs, if it wants the contract it cannot risk pricing too highly as it must assume that its competitors face no worse a cost structure than itself. A scale of probabilities needs to be developed, based on best information and experience, that estimates the likelihood of winning the contract at various price levels, and then an estimate must be made of the profitability at each of these price levels.

Other strategic factors come into play, such as how badly the exporter needs the business right now, or the likelihood that this tender will lead to other (more profitable) contracts, or the opportunities to sell add-on products such as training or management contracts.

Cost-based pricing will be explored later in this chapter. Suffice it to say here that the true cost of producing goods is often quite elusive, which leads to compromise estimates of cost with an add-on margin considered to give an adequate return on investment whilst covering attributable overheads.

In this text we should not concern ourselves excessively with economic price theories, but concentrate on the practicalities of basic export pricing. Fundamentally, if the potential price you can realize is higher than the measurable costs, then it is worth quoting and seeking business, provided that the product is available and that other more profitable sales opportunities are not being sacrificed. But bear in mind that, where importers or other distributors are part of the distribution chain, you may be looking at two levels of price setting, which are essentially interrelated: the price you will obtain as exporter, and the price your product will command in the foreign market place from the eventual user/consumer.

Some points to consider in arriving at a potential price structure are:

- Establish and tabulate all relevant foreign market data on competitive prices for similar products; this could include weight/value or volume/value comparisons. Your comparison should include both retail (where a product is resold through a distribution network) and wholesale prices.
- Identify and compare competitive wholesale and retail trade margins of profit for each market so that you can ensure that you offer competitive, but not necessarily excessive, margins. If you find your costing would enable you to offer bigger margins and still be price-competitive, then consider using the difference for sales promotional activity rather than offering excessive trade margins.
- Attempt neutrally to assess the consumer-perceived product differentiation attributes of your products versus competitors' in order to establish where in the market price rankings to target your product and meet your sales expectations. For example, if you are selling products perceived as from the top-quality source, you would probably not do yourself justice by pricing to compete at the bottom end of the market. You might achieve higher volume but no more gross profit contribution, or, perhaps, even achieve a lower volume if product purchase is associated with status factors.
- Include adequate margin over your actual production and distribution costs and those of other links in the

distribution chain to cover advertising and promotional expenses, market returns and spoilage allowances, and your distributor's costs of handling, storage and distribution in addition to the expected levels of profit contribution for the distributor, wholesalers and retailers. There may also be local sales taxes to incorporate in the price if these are not separately charged at the point of sale.

We can tabulate a reverse calculation from market sales price to the price you can charge ex-plant as in Table 16.1. Clearly, what your distributor can achieve as a local sales price in his market, less all cost factors and trade margins and less all costs of distribution to ship goods to the foreign market, governs the price you can hope to achieve as your quoted ex-plant price. And this figure, less all your costs of producing and packaging the goods for export, will give a gross margin contribution to your own company. If you are going to compete in international markets and be profitable, then obviously you must arrive at a positive contribution in this reverse calculation. If you show a negative contribution, then you would be exporting at a loss to compete with foreign market sales prices.

Marketing aspects of product pricing

In setting your prices you must work to achieve a balance between what may sometimes appear as conflicting marketing objectives. You will probably have to consider some of the following points in arriving at a pricing policy, and, whilst some considerations will apply to all markets, others may only relate to specific markets.

- What objectives are you pursuing through your export pricing policies?
  - Is the objective to prolong the survival of the company or products when it is faced with (company or industry) over-capacity, high levels of competition, or products that are in the

Table 16.1 *Elements in a pricing calculation*

The example assumes an item packed in cases of ten units per case.

Optimum assessed market price	Per unit	$ 20
	Per case	$200

Less:
– Standard retail distributor's margin (20%)	$40.00	
– Wholesale distributor's margin (10%)[1]	$16.00	
– Main distributor's gross margin (15%)[2]$	$21.60	
– Local advertising and promotion reserve (3%)[3]	$ 4.32	
– Spoilage allowance (1%)[3]	$ 1.44	
– Customs' clearance costs (3% of LDP)[4]	$ 3.39	
– Customs duties (10% of CIF value)	$10.30	
Sub-total	$97.05	
CIF price (foreign currency)		$102.95
CIF price (Sterling)[5]		£ 63.34
Less:	£ 7.00	
– International freight		
– Insurance	£ 1.35	
Exporter's FOB price		£ 55.99
– Domestic distribution costs	£ 3.28	
Ex-factory price		£ 52.71

1 10% of wholesale price of $160
2 15% of importer's price to wholesalers i.e. $144, equals $21.60
3 Based on distributor's selling price of $144
4 Generally estimated by an importer as a percentage (say 3%) of landed duty paid price or a fixed cost per unit imported
5 Exchange rate taken at £1 = $1.50

decline stages of their life cycles (possibly technically obsolete)?

Any price that covers variable costs and makes a positive contribution to fixed costs may be acceptable to the company. Some companies use this approach in export markets whilst trying to maintain an orderly marketing strategy in the domestic market, but this rarely works for long.

– Is the objective to maximize current profit from some or all export markets?

This might be an approach where there is no long term security of access to markets, or where the exporter has a protected position (possible working through a distributor who has access to scarce quota or import licences – if the exporter does not take advantage of the scarcity factor the distributor probably will).

– Is the objective to maximize sales and/or market share into some or all export markets?

In this case profit is less important than volume, and pricing will need to reflect the objectives to ensure the volume is generated.

– Is the objective to 'skim the cream' off an export market, by charging a high price to a limited customer base?

This can be a common approach with new technological developments that have particular industrial applications or consumer benefits.

– Is the objective to establish a market quality leadership position?

In this case competition should not be on price or price alone, but the marketing communications must support the quality image building exercise, so that users/consumers will pay a premium for what is seen as extra value. German household appliance manufacturers have done an excellent job building export markets at premium prices where real and perceived quality are major factors in buying decisions.

- Do you have an export marketing strategy, or are you just pursuing opportunistic openings for exports?
  - Smaller companies, and those that are relatively new to exporting tend to fall into the opportunistic category, but often fail to make the best use of their limited resources by operating in this fashion, and may achieve lower levels of profit from exports than with a clearly defined strategy targeted to a manageable numbers of markets.
  - Is your strategy a marketing strategy aimed at achieving longer-term sales volumes consistent with a market position, or is the sales strategy aimed at getting short-term, marginally costed, high volume sales to fill a production line?

- Where are you aiming to position your product in the export markets, and is price an important factor in the positioning of the product?
  - Is it a luxury consumer product that demands and responds best to a high-price image? Or is it a mass market, disposable item with a less brand-conscious target market?
  - Is it an internationally famous brand, perhaps, with a youthful cult image? Or is it an industrial product used as a component in other manufactured goods?
  - Does it have clearly perceived technological advantages or other factors that differentiate it from competition? Or is it just a regular commodity obtainable on world markets from a variety of sources with few identifiable quality or functional differences?

Price is an essential tool in the overall marketing mix, but only one factor in buying decisions, and there needs to be a

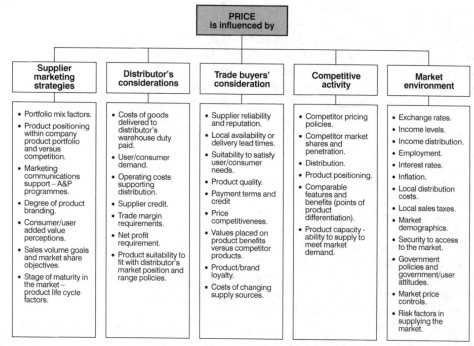

Figure 16.2 Some factors in pricing

high degree of consistency in approach to product market pricing and other aspects of the marketing strategy and programme. Figure 16.2 highlights a number of other key factors that impact on pricing decisions. The marketer must take account of what his marketing goals and objectives are in relation to factors the distributor and trade will consider in taking their decisions, and in relation to the competitive activity and general economic and social environment of the marketplace.

Price in relation to suppliers' marketing strategies

Market price structures may differ according to marketing strategies for each market, and export prices charged to each market need not be the same (although there is always a danger in a discriminatory approach to pricing that consumers or distributors with access to pricing information in other markets, and the means to purchase and import, will look for ways to buy product from cheaper sources).

The factors differentiating products within a product portfolio, or versus competitive products, might be tangible or intangible, depending on the nature of the products and thrust of marketing communication, and consumer/user needs being addressed. The more exclusive features or uses your product has, and the more these features are valued as providing benefits to the users, the greater flexibility you have as the exporter in pricing the product to sell and to yield a positive profit contribution. The closer it is to a commodity-type product, the more the 'market' dictates at any point in time what you may charge. Of course, it is not just enough that the product has value-adding features, built in by the manufacturer, and corresponding benefits; these must be communicated to the trade stockists and the consumers or users through the network of agents or distributors and through the marketing communications.

The level and weight of marketing communications support can affect how a product is priced, firstly in that from a cost perspective the marketing communications costs need to be recovered from sales over the medium to longer term, but also because with higher demand and sales the marketer often has flexibility to raise prices (unless the product is completely price-elastic, when price rises will kill demand) thereby increasing total sales revenues and profits.

The more strongly a product is branded, and the higher the level of brand loyalty, the more flexibility the marketer may have to vary pricing, and possibly the more critical is appropriate price positioning versus other competitive brands. This links with the consumer brand or product perceptions, in that the more favourable the perceptions (whether of source, quality, design, etc.) about value-adding product attributes, the more scope the marketer has to play with price as a marketing mix tool.

Price can play a major factor in achieving sales volume goals and in obtaining distribution through trade channels, as well as in contributing to achieving market share goals. So appropriate pricing structures and price positioning in the market (through distributors and trade dealers) are critical where goals are defined that are dependent on pricing strategies.

The exporter may need to consider the stage of the product in its market life cycle for each export market when developing pricing policies. Typically prices can be moved higher when a product is facing high demand (and possibly less competition) in the growth stages of its life cycle, very noticeable with high technology products (e.g. as when a new computer model is launched). A mature product may prove to be more price sensitive as a broader range of competitive or substitute products is available.

Price in relation to distributors' considerations

For direct sales or sales through agents, in-depth knowledge of the competitive market-place, the buyer and his purchase motivations and objectives, and the points of competitive advantage in your own products will help reduce the risk on underselling and achieving lower prices than the products could command.

When selling through distributors the exporter needs to control the market price positioning versus competitors' products. Many exporters have little or no knowledge of the standard margins their distributors expect to make, the local costing structures of gaining and obtaining distribution, or the customary trade dealer margins.

The distributor, in assessing demand and sales potential may not take account of the entire market, but only that part he services: many exporters have found that distributors have limited product growth by limiting distribution, sometimes turning a relatively ordinary product into a locally exclusive item that pushes local market prices up (to no benefit to the exporter).

Distributors tend to be very cost conscious. They will look closely at the product support needs, including direct selling effort and associated costs, physical distribution, merchandising for retail consumer products, after-sales service needs for technical products, and so on, and then consider just how much effort to put behind any single product in relation to how they can price it and what they expect to earn from it. As much of their thinking is concerned with short-term factors rather than investment in the future, they frequently avoid incurring costs (of distribution or product support) that will not show a return in the current year, and therefore often limit sales, service and distribution activity, looking to spread the costs of each of these over a broader product portfolio.

Supplier credit has a major influence on distributor decisions as to what products to order and promote. They typically try to minimize their personal investment and their risk associated with distribution, being reluctant to invest adequately in stock, and also to extend trade credit to a broad network of customers. Hence, all too frequently a supplier who studies trade channel distribution finds that his distributors and sub-distributors actually supply only a small proportion of potential trade channel customers or users, basically limiting distribution to those lower risk outlets.

Some distributors are reluctant to supply to sub-distributors or trade dealers, because they do not want to share the overall profit margin with another tier of distribution, in turn limiting sales. If an after-sales service operation supports the products, the more limited sales and distribution can have the effect of increasing the servicing costs per user, again acting as a negative to expanding sales. Where sales are made through sub-distributors then the export marketer should satisfy himself that margins allowed are in line with customary trade practice, to ensure a motivated dealer network.

Of course the distributor will be very sensitive to the margins he needs, but often tends to think of margins only in percentage of sales terms, rather than absolute levels of earnings, often being reluctant to accept a lower percentage margin to generate higher volume, producing more total revenue and profit. Some distributors have the attitude that they see no point in simply selling more volume (and incurring more sales and distribution costs) for little profit benefit, reflecting a common problem that they are less motivated by volume and market share than profit.

If a product is to gain support within a distributor's organization it normally needs to fit well the rest of his product portfolio, otherwise it will be neglected (possibly with potential customers not even being visited). If there is not a natural fit, and gaining distribution is seen as more of a hassle and cost, then this is likely to be reflected in the approach to pricing the product, again impacting on sales.

So the export marketer, attempting to build a market according to a marketing strategy plan, often starts with the problems of balancing the needs and pricing and profit considerations of the distributor with a whole network of other strategic and distribution considerations.

Trade buyers' considerations _____

Trade channel buyers (other than the exclusive importer or distributor) have a strong influence on the ability of suppliers to obtain distribution, as well as on final prices (price positioning) to be paid by consumers or users through the margins they include in their local pricing structures. These channels are not normally under the control or influence of the supplier, unless part of a tied distributor network, such as a franchise network. As they are not tied to the supplier, and have little if any loyalty to any of their suppliers of competing products, they are frequently influenced by factors such as:

- The reputation and reliability of the supplier and his products, and the enhancement of their personal credibility in stocking a particular supplier's products.
- Assured local availability at all times, ex-stock from the main distributor's warehouse, minimizing the capital tied up in inventories of a supplier's products.
- The match of the product profile with the needs and profile of their own customer group (retailers particularly tend to have more defined target customers nowadays than two decades ago, and also develop distinctive marketing strategies to differentiate their product and service offer from their competitors).
- Quality of the product and relative value in relation to competitive products.
- Payment and credit terms offered from the local distributor.
- Price competitiveness at the trade level, assuring trade channel dealers of fair margins, as well as price competitiveness at the resale level, offering their customers good value.
- Their own valuation of the particular differentiating benefits a supplier's products offer versus competitive products.

- The costs of changing supply sources (for example, if they have servicing expertise in the product, or supply it as part of an integrated product offer, ceasing taking supplies from one source may increase their short term costs, possibly including costs of re-training their staff in new products).

Price in relation to competitive activity

Competitors' pricing structures and policies, obviously, can influence the market pricing of an exporter's products. A competitor with advantageous cost structures might use this advantage to undermine an exporter's efforts to market in an orderly fashion, using price cutting tactics to disrupt marketing efforts. The export marketer must take account of both the competitors' current pricing and likely reactions to the exporter's products and prices.

Where competitors have strong market share positions and broad market penetration and distribution, the export marketer will have to take account of this in planning pricing and distribution policies. Alternatives might range from aiming at a niche market with higher prices, to going for a broader market at lower prices, and decisions will be influenced by a range of factors including longer term goals and product availability.

If some or all distribution channels are controlled by competitors, then that poses another problem for the exporter, who will have problems gaining distribution and penetration. That may mean forming associations with competitors, particularly filling gaps in their product portfolio, but the exporter will probably lose control over market pricing.

The export marketer needs to know his competitors' products as well as he knows his own if he is to take advantage of any pricing opportunities to position products against competitor products and obtain extra price benefit from additional value-adding product features and benefits.

Competitive product availability is a factor to consider: are there many producers of similar products or just a few? What spare production capacities do your competitors have to compete with you for exports? If you have few competitors with limited spare capacity, they may be less aggressive in exporting, enabling you to obtain better prices.

Price in relation to the market environment

The general **market environment** in each export market can also affect the exporter's pricing policies. A number of demographic, economic and legislative factors can affect pricing decisions.

- The impact of exchange rate movements on your export prices and the knock-on effect on market prices (distributors rarely voluntarily reduce prices when exchange rate movements favour them, but rapidly increase prices when adverse movements push up their landed costs).
- Levels of income, distribution of income, and other economic factors such as employment levels in the various export markets may influence product pricing decisions, perhaps depending to the extent that product demand is price-elastic, or the need to maintain volume during the down-turn or economic cycles.
- Export market interest rates, which can affect pricing decisions, as tactical opportunities can arise from either high or low interest rates (low rates might encourage sales through local access to credit, high rates might discourage sales but provide an advantage to an exporter who can provide extended credit).
- Inflation in foreign markets, which can also impact on pricing decisions, as high inflation might affect demand and encourage tactics to maintain sales, or, conversely, provide an opportunity to move prices upwards.
- Other local cost factors, such as distribution costs and local sales taxes,

both of which can affect demand and distribution.
- Demographic characteristics that impact on sales potential or distribution infrastructure needs.
- Stage of development of the market for your products.
- Security of access to market (there may be little point spending heavily on marketing communications and building market share through price discounting if importation is likely to be restricted)
- Local competition with similar or substitute products, which can influence the strategies and pricing structures the exporter elects to pursue.
- Government policies and attitudes, in that certain product categories attract attention for various reasons (for example, health and safety factors), and sometimes the product source can be a focus of attention, or the local authorities may have views on the pricing of certain product categories (sometimes recommending trade and retail price structures within a price control policy that the exporter must ensure his distributors comply with).
- There is higher risk in supplying some markets than others, and this needs to be considered in export pricing. The risk may be political, or financial. The risk may be insurable, in which case the insurance cost can be assessed and included in the price. If the risk is not insurable the exporter must then judge what premium to include in export pricing to high-risk markets.

The exporter needs to be sensitive to the disruptions frequent price changes can cause to the overall marketing strategy. In domestic marketing price is often varied for promotional reasons, usually in the form of special offer reductions. In international markets cut-price offers to importers or distributors may simply not be passed on to the consumers, and not produce the desired increase in product trial and brand awareness, or expected increases in volume sales.

It is wrong to assume that all markets are the same, and that buyers will react similarly to marketing in each market. Products are likely to be at different stages of the product life cycle in different markets. A product that is a basic item in one market might be a luxury in another market that is at a less advanced economically. Pricing policies should therefore take account for each market of the stage of the product in its life cycle in relation to the development of the market for the product.

Your policy to market pricing is also likely to be affected by the security of access to a market. Where you have continuity of access, and can make serious market development plans then it is a common approach to make serious decisions about price in relation to market positioning. But if access is seen as temporary, or in any event insecure, then the alternatives may be to sell at lower prices to achieve volume (if spare capacity exists), or to sell expensively (if buyers are willing to pay the premium) to milk the market for maximum profits in the short term. Another consideration in such situations is whether the exporter will be facing competition: for example, if product importation is subject to licence or quota, and the basis of licence or quota issue (perhaps by country of origin, or on a historical basis to a particularly friendly importer, or for a finite amount of goods by volume or value) enables the exporter to have a special advantage over competitors to supply the market needs, then price may be less of a factor and opportunities arise for higher margin sales than might otherwise accrue.

As a general rule, most international marketers and their foreign importers, distributors or direct customers prefer a good degree of export price stability to facilitate planning (in part because of the often longer lead times required to obtain competitive price and product information, and the risk of other price-disruptive changes such as those caused by fluctuating exchange rates).

Elements of price and buyer perceptions in relation to price

Export marketers need to be familiar with the principle that real and perceived values in a product can influence pricing decisions in export markets, just as they do in domestic markets. The model in Figure 16.3 illustrates various points on a price spectrum related to values the consumer sees in a product.

The various input costs total to give the basic product cost, which with scale economies may approach the long run marginal cost. Somewhere above this production cost will be the basic commodity price users or consumers would be willing to pay for an undifferentiated product. The commodity value of many products is often only small percentage margin above the cost (if it was lower then producers would cease or reduce production). The basic profit margin is shown to reflect the difference between the cost of production and the commodity price.

Most products can be sold at a higher margin as product differentiation attributes would value a product in consumer perceptions at higher than its commodity price. The market price may then be set by the supplier according to his marketing objectives and strategy. This additional margin can be termed the 'value in use' margin.

Where users/consumers place a higher value on a product than the market price, perhaps as a result of scarcity resulting from import restrictions, a black market or unofficial market (outside normal trade channels) may develop in a product, goods changing hands at more than the normal trade prices. In that case the black marketeers take the surplus margin to themselves. Where consumers buy at the market price but would be willing to pay a higher price, because they see personal benefits (perhaps not common to all users or consumers) that makes the product worth more to them, it is they who would benefit from what is termed the 'consumer surplus'.

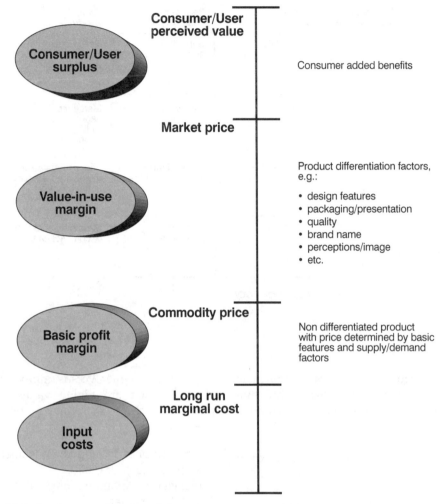

Figure 16.3 *A price spectrum model*

Where marketers recognize that there is a higher consumer perceived value in any export market than the market price this may present an opportunity to:

- increase price, taking some of the consumer surplus into the company as additional profit contribution, or to
- use price to boost penetration/consumption and sector share against competitors.

Price mapping

The previous section focuses attention on the point that the price a consumer/user

will pay for a product has little to do with a manufacturer's costs, but has a lot to do with perceptions of value in the product. The more value-added features differentiate the product from competitive products the higher price consumers/users will place on the product. A simplistic illustrative price map follows in Figure 16.4.

Exporters should prepare **price maps** for their own products in relation to competition for each foreign market (and this should be included in the annual plan for the market), with account of the value-added features/benefits (real or perceived) in each product. Usually there will be several clearly distinctive price brackets for most

Typical value-added differentiation features	Price range	Segment description	Typical products
• Hand built • High performance • Limited supply (scarcity value) – exclusive	> $100,000	Super-luxury and speciality cars	Rolls Royce Ferrari Aston Martin etc.
• Superior accessories • Lower depreciation • Quality build • Status	$60,000	Luxury cars	Mercedes Jaguar BMW Saab
• Comfort/status • Performance/power • Lots of accessories	$30,000	Larger saloons and performance cars	Those models from major suppliers aimed at the business executive market
• Economy • No frills • Reliable	< $20,000	Family small saloons, etc.	Mass market ranges of compact cars

Figure 16.4 A simple product price map: cars in the USA

product categories, representing the main product groupings of varieties with a similar mix of features and value-added benefits.

Decisions on market prices for each export market should be conscious marketing decisions under the influence and control of the exporter supplier rather than situations that arise under the control of agents and distributors.

Pricing questions and the marketer

The foregoing discussion leaves the export marketer posed with the following key questions:

- to what extent does the consumer in export markets see added value in your products?
- how important are the value-added attributes/benefits in the purchasing decision?
- what price value does the consumer put on your value-added attributes/benefits versus your competitors' products?

If you score higher versus competitors on attributes that are highly valued in the purchase decision, there may be opportunities to:

- increase price to mop up consumer surplus into your profit
- maintain price and go for greater penetration/share

If you product scores below competitors on attributes valued highly by consumers in the purchase decision, the problem may be:

- poor marketing communications taking the messages to consumers, needing review and corrective action
- lack of important value-added benefits, needing an improvement either of the product to include the desired attributes/benefits or a re-positioning of which benefits feature strongly in marketing communications

With all the variables to be considered in export pricing, you are justified in concluding that there can be no hard and fast rules or formulas for arriving at an export price. International marketers seeking business opportunities will sharpen their business disciplines and training by exposure to the procedures and processes of product costing. The time when you have to make most of your critical decisions relevant to any export deal is often when you are far away from the home office in a foreign market, unable to walk into a colleague's office to discuss the merits of the transaction under review. To make such decisions competently, you need an unusually thorough knowledge of your company, its products and all the variable factors that affect costing and pricing; and your best friend back at the home office is likely to be your cost accountant.

Exchange rate variations and price

The pricing exercise is ongoing. Changes in relative exchange rates between the home and international market will necessitate regular review. If your home currency strengthens relative to the importer's currency, yet foreign market prices are not rising, you may have to consider dropping your export price in home currency terms to remain competitive. However, if your currency becomes relatively weaker, you may be able to increase prices. Importers often take the position that they, not you, should reap the benefit of windfall gains if your currency weakens, but they rarely consider that they should take the loss in contribution if your currency strengthens, seeing the only alternative as a local price increase. Variations either way in exchange rates seem to produce demands from importers for adjustments favourable to themselves in either their cost prices or their margins and resale prices.

Many larger manufacturers avoid this potential source of conflict with their distributors and importers by quoting their ex-plant, FOB or CIF sales prices in the foreign currency and taking the currency risks themselves. In practice, the finance division will normally reduce that risk by selling the foreign currency forward as soon as a contract is exchanged and there is some certainty about when the foreign funds will be received. However, the finance department may be reluctant to get involved in pricing in foreign currencies and forward exchange dealing, taking the position that the costings are all done in the domestic currency and that it is essential to ensure a predictable profit contribution by being consistent in costing and pricing goods or services in the same currency. But that risk avoidance approach might be seen by international marketers as the tail wagging the dog!

Within the European Union more and more exporters are now opening ECU accounts, and developing costing structures that enable them to quote in ECUs. This does mean that the importers are clear on their product costs, and may make for an orderly market pricing structure. The exporter is also clear on what he will receive. The use of the ECU in trade will grow rapidly in coming years, at the expense of national currencies.

Government agencies sometimes promote the theoretically correct view that if they devalue the currency in relation to those of major trading partners exports will rise rapidly, and improve an adverse balance of payments situation. That approach fails to recognize the inherent slowness of markets in responding to many price-changing factors: buyers are likely already to have forward orders covering anticipated stock needs; and, whilst international demand may rise, it will normally take some time for supply output to rise to meet the new demand (production capacity may need to be increased).

Distributor reports

To assist you in studying competitive imports, which generally bear a direct relation to market sales, and movements in CIF values, which, in turn, may indicate likely market price adjustments, your importer should be requested to provide you with monthly reports on competitive pricing and promotional activities, including analysis of the local market customs reports showing volumes and values of imports of similar products from the alternative sources supplying the market.

Successful exporting involves considerable desk work in preparing and analysing data, including those relating to costings and prices, and planning and monitoring market activities. You may never develop as much expertise in your markets as your distributors, but you should certainly aim to have a thorough and up-to-date understanding of the mechanisms and magnitudes of trade in the market in order to present a professional image and to contribute to and manage market development. If you prepare market analyses on data supplied by your agents and distributors or other sources, then, in general, it is a courtesy to send a copy of your studies to your foreign representative, or to take the data with you for discussion on your next visit.

Export price lists

Once you have decided the price at which you wish to offer your products to your foreign customers, the next stage is to produce a formal price list. This should contain the following basic data:

- product names and/or descriptions and reference codes
- product variants
- pack sizes
- number of units per shipping carton
- package weights and dimensions
- price quote per unit to point of exchange of ownership (e.g. ex-plant, FAS, FOB port of exit, CFR destination, etc.)
- terms of sale, payment terms and conditions, insurance coverage
- warranties or exclusions
- period of validity of quotation (or date of price list issue).

You may need to include additional information particular to your company or products. When developing export terms of sale it is useful to bear in mind that just to take the domestic terms of sales is not ideal, and might subsequently prove problematic. Warranty conditions may vary for export markets, and different conditions may apply to ownership transfer, goods damaged in transit, payment, and so on, depending on the terms of sale. It is common for the goods to be sold under **Incoterms,** (an abbreviation for *International Rules for the Interpretation of Trade Terms*), and for this condition to be referred to in the seller's export terms of trade in order that buyers are clear on this point. Points of ownership transfer are commented on later in this chapter.

When you have prepared your draft price list, it is well worth passing it to colleagues in another department for their comments on the understandability of the document. If they find it too confusing, then the chances are that your non-English-speaking customers will find it equally or more difficult to interpret.

If your products do not lend themselves to formal price lists, possibly because of their commodity nature or because they are being exclusively produced for a customer, you may have to do individual costing and pricing exercises for each separate transaction or quote. In some markets it is the custom to haggle over prices and the exporter may expect to offer discounts or reductions to close a sale.

Price-controlled imports

Many developing countries have strict regulations governing the permissible retail prices for basic commodities and foodstuffs, such as bread, rice, flour and other staples. If your product is a controlled item, you need to establish if it will land and sell within the price control limits and still give the customary trade margins. It may be that all controlled items can be purchased and imported only by a specific government agency (or nominated importer).

Costing considerations ▰▰▰▰▰

Costing products is an independent exercise from pricing. The marketer will be aware that an approach to pricing which makes prices solely dependent on cost could result in poor product positioning in relation to competitive products (where the exporter faced higher total costs than competitors or required greater margins than competitive pricing might allow). Uncompetitive pricing (when all points of product differentiation and taken account of) is likely to reduce sales volumes below the level correct price positioning would generate.

That said, there are a number of specific export costs that must be included in any costing exercise, such as:

● special packaging
● additional quality control
● product specification or formulation modifications

● export administration and documentation
● financing for goods in store or transit prior to payment being received
● importer/distributor training
● customer technical support and training, and other customer service support
● allowances for the cost of the international sales department (including direct selling, sales commissions to agents, etc.)
● export marketing communications and sales promotion costs, including advertising, exhibitions, trade and consumer promotions, etc.).

Figure 16.5 illustrates how a typical costing structure is developed. Fixed costs are apportioned across the range of products according to some acceptable formula, which might relate to each product's share of turnover or other relevant criteria. Variable costs, those specific only to the actual

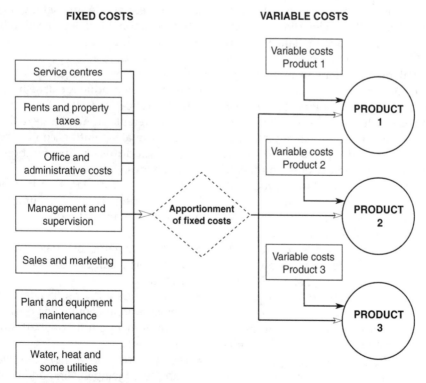

FIXED COSTS **VARIABLE COSTS**

Figure 16.5 Development of a costing structure

production of a product, can be attributed directly to the particular product.

The two main approaches to costing are normally termed **standard costing** and **marginal costing**.

Standard costing

Companies normally produce an annual budget that makes assumptions about market prices, sales volumes, production costs, overheads, marketing costs, distribution costs and so on, with the usual outcome that a system of standard costing results.

Standard costing is a system of cost accounting which makes use of pre-determined standard costs or cost estimates relating to each element of inputs for each product manufactured or service offered. Actual costs are compared with the standard costs for each time period, and adjustments might be made to the standard costs for future budgeting or planning periods where appropriate, and variances from standard costs are noted. The purpose of monitoring the variances from standard costs is so that inefficiencies can be identified and corrective action taken where appropriate or possible, otherwise there will be resultant variations in margins and profit contributions.

The cost accountant looking to establish standard costs will analyse each element of input in the categories of labour, material and overheads, and spread these costs across the planned production volume to give a standard cost per unit to be produced. Standard costs only reflect what the costs *should* be, based upon stated conditions and anticipated sales volumes. If conditions or volumes change, then the standard costs will also change. From the accountant's perspective, monitoring basic standard costs are useful in highlighting trends in prices, input costs or wage rates.

Even standard costing may not be so simple or definitive of the costs of producing and marketing a product, as there may be several forms of standard costing to consider. **Ideal standard costs** might be calculated on the assumption of one hundred per cent efficiency of all plant and equipment and labour inputs. As this level of efficiency is rarely achieved, **expected standard costs** can reflect the actual conditions prevailing within any plant, and there may be wide variations in the production of the same product produced in several plants within the same group of companies. The **basic standard cost**, which might be based on the ideal or expected or historical cost structure in a single production unit, or on an assessment of the average position across several production units, is often used as a basis for comparison with actual costs and in trend analysis.

In setting standard costs, when assessing direct material input costs, allowance is usually made for normal levels of waste. Assessment of direct labour costs frequently involves time and motion studies, the establishing of production **best practices**, and staff training to ensure work is performed in a prescribed fashion. All overhead costs (e.g. distribution, warehousing, research, personnel, engineering, design, selling, marketing, administration, legal, etc.) need to be identified and allocated across the scheduled production volume.

Consideration needs to be given to any limitations on production or selling capacity. The theoretical capacity of a plant is often quite different from the actual capacity under normal operating conditions, which might include downtime for breakdowns, shift changes, etc.

Standard costing has the advantages over just monitoring actual costs (after the events of production and sale) of:

- providing a yardstick against which actual costs can be monitored and measured
- highlighting variances (in costs and resultant profit contributions) which may result from long-term or short-term inefficiencies
- reducing the clerical work associated with the ongoing costing and cost control exercises

- providing a basis for management reporting
- highlighting areas for improvement in skills and the use and efficiency or resources
- providing a basis for product pricing that allows estimates to be made of expected profitability at any price level (and helps in formulating marketing price strategies).

These standard costs may often be used as the basis for export costing and pricing. They may be built up to include expected margins, giving a return on assets employed in the production of the products.

In some companies, price results from a serious attempt to attach a consumer or user value to the products (**market forces pricing**). But, as has been indicated in the earlier section 'Approaches to product pricing', frequently variations are adopted such as **target pricing** based on known cost factors, where target prices are set by the marketing department and compared with the costing figures and the product is deliberately positioned in relation to competitors in the market place, or **cost-plus** pricing where a margin is added to cost estimates aimed at giving a certain level of return (as a percentage of costs, sales revenues, or on assets employed in the business).

Another approach and variation on cost-plus pricing is simply to add a set percentage to standard product costs (including overheads, fixed and variable costs). Where the same percentage margin is added to all products within a portfolio this fails to reflect any differences in the consumer values placed upon the different products – some might have higher value-added benefits than others, commanding relatively higher margins for the supplier, or vice versa.

There are some situations where standard costing is not very suitable or practical, where no two products are alike, each provision of goods or services being a stand-alone project. **Full costing** might be an alternative then, where each input element

to the project is carefully assessed and its full actual cost calculated and included. But even in such cases there do tend to be a range of inputs, particularly various central overheads, where accurate cost calculations are hard to make, and a standard cost element is included.

Both target pricing and cost-plus pricing, based on company systems of full or standard costing, are common practice in international as well as domestic markets. However, in international marketing we often find that the export costings are uplifted to include factors that are specific to export without a corresponding removal of factors specific to domestic marketing. In order to help encourage the international marketer to be sensitive to what is or should be included in export costings, without attempting to turn them into a cost accountant, the next section provides some discussion of marginal costing as applicable to exporting.

Marginal costing

Marginal costing is often talked of by exporters as the answer when they are told their prices are not competitive prices, but are rarely implemented in practice (in part because it is usually difficult to pin down a company cost accountant to a definitive marginal cost figure).

Marginal costing normally follows the basic principle that not all fixed and overhead costs are attributed to products, down to the point where a fully marginally costed unit requires inclusion only of the variable cost of inputs such as materials, packaging, additional labour or utilities, and specific handling, storage and distribution costs. True marginal costing, i.e. inclusion only of variable costs directly related to the production of specific product units, is rarely practised.

Normally the accountants will work from standard costs or actual costs, and remove some of the fixed costs until a figure is reached that enables the sales contract to be concluded on a basis that shows an acceptable profit contribution.

Table 16.2 *Typical fixed and variable cost factors*

Typical variable cost factors
- Indirect labour*
- Direct labour*
- Overtime premiums
- Lost time
- Factory supplies
- Extra shifts
- Repairs and maintenance*
- Utilities (power and light)*
- Insurance on goods in production/store
- Stock financing
- Packaging materials
- Raw materials
- Spoilage
- Export distribution costs
- Export documentation costs

Typical fixed cost factors
- Office and administration overheads (including clerical)
- Subscriptions
- Production management and quality control supervision
- Rent
- Property taxes
- Basic insurances
- Research and development
- Certain utilities (phone, water, heat, etc.)*
- Standard plant and equipment maintenance*
- Sales and marketing costs
- Depreciation

*Some of the items may justifiably be treated by your accountants in either category, or as semi-variable, depending on particular company practices.

Where there are economies of scale in production then the cost of additional production units will be less than for previously produced units, in which case the long-run marginal costs may be significantly below the standard costs in a plant operating well below its capacity. Table 16.2 illustrates a typical split between fixed and variable cost factors.

If we consider further the possible role of marginal costing in international marketing, the typical company produces an annual sales and production plan and related budgets, which will aim to recover all basic costs of production and overheads over the volume of output and sales in the plan plus a margin for profit. The plan will have made specific assumptions on costs of raw materials, utilities, labour and production, distribution, marketing, general and office overheads, and so on. The standard costs will normally have been calculated on the basis of the forecast levels of production and sales, and the assumptions on costs.

The company's annual plan may have included some international sales volume. Any additional sales (over that included in the annual plan or budgets) volume may have the effect of both spreading the budgeted costs over larger output and possibly enabling actual cost per unit to drop, for example by buying larger volumes of ingredients or packaging material. Therefore, any additional margin over and above identifiable variable costs of additional goods produced for export is an extra profit contribution for the company.

You will find that an exact analysis of your true marginal cost is a frustrating study of an elusive figure, because there can be so many variables, the effect of which may not be accurately assessed in advance by your cost accountant. If you have a serious prospective export enquiry, your responsibility to the company is to negotiate the highest possible price at which you can secure the order; at the same time you should be liaising with the cost accountant to establish at what price the order is acceptably profitable. Accountants tend by nature to be more conservative than the sales personnel, and you may be amazed at how they will change their position daily – not because they are being obstructive, but because they know there are so many variables in marginal costing that a price unacceptable one week (say when the plants are running at full capacity) may be acceptable in a week when production capacity is not fully utilized.

In preparing your export costings, it will be helpful if you start at the initial planning stage by persuading your company cost accountant to identify all the fixed and variable costs separately when budgets are being prepared. Table 16.2 illustrates some typical elements of costings that may be considered as fixed or variable costs. The export manager usually has to be much more familiar with the construction and elements of product costings in his company than the home market sales manager. Generally, the accountant will be using a standard costing system for inputs and, as previously mentioned, it may be found that additional sales volumes result in lower unit costs of some inputs through increased volume usage or buying power.

Your basic aim is to reach a clear decision on whether or not to accept sales at a certain price level. The two principal steps, in summary, are:

(1) identification of the marginal cost of producing those extra units you wish to contract to sell in international markets
(2) arranging the product costing in a format that enables you to make an estimate of the profit contribution from this contract (based either on standard costing or a marginal costing basis, whichever is considered appropriate to the supply of the particular goods or services).

Bear in mind that you have a sound position for considering goods already in store or in production as marginally costed if you have the production capacity to replace them at the time they are needed for delivery elsewhere, and if they are already in exportable form (i.e. no special modifications are needed except for those that you can charge to the customer in your quotation). If modifications are needed, then that element may be marginally costed unless it really is impossible to make the modifications beyond a certain point in the production process.

Where you treat each export activity as a stand-alone project, or even where you can measure export costs and profit performance over a set time period, it can be useful to develop a profit and loss tabulation, as per Table 16.3.

Your profit estimate, or gross contribution, may be calculated simply by preparing a tabulation showing the gross sales revenue less all the marginal costs of production and specific additional costs in completing the order for export. Table 16.3 also shows a net profit, where fixed costs have been apportioned to the project. With ongoing shipments of consumer goods, it is often not seen as a worthwhile exercise to attempt a profit estimate on each transaction, but it is beneficial in the case of commodity transactions or industrial product contracts such as supplying components or capital equipment.

Another point to consider when seeking to exclude those costs you consider fixed is that in some businesses the fixed costs per unit will vary month by month if they are

Table 16.3 *Export project marginal profit and loss account*

QUARTER 3	£	£	£
Gross revenue from sales (10,000 units)			110,000
Less marginal cost of goods sold:			
Direct raw materials (£4.10 per unit)	41,000		
Direct labour (£1.00 per unit)	10,000	51,000	
Variable expenses			
Indirect labour	5,000		
Factory supplies	1,500		
Utilities	1,000		
Packaging supplies	3,500		
Storage	500		
Insurance	100		
Special quality control	200		
Spoilage/wastage	500		
Financing	1,500		
Distribution	2,000		
Repairs and maintenance	600	16,400	67,400
Contribution			42,600
Less fixed costs Quarter 3			
Export documentation		800	
Export marketing and selling		2,000	
Management and supervision		8,000	
Rent and rates		9,000	
Administrative and clerical		6,600	
Insurance		1,100	
Heat, light, power		1,300	28,800
Net profit (before tax)			13,800

treated as occurring at a point in time, yet production volumes are not the same in each month. There may be significant seasonal variations in production, and you may work with your cost accountant to assess seasonal cost factors to consider in the marginal costing process.

Marginal costs may similarly vary month by month – for example, where you are using as production inputs one or more commodities that fluctuate in price frequently, and where either you do not have longer-term contracts or your costs of replacing the commodities for regular production would be different. This is particularly likely to be the case if you have a significant proportion of an agriculturally based commodity (such as cocoa, sugar, milk or grain products) or certain metals (such as copper, gold, silver). The standard cost used by your accountant may differ up or down from the replacement cost if you have booked only commodity cover to meet the initial production plan. When you have a situation where one or more basic commodities traded freely on world markets are a major input and cost factor, then you must be extremely sharp in assessing when you may be competitive and book contracts for export deliveries. There may be seasonal swings, typical with many agricultural products, when customers look for the best deals either from the northern or southern hemisphere, and take advantage of the lower seasonal production costs.

When standard products are being produced on mass production lines, there is usually little if any variation in production or input costs from month to month; hence, the marginal cost may vary little, particularly if input supplies are well covered under medium- or longer-term contracts that reduce the effect of seasonal price variations.

The cost-plus approach to export costing and pricing

The common approach to export costing and pricing of building a cost structure to produce an ex-factory or FOB figure and then adding various margins to cover each tier in the distribution channels is illustrated in Table 16.4.

This example starts from an ex-factory price supplied to the export marketer, who then builds it up to a final retail price, based upon established distribution costs and normal trade margins for each tier in the distribution chain. The example is assuming we are shipping a consumer product, packed twelve units to a shipping case, into a market where the currency unit is of very low unit value, typical in a number of developing countries facing high inflation, etc.

By working up from an ex-factory price, allowing for the various subsequent costs and margins, we would arrive at a retail price for this product of $$4111 per unit. As the footnote indicates, this figure is unlikely to be a realistic price in a market where the currency is of low unit value. Retailers would normally round up to a convenient level to suit the local coinage or currency notes, in this case probably to $$4250 per unit. The extra margin would normally go to the retailer, who will neither sell more volume nor thank your local distributor for the extra profit per unit. In fact the product might even be wrongly price positioned in relation to competitive products!

If the marketer had recognized this situation it might be argued he should have seen where the forward cost-plus approach would take him, in this case to $$4111 per unit, and then take a marketing position to aim at a target retail price of either $$4000 or $$4250 per unit.

If you make a reverse calculation, working back from the likely alternative retail price levels, and assuming the same percentage margins at each level of the trade and for import duties and taxes (but, for simplicity, take the same clearing costs), then if you target at a retail price of $4000 your ex-factory price would reduce to approximately £22.20 (minus 3.5%), and at a retail level of $$4250 you could raise your ex-factory price to almost £24.00 (plus 4.3%). The percentage change in the ex-factory price in either case might seem small, at around 4 per cent, but this could make quite a difference to your profit contribution. If you want to target at $$4000 retail per unit then it is likely that you, the exporter, would have to adjust your price since rarely will distribution channels reduce their margins. If you target at the $$4250 price level and do not raise your own prices, then you will receive no extra thanks or sales effort from the various distribution channels that will simply mop up the surplus margin to their benefit, whereas by raising your price you have the flexibility to take a higher margin or devote additional resources to the marketing effort.

Hence, whilst this cost-plus approach to constructing export market pricing schedules is perhaps the most simple and commonly used approach, it can have drawbacks from the perspective of product price positioning and control within the foreign markets.

In your role as international marketer building a business in a tough and competitive environment you will not just be facing competition from two or three domestic manufacturers who, in the home market, coincidentally seem to have very similar prices. You have to compete head-on with

Table 16.4 *Cost-plus approach to pricing*

Ex-factory cost per case (12 units)	£23.00	
Export documentation and inland distribution	£ 2.37	
FOB UK port		£25.37
Freight and insurance	£ 2.54	
CIF foreign destination port		£27.91
CIF foreign currency (@ $$560 = £1)[1]		$$15629
Import duties, taxes, customs and excise, etc.	$$16723	
(duty at 80% CIF, other taxes at 15% of duty paid figure)		
Other clearing costs	$$ 1348	
Landed duty-paid distributor's warehouse		$$33700
Distributor's standard margin (18% on sales value)	$$ 7398	
Covering normal distribution costs of:		
● Sales and marketing		
● Distribution		
● Central overheads		
● Local promotional activity		
● Profit contribution		$$41098
Ex-distributor's price to wholesalers		
Wholesaler margin (6.4%)	$$ 2810	
Wholesaler's price/cost to retail		$$43908
Retailer margin (11%)	$$ 5427	
Standard recommended retail case		$$49335
Standard retail price per unit (12 units per case)		**$$ 4111**[2]

[1] The $$ symbol is not representative of US dollars, or any specific currency, but of a currency with low unit value in relation to sterling.
[2] The marketer will question whether the theoretically calculated retail price of $$4111 will be applied or whether it will be adjusted by retailers to the nearest local price point (e.g. $$4250), with the retailer taking the extra margin.

the major suppliers from many other nations, all seeking to enter new international markets, possibly with marginally costed products, and many of them having very different cost structures from yours.

However, in summarizing this section, the exporter should seriously consider taking a contract if:

● the price covers the marginal cost of production and distribution and any costs specifically and identifiably related to the export order
● if there is an identifiable gross margin between price and marginal costs.

At this point it is worth considering a few issues where the pricing of exports may

prove very significant to the manner in which you conduct business and the resultant sales achievements.

Parallel exports and imports ■━━

Where products are being exported by parties other than the manufacturer (such as export traders), then you have a situation generally referred to as '**parallel exports**', or even 'grey' market trade.

Sharp exporters sometimes find that they can buy a manufacturer's home product cheaper through discount wholesale outlets in the home market, especially when sales promotions are in effect, and offer these goods to importers other than the manufacturer's exclusive representative in the foreign market. The independent exporter probably has lower overheads than the manufacturer and generally sells against letter of credit, thereby avoiding the export financing costs the manufacturer may have. In addition, while the home market goods may bear an element of home market sales, promotional and distribution costs, this may be minimal during the discount promotion. The goods offered for export by the independent exporter may also be, and frequently are, in different packaging or sizes from those directly exported by the manufacturer, as the goods were clearly not produced specifically for export. They may also not comply fully with the labelling and ingredient laws of the foreign country to which they are subsequently shipped.

Similarly, where an exporter operates differential pricing policies between markets, situations may arise where customers in one foreign market can buy and import through sources in neighbouring markets more cheaply than buying through the exporter's official local distribution channels.

The net effect of parallel trade is to add a disrupting factor to the international strategy and markets the manufacturer is trying to develop, and manufacturers may find their credibility reduced both with their foreign importer and with the customers in that market. Official importers may find themselves held responsible for an incorrectly packaged and unapproved product that they have not imported, and may have some difficulty in identifying the true parallel importer because customers will frequently not disclose product sources if they are knowingly trading in parallel imports.

Manufacturers and their official sole importers may find that they have no legal recourse to prevent parallel trade, although some countries now will provide a degree of protection in recognition of exclusive distribution agreements. Local chambers of commerce and other trade associations often seek such protection on behalf of their members, who tend to be the more ethical companies in the market.

The parallel importer will also be benefiting from any advertising and promotional activity organized by the principal and official importer, yet the unofficial imports are unlikely to include any costing allowance contributing to the promotional funds. The official importer is certainly not going to pay a contribution (if one was due on their official imports) on imports not shipped through their company, even if such parallel imports could be accurately quantified.

A barrier to parallel trade exists where the importing country has specific laws relating to packaging and labelling, unit sizes, ingredient declarations and inclusion on labels of product registration details or names and addresses of importers. However, these really are only a practical barrier to trade with consumer products, and then only when the sales outlet, such as a retail store, in addition to the importer, is held liable for products sold in non-compliance with all regulations. In that case no reputable retail establishment would risk offering for sale goods clearly failing to comply with local standards and regulations. Hence, there are benefits in such regulations, which may initially appear a nuisance, in that they may assist orderly market development. Official importers who find incorrectly packaged parallel imports in any outlet can advise both the authorities and the outlet, thereby ensuring that they are not subsequently held liable for any resultant complaint involving such products.

Where the export product is marginally costed and only additions relating to the specific costs of export operations are added back into the costing formula, then it is likely that the home market priced product, even on promotion, will not prove an attractive proposition to the parallel traders. Both the manufacturer and official importer should try to avoid the consumer confusion that results when a product is found in a variety of labels and sizes, as this can seriously harm market sales, particularly in a market where consumers fear 'fake' products.

Manufacturers of component parts often find parallel trade in their products, often fostered by situations where their local distributors fail to carry adequate stocks of parts.

Cross-border smuggling

Occasionally you will encounter a situation where a low-duty country is next to a higher-duty country, or where differential prices between markets create an environment where traders or systems operate to facilitate illegal cross-border transactions into the higher-duty (or higher-priced) country.

If this is happening with your products, while you may not directly believe you are losing, your sole importer in the higher-duty country will be losing profit contributions and motivation to push sales. In addition, if you are promoting branded products through active marketing programmes, the smuggled product may result in an imbalance between where the advertising funds incorporated in product costings are earned and allocated. If all advertising funds are included by the manufacturer at source, he can reallocate some from the budget of the lower-duty country to the higher-duty country. However, if there is provision for the importers in the lower-duty country to contribute, it is highly unlikely that they will recognize any obligation to donate part of their contribution to the neighbouring market, or see any benefit from so doing. The manufacturer is more likely to optimize sales in both markets by finding a balancing formula to relate the level of promotion in both markets not to the level of shipments to the respective importers, but in direct relation to the consumption levels of the two markets, if this can reasonably be assessed.

In reality, the official importers in the higher-duty country will tend to be over-conservative in ordering, constantly fearing that the actual or potential smuggling of goods will restrict their sales. The smugglers, in the meantime, will also have an insecure outlet and tend not to satisfy all potential demand. The net result is below-optimum product sales in the higher-duty market.

One solution the manufacturer should carefully study and consider is to increase the basic export price to the lower-duty country to the point where smugglers would no longer see benefit in illegal cross-border trade for the small returns left to them. This might give more security to importers in the higher-duty market, who might then increase their orders and conduct an orderly growth programme. How much more they can sell will depend on whether the smuggled goods were reaching the consumers at lower prices, or whether the price benefit was being absorbed by the wholesale and retail trade in the form of better profit margins. In the lower-duty market, prices should not be increased to the extent that local sales decline by more than the potential net increase in the two markets added together after the change in pricing structure. Bear in mind that, since most importers work on a percentage margin on cost or sales, any price increases you pass on to them will be magnified when they use their mark-up formula of, say, 20 per cent of cost.

Some years ago such price adjustments were used very successfully to reduce smuggling of confectionery products out of the lower-duty Kuwait market into the higher-duty Saudi Arabian market, with a net overall increase in business resulting from the appointed Saudi importer's ability and willingness to import in much greater volume without fear of cheaper smuggled goods. In that particular instance, the growth in Saudi Arabia was many times greater than the loss in business for the Kuwaiti market.

You will need to consider very carefully all of the above factors and any others particular to your situation or products before implementing such changes to reduce disruptive smuggling.

If a situation exists where a country has trade barriers that limit legal import by quotas, limit imports by other licensing or currency restrictions, or do not permit any legal imports of your product, then smuggling of your product into that country may both give you the benefits of an overall higher sales volume and keep your product name in front of end users or consumers in the restricted market.

In some markets, importers make unusual or unwelcome requests to exporters, such as under-invoicing the value of goods to produce a lower duty base for the importer. Cooperation in such activities is not without some risk for the exporter, who may risk being blacklisted as a supplier. Third party inspection agencies act for a number of governments (such as Nigeria) where incorrect invoicing of prices has resulted in trade irregularities.

Many manufacturers have successfully developed contacts and tactics to supply worthwhile or potential future markets via 'the back door'. However, the marketing support the international marketer can risk putting behind smuggled goods or those that enter a market other than in strict compliance with local regulations is limited, as the exporter cannot be seen to be encouraging illicit trade (which might be the interpretation of foreign authorities who saw an active marketing programme for goods supposedly not freely available for import).

Points of ownership transfer

It is customary in the export trade to quote a price that relates to the geographical location where legal title to the merchandise changes from the seller to the buyer, and it seems appropriate to give some coverage of that aspect of exporting here since it does relate mainly to pricing aspects of exporting.

The manufacturer of, say, consumer goods, may have a standard practice of quoting 'FOB [free on board] vessel' to all his customers, because they find this an easy location to associate with transfer of title. Modern transport systems, containerized goods and multi-modal shipments result in a

wider variety of terminology and ownership transfer points, and when negotiating costs of goods and distribution costs to the point of ownership transfer (or hand-over of responsibility for onward distribution costs), international marketers will need to understand exactly what obligations and costs fall on them, the seller, and the buyer. Therefore you should obtain and study the current *International Rules for the Interpretation of Trade Terms* (commonly referred to as '**Incoterms**') published by the International Chamber of Commerce (copies are available through most chambers of commerce in the UK or government agencies will recommend other sources). It is then frequently advisable or suitable in a quotation to refer to a price in a manner such as 'Incoterms CIF' or 'Incoterms CIF plus war risk insurance'. It is customary to insert after the appropriate Incoterm the named place where risk or ownership transfers (e.g. destination).

The **Glossary** at the end of this book lists all the standard Incoterms, with explanations of their meaning in terms of transfer of ownership and seller's responsibility.

At the stage of negotiating the contract of sale, the seller should be very clear with the buyer on how each party understands the conditions of sale in relation to where responsibility for merchandise, transport, title, insurance and so on transfers.

Developing and using trade terms in export markets

The distributor who is selling through a network of sub-distributors, dealers or retail stockists will have to develop a local pricing structure that matches trade terms on offer from other distributors and suppliers to the market. Many export marketers avoid involvement in this aspect of market pricing, either because they do not feel confident to provide inputs to discussions, or perhaps because they see it as beyond their role. In this text we would take the view that it is part of the export marketer's role to establish that any local trade terms are both competitive with other suppliers, and consistent with the market pricing and distribution policies of the exporter. Hence we will provide some commentary on the typical role of trade terms in influencing market activity through the distributor.

What the trade looks at

There are various typical forms that trade terms take, outlined in Table 16.5, which also highlights the particular concerns of the local dealer or buyer, and the local distributor or company.

The trade terms in any market need to take account of:

- competitive terms on offer from other dealers offering similar products or servicing a similar customer or outlet base
- economic factors, such as the local availability of trade credit, availability of bank credit to finance the trade or users, local bank interest rates (or interest rates from other sources such as credit card providers, where the goods might be purchased using credit cards), inflation, employment levels, local levels of economic activity and business profitability, and so on
- trade dealer factors, such as strength and longevity of dealers in the distribution infrastructure – distributors will be more willing to provide trade credit to long established dealers in a stable distribution infrastructure than to new entrants in new trade channels (readers may recall the high failure rate in the early days of cash and carry wholesaling in the UK).

Credit

The credit a distributor will give is normally influenced by:

- local custom and practice of the trade
- competitive terms of trade
- cost of credit from the distributor versus alternative sources (e.g. bank)

- credit provided to the distributor from his suppliers (and at what cost)
- state of the local economy, including
  - need for stockists to extend credit or hold stock
  - employment
  - interest rates and inflation.
- strategic marketing considerations, e.g.
  - expanding distribution and/or product usage
  - pipeline stock pressure
  - expanding display
  - building market share
  - blocking competition.

The export marketer will be concerned that the distributor is providing adequate trade credit where that influences performance against marketing strategies and objectives, such as expanding product trial and distribution, or improving display for retail products.

The question the export marketer needs to address is to establish how the provision of extended credit by his company helps his market development. Many exporters are shipping goods on payment terms that range anything from 30 days to 120 days (and sometimes more). When the company gives a distributor credit, is that credit being used to finance growth of the exporter's company products, or is it being used to finance the growth of other products being marketed by the distributor? The exporter needs an insight to the practices and costs of credit provided by his distributor to users or the trade dealers. Several major multinational corporations have come to the realization that they have significant funds tied up in the provision of export credit that are in excess of the distributor's needs just to finance the holding of stock and normal trade credit needs for their products. Distributors, like any other trader, will not provide goods on credit to customers not considered credit worthy, but will sell on a cash or near-cash basis (one order at a time, perhaps), and often have a significant proportion of their turnover received in less than 30 days from invoice. The astute export

Table 16.5 *Trade terms and their objectives*

Trade term factor	Dealer's or buyer's concerns	Distributor's or company objectives
Credit • Trade credit	Obtaining maximum supplier credit. Comparing of credit terms from alternative suppliers. To finance inventories from supplier credit.	To provide minimum trade credit. To offer trade terms consistent with local trade custom and practice.
• Prompt payment discounts	Discount should be at a higher level than local bank interest to encourage early payment.	To motivate payment as early as possible and within payment terms.
Discounts • Volume discounts	To have a bonus for volume purchases. Discounts should reflect cost savings on bulk deliveries.	To motivate larger volume purchases. Particularly applied to major accounts. To reduce the likelihood of out of stock positions in the trade.
• Sliding case rate scale	Net price to reduce according to the volume purchased.	To increase trade order sizes. To reduce out of stock situations.
• Retrospective performance discounts	A reward paid in arrears for achieving agreed volumes of purchases. A reward for loyalty. An incentive to push the supplier's products.	To provide an incentive to develop an annual plan with the company, attracting more promotional activity to company products.
Minimum order quantities • Fixed case or quantity minimum order.	To avoid buying any more stock than necessary, i.e. smaller orders and more frequent deliveries.	To cover minimum costs of servicing an order (sales and distribution costs). To maintain stocks in the pipeline, rather than allowing the trade to run out through placing small orders.

marketer should look to collect information that shows the distributors' cash flow profile, in order to use this as appropriate in negotiations.

The export marketer and his distributors should recognize the time value of money in all transactions that extend credit at any level of the distribution chain.

Guidelines for credit

There are a few basic guidelines that the export marketer might like to bear in mind, when being pressured to extend the exporter's credit to the distributor or direct customer even further (perhaps from 60 to 90 days). The local distributor might also apply these to his own market operations.

- Do not extend credit if you do not have to – encourage the distributor or direct customer to look for local finance for imports
- Credit check before you extend credit (to end users, distributors and foreign countries)
- Take trade references
- Avoid extending credit beyond the normal level of stock cover carried by the trader.
- Enforce your payment terms.

Discounts

Discounts are a tool for use in trade dealer and account management and are normally related to:

- the need for improved cash flow
- influencing sales volumes through
 - maintaining distribution
 - expanding the base of distribution
 - minimizing out-of-stocks
 - building market share
 - dealer or account stock holding policies.

Many distributors (and even some export suppliers!) offer discounts not related to any of the above, but as:

- an incentive to buy (not specific to volume performance or marketing objectives)
- custom and practice for a particular account.

Discounts given without specific contractual performance conditions are hard to remove and non-motivational in building sales volume and market share.

Types of motivational discount

There are two main types of motivational discount (with various application formats) used by distributors in many markets and

Prompt settlement discounts	• Designed to improve cash flow. • Will not produce the desired result unless it is greater than the alternative source of financing trade credit, i.e. the retailer's bank interest rate.

Performance discounts or rebates	• Decreasing price with increasing order volumes: this recognizes the savings on distribution and marketing costs and should not be higher than these savings as otherwise you are sacrificing margin.
	• Performance rebates at pre-agreed rates geared to annual performance
	 – at fixed absolute levels
	 – for an increase on the previous year's sales
	 – as an achievement against target.
	• Sliding scale quantity discounts, e.g.
	    0–49 cases £100 per case
	    50–99 cases £ 96 per case.

designed either to improve the cash flow or to encourage increased sales and loyalty. There are prompt settlement discounts and performance discounts or rebates.

To be controllable and motivational discounts and rebates should be for specific performance achievements, and be retrospective rather than 'off invoice' except where related to a sliding case rate scale.

Minimum orders

The basis of calculating a minimum order is normally to set it at a level where the margin contribution will at least cover the direct costs of distribution and servicing the customer account. It is very common for distributors not to know servicing and distribution costs, and therefore to set minimum orders too low, with the result that many orders are actually loss making.

The export marketer may find benefit in working with his distributors to investigate this aspect of trade terms where it is in use, to ensure firstly that minimum orders are at a viable level in general, and secondly that his own products are not disadvantaged by any minimum order applied across a broader product range. It may happen that small orders for the exporter's own products do not make a worthwhile order or delivery on their own, effectively limiting product trial and distribution opportunities. Whilst it is never viable to supply all potential customers, there may be ways of tackling this, possibly through a small order charge, delivery by couriers or postal systems rather than by trucks (where practical for the product), or developing a network of sub-distributors.

If orders are collected on call visits, and if the frequency of visit to an account is too frequent, this encourages the placing of small orders at or close to any minimum as the customer feels a need to give the salesperson an order – the reward for the visit. It is commonly found with many distributors that rather than under-call they tend to over-call on their network of customers. Many have not been exposed to best practice in

sales journey planning, and salespersons have the habit of calling on all customers at equal frequency (say monthly) rather than relating the frequency of calling to the volume sales potential. An excuse for salespersons over-calling is often that they are in the neighbourhood anyway, or that they were looking to collect payment for a previous delivery (personal collection being a common, if technically inefficient, practice in many markets where the post is not reliable or trusted, or where this is trade practice).

Guidelines for establishing minimum orders

From the practical perspective the export marketer might assist his distributors develop an approach to minimum orders using the following guidelines.

- Calculate the cost of distribution and related sales and marketing costs, and estimate the optimum minimum order to cover these.
- Set call frequencies at time intervals to justify orders of the optimum minimum
- Smaller outlets will need to review stock cover in line with prescribed minimum
- Trade credit can be used to finance an increase in stock holding

The objective is to use trade terms fairly and equitably to motivate growth in volume and distribution.

Further reading

Sales Management. Chris Noonan (Butterworth-Heinemann 1998). Chapter 15: Territory management; Chapter 17: Sales management control; Chapter 18: Trade development

Global Marketing Strategies. Jean-Pierre Jeannet and H. David Hennessy (Houghton Mifflin 1995). Chapter 13: Pricing for international and global markets

Export Strategy: Markets and Competition. Nigel Piercy (George Allen & Unwin

1982). Chapter 8: Price policy; Chapter 9: Export pricing; Chapter 10: Non-price competition in exporting

Marketing Management – Analysis, Planning, Implementation, and Control. Philip Kotler (Prentice Hall – 8th edition 1994). Chapter 19: Designing Pricing Strategies and Programmes

Marketing – An Introductory Text. Martin Christopher and Malcolm McDonald (Macmillan 1995). Chapter 12: Pricing Strategy

The Marketing Book. Edited by Michael J. Baker (Butterworth-Heinemann, 4th edition 1999). Chapter 18: Pricing

International Marketing. Stanley J. Paliwoda and Michael J. Thomas (Butterworth-Heinemann, 3rd edition 1999). Chapter 10: Pricing, credit and terms of doing business

International Marketing – A Strategic Approach to World Markets. Simon Majaro (Routledge, 3rd edition 1991). Chapter 7: Pricing in World Markets

Checklist 16.1
Pricing and costing considerations

Action points

Pricing

Examine your export pricing practices. Are they based on:

- domestic-plus?
- cost based (percentage margin mark up)?
- market forces pricing (including price-taking)?
- target pricing?
- price-taking?
- pricing for value?
- tendering sealed bids for contracts?

Are pricing practices consistent with your marketing strategies:

- market spreading/concentration?
- market positioning/segmentation?
- planned export market development versus opportunistic exports?

What factors and product differentiation attributes act to reduce your need to compete on price alone:

- quality/service/delivery/payment terms?
- design/functionality/technology?
- brand awareness/positioning/loyalty?
- consumer/user perceptions and intangibles?
- costs to buyers of changing suppliers?
- other (list)?

What market information is available to consider in relation to price setting:

- competitive pricing levels and structures in target markets?
- competitive market shares and market segmentation?
- trade margins in the distribution chain?

What regulatory restrictions limit your price flexibility in each market?

- *list by market*

Are price differentials between markets:

- desirable?
- practical?

Checklist 16.1 (*Continued*)

Are export marketing objectives best served by pricing in:

- domestic currency?
- destination market currency?
- third country currency?

Price mapping
Have you developed price mapping charts for each market?

- develop a separate price map for each trade sector/channel
- develop a market price band map from field survey data
- plot the actual position of competitive brands
- plot the actual position and ideal position of company brands
- use data to develop marketing strategies to address/ correct variations of actual prices in relation to the target position.

Costings
Is the company's normal export costing practice based on:

- standard costing?
- full costing?
- marginal costing?
- other (identify)?

What approach to costings is most relevant to your marketing strategies and objectives:

- standard costing?
- full costing?
- marginal costing?
- other (identify)?
  (note which approach to costing is preferred for each target market)

Identify and list the elements of your product costings:

- fixed costs
- variable costs
  (relate these to full and marginal costings)

Identify and list the special costs incurred in fulfilling export orders e.g.:

- special packaging
- product modification
- extra quality control
- export documentation and administration

Checklist 16.1 (*Continued*)

	Action points
<ul><li>financing of goods in store and in transit</li><li>customer technical support and training</li><li>export direct sales costs</li><li>export communications (including marketing and promotions)</li><li>export distribution</li><li>other</li></ul> What factors limit your price change flexibility? <ul><li>list factors</li><li>note any special costs incurred in changing prices</li></ul>	

Checklist 16.2
Other market considerations in pricing

	Action points

◆ **Marketing strategies**

- portfolio mix factors
- positioning within company portfolio and versus competition
- marketing communications support
- degree of product branding
- consumer/user added-value perceptions
- sales volume and market share goals
- stage of maturity in the market and product life cycle

◆ **Distributor's considerations**

- user/consumer demand
- costs of goods ex-UK
- import duties and taxes
- trade margin expectations
- operating costs distributing the brand
- net margin requirements
- product fit with distributor's market position and range

◆ **Buyers' attitudes, considerations, acceptance**

- supplier reliability
- local availability or delivery lead times
- suitability to satisfy user/consumer needs
- payment terms
- price competitiveness
- product benefits versus competitor products

◆ **Competitive activity – target segments and price**

- pricing policies
- market shares, penetration and distribution
- product positioning
- comparable features and benefits
- production capacity – ability to meet demand

◆ **Market environment facing target segments**

- income levels and income distribution
- employment
- interest rates and inflation
- local distribution costs
- sales tax, import duties, exchange rates, etc.
- market demographics relevant to product
- security of access to market
- government policies and user attitudes

Checklist 16.3
Trade terms and customer credit

Action points

Trade credit

◆ Do current distributor trade terms in each market take account of the following:
  ● local custom and practice of the trade?
  ● competitive terms of trade?
  ● cost of credit from the distributor company versus alternative sources?
  ● state of the local economy
    – need for stockists to extend credit or hold stock
    – employment
    – interest rates
  ● strategic considerations, e.g.
    – expanding distribution
    – pipeline stock pressure
    – expanding display
    – building market share
    – blocking competition

Discounts

◆ Are discounts used as an effective tool in account management and in relation to:
  ● the need for improved cash flow?
  ● building sales volumes?
  ● expanding the brands distribution base?
  ● minimizing out-of-stocks?
  ● building market share?
  ● account stock holding policies?
◆ Are all discounts and performance allowances related to specific (contractual) performance conditions?
◆ Are there any instances where discounts and allowances are offered as:
  ● an incentive to buy without volume or other performance requirements?
  ● custom and practice for a particular account?
◆ Are trade terms used fairly and equitably to motivate growth in volume and distribution?

Checklist 16.3 (*Continued*)

	Action points

◆ Is the time value of money recognized in all transactions that extend credit at any level of the distribution chain?

Types of motivational discount

◆ Are your distributors using any or all of the following effectively?
  ● prompt settlement discounts designed to improve cash flow
  ● performance discounts
  ● decreasing price with increasing order volumes:
    – performance rebates at pre-agreed rates geared to annual performance
    – sliding case scale quantity discounts

Minimum orders

◆ Does the gross margin contribution on a minimum order cover the direct costs of distribution and servicing the call?
◆ Are call frequencies calculated on the basis customers should be able to order at least an economical minimum order each call?

Credit control

◆ Are all new customers subjected to a credit check?
◆ Are trade references taken on new customers?
◆ Are agreed payment terms strictly enforced with all customers?
◆ Are there instances of credit being extended beyond customers' normal levels of stock cover required to meet usage or sales in the interval between orders.

17

Packaging for export _____

 In this chapter we will look at some aspects of product packaging that should be considered when products are being designed and offered for sale in export markets. The aim is to help the export marketer to prepare product for export, minimize the risk that product will be damaged in transit (resulting in customer dissatisfaction), and ensure that the marketer has taken account of all the packaging requirements to comply with local regulations in foreign markets.

Export packaging serves both as a means of protecting product from damage in transit and storage, and as a marketing communications vehicle, conveying product information to distributors, users and consumers. Consumer product companies tend to be more conscious of the opportunity to use packaging as an additional way of communicating with the target market consumers. Many suppliers of industrial products make minimal use of the packaging to convey product messages or to promote branding. This chapter will look at the role of packaging and its communication opportunities.

Export packaging has a number of functions and objectives. It must:

- ensure that the product arrives in the market and with the final end user or consumer in as good condition as it leaves the exporter's factory, and be:
  – in perfect working order and without physical damage of any form
  – free from heat, humidity, infestation and other climatic damage
- comply with all laws, rules, regulations or trade conventions that apply to the packaging of goods for sale in that

market, and to the international carriage of such goods (e.g. goods considered to be dangerous)
- identify the product clearly to the end user in the export market and relate to local culture (particularly in the case of consumer products) so as not to be considered offensive or unacceptable in any aspect of presentation or design
- comply in each and every respect with the specifications and requirements of the importer agreed upon at the time of concluding the supply contract
- facilitate ease of handling and storage in transit and in each of the distribution channels, and also in the environment where the product will finally be used.

Figure 17.1 illustrates diagramatically some of the key considerations the marketer should take into account when designing the export packaging, and when referring to packaging I am including not just any outer export shipping cartons but also the inner packaging offering immediate protection to the goods. The following sections will give expanded commentary on these packaging considerations.

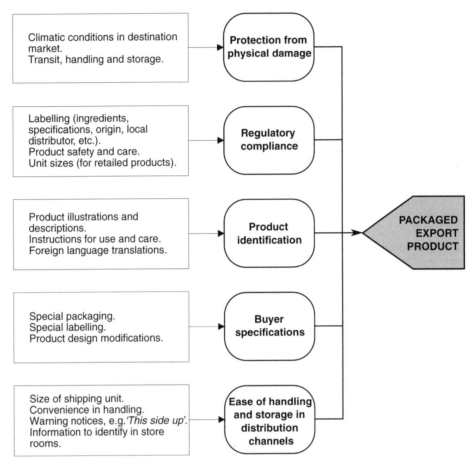

Figure 17.1 *Some considerations in export packaging design*

Physical suitability

The transportation of an export order from the supplier to the final customer is likely to involve several modes of transport (truck, air, sea, road, rail), and many rigours not encountered in a home market sale. Goods may be containerizsed for part of the journey and shipped loose for another part. There could be a variety of climatic variations to take account of, and probably much rougher handling and storage conditions than your product faces at home. Packaging design and structure need to reflect the factors of:

- transport mode
- manual or mechanical handling

- perishability (such as effects of climate, i.e. heat and humidity)
- nature of the goods (would they be classed as 'dangerous'?)
- communication with the user/consumer.

Physical protection during transportation and handling

Goods shipped internationally are frequently handled in transit more than those shipped domestically, and those handling the goods may not have a direct interest in their care, i.e. they are not directly employed by either the supplier or the customer. Also the handling may often be rougher. Protective packaging needs to allow for both these scenarios. Goods that start their journey on pallets may reach a point of the journey where the pallets are split for ease of handling or transhipment, such as in warehouses where forklift trucks are unavailable. In that case once the strength of the protective pallet is removed the shipping cartons may need additional strength to survive direct handling through the other stages of distribution.

It is useful to start by assuming that your export packaging needs to be much stronger and more durable than packaging used domestically. Normally it is easier for the export supplier to strengthen the outer shipping cartons than inner boxes surrounding individual product units. First, examine the outer case or carton in which the products are shipped domestically. It may be that either the weight of the carton board used, or the packaging configuration of individual units can be varied in order to reduce the risk of damage. Carton dividers or various polystyrene fillers may help provide extra strength and protection from physical damage, particularly where the goods are susceptible to damage from vibration or shaking. Sealing the carton with tape in addition to normal gluing may also reduce risks of physical or climatic damage.

The individual unit of the product may need its own extra protection. For example, if there is a risk that the product could rust in transit, it may need protection in the form of a moisture barrier such as an impervious sealed polythene film wrapper round the unit container. It may benefit from polystyrene corner protectors to prevent physical damage. Consumer durables are likely to need more protection than many industrial components, since unsightly dents will make the product unsaleable, but many hitech components are susceptible to moisture and vibration damage particularly.

Perishability – heat and humidity protection

Perishable foodstuffs, some toiletries, cosmetics, medicines, many canned goods, consumable photographic products, some hi-tech products and a broad range of other consumer and industrial goods require careful attention to adequate protective packaging to prevent heat and moisture damage that could result in mould, corrosion of metal containers or working parts, or general malfunctioning or deterioration. In addition, a food product may be subject to insect infestation in transit or before sale in the foreign market. Good sealing on the outer carton is the first stage of protection. A polythene heat-sealed over-wrap may be considered necessary for some products. Inner cartons can likewise be protected by a shrink-wrapped polythene cover. Impregnation of cartons may assist in reducing infestation by insects if the chemicals are food-safe. The final product within the display box, such as a cereal, may need to be foil-wrapped to protect against heat, humidity and insects.

If you are exporting perishable products many of your export markets will not yet have all the sophisticated and hygienic storage facilities of the home market. There may be a shortage of refrigeration and pest control equipment, and even distribution channel outlets with air conditioning in hot countries may turn it off overnight to cut operating costs. If you, as the supplier, do not recognize and protect against known risks, your product sales will suffer in the market.

Be aware of the potential problems facing your products and seek the advice of professional packaging scientists, either at your home office or through the service of your packaging supplier.

Products shipped and distributed with inadequate protection to ensure user or consumer satisfaction may reach the final user in a condition that risks the goodwill of the exporter. Dissatisfaction with a product's condition opens an opportunity for a competitor. Since inadequate product protection through packaging also gives foreign market distributors an excuse for unsatisfactory sales performance, it is essential that an exporter efficiently audits

A case example – confectionery to Hong Kong

As an illustration of a situation where packaging affected market sales drastically, there was a confectionery product being marketed in Hong Kong, where the climate varies from unbearably hot and humid to pleasantly temperate. After launch, this product had excellent sales, especially at Chinese New Year. In the normal air-conditioned supermarkets the product was well stored and displayed, and sales were consistent all year. In the more open street-side traditional stores, sales were voluminous in the first gift-giving season after product launch, and barely slowed down into the hot and humid summer. However, the second gift season resulted in a dramatic decline of sales through the non-supermarket outlets, despite trade and consumer acceptance for the product. Extensive store checking and product sampling revealed that, although the product was well distributed and displayed, product off-take had dropped because the particular confectionery item had a light, aerated centre, which collapsed under humid conditions to a chewy ball – not what the consumer expected. The alternatives here were:

- to improve the packaging to be suitably heat and humidity proof
- to limit distribution to air-conditioned stores
- to introduce a new and better product freshness and uplift policy for the damaged product.

In fact, the practical solution was a combination. It proved impossible adequately to package the confectionery product to give total heat and humidity protection at any reasonable cost. The outer display box could be wrapped with a polythene over-wrap to reduce humidity damage while goods were stored. In addition, the distributor had to persuade the small stores to treat the product as a gift-giving seasonal item only, so that consumers could be guaranteed the quality in the cooler weather, and introduce a product return policy. In the height of the hot and humid summer season, sales were restricted to air-conditioned stores, which, although it caused a short-term drop in sales into outlets, resulted in consumers knowing that the product was available through non-air-conditioned outlets only in the cooler season. Special gift packs were developed where a multiple of individual packs was placed in a decorated tin container, giving added protection. The result was that, in the following gift-giving season, sales volume again escalated to new peaks because of increased and renewed consumer satisfaction.

and monitors the suitability of his packaging to provide requisite physical protection.

Rules and regulations ▬▬▬

A host of regulations govern trade and the distribution of goods within markets and across borders. In the UK exporters will find that all relevant information can be obtained through the Department of Trade and Industry export services sections (readers in other countries should first approach their government export services departments for assistance, or other sources such as those detailed in Chapter 3, Desk research). Some key aspects of regulations are worth considering here.

Label information

You should consider what the authorities in the foreign market may wish to be made known about the product when it is offered to the public. Rules and regulations frequently act as non-tariff barriers to trade and, in practice, are more visible when applied to consumer goods than to products for industrial processing.

The regulatory authorities do not usually get too involved in regulating outer packaging such as cartons, beyond simple specifications perhaps on print size, language and basic data you should incorporate (such as name and address of manufacturer, name of contents and number of units contained therein). Manufacturers usually have more data they consider necessary for inclusion, such as expiry dates of perishables, indications about the correct side to face up, and so on.

On the individual product unit offered for sale, it is normal to find additional and specific regulations relating to:

- ingredient specifications and composition
- manufacturer and country of origin
- shelf life expiry dates

- manner of usage
- product representations
- product registration details
- importer's name and address
- language of labelling.

Regulatory authorities will also generally regulate the location and size of print for all compulsory information. For example, you will often see references to the main panel incorporating much of this information, and that can be taken to mean the side of the box displayed towards the consumer at the point of sale.

Language

If two or more languages are used, then the usual rule is that the local language must be in print at least as large, and appear on the same panel location, as the foreign language.

The practice of requiring the use of the local language on product labelling and on any other information or instruction sheets has grown rapidly in recent years as more countries have felt the surge of nationalism, and as consumer protection has come to the fore. Most marketers will see this as both beneficial and reasonable, although imposing more demands upon the production and planning departments. Some companies respond by designing one multilingual label for their major markets (e.g. incorporating Spanish, French, English and German). There is the risk that a cluttered label leaves a confused image with the consumer, and two languages are considered by many exporters as the limit on a label. (It is more practical to incorporate more languages in an instruction booklet of the kind normally accompanying most consumer durables.)

The more product variants or product pack sizes and labels you are obliged to have, the more strains are placed upon your production, planning and inventory control departments if you are producing consumer goods. If, however, you are selling bulk products or industrial products, you may be able simply to store the standard product in unlabelled form until you know to which market it will finally be shipped and then label it accordingly, reducing your inventory of different pack sizes, designs, labels or finished goods and related working capital.

Label approvals

The technical terms permissible in obligatory ingredient or component declarations may vary from country to country. In some instances product labels may require prior approval in the destination market prior to product import or distribution. It is essential that you obtain copies of the respective regulations for each market in which you offer products for sale and ensure compliance. Translations may be available via your embassy, distributor or agent, and it is always wise to confirm the acceptability of labels by sending samples to your agent or distributor for comments and perhaps their help in seeking any appropriate local approvals prior to printing.

Agencies involved in labelling approvals may include any or all of the following:

- health departments
- consumer affairs bureaux
- weights and measures departments
- price control agencies
- import control agencies
- government analytical laboratories
- customs and excise authorities.

Apart from assistance from your agent in labelling matters, you may feel more comfortable if you establish a relationship with a suitably qualified lawyer in the export market.

Dangerous goods

Customs authorities or other regulatory bodies specify the nature of packing, shipment, and handling and storage that apply to goods considered 'dangerous'. The carriers can usually give specific advice and guidelines applicable to their routes and mode of transport (air, sea, road, rail), or in the UK information will be available through the Department of Trade and Industry. Substances including explosives, poisons, chemicals, gases, inflammable liquids and solids, corrosives, radioactive materials, and other products considered a hazard whilst in transit or store are subject to regulations.

If the product or container is susceptible to expansion or contraction as temperatures change, or to become a fire or explosive risk, packaging may have to allow for potential volume changes or risks. If the product is combustible or explosive under conditions of movement, vibration or temperature, the goods may need to be shipped at controlled temperatures and in a movement-free environment. If the goods can contaminate others, they may need separate storage or container facilities.

Packaging should be both resistant to its contents and to the environment encountered in store or transit. Various guidelines, regulations and codes exist, such as those of the International Air Transport Association and International Maritime Dangerous Goods Codes.

Clearly, each stage of packing should bear suitable and clear labelling instructions on handling, storage and action to be taken in the event of possible emergencies. Some products may simply be unsuitable for shipment by a particular mode of transport.

Product identification and positioning

Quite apart from the official rules and regulations governing your product labelling, your first concern as an international marketer is to ensure instant product recognition at each stage of the distribution chain and by the final user at an industrial location or the consumer at the point of sale, and to design the packaging to convey your quality image, in addition to protecting the product.

Communication with distributors, users and consumers

There is a key potential role for packaging as a media for communicating messages about the product and the supplier to each level of the distribution chain down to the final user or consumer. The exporter might like to audit his packaging and see how well it is used or how it could be used better to promote product and company information and to distinguish the products from competitors' products.

Where possible, use a distinctive name or description of the product in the local language, or develop a pack design or representation in a form with strong local recognition potential. That will be beneficial, particularly for a product being launched into a country where the written language bears no relationship to your own, such as Thai, Arabic, Chinese and Japanese.

Local culture

There are cultural aspects of packaging that must be considered along with the objectives of international brand recognition. Generally you will find it easier to add something to a culture than to change something within that culture. This is often found to be the case when marketing consumer products. During the early efforts of the fast-food chains to establish themselves in Southeast Asia, the hamburger and pizza organizations seemed to find it easier to gain acceptance than the fried chicken operations. The consistent response to travellers who asked friends and associates why this might be the case was that the Chinese had been cooking chicken in their own traditional way for many generations and preferred its taste to the fried form (although more recent developments across Asia show that all the major fast food formats can achieve good acceptance and market penetration).

The export marketer should seek to identify, and allow for any particular cultural factors that could influence packaging design, such as:

- **local attitudes**
- **local superstitions** (including about symbols used in names or marketing communications)
- **local reactions to words** (brand names, when pronounced by foreign market consumers, may have unacceptable sounds or meanings)
- **colour.**

Chinese communities historically favour red and gold for packaging gift-type items, and white is seen as associated with death and unhappy events. So it may be quite inappropriate to have an expensive gift perfume boxed in white. Even the shade of a colour can significantly affect attitudes and sales. On one occasion, when designing a gift box for confectionery scheduled to be launched one Chinese New Year in Hong Kong, a principal and his distributor had made a provisional decision in favour of a particular shade of red. However, as a quick check, since they knew how important it was to get the right shade, they took a group of the clerical staff in the distributor's office and walked them, one by one, past the alternative shades being considered, seeking an instant comment on preference. It may not have been a very scientific test by research standards, but the response was unanimously against their choice and in favour of an alternative.

Forgeries

International marketers of branded goods are frequently plagued by rough copies of their products or packaging in developing markets, and often the copies try to use a crude variation on the foreign brand name, which, in any event, most of the local customers can neither pronounce nor read correctly. This problem is more evident with consumer products, but many manufacturers of industrial products or spare parts for equipment (e.g. automotive parts) have faced this frustrating source of misrepresentation and competition, which can only harm a good brand name when substandard forgeries penetrate a market. Every traveller has seen poor copies of Cartier watches and Gucci accessories that come out of the Orient. Local manufacturers will always seek a quick profit if they find they can produce a cheap copy without much capital investment. So anything you can do to make the copying process both difficult and risky (by enforcing trademarks, unique brand features, patents and copyrights) should be done; this will assist the brand development of the original item, because sales are likely to be significantly reduced if consumers come to fear that their purchase could be a forgery. Distinctive packaging, even for certain types of industrial goods likely to experience copying, can add another cost factor into the equation that might reduce forgery.

Copying may be a form of flattery, but if your distributor of fashion accessories is an exclusive retailer, they will justifiably be upset if the street vendors are offering close copies at vastly reduced prices.

Purchase motivations

Packaging can play an important part in positioning products in relation to competitors' products and consumer expectations. This is more commonly the case with consumer goods, and we are all familiar with the marketing practices that attempt to create an element of exclusivity to products through sophisticated and expensive looking packaging.

Market habits and purchase motivations can be important considerations at the stage of packaging design. For example, gift giving in Japan is a major event at certain times of the year, when retailers devote much of their display space to suitable gift items. Since the gift should not put an obvious value upon a person's friendship, it is less acceptable to give a standard retail item, such as a regular-size bottle of Scotch whisky, than to give a specially packaged and sized item where the inherent value is disguised, say the same Scotch but sold in an elegant crystal or earthenware decanter. Cosmetic and toiletry items could be in elaborately designed multiple-product gift boxes rather than sold in the normal single-item form.

The exporter must consider most carefully for each separate market:

- who will buy the product?
- what will be the likely purchase and use occasions?
- when and where it will be purchased?

Your knowledge and judgement on these matters should be incorporated in the design of the packaging.

Above all, be flexible, because what may be a mass market line in one country may be best sold as a luxury in another.

If you are not limited by a prescribed international brand image (more usual for a consumer product), then pay heed to the local advice from distributors and advertising agencies on aspects of packaging and presenting your product, including acceptable unit sizes, shapes, design, logos and labelling. However, with the increasing momentum behind globalizing brands, aided by liberalization of trade and the proliferation of multinational corporations and mega-mergers, there is a lessening of flexibility to develop independent local marketing strategies in many product categories.

Product use information

In many foreign and developing countries, industrial product users and consumers are constantly being bombarded with new products and product concepts that may initially be outside their experience. Apart from packaging to ensure recognition of a particular brand and to establish a market position for that brand, it is important to ensure that the descriptive phrases used in labelling or advertising the product tell the consumer what to do with that product or how to use it correctly and safely.

With a breakfast cereal, you may need to illustrate the eating occasion along with the need to add milk. Other convenience foods may need more elaborate illustrations of how the product is prepared. Household cleaning items may need fuller descriptions on applications if they are new products to a market. Consumer durables and many industrial products should have comprehensive and extra instructions on use, care and maintenance, and safety, as in the case of electric drills or other tools aimed at new DIY markets or industrial machinery replacing manual processes.

Opportunities to promote industrial products through packaging

Whilst consumer marketers often give considerable attention to using packaging as a means of product identification and communication, many industrial product marketers will find scope to improve marketing communication messages on packaging. There are still quite a number of products that are used in trade outlets or as ingredients or components and that bear little information on packaging other than a supplier's item code number. This can cause confusion to persons handling or seeking to obtain the products. The item code a supplier allocates a product is unlikely to suit the user or distributor, who will probably allocate another item code for stock control and warehouse storage purposes. A person wanting a particular item may well know it by name and specify another product it is needed for (e.g. 'Have you got a widget for an XYZ motor?'), but that request may simply start a search through computer lists or catalogues to find which item number matches the requirement. In many instances there is scope to include a product description on packaging, in addition to any other catalogue or supplier item number, facilitating retrieval to meet user requests.

Many industrial products are poorly branded or fail to promote to the best advantage the supplier's name and goodwill. One of the common arguments for this is the costs of printing, and the rapid discarding of product packaging in the use environment. Whilst these points may be true, in many instances the person using a product is not the actual buyer who places orders. A buyer who has alternative sources of products may be motivated not just to buy on price where a product is customarily requested internally by name, e.g. 'Can you order another five gallon drum of that SuperClen floor cleaner?'. Typically a buyer is likely to assume that, where a product is requested by name, it is found acceptable in use. Actual users who become used to a particular product, such as the SuperClen factory floor cleaner, are likely to find fault with alternatives, putting more pressure on the buyer to use the favourite brand.

Some industrial products can convey a branding message through the shape of packaging or product containers, or through packaging design factors. For example, rather as Coca-Cola has product identification through the bottle shape, other products can be distinguished from competitor products through the shape of packaging or containers. Product packaging such as cartons can be distinguished by company or product logos or other form of distinctive design that makes a product stand out in the store room, e.g. stripes on the boxes rather than plain cartons.

A thorough and professional approach at the stage of designing product packaging and literature will reduce the risk of lost sales because of consumer ignorance of the product.

Customer's specifications

The export customer or product distributor may well have established during the negotiation process certain particular packaging or product requirements for his market, and apart from the exporter complying with special requirements the customer also has the right to expect the use of suitable protective packaging to ensure goods arrive with the customer in the condition they leave the exporter's factory.

Customers will expect:

- packaging that meets special **specifications** included with orders
  - check whether variations from standard packaging are specified (e.g. importer's names and addresses, changes to ingredient declarations)
  - ensure packaging meets any requirements within a letter of credit
  - look for requests to make modifications in unit size of products, or configurations in multi-unit cartons
- packaging in line with the custom of the trade
  - packaging that is adequate to ensure that the product arrives safely at its destination and suits the mode of transport used
  - packaging that complies with rules and regulations in the receiving country for the particular product.

The rule for the exporter is to check with the customer on all points concerning each order, and to issue an order acceptance and confirmation that not only details the packaging but also the volume, value and method of shipment, and other specifics relevant to a particular product.

Some requests you may be able to comply with; others you should not comply with if they put you at risk of being in breach of regulations or otherwise acting incorrectly. It is well known in developing countries that importers may request changes in labelling or product descriptions to enable an otherwise restricted product to enter the country, or to enable importers to pay a lower import duty by it being reclassified. If your product contains a non-approved ingredient or colour and you cannot change your ingredient to an approved item, then do not risk a false or incorrect label declaration at the request of an importer.

If your industry and product have an acceptable standard form of packaging, for example a certain type of bag for an agricultural product, then your shipment should be at least as well packed. If your shipment of, say, milk powder in bulk 25 kilogram bags uses only 2-ply bags when the normally accepted bag is a 4-ply unit, then your customer may have grounds for complaint or claim. (Insurers might also consider inadequate packaging as grounds for disputing a subsequent claim.)

Similarly, consider at this point the mode of shipment. If you are offering to deliver goods that normally require refrigeration and the product arrives unrefrigerated, then your customer may have a basis for claiming that any CIF quote you sold against was fairly assumed to be commensurate with the product requirement of refrigerated stowage in transit, and claims may ensue or your bills may not be paid.

FOB and CIF price quotations customarily include suitable export packing unless otherwise specified. Examples of phrases typically used in an exporter's quotations might include: 'goods packed for export in heavy-duty cases, with supporting dividers, and individual product units are polythene over-wrapped', or 'goods are supplied in standard domestic market cartons and packaging, but may be protectively packed at an additional charge of £20 per 50 units in specially constructed wooden crates'. Your price list should summarize your standard terms and conditions of sale, along with notes on packaging for export, to reduce the risk of complaints by customers that they were insufficiently informed of your practices and procedures.

In summary, check the initial order, the shipping documents and the payment documents to ensure that at each stage you are fully in compliance with instructions concerning the type, quantity, quality and packaging of goods ordered by your export customer.

Packaging and freight ▪▪▪▪▪▪

The mode of packing for export – for example, whether the goods are palletized or containerized or simply shipped loose stowage – may make a difference to freight and handling charges. Also, the weight and dimensions of cartons may affect whether you pay freight by volume or weight measure. The general principle, both to reduce the risk of damage in transit and to minimize freight costs, is to make the packaging a precise fit at each stage of packing; i.e. product into initial inner container; inner container into multi-unit (or single-unit, as appropriate) outer container. Efficient choice of the most effective form of protective packaging to minimize size, weight and general bulk may even result in a faster form of shipment such as air freight becoming a cost-effective mode of transport.

Of course, the mode of shipment will also depend to a degree on the value of the merchandise being shipped: the smaller the ratio of freight costs to market value, the more attractive it will be to exporters and importers to consider faster, if more expensive, modes of shipment.

If the exporter is to receive a clean bill of lading at shipment, then the packaging must have at least been adequate to ensure no visible defects or damage when goods were loaded onto the vessel. Goods shipped in sealed containers may result in the issue of a bill of lading bearing a note such as 'a container said to contain 500 cartons of canned soup' without reference to the goods being received in good order as they cannot easily be checked.

Facilitating ease of handling in distribution channels ▪▪▪▪▪▪

The exporter sitting back in his home office and planning market developments needs to give some thought to any factors that can ease the handling of products in the distribution chain. A good starting point is usually to visit sample outlets in the distribution chain, including the distributor's warehouse, customers' premises, and the final place of product use. Attention may need to be given to:

- size of product packs
- convenience of handling
- clear warning notices
- contents identification.

Size of product packs ———————

Customarily companies design products and related packaging to suit the domestic market. People handling the bulk products are typically aided by mechanical handling equipment. When outer shipping units, such as pallets, are broken down and goods handled manually, that will normally be done by people in good health and of a much larger physical size than those in most of the developing world. If fluids are normally packed in 25 litre drums, or solid items are packed in relatively large weight units, will local personnel in the foreign market find it easy to handle and move product without the aid of mechanical equipment, often not available, or only in limited supply? If your products are packed in too large a sized unit to be easily handled by a single person of smaller size than would be expected to handle it in your domestic facilities, then buyers might bias purchase decisions towards smaller sized units available from your competitors.

Convenience of handling ———————

Some products that are of a size that allows physical handling (without mechanical aids) are packaged in cartons or containers that do not make handling easy. The design of larger containers could be studied for opportunities to incorporate some form of hand holes to serve as lifting points. The strength of cartons can be checked to ensure they will not collapse when packed with product and lifted.

Size, commented on in the previous section, can be a factor in convenience of handling. Size might be looked at in relation to the way the carton must be lifted, e.g. a wide package that must be lifted in a flat horizontal fashion, or a tall carton that must be carried erect, may present problems for the package handler to carry and manipulate. Logistical problems in moving packages should be identified and addressed with consideration to the handlers in the export environment.

Containers used for fluids should incorporate strong handles for ease of lifting and use. If possible spillage at the point of use should be avoided through inclusion of a pouring spout or lip located on the container at a point where the pouring action can be controlled.

Clear warning notices

All packaging should show clearly any warnings that might be applicable to the contents, such as whether dangerous goods are included, if there is a right side up for the carton or container (very important for many fluids or products where handling or storing incorrectly would result in delicate components of products being crushed by the weight of other parts of the product).

Warnings should include both words and diagrams, and be in a format ensuring understanding in the receiving market. 'This side up' in English may be of little help to an illiterate product handler in a developing market. A range of warning signs are promoted for international packaging communications and understanding.

Because cartons are often stacked high in many less sophisticated warehouses where warehouse racking is not available, if there are weight restrictions on the load a carton can tolerate without damage to the contents the exporter might consider it useful to state this in some format on cartons.

Contents identification

As has been mentioned previously, apart from any supplier's product identification codes, cartons should also show the usual product name, or, in some instances where it will make identification easier in the distribution chain or use environment, a diagrammatic product illustration. The number of individual units contained in a shipping carton should be noted on the carton also, for ease of stock checking.

In summary, the packaging of a product can usefully communicate a range of product information, any relevant warnings, and provide an opportunity for displaying marketing messages promoting the company and the product.

Further reading

Export Trade – The Law and Practice of International Trade. Clive M. Schmitthoff (Stevens – 9th edition). Chapter 6: Invoices and Packing

International Marketing. Stanley J. Paliwoda and Michael J. Thomas (Butterworth-Heinemann, 3rd edition 1998). Chapter 9: Product Policy Decisions

Checklist 17.1
Packaging considerations

	Action points

- Does the product packaging provide protection against the particular risks to the product?
  - *List the risks*
- Does packaging comply with the custom of the trade?
  - *Identify standard practice*
- Does the packaging comply with the rules and regulations of each destination market in respect of labelling?
  - *Identify for each market in respect of: unit sizes, specifications, ingredients, formulation, composition, country of origin, expiry dates, manner of usage, product representations, product registrations, importer identification, language, other*
- Does the product or packaging require specific approvals or registration prior to distribution?
  - *Identify approving agencies*
- Are your goods likely to be classified as dangerous?
  - *If so, obtain specific advice on packaging for safe transport, handling and storage*
- What scope is there to develop packaging to promote the identity of the manufacturer or product?
  - *e.g. use of product illustrations and descriptions, instructions for use and care, foreign language translations of information*
- What cultural factors should be considered in designing packaging and labelling (and marketing communications)?
  - *Identify and list*
- Is there scope to improve the ease of handling and storage of the product, such as through packaging that:
  - provides a convenient size of shipping unit
  - is easy to handle
  - provides clear warning information on how to handle and store the product – gives information to aid identification of the product in store rooms.
- Has account been taken in packaging design of:
  - who buys the product?
  - where it is purchased?
  - why it is purchased?
  - when it is purchased?

Checklist 17.1 (*Continued*)

	Action points

• Has packaging design taken account of essential product use communications (the extent of which may vary between markets)
   – on unit packaging?
   – on supplementary literature?
   (Note any special market requirements)
• Have packaging design and configuration taken account of freight costs by preferred mode of shipment?	

Part Four

Marketing Communications

18

Developing the communications strategy

In this section we will discuss marketing communications, and aspects of their use in support of exporting and market development. Specifically in this chapter we will look at:

- the marketing communications mix and its role in the marketing strategy
- the way perceptual and factual communications impact on the consumer or user, and
- how marketing communications work.

The aim is to give the export marketer an insight into the general subject of marketing communications, and to recognize the importance of marketing communications, in whatever forms are appropriate, in the implementation of a marketing strategy.

Advertising and promotion are a fundamental part of the marketing activity for most companies in their domestic markets, but for most exporters a much lower priority is given to marketing communications in international markets, in part because of budgetary constraints, and perhaps also because of the relegation of export market development to a secondary role in relation to domestic markets. Exports are often sales driven ('Where can we sell more of what we make?') rather than market driven ('What are the needs, wants, and opportunities in the markets?'). In this chapter we will review the role of marketing communications within the marketing mix, and develop an approach to formalizing thinking and planning for international marketing communications.

In Chapter 10, Developing an export strategy, Figure 10.8 highlighted the stages in strategy planning as:

- developing a portfolio plan
- breaking that down to detailed plans for individual brands or products (with attention to the marketing mix factors – product, price, place, promotion, people, processes)
- developing a communication strategy to support the marketing strategy.

From this earlier example we can develop a model, Figure 18.1, that highlights the key role of communications strategy in influencing sales and financial performance in the marketplace.

The communications strategy, when supported by the field sales activity needed to generate customer orders through direct

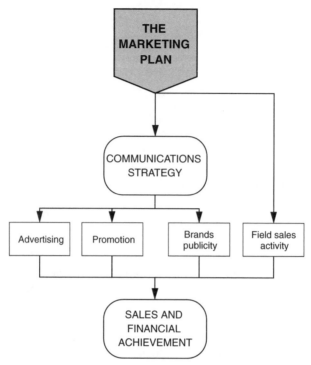

Figure 18.1 *The role of communications strategy in influencing achievement*

customer contact (or, in some cases, telephone contact or mailshots), leads towards the achievement of the sales and financial goals. If there was a reliance on field sales activity alone without a supporting communications strategy, or vice versa, then achievements against plans might be suboptimum, or the plans themselves might reflect a shortfall against potential for the products.

Typically field sales activity in export markets will either be through the direct selling activities of the exporter's (manufacturer's) international sales and marketing team, or their appointed agents or distributors. The marketing communications messages, supporting the brand or products, are typically carried to the user or consumer through:

- advertising
- brands publicity
- promotional activity.

We will discuss each of these in subsequent chapters.

The marketing communications mix

In developing international marketing communications the marketer needs to recognize that universal communications formats may not be suitable. Just as the marketing objectives may vary market by market, so the communications mix best suited to promote the achievement of objectives may need to be varied between markets. The marketing communications mix consists of a mixture of **personal** and **impersonal messages** (Figure 18.2), and the balance of communications in the mix will vary by market according to:

- the availability of media in the various markets
- the power of the individual communication options in influencing purchasing decisions
- the available budgets and costs of the communications options
- the marketing objectives for each market

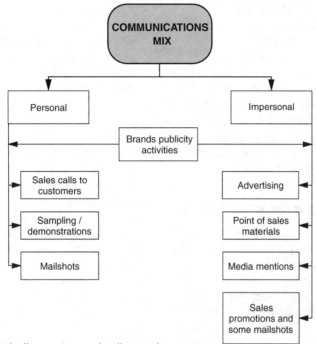

Figure 18.2 *The marketing communications mix*

(for example, market in-depth penetration, niche marketing, skimming profit, etc.) and product investment strategy (governed in part by the stage a product is judged to be at in its life cycle in any market)
- the security of access to the markets (for example the risks of political or economic upheaval disrupting orderly market development).

Brands publicity activity can bridge the gap between personal and impersonal communications, as will be discussed later. Here some additional commentary will concentrate on the main personal and impersonal marketing communications.

Sales calls to customers

The direct sales call on the customer is the most personal form of communication available to the marketer. In most markets agents and distributors will have a sales team promoting the products they represent. From the exporter's perspective the main

problems in relying on an agent's or distributor's sale team are:

- getting a reasonable share of the time spent with any customer or prospective customers (where the representative may have several products to promote to the same contact)
- developing a sufficient level of product knowledge and expertise within the sales team
- the limited professional selling skills often encountered within the sales teams of agents and distributors.

If the market sales team is a major means of customer communications then the export marketer needs to give time and budgetary support to ensuring this communications vehicle is effective, including:

- providing specific training in all aspects of the products (e.g. design, formulation, uses, product features and related customer benefits, and product care or servicing) – this training might include visits to the exporter's manufacturing

locations, suitable video films of manufacturing processes and product use and applications, etc.
- developing sales literature that is comprehensive and comprehensible both to the sales team and customers, with a focus on customer benefits to each level in the buying process, e.g. buyers, influencers, specifiers and users.
- providing direct training in best practice selling and negotiating skills.

Product sampling or demonstration

Product sampling and demonstration is another key form of personal communication. It presents an opportunity to show the features and benefits of the product to the prospective buyer, and lets the customer personally experience or try (particularly in the case of a technical product) the product. Some products are best demonstrated in the environment where they would actually be used. With technical products it is important to ensure that all levels in the buying chain (buyers, influencers, specifiers and users) are exposed to demonstration, otherwise those not party to the presentation and demonstration are likely to raise objections, possibly not truly related to the suitability or performance of the product but more to the internal company politics of them not being involved in the selection and buying process.

A few guidelines for the export marketer to consider when planning product sampling or demonstrations include:

- give particular attention to selecting product demonstrators if they are not permanent members of your agent's or distributor's sale team – ensure they have the personal qualities, experience and skill to relate to your prospective customers or product users
- provide specific training in the products, particularly focusing on customer benefits derived from the key product features, and ensure they can deal with questions on product handling, maintenance, general care, etc.

- if the product has any potentially risky aspects of its use, then ensure they are well versed in safety-in-use aspects of product knowledge, and only demonstrate it in environments where nobody is at risk.

Mailshots

International mailshots are becoming an increasingly used means of direct and personal marketing communications, especially as directories and databases make it easier to identify and target buyers and users. Poorly targeted mailshots are costly and produce little response. A well-targeted mailshot can be an effective means of communicating personally with the trade buyers, end users or consumers. A mailshot is most appropriate where the number of potential customers is limited, and where they can be identified against relevant criteria and from information sources (e.g. existing customer or contact lists, specialist directories, database information services, etc.).

With consumer products the recipient of a mailshot might be both the buyer and user, but with industrial products it is advisable to target each person in the buying chain, the buyer who places the order, the technical person who specifies products for use in the company, and the person who actually uses the product in his everyday job. The information each may need might vary according to their particular emphasis in evaluating and selecting products. The buyer is likely to have concerns over price, availability, aesthetic design, and warranties in particular; the specifier and the user are likely to have less concerns over price and more about suitability for use in the work environment (functionality), reliability, maintenance requirements and costs (and availability of spares or service), ease of use and maintenance, staff training requirements, safety, and technical performance.

Mailshots can be personalized to the recipient's needs and interests, or a standard item of product promotional literature might be accompanied by a customized letter. When designing international mailshots:

- ensure the mailshot literature is designed to make an impact in the shortest time, so that recipients are encouraged to read on in spite of the volume of mailshots received
- focus on key product messages, such as its benefits in use (to buyer, specifier and final user), availability, comparable performance with competitive products or other performance standards, technical specifications, service requirements, etc.
- keep the messages brief, basic and comprehensible (do not expect the buyer to have to partake in mental gymnastics to understand the messages)
- preferably use the language of the recipient
- show product illustrations (photographs are better than line drawings), preferably in a typical use environment
- explain where the product can be purchased, and motivate action by the recipient to call for a demonstration, sales visit, or to discuss further the relevancy of the product to his needs (e.g. reply paid postcard to be returned to the supplier or his local agent or distributor).

Advertising

Advertising is an impersonal means of communicating with prospects and customers as it is not personally addressed or directed to any one individual, but communicates product promotional messages through mass media. Whilst advertising messages may be quite specific in presenting product features and benefits, they are often widely broadcast to, or read by, a much wider audience than would be in the target market segment of users or consumers. Advertising a technical product in specialist media, such as technical trade journals, will target a particular group of users or consumers better than advertising a similar product through mass media such as broadsheet newspapers, television or radio. Marketers advertising their consumer products that have broad appeal are more likely to prefer mass media communications where the target sector cannot be reached cost effectively through a more focused means of communication.

Selecting media in foreign markets is often more difficult than in the domestic market, as the marketer may have less relevant and meaningful information upon which to base a selection. Once users or consumers in the target market segment are defined and identified then marketers will commonly evaluate alternative media for advertising on a range of criteria, including:

- **size of circulation or audience** – but size of audience alone is insufficient as allowance must be made for the *quality* of the audience, i.e. how many in the audience fit the target market consumer or user characteristics?
- **media *quality*** – some media or publications have more prestige with their audiences or readers than others (possibly because of editorial policies or content), and advertisements might have more attention paid to them
- **cost per thousand** to reach the target group (users/consumers) covered by the particular media – decisions based on cost alone risk making assumptions that all people in the audience are serious prospective customers, and might also be made without any measure of the media's effectiveness in producing tangible sales results or other intended responses
- **budget constraints** (funds available to support the product with above and below the line marketing activity, including communications)
- **creative constraints** – some products might lend themselves better than others to promotion through particular communications media, i.e. radio is a growing media in many markets, but

often presents headaches to the creative team in devising an advertisement to communicate appropriate messages where a product cannot be seen

- the **reach** of the selected media versus the **frequency** of exposure to the message – here the considerations focus on whether it is better to reach a very broad base of potential users/consumers who might only be exposed to the advertisement once or few times, or to whether it is better to reach a more limited number of prospective customers but with a greater frequency of exposure
- **lead times** to mount an effective campaign – in some situations time is of the essence, such as in countering competitive activity or where the market is seen as very dynamic (possibly with rapidly changing tastes and preferences, or a rapid rate of product innovation).

In developing nations another factor sometimes must be considered in making a choice between media – the certainty that the advertisement will appear as scheduled. Over the years many exporters have experienced problems getting confirmation that all paid for advertisements are featured on time or at all in markets where there is no independent auditing of advertising! Posters may not appear on poster sites, or the sites might be hijacked by unauthorized bill posters. Television or radio advertisements have been known not to be broadcast at pre-booked times, which is a particular loss of exposure if an advertiser was paying for fixed time or peak spots (sometimes power disruption affecting broadcasting or reception has been used as an excuse). The security of knowing that an advertisement will be featured in the right place and at the right time, and reaching a prescribed target audience will influence decisions on media selection in developing markets.

Point of sale material

Point of sale material is also not targeted to any specific customer and is therefore impersonal. But it does attempt to influence any prospective customers who are at the place where sales transactions occur (i.e. at a trade counter in a wholesale distributor's premises, or in a store displaying a consumer product). Marketing messages featured on point of sales material are necessarily generic in aiming at the widest possible range of prospects with a simple message. Point of sale material, whilst an impersonal communication, can be a useful marketing tool in that:

- effective use of point of sale material can increase volume sales significantly
- it can be short-term or permanent, but ensure that the material is relevant for how you want to use it
- the incremental sales gain far outweighs the initial costs
- it should always be used to support above-the-line (media) campaigns to present a final motivating message where the prospect sees the product on sale.

Unsightly or damaged point of sale material probably does more to hinder than promote sales: encourage distributors to replace damaged point of sale material, and to remove promotional material when the promotional feature ends.

Point of sale material is often wasted, in that many distributors receive it from the export suppliers, but do not implement an effective distribution and use programme through their sales teams, leaving much material to become obsolete in storerooms. Distributors and agents in foreign markets will often benefit from training in effective use of point of sale material. They need to understand that:

- it is a useful, and sometimes vital, tool in the selling and communication process, in that it both gives a sales person a talking point during a sales presentation, and provides a motivational message to new and current customers, prompting product trial or building brand loyalty

- it is costly to design, produce and distribute internationally, and is wasting scarce budgetary resources if not used effectively
- it acts like a silent sales person when prominently featured in outlets that stock and display a supplier's products, reminding both staff and customers of the product at the moment when a selection is being made (and this is just as applicable to industrial products distributed through trade suppliers as for retail products)
- the presence of some point of sale material (such as a sign promoting an outlet as an exclusive stockist or product service specialist) can add status to the outlet, drawing more customers to the location
- their sales teams might need training in placing point of sales material at key locations at a customer's premises.

Media mentions

Companies frequently seek favourable editorial comment in various media, since such independent comment can have a significant influence on prospective customers (or support the earlier decisions of existing customers for the product) who might be sceptical about claims in paid-for advertisements. Obtaining media mentions is normally part of the brands publicity activity supporting the mainstream marketing communications.

In export markets, where a product or company might be less well known, without a hard core of loyal customers, editorial media mentions can be a powerful tool in promoting trial and confidence in a product or a company. Export marketers often devote little attention to obtaining favourable media mentions in their markets, perhaps because they lack the detailed knowledge of, and contacts in, the media. Whilst building the media contacts can be time consuming, limited budgetary resources for advertising can be supported by effective brands publicity activity promoting edito-

rial coverage of products, sponsorships, and other newsworthy items.

The agent or distributor is often best placed in his own market to develop editorial media contacts, but larger companies might have internal specialists who can develop a strategy that supports mainstream international marketing activity and material for circulation.

Sales promotions

In general sales promotional activity is impersonal in that it is focused on a product or targeted to a group of customers meeting certain broad criteria, and is not addressed personally to identified individuals.

The effectiveness of sales promotional activity is often questioned by marketers. This questioning attitude is probably even more valid when export promotions are run in remote markets. Distributors, charged with promotion implementation, often have no personal financial involvement in funding promotions, and have no personal risk should a promotion be ineffective. Chapter 21 will develop an approach to planning and implementing export promotions that focuses on:

- having clear promotion objectives agreed in advance
- tight budgetary controls
- selection of promotional formats most suited to achieving the objectives
- effective monitoring of promotion achievements and comparison with objectives.

Perceptual and factual impacts of marketing communications ▬

Marketers are always looking for new ways to communicate with their target customers. The main means of communicating marketing messages are illustrated in Figure 18.3, and can be divided into two categories, **perceptual** and **factual** messages.

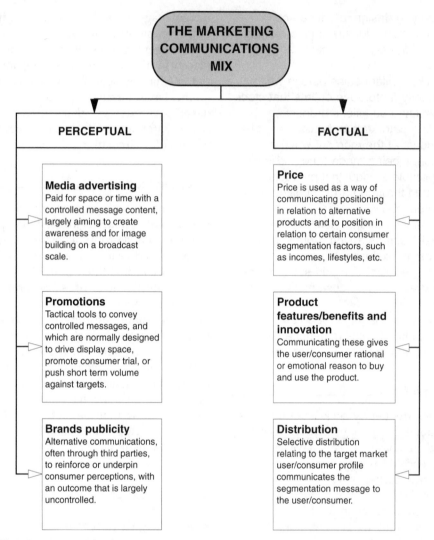

Figure 18.3 *Perceptual and factual impacts of marketing communications*

Perceptual messages are usually concerned with the motivations and influences that encourage purchase and trial, or product loyalty. These messages might include a playing to people's aspirations, peer group acceptance, street credibility, and self image, to list but a few. The factual messages convey specific information about a product, such as its price and its price positioning in relation to competitive or alternative products, its features and their benefits to users, and the distribution pattern also conveys factual messages about the product's positioning and target con-

sumer profile (an exclusive product, such as a designer perfume, would normally be in restricted distribution in outlets whose customer profile matches that of the target consumers – mass distribution through supermarkets would convey a wrong message about both its positioning and target market).

From the perspective of international marketing there are a number of points to be considered about perceptual and factual aspects of marketing communications if the marketer is to be in control of his marketing strategy for a product.

Media advertising

The advertiser needs to check that the perceptions he wants to create are conveyed in a manner understood in each market, and that the imagery used to convey these perceptions are culturally and socially acceptable.

Advertisements designed for the domestic market may not suit some or all of the export markets. Imagery may have different meanings or impacts. An advertisement designed to show the international acceptance of a product, and featuring actors from a number of different races or nationalities, might cause offence in a market where there are local negative attitudes towards a particular race or nationality. Advertisements featuring persons in sensual situations are likely to offend Muslim sensitivities in many markets. Imagery that promotes a feeling of well being or peer group acceptance when smoking cigarettes might not be acceptable to advertising standards authorities in many markets.

Promotions

The suitability and acceptability of promotion formats designed to communicate perceptions about products also needs to be checked for each market. Gifts for buyers might not be acceptable to some organizations. The exporter may need to satisfy himself for some markets that the intended beneficiary actually does receive the benefit of promotions.

Brands publicity

Whilst brands publicity activities, whether sponsorships or editorial commentaries or other formats discussed in Chapter 20, can be powerful tools supporting the main thrust of media communications, it is important to check the local suitability of an activity as a means of creating the right positive perceptions. For a cigarette company to be sponsoring a school activity, such as a sports day, might cause a negative

backlash from local authorities concerned with a rising trend in young persons smoking and the long-term associated health risks.

Price

It is just as important for the export marketer to be in control of the price and relative price positioning of his products in export markets as the domestic marketer is in the home market. Sadly, many exporters do not have much or any control over export market pricing structures or positioning, since they do not control the prices or margins of their distributors or other tiers in the distribution chain. Since price communicates factual messages concerning positioning (often in relation to competitor products, consumer incomes and lifestyles), and often also implies value in terms of source, reliability, quality, and so on, the export marketer needs to work with distributors to ensure correct positioning whilst also providing each tier of the chain with a fair margin.

Product features and benefits

Since user or consumer needs from a product might not be the same in all export markets, factual communications about features and benefits should focus on local needs. Design factors (colour, shape. etc.) and ease of use might be key benefits in power tools sold in developed markets, but in developing markets their needs might focus more on reliability, ease of maintenance, longevity, and durability in tough working environments (motors not clogging with sand!).

Distribution

Whilst in the home market the marketers might find it relatively easy to identify selected outlets that have consumer profiles matching those of the product, in many export markets the export marketer does not have this information, and is reliant on a distributor to obtain distribution, where often the distributor fails to communicate much about the outlets he covers.

Part of the distribution planning process with distributors must focus on the importance of categorizing other outlets in the distribution chain, or prospective and current customers, in order that actual distribution sought matches perceptional aspects of the marketing communications.

The exporter needs to train the distributor in the importance of matching distribution to target market user or consumer profiles, as a mis-match causes confusion to prospective customers, and part of this training may involve conducting an audit to classify all users or trade outlets. For example, a premium priced whisky stocked by a neighbourhood bar serving local working persons might not sell at all and cause the bar owner to de-stock on other company brands more suited to his outlet; but, also, consumers who were aware that the product was available in almost any outlet might stop consuming it as it had lost its perception of up-market exclusivity in their eyes.

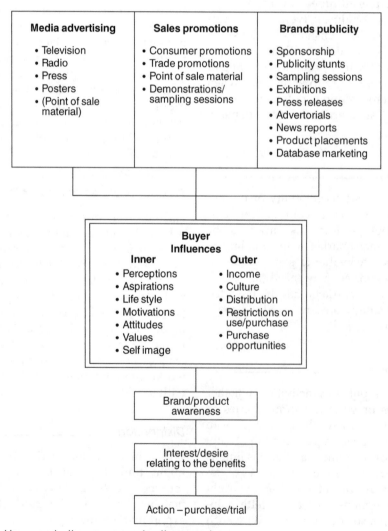

Figure 18.4 How marketing communications work

How marketing communications work in the market

We can illustrate diagrammatically, as in Figure 18.4, how marketing communications work. This diagram breaks down the means of communicating into brands publicity, sales promotions and advertising. Some forms of marketing communication might fall into more than one of the main headings, depending on how it is intended to be used or to work, i.e. point of sale material might be either under media communications (in that it is a printed communication) or a sales promotion format (in that it is only placed at, and effective at, the point of sale). Similarly, sampling sessions can either be considered as a sales promotion activity or a brands publicity activity. The three main means of communicating can each work on the buyer and the main factors that influence buyer behaviour – called here the **inner** and the **outer** influences.

The **inner influences** are very personal, such as self image and motivations, and some are often conditioned by environment and culture, such as attitudes and values. The buyer's aspirations, lifestyle and perceptions of a product will also all have an influence on purchasing decisions.

Outer influences are those external factors that have an influence on buying decisions, the most obvious being the prospective buyer's income. The culture plays a part, in that a product alien to a particular culture will often have more problems gaining acceptance and trial.

The intention of media communications is to lead the buyer along a chain, initially creating an awareness of the brand or product, then arousing desire in relation to the real and perceived product benefits, and finally prompting favourable action to buy and try the product.

The export marketer can build on his understanding of how communications

work to develop a communications strategy, through available media supported by promotional activity and brands publicity, that will focus on both the inner and outer influences on target buyers. The principles apply to industrial just as to consumer goods. With industrial goods the key outer influencing factor might be a budget rather than a personal income, and, whilst personal life style might be less relevant as an inner influence, media communications can play to an appropriate mix of other inner influences. For example, a buyer of pumps will have perceptions about the product (its source, design, quality, reputation, etc.), have his own self image as a professional buyer (possibly that he is a tough negotiator who knows quality), and have motivations such as keeping the users in the factory satisfied because the product works reliably and cost effectively. Marketing communications can then be designed that address this mix of influencing factors.

Further reading

Marketing Management – Analysis, Planning, Implementation and Control. Philip Kotler (Prentice Hall, 8th edition 1994). Chapter 22: Designing Communications and Promotion Mix Strategies

Marketing Communications. Colin J. Coulson-Thomas (Butterworth-Heinemann 1983). Chapters 1, 6, 7, 8, 9, 10, 11, 12, 13

Marketing – An Introductory Text. Martin Christopher and Malcolm McDonald (Macmillan 1995). Chapter 13: Communications Strategy

Essentials of Marketing. Geoff Lancaster and Lester Massingham (McGraw-Hill, 2nd edition). Chapter 11: Marketing Communications

The Marketing Book. Edited by Michael J. Baker (Butterworth-Heinemann, 4th edition, 1999). Chapter 21: Promotion

Checklist 18.1
Marketing communications

Action points

Have you developed a communications strategy to support the marketing strategy for each export market, covering as appropriate:

- advertising?
- promotion?
- brands publicity?
- field sales activity?

Which market factors will affect the balance of the communications mix in your individual markets:

- availability of media?
- local power of individual communications options to influence decisions?
- available budget versus costs of communications options?
- marketing objectives?
- security of access to markets?

Which communications mix options best suit your objectives and marketing strategies in individual markets:

- Personal
    - sales calls to customers?
    - product sampling or demonstration?
    - targeted mailshots?
    - personally focused brands publicity activity?
- Impersonal
    - media advertising?
    - point of sales materials?
    - media mentions?
    - sales promotional activity and/or targeted mailshots?
    - general brands publicity activity?

Checklist 18.1 *(Continued)*

	Action points

Which ways to communicate perceptual and factual marketing messages will impact most effectively on target groups in your markets:
 	
 • Perceptual
   – media advertising
   – promotions
   – brands publicity
 • Factual
   – price
   – product features/benefits and innovations
   – selective distribution in outlets serving the target markets of users/consumers	

19

Advertising in the marketing communications mix _____

In this chapter we will be looking at advertising within the marketing communications mix, with specific attention addressed to:

- its role and its effects on consumers and market sales activity
- factors to consider in deciding whether advertising is appropriate to markets
- marketing communications objectives in relation to the consumer purchasing process
- questions for the marketer to consider in developing an advertising plan
- a process for preparing an advertising brief for an agency
- techniques for testing advertisements
- factors to consider in selecting advertising media.

The aim will be to give the export marketer, who may not have worked in domestic marketing, a better understanding of the workings of advertising in the marketing mix, and to be better prepared for dealing with advertising agencies in export markets, with a view to improving the effectiveness of the advertising against its objectives and the use of budgets.

The traditional approach to export marketing communications in many organizations has been to focus on media advertising. Budgets have often been committed without clear definition of the marketing objectives to be addressed, or with too little research into the market and users or consumers. Without clear marketing objectives and a good level of knowledge of the target market it becomes difficult to establish clear **quantitative** and **qualitative** objectives for a media campaign, or to design media communications that will address the objectives. Advertisers might then be in the situation of developing materials that seem aesthetically pleasing to them, and that provide a lot of information about products that they consider important, but have advertisements that do not produce the desired response.

We will look now more specifically at the role of media communications in the marketing communications mix and at developing advertisements that address specific objectives set by the international marketer for his markets.

The role of media communications ▰▰▰▰▰▰▰

When designing media communications for export markets the marketer should be clear on the objectives of the media campaign. Often the easiest option is to adapt domestic advertisements (whether for printed media or for television), but that might not be appropriate if the domestic market is more developed or sophisticated, and the domestic media communications have objectives that differ from those for the export markets. We should be clear what we can expect media communications to do for the company or the product, and define our objectives before developing the strategy or designing the visual, audio or written communications.

The media communications can be directed to both users/consumers or trade channel distribution outlets, such as retailers or wholesalers. Media communications aimed at consumers or users, in whatever format, primarily serve four key functions, illustrated in the following boxed list.

Trade channel communications _____

Distributive trade channel media communications specifically can:

- provide product information on source, heritage (company or product historical credentials), product performance, product use, care and maintenance or servicing, recommended trade pricing structures, etc.

The key functions of media communications

1 Informing prospective users/ consumers of what is on offer:
  - the range of product choices
  - how they are used/consumed
  - promoting responsible use/ consumption
  - new product innovations
  - where to buy and what to expect to pay
  - inter-product comparisons

2 Long-term brand building:
  - communicating product features and benefits to consumers
  - creating favourable brand images and consumer perceptions
  - brand positioning within the company portfolio and competitive market and product environment
  - building recognition of the company name when appropriate

- building-long term brand loyalty, endorsing the product selection

3 Developing positive attitudes:
  - towards the company and the products
  - countering negative lobbies or voices (including adverse media coverage)
  - overcoming prejudices towards the industry, company, etc.

4 Short-term tactical support to promotions and brand positioning:
  - promoting the achievement of specific marketing and sales objectives
  - targeting specific consumer groups
  - targeting specific outlets or trade channels
  - defensive or blocking campaigns to counter competitive activity

- promote special trade offers and inform about promotional programmes including media advertising
- provide feedback on the product's sales performance and work to promote good stock control and limit stock-piling or stock shortages
- build long-term trade channel loyalty through good communications and trade support
- promote better product category management (including sharing information on stock and sales).

Trade channel communications are an important marketing tool in building firm relationships with product distributors and stockists. Some companies make their products available to any potential trade outlet, but many suppliers (especially where the product has a niche market, 'exclusive' image or servicing needs) limit distribution to appointed dealers. Whilst in domestic markets it is common to develop good trade communication packages, including training materials where relevant, in export markets exporters often neglect the tiers in trade channel distribution below the main importer (relying on their appointed distributors to be the driving force in building the business), and lose the opportunity to build trade loyalty, commitment, and a partnership throughout the supply chain. Export marketers should give attention to developing trade channel communications suited to each market's needs and trading environment, just as they address media communications aimed at consumers.

The effects of advertising

Advertising impacts on both the product users or consumers and on the trade channels distributors and stockists. Figure 19.1 illustrates typical ways advertising can influence consumers and sales activity. The effects on users or consumers can drive demand; the effects on sales activity can drive supply through trade channel outlets, ensuring that distribution is available to meet demand in locations suited to customer purchasing practices. In markets where a manufacturer is known and strong, new products can often be distributed

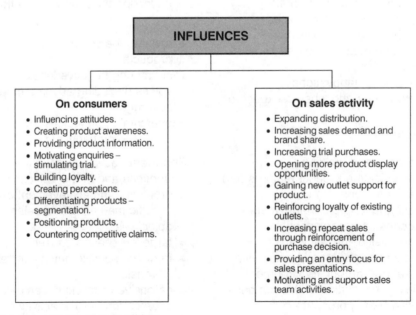

INFLUENCES

On consumers
- Influencing attitudes.
- Creating product awareness.
- Providing product information.
- Motivating enquiries – stimulating trial.
- Building loyalty.
- Creating perceptions.
- Differentiating products – segmentation.
- Positioning products.
- Countering competitive claims.

On sales activity
- Expanding distribution.
- Increasing sales demand and brand share.
- Increasing trial purchases.
- Opening more product display opportunities.
- Gaining new outlet support for product.
- Reinforcing loyalty of existing outlets.
- Increasing repeat sales through reinforcement of purchase decision.
- Providing an entry focus for sales presentations.
- Motivating and support sales team activities.

Figure 19.1 The effects of advertising

rapidly through existing trade outlets because of the supplier's image and reputation with the trade, and then media support can be used to pull product through by creating consumer awareness. In export markets, whilst traditional approaches to marketing encourage building a viable distribution base before commencing mainstream media advertising, it is often difficult to obtain broad distribution for relatively unknown products or suppliers. That can pressure an export marketer to invest earlier than he might like in advertising as a means of encouraging the trade to stock the product. As distribution is a key factor in obtaining sales volume, the marketer will need to consider how he can use trade advertising and promotions to promote distribution, or to what extent he must invest in consumer advertising in advance of an adequate base of distribution being obtained in order to also encourage trade outlets to stock the product.

Should we advertise?

For the export marketer there are three main areas to consider in advertising in any of his markets.

- Firstly, he needs to know information about the market segments in relation to his products or product portfolio.
- Secondly, he needs to be clear on where the product stands in its life cycle in each market (which may vary between markets) in order to take decisions on levels of investment in marketing communications.
- Thirdly, he must consider the source and level of any budgets available for marketing communications.

Figure 19.2 illustrates some of the main questions that will arise in each of these categories of considerations.

FACTORS IN A DECISION TO ADVERTISE

Portfolio plan and segmentation factors

- Do we know enough about the product to develop a focused media campaign?
- Can the consumer segment (as defined by relevant consumer characteristics) be separately targeted through media?
- Can the trade channels be targeted through media?
- What are the portfolio plan objectives for the brand? Do these include development through mass media or selective media?
- Is there a unique consumer brand proposition lending itself to media communication?
- Can the responses of trade channels and consumers to marketing communications be measured?

Investment classification factors

- Which stage of the product life cycle do we judge the brand to be at:
  - launch?
  - seed?
  - invest?
  - maintain?
  - harvest?

Budget levels

- Do the potential volumes produce and A&P budget at a threshold level to permit media support in any effective way?
- Do budget levels permit development of local creative inputs – e.g. films/videos, press or posters?
- Are the budgets at such a low level that focused support through promotions are more suitable to the brand objectives and volumes?

Figure 19.2 Factors in a decision to advertise

Advertising needs to be focused on a target group, so the marketer needs to be clear on who is his target group and how they can best be reached (what media are available and suitable). The core product message needs to be developed and communicated in a way that is meaningful to the target audience. Another consideration will be the ability of the marketer to gauge the effectiveness of advertising on the consumers or trade. Another area of consideration illustrated is whether the product is in a growth sector of its life cycle, and worthy of an investment strategy, or whether it is in decline and profits should be harvested.

Marketing communication budgets always seem too small to achieve the objectives or to make an impact on the market place. Decisions will have to be taken on the best use of budgets, e.g. the balance between media, promotions or other activity such as brands publicity. Whilst one market with growth potential may not generate sufficient advertising revenues within product costings to be self sufficient, funds can always be transferred from other markets where there is a lower level of advertising and promotional activity than the funds accruing would permit (often where products are in the maintenance or harvesting stages of their life cycles).

Marketing communications in relation to consumers

Consumers are constantly bombarded with media messages and other forms of marketing communications, even in less sophisticated markets. In highly developed markets the range of media the average consumer is exposed to may be broader than in less developed markets (where personal ownership of televisions may be rarer, and expenditure on printed media such as newspapers and magazines may be less). But whatever the range of media, marketers find ways to communicate: where television and magazines are less available, posters and cinemas are often used more intensively. Figures 19.3 and 19.4 show the processes the users or

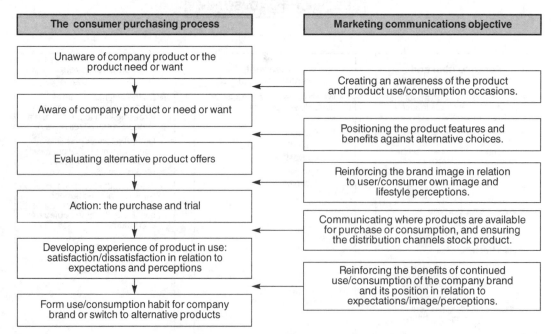

Figure 19.3 Marketing communications objectives in relation to the consumer purchasing process

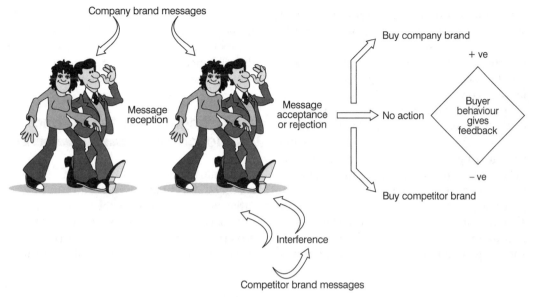

Figure 19.4 *Brand messages and the consumer*

consumers are going through when exposed to marketing communications.

Figure 19.3 shows the consumer starting from a position of unawareness about a product or the need for a product, and then moving through the stages of building an awareness of a product or product need or want, then considering the alternative product options available in the market, before trying the product or making a purchase.

As experience of the product builds through use, the customer also builds a level of satisfaction in relation to their earlier expectations or perceptions. If the user or consumer is satisfied they will form a preference for the company product, and become a regular user, otherwise they will switch to alternative products. The right hand column of the illustration highlights the typical marketing objectives a supplier will have at each of these stages in the purchasing process. This will indicate to the marketer that different marketing communications messages may need to be developed and promoted according to where the target consumers are in the purchasing process. At the earlier stages of unfamiliarity with the product, and perhaps no clearly defined need, the advertisements may focus

more on promoting features and benefits, and highlighting the products compatibility with the target consumers' life styles. After a product has been purchased and tried, messages often focus more on reinforcing satisfaction with use.

Figure 19.4 illustrates the chain of communications and subsequent responses when the user or consumer is bombarded by, or even gently exposed to, advertising messages, whether in the form of mainstream media campaigns or lower key brands publicity activity. The effectiveness of a communications campaign can be judged by the resultant behaviour of the users/consumers, i.e. to buy the company product, or show preference for a competitor product, or to take no action at all. The company's advertising effectiveness can be judged over time according to how the consumers react – if there is a measurable move towards purchasing company products then the messages are working, but if there is no move towards company products or a switch towards competitor products then the messages of the media communications need review.

Company media messages will be reaching the target customers along with competitors' product messages, and whilst some messages from competitors might be supporting the general building of a market for the products, more specific messages will be encouraging the target consumers to favour competitors' products. There will also be a lot of other information circulating in the market place (shown in the diagram as 'interference'); some will be positive encouraging expenditure but on other products, and some may be negative types of information, e.g. discouraging use of the products in some cases (e.g. tobacco and alcohol), or possibly government messages encouraging saving rather than consumer spending (where consumer demand is pro-

moting inflation). When designing media messages account needs to be taken of the competitors' messages and any general 'interference' in an effort to ensure yours is the stronger and more influential message.

Budgeting for advertising and promotions

Customarily marketers build in a margin to costings for marketing communications, often referring to it as the A & P reserve (advertising and promotion reserve). The advertising and promotions contribution is typically accrued either as a percentage

Advertising – the questions	
● Why are we advertising?	– *define the objectives*
● Whom are we targeting?	– *specify the target market clearly*
● What is our message?	– *does it relate to both the target market and the brand perceptions we are promoting?*
● What media are available in the market to communicate with consumers?	– *if conventional media are unavailable or restricted, what alternatives exist or can be developed?*
● Where should we advertise?	– *will the target market get the message and how often?*
● How will we communicate our message?	– *will it be meaningful and relevant to the target audience?*
● When will we advertise?	– *are there special seasons/occasions that dictate a prime period?*
● What is the budget?	– *how are we limited in reaching our objective and target market?*
● What is our media schedule?	– *can we put the fine detail to the campaign?*
● Can we control the budget?	– *have we a way of monitoring budget and schedules?*
● How can we measure the campaign effectiveness?	– *are there quantitative measures of performance against objectives?*
● What have we learned from the campaign?	– *can we evaluate response and effectiveness in a way to aid future planning?*

related to the sales volume (sometimes calculated as a percentage of the standard cost of producing a unit, or more commonly calculated as a percentage of the company's sales revenue per unit), or a fixed sum per unit. This type of approach gives a simple formula for estimating the funds that can be spent on marketing communications and related promotional activity for any given level of sales volume that is forecast or achieved.

If sales volumes were the sole determinant of the level of marketing communications spend then there is an assumption that sales is the stimulus with marketing communications the response, whereas logic dictates the reverse is the case. The marketer must be clear on his marketing objectives for each product or brand in each export market, and develop a marketing communications strategy appropriate to those objectives, i.e. that will actively promote the achievement of those objectives. That may mean that the standard system used by many companies of having one export price list for all markets, with a similarly fixed accrual level of reserves for advertising and promotion, is too simplistic. Export prices may need to be varied market by market, with the objective of achieving correct market positioning relative to competitor products in each market, and with suitable funding included for marketing communications. Also clear strategic decisions need to be taken on which products within a company's portfolio are to be treated as investment products and in which export markets they will be promoted more heavily, because those products may need far higher levels of advertising and promotion support than can be levied in an advertising and promotion reserve during the investment stages of brand building.

Whilst typically advertising and promotion accrual reserves are built in to standard costings at levels of 3 to 5 per cent (occasionally a little higher for some products that require heavier marketing communications support, as with some fast moving consumer goods), expenditure dur-

ing the investment stage of a product's life cycle might run in the range 10 to 30 per cent over limited time periods for some products.

There need not be a direct relationship between the budgeted advertising and promotion reserve accrued in the accounts as sales are achieved and the expenditure on a product or brand, as money may be transferred from products at the **seed** or **harvest** stages of their life cycles to other products or brands considered to be at the **investment** or **maintenance** stages in their life particular cycles.

Depending on the exporter's approaches to product pricing and marketing communications, advertising and promotion reserves might be accrued for all the export markets by including the appropriate level of reserve into costings for accrual on export sales to all the active export markets, or the advertising and promotion reserve might selectively only be included in the costings for export markets where the marketer expects to be active with media communications and promotional activity.

Another consideration for the marketer is that any advertising and promotion funds accrued need not always be spent in the market that generated the sales volume producing the funds available for marketing communications. Funds generated in one market might often be used more effectively in another market. For example, if you make periodic opportunistic sales into some African markets, where you cannot plan for orderly growth and ensure a regular level of stock available in the markets (possibly because of the irregular availability of import licences or foreign exchange for imports), then you might be wasting scarce reserves for long-term brand building by using them in those African markets producing these opportunistic sales.

As a general principle funds are best spent in markets where you can plan an orderly marketing strategy, with assured continuity of supply of your products to the market. That does not mean that you should cut any advertising and promotion levy from your pricings for sales to the opportunistic markets, as the deciding factor in your costings and product pricing should not be whether or not you will be supporting a product with a programme of marketing communications, but at what price level can you achieve the opportunistic sales. Too many exporters tend to treat un-forecast opportunistic sales as a bonus, and therefore are more willing to drop prices to obtain the extra sale, often effectively treating their product as a commodity, rather than focusing on selling the added value features and benefits of their products.

A task approach to marketing communications budgets

For those companies that have the volume of export sales that warrants a serious approach to export market management, and the resources to actively manage export markets, the marketing communications strategy for each market can be looked at on a task basis of assessing and listing each marketing communications task judged necessary to foster achievement of the broad marketing objectives. A task approach to allocating marketing communications budgets will work on the basis that the marketer clearly defines the communications objectives and their desired response, both in consumer behaviour and sales results.

Each task identified as necessary to achieve the objectives is then costed, and cumulated to a total marketing communications budget. This may then be compared with the level of advertising and promotion reserves earned or expected to be earned by current or projected sales volumes. A deficit indicates that investment funds must be transferred from other sources. A longer-term return on investment approach may then be taken to evaluating the investment decision, i.e. how long before the level of advertising and promotion funds included in product costings and accruing from sales will be at a level for the brand to be self supporting?

All decisions on marketing communications must reflect the level of competitive activity on competitive brands and directly substitutable products.

Developing an advertising brief

Export marketers who need to develop media communications in a foreign market need to be familiar with the process of briefing advertising and other promotional agencies (including public relations and sales promotions agencies), and to develop a systematic approach to the agency briefing process in order that they can both expect proposals to match the media brief, and be able to make comparisons between alternative proposals or alternative agencies (where they are looking to appoint a local agency).

Developing the communications strategy can involve the marketer in quite a lot of time liaising with, and briefing, the various agencies involved. Typically industrial products exporters take a more simplistic approach to marketing in export markets, focusing more on direct promotion to the end user market. Consumer product manufacturers might need to be as sophisticated as in the home market, where they will probably have a briefing process as in Figure 19.5.

The purpose of the **advertising brief** is to:

- develop a clear statement of the requirement, clarifying the inputs required from all involved, and develop objective inputs into a consistent brief
- provide to the agency or other resource provider the basic information needed to develop a proposal
- ensure there is a commonly communicated (and understood) brief that will enable subsequent proposals to be filtered and evaluated against common objective criteria.

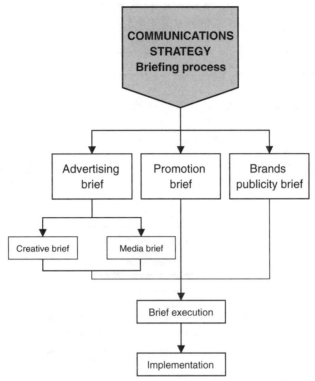

Figure 19.5 *The communications briefing process*

The marketer should:

- be specific in the tasks to be addressed
- say what must be avoided (any taboos, or corporate guidelines that must apply)
- leave ample room for creative ideas from the agency.

A typical advertising briefing process is illustrated in Figure 19.6. The marketer will prepare a brief, and that document should include and clarify any relevant information about his company's procedures for evaluating proposals or organizing its media activity and its expectations from the proposal and the resultant advertising campaign. At this briefing stage consideration needs to be given to how the marketing and promotion of a product will dovetail with other products in the company product portfolio and specific information relating to the particular brand or product (i.e. its brand objectives, segment information on target audi-

ence, focus of the media message content and its expected impact or response on the target audience). The agency will then respond by preparing some appropriate alternative executions for the export marketer to consider, and these proposed executions can be measured and monitored against the objectives set out in the initial brief and any other information provided in the briefing process.

If the marketer needs additional guidance in developing a brief for an agency, then Figure 19.7 shows how the brief might be structured.

Guidelines for an advertising proposal

When the export marketer has requested an advertising agency to prepare a media proposal he will need a framework of things to look for in reviewing the proposal. The

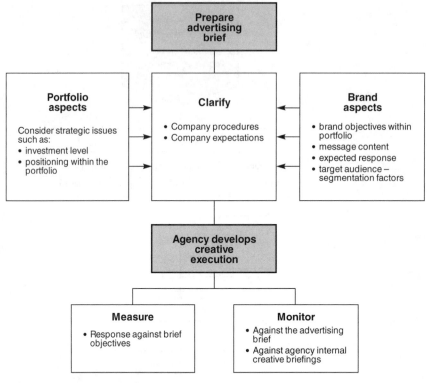

Figure 19.6 *The advertising briefing process*

review of the proposal should at least follow the guidelines listed below.

- It should meet the advertising/media brief, addressing all the issues raised.
- Objectives of the advertising proposals and media campaign (qualitative and quantitative) should be clearly stated, including time frames to achieve objectives.
- It should provide details of the proposed utilization of budgets between the various media proposed (including all commissions, any taxes, etc.).
- All costs of the package, including creative and materials costs and possibly costs associated with usage in other markets, should be identified and listed (emphasis to the agency that you want no hidden costs not listed within proposals).
- All the 'visuals' proposed should be illustrated, such as with story boards.

- The product 'messages' should be detailed in respect of:
  - content
  - mediums of communication
  - intended impact.
- The testing of concepts, if appropriate, should be detailed, and costings for testing included.
- Performance measures or standards of performance should be clarified and detailed (addressed to the objectives).
- Evaluation processes and techniques to be used in assessing the effectiveness or impact of proposals and media campaigns, and their timings, should be detailed.
- The specific responsibilities for each stage (planning, production, implementation, media booking, measurement and control) should be identified and detailed, with time frames.

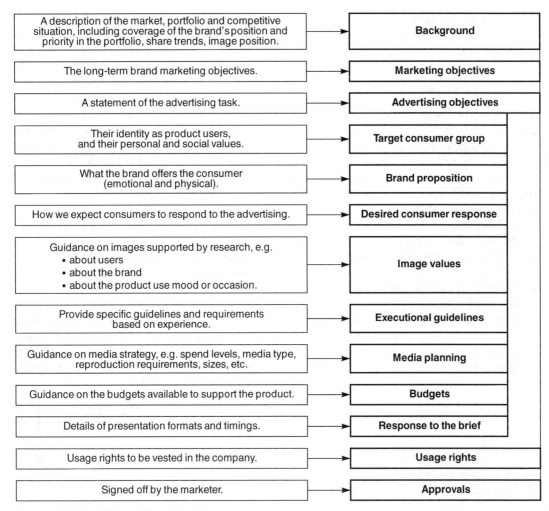

Figure 19.7 *The advertising brief format*

Concept testing advertisements ■

To minimize the risk of media activity failing to achieve its aims, as part of the brief and at the stage when the agency is developing the advertising proposal, the export marketer can make use of **concept testing.** The purpose of concept testing is to ensure judgements for selection and development of media activity are based on objective data related to product marketing and communication objectives.

Concept testing serves the functions of:

● providing a basis for objective selection of specific ideas

● providing reassurance that ideas are compatible with consumer or trade expectations for the product/brand
● supporting activity and expenditure proposals, and the marketer's budget requests
● reassuring colleagues and other involved departments that an activity or message is right for the brand and will promote achievement of marketing objectives
● providing a clear direction for actual detailed final briefs, resultant proposals, and the execution of marketing activity
● enabling qualitative and quantitative expectations to be assessed and standards of performance agreed

● serving as an additional source of knowledge for refining executional techniques.

Testing techniques

The company has to decide, at the time of developing briefings, what responses to an advertisement will be considered as indicating an effective advertisement in line with pre-stated objectives, and then must attempt to assess the likelihood of an advert producing the desired result. Figure 19.8 illustrates typical techniques used for testing advertisements. These techniques can conveniently be divided into two categories:

● **pre-testing techniques** – those techniques that can usefully provide information to help evaluate alternative forms of concepts and advertisements prior to them being used in media campaigns

● **post-testing techniques** – those techniques that can be used once the target audience is exposed to media campaigns to judge the effectiveness of the advertising concepts and messages in promoting the desired reaction.

The testing techniques used with concepts and advertisements are not an exact science. Marketers do encounter problems in media experimentation and testing, and these often revolve around:

● setting valid objectives for a proposal or campaign
● controlling and designing tests
● interpreting the data produced by tests.

Because tests might not be easy to measure and monitor that should not be used as an excuse not to conduct any testing but just to rely on judgement and 'gut feel'. Any serious quantitative or qualitative test data

Pre-testing techniques	Post-testing techniques
Checklists: company's internal list of elements to be included in an advertisement and against which proposals can be judged – this assumes the list is relevant to the objectives and comprehensive.	Enquiry tests: monitoring enquiries/sales by advertisement used and by media.
Consumer juries: a group of prospects is asked for assessment and comments to gain an insight to their understanding of an advertisement and likely response – but it depends on a jury's verbal comments and is not fully objective.	Recall/recognition tests: surveying consumers to see recognition/recall of advertisements and their message impact and interpretation.
Enquiry tests: alternative advertisements are used in alternative media or regions, and quantity of responses measured through prospect enquiries – but it is difficult to measure the quality of enquiries without further work (good for mail order).	Consumer audits: auditing a random group of consumers to see their product purchases/patterns/attitudes, etc. before and after an advertisement or campaign.
Laboratory measurement devices: prospects' physical responses are measured in a controlled environment – sweat reaction, blink rate, pupil dilation, etc. Whilst objective and controlled, relative sales effectiveness is not measured.	Retail audits: monitoring response to advertisements through effects on retail stock holding, stock purchase, and offtake
Experimentation: different advertisements and ideas may be tested in different regions or media, or to different market consumer segments, and response measured through sales data.	

Figure 19.8 Techniques for testing advertisements

will aid judgements and reduce the risks that media campaigns are inappropriate for the objectives or ineffective in promoting their achievements. Cultural differences between markets make it particularly important that advertisements for use in export markets are carefully designed and tested, especially where the products involved are consumer goods and the media are to be mass media such as television, press and radio. Industrial products feature less in mass media and rather more in trade press in most markets, and the messages being communicated are often much more basic than with consumer goods, focusing more on communicating product benefits than life style factors involved in purchasing decisions.

Selecting the right media ■■■■■■■

Selecting media may seem straightforward but there are a number of factors to consider if a limited budget is to be used effectively. In the home market the marketer has much broader personal experience, and often more data is available about the reach and effectiveness of various forms of media. In export markets less data may be available (although developed markets will have just as much sophisticated data as the home market, if it is accessed), and comments from agents and distributors might have to be taken with some reservations, as it is not usually their own funds that are being committed, and their own motivations in making media recommendations might not always coincide with those of the exporter. The export marketer should consider eight main factors in selecting the right media mix for advertising a company product, as detailed in the inset list.

The typical advantages and disadvantages of the normal range of mass media used in marketing are illustrated in Table 19.1. Marketers are constantly looking for new ways to reach their target audience, creating opportunities for new media promotional activity, such as through comput-erized data information services, electronic mail, faxes, as well as through the means of direct mailshots to targeted groups. Whilst mass media may seem more suited to consumer goods there has been a growing use of media such as television and journals in some markets for corporate image promotion by large conglomerates. This corporate advertising, often focusing on building credibility and corporate identity, then helps sell the products of their group of companies, which might be a mix of both consumer and industrial products.

Guidelines for developing cross cultural local media communications ■■■■■■■

If you are developing local media communications, possibly for use in more than one market sharing the same language or culture, then the following guidelines may assist design, depending on which have an applicability for the communication being developed.

- Show the product clearly with good photographic representations.
- Avoid abstract copy themes that may be difficult to comprehend in different cultures.
- Keep copy simple, brief, meaningful (to the reader/viewer/listener).
- Recognize the limitations of the recipient's attention span at the time and place the message will be communicated.
- Take account of the recipients' current level of interest in the product or alternatives, and their experience in its use or consumption occasion.
- Be sensitive to local attitudes, sensitivities, and cultural norms (try to establish if there are any local taboos that might limit how you advertise or present products or concepts, e.g. using bathing beauties to demonstrate products).

Eight key factors to consider in selecting advertising media

1 Portfolio aspects of segmentation, e.g.:
   - price positioning within the company product portfolio and in relation to competition
   - consumer characteristics of the product/brand
   - stage in the product life cycle (launch/seed/invest/maintain/harvest).

2 Budget levels in relation to media threshold levels and costs of medium as a viable choice to reach a target audience, e.g.:
   - high budget
     - television/press offer wide media possibilities for consumer goods to reach a broad consumer segment
     - support can be provided by sponsorships, trade promotions, merchandising and display activity (according to what best suits the products and marketing objectives)
   - low budget
     - cinema/magazines offer narrow media possibilities to reach more limited (or focused) consumer product segments
     - support can come from public relations activity, trade promotions, direct marketing, sampling/demonstrations.
   - cost effectiveness
     - this is often measured according to the cost per 1000 people or target prospect market reached (this is a simple measure that assumes all the audience for a media are prospects, and does not produce a measure of effectiveness, i.e. cost per sale).

3 Media availability, e.g.:
   - range of media available (often limited in less developed markets)
   - regulatory or legislative restrictions on media use by products (some products, such as tobacco and alcohol, are limited in certain markets as to what media they can use for advertising).

4 Media characteristics, e.g.:
   - geographical coverage
   - audience mix or special group coverage
   - frequency of audience coverage
   - physical limitations such as size, colour, visual limitations for printed media.

5 Compatibility with brand image, e.g.:
   - media quality image
   - profile of media audience compared with that of the products (such as an orientation towards fun/youth versus traditional/conservative
   - medium popularity within the target group.

6 Media coverage of target group, e.g.:
   - what proportion of the target group actually see/receive the message placed with each of the alternative media.

7 Creative suitability of each of the media
   - can the chosen media meet the creative requirements in terms of communicating brand image, perceptions, usage moods (if applicable), brand message/proposition, etc.?

8 Media reach versus frequency factors:
   - the marketer must consider whether to focus on a wide audience (**reach**) or a narrow audience (**frequency**) – if all prospects are equally likely to buy then 'reach' may be the main criteria, but where only a limited group of consumers seeing the advertisement are likely to respond then frequency may be more important.

Table 19.1 *Comparisons of advantages and disadvantages of major media*

Media	Advantages	Disadvantages
Television	• Large target audience. • Product can be shown to demonstrate its use and key benefits. • Messages concerning usage moods and perceptions can be communicated visually. • Advertising information is received in a relaxed environment.	• Commercial breaks may be seen as a nuisance and avoided. • Suitable for mass market consumer goods but not usually suited to specialist industrial products with very limited target group. • Large budgets needed.
Cinema	• As above, but small audiences, but can suit certain products aimed at cinema going segments, e.g. youth. • Cinema remains popular in many developing markets where television ownership is not yet widespread. • Suits products with smaller budgets.	• Position of advertisements in relation to film may affect numbers seeing advertisements.
Radio	• Seen as an intimate media by many listeners (illustrated by growth in popularity of phone-in talk shows in many markets). • Some segmentation possible through fragmentation of audiences (wide range of stations serving smaller defined target groups in many markets). • Often has a low cost (but offset to a degree by need for higher frequency)	• No visual communication or impact. • Mood expression difficult. • Usually small fragmented audiences. • Suspect retention level dictates high frequency.
Newspapers	• Flexible timing (space bookable at short notice). • Products can be shown in illustration form. • Technical information can be communicated and studied at leisure. • Read by large audiences.	• Short life span of newspapers. • Advertisements often glossed over too quickly in busy reading situation. • Messages normally need to be very simple. • Not usually good for communicating consumption/ usage moods.

Table 19.1 *Comparisons of advantages and disadvantages of major media* (Continued)

Media	Advantages	Disadvantages
Posters and outdoor advertising, e.g.: transportation	• High exposure to travelling public. • Lower costs than some media. • Illustrative (but keep simple). • Segmentation by area may be possible, and by some other target groups (e.g. users of categories of transport).	• Must be a simple message. • Needs to be particularly eye catching and memorable. • Bad weather reduces impact.
Magazines	• As above, but longer life spans than papers. • Consumers conditioned to seeing advertisements, and often to reading them. • Often scope for editorial comment or placement of advertisements near relevant editorial features. • Read at leisure. • Often passed round several readers. • Photo print quality superior to newspapers – more impact. • Can often convey moods better than newspapers.	• Advertisement positioning may be important – some sections of magazines may be glossed over if not relevant to readers' interests. • Some people buy magazines just to read certain sections. • If many advertisements are carried it can be difficult for anyone to make a particular impact.
Newspaper supplements	• Large circulation. • Normally read at leisure (not disposed of with the newspaper).	• Not passed round as much as magazines, nor usually kept as long. • Read very selectively because of general content nature.

• Keep technical jargon to a minimum as this may not be understood by non-experts.
• Inform the target audience of manner of product use or product consumption occasions, alternative modes of consumption, value-adding production techniques or special product attributes (source, relative performance versus competition, etc.).
• Outline consumer benefits (performance/strength, quality consistency, reliability through heritage, price, value for money, and image perceptions, etc.)
• Communicate who makes the product, where it is produced, and where to obtain it (and how to obtain more information or see a demonstration).
• Create brand awareness through promotion of the brand name with its unique brand proposition.

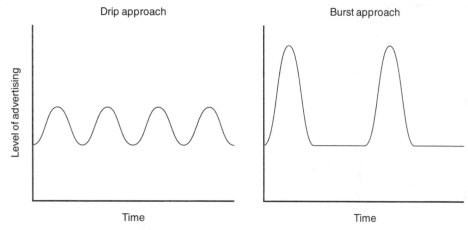

Figure 19.9 *Patterns of advertising campaign timings*

Campaign timings ▬▬▬▬

Two common approaches to media campaign planning over time, illustrated in
Figure 19.9, are the **drip** approach, and the
burst approach. As the diagram illustrates:

● the **drip** approach is to spend the
  available funds to a more regular pattern
  over a longer time period, and drip
  advertising suits non-seasonal products
  or a maintenance marketing strategy for
  well established products
● the **burst** approach is to put the
  available funds behind the product with
  short, heavyweight media campaigns at
  key time intervals, and under burst
  advertising it is normal to focus on key
  selling seasons, and that approach may
  also suit combating competitive activity
  or a development style of marketing.

The export marketer will need to decide
which approach to media advertising best
suits his markets, objectives and budgets,
and to be clear on any seasonal sales pattern
in each of his export markets when planning
the timing of marketing communications, in
order that any advertising campaigns maximize the return from the investment in the
media. Where distributors are being used in
export markets it becomes important to

have access to their local sales data in order
to identify seasonality, rather than just relying on the pattern of export shipments (as
there may be variations between the pattern
of shipments and the pattern of actual sales
in the export markets, if distributors do not
have good stock and order controls).

Where budgets are very limited, but
media support is judged necessary, it
becomes even more critical to think carefully
about the timing of media activity to provide maximum support for the product and
the accompanying trade sales efforts. For
most products a certain level of frequency of
advertising is necessary to create awareness
and produce the desired positive responses
from users or consumers. The drip approach
is unlikely to create much impact when
budgets are very small, and a focused effort
through shorter more intensive bursts has
often been preferred, particularly in the
upswing of a key selling season.

Media schedules ▬▬▬▬

If the marketer has appointed advertising
agencies in export markets then he will
need to develop media schedules to control
the booking of advertising and to assist in
the planned integration of supporting sales
and promotional activity. The agent or

Media schedule: *Press*

Period:
Market:
Product/brand:
Distributor:
Advertising agency:

Proposed/booked:
Currency:
Date prepared:
Revision number:
Prepared by:

Publication	Copy	Size, colour, position	Basic rate	Number of insertions	Total cost with discounts	Readership reach	Cost per 1000 reach	J	F	M	A	M	J	J	A	S	O	N	D

Figure 19.10 *Model media schedule control forms*

Media schedule: *Television/Radio/Cinema*

Period:
Market:
Product/brand:
Distributor:
Advertising agency:

Proposed/booked:
Currency:
Date prepared:
Revision number:
Prepared by:

TV/radio station or cinema company	Total audience reach	Length of spot	Total spots booked	Cost per 1000	Total cost after discounts	J	F	M	A	M	J	J	A	S	O	N	D

Figure 19.10 (Continued)

Media schedule: _Posters_

Period:
Market:
Product/brand:
Distributor:
Advertising agency:

Proposed/booked:
Currency:
Date prepared:
Revision number:
Prepared by:

Poster company	Poster size	Number of sites	Total cost	Cost per site	J	F	M	A	M	J	J	A	S	O	N	D

Figure 19.10 (Continued)

distributor would normally be involved, if not at all points of the briefing and planning stages, at the implementation and monitoring stages.

- press
- television/radio/cinema
- posters.

There is no particular model format for a schedule, so its design is flexible to suit the needs of the individual company and its control of media communications. Figure 19.10 illustrates a typical simple format.

Further reading

Marketing Management – Analysis, Planning, Implementation and Control. Philip Kotler (Prentice Hall, 8th edition 1994). Chapter 22: Designing Communications and Promotion Mix Strategies

The Effective Advertiser. Tom Brannan (Butterworth-Heinemann, 1993). A short but excellent exposition within the CIM Marketing Series)

The Marketing Book. Edited by Michael J. Baker (Butterworth-Heinemann, 4th edition 1999). Chapter 21: Promotion

International Marketing Communications. Tom Griffin (Butterworth-Heinemann 1993)

Action points

Product background
Product's historic performance in the market:

- narrative history
- historical statistical performance.

Market history:

- portfolio and competitive situation.

Brand history:

- state of development
- current share and trend
- competitive positioning
- position and priority in the portfolio.

Product/brand long-term marketing objectives
Market position:

- product positioning within the product category
- price positioning.

Specific advertising objectives
- product's long-term mission
- product's importance in company portfolio
- specific current advertising objective.

Target group
Relationship to your brand:

- identity as product users
- personal and social values.

Brand proposition
- the promise the product gives the consumer
- physical product attributes (real benefits)
- emotional product attributes (perceived benefits).

Checklist 19.1 (*Continued*)

Desired consumer response
Attitudinal and behavioural changes or improvements desired from media campaign:

- current feelings about the brand?
- desired feelings about the brand?
- desired thoughts about the brand?
- desired action when next choosing a product from the category?

Image values
Based on qualitative research and monitored by brand tracking studies, clarify:

- the user imagery to be developed
- brand imagery
- mood and occasion of use or consumption.

Executional guidelines
What guidelines can you give an agency covering:

- previous experience of media in markets
- mandatory requirements of your company.

Media planning
Provide or look for guidance about:

- types of media to use to achieve objectives
- campaign timings
- budget levels
- production of media materials.

Budget
- creative inputs
- supporting materials
- implementation costs (including human resources)
- performance monitoring and evaluation.

Response to the brief
Clarify to an agency when and how they should respond to a brief with proposals.

Usage rights
Clarify for an agency whether advertising materials will be wanted for use in other markets and ensure any appropriate copyrights are vested in the company, and international rights for actors' or models' services are at minimum cost.

Checklist 19.2
Advertising proposal

	Action points

• Does it meet the brief, addressing all issues raised?
• Are the objectives of the project (qualitative and quantitative) clearly stated, including time frames to achieve objectives?
• Does it provide details of utilization of budgets between mediums?
• Are all costs of the package, including creative and materials costs, identified and listed?
• Are 'visuals' illustrated?
• Are 'messages' detailed by:
  – content
  – mediums of communication
  – intended impact?
• Are appropriate concept tests detailed?
• Are performance measures or standards of performance clarified and detailed (addressed to the objectives)?
• Are evaluation processes, techniques, and timings detailed?
• Are the specific responsibilities for each stage (planning, production, implementation, media booking, communication, measurement and control) for each party identified and detailed, with time frames?	

20

Brands publicity

 In this chapter we will continue looking at ways of promoting products, with a focus on **brands publicity** activity. That term is used rather than the traditional term of public relations, since brands publicity as presented here includes public relations and a much broader range of activity communicating brand messages by means other than traditional advertising and sales promotion.

The aim is to highlight to the export marketer that:

- there are many opportunities and ways to promote products other than just media advertising and promotions
- and that pre-determined messages can be designed for communication through non-conventional media that focus on a particular target group or address a particular issue or problem.

Apart from media advertising, users or consumers and trade channel outlets can also be communicated with, and motivated by, **brands publicity activity**.

> **Brands publicity can be defined as marketing activity that communicates predetermined brand messages to specific people by means other than conventional media advertising or sales promotion.**

Communications may be either personal or impersonal (see Figure 18.2), and brands publicity activity can fall into either category.

- Brands publicity activity is more than public relations, and can typically be developed as a long-term core communications programme that aims to affect positive brand awareness, brand (or company) image, and consumer attitudes.

Using brand publicity activity ▬

In the marketing mix brands publicity activity can be developed to serve several key functions, such as:

- reinforcing the brand messages being given by all other means (advertising and promotion, word of mouth comments between consumers)

- creating product/brand/company awareness
- stimulating product trial
- developing and maintaining loyalty to the product
- creating a perception that relates to use of a product
- countering any negative publicity or attitudes that might develop.

There are several reasons the marketer might choose to support media advertising with **brands publicity** activity, depending on the market and the marketing objectives, including the following:

- Brands publicity works at a different level than the direct sell of media advertising or personal selling. It can be geared to play to emotions such as empathy, peer group conformity, self choice and individuality, and third party endorsement.
- Brands publicity activity is usually more low key and less direct than media advertising, and the understatement of promotion through brands publicity activities often suits higher priced, lifestyle and aspirational products.
- Brands publicity activity, as a lower key form of promotion, opens up opportunities for the consumer to make a personal discovery of the product rather than feeling 'pressurized' through media advertising or approaches by a salesperson.
- By presenting the 'facts' about a product indirectly through third party testimonials or media editorial commentary the consumer can feel justified in making the choice in favour of a product, and satisfied that the decision to buy it and try it was personal choice.
- Where the brand proposition or other advertising messages are being misunderstood, supporting brand publicity activity can be a more subtle, and therefore a more believable and acceptable way of correcting product misconceptions than direct advertising.

- Some forms of brands publicity activities can be structured to be a less confrontational way of influencing potential consumers than direct advertising or personal selling.
- Where advertising restrictions limit or inhibit the marketer's ability to advertise directly (as with alcohol and tobacco in many markets, or professional services, or products controlled in some way, i.e. prescription medicines), brands publicity opportunities can be sought and developed which are acceptable and effective in supporting and developing product awareness and trial.
- Brands publicity activity can usefully support the brand building of normal advertising and promotional activity. The export marketer benefits when his brands are strong in the markets, and the consumer develops a confidence in a strong brand that promises consumers reassurance in its consistent quality and the personal and product benefits to be expected.
- Word of mouth is known to be a very effective method of building brand preferences (though not necessarily the most cost effective) and brands publicity activity can work on developing favourable word of mouth commentaries from satisfied consumers to prospective customers – start a favourable product rumour and you start a rush to try and buy! As every marketer knows, bad word of mouth against you is a fast way to lose brand loyalty, and brands publicity can work to counter negative comments and attitudes in a more believable way than direct advertising!
- As illustrated earlier in Figure 18.4, brands publicity can work particularly well on the inner buying influences.

Brands publicity opportunities ▬

The scope for brands publicity is wide, as illustrated in Figure 20.1. Within this range of activities consumer goods and industrial

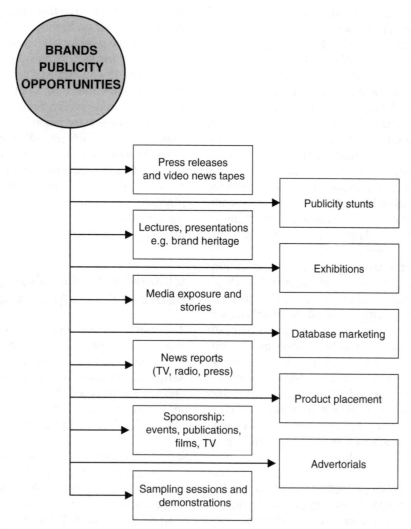

Figure 20.1 *Brands publicity opportunities*

goods manufacturers can find opportunities to promote using brands publicity, either to support other advertising or promotional activity or as the sole means of promotion.

The suitability of any type of brands publicity activity for international markets will have to be judged by the export marketer on a market by market basis. In some sophisticated markets industrial users or consumers of speciality products might be targeted very tightly through database marketing and direct mailshots; but in others general sponsorships of events might prove the most opportune way of commu-

nicating. In developing countries some consumer goods benefit greatly from many low cost sponsorships of local activities, like school football leagues and other sporting or local cultural events. Publicity stunts such as using hot air balloons in the shape of products or featuring product logos have been successfully used by many marketers in markets where such an activity is rare and attention-getting. Product placement in locally made television programmes or films can be influential in promoting consumer goods, and exposure at key local trade exhibitions can benefit industrial products.

Advice can be sought from the local agents or distributors as to what forms of brand publicity are likely to be effective, and they may have local contacts with media or public personalities who might be used in product endorsements. But the marketer must avoid being led into sponsorships of favourite charities or interests of the agent or distributor, and only engage in activity where it clearly reaches the target market, has measurable costs that can be estimated in advance (in order that the alternative brands publicity opportunities can be compared for cost effectiveness in communicating with the target group) and tangible product promotional benefits.

As part of the marketing communications planning process the international marketer should survey all the local opportunities for brands publicity in each of his markets, and develop a programme either to support mainstream marketing communications (advertising and sales promotions) where these are used or as an independent means of developing and communicating product messages where there is no other marketing communication activity. Like sales promotions (covered in Chapter 21) brands publicity activity can be:

- very flexible and adaptable in terms of tackling specific issues or supporting mainstream marketing communications at a national or local level
- capable of specific action through a specific focus
- implemented at relatively short lead times (compared with television advertisements)
- inexpensive and cost effective means of promoting products
- adapted to large and small markets, major or minor products or brands.

A disadvantage can be the difficulty in measuring the results of brands publicity activity in generating sales when it is part of a broader marketing communications programme, and the inability of the marketer to control the way brands publicity messages are passed on through third parties. The risk in solely relying on brands publicity activity is that, unlike paid for advertising where the marketer controls the messages passed to consumers, the outcome of brands publicity is often outside the control of the marketer – he can influence product messages but not control how they are passed on through the chain (such as through editorial commentaries or news features) to consumers. This weakness does not negate the value of brands publicity in reinforcing or underpinning consumer product perceptions through the use of a third party in communicating supporting messages.

Guidelines for developing brands publicity messages

The marketer developing brands publicity messages as part of his communications mix, should recognize the volume of marketing communications in the marketplace, and the interference effect this will have on his own messages. Some guidelines for developing brands publicity messages are:

- keep the message simple in content and style – the more complicated the message the greater risk it will be distorted or diluted on communication through the chain to the consumer
- make it relevant to the users/consumers so that they want to pay attention and receive the content of the message
- try to minimize the risk of external interference when delivering the message through brands publicity activities so that the attention of the intended audience is not distracted from the message being communicated
- reinforce the message by communicating it regularly and through various mediums to increase the likelihood it is correctly received and acted on
- think about your competitors' reaction to your brand publicity activities and how to neutralize them, since they are not likely to ignore your efforts.

Brands publicity in relation to public relations ▰▰▰▰▰▰▰▰

Brands publicity and public relations are both parts of the communications marketing mix but vary in their role and the message they communicate.

● Brands publicity is geared to conveying a specific brand message, e.g.
that use of a brand fits naturally with certain lifestyles, demonstrated by opinion forming famous persons seen to lead that lifestyle and choosing the brand, or through promotion at events associated with that lifestyle
or
the quality of the product is superior to a competitor's product, as demonstrated by independent experts or testing.

● Public relations is geared to conveying a company message, which may use brand activity to support it, e.g.
that the company is a major international producer and distributor of quality products, demonstrated through the portfolio of brands marketed or particular brand successes
or
the company is committed to environmental issues, demonstrated by new recyclable packaging, or a windmill power generating project.

If the international marketer is using independent experts or third party testimonials to promote a product in any markets then, of course, the experts or endorsees should be known to, and have credibility with, the local population (although not necessarily themselves be local persons – but a mix is often effective). It is always important that any personalities used in advertising or promotions are 'clean' in that they have no negative aspects to their personalities or records as any adverse publicity concerning the personality can rub off on the product or company. Similarly, it is often better to use personalities who have some proven

longevity in their field of fame or expertise, rather than just being the 'flavour of the month' type of personality who has a fickle following, as interest in the product might wane as quickly as the personality's fame.

Carrying the brands publicity message ▰▰▰▰▰▰▰▰

The brands publicity message is carried through **direct** and **indirect** mediums. Whilst the advertising message can be more controlled and predictable in its outcome (as the message is designed and developed by the company, and can be tested in advance for its impact and effectiveness), brands publicity messages are often both less controlled and predictable (as they may be passed on through third parties who are not in the direct control of the company), requiring great care in developing the message and medium to minimize the risk of conflicting messages. Figure 20.2 illustrates a matrix of controlled and uncontrolled messages.

The diagram shows two axes – **controlled** and **uncontrolled** messages, and verbal and visual communications opposite written and verbal communications. Controlled messages are those prepared by the marketing company and carried to users or consumers through the media listed in the lower half of the diagram.

Uncontrolled brands publicity messages are illustrated in the upper half of the diagram, and whilst the marketers might try to influence the message, its final form is outside their control as it is communicated through third parties who are neither paid to broadcast or communicate a set message and who are not within the direct sphere of the company's influence (nor are they employees, salespersons, paid product endorsers, etc.). Every marketer dreads negative brands publicity messages carried through rumour or media, as it always seems that negative messages travel faster, further and with more force than positive messages.

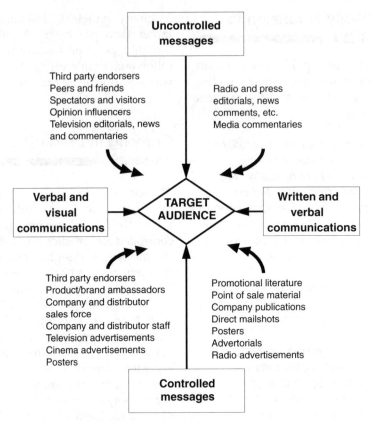

Figure 20.2 Controlled and uncontrolled brands publicity and advertising messages

Some of the controlled messages are advertisements, paid for by the marketing company, and usually carried in television, radio or press advertisements, or possibly through posters or advertorials (posters might be treated as written or visual communications, or a combination). Other controlled messages are of the brands publicity type, where they are carried by persons or media under the direct influence of the company. Persons carrying brands publicity messages are typically sponsored product endorsers (possibly full time brand ambassadors or brand promoters, demonstrators, public personalities paid to promote or endorse products), company staff and salespersons, distributors' staff and salespersons. Media carrying brands publicity messages (but which are not direct advertisements) can include company literature and company publications (even company accounts

booklets, or company notepaper may promote product messages), point of sale material (a standard sales promotion tool), and direct mailshots.

From the perspective of international marketing the marketer should consider and develop a brands publicity programme to support his media advertisements for each market, to expose his customers (trade or final users) to another powerful source of influence, one that can often promote messages that last longer than advertising messages and helps build product loyalty.

Brands publicity timing

Using brands publicity activity in support of brand marketing is a continuous and integrated process with the mainstream advertising and promotional activity. The brands publicity schedule should be linked with the advertising and promotion timing schedule whilst additional brands publicity activities can also go on outside this timetable.

Brands publicity may be based on a promotion or an event that is either newsworthy in its own right or where news can be created. Brands publicity activities in themselves may also have media or promotional support, e.g. a sponsored sporting activity or charitable money raising programme. For each market the international marketer should attempt to identify brands publicity opportunities to support the mainstream marketing activity at the time of preparing the marketing plan, and cost the opportunities in order that decisions can be made as to which opportunities fall within budgetary limitations or offer the best value for money. Apart from the pre-scheduled brands publicity activities supporting advertising and promotions there will always be scope for opportunistic publicity, and the international marketer can work with the distributors to take advantage of these. Some opportunities will have little if any cost, such as simple press releases promoting sponsored events, special promotional activities, and new products. There may be opportunities to link with customers in promoting products along with a customer's promotion of its own activities.

Typical brands publicity opportunities supporting media advertising include:

- press releases
- news releases
- linked events
- demonstrations, product samplings, and other in-store activity supporting retail products.

Brands publicity opportunities supporting promotional activity often include:

- press conferences and releases announcing the promotions
- personality launches that attract publicity
- linkage with major local events (e.g. festivals, cultural programmes), association with local interest issues or concerns (e.g. environmental or social issues).

Further reading

Marketing Communications. Colin J. Coulson-Thomas (Butterworth-Heinemann 1983). Chapter 14: Public Relations

Marketing Management – Analysis, Planning, Implementation and Control. Philip Kotler (Prentice Hall, 8th edition 1994). Chapter 24: Designing Direct Marketing, Sales Promotion, and Public Relations Programs

Public Relations Techniques. Frank Jefkins (Butterworth-Heinemann, 2nd edition 1994). The interested reader will find much of this text useful reading

Sponsorship, Endorsement and Merchandising. Richard Bagehot and Graeme Nuttall (Waterlow, 1990). Chapter 1: How Sponsorship Works. The book is a quite detailed text on many aspects of negotiating and managing sponsorship, and will prove useful to those marketers who need a more in-depth knowledge

Sponsorship – What it is and how to use it. Steve Sleight (McGraw-Hill, 1989). A useful introduction to many aspects of sponsorship

Action points

Identify brands publicity opportunities, e.g.:

- press releases and video news tapes
- promotional lectures and presentations (possibly promoting brand usage or heritage)
- media exposure and stories of local interest
- news reports (television, radio, press)
- sponsorship of events, publications, films, television programmes, etc.
- product demonstrations or sampling sessions
- publicity stunts promoting products
- exhibitions
- database marketing (mailshots or telephone)
- product placement (i.e. in films, television programmes, with local personalities at public events)
- advertorials
- other opportunities (identify and list)

Develop a brands publicity action plan to support media advertising and sales promotions, giving attention to the points and stages listed below:

- develop an activity profile, i.e. which brand publicity means best suit the products and markets
- identify the available resources to implement the programme, analyse resource inputs needed (from the company and/or distributor)
- develop product/brand information packs
- prepare agency briefs (or freelance briefs) if an agency is needed to organize or develop activity
- develop an activity calendar (linking as appropriate with media and promotion calendars)
- develop media placement and medium usage schedules
- develop editorial briefs as required for the main media (television, radio, press)
- plan and schedule activity materials production using a calendar

Checklist 20.1 (Continued)

	Action points
<ul><li>dispatch activity materials and provide plans and calendars</li><li>set up media/promotional planning meetings</li><li>set up supporting personal appearance schedules for third parties involved in activity promotion and sponsorships</li><li>monitor media for exposure</li><li>monitor reaction of consumers to brands publicity activities</li><li>evaluate activities and measure performance achievements against objectives</li><li>report on activity and assess suitability on a post-activity basis</li><li>identify any problems in brands publicity strategy and activity and make corrective action plans.</li></ul>	

21

Export sales
promotion _____

 This chapter will focus on sales promotions as a means of developing
product markets and supporting the marketing communications activity.
We will look at:

- the role of sales promotions in the marketing mix
- developing a more formalized approach to selecting and planning promotions, as part
  of an integrated annual marketing communications plan
- some of the main ways of promoting products (both industrial and consumer
  products)
- developing promotional briefs for internal use or in liaison with agencies
- setting up and monitoring key account promotion plans.

The aim in this chapter is to highlight to the export marketer that he must start by
identifying exactly what objectives are to be addressed through promotions, and that
there are invariably a range of promotion options that can be used to assist in achieving
particular promotion objectives supporting a marketing strategy.

The need to advertise and promote will
depend greatly on the type of product you
produce and offer for sale, and the degree of
security your products have in respect of
import controls such as import licences and
quotas. If there are import limits in respect of
volume or value, then the level of expenditure should probably be no higher than is
necessary to move the volume of imports
through the distribution pipeline either
within the limits of shelf life (if a perishable
product) or before the next quota issue.

An industrial product may need a very

different approach from a consumer product, and a consumer durable product will
need a different programme from nondurable items. One chapter cannot cover
this vast subject, but it may serve to provide
an outline of facets to consider. In this
chapter I will look at some of the typical
ways of promoting industrial and consumer
products. We will then look at the promotion planning process, discuss the role of
promotional activity, give examples of types
of promotional activity, and relate this to the
export environment.

Promoting industrial products ▬

Industrial products (often including services such as consultancy) may need a somewhat different emphasis in marketing from consumer products. Typical media used in promoting industrial products include:

- trade journals and buyers' guides
- direct mailshots
- advertising
- trade shows
- exhibitions.

Trade journals and buyers' guides ──

Industrial products often benefit most from advertising and editorials in local or international trade and technical journals. They need to be promoted to a particular market, such as the buyers of processing companies or the manufacturers of machinery or industrial plant and equipment.

Listings and advertising insertions in buyers' guides aimed at a particular trade sector, such as the construction industry, are extremely good at eliciting response, providing the insertion is very clear:

- in describing what you are offering
- in summarizing the product's uses, and
- in stating who to contact at the manufacturer's office to obtain specification details and price quotes.

If you promote through a regional guide or journal, then you should list the local importers who carry stock or handle market sales efforts.

There are so many new trade and regional directories coming on the market that you need to research who is producing the directory and its circulation. A phone call to trade or professional associations or chambers of commerce will usually help you establish which directories they value and to which they subscribe. You could also ask a few buyers of your products in the home market which international directories they would refer to in seeking such products.

Then call the publishers of those directories to obtain international circulation data by market.

Direct mailshots ─────────────

Direct mailshots are frequently criticized for a low level of response, often only in the 1 to 2 per cent range. However, they can be a far more effective tool in promoting industrial products than consumer goods, because with industrial products it is often easier to target the buyers and users. International trade directories often provide an excellent source of information on contacts for direct mailshots. In some markets mailing lists can be purchased that focus on particular target groups. With industrial products it is important to target each of the influential persons in the chain leading to buying decisions, i.e.:

- the buyer who places the purchase order
- the engineer or researcher who might specify products
- the individual or manager of the department that will use the product.

Advertising ───────────────

Advertising for industrial-type products will generally convey a different message from that for consumer goods. Often the advertising copy needs to elaborate on technical specifications and applications data so that a potential buyer can quickly identify a use or need or potential opportunity. In addition, the buyer must be encouraged to contact the manufacturer or his agent for further specific data relating to use in their plant or industry. It is therefore common to include some form of customer enquiry form.

A few guidelines to consider in preparing your industrial product advertisement are:

- show the product clearly
  - with a good product photograph in preference to line drawings whenever practical

- avoid abstract copy themes
  - because a busy buyer normally only skims through journals and has little time to interpret vague advertising
- keep the copy as brief, simple and meaningful (to the buyer) as possible
- inform the reader of the product's uses and applications, basic specifications and performance details
- outline the benefits to the buyer and user of incorporating your product in their processes or finished products. These may include:
  - price, availability, performance and yield improvements, economy of energy use, safety, quality control, technological advantage, increased user or consumer acceptance through incorporation of a product with its own market acceptance (such as certain artificial sweeteners used in soft drinks, and Dolby noise reduction systems used by many leading hi-fi product manufacturers)
- tell the buyer who makes the product and where they can get more information and see local demonstrations
- create brand awareness
  - promote the product's brand name or the supplier's corporate name wherever possible, to build goodwill to the product or company.

Trade shows

Exposure at trade shows can be very valuable because these shows tend to attract the specialist buyer or technical personnel such as researchers or production personnel. In recent years, however, many minor trade shows have been promoted, and one must question the benefit of these shows to any except the professional show organizers. Carefully evaluate which of the major shows around the world are considered by your target audience as worth attending. A considerable number of buyers and technical persons travel to the major international and regional trade shows, but local shows are often poorly attended, in part because some

of the motivation in making a trip to a major show, say in the USA or Europe, is to meet old contacts and have a pleasant overseas trip on company expenses.

Usually the least expensive trade promotional efforts occur when your embassy in the foreign market puts on a mini-trade show and hosts local buyers and company representatives. Before you involve yourself in this, and possibly send representatives and samples, ask for a list of who will be invited and expected to attend.

The costs of participating in some international trade shows may attract subsidies from a government or trade agency concerned with export promotion (such as the Department of Trade and Industry, often linking with local chambers of commerce), but these are normally only partial subsidies for the total cost of booths, travel and samples. The costs of attending a small regional show are likely to be more per attendee or per lead generated than participation in a major show, such as the Anuga or Sial food shows in Europe.

Once you have made the decision to display at a trade show, then it is wise to advise all your existing agents, importers and buying contacts of your planned presence and booth number so that any contacts planning attendance at the show may schedule a visit with you. Your booth needs to be staffed with personnel fully competent to answer technical questions and to give firm price quotations to potential customers. Plenty of trade literature and relevant samples need to be available, and you should have a system for recording who has visited your booth so that you or your importers can follow up in each market to develop business.

Later in this chapter I will expand on managing attendance at exhibitions.

Videos and information packages for computers

The growing use of video as a means of marketing communication provides an excellent opportunity to make low budget videos for screening at user or consumer premises, particularly where an educational input is needed to brief potential users and consumers on product range, new product developments and innovation, product applications and uses. Many industrial products have a technical aspect that can be demonstrated through a video that might show how the product is used in its normal use environment, how it is built or constructed, and possibly how easily it can be maintained or serviced. A video can be a far more powerful means of communicating than a product brochure.

With growing use of computer graphics in industry there will be an expansion in use of this media in marketing communications, as companies find ways to promote to end users, both through direct contact that delivers information on disc for loading onto computers at client premises, and through the growing network of product information services that can be accessed directly via modems.

The Internet offers perhaps the greatest opportunity to promote products internationally at an affordable cost, as commercial and home use of computers expands, and technology develops and adapts in ways that open opportunities for every business and consumer to have access to the Internet. Many businesses already promote via the Internet web sites, but this will grow exponentially in very few years. Curiously, it is often the customer pressurizing suppliers to make use of the Internet as a communication and promotion aid, as well as providing a means of rapid ordering. Readers are encouraged to explore this medium, and to ensure that they do not lag behind in the use of technology to communicate, promote and access customers and markets.

Promoting consumer goods ▄▄▄

Whilst the range of advertising and promotional activity supporting consumer goods may be well established and familiar to most international marketers, the mix may vary between consumer durable and non-durable goods, so I have separated those sectors for brief comment here.

Durable consumer goods _____

These can generally be promoted and advertised in a similar fashion to the domestic market programme. However, for developing markets where you are trying to establish a need and create demand, you may need to give emphasis to product use and applications. You can possibly take advantage of your international reputation to make the consumer feel secure with the expected quality and performance. If the item may need any spare parts or servicing, it is essential that the potential buyer knows what local support services you or your distributor can offer and where these will be made available.

Lifestyle advertising is much used to promote a developed-market product in the less developed countries – advertising copy or illustrations show potential users how 'the other half' lives. Consumers all round the world desire to improve their standard of living and are heavily influenced by exposure to western films and journals (much to the frustration of governments seeking to limit western influence or control imports).

Consumer durables also benefit from promotional activities that emphasize convenience and labour-saving aspects. Even in so-called 'developing' nations (notably in some countries in Latin America and Asia), more and more family units are finding it necessary for both husband and wife to seek employment, either to supplement the family budget or because modern living leaves the wife with less demand on her time from domestic chores and more of a feeling of self-worth and desire to contribute to society by pursuing a career.

Because many of the durable products being promoted internationally may be aimed at consumers who are less familiar with usage than the home market consumer, it is essential that instruction leaflets are translated into the local language of the foreign market. The consumer must not be exposed to any risk of incorrect use or assembly through inadequate instruction, and the authorities in the foreign market may have regulations concerning prior approval of any packaging or instruction literature. For example:

- If the item is electrical, then it should be already adapted for use at the correct local voltage and current strength.
- If the item is for regular use in hot and humid climates, then it is essential you have thoroughly tested its ability to perform under such climatic conditions, and that it will neither rust nor malfunction because some part corrodes or expands.
- If the product is going to be subjected to heavy duty use in adverse conditions (such as some agricultural machinery or other industrial equipment) its ability to withstand the rigours of everyday use in the foreign market environment must be tested.

Your company's reputation will take longer to repair than the product if early shipments do not perform in line with your advertising claims or consumer expectations.

Durable consumer products can often be promoted in a similar fashion to non-durable consumer products. Frequently used promotional techniques for consumer durables include:

- television and radio advertising
- poster campaigns
- advertisements in newspapers and periodicals aimed at the target market
- in-store promotions and demonstrations
- displays and exhibitions at consumer and trade shows
- consumer competitions using the promoted items as prizes
- piggyback promotions, e.g. 'buy a refrigerator and get a free coffee percolator'.

If you decide with your distributor to run any in-store or consumer promotion, then it is essential to keep the programme administratively simple so that your distributor can successfully handle it with limited resources.

Branded non-durable consumer goods

Items such as toiletries and foodstuffs often take a number of years to develop to maturity in a market, partly because in many cases the importer is initially facing limited sales opportunities to the more affluent element of the local population. However, displayed distribution will create interest and desire among a much wider population, because in many of the developing countries the young people tend to spend many hours simply window-shopping and admiring the products they would like to have (and see advertised in international media, including films and magazines).

Some of the promotional techniques used successfully with non-durable consumer goods include:

- media advertising (radio/television/cinema/press)
- posters, either static or mobile sites, such as on vehicles or balloons (posters are particularly favoured in less affluent markets where few own televisions)
- magazines, particularly those with 'lifestyle' image
- co-operative advertising, where certain key accounts share the advertising costs, promoting their own sites along with the product
- in-store demonstrations and promotions
- couponing
- consumer competitions involving purchase requirement (where legal)
- retailer competitions related to sales volume or feature displays
- point of sales material, e.g. window stickers, window posters, feature display cards, shelf-talkers, counter display cards, promotion leaflets, etc.

Advertising

It is essential that you seriously assess your sales potential for the product and the degree of security with which you can import before committing yourself to an advertising budget.

Consideration must be given to the level of effective distribution and product display achievable and to consumer spending power to ensure that you do not overspend at too early a stage of market development or penetration. Advertising agents will generally propagate the pulling power of advertising through media, perhaps with some merit, but at an early stage of market penetration with consumer non-durables many exporters find the first priority to be obtaining displayed distribution of the product.

Media advertising should be in the local language to reach the target market effectively. Some countries actually require this and even that films intended for use in their market should be locally produced. That adds greatly to the cost of a programme, and the international marketer initially is better advised, where practical, to devote more of the limited budget to actual advertising and less to producing costly and fancy films. A thorough review of your domestic advertising films may well reveal some that are suitable for use in foreign markets initially, even if they are considered old for the home market, for a very low expenditure on local language voice-overs. In fact once you establish a track record for achieving export sales, it is worth making the case to the domestic marketing department that consideration be given when new films are being produced either to producing an international version at the same time for nominal additional cost, or to making a modified version with minimal need for lip synchronization with foreign language voice-overs.

When you finally start a media programme in any foreign country, it is sensible to appoint and work with a local advertising agency or affiliate of your domestic agency.

There is no substitute for local experience and knowledge, in addition to local monitoring and controlling of advertising schedules to ensure that programmes booked actually are enacted by the television or radio station.

The local agency may offer comment on culturally unacceptable aspects of your home market films, possibly for racial reasons or as regards public standards.

Consumer promotions

Apart from media advertising, consumer promotions can greatly contribute to product trial and awareness in many developing markets. However, all too frequently the cost of the promotion outweighs the benefit to the manufacturer.

To the professional marketer, the purpose of a promotion is not just to demonstrate use of a budget, but to use that budget as a scarce resource and maximize **display, distribution** and **consumer trial**. It is essential for forward planning purposes to make the most accurate possible post-promotion estimates of the results achieved under each of these categories. Many a consumer marketing manager has organized worthwhile promotions, such as a redemption offer, only to find the retailers and distributors making no special effort to promote it with extra display features. Hence, in the early stages of market development in new markets consideration must be given to the order of priorities – get the distribution, then the display, then motivate the offtake. The three are not mutually dependent, of course, but the most effective promotion is likely to be one that tackles all three response areas.

The first stage is to assess your potential distribution outlets. Surveys may already exist for the local market showing, say, the locations of each suitable target retail outlet, whether for food products, toiletries, electrical goods, etc.

If such information is not readily available (as in a number of developing markets), then there may be relatively inexpensive ways to build your own list. You and your distributor may feel that the priority is to tackle the major cities. In that case you could hire college students at low cost in vacation periods to make a comprehensive street-by-street survey of all outlets currently selling similar or competitive products. Some basic follow-up to check on the students' report sheets will enable you to assess their accuracy. To my pleasant surprise, when I have used college students to compile an outlet database in several foreign markets, field follow-checks indicated that the students have been 80–90 per cent thorough, which is surely far better than having no decent outlet base. Frequently the distributor will be able to identify many new outlets and potential customers for other products he represents from your survey, and it is therefore worth trying to gain commitment by conducting the survey on a cost-sharing basis.

Once a basic survey of target outlets exists, a distribution objective for a specific promotion can be set and then monitored by subsequent retail checks. Plan and provide simple point-of-sale material that will not offend a retailer or obstruct his customers, yet will gain attention at the display point. For example, in markets where many retail outlets are open stall street-side shops, stickers and hanging display cards often have more permanence than larger posters, which either are torn down or obstruct the retailer's limited sales area.

Since the salespeople in many markets are on commission, and may be reluctant to give time to installing display material, it may be beneficial to have a salesperson's bonus for each outlet accepting display material, or a competition for the best displays on each sales territory.

Another key objective is the retention of feature displays for the duration of a promotion. Ideally some form of special display box could be located at the key sales point. A dealer display competition is one way to motivate this. There are various approaches to this; you can experiment and find which is effective for each market and distributor. Some examples include:

- the sales supervisor can give instant prizes (such as a discount voucher for next purchase) to retailers featuring the key point display during random store checks
- a salesperson photographs displays and submits the photographs for judging. The winning retailers receive a worthwhile prize for display originality or prominence if they still have the display in place when the supervisor calls to award the prize.

Display retention can be assisted by clearly communicating to retailers the media advertising programme supporting the promotion.

The leaflets for competitions or premium offers must be clearly displayed in the retail outlets during a promotion. These leaflets should be in the local language and explain the rules and procedures for entry simply.

In many developing markets the international marketer is not dealing with the degree of retailer and consumer sophistication found in the home market. Define and quantify realistic and achievable marketing objectives, and make a specific plan with your distributor to achieve growth under each criterion. Ensure that your plan considers each variable that can influence the outcome of the promotion. Subsequent sections in this chapter deal with developing promotion objectives and a sales promotion plan.

In-store demonstrations

These have been mentioned in passing as an aid to consumer trial. Attention needs to be given to the cost-effectiveness of such promotional techniques. Frequently it is found that the demonstrators are not very effective and have little product knowledge. The costs of the wages and sampling programme are often greater than the additional gross sales revenue achieved. Therefore, if you feel that your product merits experimentation with sampling and demonstration programmes in order to increase consumer trial

– it may be the only way to motivate a major store to give you a feature display space – then do take the extra time needed to select and train your demonstrators.

Creating impact at the point of sale

Rather than reproduce material here, I would refer the reader whose products benefit from point of sale merchandizing and promotion activity to read Chapter 20 in my companion CIM volume, *Sales Management* (Butterworth-Heinemann 1998). Within this text I will limit coverage to a few key points, with the note that it is becoming increasingly important for market-led international suppliers to find ways to communicate with their customers at the point of sale in all their destination markets:

- to support the heavy investment in local advertising and other promotional activity
- to differentiate and highlight their product among the proliferation of brands on offer
- to ensure that they receive optimum display exposure within the space management programmes of their retailers and trade channel outlets.

In domestic markets many suppliers of consumer goods devote considerable marketing and sales resources to merchandizing with the objective of creating impact at the point of sale. In export markets this aspect of promotion is often either neglected, as distributors see it more as a cost than a benefit, or poorly pursued. Product display often receives very little attention from distributors' sales teams who are rewarded significantly by commission, and are selling a multiplicity of products. Their natural reaction is to pursue quick orders across their portfolio of products, and not to devote too much time to any single principal's product. The net result is that merchandizing at the point of sale is neglected, and sales of those products that need point of sale merchandizing support and promotion are below potential.

There is no simple answer to this problem. The export marketer can work at several levels to encourage attention to merchandising.

- Produce products in packaging that suits the way the trade channel outlets like to display product.
- Produce a range of point of sales material that is easy to use, impactful, and appreciated by the retail customers or trade channel dealers.
- When working with distributors' salespersons, focus training on point of sales merchandizing.
- Develop incentive schemes for the sales team of distributors that rewards effort and achievement in display and merchandizing activity.
- Encourage distributors to introduce the issue of display and space management into discussions and negotiations with major accounts, including providing display incentives and sales performance related rewards in addition to normal pricing structures (e.g. annual rebates for achievements over agreed targets, and/or for maintaining agreed display standards). As the major retailers and dealers improve the quality of their display, so this puts pressure on the smaller retailers in the market.

A DEFINITION OF MERCHANDIZING

Merchandizing can be defined as the physical placement of a product in a store in a location that is easily identifiable and accessible by the consumers, and enhancement of the display with relevant point of sales material, enabling consumers to make better quality purchasing decisions, thereby maximizing sales through the quality, impact and location of the product display.

Your distributors may need support and training in good space management principles at the trade channel level aligned with good inventory management in their own operations. Quite commonly they do establish a clear space for a principal's products in key retail outlets, but then on a store audit the principal may find that the top selling products are out of stock, and the space filled with less voluminous products (with a net loss in revenue). The distributor's sales team may believe they have done a satisfactory job blocking a display space, and not understand the need to focus on the top sellers, and not appreciate the loss of revenue from poor stock management.

Point of sale material

Point of sale material can play an important part in the promotion of consumer goods, and to a lesser degree can play a part in highlighting industrial products either at dealer premises or at sites where products are in use. It can be either temporary promotional material to support a particular campaign or activity, or permanently located such as signs showing a distributor stocks a certain product range. Common formats of point of sale material include: brand signs exhibited outside the premises of product stockists, window stickers, window posters, price cards, feature display cards, shelf-talkers, counter display cards, special product display stands, product dispensers, pennants, promotion leaflets, etc. Basically anything that draws attention to a product at the place where products are sold or consumed (such as ashtrays promoting a brand of alcohol in restaurants) can be considered as point of sale material.

The effectiveness and role of point of sale material are highlighted when the marketer and his distributors recognize that many users and consumers do not make a final product selection until at the point of sales, i.e. a retail store or trade supplier of products. Whilst some products are largely purchased on impulse (such as confectionery and snack products), and the purchase decision is highly influenced by the location

and quality of display and related point of sale material, other products are planned purchases. Even where a planned purchase is made, the particular selection of the product variety or brand may not be made in advance, and the decision can then be influenced by point of sale material strategically placed and serving to inform about a product and motivate selection, generating incremental sales.

It is customary in export marketing that point of sale material is designed and supplied by the manufacturer, but distributors need training in its placement and beneficial use if limited budget resources are to be used effectively. Many an export marketer has been shocked and disappointed to find stocks of expensive, but often out of date and unused, point of sale material accumulating in distributors' warehouses.

When developing point of sale material for foreign markets:

- check that items supplied are practical for use by the sales team in the market and for placement at product sales locations
- use local languages on point of sale material wherever possible
- focus on simple product related messages (highlighting product benefits)
- agree quantities of each item to be supplied with the distributor, with some estimate of expected placement sites within each type of trade channel (to minimize or avoid wastage).

The messages that this short commentary on basic product promotion should leave you with are the following:

- To be successful in a remote market where you have little direct control over a distributor, limited market strength with retailers and little consumer awareness, keep promotions simple and set fundamental objectives that are accepted by all parties as both achievable and measurable.
- Plan each aspect of a promotion in detail with your distributor to give a

measurable sales benefit for each pound spent. Discussions of 'intangible' benefits at a post-promotion review are often just an excuse for having designed a poor promotion or failing to seek tangible, quantifiable results.

● Measure the quantifiable benefits to your distributor and advertising agencies so that successful aspects can be incorporated in future promotions, and ineffective elements can be discarded.

Export sales promotion ▬▬▬

Whilst the previous sections introduce aspects of product promotion that might apply to industrial or consumer goods it is important that the export marketer develop a formalized approach to promotion planning. This section will focus on aspects of promotion selection, planning and evaluation, and encourage allocating limited export promotion budgets to activities that produce measurable results.

Both advertising and direct sales promotional activities play a role in developing international markets and may be targeted to one or more of the strategic areas illustrated in Figure 21.1, depending on your assessment of the priorities at the time. In this section I will focus on non-media sales promotion activity.

Sales promotion activity is, in the main, a shorter-term tactical weapon in the international marketer's armoury. It has the

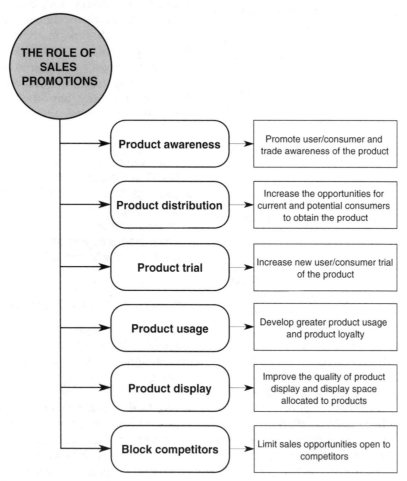

Figure 21.1 *The role of sales promotions*

advantage of being flexible in timing, purpose, direction of effort, and manner of implementation. It can also be very cost effective. Many forms of sales promotion need very short lead times to plan and implement, and can supplement other advertising and marketing activities.

For a mature brand in any market the long-term benefit of continuous sales promotional activity, particularly if primarily price promotion, is questionable, since it is unlikely to cause many new customers to try the product rather than encouraging existing customers to 'stock-up' at discounted prices.

Advertising is normally more costly than other forms of sales promotional activity and takes far longer to plan and develop. In general advertising is used to support the main strategic thrust of the marketing programme by creating consumer/user awareness in the target market sectors, developing a brand image, assisting in the creation of market segmentation, and creating, developing or reinforcing consumer perceptions – all of which are aimed to expand sales within the target group, increasing penetration and market share.

Definitions

At this point we should attempt to clarify our definitions of sales promotions and advertising.

- **Sales promotions** can be considered as all supplementary selling and marketing activity that is neither direct media advertising nor direct selling, but which co-ordinates personal selling and advertising into an effective persuasive force. (Promotions may be supported by advertising.)
- **Below the line promotions** are normally considered as all non-media promotion, historically derived from promotional and advertising expenditures that were not subject to commission compared with above the line activity that was.

- **Advertising** can be seen as all mainstream marketing communications promoting or concerning a product, normally subject to booking commissions, placed with mass media or specialist media, including television, cinema, radio, press, general and technical or specialist journals, posters, etc.

Using promotions in the marketing communications mix

Sales promotional activity is a key flexible and, if well planned and managed, cost effective means of communicating product information, benefits and other marketing messages to both the distributive trade channels and users and consumers. The international marketer should adopt an integrated approach, linking above and below the line promotional activities to complement and support each other in the communication mix, ensuring promotional activities geared to any one of the exporter's portfolio of product or brands are:

- not in conflict with the objectives or activity supporting another product or brand at the same time period
- supports (in terms of objectives, focus and timing) other mainstream marketing communications (e.g. media advertisements and campaigns) or brand publicity activity and objectives.

Advantages of sales promotions

The main advantages in using sales promotional activity, either alone or to support mainstream marketing activity and communications, are:

- very flexible and adaptable in terms of tackling specific problems or supporting mainstream marketing communications at a national or local level
- capable of specific action through a specific focus and structure

- relatively short lead times to design and implement (compared with media communications)
- often easier to monitor the effect or tangible results
- economical and cost saving, possibly with economies of scale
- can be adapted to large and small markets, major or minor products or brands.

The key to successful use of a sales promotion is to be very clear on its objective, and then design a promotion that is:

- narrow in its focus of objectives
- simple to comprehend and implement (by the salespersons responsible for implementation and participants)
- simple to measure and monitor.

Figure 21.2 illustrates the typical planned effect of a sales promotion. This assumes that the actual promotion is run for a limited time period, e.g. from time A to time B. If the promotion is successful, then:

- the promotion should increase sales above the level that would occur without a promotion

- sales may remain higher than normal for some period after a successful promotion particularly if new customers have been won to the brand
- the cost of the promotion can be compared with the additional gross sales revenue during the promotion and in the post-promotion period, and with the additional gross profit contribution from incremental sales during the promotion and in the post-promotion period.

A decision-making framework for evaluating promotion options _____

In order to ensure that the most suitable promotion is selected to address an issue, problem or objective a decision making framework is developed in Figure 21.3. The international marketer might find it useful to adopt this framework when evaluating the options for his products, whether industrial or consumer goods.

Types of sales promotions _____

The type of sales promotional activity the international marketer might choose will depend on the type of product being sold, the objectives of the promotion, and who is

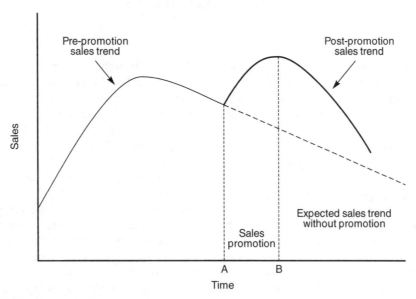

Figure 21.2 The impact of a sales promotion

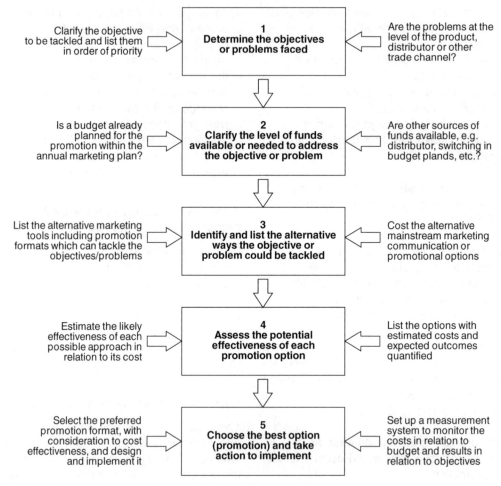

Figure 21.3 *The decision-making process for promotions*

to be influenced by the promotion (trade buyer, user, consumer). Consider which of the following types of promotion might offer potential for your products in foreign markets, and incorporate them in the annual promotion planning activities. The main types of promotions include those listed in the box.

The range of promotional activity illustrated in the list can be divided into those most suited to promoting sales through the various trade channels distributing the products, and those most suited to promoting sales to users or consumers. Some of the promotion formats are adaptable either to the push of sales through the trade or the pull

of sales through consumer demand. Table 21.1 illustrates the typical suitability of the various promotion formats for **trade-push** or **consumer-pull** promotion objectives.

As a rule, an integrated sales promotion programme will run parallel to the main media communications programme, if one is in place, and support its objectives, but also works at a lower level on key tactical objectives, with a mixture of both '**push**' and '**pull**' promotional activities. Appendix 21.1 illustrates a range of typical sales objectives tackled through sales promotional activity, and indicates some of the promotion formats that can be used to tackle each objective.

Company credit cards	mainly offer scope for retailers of goods and services, some franchised businesses and providers of services such as accommodation (hotel chains), where the company is seeking to build customer loyalty.
Consumer price promotions	(including multi-packs for some lower value retail goods) are aimed to boost trial, entice consumers away from competitors, develop brand loyalty or encourage consumer stocking up with extra product.
Consumer competitions	are normally designed to increase display, trial, usage, loyalty and brand awareness.
Consumer premium offers	usually offer low cost items in exchange for a number of product labels or other evidence of product use and a reduced price for the premium item, are also aimed at increasing trial, display, usage and product brand awareness.
Couponing	is a promotional format used with either durable or non-durable products, to increase trial and repeat purchase, or to promote linked sales of other products in the supplier's product portfolio.
Dealer competitions	can help to expand distribution or, if aimed at retailers, to increase and improve display, and might possibly be managed by the exporter or a main distributor.
Direct mailshots	have proven benefits, albeit often with low response rates, where the target market of potential users or consumers can be readily identified by job, economic status or other measurable criteria (such as doctors, architects, credit card holders, etc.).
Display bonuses	are usually used where goods are offered for sale through retail distribution channels, and provide a reward to a trade outlet for an agreed display layout or space allocation.
Distributor sales force incentives	are excellent means of directing sales effort to areas needing corrective action or special effort (including new products).
Editorials/advertorials in special magazines and journals	are useful to promote specialist products direct to the target user or consumer, and are usually aimed at particular market sectors.

Exhibitions	particularly offer scope to promote industrial or consumer durable products, such as plant and equipment, household durables, ingredients and components, new technology, services, etc.
Free product trial periods	have scope for industrial products and some consumer durable products, the assumption being that trial at the place of use will result in a confirmed sale.
Gifts for buyers	are useful tools to promote product trial, and whilst gifts for trade buyers are perhaps frowned upon in many of the developed nations, they are a useful promotional activity in many market sectors to gain product trial or approval listing, and also offer scope for products sold through retail channels (e.g. free travel bag with purchase of multiple toiletry items).
Introduction incentives	are much used where specialist services are being marketed (e.g. financial services, home improvements, products or activities requiring an annual membership or subscription).
Lectures, film shows, etc.	are particularly useful where an element of training or education is needed in promoting the product to the potential end users.
On-pack give-aways	are commonly used to promote consumer products, where the free item might either relate to the main product (e.g. a free razor with a pack of blades, or hair conditioner with shampoo) or be a new product aimed at the same target market.
Performance rebates or allowances	encourage buyers to support one manufacturer rather than competitors
Personality promotions and sponsorships	offer considerable scope with many products to obtain and use the endorsement of famous personalities publicly associated with the products or services (it being essential personalities involved in sponsoring products are unlikely to do anything to bring the brand name into disrepute).
Point of sale materials	draw attention to products in sales outlets, possibly highlighting the location or product features and benefits.

Promotional aspects of packaging	can enhance presentation through design, presentation of information or illustrations of use and applications, convenience for display, and creating a unique brand identity and impact at the point of sale.
Product merchandising	is often undertaken for products distributed through retail channels by field salespersons or specially trained merchandisers, and can be very effective in creating product awareness at the point of sale, particularly ensuring product is correctly priced, neatly displayed, and highlighted to potential consumers through the use of appropriate point of sale material.
Product sampling programmes	are normally used (mainly with non-durable goods) to increase product trial and entice consumers away from competitive products.
Product training programmes	are normally aimed at increasing the knowledge and expertise of product distributors, enabling them to sell with increased confidence and to offer their customers better support.
Product use demonstrations	create awareness of product features and benefits and encourage product trial by potential users, often highlighting to them the ease of use of the product.
Prompt order bonuses or discounts	encourage the early placement of orders after submission of quotations or demonstrations.
Public relations activities	can be a powerful tool in creating awareness, product trial, and developing a favourable brand image, and have grown in use and importance as a supporting activity in the sales and marketing programme of many companies.
Sales promotional literature	offer a way to gain attention from trade buyers whilst creating desire and confidence in the supplier as a product source by presenting product features, benefits and applications to buyers.
'Tie-ins' with local special events	can offer a powerful promotional vehicle in some markets, e.g. carnivals, sports functions, and charity activities.
Trade price discounts	to distributors or users encourage stock purchase and increase in stock held in inventories.

Trade channel (dealer) margins	can be adjusted for a specific period or sale to motivate trade buyers to support a product through increased sales activity.
Trade stock bonuses	(sometimes referred to in marketing jargon as 'dealer loaders') can be used to widen distribution or boost stock levels in the distribution chain, e.g. one case free with a ten case order.
Trading stamps	or similar incentives are aimed at repeat purchase and building loyalty to a product or trade channel issuing the stamps.

Table 21.1 *Suitability of promotional activity to trade and consumer selling*

Type of promotion	Trial e.g. new products	Loyalty e.g. established products
Trade-push		
Dealer competitions	✓	✓
Dealer margins	✓	
Direct mailshots	✓	✓
Display bonuses	✓	✓
Distributor sales force cash incentives/competitions	✓	✓
Exhibitions/trade shows	✓	
Gifts for trade buyers	✓	
Lectures, slide or film shows, videos, etc.	✓	✓
Performance rebates or allowances	✓	✓
Product demonstrations	✓	
Product training programmes	✓	
Prompt order bonuses	✓	
Public relations activity	✓	✓
Trade credit extensions	✓	✓
Trade magazines or journals	✓	✓
Trade price discounts	✓	✓
Trade sales literature	✓	
Trade stock bonuses (dealer premiums)	✓	✓
Consumer-pull		
Consumer competitions	✓	✓
Consumer exhibitions	✓	
Consumer magazines or journal features/advertorials	✓	✓
Consumer premium offers (self-liquidating promotions)	✓	✓
Couponing	✓	

continued overleaf

Type of promotion	Trial e.g. new products	Loyalty e.g. established products
Customer price specials (e.g. 2 for 1)	✓	✓
Direct mail shots	✓	
Free product trial periods	✓	
Gifts for buyers	✓	
Introductory incentives (e.g. for introducing new customers)	✓	
Lectures, slide or film shows, videos	✓	
Multiple packs (banded packs – same or different products)	✓	✓
On-pack give-aways	✓	✓
Outlet in-store merchandising	✓	✓
Personality promotions/sponsorships	✓	✓
Point of sale material	✓	✓
Price reductions – store price cuts	✓	✓
Product sampling	✓	
Product use demonstrations	✓	
Prompt order bonuses	✓	
Public relations activities	✓	✓
Packaging, e.g. for special promotions	✓	
Product information leaflets at point of sale, etc.	✓	
Recyclable containers (re-usable bottles or product containers)		✓
Tie-ins with special events	✓	
Trading stamps and similar incentives	✓	✓
Warranties of satisfaction	✓	

The following example form (Figure 21.4) can help in identifying, listing and evaluating promotion options. Notes can be made under the various criteria relevant to selection of a promotion.

The advertising and promotion plan

The preparation of an annual advertising and promotion programme is an essential process in planned market development. It may be an internal control and requirement from the international marketer's superiors, and it should not be prepared in isolation from the distributors, who will have significant experience and local market knowledge to contribute to the document (and far greater commitment if it is also their plan). As with most marketing programmes, subsequent developments often cause changes from the outline; such change need not signify a bad plan, just the need to adapt flexibly to any short-term or unforeseen circumstances.

The final version of the **annual promotion programme** should include relevant comment on such topics as:

- the timing of promotions for each product, taking account of seasonal factors such as gift-giving periods and vacations
- the objectives of each promotion or promotional activity, and the ability to control and measure performance against objectives

PROMOTION OPTIONS FORM						
General promotion focus/objective						
Timing:						
Budget:			Budget source:			
ALTERNATIVES	Specific sales objective	Budget cost	Lead time	Ease to implement	Ease to control	Measur-ability of results
TRADE SALES (PUSH)						
1.						
2.						
3.						
4.						
5.						
6.						
CONSUMER SALES (PULL)						
1.						
2.						
3.						
4.						
5.						
6.						

Figure 21.4 Basic form for evaluating alternative promotion formats

A case example –
attempting to use promotions to clear
stocks

A distributor of an international brand (but not the market leader) of sports products had placed his orders on his principal for the season's requirements of skis. There were few outlets for skis in the market, approximately one hundred in total, including some sales through ski training schools.

In the skiing season snow fall was unusually low, whilst at the same time there were early signs of economic recession. Skiing activity fell to a lower than normal level. The result was that the distributor involved failed to sell his stock into the trade outlets in the volumes required to clear stocks.

When the next ski selling season started the distributor decided first that he should clear the previous season's stock. His approach to this was to offer it into trade outlets (sports shops, etc.) at a discount of 25 per cent. His idea was then to sell in his new season's line on the next sales visits by his sales team. The sales team were also allowed to grant extended credit of 90 days (the normal being 30 days) to encourage the trade channel outlets to stock-up with the old model skis.

On the next sales calls made by the distributor's sales teams they faced considerable trade negativity. The general complaint was that the stock they had bought in (and many had additional stock from the year before) was not selling in the face of the competitor's new range.

This is an example of a promotion that not only failed to solve the initial excess stock problem, but also disrupted orderly marketing and the current product marketing strategy. The key points here perhaps are:

- the ski distributor saw his problem only at the level of his own inventories, and set an objective only to move stock into trade channel outlets
- that discount promotion did nothing to promote sales to end users (skiers) as there were no conditions put upon the discount (i.e., in-store price reductions, special displays, etc.)
- the discount offered was seen by the trade as extra profit for them, since they had no particular loyalty to the brand or motivation to invest in its promotion
- when the old model skis were failing to sell out, the distributor was having trouble collecting against his invoices for those goods, as some traders separated them in their minds from the normal business and declined to honour payments within the agreed (extended) terms.

The result of the promotional tactics adopted for the distributor was not one, but two poor selling seasons, as he wasted considerable time and resources clearing the problem, by having to offer additional promotional support to sell stock out of the trade channel outlets. Some stock had to be taken back (and offered very late to training schools), to clear pipeline stocks in key outlets in order to move new models into the pipeline.

The main learning point is that the distributor had failed to think through his problem and clarify what objectives he wanted to achieve through promotion, and then to ensure that each sub-objective was addressed. If he believed that the stock problem should be addressed through a promotion through retailers then he could have designed a multi-level promotion, such as:

- a 'sell-in' special offering product that would be re-sold to the consumer at a discount (of, say, 20–25 per cent off normal retail prices), but guaranteeing the retailer's margin (unless it was agreed that they would take a lower absolute margin per unit in order to increase volume)
- special feature displays or tie-in promotions with other products that would focus consumer attention to the offer within the store
- store sales personnel might be invited to join in a competition (where store owners/managers were agreeable) possibly with points towards prizes for sales achieved, so that store sales personnel were motivated and rewarded for extra sales a activity
- to differentiate the promotion between various competing stores the structure could be varied within similar cost levels, i.e. some stores might purely give a price discount, others might offer another 'free' item of similar value to the discount allowed with a set of skis, such as ski protective carrying bags.

An approach such as this would be expected to be more successful than that adopted. Also, it is likely that the distributor would not have needed to give extended credit on the stock sold in, as accompanying promotional activity was designed to move stock through and out of the retail pipeline with consumer sales. When additional credit is given in some circumstances the trade come to assume in can be negotiated or taken in all circumstances.

Subsequent discussion with the distributor showed that another alternative would have been to offer the old model skis to the ski training schools at a discount, as those outlets were not 'fashion conscious' and pressured to use latest models for training, but were more oriented to cost-saving factors.

A case example – promoting confectionery in Singapore

A confectionery manufacturer was finding sales in Singapore were stagnating. A review of distribution and sales activity showed that the outlet base stocking product was only around 300 stockists, including the major supermarket outlets, and most general food stores, and hotel foyer outlets. Distribution was focused primarily on the key shopping, tourist and business districts. There was a weakness of distribution in the numerous street-side neighbourhood stores serving the local communities. The primary objectives of a sales promotion were:

- to expand retail distribution into neighbourhood stores
- to gain prominent display at the key selling points
- to retain display for long enough to create consumer awareness of new distribution points, thereby generating a sufficient level of ongoing sales to encourage the new stockists to retain the confectionery range in stock and displayed at a key selling point within the stores.

The promotion to meet these objectives included several tiers or sub-promotions, as follows:

- New stockists were offered an introductory bonus of one free box of product with ten boxes of assorted products (at least five items from a range of fifteen, but with the focus on the top sellers).
- New and current stockists were encouraged to give a key site prominent display as part of a competition. The competition required the retailer to display the product prominently for four weeks. When the display was placed, in an attractive special display box, supported by other point of sales material (particularly hanging display cards to catch attention on the street side from passers by) the salesperson took a photograph to enter a weekly draw.
- For each special display the salesperson received a sales incentive, to encourage effort and reward success. The salesperson received an additional cash reward if one of his customers won an award in the weekly draw.
- A weekly draw was conducted by the local newspaper, who featured the winner in a photo-shot (a motivator, whilst also ensuring credibility that the competition was honest). The weekly winner would receive S$250 cash if, when the sales manager called to give the prize, they still had the special display as located in the photograph. Each shop would remain in the draw for the full four weeks, to motivate display retention.
- Consumer advertising was increased during the four week promotion period to motivate increased trial and offtake, and as a reinforcing measure for the new retail stockists to see extra activity.

The promotion increased distribution by two-thirds, and generated a worthwhile ongoing increase in sales, also opening new outlets for other of the product ranges handled by the local distributor.

- special promotional media support or general media support (bear in mind that, if there is a clear seasonal sales trend, a pound spent in the peak sales period generally creates a greater impact on sales than a pound spent in the low period)
- promotional aids (such as sales literature and point of sales materials) and other materials needed to support the promotional activity, including preparation lead times

- special packaging requirements and production lead times
- manufacturing, shipping and other distribution lead times for special promotional goods.

Promotion planning

Each separate promotion programme should have a fully detailed written plan, in addition to the outline annual plan referred to above, incorporating such information as:

- budgeted expenditure in total and by item of expense
- objectives of the promotion
- lead times for preparation of each aspect of copy and artwork connected with design of packaging, display material and media advertisements
- production quantities of each item of advertising and display material, packaging and product
- all rules applicable to any competition, e.g. competitions direct to consumers, retailers and distributor salespersons
- comment on the legality of a promotion in the foreign market and any regulatory approvals needed to run the promotion (e.g. lotteries may require an approval)
- criteria to measure promotion success and a programme to evaluate success.

The planning stage must ensure adequate lead times for all preparation and production of each special aspect of the promotion, including artwork, schedule advertising, packaging and production of merchandise, even though there may be an element of flexibility in the final promotion dates. Your distributor and advertising agency should be kept fully apprised of all aspects of planning, and be clearly briefed on their respective responsibilities, although the international marketer's job will include monitoring the performance of their respective contributions within the plan time-span.

Figure 21.5 illustrates some key stages in promotional planning that you might find convenient to elaborate on and adapt to your own planning process.

Preparation of your annual marketing plan in a simple schematic may assist control of the various stages in implementing the marketing programme. In the plan in Figure 21.6(a) export promotions for a toiletry range sold into Canada give the base for the matrix. There are two main promotions within the budget for the year.

First, there is a summer 'travel kit' promotion, which could be a four-item assortment with a free toiletries bag for the consumer. This is supported by magazine advertising in 'lifestyle' image journals. To get the product in displayed distribution, the display period is preceded by a 'dealer loader' promotion (say, one box free with twelve) to fill the pipeline with stock, and a salesperson's bonus competition. Secondly, there is a Christmas promotion as the main event of the year, based on the marketing experience of the international marketer that toiletries are popular gift items. This is supported by television advertising, magazine advertising, feature displays, dealer loaders, salespeople's incentives, and competitions for best displays. The summer promotion would concentrate on summer skin-care items, such as suntan oils and lotions, and after-sun treatments. The winter programme would concentrate on colognes, perfumes, aftershaves and similar items, and complementary luxury products.

The basic planning principle applies as much to industrial products as to consumer products, but several markets might be linked together for the purpose of promotion planning where they share common activity, such as regional exhibitions. Figure 21.6(b) illustrates an outline promotion programme for navigation equipment, where the size of the markets does not warrant great detail at the level of each market, and the main forms of promotion are through exhibitions and event sponsorships. In this example most activity is concentrated in the spring and summer and particular attention is given by the company, in view of the technical nature of the products, to distributor and agent motivation and training through conferences and factory visits (linked for economy with major exhibitions).

These examples, of course, are not all-encompassing. Every product has promotional techniques to which it best responds, and every company has product attributes and benefits that its own experts and mar-

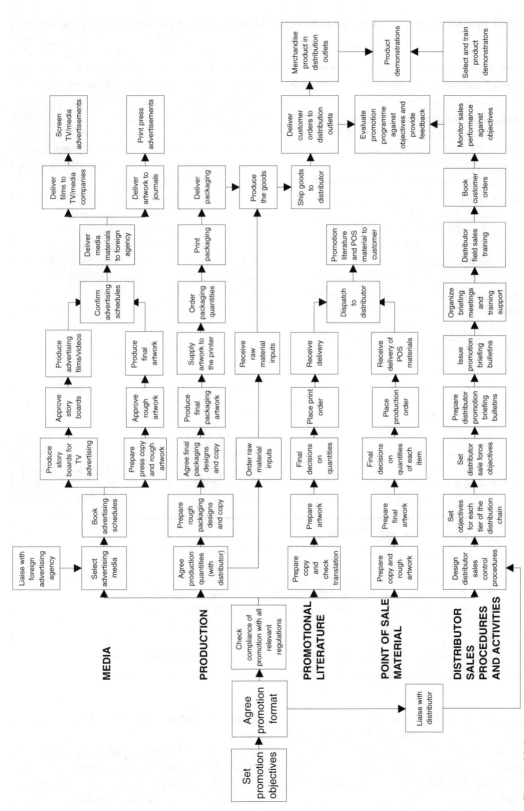

Figure 21.5 *Key stages in organizing an export sales promotion*

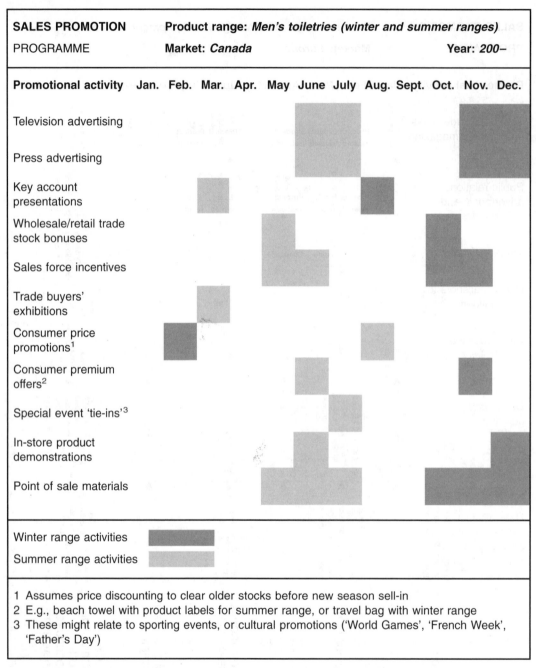

Figure 21.6(a) *Outline of a consumer product sales promotion programme*

keting team best know how to exploit. Liaison between the international marketer and the domestic marketing team will promote a cross-flow of ideas and experience to the benefit of the export marketing programme.

Setting promotion objectives

As with all sales and marketing activity in the domestic market, any forms of promotional activity in an export market should be carefully thought through and have clearly

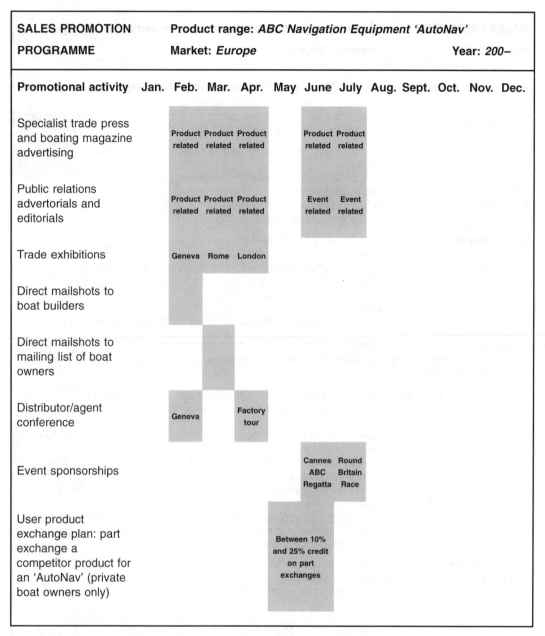

Figure 21.6(b) *Outline of a specialist product sale promotion programme*

defined and measurable objectives. (This has been mentioned at several points within this chapter, but I make no apology for the emphasis because a plan without objectives is like a balloon without air – going nowhere!). These must be communicated to, and agreed with, all the parties involved in planning, implementing and managing the promotion, with particular attention to the agent or distributor.

Most marketing activity is geared to objectives within the general categories of:

- increasing market penetration and share (including stealing sales from competitors)

Promotion objectives for a men's personal care range

Distribution objective: increase in distribution from 20% to 30% of all outlets stocking the product category
Method:
  – salespersons' new account incentive bonus
  – new retailer bonus of 2 free packs for each case of 12 packs ordered (applicable to all size and range variants).

Display objective: 50% of stockists with feature display (say, 15% of all outlets)
Method:
  –point of sale display material and product feature boxes
  – media support on television and in press
  – dealer display bonus or competition
  – salespersons' display competition.

Consumer trial: 20% increase in consumer trial
Method:
  – consumer premium offer (label redemption programme)
  – advertising support on television and in press
  – point of sale material and leaflets
  – feature displays in retail outlets
  – in-store demonstrations and sampling in 50 main outlets.

Promotion objectives for ABC navigation equipment 'AutoNav'

Distribution objective: appoint agents/distributors, with after-sales support facilities, in 4 additional European Union markets, to complete coverage of EC
Method:
  – participation in key European boat exhibitions, actively seeking new agents/distributors
  – providing specialist training in products, sales and service to new agents/distributors
  – market visits by international marketing executives to identify and establish credentials of potential agents/distributors
  – advertising and editorial coverage in selected trade journals, focusing on the hi-tech nature of products, encouraging potential distributors to contact the company.

Consumer use objective: increase European market penetration and share from circa 5% to circa 8%
Method:
  – participation and sales promotion at three key European boat exhibitions
  – sponsorship of two key events, one power boat, one yachting, promoting the product name to the boating fraternity
  – product advertising in specialist boating magazines, supported by editorial and advertorial coverage of both the products and the sponsored events
  – expansion of distribution network to all European Union markets, with local service centres in main ports in each market, increasing sales opportunities through expanded sales/service network
  – direct mailshots to all boat builders and all boat owners listed with national associations and highlighting product features and benefits, distribution and service network and support, and special part exchange arrangements for competitor products.

Figure 21.7 Draft promotion objectives

- increasing product distribution
- generating additional display activity (for consumer goods)
- increasing product trial by potential users
- creating or developing brand awareness and building consumer loyalty
- limiting sales opportunities open to competitors by filling the distribution channels with stock and encouraging users or consumers to 'stock up' in anticipation of future needs.

Within these overlapping categories the international marketer should be able to set specific objectives such as:

- number of additional units targeted to be sold by market or trade channel, or number of new users expected to result from the promotion
- number of new stockists to be added to the distribution network
- increase in market share
- measurable increase in brand awareness (in response to market research activity)
- measurable improvement in product displays (for consumer products) within retail stockists, and so on.

Figure 21.7 illustrates a draft of an elementary promotion outline with quantified objectives, and this can be refined and expanded as experience permits and circumstances require.

The objectives and the methods to motivate results are obviously interrelated, and from this outline plan the full promotion can be planned in detail to ensure timely production of all display material and sales aids, and the booking of media spots. Remember:

- if the promotion has worthwhile objectives, then it is worth thorough planning
- if it is worth the budgeted expenditure, it is worth the management time and effort training the distributors' sales personnel to ensure effective implementation

- if achievement of the objectives is important to sales development, then the results are worth monitoring and quantifying.

For consumer goods the marketer should visit the market during the promotion period to conduct extensive random checks on display and distribution and to assess the effective use of point of sale and quality of feature displays.

Appendix 21.1 at the end of this chapter illustrates a range of typical promotion objectives alongside some of the typical promotion formats that are used by marketers to address the objectives. It can be a useful exercise to prepare a similar type of list specific to your company and products, where you can draw on experience to relate promotion formats to your typical objectives.

A promotional brief format

It is customary in the more sophisticated marketing organizations, particularly those marketing fast moving consumer goods, for a **promotional brief** to be prepared, normally the responsibility of a product manager or other senior marketer. It should communicate specific objectives and criteria for judgement concerned with the development of consumer and trade promotions as a tactical tool. A typical promotion brief framework is illustrated in Figure 21.8. The export marketer might choose to develop an approach to formalizing his promotional briefs for major products in major markets.

Evaluating and monitoring promotions

Often the means do not exist in developing markets for sophisticated measurement of results against objectives, but that is a poor excuse for not attempting a basic post-promotion (including advertising) evaluation. Clearly, as the international marketer in charge of a market you want to be able to see a rise in sales during marketing activity (whether advertising or promotional in

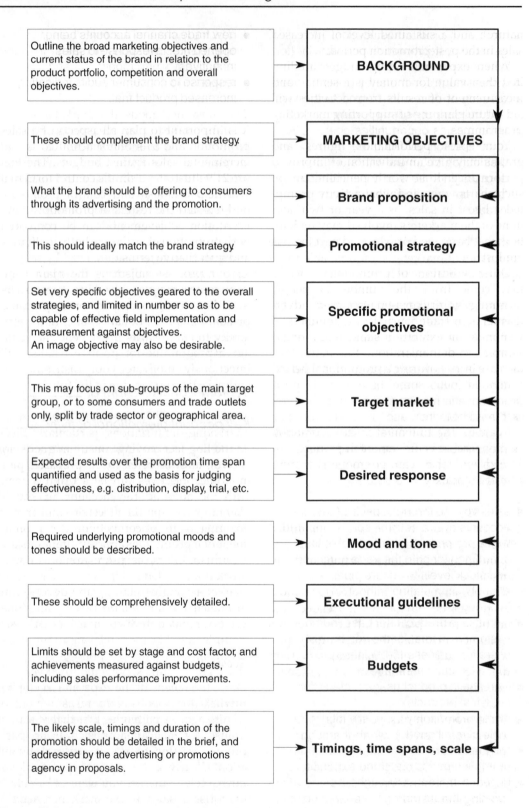

Outline the broad marketing objectives and current status of the brand in relation to the product portfolio, competition and overall objectives.	**BACKGROUND**
These should complement the brand strategy.	**MARKETING OBJECTIVES**
What the brand should be offering to consumers through its advertising and the promotion.	**Brand proposition**
This should ideally match the brand strategy.	**Promotional strategy**
Set very specific objectives geared to the overall strategies, and limited in number so as to be capable of effective field implementation and measurement against objectives. An image objective may also be desirable.	**Specific promotional objectives**
This may focus on sub-groups of the main target group, or to some consumers and trade outlets only, split by trade sector or geographical area.	**Target market**
Expected results over the promotion time span quantified and used as the basis for judging effectiveness, e.g. distribution, display, trial, etc.	**Desired response**
Required underlying promotional moods and tones should be described.	**Mood and tone**
These should be comprehensively detailed.	**Executional guidelines**
Limits should be set by stage and cost factor, and achievements measured against budgets, including sales performance improvements.	**Budgets**
The likely scale, timings and duration of the promotion should be detailed in the brief, and addressed by the advertising or promotions agency in proposals.	**Timings, time spans, scale**

Figure 21.8 A framework for developing a promotional brief

nature), and a sustained level of increased sales in the post-promotion period.

Where export marketing budgets are limited then value for money is essential, and measurement of results from activities will aid future planning of supporting marketing programmes.

Your sales performance figures and graphs may give an indication of improved performance. It is worth pencilling in on such charts when and what activity prompted a boost in sales, as a year or two later none of the marketers involved may remember what happened or why, and past lessons are lost.

Other indicators of promotional success may come from: the number of people returning enquiry cards in response to advertisements in trade journals; the numbers of visitors at an exhibition stand requesting a sample or demonstration; the percentage increase in sales during a promotional period compared with some base period; post-promotion performance exceeding the forecast trend line, etc.

Evaluate the outcome of the promotion against the specific quantified objectives agreed and that can be measured from available data, e.g.:

- sales volume through specific (key) accounts over a set time span compared with a pre-promotion comparable time span (monitor both the trade purchases and stock levels to ensure pipeline stocks are not accumulating without an increase in throughput)
- increase in product user base (number of customers in total, or the numbers of users for business-to-business products within the customer base)
- increase in product usage (notably for industrial products)
- increase in display facings in monitored outlets (retail goods)
- increase in product distribution over the promotion period, i.e. trade stockists
- increase in product throughput of sub-distributors during the promotion period

- new trade channel accounts being opened (i.e. in response to sales incentives)
- response to consumer audits indicating increased product trial.

It is important to plan all aspects of a sales promotion and to monitor actual costs and incremental sales against budgets. The Figure 21.9 illustrates a simple control form that will help establish and control promotion budgets and the results of promotions, and promotion achievements can be compared with promotion objectives in both qualitative and quantitative terms.

Your professionalism as the main company representative with whom your distributor has relationships in preparing and presenting promotional plans, and your ability to successfully implement and manage a programme for positive results, will infectiously motivate your distributor to enthusiastic co-operation in the future.

Key account promotional activity

At the key account level in any market very specific (and more easily measurable) promotional objectives can be set and agreed with the account. Key account activity is likely to have spin-off effects on some minor accounts aware of competition and promotion, but if promotions are only offered to key accounts there is the risk of minor account alienation.

A key account objective planning form can be used as a control document, and one format is illustrated in Figure 21.10. This example might be more relevant to products resold through other distribution channels, such as retail outlets, but a modified version can be designed by the export marketer to suit his own products and markets.

This example highlights the current status against key result factors such as product listings, distribution, display, sales volume, and then notes the planned promotional activity focus (e.g. display or price oriented promotion) and the expected incremental sales the promotion should produce.

Local promotion design and control form					
PROMOTION FORMAT					
Objectives Qualitative Quantitative			**Achievements** Qualitative Quantitative		
Implementation dates:			Budgets:		
	Lead time	**Dead-line**	**Budget**	**Actual cost**	**Notes**
Check legal compliance					
Literature and POS materials ● Design/artwork/copy ● Set production quantities ● Source/order ● Distribute to sales force ● Distribute to trade channels					
Media ● Agree budget splits ● Select appropriate media ● Design artwork/copy ● Creative execution ● Production of materials ● Schedule media placements					
Sales implementation ● Set sales/other objectives ● Design control procedures ● Prepare sales instructions ● Conduct sales force briefings ● Conduct field sales training ● Book promotional orders ● Monitor performance					

Figure 21.9 *Sample form to help promotion budget planning and control*

ACCOUNT OBJECTIVE PLANNING FORM	Listing		Distribution		Display		Volume		Promotional activity		Promotional increment (volume/value)	Action by
ACCOUNT	Current	New	Base	Objective	Base	Objective	Base	Objective	Display	Price		

Figure 21.10 *Key account objective planning form*

Account promotion programme: control form					Cost factors								Post promotional analysis		
Brand/pack	Promotional activity	Promotion dates	Normal period unit sales	Target promotion unit sales	Normal unit cost	Promotion unit cost	Other fixed costs e.g. adverts	Budget promotion unit cost	Normal retail price	Promotion retail price		Actual sales	Actual total costs	Actual cost per unit

Figure 21.11 A control form to monitor key account promotional activity

An alternative way of planning and monitoring key accounts promotional activity in terms of the sales and cost is illustrated in the form shown as Figure 21.11. This control format, which might be adopted by distributors in the foreign markets, is particularly suited to products that are sold through retail trade channels or could be adapted to suit products sold through other distribution channels such as wholesalers or sub-distributors.

Guidelines for developing promotional materials ▬▬▬

The trade buyer, consumer or user is normally only exposed to the promotional visual communication for a very short time, and must absorb the communication content and message and normally move to an action phase within that time. The basic selling principles of getting **attention,** creating **interest,** generating **desire and** provoking **action**, should be applied to designing sales literature and point of sale material.

If sales literature is to be used internationally, either in English or with foreign language translations, then it is wise to keep sales literature straightforward, clear, concise, informative, meaningful, and motivational. Good practice guidelines for the design and message communication of promotional visual aids include the following points.

- Keep the message simple:
  - avoid jargon or communicating message content outside the experience of the audience.
- Ensure the choice of print shades and colours make the message legible and impactful.
- Focus design on impact and suitability of material/visual aid for designated location:
  - ensure it is hangable, fixable or self-supporting if point of sale (POS) material, and of suitable size to make an impact without obstructing venue activity.

- Promote the brand and the brand proposition at least equally with any supporting promotional activity (e.g. premium product) – avoid making the brand a secondary factor to the promotion except in the case of event sponsorships.
- Focus on the brand benefits and additional promotional benefits that give a reason to buy or try now.
- Relate the promotion to product use venues and use occasions in a way that promotes trial or builds brand loyalty:
  - if premium items are being used (given free or offered at reduced prices) they should be synergistic with the product, e.g. if promoting scotch whisky perhaps use glasses, place mats with Scottish scenes, etc., or if promoting fire extinguishers possible premiums might include fire warning notices, smoke alarms, fire blankets, etc.
- Design your sales literature so that it:
  - presents the product features or attributes clearly
  - details the benefits to the users/consumers
  - gives confidence in the supplier as a source of quality merchandise and efficient after-sales service (highlight any international sales and service support network)
  - identifies product uses and functions (often pictorially)
  - instructs how a product can be used (safely)
  - outlines product specifications relevant to the purchase decision
  - illustrates the product, preferably in photographic rather than diagrammatic form
  - presents information in such a fashion as to answer most user/consumer queries
  - generates desire to the point where the potential buyer seeks a sample, demonstration, or product trial, or purchases the product at once.

Financing advertising and promotions

There are two main ways to generate the funds needed for advertising and promotional support:

1. making an advertising reserves provision within product costings and include this within the FOB/CIF price, or
2. making a levy on distributors, possibly an additional charge levied in the foreign market and allocated to and advertising and promotion account, perhaps held in escrow and against which valid charges can be claimed (an approach commonly adopted by international franchisors).

The former is the more common approach, in that the exporter feels more comfortable that he has control over funds and marketing programmes, but has the disadvantage that the advertising and promotion funds, which may largely be spent within the foreign market, attract import duties and any foreign market sales taxes. Both these approaches to funding marketing programmes warrant further commentary, as follows.

Advertising reserves

If your products need promotional activity to create or maintain demand, then you need to incorporate a budget for such activity in your costing programme. The simplest system is to build in a percentage of the ex-plant or FOB price, which need not be the same percentage for each market if expenditure will be at different levels in each market. Some markets may actually develop through a lower price and less promotional activity, particularly if consumer spending power is low. Others may need heavy media support to aid efforts to gain market penetration through display and distribution.

A fundamental concept in marketing is to push your strengths. That may be liberally interpreted in international markets as placing emphasis on the markets and products with the most potential, where potential may be measured in such terms as:

- consumer incomes and spending power
- population size and growth
- assessments of market sophistication in matters of distribution or consumption
- cultural acceptance of your products (the market possibly already being developed through competitors' activities)
- freedom from import or exchange controls.

Where there are clear risks to your market development programme, such as unstable governments and arbitrary changes in regulations, or where you can clearly see that developing a consumer franchise is a major long-term project, then, although you perhaps should not abandon the market, you might be wise to allocate very limited promotional funds in the initial stages. In fact, in such situations there is frequently merit in seeking contributions from your importer, within the limits of acceptable market prices, to use on limited-scale local promotional activity.

As the timing of promotional expenditures may not be directly related to when the funds are earned from product sales, a system should be agreed with the company accountants whereby accruals for advertising and promotions are noted separately in the accounts as a reserve and not be allocated back to profit if not dispersed in the same period as the accrual is earned.

Distributors' contributions

In addition to the margin international marketers include in their prices as an advertising reserve, it is often possible and beneficial to request distributors to incorporate a **local reserve** for advertising and promotion. Such a local reserve has the practical benefit that it commits the distributor more fully to promotional programmes and their measurable success, and it may also mean that less total import duty is paid on that element of the FOB price that would form the manufacturer's reserve. The higher the rate of import duty, the greater the benefit in incorporating the advertising reserve at the distributor's end of the transaction.

As a practical matter, the international marketer may well find that more control problems occur with the element of advertising and promotional funds reserved by the distributor. Some distributors become reluctant to commit themselves to promotional programmes because they do not want to spend local advertising reserves; they may hope to incorporate unused reserves into profits at the end of the year, especially if they have not agreed to reserves being carried forward into another financial year. Distributors are likely to be much more co-operative in the accrual and use of local reserves where they clearly feel secure in their distributorship, as insecurity tends to bring out short-term profit maximization attitudes.

Occasionally an importer wants to draw against the advertising reserve to cover adverse currency fluctuations, while not wanting to reciprocate by contributing extra to the reserve when the currency strengthens. That factor may be removed by the exporter taking the currency risk and pricing only in the foreign currency.

Careful budget planning is essential if you are neither to over-invest in promotional activity nor to fall out with your distributor over sources and uses of funds. Chapter 7, Agency and distributor agreements, has indicated that at an early stage some clear contractual basis could be given to the mutual obligations of the parties in respect of advertising and promotion, including the respective contributions and the mechanics of management control over planning and disbursements against accrued reserves. In the final analysis, only mutual confidence and mutual business benefit will produce co-operation without conflict.

Exhibitions

These have been mentioned earlier in this chapter, and at this point it is perhaps worth giving some additional coverage to this aspect of international marketing, particularly for those readers who have not yet had personal experience of participation in foreign exhibitions.

Exhibition planning and management are time-consuming activities, and the international marketer will face far more frustrations and problems if the exhibition is actually based in a foreign market. Therefore you will need to concern yourself with:

- selecting only those exhibitions that are anticipated to meet exhibition objectives as part of the overall sales and marketing strategy
- setting exhibition objectives
- planning the details of attendance at the exhibition (of both support personnel and equipment, including samples, literature, etc.)
- organizing post-exhibition follow-up with contacts made.

Exhibition objectives

As a starting point it is essential to define your exhibition objectives clearly so that you then participate in only those exhibitions likely to reach the right audience. Some typical objectives might be:

- to identify potential agents or distributors
- to expand exports by finding new foreign direct importers (for either consumer or industrial products)
- to solicit immediate export orders
- to maintain contact with existing foreign agents/distributors/customers in a forum that enables many contacts to be seen in a short space of time
- to test acceptability of, and obtain feedback on, products or services
- to introduce new products or technology to international forums (whether new

contacts or existing agents/distributors/customers, who can be briefed on applications and operations of new products through demonstrations and presentations)
- to work with another exhibitor on a cross endorsement basis, i.e. where the other exhibitor uses the exporter's product as a component, such as a vehicle manufacturer who specifies the exporter's automotive parts as original equipment in its vehicles.

As a supplementary exhibition activity, exhibitors have the opportunity to update themselves on competitive activity and products, learning of their prices, promotions, new developments, and marketing activities. Of course the exhibitor is exposed to the same scrutiny, but can certainly train those managing the stand to be conscious of what information should be dispensed freely and what should be treated as more confidential for limited circulation.

Which exhibition?

As previously mentioned, the numbers and frequencies of exhibitions seem to be proliferating. The international marketer may have the options of trade-only exhibitions, aimed at international buyers for the particular product group, or consumer exhibitions (often promoting products with an international 'lifestyle' theme). As the export marketing budget is probably quite limited, and human resources even more limited, selection of the exhibitions to include in the marketing programme might take account of such factors as:

- cost of participation (either total or per attendee)
- location (proximity to the exhibitor's centre of operations)
- facilities for the shipment and importation of product samples and literature
- relationship between the company's products and target market and the known parameters of the exhibition's

visitor profiles (job functions, industries, interests, nationalities, etc.)
- international reputation of the exhibition
- quality and quantity of other exhibitors (named exhibitors who will be a draw to visitors)
- competence of exhibition promoters and managers
- timing of exhibitions in relation to company sales cycles or new product launches
- suitability of the exhibition facilities for the display and demonstration of the company's products.

Exhibition planning

Successful exhibitions do not just happen; they are the result of long and careful planning. The international marketer will presumably not be alone in the exhibition project, but part of a company team, and with that in mind a few guidelines might be helpful.

- It is preferable to delegate overall exhibition project responsibility to one person, who should be given full access to budgets, and the necessary resources of people, time and money, and report to the head of the international division (export director or other top manager) on project matters.
- Book your participation as early as possible to ensure choice of site within the exhibition complex (cancellations may incur penalties).
- Prepare a list of all necessary stand equipment (samples, literature, sales aids) and establish what the exhibitor will provide and what you must provide (e.g. if any special equipment is needed such as chilled storage, rotating stands). You will want to know locations of facilities such as electricity and water if needed for demonstrations.
- A critical path plan may help you ensure all deadlines are met, particularly if the exhibition materials must be shipped and cleared through customs. The longest

lead time to produce any particular item needed at the exhibition governs the entire timing schedule for the project.

- Plan the manning of the exhibition stand, using personnel familiar both with products and international marketing. Where products are of a low technological nature, and perhaps demonstrations of applications are quite basic (as with some food products and household electrical items), local demonstrators may be available. Interpreters may need to be hired in some instances. You should have enough personnel available to rotate staff every few hours whilst providing a high standard of company expertise into contact discussions.
- Promote your participation: notify your existing agents, distributors and customers of your participation in any exhibition through personal letters or advertisements in international trade journals.
- Ensure you have adequate supplies of promotional literature and product samples to meet anticipated needs. There is no need to give expensive sales literature to casual browsers, but at the same time I am always amazed at how many exhibitors run out of promotional aids part way through exhibitions. If interest is aroused with a prospect and you cannot provide all the information, an opening is made for a competitor!
- Have a system for recording who visits the stand and the nature of their enquiry (pre-printed enquiry cards are a help).

Exhibition follow-up

The major post-exhibition problem encountered by most exhibitors is follow-up on leads and contacts generated. Some of the enquiries may have been of a very general nature, needing conversion to a specific product or service. Others will require technical data from other departments. Some may need follow-up visits and meetings;

others just need postal (or facsimile or telex) communication. After the exhibition the international marketer in charge should:

- quantify results in terms of leads generated and orders taken in relation to exhibition participation costs (including the cost of management time)
- analyse enquiries into priority groups according to exhibition objectives, and set a timetable for follow-up visits, demonstrations, sample dispatch, etc. (it is useful to develop a simple follow-up control form to ensure action is happening)
- commit suitably qualified (technical) personnel to pursue leads.

The amount of post-exhibition follow-up will depend on the objectives and nature of the products, and the resources (particularly sales personnel) available to you.

Further reading

Sales Management. Chris Noonan (Butterworth-Heinemann 1998). Chapter 20: Merchandizing at the point of sale

Marketing Management – Analysis, Planning, Implementation and Control. Philip Kotler (Prentice Hall, 8th edition 1994). Chapter 24: Designing Direct Marketing, Sales Promotion, and Public Relations Programs

Public Relations Techniques. Frank Jefkins (Butterworth-Heinemann, 2nd edition 1994)

Marketing Communications. Colin J. Coulson-Thomas (Butterworth Heinemann 1983). Chapter 18: Sale Promotion.

The Marketing Book. Edited by Michael Baker (Butterworth-Heinemann, 4th edition 1999). Chapter 22: Sales Promotion

Below-the-line Promotion. John Wilmhurst (Butterworth-Heinemann, 1993)

Successful Exhibitions. James W. Dudley (Kogan Page, 1990)

Appendix 21.1 Typical focuses of sales promotions – examples ▬▬▬

Promotion focus/ objective	Promotion format
Trade channel pipeline stocks too low.	● Performance rebates – higher margins with higher sales. ● Trade stock bonuses, e.g. 1 free with 10. ● Dealer margin increases. ● Distributor sales force incentives.
Trade channel pipeline stocks too high.	● Dealer sales competitions. ● Product training programmes. ● Feature display bonuses. ● Price cut specials. ● Point of sale material – product information, promotion information. ● Local advertising or product/promotion. ● Personality promotions – endorsements, brand ambassadors, etc. ● Couponing. ● Tasting/sampling promotions. ● Consumer specials: banded packs, etc.
Trade credit/debt reduction.	● Early settlement incentives, greater than alternative financial sources. ● Increasing scale of performance rebates, etc. linked with prompt settlement, or non-delivery sanctions for non-payment. ● Dealer loader premium offers geared to cash with order/delivery. ● Distributor sales force commission claw-backs or penalties for non-settlement of accounts. ● Positive distributor sales force incentives for debt collections (usually with supply sanctions for slow payers).
Weak trade product knowledge resulting in lost sales opportunities or customer dissatisfaction.	● Product training seminars, videos, films, etc. ● Field sales team/brand ambassadors working in outlets. ● Trade product literature. ● Trade magazine editorials/advertorials. ● Product information leaflets at point of sale.

Promotion focus/ objective	Promotion format
Inadequate product display.	<ul><li>Display incentives.</li><li>Sales performance rebates, etc. motivating display at key sites.</li><li>Dealer display competitions.</li><li>Point of sales material.</li><li>Consumer promotions motivating off-shelf feature displays.</li><li>In-store product merchandising teams.</li></ul>
Increasing product market share.	<ul><li>Performance rebates and allowances, quantity discounts, etc.</li><li>Trade credit extensions.</li><li>Trade stock premiums – dealer loaders.</li><li>Dealer competitions.</li><li>Distributor sales force incentives/competitions geared to volume and display.</li><li>Consumer premium offers.</li><li>Consumer competitions.</li><li>Price promotional price specials.</li><li>Tie-ins with special local events.</li><li>Sponsorship activities by local opinion formers/leaders.</li><li>Price reduction offers.</li><li>Couponing.</li></ul>
Defending against product sales/share erosion from competitive activity.	<ul><li>Dealer stock incentive promotions – dealer loaders.</li><li>Dealer competitions and gifts.</li><li>Distributor sales incentives geared to volume and display.</li><li>Consumer price specials, etc.</li><li>Couponing.</li><li>Improving in-store display through point of sales material and merchandising.</li><li>Point of sales materials</li><li>Sampling/demonstrations/brand ambassadors.</li><li>Advertorials in trade and consumer magazines.</li><li>Direct mailshots to selected target persons.</li><li>Sponsorships by opinion formers/leaders.</li><li>Tie-ins with special local events.</li><li>Consumer loyalty promotions – e.g. collectables, premium offers.</li></ul>

Promotion focus/ objective	Promotion format
Developing brand loyalty.	• Trade advertorials. • Dealer gifts on a build up/collectable basis. • Distributor sales force competitions with a build up/collectable element, e.g. points against gifts. • Consumer magazine advertorials. • Personality promotions/sponsorships. • Point of sales material prompting repeat use. • Consumer premium offers with collectable element (self-liquidating promotions). • On-pack give-aways. • Price incentives – e.g. multiple purchases at reduced prices. • Couponing.
Increasing consumer product trial.	• Dealer/outlet sales incentives. • Inter-dealer/outlet competitions. • Special consumer prices for limited period. • Point of sales material. • Consumer product information literature. • Consumer information videos shown at outlets. • Key site display. • Sampling. • Visits to outlets by brand ambassadors/ personalities. • Demonstrations. • Direct mailshots to opinion formers in target market sectors. • Couponing. • Trial size with established product and variations. • Feature displays linked to buying incentive, e.g. special trial price. • Cross product trial offers ('piggy-back' promotions).
Building a customer/ prospect database.	• Coupons on trade magazine advertorials inviting application for vouchers, etc. • Prizes to persons who make productive introductions of new prospects. • Free draws for product prizes, etc., possibly connected with a trial promotion such as sampling or product purchase. • Data collected from other forms of consumer promotions and competitions with a write-in element.

Promotion focus/ objective	Promotion format
New product launch.	<ul><li>Initial order special allowances in price terms or bonus product.</li><li>Extended trade credit for new products.</li><li>Trade sales literature.</li><li>Dealer/outlet sales competitions.</li><li>Product introduction seminars.</li><li>Sponsorships and outlet visits by personalities.</li><li>Advertorials.</li><li>Point of sales material.</li><li>Sampling/demonstrations.</li><li>Feature displays, possibly with display allowance.</li><li>On-pack premium offers (give-aways).</li></ul>
Increase sales force effort.	<ul><li>Sales bonuses for new account opening.</li><li>Performance related volume sales incentives (commissions).</li><li>Bonuses targeted to specific sales force objectives, i.e. particular brand distribution and display objectives.</li><li>Sales training and product knowledge training.</li><li>Appropriate product literature.</li><li>Appropriate point of sales materials.</li><li>Bonuses for achievement of specific display objectives (on-shelf facings or feature displays).</li><li>Trade and consumer promotions that focus attention and activity on achieving extra sales effort and volume.</li></ul>

Action points

Agree and set promotion objectives
Consider alternative promotion formats against:

- promotion objectives
- budgetary limits
- sales force resource limits
- planning and implementation lead times

Check applicable regulations on promotion formats

Fix quantities of special:

- product
- packaging
- sales aids/promotional literature
- point of sale material

Design copy and artwork for:

- special packaging
- promotional literature
- point of sale material
- other sale aids

Order production quantities of:

- special packaging
- promotional literature
- point of sale material/other sale aids

Develop supporting media campaigns:

- Prepare copy and artwork and storyboards for press and other media campaigns
- Instruct advertising agencies to prepare final media campaign material
- Book media advertising schedules

Checklist 21.1 (*Continued*)

	Action points
Sales management of promotional activity	

- Design procedural systems and controls
- Prepare promotional communications to the sales teams, e.g. bulletins and procedural instructions
- Distribute sales team allocations of promotional literature, sale aids, and point of sale material
- Conduct sale team briefings
- Conduct sales team field training
- Set objectives for each customer
- 'Sell in' promotion to customers
- Distribute promotional product to customers
- Conduct in-store promotional merchandising
- Measure performance against promotion objectives
- Prepare a post-promotion evaluation

Checklist 21.2
Export sales promotion

Action points

Develop an annual 'advertising and promotion plan' including:

- budget details
- advertising and promotion objectives
- media support
- timing and lead times for preparation and implementation
- special packaging requirements
- promotional aids and materials requirements
- legal approvals of promotion regulatory compliance
- implementation (including training) programme
- post-programme evaluation against measurable criteria

Media in marketing communications and promotion mix

- ◆ **Advertising increases demand and distribution by:**
  - illustrating product use and applications
  - emphasizing after-sales service
  - demonstrating product attributes and benefits
  - creating brand name awareness
  - creating or emphasizing market positioning. Check that your local advertising addresses these points.

- ◆ **Advertising media commonly used can include:**
  - television
  - radio
  - lifestyle journals and special interest magazines
  - cinema
  - press
  - POS material and trade/consumer information

Promoting industrial products

- ◆ **Media frequently preferred include:**
  - trade and technical journals
  - international buyers' guides

- ◆ **Advertisements should include:**
  - brief technical description and specifications
  - product illustrations
  - product attributes
  - product benefits
  - sources of product
  - after-sales servicing facilities and availability
  - source of further information

- ◆ **Promotion of industrial products is common through:**
  - specialist trade shows
  - national and international exhibitions

Checklist 21.3
Promotion formats

Action points

The selection of a promotion format will depend on the nature of goods (industrial or consumer) and a clear definition of the objective of the promotion.

◆ **Typical promotional formats include:**
- Brands publicity and public relations activities
- Company credit cards
- Consumer price promotions
- Consumer premium offers
- Consumer competitions
- Couponing
- Dealer competitions
- Direct mailshots
- Display bonuses
- Distributor sales force incentives
- Editorials/advertorials in special magazines or journals
- Exhibitions/trade shows
- Free product trial periods
- Gifts for buyers
- Introduction incentives
- Lectures, slide/film shows, videos
- On-pack give-aways
- Performance rebates or allowances
- Personality promotions and sponsorships
- Point of sale material
- Promotional packaging
- Product merchandising
- Product sampling programmes
- Product training (e.g. distributors)
- Product demonstrations
- Prompt order bonuses or discounts
- Public relations activities
- Sales and promotional literature
- Tie-ins with special events
- Trade price discounts
- Trade stock bonuses
- Trading stamps and similar incentives

Checklist 21.4
Exhibition planning

Action points

Select the exhibition

Consider:

- access to public transport (road/rail/air)
- proximity to customers/markets
- reputation of exhibition
- competence of organizers
- compatibility of visitor profile with target market profile
- timing

Objectives

Set objectives:

- obtaining orders at the stand
- product launch
- contact with existing customers/distributors
- identifying new customers/agents/distributors
- general marketing promotion
- market evaluation
- evaluation of competitive activity
- other (identify)

Planning

Set budgets:

- participation fees
- stand design costs
- delivery/handling/storage of exhibits, etc.
- hire of furniture, telephones, etc.
- stand cleaning expenses
- sales promotion literature and other aids
- samples
- foreign language interpreters
- locally hired demonstrators, etc.
- staff travel and subsistence expenses
- advance publicity and public relations
- insurance of exhibits, etc.
- customer hospitality
- others (list)

Checklist 21.4 (Continued)

Facilities check:

- electricity supply sources
- lighting
- stand location (proximity to traffic flow, competitive stands, etc.)
- ease of access for bulky exhibits
- catering
- security
- communications (telephones, fax, telex)
- other (list)

Action:

- develop a critical timetable
- appoint an exhibition project leader
- book the exhibition stand
- decide on exhibition theme
- design stand and place order
- design all promotional literature and place orders
- decide on exhibition manning requirements
- book hotels and travel for company personnel
- book hospitality suites
- plan and book advance publicity
- notify existing and potential customers
- prepare and implement public relations campaign
- prepare exhibits
- ship exhibits to the exhibition
- prepare and ship samples to exhibition
- hire interpreters and local support staff
- prepare stand manning rota
- check despatch of all equipment, materials, etc.
- other (list)

Post exhibition

- compare achievements with objectives
- compare budgets with actual costs
- prepare and implement a contact enquiry follow-up programme
- evaluate competitor and market information obtained

Part Five

Regulatory and Legal Aspects of International Marketing

22

Regulation of trade

 Whilst the concept of free trade is commonly advocated in political circles, particularly in the developed nations, international trade is still regulated by a variety of means that the export marketer must understand and work within. This chapter will discuss some of the main means of regulating trade, with the aim of giving the export marketer an understanding of these controls, how they are often applied, and hence to ensure that account will be taken of the impact of any controls in export markets when developing marketing strategies and planning marketing communications support. It will also touch on some other points where law may apply to international trade.

In spite of the efforts by governments to encourage and increase international trade both exporting and importing nations generate a host of rules and regulations pertaining to the conduct of trade. Those that involve only reporting the numerical details of transactions are a limited inconvenience, and one that can equally benefit the export marketer when it comes to doing desk research. Export or import licences or quotas or other specific restrictions impose additional rules on the game of international trade and marketing, rules that are not interpreted by independent referees. Some of these restrictions are examined here in so far as they may have an impact on orderly marketing. Figure 22.1 illustrates that typical government controls fall into categories of licensing, quotas, foreign exchange controls and data reporting (normal through documentation lodged with customs and excise departments).

Export licences

Many governments impose requirements for export licences for certain categories of goods or for goods intended for certain destinations. These regulations will vary from time to time, and it is essential that you obtain full copies from the government trade or external commerce departments, or through your export trade association (the Export Licensing Branch of the Department of Trade and Industry in London may assist UK exporters). Banks and chambers of commerce are also generally familiar with export documentary requirements – the banks especially, as they may have reporting requirements, particularly in respect to foreign receipts of funds.

Non-compliance with any special export regulatory requirements will probably carry fines or other penalties, and you, the exporter, will not be able to claim igno-

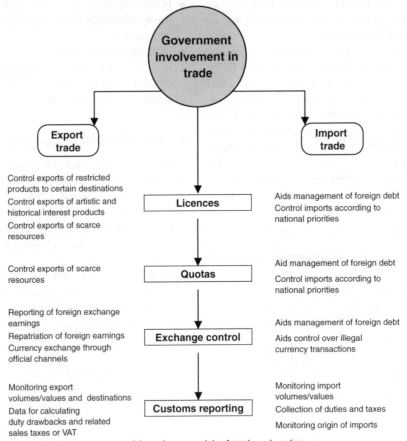

Figure 22.1 *Aspects of government involvement in foreign trade*

rance as an excuse. If forms are required, the appropriate government trade or regulatory department will have these. If an export licence is required, then the forms should be returned and approved prior to your acceptance of a firm order. Otherwise provision should be made in your offer by a clause such as 'subject to receipt of all necessary export permissions or licences'.

Export licences may typically be required for goods in any of the categories of:

- military or defence products, or products of a similar nature such as communications equipment
- products, such as computer hardware and software, that could aid the economic development of political adversaries

- items of unusual artistic or historic value, such as works of art, antiques, precious metals and jewels
- certain agricultural commodities or live animals
- raw materials or commodities that are available in only finite quantities, such as oil and scarce minerals and metals.

It is essential that all applications and certification supplied as part of the licence application are accurate and truthful. False applications or breaches of licensing regulations are generally treated very seriously.

The export licence may not be transferable from one party to another, or from one destination to another, and may be valid for only a limited period. In addition, it may restrict transhipment or shipments that the seller has any reason to know or suspect are going to be reshipped to an unapproved destination.

In some countries, regulatory bodies require an export licence application to be made only by a direct manufacturer, and may choose not to grant licences to forwarding agents or other middlemen. There will frequently be a requirement for subsequent proof that the merchandise licensed for export went to the specified customer and destination, and was not just held in bond for later onward shipment to unauthorized destinations.

Export quotas

Quotas on exports of a product will normally be introduced only if the authorities see it as a scarce resource, and possibly a non-replaceable resource. A global quota could be allocated, or a specific quota by destination. The quota could be open for any person to make application, or it could be limited to manufacturers or other registered exporters.

Import licences

Although there have been moves to promote a freer attitude to international trade, many countries, both developing and highly developed, still operate a system of import licensing, particularly for products seen as non-essential to the economy. This is usually a means of controlling imports in relation to several factors:

- the importing country's ability to meet its commitments to provide the necessary foreign exchange for imports in a timely and orderly manner
- the importing country's assessment of its import priorities (for example, basic foodstuffs will generally be high on the list and luxury items much lower)
- exercising control of legitimate imports in order to identify, reduce or eliminate illicit imports resulting in black market transactions

- restricting imports of products that are freely available from local sources or production
- limiting imports of products where there is a local fledgling industry seeking protection in order to build its market and acquire production skills.

Basis of allocation

Import licences may be issued in any of several ways, depending on the preferences of the issuing authority or the strength of any special interest or lobby group that can influence the method of issue. There are three common systems for allocating licences.

- ***First come, first served***. This literally means that applications are accepted and processed in strict order according to the date of receipt. Licences are allocated accordingly until the quota, if one is in force, is fulfilled.
- ***Licence issued to historical importers***. This method recognizes long-term special interest groups, such as a wine importers' association. Those importers who were in business prior to the introduction of a licensing system are protected by having first access to licences, and any quota is allocated according to some formula worked out with the importers to give each a quota share relating to the existing level of business in an agreed base year. This system has been strongly operated, and equally strongly protested by potential new importers, by the United States Department of Agriculture in allocating import quotas for cheese and dairy products.
- ***Licensed end user***. If licences are issued for the import of any raw materials or special inputs or components for a manufacturing process, then it is common practice to issue the licences only to the legitimate end user of the raw material or imported inputs. This lessens the risk of a legitimate user being exploited by

inflated prices imposed by middlemen. However, if the end user holding licences actually does not utilize their imports or allocation, but has the right to resell any surplus, then they can take advantage of any competitor short of their requirement. Some countries attempt to counter this problem, but all too often with limited success.

Many developing nations that choose to exercise exchange control and import licensing procedures also have a priority list both of importable products and of recipients of the available import licences. Licences are frequently allocated to persons with connections or influence with government officials, and the person who may be allocated the licence as a favour may have no real interest in handling imports.

It is of fundamental importance in appointing an importer or agent, in a country with any form of control on imports or foreign exchange, to satisfy yourself that your appointee can obtain all the necessary permissions governing importation of your products and in sufficient quantity. This may mean you need an importer with demonstrable political connections as well as the financial strength to pay for goods ordered and shipped. In such a situation it is also necessary to form a view of the longevity of your secure operations, because a change in government might mean your favoured importer is no longer favoured. Your agency contract may beneficially contain a clause that the contract may be cancellable if the importer fails to obtain necessary licences within an agreed time period.

Transferability of licences

If licences are transferable from the original holder to others, then there will probably be a market value to the licence, and persons may be persuaded to sell their licence for a fee or share of profits on goods imported. If licences are transferable under any legal arrangement, then both the exporter and importer should establish who holds licences and for what values or volumes so that, if business develops, attempts may be made to 'purchase' additional licences.

Other rules may also apply to the issue of licences or exchange control, such as limiting an application in one year to the actual value or volume allocated or imported in a previous year. If any rules such as that operate, then a licence holder, even if they have the right to transfer a licence, will want imports in their name so that they have the right to re-apply the following year.

Import quotas

In general, allocations of quotas and licences go together, and much of the preceding section applies. If a quota is going to be issued, it is better for export marketers that it be issued to specific persons or companies, with whom they can (or may plan to) develop a satisfactory working relationship to supply a quota holder's requirements.

However, a situation occasionally arises where a global quota is allocated, and the only rule is that anyone may import against the quota on a first come, first served basis. Exporters really should avoid participating in quota races, and limit activity to situations where the risks are calculable, such as where a specific importer has a known quota or licence and fulfilling it comes down to good old-fashioned price and quality competition matched by prompt delivery.

Exchange control

Either or both exporting and importing nations may have regulations pertaining to foreign currency exchange control.

Outward exchange control

The exporting nation is not likely to discourage exports, except of scarce resources, but may require that:

- all foreign earnings be reported
- foreign exchange earnings be 'exchanged' at official banks and at official exchange rates
- no foreign exchange may be held in offshore accounts.

Exchange control in the exporting country also helps authorities ensure that exports are being paid for in a timely fashion. Authorities may even limit the time period of payment, say to less than 180 days, to balance inflows of foreign exchange with outflows required for imports. Additionally, the central bank of the exporting nation may be seeking to satisfy itself that any reported commissions and fees to foreign concerns are strictly for legitimately supplied services, and not just a ruse to bank funds offshore in a stronger currency.

Inward exchange control

Exchange control in the *importing* country will aid in restricting the importing nation's indebtedness, and reduce the volatility of exchange rates.

In a number of developing nations regulations may operate that require the importer to deposit a portion of the value of any specific licence issued or pro forma invoice, so that the central bank can monitor foreign currency commitments and ensure that the importer is not entirely dependent on foreign credit sources for expansion. The length of credit terms or the portion of the invoice value that may be on extended terms may also be limited. Some nations impose regulations that, prior to importing certain goods, the importer must either pay by letter of credit or deposit part or all of the full invoice value in the banking system, thereby restricting to some degree increases in the supply of international credit putting pressures on the domestic money markets.

Exchange control and licensing requirements, and the presentation of acceptable import authorizations or documentation to customs authorities, may also help reduce

illegal imports or illegal currency transactions in a country that does not have a strong domestic currency and that needs strict control of imports and exchange transactions.

Customs controls and reporting ■

Monitoring export sales

Most exporting nations have very strict regulations on reporting exports by volume, value, product type and description, and destination, with penalties for false declarations or non-compliance with the rules.

Exporters requiring specific information on reporting procedures and documentation for their products should first contact the local office of the customs authorities, whose personnel are always most co-operative, especially in aiding the new exporter to understand current procedures.

Exporting customs authorities will normally require information covering the value of the consignment, and the product description or specific formulation or composition of a product if it is open to interpretation as to which customs category the export should be allocated to. The exporting customs can provide full lists of the custom classification numbers for all product categories, and may assist in deciding which is a relevant reporting category if they are provided with a sample and formulation for any product. Product descriptions on all documentation should match up with each other and with product labelling, and the export declaration will require the shipper to note the appropriate export numerical classification agreed with customs.

Duty drawback

If there is a duty drawback system in the exporting country applicable to the element of a formula or consignment that is re-exported, then the exporting customs records by category and product formulation will be supporting evidence for the exporter to reclaim previously paid duties. Similarly, if there are any other systems of subsidy on certain categories of exports, the export customs documentation will provide the basis of proving a claim for reimbursement under the export subsidy programme operated in the exporting nation (for example, the system of subsidies operated within the European Union for various agricultural products).

Monitoring imports

The customs authorities of the importing nation have the principal duties of ensuring that:

- import duties and taxes are paid at prescribed levels
- requisite licences and permits are correctly available and applicable to the specific consignment
- merchandise reported on the shipping documents is the actual merchandise in the consignments, i.e. that contraband or goods of more value than those on the invoice are not contained in the consignment, possibly in fake packaging.

Some importing nations require a proof of **fair market value** to establish that the product is not being dumped cheaply in their market, thereby undercutting local producers. In such situations the exporter should seek the authorized certification to be exclusive of any local sales taxes. The importing nation may even have a system of charging duties on the basis not of the actual invoiced value, but of the exporting nation's fair market or other value. This is a practice adopted by some nations that have ongoing problems of either under-invoicing, in order to pay lower duty, or smuggling. During a period when Indonesia had no formal import exchange controls, it did have high import duties with the aim of limiting imports, and was for many years plagued with incorrect documentation in the form of under-declaration of prices on invoices for re-exports of products from neighbouring

countries. Their answer to the under-invoicing (where the importer actually paid not just the face value of the invoice included with the consignment, but also the requisite difference against a separate invoice) was to establish duties based upon arbitrary sales values of similar products on the Singapore wholesale market. This is a cumbersome system, but may be encountered from time to time in developing nations.

In most instances the product classifications of the exporting and importing nations used on their respective customs declarations will match if the two countries use standard classifications such as that used in the European Union (Harmonised Commodity Descriptions and Trading System).

Bonded goods

Goods that are held in a bonded warehouse by either an exporter or importer may require different documentation. It is a common practice to hold goods in a bonded customs warehouse if the level of import duties or other excise taxes is high in relation to the value of goods. Liquor is an instance where most importers leave their imports in bond until actually needed for imminent sale.

Goods shipped on a **through bill of lading** are normally treated as in transit, and may be held in bonded warehouses or other specially designated areas until shipped on to the ultimate destination. They do not normally incur any import duties or related taxes at the transit points so long as no customs import entries are filed. Control of goods in transit is very strict to ensure that there is no tampering with the product or falsification, and containers are normally custom-sealed.

Sales and value-added taxes

More and more countries are developing systems of either sales or value-added taxes. On the other hand, goods exported are not normally liable to the domestic taxes operating in the exporting nation or, if these have been prepaid, then claims for relevant rebates may be filed according to the local procedures. Without a system of rebates, the exporter would be at a competitive price disadvantage with foreign exporters quoting from countries without a sales or value-added tax structure.

The paperwork burden ▬

The need to report exports or file claims for rebates will again add to the administrative burden of the exporter. However, a little practice in the completion of the forms, and the introduction of a standard administrative system to prepare claims as each shipment is effected, will help to prevent the task becoming a problem.

As the department makes full use of computerization, it is an easy matter to prepare a program that calculates the relevant rebates relating to each formulation and shipment. It may be that the procedures specify that only a certain group can file for rebates, for example manufacturers rather than export traders (since the manufacturer is the person who actually used the taxable ingredients). Alternatively, there may be a registration procedure, as with the European Union dairy exporters, whereby a licensed trader can register to be eligible to file export subsidy claims. Exporters should ensure that they have filed any registrations applicable to their subsequently being eligible for any export rebates or subsidies. As previously mentioned, the export customs entry documentation will normally be a prerequisite in filing such claims.

Proof of origin ▬

The major reasons why an importing nation may require proof of origin of merchandise are:

- if there are any systems of preferential tariffs operating in favour of certain nations, such as the historical British Commonwealth preferential treatment of goods imported from other member nations, and those operated within the Association of South East Asia Nations or the Latin American Free Trade Association, and other regional political trade associations
- where there are embargoes on trading with certain nations for political reasons
- where there are health restrictions on imports from certain sources – say because of fears of pestilence, including foot and mouth disease with cattle, associated with agricultural imports from a number of sources. In fact, products from sources not considered free of such risk will normally not be importable.

Under a preferential tariff system, goods that are simply re-exported, or where a large part of the components were from outside the region or association treated preferentially, may not benefit from application of the preferential import tariffs at the importing nation's customs, even though such goods may still be eligible for duty drawbacks in the exporting nation.

Usually a **certificate of origin** must be certified by an independent office, such as the local consular services of the importing nation, or a chamber of commerce may be authorized to sign certificates.

In addition, some importing nations request other certification under such headings as **certificates of free sale**, which are intended to show that the products are generally acceptable as safe and freely available in the exporting nation, and are not an inferior product being 'dumped' on the importing nation.

With the growth of fraud through export transactions, such as the under-invoicing to avoid duties, and over-valuing goods to by pass currency controls by taking funds out of a country, governments in some countries have introduced pre-export inspection schemes to examine export consignments, and satisfy themselves that contents of consignments are as declared, as well as being fairly priced for export. Various companies administer these schemes on behalf of foreign governments, and specific information will be obtained through desk research and through UK export agencies such as the Department of Trade and Industry.

Government involvement in regulating the flow, volume, value and nature of goods traded for export or import will not suddenly disappear; indeed, the trend has been towards more rather than less regulation, to the frustration of exporters.

Therefore, in your role as export marketer, you must not only become familiar with the applicable rules and regulations of all the countries with which you are trading, but also understand the interpretations put upon regulations. It is the manner of interpretation of rules and regulations that often enables trade to take place even in difficult circumstances. To operate within the rules and regulations yet use them to your advantage wherever possible requires flexibility and adaptability as key attributes in successful export marketing.

Other legal considerations in international trade ■■■■■■■

International corruption

To obtain business in many developing nations, especially government-related or approved contacts, it is necessary to have the right contacts, frequently connected with government departments and senior officials. Direct bribery has been a common and accepted practice in many nations to smooth the way to major contracts that involve multinational corporations and local officials. Incentives have been expected and provided for a range of services, from approving major construction bids to just clearing a container promptly through a congested port. Pressure has grown within many major western countries to cease corrupt practices used to obtain or retain foreign business. It has been considered socially unacceptable to encourage the accumulation of vast wealth by a few persons in power in nations that generally have intense poverty and inequality of distribution of wealth.

Governments such as those of the United States have tended to legislate against the provision of benefits to individuals in government service in foreign nations, under threat of severe penalties on companies and individuals. The USA introduced the Foreign Corrupt Practices Act in the late 1970s; its enforcement has resulted in many senior industrialists arguing that major contracts were being lost to other more liberal nations. European governments, for example, have been less inclined to restrictive domestic legislation.

While it may be hard or impossible to change the cultural traits of officials seeking advantage in any nation, the international business executive must comply with the laws in both their own and the foreign nation in respect of conferring benefits upon individuals. He must also be very sensitive to the potential damage to his good name through adverse publicity in the event of any scandals arising from dealings.

Compensation on terminating agreements

Before granting any foreign party any special or exclusive rights in respect of products or markets, it is necessary to check with lawyers in that country about any future restrictions that the agreement may impose on the exporter's rights. For example, a number of countries (including those of the European Union) require that, in the event of termination, a distributor or sales agent is entitled to compensation, which may include ongoing sales commissions from sales to customers they introduced to the principal, or compensation for other lost earnings or potential earnings, or for investments required to be made by the principal for the distribution of the products.

Local market laws may also limit the degree of exclusivity the principal can demand in an agency or distribution agreement. While it might be acceptable to require an agent not to represent any similar product directly competing with that of the principal (say, another electric toaster), it may not be acceptable to require the agent not to represent any other items in the general product category (say, electrical household goods).

Restrictive practices in the European Union

The theory of trade within the European Union has been that differences in offer price at the border should reflect only differences in cost structures, possibly related to marketing and distribution, local sales taxes or other distinguishable factors. Articles 85 and 86 of the Treaty of Rome are intended to limit activities that could distort or restrict competition within the Union. Article 85 specifically deals with:

- price-fixing or quantity-fixing agreements
- controlling or limiting production, markets, technical development or investment
- sharing markets or supply sources
- applying unequal terms to equivalent transactions between parties within the Union
- imposing onerous terms into agreements that have no relationship to the core subject of the agreement.

Article 86 takes these points further to prohibit the abuse of a dominant position within the European Union to restrict or distort trade.

The application of these articles to trade agreements is very wide, covering exclusive distribution agreements, horizontal and vertical marketing arrangements, market-sharing and price fixing agreements, various forms of co-operative marketing arrangements, joint ventures, patent and trade mark user and licensing arrangements, and the growing franchising of business formats and trade marks and licensing of technology.

Of course there are procedures for registering agreements, and obtaining either individual or block exemptions for certain activities. Exclusive agency and distribution agreements may be exempted in some

circumstances, such as where an agent accepts no commercial risk and is effectively an extension of the manufacturer's marketing organization only, or where a distribution agreement between two parties applies to defined territories and there are still alternative ways (through parallel imports) a customer could obtain the goods within the Union.

The export marketer should have some awareness of, and familiarity with, these and other relevant regulatory controls that might impact on inter-European marketing and foreign market development.

Jurisdiction of laws governing contract and performance

Since the contract between the buyer and seller may involve the laws of two countries, and any dispute may present serious difficulties in court litigation and resolution, avoidance of serious conflict is the first rule. Although a contract may state that the laws of one or other country will apply to litigation, that in itself may become an issue of dispute consequent upon any other disagreement, and a court in one country cannot practically expect to understand and interpret the laws of another.

Attempts to reduce conflicts arising from international sales have been made in establishing uniform laws governing international sales and the formation of contracts, with a number of nations adopting recommendations from international bodies. Generally a contract for sale of goods is governed by the laws of the country designated to hear disputes according to the contract. If no country is designated, then the Hague Convention on the Law applicable to Contracts for the International Sale of Goods recommended that the laws in effect in the country of domicile of the seller be used, unless the order was specifically received and accepted in the buyer's country, in which case a dispute should be heard in and according to the laws of the buyer's place of domicile. The European Union Convention on the Law Applicable to Contractual Obligations similarly approaches the treatment of contracts by allowing parties to have freedom of choice in agreeing the law to be applied to matters concerned with the contract, and where no proper law has been nominated by the parties then the law applied should be that most closely connected with the contract. Under the European Union Convention the parties cannot contract out of the mandatory provisions of the law of a particular country if all the other elements at the time of the selection are connected with that country.

Since there is no overriding international agreement on laws of trade, an agreement between parties should not only identify what laws will apply but establish the enforceability of any decision. This principle is just as applicable to establishing export terms of trade when making a sale to a foreign customer as it is to a representation agreement such as for an agent or distributor.

Illegal contractual terms

Clauses should not be included in an agreement that are not in compliance with the laws of either country. An exporter or international contractor who suspects or knows that aspects of their contracts or business relationships may breach the law of their own or another country that is party to the contract should seek advice from their lawyers on their corporate and personal risk and exposure. While the foreign country may have no direct legal recourse against the exporter or contractor, if it identifies activities it considers illegal in its nation, it may take local action against any assets or investments in its country or jurisdiction, such as confiscating goods in transit.

Litigation

As soon as the risk of litigation becomes apparent, the export marketer should consult the company lawyer. The first issues will be where the litigation can or should take place, or whether or not any practical

steps can be taken to avoid it (such as arbitration). If the litigation will take place in a foreign country, then clearly it will be necessary immediately to consult and retain a local lawyer to ensure proper drafting of pleadings, the taking of depositions, and the conducting of subsequent court cases. By consulting a lawyer early, the exporter may avoid the risk of unintentionally issuing any communications that may subsequently be used against them.

It will be hoped by the exporter that the other party, the buyer, will submit to the jurisdiction of the seller's courts, i.e. the courts and laws of England for a United Kingdom exporter. That may have been stipulated in contracts: if not, it might be that English courts would assume jurisdiction if the buyer is in the country or where any of a number of legal situations are deemed to apply (perhaps where the buyer maintains a place of business or has trading activities within Great Britain).

Within the European Union, the Brussels Convention on Jurisdiction and Enforcement of Judgements in Civil and Commercial Matters discourages shopping around between countries in the hope of favourable attitudes or outcomes, since judgements in one contracting state will in general be enforceable in another. The Convention has adopted the fundamental principle that only one court is competent to hear claims in civil and commercial cases, and that is the court of domicile of the defendant.

Arbitration

Most agency and distribution agreements, and many other international agreements, have a clause or section dealing with arbitration, whereby parties to the contract seek to resolve a dispute without resort to litigation. That clause will normally show where and how such arbitration should take place, including reference to any standard rules of arbitration of a national or international association, such as an international chamber of commerce. If there is no clause to the contrary, then it might reasonably be concluded that the parties were accepting that the laws of the country where arbitration was accepted to take place also applied to the overall contract, unless the arbitration was to take place in a third country purely for mutual convenience.

No single set of arbitration rules is universally applicable, but some of the major groupings the export marketer may encounter include those of:

- the International Chamber of Commerce Court of Arbitration
- the London Court of International Arbitration
- UNCITRAL conciliation rules (United Nations Commission on International Trade Law)
- American arbitration.

Arbitration associations generally have a panel of persons qualified to assist and act as arbitrators, the fundamental prerequisite being that arbitrators are impartial and conducting arbitration only in accordance with the procedural rules agreed as applicable.

The basis of international trade is goodwill; if arbitration and litigation must be resorted to, then there will be a loss of that goodwill. Incorporating a multiplicity of arbitration and litigation clauses into a contract does not absolve export marketers from their primary responsibility – to do their homework thoroughly. Research, study, preparation, negotiation, goodwill, mutual profit opportunities, are all key to the successful outcome of an international business relationship. A contract entered into without thorough preparation and mutual understanding of each party's business objectives, capabilities to perform and market conditions starts from a weak base.

Further reading

Export Trade – The Law and Practice of International Trade. Clive M. Schmitthoff (Stevens, 9th edition 1990). This standard reference work contains a range of chapters that offer a thorough background to many aspects of international trade. Chapter 13: English Law and Foreign Law; Chapter 14: Unification of International Sales Law; Chapter 31: International Commercial Arbitration; Chapter 32: International Commercial Litigation; Chapter 35: Government Regulation of Trade

Principles of International Physical Distribution. J. G. Sherlock (Blackwell – Institute of Export, 1994)

Principles of Law Relating to Overseas Trade. Nicholas Kouladis (Blackwell Business, 1994). The entire book is relevant reading on legal aspects of international trade to the reader with a need for more knowledge, or as a reference book.

Checklist 22.1
Regulation of trade

Action points

Do your products require export licences to:

- all countries?
- some countries?
  (*identify and list*)

Are any export quotas applicable, and if so:

- to which markets?
- in what quantities?

What domestic exchange control regulations exist covering goods exported and the disposition of funds?

Identify and list which of your foreign markets operate:

- exchange control regulations
- import licensing
- import quotas

Are your products eligible on export for:

- duty drawbacks?
- rebate of sales, value-added or excise taxes?

Do any of your export markets have laws or regulations that offer protection for agents or distributors?

- compensation on termination of agreements?
- legislation governing agency/distribution agreements?

Do your agreements have clauses that cover:

- arbitration in the event of disputes?
- which country's laws apply to interpretation and enforcement of the agreement?

23

**Intellectual
property protection** _____

 Ownership and protection of a company's intellectual property are fundamental aspects of international market development in most product categories, whether it is patents, trade marks, copyrights or distinctive designs, or simply confidential commercial know-how that can be exploited commercially as long as it can be kept confidential to the originator. In this chapter we will introduce the export marketer to the subject of intellectual property protection. The aim is not to make the marketer into a do-it-yourself lawyer, but to equip him:

● with sufficient knowledge to hold meaningful discussions with company lawyers specializing in intellectual property protection,
● to enter negotiations with foreign agents, distributors, licensors or franchisors with some knowledge of what must be protected and how to protect it through registrations and agreements.

Protection of your company's trade marks, patents, copyrights and other intellectual property is an essential step in preparing for international business opportunities. These may often be assets with vast monetary and intangible non-monetary values. The purpose of this chapter is to cover some key principles and not to make you into a patent or trade mark lawyer, since this is a vast and complex field of law with many changes, notably in the European Union, over recent years.

Suitable protection and use of intellectual property rights can be a fundamental aspect of assisting professional international marketers to achieve their global marketing objectives. Whilst developing an active protection programme may not be cheap, Figure 23.1 highlights what intellectual prop-

erty the marketer might want to protect, outlines some typical situations when protection would be advised, and the main means of protection available.

The owner of intellectual property rights is able to restrain others from doing certain things whilst exploiting the rights himself commercially. Infringement of rights in any of these areas of intellectual property may be actionable through the courts of countries where infringement can be proved.

Such protection may not be possible or necessary if you are selling a bulk commodity or generic products such as industrial construction materials, but it is advisable for most consumer branded products or exclusive processes or technology, or to protect computer software and creative works. Occasionally a company may take the position

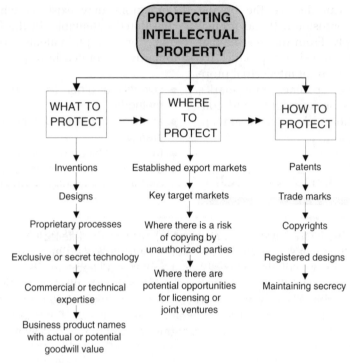

Figure 23.1 *Protecting intellectual property*

that their process is better not patented as that will give competitors more information than they are otherwise likely to obtain. That is more likely to be the case with an exclusive formulation or processing technique rather than design of equipment.

Registration of patents, trade marks and the company's other intellectual property should advisedly be in the name of the original owner (the company), rather than a local agent, representative, associate company or licensee (any of which might subsequently change ownership). It may then be sub-licensed with any appropriate rights granted to a foreign subsidiary or affiliate or licensee, giving maximum protection to the rights of the registrant (possibly with termination rights should ownership of the licensee company change in an unapproved fashion).

Readers might benefit from obtaining (from such sources as Her Majesty's Stationery Office in the United Kingdom) copies of domestic laws and regulations con-

cerned with patents, trade marks, copyrights and industrial designs, and familiarizing themselves with the domestic and European legislation as that will provide an excellent background understanding to the subject of intellectual property protection.

A product may have a long life span, and different intellectual property rights might apply at different stages of the product development, possibly with several property rights applying at one time. When the product is at the embryonic development stages ideas and concepts might be protected by secrecy and laws governing confidentiality. When working models are produced patents might be applied for. When the product is marketed it might be protected by the existing patent and a trade mark applied to the product and giving it a distinctive recognizable identity in the market place. Once the product is well established it can be further protected and laws concerned with **passing off** (that is where other products using designs, logos, trade names, etc. that can deceive the buying public and cause confusion with the original product) may apply. From this we see that when it comes to licensing a product we may have several forms of intellectual property with a licence – patents, trade marks, registered designs or copyrights, and confidential information such as technical manufacturing processes.

Patents

Traditionally a patent is protected only in the territory where the patent application has been filed and accepted. Therefore, separate registration is necessary for each country where it is felt protection may be required for either marketing or defensive purposes. Various degrees of protection are available, depending on whether a patent is applied for to protect an original invention or process, or whether protection for a design or technical improvement is being sought.

It is usual to seek assistance of a specialist patent and trade mark lawyer with an international network of associates in assessing the elements of a design or process that may be unique and protectable because of the degree of originality, and to handle the mechanics of protection in foreign territories.

Basis of patentability

A patent for an invention will normally be granted only where it satisfies certain conditions:

- it is novel, not forming part of the present state of the art in its area of application
- it is commercially exploitable and has demonstrable industrial applications
- its newness involves an identifiable inventive step, not something obvious to a person skilled in the subject matter to which the invention applies.

Limitations may exist on what might be considered patentable. In the United Kingdom, for example, patents would not customarily be granted in respect of:

- scientific or other discoveries, theories or methods
- any work considered to be artistic or creative
- the presentation of data and information
- schemes, rules or methods for performing a mental act, playing a game, or doing business.

However, copyright protection might cover some of the foregoing.

Patent applications must be accompanied by detailed specifications and descriptions of the invention, including relevant drawings, and the descriptive material must be sufficiently clear to enable any person skilled in the art of the particular subject matter to interpret it and reproduce the invention. It is just this need for detailed disclosures that makes inventors and proprietors of exclusive processes (as distinct from new products) reluctant to file for patent protection since that might open opportunities for competitors to 'design round' the patent and reduce the effective exclusive life (and possible licensing earnings potential from royalties) by speeding competitive research into improvements and making the process prematurely obsolete.

Some companies that prefer not to apply for patents covering industrial or technical processes, believe that their best protection from copying by competitors or 'designing round' the patent is to rely on secrecy. Whilst this is an understandable approach, each situation must be considered separately in case laws of confidence might prove a weaker protection than a patent. Protection may also be available where elements of product design are eligible for protection.

Under guidelines of the International Convention for the Protection of Industrial Property (Paris 1883) – now subscribed to by some 114 countries – a person filing in one territory may have a priority right in filing in another territory participating in the Convention and accepting its guidelines, but such a priority period normally only extends for one year from the date of application in the original territory.

This Convention broadly offers the following protection:

- All persons and businesses having residence or commercial establishments in a country have the same rights as nationals without discrimination.
- Within twelve months of filing an application in one convention country, a business or person has priority to file applications in other convention countries; the priority date is the first date of application in the original country where an application was filed.
- A 'grace' period is granted for the payment of renewal fees by original registrants.
- Temporary protection may be granted to patentable inventions exhibited or demonstrated at international shows.

Some countries have rules that limit patent applications if there is publication of data or production of items prior to filing for the protection. Others allow for filing within a period of, say, one year from first publication or production or sale of the item, as in the United States. This one-year 'breathing space' during which a party can file a patent application in other countries after first filing in the home country gives the inventor or marketer time to assess the real commercial potential in markets before rushing off on an expensive mass registration process.

Apart from the rights and protection provided by the various patent conventions, major industrial countries have occasionally entered into bilateral agreements with other countries not members of an existing convention. Also, within Europe the members of the European Union are moving away from the system of separate registrations in each member state to introducing a registration process covering the entire European Union. The European Pat-

ent Convention permits the application of a bundle of patents covering a number of member states. The development of a single community wide patent will prove most popular.

The right to apply for a patent rests either with the inventor or with the party who can claim ownership, such as an employer if the invention was made specifically in relation to the terms of employment. Processing patent applications takes so long (frequently several years) that there is always the danger that another similar patent application is in the pipeline ahead of yours.

Quite apart from the protection afforded to a design, product or process by a patent, the inventor may have other more basic copyright protection of his plans, drawings, designs and specifications.

Provisions within the United Kingdom patent laws and European Union laws allow a person to apply for a compulsory licence to work a patent once a period of three years have passed from the patent being granted and where certain conditions can be demonstrated to exist, such as that the patent owner is failing to meet demand on reasonable commercial terms.

Contesting patents

In a number of countries a patent might be contested in several circumstances, such as:

- where the invention was not patentable in the first place, perhaps because it
  - failed to satisfy the criteria of novelty,
  - was not capable of commercial exploitation, or
  - failed to provide a new inventive step not apparent to persons skilled in the art
- where the patent was granted to a person not entitled to be granted the patent
- where the submitted specification of the patent does not disclose the invention sufficiently clearly for a person skilled in the art of the subject to perform the invention

- where an amendment to a specification has been wrongfully allowed that extends the protection conferred by the patent
- where a specification of the patent extends beyond the disclosures of the original patent application, and where the patent applicant may in effect be modifying the specification to include later improvements or developments. Subsequent improvements and developments must be the subject of separate new applications, which may be granted priority back to the original application filing dates of the first specification if made within 12 months.

European patents

The introduction of the concept and practice of European patents, recognized in the United Kingdom through the Patents Act 1977, gives all the same rights and remedies in the United Kingdom to a European patent as if the patent was first registered in the United Kingdom. Similarly, within the European Union it is intended under the Union Patent Convention that all rights, powers, obligations, remedies, liabilities, restrictions and procedures provided for by or under that Convention shall have legal effect in each member state of the European Union, and patent applications can be filed at the European Patent Office in Munich or at any national patent office.

Trade marks

As incomes around the world rise and more people have the opportunity to visit other countries for business or pleasure purposes, so the value of international trade marks becomes more apparent to the international marketers as they are closely associated with business goodwill and reputation, and are often seen by the public as indicating quality and source of a product. Travellers

may feel more secure buying a product they are familiar with back in the home market, and the youth of the world may wish to consume or wear the products made fashionable in films and other international media. There has been much opposition in some developing countries to the spread of western youth culture to their own youth, but it is a trend that has not yet lost momentum.

For a trade mark to be registrable in most countries it should not be a proper noun or be misleading, but should be distinctive and used in the course of trade. An invented word is often easier to register, and nowadays not only do product marketing managers spend time trying to develop potentially registrable trade marks to associate with their products, but many specialist agencies concentrate on the creation of names that are both registrable and distinctive and also are capable of forming a consumer association between a product and its brand name. A registrable name in one country may not be accepted in another if it fails in the eyes of the local trade marks office to meet its criteria.

It is common for trade marks to consist of, or include, designs or logos, and this may present problems independently from a name. A design in one country may not be acceptable in another: for example, a fruit illustration might not be permitted for inclusion in a design in one country if it is considered misleading of the nature or the content of the product (i.e. purporting to consist of natural ingredients when it does not).

In the United Kingdom the 1994 Trade Marks Act harmonizes UK law with that of the broader European Union, and some extensions of coverage result, for example:

- smells, colours, and sounds may be protectable within the UK and European Union where these can be represented graphically
- some geographical names may be protectable as registered marks where they acquire a distinctive character

- the shape of products may be protectable under the recent Act except where
  - the shape results from the nature of the products
  - the shape the is needed to obtain a technical result (i.e. concerned with product performance)
  - the shape adds significantly to the value of the goods.

The role and value of trade marks

Trade marks serve to identify a product through the use of distinctive product names or logos commonly associated with the product or its producer. Manufacturers strive to develop recognition of the trade mark associated with their products and to establish a particular reputation for quality, service, reliability and product perceptions.

The applicant for registration of a trade mark is generally the company or person planning to use it, although a subsequent registration might be sold or its use licensed, subject to a registered user agreement in a form acceptable to the registering authority.

In many countries, ownership of a mark is limited to a particular product category. In the United Kingdom, for example, some thirty-four product categories are distinguished along with eight service categories; the same name can be applied to different products in different categories, and the mark owned by different manufacturers.

Trade mark applicants traditionally seek registration for use in as many classes of goods as they can practically hope to justify, and wait for other parties to oppose registration in any particular class (perhaps for lack of use) subsequently. Applications may be opposed or rejected on the grounds of similarity or confusion with another mark, or because the mark or design is not sufficiently distinctive or original. If there are subsequent changes in ownership of the company that has registered trade marks and patents, then the new owners need to ensure that the acquisition includes the transfer of ownership of all such intellectual property rights.

Who can register a trade mark?

Anyone can apply to register a trade mark, but prior use of a trade mark in a territory is often taken as giving a priority claim to protection and registration. As with patents, trade marks generally require a separate application to protect the mark in each separate country. In the United States, the user of a mark in one particular state may have protection without registration within that state by demonstrating an active sales history prior to another user of the same trade mark or name offering the product for sale in the particular state. If priority of use is the accepted criterion in any market, and the exporter can demonstrate the first usage and regular use of a product freely sold in the market, they may have a basis for protection against infringement, even if no formal application for a registration is made. In other countries, the basis for protection and ownership is the first application to register the mark.

It is usual for trade mark registrants to be required to prove continuing use to register and keep a trade mark. This puts pressure on multinational corporations to ensure that goods are distributed in countries where they have registrations to protect or retain. Sometimes use of a trade mark can be demonstrated just by shipping occasional token quantities of appropriate products to a market, perhaps to an associate or friendly company (such as a distributor of other products in the company's product portfolio), with an invoice that establishes a commercial transaction. Ownership may be based on uncontested use for a given period.

The system of giving a registration to the first applicant for a mark has proved detrimental to some multinational corporations with international brand names, who find a local person or company has already filed for their trade mark in any market. The exporter could be forced to negotiate an agreement to use what they viewed as their own mark, or to create another brand identity that may take more time to develop. If the trade mark is lost to a third party that could reduce opportunities to license it and reduce the value to any licence of other intellectual property that should normally include the trade mark. If an international company with strong brands has to buy back its own trade names in order to own the trade mark rights, this adds to market entry costs, but could be much cheaper than the alternative of trying to establish new trade marks through heavy advertising and promotion.

Trade mark protection programmes should be developed where a company may:

- directly export products to foreign markets
- commence local manufacturing or marketing through branches or subsidiaries in the future
- license manufacturing and/or distribution of branded products or services
- feel threatened with potential misappropriation of a trade mark already protected in the home market, or piracy or local misuse (on inferior products) by enterprises in the foreign market.

A case example – The Body Shop International

The Body Shop International plc grew in its early years through the mid-1980s primarily within the United Kingdom. It had a very successful format and product range that suited franchising, and that route was pursued aggressively and successfully. The international strategy was to pick off key markets where they could expect to build a similarly successful franchised operation. Early foreign ventures were in some European, Middle Eastern and Asian markets.

Research showed that two key markets should be Japan and the United States, both large consumers of skin and hair care products, and markets where the company's social marketing concerns would be valued and relevant to consumers.

Research into trade mark ownership showed that for both Japan and the United States an American company had a prior registration and usage of the trade name of 'The Body Shop', preventing the UK company of that name using and exploiting the mark in those two key markets. The particular American company had actually been using the name for quite some years, although it was a small producer and distributor of similar products.

The only practical alternative to the UK company (other than using a different trade name for those two markets, which would dilute its global brand image) was to negotiate a deal that gave it the trade mark rights to the name in the United States and Japan. In this situation, whilst the problem might not have been avoided, in so far as the United States company had a long track record of trading with the name, it was still a costly exercise to acquire it for the UK company.

The normal practice where a new name is being developed that might have international brand potential is to attempt to research and develop a brand name that is unique, and that is certainly not protected in major markets of the world.

Both the United States and the United Kingdom have traditionally favoured systems where ownership is based on uncontested use and registration for a period of time. Use of an unregistered mark by one party does become an obstacle to another party subsequently seeking a registration of the same mark.

It may be possible to seek registration for a mark purely for use in export markets, if no other party can show a prior proprietary right to that mark for those export markets.

International conventions

The International Convention for the Protection of Industrial Property affords trade mark protection in the same manner as for patents, including:

- the right to equal treatment with residents and nationals in the foreign country without discrimination in registering and protecting trade marks
- a six-month priority period after first registering in the home country to file for registration in the foreign country
- the proprietor of a registration in one convention country in principle being able to seek the same protection in other convention countries in the registration's original form
- registration not being cancelled for non-use until a reasonable time period has elapsed and a defence may be made of special circumstances preventing use
- renewal in one convention country not obligating the mark's proprietor to renew the mark in other convention countries
- the possibility of claiming in another convention country that if registration were granted to another party it would cause real confusion with a similar or the same mark previously registered or used in a different convention country. Such a claim may have time limitations to proceed with a claim or attempt to block the foreign registration attempt.

Cultural considerations

Occasionally a trade mark accepted and established in one country might prove unsuitable for use in another. The actual word, its pronunciation, spelling or accompanying designs may have some unacceptable local connotations, or prove difficult for customers to pronounce. Multinational companies choose trade marks and brand names with great care to minimize this risk. Occasionally marketers find another local name is coined for the product by the local users or distributors, and in these situations the trade mark proprietor may want to consider whether the local name should be registered and incorporated in the product literature or on packaging materials.

Occasions may arise where a trade mark becomes commonly associated with a whole range of products in a category (e.g. 'Hoover' to refer to any vacuum cleaner, 'Vaseline' to refer to any petroleum jelly, and 'Coke' to refer to any cola type of soft drink. Trade mark proprietors need to be sensitive to that situation, and take appropriate action, as misuse might eventually result in the trade mark being lost if it is considered to lose its distinctiveness and becomes generically descriptive of a product type or category rather than a single manufacturer's brand.

Cancellation of trade marks

A trade mark registration might be cancelled for a number of reasons, including:

- if the mark is left unused for a set period of time (within five years of registration within the UK), unless the proprietor can defend its lack of use to the satisfaction of the trade mark registrar
- for certain registration categories, even though it is used in at least one category (since many manufacturers register a mark in as many categories as they can as a defensive move)
- that it has ceased to be considered distinctive, perhaps because it is thought

A case example –
Yoghurt trade mark licensing

A brand leading manufacturer of yoghurt decided to seek international licensing opportunities, since it was not practical to physically export product to distant markets because of shelf life limitations and the low value of ingredients in relation to international freight and distribution costs.

A number of markets where targeted, amongst them Canada. A potential licensee from Canada visited the company's UK premises. Whilst no commitment was made by either party at this meeting, it was agreed to hold further contact and discussions. The UK manufacturer checked its trade mark files to note that the brand name was not protected by trade mark in Canada, and started procedures to file for registration.

Some weeks later the company's export marketing director scheduled a visit to the prospective licensee's premises in Canada. Whilst there, at a point in the meeting papers on the desk of the prospective licensee were disturbed, and the export marketer noticed, to his surprise, that amongst the papers was an art work quality reproduction of his yoghurt logo including the brand name.

The meeting ended without a commitment from the yoghurt manufacturer, and subsequently the export marketer started investigations into progress for his company's trade mark application. It was soon discovered that the prospective licensee had filed an application in his own company's name just days before the application from the original UK company was received at the Canadian Trade Marks Office.

Clearly, the value in a licence to manufacture the yoghurt would have been greatly diminished where the manufacturing know-how licence was not accompanied by a trade mark licence, and the prospective licensee would have had scope to pressure the original UK mark owner to grant manufacturing and know-how transfer licences to his company rather than any other (since he would own the Canadian trade mark).

The exporting company, whilst having no formal confidentiality agreement or other protection in place to prevent an infringement by the prospective licensee, did have correspondence and documentation showing the parties were in discussion about the grant of a licence that would incorporate a brand trade mark licence.

The lawyers were, in this case, able to resolve the problem to the benefit of the UK company without an expensive law suit. The learning point being the need to actively protect intellectual property in timely fashion to maximize potential returns from future trade and licensing, and to enter confidentiality agreements with 'no pre-emptive application and registration clauses' at an early stage of negotiations with prospective foreign partners, whether agents, distributors or licensees.

to have become a generic term used to describe all similar products

- if a party can justifiably claim to be entitled to a registration in a particular category because the existing registrant does not market goods in that category (and a new applicant for registration may be able to demonstrate that sales have taken place over a period of time using the mark without it being contested)
- if a trade mark is subsequently considered to cause confusion with another (previously) registered mark, or where the mark is considered to mislead the consuming public about the quality, source or nature of the products with which it is associated
- if a mark has been used by a proprietor in a manner different from that in which it has been registered (so beware of 'jazzing up' the presentation of a trade mark to reflect changing market perceptions if that breaches present registrations).

Copyright ▰▰▰▰▰▰▰▰

Copyright is perhaps one of the more difficult areas of intellectual property to protect in an international context. Although many nations subscribe to copyright conventions, providing rights and protection, in many markets it is difficult to trace and prosecute infringers and producers of pirate material. Primarily copyright protection is designed less to stop other persons using a work than to ensure the originator or creator of the work receives some reward for their input of skill, artistic and creative abilities and general intellectual property. Copyright law has adapted to changing technology over the years, and, whilst initially protecting written communications, has encompassed films, photographs, sound recordings, broadcasting in its many forms, and computer software including computer games, and it will, no doubt, continue to adapt to other future developments.

Nature and ownership of copyright ___

The ownership of copyright in a work gives the owner the exclusive right to do, and to authorize others to do, certain things in relation to that copyright work, such as to reproduce it if it is a written or literary work, or perform it if it is a play or musical work. The copyright might belong to an individual person or group of persons or to a company, and might apply to either a published or unpublished work. Under traditional British copyright law (the current relevant Act being the Copyright, Designs and Patents Act 1988) and that of many nations, protection may extend for fifty years after the work was created or after the death of the author or originator of the work. Most countries have basically similar protection.

Copyright generally applies to works of literary, artistic or creative merit, skill and originality (such as: books; plays; music; films; cable, sound and television broadcasts; poems; works of art) which nowadays must be considered to include computer software and video games. The ability to exploit intellectual property rights is fundamental to promoting investment in creative fields. A 'work' need not be of demonstrable merit, it merely needs to be the result of the originator's own effort and skill in producing something tangible. (An idea is not copyrighted.) Whilst many copies are legitimate (where they are for personal or research use, for example) work copied without the owner's permission for non-legitimate purposes may generally be seen as an infringement.

Where work that is protectable under copyright is developed by an independent third party (not an employee of the company contracting for the work) the copyright in the work is owned by the originator (developer) of the work, for example, a consultant agency or software producer, except where there is a specific contractual agreement between the parties that copyright will be owned by the party commissioning, and paying for, the work. Where work that relates to employment is produced by an employee in the normal course of his or her employment, then any copyright will normally be vested in the employing company.

As with patents and trade marks, international conventions, such as the Universal Copyright Convention and the Berne Convention, offer protection against illegal copying and redress for infringement in nations that are signatories to the Conventions.

Industrial designs

United Kingdom Acts applying to designs include the Registered Designs Act 1949, the Design Copyright Act 1968, and the Copyright Designs and Patents Act 1988. Similar protection is provided for in many markets, and the international marketer concerned with designs will need to investigate, understand and comply with regulations in each market, probably using the services of suitably skilled lawyers.

In the United Kingdom original functional designs may be registered and protected. The Copyright, Designs and Patents Act 1988 gives the owner or originator an opportunity to protect a three-dimensional design of an object for a period of up to fifteen years against copying through a **design right**. Visually attractive designs that are applied to products can be protected as **registered designs** under the Registered Designs Act 1949.

Ownership can be transferred to another party, assigned, or a licence can be granted to a party to perform or do certain things with the copyrighted work. This gives some measure of protection in respect of exclusive product designs, but equally may be difficult to enforce: the copyright owner must demonstrate that their design was first in the market and also that it was actually and deliberately copied.

Creators of designs should ensure that they sign and date all new and original designs, keeping the originals safe in case of any future disputes with other parties where they market similar competitive products at a future time. Whilst design rights might apply, in some cases it may be appropriate to file for a registered design. Companies should ensure that their employment contracts entitle them to claim ownership of designs produced by employees in the normal course of their employment.

Registration in the United Kingdom may provide protection in some countries that recognize United Kingdom registration, or a basis for filing for protection in other member states of the International Convention for the Protection of Industrial Property. A separate application must be filed in each member country where the owner wants registration within six months of an application being filed in the home market.

Confidential information

Confidential information can be protected by laws that prohibit breach of confidence, and persons who have received confidential information can be restricted from passing confidential information to unauthorized persons or making use of the information. Laws of confidence can protect ideas, such as when a project is in an embryonic stage of development, as well as tangible intellectual property, and these laws are an important adjunct to other registration or protectable intellectual property rights. It is important to make an obligation of confidentiality explicit in respect of information not in the public domain and the release of which would be injurious to the owner.

International marketers concerned with discussions on licensing and joint ventures often enter into confidentiality agreements at an early stage of discussions with potential partners to protect any commercial data or ideas not otherwise protected from unauthorized commercial exploitation by their contacts. When preparing a confidentiality agreement, the structure of which should be checked with any local laws governing confidentiality in the appropriate market, detail:

- the duties of the recipient of confidential information to store it safely
- the obligation not to release any of it to unauthorized third parties
- the obligation to protect it from unauthorized copying, theft, etc.
- the obligation to indemnify the owner of confidential information for any costs or losses incurring from unauthorized release, copying, or access to information, whether as a result of a deliberate action by the recipient or negligence.

It can be useful to:

- detail who may see confidential information (by name and position)
- mark any data passed in confidence as 'confidential'
- mark any documents that should not be copied accordingly on each document.

Intellectual property in the European Union

With the development of the European Union it is logical that the differing laws covering intellectual property should be harmonized to give greater pan-European rights and protection to owners of intellectual property. The direction of European Union action has been towards:

- harmonizing the differing laws of the various member states
- giving Union-wide rights on intellectual property
- simplifying the Union-wide registration of registerable intellectual property rights, i.e. that registration could be sought with one single application
- applying the principles of the Treaty of Rome to the use and exploitation of intellectual property rights.

European patents

Grants covering patents can be obtained under the European Patent Convention,

which effectively provides a bundle of national patent rights, or under the 1975 Union Patent Convention a unitary patent covering the European Union can be applied for. Trade marks present a greater problem as similar trade marks may be registered and used in different countries by different mark owners. New trade marks may not suffer this disadvantage and prove easier to register across the European Union. As the European Union expands through new membership of a broader based European Union the new members will need to bring their laws into line with Union law.

Whilst intellectual property rights can be acquired for the European Union their use must avoid unacceptable restrictive trade practices (Article 85, Treaty of Rome) and abusing dominant market positions (Article 86, Treaty of Rome).

Trade marks in the European Union

It has long been the intention that there should be a European Union trade mark, but this will take time as it means work towards harmonizing national laws and will present difficulties where similar marks have been registered by different owners in different markets. When developing new marks for Europe marketers have the opportunity to select trade marks that do not conflict with existing registrations in any member state.

Copyright and the European Union

Historically copyright has varied considerably within the member states of the European Union. Union law takes precedence against any inconsistencies in national law of member states, and the European Union recognizes intellectual property rights as a form of property. The application of laws must also look to comply with clauses in the 1957 Treaty of Rome, particularly those concerned with freedom of movement of goods (Articles 30–36), that concerned with prohibiting restrictive trade practices (Article 85), and that concerned with preventing the abuse of dominant trade positions

(Article 86). Copyright licence agreements may grant rights to licensees in individual member states that effectively provides a licensor with control over markets.

Infringement of patents, trade marks and copyrights ▰▰▰▰▰

If a trade mark or patent is infringed, the infringer risks a suit for damages and an injunction to prevent further use or abuse of the registered mark, design or process. Even if the alternative design or mark is not identical to the registered and protected item, there may be a case of 'passing off'.

Patent infringement

A patent infringement might be considered to occur where the invention has a currently valid patent registration in the country of the infringement (i.e. it has not been cancelled, withdrawn for any reason, or lapsed), and one or more of the following conditions prevail:

- an unauthorized party manufactures, distributes or markets the patented product
- an unauthorized (unlicensed) party uses a patented process
- a party uses, imports or disposes of any product that has been obtained through the unauthorized use of a patented process
- a person supplies an essential element of an invention knowing that it will be used in an unauthorized version of a patented product or process.

The patent owner can bring proceedings for infringement through civil courts, seeking redress through:

- an injunction restraining the infringer from continuing to infringe the patent
- an order causing all the unauthorized product to be delivered to the patentee or that all infringing product be destroyed
- damages in respect of the infringement

- an account of the infringer's earnings and profits resulting from the infringement
- a declaration from the courts that the patent is valid and has been infringed by the defendant.

Bear in mind that legal actions are both expensive to pursue and slow to progress, as well as being difficult to control in foreign territories. They can also be counterproductive if you have scarce management resources, because they are very distracting to managers who must devote the time to progressing infringement suits rather than market development.

Trade mark infringement and passing off

Most exporters of branded products to foreign markets have seen cases of copies based on their trade mark or concept. Sometimes the forgery is very poor, and some persons may say there could be no confusion. From the marketer's viewpoint, any copy can cause confusion and risk the loss of customers who become uncertain over quality. Goodwill in the trade marks can be seriously damaged. Copies particularly develop in those countries with less enforcement of some aspects of commercial law, and where they are developing an industrial base mostly of small, labour-intensive entrepreneurial owned manufacturers. The Orient is full of copies of designer leather accessories, watches and electrical sundries. Even books have been copied in total, ignoring international copyright laws.

Within the European Union customs officers have powers under anti-counterfeiting regulations to seize goods that infringe trade mark rights. Owners of intellectual property rights are finding that legislation is moving in their favour to provide additional protection and remedies where infringement is identified.

The similarity between the real and fake item may be in such general matters as overall impact or image, pack shape or colour, or a local name in similar style to the foreign name, which causes confusion with persons of limited literacy. In a 'passing off' case it is not always necessary to prove either that fraud did take place or that particular consumers were deceived, only that deception might result.

An infringement may occur where the unauthorized party uses the actual registered form of the trade mark, either on a direct copy of the genuine product to which it is normally attached (probably a deliberate infringement) or on another product in a category to which the trade mark registration applies.

Where a possible infringement is identified the trade mark owner's main concern is the protection of the business's goodwill and reputation, the first action is often for the trade mark owner to issue a formal warning, drawing the infringer's attention to the appropriate trade mark registration. Sometimes a visit from the exporter's agent to the infringer can help in warning them of an awareness of their activities. This may be all that is needed to warn the infringer off their course of action, especially if infringement was accidental. If the warning is not successful in stopping the infringement, then an injunction may be sought to prevent further use and any appropriate damages through suit. Redress might extend to the seizing and destruction of offending products and packaging materials and related product literature.

From a practical point of view, any international representatives of a corporation should make a special effort to identify any possible trade mark infringements in those markets to which they travel, and ensure that prompt action is taken where any threat to a registered trade mark is found. The trade mark owner should not rely solely on the local agent, distributor or licensee to police the market, reporting potential infringements, even where an agreement calls for them to do so. The local representative may not be sufficiently familiar with trade mark law and practice to recognize and be concerned over potential 'passing off' infringements, or may simply be accustomed to accepting copying in his local market.

Defending a trade mark or suing to prevent infringement in a foreign market is both costly and time consuming, and the best approach is a thorough programme of intellectual property protection, with an automatic system to alert you to renewals and defence procedures such as making regular deliveries and sales of registered items to avoid a claim of non-use.

You could usefully build a file record of all marks observed on your travels that closely resemble your company's, on both similar and different product categories. You should occasionally review your findings with the trade mark lawyer in case of potential problems.

Copyright infringement

In seeking to enforce copyrights internationally, the export marketer should bear in mind that there may be cause for action against both persons making the copies and persons who commission or knowingly market the copies. However, it will be harder to enforce action against end users or distributors who unknowingly have purchased or used illegal copies, except perhaps by having any such copies that may be recovered destroyed.

As copyrights are separately protectable in each country, it could be that a legitimate copy in one country may be breaching the copyright elsewhere if it is sold into a market where another party has a right such as a licence on the copyright.

A person may be infringing a copyright in a copyrighted work when they:

- reproduce the work in any form, such as taking unauthorized photocopies
- act to publish all or part of the work
- make an adaptation of the work, which, in turn, they might copy, publish or distribute, or claim copyright to
- import a copyrighted article into any territory without the copyright owner's

express consent or the consent of a party with a licence to the copyright in that territory

- offer for sale or trade any copyrighted work in a place where the making or reproduction of the copy offered for sale would have breached local copyright ownership
- permit a public performance of a work without the specific approval of the copyright owner or licensee.

Where an infringement of copyright is judged to have occurred the copyright owner or an exclusive licensee may issue suit against the alleged infringer and seek an injunction preventing continuation of the infringement, destruction of any offending articles, such as unauthorized copies, and such damages and account of profits as a court considers appropriate for the infringement. Action must be taken in the country where the infringement occurs. Whilst piracy and counterfeiting of copyright works may come within criminal laws as well as within civil laws in some countries it is usually difficult pursuing actions in some foreign markets.

Compliance with local market copyright protection procedures will make enforcement and control over potential royalty earnings that much easier. Some countries, such as the United States, may wish a copyrighted work to be registered, and your lawyers should advise you on your own specific protection programme, particularly if you are likely to want to grant any licences in connection with copyrighted works. A copyright licence goes beyond just giving permission to use or quote a work or to perform a play, and may very likely transfer certain property rights in a specific market.

Licensing patents, trade marks and copyrights

Licensing arrangements will be explored more fully later in this text, but some commentary specific to intellectual property is relevant here. A proprietor of a trade mark, patent, copyright or business format may license its use to a licensee or franchisee in exchange for fees, royalties or other considerations. This is becoming particularly common with lower-value consumer items, such as beverages and fast foods, that would not bear the shipping costs or delays. A licence can also be issued to a subsidiary of a parent multinational corporation; in fact, the parent company is advised to own all its international marks in its own name and to create sub-licence or 'user' agreements as appropriate with associates, affiliates and joint venture partnerships in order to retain full control of the use of the mark or design. The registered user may have rights to defend the marks against local infringement. If you plan to license any trade marks or patents, then close attention to your registrations is fundamental for an international brand, because without the registered trade mark you may have little of commercial value for either you or your franchisee to exploit.

Licensing patents

Because the patent, or application for a patent, is personal property, the rights to it can be transferred through:

- mortgage
- assignment to another party
- a licence to work the invention that is the subject of the patent or patent application (or a sub-licence, if that is permitted in a licence).

The transfer of the property in a patent must be effected in writing and signed by the parties to the transaction.

Whilst a patent can be exploited by a licence, a product or process does not need to be patented for licences to be granted or sold. Many licensing arrangements nowadays are actually only licensing a system of conducting business – the 'business format' franchises offered by many franchisors of small business units.

In some instances compulsory licences can be granted to patents, usually after they have been registered for several years and in circumstances where they are judged not to be worked properly (i.e. demand is not being met, or the patent is not being commercially exploited, or where a patent owner is judged to be abusing a dominant position). Where a compulsory licence is granted the patent owner will customarily receive reasonable royalties or other remuneration.

Trade mark licensing and user agreements

Where a licence is granted to use a trade mark it is essential that the terms of the licence clearly restrict the licensee to use the mark only for the products designated in the category in which the original registration was effected, and in the designated fashion of the registered mark. Generally a trade mark licence accompanies the provision of other intellectual property, such as a business format, patent or know-how. Normally the licence to use a trade mark on approved products in exchange for royalties, or even a standard user agreement without payment, will contain restrictions concerning the quality control standards applied to the products and/or their manufacture.

Where a 'user' agreement is arranged in a particular foreign market, care must be taken over shipments into that market by registered users or exporters in other markets, especially where the parallel imports are through a party other than the registered user, in order to avoid risks of invalidating a trade mark or user agreement in the importing market. As a general guideline, where goods of the same brand or trade mark are being imported from different sources, it is better for all imports to go through one registered user, but this can often only be practically organized if all the sources are affiliated.

When granting a licence it is customary for a licensor to seek to restrict the licensee to use the trade mark for the manufacture and/or sale of goods only within a prescribed territory. The licensor may also seek to protect users of the trade mark in other territories by restricting exports bearing the trade mark. Similarly, where a trade mark is owned by a proprietor in one country, they (or their registered user) can restrict imports into that country from sources other than the actual owner in that country.

Once a licence is granted to a licensee in a territory to exploit a trade mark, the licensor may find that, if they grant exclusive use to the trade mark, they may not have the right to ship goods into the territory themselves. At the stage of negotiating the licensing agreement, some licensors reserve the right to supply goods into a licensed territory either where a licensee fails to develop a market (possibly not meeting minimum performance standards) or where an unforeseen catastrophe disrupts supplies (such as a factory fire).

Within the European Union different regulations apply to licensing to avoid restriction of competition. The owners of trade marks do not have the right to restrict other independent distributors in one member nation from shipping goods into another member nation, or to stop import of goods legitimately using registered trade marks.

Assignment or license of a copyright

Copyright can be transferred by various means, including assignment or the granting of a licence. Restrictions can be set governing the transfer of copyright, such as:

- the transfer of copyright can be limited to one or more of the class of acts to which the copyright owner has exclusive rights (e.g. a person might be granted exclusive film or broadcasting rights, but not the publishing rights to the written format of a work)
- copyright might be assigned or licensed in one or more of the countries in which the proprietor has copyright protection

- the assignment of rights might be for part of the period for which the copyright is to subsist.

In practice, licensing agreements often involve the transfer of intellectual property in more than one category of patent, trade mark and copyright or design, hence the complexity of many international licensing or franchise agreements.

Patent and trade mark law may seem rather complicated, but it is an area in which the export marketer may have frequent cause for concern, either because of potential infringements or because of the need to obtain registrations. I would recommend that you do not become your own lawyer but sit down with the company patent and trade mark lawyer and obtain an understanding of the principles.

Further reading

Export Trade – The Law and Practice of International Trade. Clive M. Schmitthoff (Stevens, 9th edition 1990). Chapter 19: The Competition Law of The European Community and The United Kingdom

Intellectual Property. David I. Bainbridge (Pitman, 2nd edition 1994). A specialist text of use to the reader who needs a much more in-depth coverage of the subject matter of intellectual property.

UK Trade Marks Act 1994 – A Practical Guide. J. Groom, R. Abrett, J. Pennant and A.Y. Spencer (The Institute of Trade Mark Agents)

Patents, Copyrights and Trademarks. Frank H. Foster and Robert L. Shook (Wiley)

Checklist 23.1
Protecting your intellectual property

Action points

Identify and list the valuable intellectual property you have that warrants protection through registration or secrecy (non-disclosure) in domestic and foreign markets

- patents
- trademarks
- copyrights
- industrial designs
- proprietary processes, technology and products
- confidential commercial (business format) expertise.

Are there any local names for your products in foreign markets that might benefit from trade mark protective registration in that market?

- *(identify and list)*

Prepare a matrix chart that shows:

- on the vertical axis detail
  - the markets you already export to
  - your key target markets
  - markets where there is a risk of competitive company product copies (manufactured or marketed)
  - markets with licensing potential.
- on the horizontal axis detail your existing registrations by market for patents, trade marks, copyrights, industrial designs.

Use this chart to make a positive programme of intellectual property protection in priority markets.

Conduct an internal trade mark audit

Obtain samples of all company paperwork (letter headings, and all marketing literature and packaging materials) that contains any representations of company brand names, logos, designs, trade marks, etc. (for the domestic and all foreign markets) and

Checklist 23.1 *(Continued)*

	Action points

make comparisons of style and formats actually used versus the strict form covered by registrations:

- list all variations of brand and trade names and marks on any company literature from the correct style and format
- prepare an action plan to standardize internationally the use of brand names, logos, trade marks.

Do your agent–distributor agreements and licensing agreements contain clauses that:

- restrict your foreign market associate from applying for local pre-emptive intellectual property protection of your patents, trade marks, copyrights, etc.?
- impose confidentiality restrictions on agents, distributors and licensees restricting use of confidential commercial and technical data or its passing to unauthorized third parties (possibly with penalties for loss of sales, profits, etc.)?
- require your foreign market associate to support your applications to register intellectual property in your name in the foreign market, and to defend it against infringements?
- require your foreign agent, distributor or licensee to alert you to all potential infringements of your intellectual property?
- give you the freedom to defend against infringements or cancellations of intellectual property at your option (rather than having a contractual obligation to defend in all cases)?
- provide for trade mark user agreements in the foreign market where appropriate?
- provide you with options to amend or renegotiate the agency or distributor agreement should your marketing needs subsequently indicate a move away from direct exports to foreign market licensed manufacture?

Part Six

Developing Markets Further

24

Foreign branches
and subsidiaries

 In this chapter we will start to explore some of the alternatives to direct exporting through an agent or distributor. There are a number of options, and it is common that exporters develop to adopt one or more of these options. Often they have problems choosing the timing of pursuing an option, such as a subsidiary or joint venture, or enter the new stage without an adequate strategy or plan. The costs of poorly planned and managed expansion ventures can be high, both in terms of finance and the management resources involved. In this chapter we will:

- look at some of the options available to the exporter to pursue greater growth through commitment to expansionary ventures in foreign markets
- review some of the issues and problems involved in setting up a direct operation or joint venture in a foreign market.

The aim is to encourage the export marketer to keep an open mind for expansionary opportunities, but also to alert him to the needs for careful planning and correct structuring of the venture to achieve its potential and the company's objectives within a market.

As international business for an exporter grows and certain markets come to be especially significant, it is a natural progression to consider ways of increasing foreign market penetration, distribution and effectiveness of management control. Table 24.1 summarizes the main options diagrammatically, grouping them into four stages of export organizational development. It is not intended to imply that any company goes through each of these stages, or that they are mutually exclusive (some of the development options could readily fall into more than one stage), but it is common for the export marketer to start off in Stage I with basic physical exports through direct exports or agents, to progress as experience is acquired into some of the Stage II or Stage III options, and eventually, as the level of trade becomes significant, to follow one of the Stage IV options. Any of these stages might be missed if marketing circumstances dictate an early move to a higher stage, such as to a foreign subsidiary or licensing arrangement.

This part of the book addresses some of the alternatives to direct exports not previously covered. This chapter looks at branches and subsidiaries together, as they both involve direct company activity in the foreign market. Chapter 25 considers various joint selling options. Chapter 26 explores licensing arrangements in greater depth.

Setting up a local branch or subsidiary to manage the company's marketing and distribution directly is a logical option, although the benefits are often more clear to management than the problems that will subsequently be encountered by the person charged with responsibility to implement the plan. Equally, there may be inadequate information on the respective alternatives of:

- a branch
- a local distribution company
- a subsidiary company of the parent
- a joint venture
- a licensed manufacturing facility
- a franchise marketing arrangement
- strategic alliance opportunities.

While it is not possible in a work of this nature to explore the problems and alternatives on a country-by-country basis, it is possible to raise some warning flags and discuss some issues.

When considering direct involvement in any foreign market, it is essential to review your thoughts, objectives and alternatives with both a local lawyer and an accounting firm. In fact, many auditing firms are multinational and will be able to give great assistance, even through the home office initially. Some international auditing firms publish excellent booklets on specific aspects of doing business in foreign markets, and you can obtain these by calling their local office.

Table 24.1 *Some of the options in international market development*

Stage I	Stage II	Stage III	Stage IV
Direct company export team	Group marketing	Foreign branch	Foreign subsidiary
Export agents	Joint marketing company		Foreign joint venture
Export management companies	Consortia		Foreign licensing company venture
Trading companies			Strategic alliances
Trade association sales promotion organizations			
Rationale	**Rationale**	**Rationale**	**Rationale**
Direct exports from home market factories through export sales operations based in the home market, working through a network of agents or distributors in the foreign markets. The aim is market penetration with minimum investment.	Shared marketing operations with other group companies or joint marketing with non-competing compatible businesses (as in consortia). Key objectives are often to spread operating costs and share expertise whilst gaining market entry.	Direct export from home factories, but with marketing normally controlled by local foreign market branches staffed by experienced company managers (either expatriates or local).	Local manufacture of products in the foreign markets (or local provision of services), with objectives of depth of market penetration and competing with local companies on an equal basis, normally with economies in production, supply, operating and marketing costs.

Branches ▬▬▬▬▬▬

Once the export marketer's business to a market becomes significant and still demonstrates growth potential in a politically stable environment, the idea of a foreign branch with a resident representative is often envisaged as an attractive progression. The first approach is usually just to transfer someone from the home staff, give them a secretary and small office, and leave them to develop more effective and aggressive marketing programmes through a network of distributors. The thought is that the branch should purely handle sales and marketing, and not actually take title to goods with subsequent distribution responsibility for the merchandise. Local reasons why the company does not want to handle physical distribution, may include:

- it would involve a commitment to more than just a branch office facility
- large amounts of working capital would be required for inventories, equipment and staff supporting actual physical distribution
- a significant level of staffing would be required, with the accompanying legal and moral responsibilities and significant training needs
- a full subsidiary might attract a differing tax basis than applied when there was just a resident representative covering, probably, the local region.

Benefits of branches ─────────

Major benefits of establishing a foreign branch office include:

- increased control over marketing and distribution
- greater in-depth market knowledge and an opportunity to increase market penetration
- opportunities to acquire specific market experience prior to market expansion through subsidiaries or joint ventures
- opportunities to recruit and develop local

support staff to form the nucleus for further expansion.

The branch marketing office system is a well tried and proven technique for increasing control over management and marketing of distributors with minimum commitment and investment by the parent company, and it should be considered as the first stage. A local representative will learn far more about their markets than the home-based representative can ever expect to learn with their perhaps twice-yearly trips to the distributors.

There are also significant political benefits and business merit in recruiting some local staff to assist in the marketing aspects just as soon as the branch can justify expanding. Having local management employees demonstrates your commitment to training the local talent in your products and foreign management techniques, and adds to the effectiveness of the branch with the input of local cultural knowledge on business practices, language and local marketing.

The local branch sales and marketing office gives a breathing space for the manufacturer to work for greater market penetration without major commitment, while learning the mechanics and skills of actually running a business in that market. In any case, the original distributor agreement may still have some time to run before the manufacturer's branch could legally assume a role as distributor.

It would be common for the branch in, for example, Singapore or Bahrain also to assume regional responsibility over Southeast Asia or the Middle East. The costs of travel within the region would be far less than sending other persons out from the home office, and visits to any one market would become much more frequent, according to the estimated business potential.

Branch office location ─────────

In order for the branch manager to function independently in the foreign market, it is wise not to accept the kind offer of your local distributor to use an office at their facilities. Maintaining independence generally proves critical to developing and implementing programmes, or to putting pressure on a local distributor to perform.

In most markets there is no shortage of office space, but if you feel the need to have shared facilities it would be better to, say, rent space from your advertising agent or auditor, partly because such agencies are more used to client/agency relationships where there is both a closeness and a separation of interests. Working out of a distributor's office would greatly limit the privacy of communications with the home office, since customarily much of the communication is on the telephone or by facsimile transmission.

Initially all the local office need be is one room, a couple of desks, filing cabinets, computer, telephones, telex, facsimile machine, and a competent secretary to support the manager. To make it a plush, prestigious establishment in the first year is unnecessary; the kind of person who is most successful at running such small-scale branch offices does not generally need to satisfy an ego with ostentatious trimmings, because they are usually a more down-to-earth, 'hands on' performer.

Compliance with local regulations

It is essential to study, understand and comply with all local laws dealing with establishing a branch office in the foreign market. For example, the regulations applicable to obtaining a visa and work permit for the transferring branch manager may be much less rigorous if you are basing a regional representative in the market rather than someone with responsibility for only one market, where the authorities may feel you should hire only a local person.

Within the European Union there is free transfer of labour between markets obviating the need for special work permits and visas. In many other countries, including the United States, there are restrictive procedures to be complied with, sometimes resulting in requirements that local employment be created in return for the issue of a visa and work permit.

It may be that the branch should not generate a local profit but should be only a cost centre; any other situations might involve compliance with numerous other legal and tax regulations and reporting formalities. Your accountant and lawyer in the market will be the keys to minimizing formalities.

Bear in mind that, once you establish a branch, you will have a business entity that can be sued in most markets.

Branch managers ▄▄▄▄▄

Conditions of employment

A discussion of branches would be incomplete without a mention of aspects of selecting and rewarding branch managers, since they are the key to achieving objectives.

Before selecting and sending out someone to an alien culture, the exporter owes it to them fully to research local living conditions, including:

- salary structures
- taxation
- schooling and medical facilities
- expatriate living conditions in the local market
- fringe benefits.

You need to satisfy yourself that the selected branch manager has the independence of personality to survive the inevitable trials and frustrations that will be encountered, especially in the formative year. It might be that the appointee branch manager and his or her spouse both receive language training in the foreign market language if they do not already have a familiarity, as the inability to communicate even in basics usually proves a major inhibitor to progress and a stumbling block to social integration in the community.

The family circumstances of the individual may have a strong bearing on their ability to perform. If they are married, then their spouse will need to be equally independent in order to cope with the periods when the branch manager will be travelling within the region and with the other frustrations of living in a city where all the home comforts may not be so readily available, or where the climate may present its own adverse reactions. In some foreign postings account must be taken of the special local risks and hazards to individuals from local circumstances, such as high crime or political instabilities, where it might be intimidating for a spouse to go shopping alone and may require home help.

The expatriate will expect to be on a clear contract specifying their terms and conditions whilst abroad, and protecting their position and rights within the home organization to give a secure future. Where the employee's base might normally be deemed as in the UK, they may benefit from protection provided by the United Kingdom Employment Protection Act (1978) and subsequent legislation. Locally recruited staff need only be on local contracts complying with the practices of the foreign market in terms of salary and benefits (but, as mentioned subsequently, these can be restrictive).

The company that moves someone abroad has a strong responsibility for their welfare, career development and morale, because that person is outside the mainstream of company activity. Most companies with expatriate staff soon realize the benefits in terms of morale and performance of keeping very close liaison with expatriates, and a noticeably paternalistic approach to dealing with such employees frequently develops. After someone has learned the workings of a market or region and the local language, it is expensive if they are poached away by a competitor, but fortunately that happens rarely.

Remuneration of the branch expatriate manager may be significantly higher than for a similarly evaluated position back home. An expatriate sacrifices the home comforts to improve their financial position,

after tax, and generally accumulate capital. The personal attributes and skills required must result in a higher monetary valuation in the particular circumstances, because they must be decisive and independent, and able to cope with the most varied frustrations, from the inability to get the telephones to work to threats that they will be imprisoned because the tax returns are late. Benefits to an expatriate branch manager will normally include:

- company vehicles
- possibly cost-of-living allowances (if that is not assessed in the basic compensation)
- free medical insurance cover
- contributions to the continued education of children of school or college age back home, or contributions to education fees if suitable educational establishments are available locally
- continuity of membership of home company pension or profit-sharing plans
- housing or rent allowances
- disability or life assurance cover, bonus and incentive schemes
- home leave
- attention to any locally necessary personal security protection for the family (in markets where foreign individuals face personal risk).

Surveys of the level of remuneration and benefits for expatriates in certain markets may be available through auditors, international management consultants or multinational banks, which generally have considerable experience in these areas of operation.

Developing and integrating the branch manager

Do not send someone abroad until all the details are worked out and mutually agreed, otherwise you risk major morale problems if they feel they are being forgotten or exploited. In fact, it is wise to include a period back at the home office each year (say, one or two weeks), just so that they feel an integral part of the team and no 'them and us' attitudes develop. There will be an ongoing need for personal training and development in managerial job related skills and company and product knowledge if the person is to promote the company philosophies and products as part of an internationally co-ordinated programme in their foreign market.

Equally, there is a limit to the time an expatriate manager can be based on assignment in a market and still function effectively as an extension of the home team. Many companies have concluded that three to five years is the limit, and have developed policies of repatriation after a term overseas, with a home office assignment for a period before a further overseas posting. Some expatriate managers get to like the lifestyle overseas and perhaps resist coming home, but in general the company will benefit more in the long term from a clear and accepted rotation policy.

The contract terms should satisfy the person that the company is fair, generous and concerned over their well-being. The company should demonstrate sensitivity, professionalism and clarity of thought. Issues such as repatriation at the end of the contract period or on termination of a contract should be addressed. Also, corporate limits on the branch manager's authority and power should be identified (the branch manager possibly acting as agent of the home company in some situations), and any necessary local powers of attorney raised, such as to operate a local business bank account, or to commit to renting local business premises or residential premises in the company's name. Various bonds, indemnities or insurances may be needed.

Apart from the earlier suggestion that advice relating to the specific employment of expatriates may be obtained via banks or international auditors, do not overlook the old standbys for general information such as your embassy or local chamber of commerce branch in the market (for example, British or American chambers of commerce branches are found in many foreign markets). Another useful source of information will be the personnel director of any other company that you know that has a foreign branch in the market.

Contacts will be most helpful in assisting you to identify parameters for rewarding expatriate staff and with practical advice in establishing your local office.

Foreign legislation

Earlier reference has been made to the need to ascertain the legislation, rules and regulations applicable either to basing an expatriate branch manager in a foreign country or to opening and operating an office there. A regional office and staff may receive different treatment from an exclusively local market office, in terms of the issue of work permits or taxation of the individuals or operations. The export marketers investigating direct expansion into foreign markets by branches, subsidiaries or associate joint ventures will have to focus some research into regulatory aspects concerned with:

- corporate law
- foreign investment and taxation of local business ventures (particularly those with a foreign investment)
- and relevant employment law.

A number of questions should be put to the lawyers and auditors you plan to use, including the following:

- How will income and associated benefits of expatriate staff be treated for taxation purposes?
- What restrictions may apply to travel in and out of the base market and region?
- What tax treatment will the branch attract? Will it be accepted as a non-profitable cost centre on remittances from the parent, or will it be assessed in some way as if it generated local profit, possibly with home market dispatches to the market being assessed as if they

were actually made by the branch at an arbitrary profit level?

- Does the expatriate need any specific licences or permits to open and run a non-trading branch?
- What local labour laws apply either to the expatriate or to locally recruited staff?
- Will there be regulatory problems in importing samples of merchandise or advertising materials for examination by the branch? (Although customs duties may be normal and acceptable, if other local agencies concerned with product approvals or censorship of advertising materials become involved, samples can sometimes be held up for months.)
- If the branch develops to handle distribution, what will the tax treatment be then, and is there any risk either of taxation on parent company profits or of an examination of inter-company pricing mechanisms and practices? (Some countries feel that they are exploited by multinationals that prefer to take the bulk of profits at home on exports and leave little for the locals to tax.)
- What regulations or restrictions apply to any management contract between the parent and branch or subsidiary where charges are levied for services provided from the home base? (Many countries have regulations limiting such activities, because they again may be seen as a way to repatriate profits.)
- What restrictions apply to royalties on trade mark or patent user agreements (or other intellectual property) between parent and subsidiary or branch operations? (The same comments as above apply.)

These are just a few of the most basic questions that need study. In the final analysis, the objective is to increase sales and profits when a branch or subsidiary is established; if the local laws are going to be so restrictive that there is no net benefit to the exporter, then the establishment of the branch must be questioned. The local legal and financial advisers should be clear that their roles are to assist with opening a branch geared to minimum local tax liabilities and impact of rules and regulations upon both the branch and the foreign parent, consistent with the company's objectives of increased sales volume, market share and penetration.

Subsidiaries and joint ventures ■

In order to achieve greater control over sales and distribution, and possibly to handle local manufacturing, assembly and packaging, some manufacturers set up a foreign subsidiary, or possibly a joint venture operation with local interests if the rules of the country restrict foreign ownership of equity in local operations (many developing countries limit foreign ownership to below 50 per cent). But bear in mind that a foreign subsidiary or joint venture will be incorporated under the laws of the country where it is operationally based; whilst that may have benefits in terms of equal treatment with local companies, it may also expose the company to undesirable reporting requirements.

Within the European Union it has long been planned to have a system of European companies, which will benefit by treatment in all Union countries as if they were a national company. But progress towards this goal is likely to be slow.

Why consider subsidiaries and joint ventures?

Setting up a foreign subsidiary or joint venture company will involve considerable time and expense, and it is important to fully understand your own reasons for seeking to take either route, other than just a corporate ego trip to attach the claim 'multinational' to your operations. Some of the more common reasons for considering a foreign subsidiary include:

- **Capacity limitations**. When your domestic plant is operating at or close to capacity, and the options are to expand domestically at the existing site or to develop a new site, then consideration should be given to where the sales from the new facility will actually be made.

- **Protection**. Building a manufacturing facility in a foreign market may enable you to seek protective import restrictions to block out competitive products totally or partially through import licensing controls and duties applied to your product category.

- **Competing on equal terms with locals**. The foreign market may already have excessive and punitive import barriers, either to protect a developing local industry or to limit foreign exchange outgoings. Market development may therefore already be hampered or at an impasse unless you do put up a local facility.

- **Greater market penetration**. Foreign trading subsidiaries may enable much greater market penetration than working only through a local distributor, partly because consumers may respond positively to knowing the manufacturer is there to stand behind their products with warranties.

- **Locally available inputs**. Certain basic ingredients or raw materials may be less expensively or more abundantly available locally in the foreign market, reducing the costs of the finished products.

- **Benefit from regional economic groupings**. A plant in one foreign market that is a member of a regional economic association of geographically close or culturally similar nations, such as ASEAN (Association of South East Asian Nations), CARICOM (Caribbean Common Market), EC (European Union), may benefit from trade preference arrangements in shipping to the other members of the association. It is essential for the plant to be established in the member that offers the greatest benefits to the manufacturer in terms of taxation, security and availability of materials and skilled labour.

- **Pressures to commit to local investment**. There may be pressure from the foreign country to aid the balance of payments and provide local employment and labour force skill development opportunities.

In essence, exporters seeking to set up a foreign branch or subsidiary or joint venture should satisfy themselves that there are clearly ascertainable economic and political benefits to the home company in establishing the foreign operation. Clearly it is wiser to focus on politically and economically stable foreign markets for direct investment.

If the benefits are seen to exist, then the next stage is to consider the financing. Some factors to consider in this respect are as follows:

- **Sources of capital**. Can some or all of the capital requirements of the foreign venture be raised from sources in the foreign market; if so, on what terms and conditions?

- **Limitations on equity participation**. What maximum share holding can the parent company hold? If it is less than 100 per cent, are there systems of pyramiding by inserting holding companies above the operating company in order to gain more effective control of assets, management and profits?

- **Local investment incentives**. Are any investment, land or equipment loans or grants available to induce the parent to enter manufacturing in the market?

- **Import permits for inputs**. Will the foreign subsidiary or corporation receive all necessary permits to import needed plant, equipment and raw materials, and what ongoing guarantees are given in this respect?

- **Tax treatment of earnings**. Will earnings from the subsidiary or joint venture receive any favourable tax treatment ('tax holidays' may be available), and will earning be freely remittable to the foreign parent? Many corporations invest in a country only to find at some later time that regulations are imposed limiting their right to repatriate profits (such as that profits can be repatriated only to the level of the initial investment capital).

- **Contributions of plant to capital**. Will plant and equipment (especially used plant and equipment from the parent) be eligible to be considered as the parent's contribution to the capital investment?
- **Returns on the investment**. Does the expected level of return on the foreign investment equal or exceed the level of return on capital being achieved in the home market, with any assessed adjustment for the higher risk factor?
- **Management control of the venture**. What local rules exist on the structure of management and boards of directors? The parent company will clearly want maximum management control to protect its investment, particularly at board and senior management levels.
- **Discrimination against foreign ventures**. Will any rules or regulations in existence or planned discriminate in any way against wholly or partly owned foreign corporations, for example in tendering for government contracts?
- **Charging royalties and management fees**. Can royalties and management fees be charged for provision of know-how and services from the foreign parent company and repatriated freely?

If the answers to these basic questions are favourable, and the financial and marketing considerations indicate that a subsidiary or other form of joint venture or foreign operation should be set up, then the next stage is to look at finding the partner and the staff to run the venture.

Selecting local partners

It is essential that the local partner be financially sound and generally able to make a positive contribution to the business, even if that is only in terms of political

contacts who can issue all the relevant permissions needed to operate.

The manufacturer should be wary if the partner does not actually want to contribute investment funds to the project but just receive their stockholding as a gift in exchange for the use of their name. Traditionally, such partners feel little commitment because they have little or no investment at risk.

The costs and disruption to markets and marketing of separating from a joint venture are high. Risks of incompatibility may be reduced if the partners share information, reach common decisions, and avoid unilateral decisions that affect the joint venture business. Some key points in successful joint ventures include:

- neither partner should try to dominate or exercise unreasonable control
- both partners must be prepared to support the venture with all reasonable resources, including finance, technology, managerial and technical expertise
- the venture should be allowed to develop without the imposition of the culture of either partner (developing its own style and culture that gives it an independent identity)
- unfair restrictions should not be put upon the joint venture that limit its growth potential to the detriment of the joint venture or benefit of either partner (e.g. geographical limitations that stifle growth and achievement of economies of scale, or product sector limitations that discourage innovation)
- both partners should co-operate fully with the joint venture management, ensuring that there are three way formal and informal communications.

Where one party attempts to dominate the management and decision-making processes, or impose its culture, then there is increased potential for conflict and collapse.

Once again, the best advice on local partners and methods of operation may come from banks, embassies, accounting firms, other government commercial agencies, and possibly chambers of commerce. Extensive research is advised because, once the local company is registered and operating, changes in partner are virtually impossible. The export marketer concerned with finding and selecting partners will find some useful guidelines in Chapter 26 dealing with licensing arrangements, and much of the earlier commentary of Chapter 5, Identifying and selecting agents and distributors, is also relevant.

Local investment aid

Most foreign countries wishing to encourage investment will have a specific government agency charged with providing advice and assistance to the visiting manufacturer. In fact, financial help may be made available either directly or indirectly, including:

- reduced taxes or tax holidays for some finite period
- land grants or subsidies
- employment and labour grants to encourage training of local labour
- foreign trade zones enabling the manufacturer to avoid local taxes and duties on goods destined for re-export
- priority in obtaining import permits for essential plant, equipment and raw materials (it is vital that the manufacturer is fully satisfied that all plant, equipment and raw materials not locally available may be imported without undue delay or restriction).

Local staffing

As you progress down the road to entry through either a subsidiary or joint venture, you will need to study the local labour market and conditions affecting recruitment, training and employment of staff, including all minimum wage laws and rules relating to unions or job security.

In general, employees recruited in the foreign market as direct employees of the foreign venture will require only local con-

tracts of employment complying with all the local rules and regulations of employment. Only your (few) transferees for senior management posts may either have a claim to, or expect some treatment that reflects, home market or home company practice. In some markets, once you employ a person, they have a high level of security and legal benefits, and it may be extremely difficult to terminate even the less-than-satisfactory performer. Also, a number of countries, such as some in the Orient and Mexico, have a practice of paying a thirteen-months' salary to employees, and that should be identified before going into any costings, along with any financial obligations upon redundancy or for social security programmes.

Reporting requirements

The domestic legal and financial departments should be fully involved at every stage of a study on any foreign investment, because the formation of such a venture may have legal reporting requirements or restrictions on the activities of either the foreign or domestic corporations or on the management of either. The Foreign Corrupt Practices Act in force in the USA in the 1980s was a major deterrent to foreign investment and marketing decisions of domestic United States corporations, which feared to operate in the accepted manner of many developing nations and were thereby disadvantaged compared with European or Japanese groups in many instances.

Equally, if parts or equipment are being provided from the parent to the subsidiary in the foreign market, there is a strong likelihood that the internal revenue authorities in the foreign market will at some time investigate the inter-company pricing structures, possibly in an effort to demonstrate that these goods are being overpriced as a way of repatriating additional profits.

Strategic alliances

Recently marketers will have been made aware of the growing trend for **strategic**

alliances between businesses that they feel have opportunities to exploit in partnership. This involves the partners pooling agreed resources, and each partner brings certain particular expertise or inputs to the alliance that complement those of the other partners. Some of the visible strategic alliances that everyone is exposed to are those between airlines that have particular regional strengths who co-operate to promote greater passenger load factors on each others routes, and those between airlines and hotel groups and car hire operators.

Typical strategic alliances have a basis in sharing, and three main formats are:

- distribution alliances
- technology alliances
- production alliances.

Distribution alliances

The common pattern here is that a company with product strength but a distribution weakness forms an alliance with another partner that has distribution strength without conflicting products. At one end of the spectrum these alliances may include a specific joint company set up by the partners as part of the alliance, but in its simplest form it can simply be exclusive distribution arrangements.

- Coca-Cola makes some of its portfolio of beverage products available to and through McDonalds fast food group in a relationship that assures McDonalds that it has a level of exclusivity amongst the fast food giants.
- Some leading airlines with regional strengths have banded to form alliances, one being the *Star Alliance* that includes Ansett, Air Canada, Lufthansa, South African Airways, SAS, Thai Airways, United Airlines, and Varig. They have extended their alliance to include hotel groups and car hire companies. Passengers share in the benefits in that they can accrue mileage awards when travelling with any of the alliance partners.

Technology alliances

Market access can be gained in some strategic alliances by exchanging technology. This kind of alliance has been developed in the computer industries, with hardware and software companies, in information technology, in the motor industry, with biotechnology companies, just to highlight a few areas. Partners look for benefits that develop increased revenue flow and profits through more rapid innovation, quicker and more cost effective access to, and distribution in, markets, and opportunities to mutually exploit markets with partners.

Production alliances

Common forms of production alliances include examples of where end product manufacturers forms strategic alliances with component producers, helping those producers become more innovative and efficient, while assuring itself of continuity and quality of supply. This has been common in automotive and electronic industries. In the automobile industry, where new model development costs seem to grow exponentially, manufacturers are co-operating in alliances to share development costs and then marketing what are fundamentally the same designs under their various brands. Readers may recall that, in the late-1990s, prior to the take-over of the UK's Rover car group by BMW of Germany it had a successful alliance with Honda. When there are significant changes that alter ownership, performance, or strategic directions of either party then joint ventures suffer and can be difficult to unravel without major disruption to markets.

Strategic alliances need not just apply to companies that are actual producers of products, but can also apply in business to business and service sectors. Utility companies are finding scope for co-operation in many markets, whereby they can increase profits and offer a better service more cost effectively through co-operation in some aspects of product distribution, marketing and customer service. Suppliers of technological products that require after-sales servicing are co-operating in joint companies and alliances that provide a better quality of service support to a range of products that compete for retail sales. There is often scope for alliances in smaller less developed markets where similar levels of co-operation may not be necessary in the larger markets.

Problems with alliances

Some of the points raised in the section on Joint ventures (Selecting local partners) apply equally to strategic alliances. Care in structuring the strategic alliance may minimize the risks of subsequent problems that arise from:

- conflicting management objectives
- imbalance in partner contribution
- imbalance in partnership benefit
- management relationship problems.

In many instances, simple marketing alliances lead to cross shareholdings as the partners recognize that their businesses are becoming more interdependent.

With the growth in global brands, the need for larger scale production and sales to recover ever-rising product development costs, the growing complexity of technology, and a trend towards greater convergence of consumer needs in many markets, there is likely to be a growth in strategic alliances.

As companies gain experience in working together the success rate should rise, but the starting point must be mutual trust and intensive networking between various layers of experts and managers in the partners.

Most developing nations are actively seeking to encourage investment that creates employment opportunities, and discussions with your own country's international agencies concerned with aid programmes will yield considerable practical advice on the climate for investment and the expected security. Lines of credit and special aid packages may be available through either domestic institutions (e.g. UK banks) or international institutions such as the European Union Commission programmes.

Further reading

The Law and Practice of International Trade. Clive M. Schmitthoff (Stevens, 9th edition 1990). Chapter 17: Branch Offices and Subsidiaries Abroad, Foreign Acquisitions; Chapter 18: Joint Ventures and Other Forms of Joint Export Organization. The European Economic Interest Grouping

International Marketing. Stanley J. Paliwoda and Michael J. Thomas (Butterworth-Heinemann, 3rd edition 1998). Chapter 7: Market entry strategy decisions 2: investment

	Action points

Branches

Consider branches as suitable options when you want:

- minimum commitment of resources
- limited marketing support
- avoidance of tax and control problems over subsidiaries and other ventures.

Benefits of branches:

- increased control over marketing and distribution
- greater market expertise
- increased market penetration
- opportunity to develop local support staff.

Legal and financial considerations for branches:

- tax treatment of remuneration of expatriate personnel
- any restrictions on freedom to travel
- tax treatment of earnings of branch and parent
- licences or permits to operate as a branch
- local labour laws applicable to local staff
- import restrictions on advertising materials and products.

Subsidiaries and joint ventures

Factors that might encourage your foreign market development through subsidiaries or joint ventures:

- domestic capacity limitations
- protection through import restrictions
- to compete on equal terms with locals
- greater market penetration
- cheaper local inputs (labour, materials)
- benefit within regional economic groupings
- foreign government pressures to invest locally.

Checklist 24.1 (*Continued*)

	Action points
Some financial and regulatory considerations: ● sources of capital ● limitations on equity participation ● foreign market investment incentives ● foreign market employment incentives ● import permits for inputs ● tax treatment of earnings ● contributions of plant to capital ● comparative returns on investment opportunities ● inter-company pricing considerations ● restrictions or controls on management participation or contracts ● any controls or restrictions on management fees and royalties ● discrimination against foreign owned ventures ● local employment regulations ● foreign market export incentives ● corporate reporting requirements.	

25

Joint selling organizations

 In this chapter we will continue to explore other routes to international market development, such as:

- shared foreign market sales offices
- selling trading companies
- selling through export management companies
- export trade associations
- group marketing companies
- consortia.

The aim will be to illustrate that there are profitable options to direct exports that the exporter might explore as international business for his products develops.

External independent organizations

There are various ways manufacturers can benefit from concentrated export activity yet share the cost of operations through joint export marketing companies. Typical joint selling organizations include those covered in the following sections.

Shared foreign sales offices

A number of companies can combine to share the costs of a resident manager or sales office in a foreign market or region. The individual companies would need to feel that each would receive a fair proportion of time and attention. Ideally, products represented should be complementary rather than competing, so that they could possibly be marketed in a similar fashion

or to similar outlets. For example, a combined foodstuffs operation could represent, say, a confectionery line, a pet food line, canned fruits and vegetables, a soup company, and so on, all marketable to the region or market's food outlets yet not conflicting.

However, it is not common for quite independent companies to band together in this fashion commercially, possibly because of concern that they will not get a fair share of the resources, or that costs are not fairly allocated, or simply that they might just as well conduct sales and marketing matters through their own appointed distributor.

Trading companies

An alternative approach is to appoint as export representative an independent trading company that has its own overseas branches or associates in a number of countries. A number of such trading companies have grown up mainly out of the major trading nations, including Britain, the United States, the Netherlands, Denmark, France and Switzerland. They are traditionally centred more on activities in markets where their mother country had strong traditional trading, political or colonial interests.

The trading company might require an exclusive representation agreement either for specific markets in which it operates, or across all of the covered markets, and would generally handle sales and marketing operations by buying the products through the mother country's home office and acting as exporter to the foreign market, where it would then import and distribute merchandise. The home trading office might recover costs by building in a margin to the export price, or by charging a commission.

In some instances a foreign branch of the trading company acts as buyer on its own account, dealing directly with the manufacturing exporter, and normally seeking a local distribution exclusivity. In that case the exporter would normally negotiate and enter an agreement just as with any other distributor. The foreign branch could incorporate its requisite operating and profit margins in local pricing structures. Various problems arise in that each of the branch offices of an international trading company makes its living in its particular local market, often needing to sell quite a vast range of products from the developed nations to support its operations in a less developed market where consumers have limited cash resources. This tends to result in little attention to the active marketing and promotion of any single product line.

The number of manufacturers operating on a multi-market basis through the major international trading companies may have declined recently, but this has been a traditional way of exporting over the years, particularly for smaller companies and in times when international travel was more arduous and time-consuming.

Exporters looking for opportunities to sell into the Japanese market have historically found that the best route was to sell through a Japanese international trading company. These companies operate on a very large scale, and have representative offices all round the world in nations where they have enough trade to justify an office. They may function as sellers of Japanese products, and buyers of products for export to Japan. Frequently in Japan they simply act as importer rather than distributor, and re-sell goods to another company that acts as main distributor. The Japanese market tends to have several tiers in the distribution chain in many product categories, and the trading company usually has close affiliations (such as through cross share-holdings or other financial ties) with a pyramid of companies that are operating at each level in the distribution chain. Whilst a multi-tier distribution chain adds to distribution costs, as well as to problems of orderly market management, many exporters that are not large enough to make alternative arrangements (i.e., branches or joint ventures, etc.) must live with the cultural distribution process.

With the break up of the former Soviet Union in the 1990s a number of trading houses have developed that specialized in supplying to Russia and Eastern Block markets. Many exporters have preferred to use these companies rather than attempt direct sales and marketing into some very volatile markets. Exporters have normally sold to the UK trading company, who then ship and resell into the market. This has minimized the risk of payment problems. The often-convoluted distribution infrastructure for an exporter's products into Russia and other emerging eastern markets has frequently remained quite a mystery to the western marketers. Over time these markets should develop more formalized and traditional distribution infrastructures that will enable the exporters to work in more traditional manners, and with serious marketing plans. Meantime, exporters are often achieving significant volume, albeit in an opportunistic fashion without any sophisticated marketing planning.

Export management companies

A variation on the export trading company with its own overseas distribution operations is the simple export management company, which operates from the home market but sends its representatives to visit potential customers in the foreign markets at regular intervals.

In the United States there are quite a number of export management companies. They may commonly sign a sole export agreement with a manufacturer and act rather like the manufacturer's export department in seeking to promote sales. Their operations may attempt to cover the world, or just certain regions. They may work on a commission on sales only, or charge a fee, particularly in the initial stages. Some of them will take title to goods before exporting them, and in that case will generally build their required margin in the uplifted export price to the customer. Some export management companies will also extend credit to customers and have the freight advantage of pooling shipments of different products to the one market or customer. Some export management companies will also undertake all the export packing and documentation required on behalf of the manufacturer.

In the United Kingdom export management can be found that provides all or some of the above export support services. In some cases the manufacturer just prefers a more limited service with an export agent based in the home market, but who travels to the foreign markets on behalf of all his client companies and focuses on soliciting orders on a commission basis.

An export management company may provide a useful service to the smaller manufacturer, particularly one supplying a specialist trade sector, such as, say, hotel supplies. The general disadvantage is that most such companies are small in staff and turnover, and do not know a manufacturer's

products as well as the manufacturer. It may be that a joint arrangement could be set in operation, where the manufacturer handled the product enquiries but the export company could assist with desk and market research to identify potential contacts and physically handle the movement of goods and export documentation.

Trade associations

Another newer development that is gaining momentum in some countries, particularly over the last decade, is the formation of export trade associations of manufacturers or primary producers in an industry.

Trade associations are not new. What is newer is their greater activity in international marketing and promotion, particularly in generic advertising of industry products in international markets, and organizing promotional activity on behalf or participating members, such as through special national weeks in foreign retail store groups. They also often develop a generic marketing symbol designed to attach a national identity and quality image to the product of the promoted category.

Some such organizations from around the world have been opening foreign offices to promote their industry's products and exports in more aggressive fashion. Some of these organizations have received significant support from their government trade agencies. Examples of such organizations include Food from Britain, Foods and Wines from France found in several countries; and others such as coffee growers' associations, fruit marketing operations, wool marketing groups, and a host of others mainly geared to promoting primary producers and processors.

These associations have demonstrated considerable effectiveness in many markets, mainly concentrating on generic marketing and support programmes for a manufacturer's own export efforts. However, they do sometimes work by seeking orders and allocating these between manufacturers according to some prearranged formula considered fair by the participants.

Generally trade associations do not seek to take title to goods or handle export or distribution procedures, but they will work to assist in distributor training and motivation, along with attention to consumer awareness programmes through general product promotion and product publicity. Their real benefit is in pulling together a group of diverse manufacturers and exporters to jointly promote their exports as part of a co-ordinated and consistent strategy.

In some industries it has proved difficult to promote exports through specialist trade associations. Inter-company rivalries often dominate discussions and attempts to allocate resources or the structuring of marketing plans.

Group marketing companies ▬

As multinational corporations become more dominant in world business, and as national companies diversify in the range of products manufactured and sold, there has been a growth in the number of companies seeking to concentrate their export effort.

One approach is to set up a single group export division, which may even be a separate legal corporate entity set up to manage group international marketing.

Benefits in integrating resources _____

In some countries a separate export corporation may have tax benefits aimed at aiding export activity, such as deferred taxes, or taxes due only when dividends are paid to stockholders, or even reduced taxes. Ireland, for example, for many years gave long-term 'tax holidays' on corporate profits that were exclusively the result of export activities. The USA in the mid-1980s introduced a system of Foreign Sales Corporations. Clearly, any company that has a significant level of export activity or international profit earnings

should review the optimum corporate structure with the corporate lawyers and financial division. Additional access to government grants, aid or credit for export activities may be available.

Particular benefit to the multinational or multi-product group with separate export management teams comes from the synergy that may result from export management activity within and between the members of a group all being concentrated with optimum use of specialist skills and reduced duplication of effort by forming a group export division. However, the initial reaction from the individual companies is that each of their product ranges needs specialist knowledge and attention, and they need to control their own destiny. That does not necessarily negate the benefit of a group operation.

Individual marketing people can be assigned to concentrate on particular products or groups of complementary products, but the group as a whole may benefit from synergy through:

● avoiding the duplication of costs and personnel of several shipping and administrative departments
● taking advantage of any tangible tax benefits or other clear financial considerations, including lower interest funds or grants for export development
● spreading workloads if there are seasonal aspects to any of the group's products in a diversified multi-product group (the products may have different seasonal peaks, such as a range of summer beach accessories and a range of toys with heavy Christmas demand)
● optimizing the use and disposition of management and marketing skills
● co-ordinating marketing programmes between product groups in each foreign market, maximizing inter-product benefits and promoting a stronger corporate image
● producing greater negotiating strength with shipping lines on freight rates and rebates, and also with marine insurance companies.

Where group exports are combined, particularly with differing seasonal export trends between product groups, a consolidated shipping department would have a more balanced workload. While products may differ greatly, the mechanics and administration of shipping those products generally differ little, and, as each separate shipping department would be geared in staffing levels to handle peak loads, consolidation should significantly reduce supervision and clerical staff levels, and enable additional investment in computer-ized and other mechanical aids to be justified.

Some organizational alternatives

The sales and marketing organizations could be structured either with geographical emphasis – say, each regional manager handling all the group products to a region (see Figure 25.1) – or with emphasis on compatible products – say, one manager is responsible for foodstuffs, another for cosmetics and toiletries, and so on (see Figure

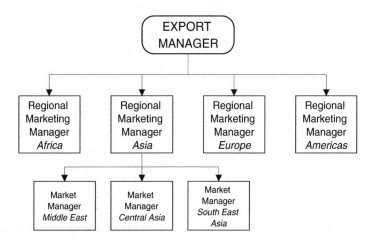

Figure 25.1 *Group export marketing organization: geographical responsibility format*

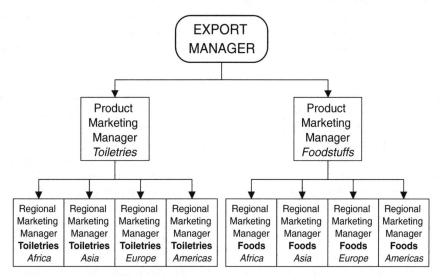

Figure 25.2 *Group export marketing organization: product responsibility format*

25.2). If the volume of exports in any product category is or becomes large, then many exporters' experience has led them to favour the product range specialization, with a network of regional managers for each separate product category or group, possibly with a product group export senior manager or vice-president, all reporting to the president or general manager of the international division.

When business develops to the stage of overseas branches, subsidiaries and affiliates, these also would logically report to the international division, which would either draw on specialists from specific production or research divisions, or have its own core management team to cover the main management disciplines.

A single group international division may also provide benefit in such aspects as handling imports of raw materials used in separate operating divisions. One company might be selling into a market that also supplies a raw material to a group member (or possibly of interest to another friendly manufacturer, enabling barter or countertrade to develop). If there are any currency exchange problems in obtaining payment for exports to that market, then it may be possible to use the locally accruing funds to pay for necessary raw materials. Liquor, for example, might be sold into a country that could supply fruit for a canning division. This type of arrangement might also have savings in respect to costs of letters of credit, foreign exchange transactions or other financing.

In a group where there are several companies or divisions each separately operating an export department, a chief executive might find benefits in having a group-wide study done to identify synergy and savings. Some group export organizations have even found that they could beneficially become involved in major international barter and countertrade operations as a way of penetrating otherwise hard-to-enter markets, supplying their goods for barter products that could be resold in western markets. **Countertrade** is an aspect of export activity

we will not cover within this text, but only make the point that where companies develop through countertrade it is essential that the product they receive as countertrade for their own goods or services must:

- have a ready market either within the United Kingdom or elsewhere within markets to which the countertrade goods can be cost-effectively shipped
- be freely tradable, i.e. not significantly restricted through licensing or quota restrictions in those countries where the goods are marketable
- have a measurable value in that its market value will not be subject to wide fluctuations for reasons outside the control of the partner accepting goods as countertrade payment
- be of measurable and consistent quality to ensure that they meet an acceptable international standard and are therefore tradable (the exporter should have a right of acceptance or rejection of goods on grounds of clearly defined quality standards).

Consortia

In the construction and engineering industries, it is particularly common for companies to co-operate in preparing bids for major projects, such as for the building of a power station in a developing country or a dairy processing plant, which would require two or more companies to co-operate to act as a single entity or bidder in tendering for the project. A consortium may consist of companies from several different countries or from one nation, but each would have a specific and different contribution to make to the project. The range of skills under such a contractual obligation might include:

- architectural and engineering design
- construction and installation of plant and equipment
- plant commissioning and operations advice

- quality assurance control and technological support
- finished product distribution
- training
- ongoing operational management.

Many such consortia are formed with the active encouragement of governments at home and abroad – especially in developing countries needing aid in planning and implementing projects that utilize untapped resources – and with the blessings of international agencies and banks, which may be providing finance.

In structuring a consortium to bid for and undertake a proposal, consideration needs to be given to whether a partnership or separate corporation best suits the aims and objectives of all concerned. There must be clearly defined contribution responsibilities, obligations and duties, as well as financial structures and profit-sharing plans.

Performance bonds

If there are performance bonds to be placed, as is normal for major consortia projects, or there are liabilities in the case of failure to perform to contract or to complete on time or to agreed standards, or in respect of subsequent maintenance or faults that develop, then the risks need to be identified in advance and fairly apportioned in an agreed manner between the partners.

Warranties

The project will undoubtedly involve warranties, either on project or plant performance or resultant yields of output, and the parties in the consortium responsible for each aspect must, as part of the consortium, honour its warranties.

Insurance

If there is support from the government in the base country of the consortium, then some insurance or underwriting of the consortium project, costs, risks or profits may be available from government or international agencies (such as Export Credit Guarantee Department cover in the United Kingdom), including underwriting the risk of default by the foreign party to meet its financial obligations and commitments at any stage of the project.

Generally it will be found advantageous in any major consortium project to appoint an independent chairperson from outside the group of partners to maintain balance and resolve disputes that might arise between the partners. Clearly any internal disagreements should be kept from the notice of the foreign contracting party, and the independent chair might, under the terms of the agreement binding the partners to each other, have the final say in resolving internal problems.

Consortia of partners who have previous experience working together, not necessarily in a joint bid for a project but possibly in a buyer-supplier relationship, may well operate more smoothly. Parties thinking of forming a consortium may initially benefit by seeking association with complementary skill-contributing enterprises with which they have had previous satisfactory working relationships.

Further reading

Export Trade – The Law and Practice of International Trade. Clive M. Schmitthoff (Stevens, 9th edition 1990). Chapter 18: Joint Ventures and Other Forms of Joint Export Organization. The European Economic Interest Grouping; Chapter 19: The Competition Law of the European Community and the United Kingdom

26

Developing markets through licensing and franchising

 In this chapter we will explore another approach to expanding international business, through the licensing of patents, trade marks and other intellectual property. Whilst some large companies have much experience in this field, many smaller companies have opportunities to develop markets through licensing but are reluctant to venture forward with this approach often because of a lack of understanding. We will look at:

- what licensing and franchising is about
- some of the many situations a company may face where licensing or franchising could offer an alternative route to market development
- how the parties to a licence or franchise agreement can benefit from the arrangement
- factors to consider in identifying partners
- inputs of the parties into a licence or franchise arrangement
- financial aspects of franchising and licensing
- structuring a licensing agreement.

The aim is to provide the export marketer with sufficient understanding and confidence to seek out and address licensing and franchising opportunities, and to develop a strategic approach to these opportunities in marketing planning.

Apart from developing international markets through direct exports, another approach to expanding international markets is to license or franchise another party in the foreign market to manufacture, pack and/or distribute the product to the market in exchange for fees or royalties, which are often related to the volume of sales. Here we shall review some of the factors manufacturers might consider in assessing if their products are suitable for such an arrangement. They will have to identify unique attributes of the product, process, brand name or business format, and the benefits to both parties of a licence or franchise agreement.

An introduction to licensing and franchising ▬▬▬▬▬

Franchising and **licensing** are both routes the marketer can explore to expand his business or product sale. They both have some points in common, for example:

- there is something the franchisor or licensor has the ability to grant rights to
- the franchisor or licensor can restrain unauthorized parties from infringing his rights
- someone wishes to acquire those rights with some degree of exclusivity or protection from unauthorized competition.

Figure 26.1 illustrates what intellectual property a licensor or franchisor might typically own and grant rights to another party to exploit in foreign markets.

In most of the subsequent sections of this chapter we will primarily focus on licensing in its broader sense, treating franchising as a special case of licensing, and particularly commenting on aspects of international licensing, since marketers are often concerned to enter international markets through licensing.

What is licensing? ▬▬▬▬▬

Licensing is the grant of permission, usually for a payment of a royalty or fee, by the licensor to the licensee to exploit some form of intellectual property right such as a:

- patent
- trade mark or service mark
- copyright
- design
- secret know-how.

Licensing typically takes one of three forms: a technical licence, an artistic licence, or a commercial licence. These might be defined as follows:

1 **Technical licence** where the grant is to copy a product or process, such as reproducing goods to a licensed design (e.g.

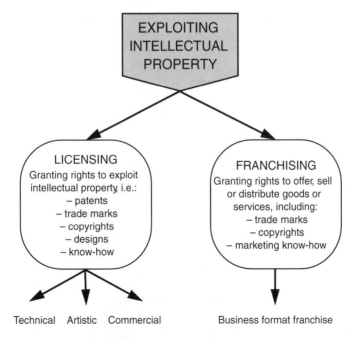

Figure 26.1 Exploiting intellectual property

patent), or adopting a licensed manu-facturing process.

2 **Artistic licence** where the grant is to copy or reproduce something considered as having artistic originality (often a copy-righted work), e.g. plays, music, literary works.

3 **Commercial licence** where there is a copy of the licensor's business using the name associated with the licensor's own com-pany, allowing the licensee to benefit from the goodwill associated with the licen-sor's business including using the trade mark (this would be considered a fran-chise when in a sophisticated form, where all aspects of the business format are licensed, including the manner of promot-ing product distribution, trade marks, business systems, etc.).

Some licence agreements might include more than one of these forms, for example, where both the rights to manufacture a product and the trade mark normally asso-ciated with the product are licensed.

What is franchising?

Franchising is primarily a sophisticated form of licensing, where the franchisor usually retains a considerable control over the market development, franchised opera-tions, and development of goodwill asso-ciated with the goods or services.

- Franchising is the granting of rights to offer, sell, or distribute goods or services under a marketing system devised by the franchisor, often presented as a complete business format.
- The franchisee's business is normally promoted using the franchisor's trade marks, advertising expertise and promotional support, with the franchisee benefiting from the goodwill associated with the franchisor's products, corporate image, business format and good name.
- In a typical business format franchise, as far as the customers of any outlet are concerned the franchised outlet has a

consistent image, range, style and system of operating (franchisor 'quality control') as all similar franchised outlets, and the franchisee has no independent identity from the franchisor and other franchisees.

- The franchisor customarily provides a significant level of initial and ongoing control and support, including:
  - operating systems, management controls and performance monitoring
  - marketing advice and support
  - staff training
  - location assistance.
- The franchisor typically receives his rewards through either:
  - a system of fees related to sales (often a percentage of turnover)
  - profits from sales of goods sold to the franchisee, who must buy the goods exclusively from the franchisor or his nominees.

Typical examples of franchising are found in fast food restaurants, quick printing, high street niche retailing ventures, hotels, car hire, and car distribution.

In foreign markets it is quite common for a franchisor to sell the master franchise for a country (or part of the foreign market through area franchises). The selection of the master franchisee for each market is key to the subsequent success of the venture as the head franchisee must be able to do every-thing in his market in providing franchisees with the support and active management that the franchisor does in the home market.

Main differences between licensing and franchising

In very broad terms licensing could perhaps be described as the transfer of proprietary intellectual property (usually including at least some of which is protectable through registration) from one party to another, whereas franchising is normally a more limited aspect of licensing, often focusing in large part on the transfer of commercial

Table 26.1 *Main differences between licensing and franchising*

Main differences between licensing and franchising	
Licensing	**Franchising**
In licensing it is common to grant a licence connected with a product, such as to use a patent or technology to produce and market a product (including a copyrighted work).	A franchise is usually an all-encompassing business format, including trade marks, intellectual know-how, operating systems, and the franchisor's goodwill, but frequently does not involve product manufacturing.
A licence to a patent is often granted for the outstanding patent life, perhaps up to 20 years.	Business format franchises are usually granted for around five years (renewable upon agreed terms and conditions).
Normally few companies might lay claim to a licence to an industrial process (which would involve high levels of capital investment).	Many companies or individuals might be eligible for a franchise of a business format (often with little capital investment).
A licensee is likely to be selected according to criteria related to their performance and experience in existing areas of business related to the subject of the licence.	A franchisor typically selects franchisees according to experience of the kind of franchisee likely to be successful, and prior experience of the business or market may not be a prerequisite.
A licence to technology might just apply to the state of the art at a point in time, and need not include the subsequent provision of developments and improvements.	In franchising, systems are developing rapidly and changes are incorporated into the system operated by existing franchisees so that all benefit and a strong corporate image is maintained.
The licensor may have limited rights or no rights to exert operational control over a licensee.	A franchisor usually exerts a high degree of operational control over the running of a franchised business.
A technology licence may not make public acknowledgement of the existence of a licence or recognition of the licensor.	A franchise is normally overtly promoting the trade names and goodwill of the franchisor.
Potential licensees normally have considerable scope to negotiate agreements that depend greatly on their individual strength and the potential for the licence in their market.	The franchising of a business format usually involves clearly defined terms and conditions common to all franchisees and embodied in a standard form of franchise agreement.
An industrial licensee will normally have considerable business experience, particularly in the markets of the licensable subject matter.	Franchisees tend to be new into the franchised business, with some capital but a strong need for guidance from the franchisor.

know-how or skills supporting a product or trade name that has a value through the goodwill built up internationally by the franchisor. Some of the more significant differences between licensing and franchising are illustrated in Table 26.1.

Whether your particular interest is in intellectual property licensing or in business format franchising, much of the commentary of this chapter should prove useful to increasing awareness of the mechanics, problems and opportunities.

Why consider licensing?

Direct exports do not always suit each product or its target market, and the export marketer may seek to license or franchise their intellectual property (normally consisting of products, technology, trade marks, copyrights or business format) for a number of reasons, which broadly fall into the general categories of:

- the nature of the product
- the foreign market environment
- other factors restricting exports or direct foreign investment, or pressures to increase foreign earnings.

More specifically, the particular reasons or circumstances that often precipitate consideration of licensing as an alternative to direct exporting include the following:

- **Short shelf life products**, where the balance of shelf life on arrival in the destination market might inhibit effective distribution and marketing.
- **Delicate products**, unable to withstand the rigours of international transport.
- **Product life limitations** before obsolescence or consumer/user tastes or needs change.
- **Freight costs**, where these are high in relation to the value of the final product on the foreign market.
- **Product modifications**, where product preferences or tastes of the foreign

market or its regulations require the manufacturer to modify the design, construction or functionality of a product.
- **Restrictions on investment**, such as limits on equity participation inhibiting the foreign corporations from involvement in direct investment.
- **Restrictions on repatriation of profits**, from investments in the market by foreign corporations.
- **Import restrictions** may exist that limit development through direct exports from the supplier.
- **Management control restrictions,** where the foreign corporation cannot exercise management control in subsidiaries or joint ventures.
- **Local business practices** that may prompt the foreign company not to want to invest directly in a market.
- **Limited foreign market customers** who exert pressure on a licensor to provide technology transfer in exchange for ongoing product purchases or risk loss of markets to other suppliers.
- **Component products** that form part of a complementary product or process.
- **Forming local distribution links** that can provide effective distribution or after-sales service support in the market.
- **Access to raw materials or essential inputs**, where a local foreign market company controls access to these.
- **Lower cost of inputs** available in the foreign market.
- **Linking licensed products with local products,** where the licensed product might be a component.
- **Economic pressures to manufacture locally**, exerted by foreign government authorities.
- **A need for local entrepreneurial involvement.**
- **Limited capital resources** in the exporting company to enter foreign markets with company owned subsidiaries, branches, joint ventures, or acquisitions.
- **High research and development costs**, where licensing might speed

investment recovery before product obsolescence occurs.

- **Export restrictions** that prevent the domestic manufacturer from shipping directly to certain destination markets.
- **Competitive market development**, such as blocking a competitor from entry or further development in a foreign market.
- **Reciprocal licensing opportunities**, where a foreign company has a product or technology that could be used by the company in its domestic markets or manufacturing operations.
- **Unused intellectual property**, for example, where a product or technology has diverse applications in areas where the company has no direct involvement.
- **Time constraints on penetrating a market**, where the company needs to act quickly to take advantage of opportunities of block competition.

In essence, if a manufacturer or trading business sees obstructions in the way of effectively and competitively building an ongoing international market for their goods or services, or utilizing the strength of their brand name, or the international recognition and incorporation of their special process by potential users, then they should consider the opportunities offered by licensing.

Why consider franchising? _____

Franchising can offer a route to market expansion where:

- you have an identifiable product range or service capable of sales expansion through distribution expansion
- the company has a strong brand franchise and user/consumer goodwill
- the company has insufficient capital to expand through its own resources (at a pace of expansion that will keep it ahead of competitors)
- there is an identifiable (unique) business format (system of operating, managing

and promoting individual distribution centres)
- distribution outlets will benefit from entrepreneurial management by individual owners rather than company ownership
- quality control of products and service at all distribution centres can be maintained to consistently high standards
- the company can standardize its operating systems, business format, etc. and communicate these to franchisees through training
- the company does have the financial and human resources to provide the support need to franchisees and to control the business to set standards

What can you license or franchise? _____

A company will generally grant a licence (or franchise) that gives the other party exclusive or non-exclusive commercial exploitation rights, possibly with geographical or other limitations or restrictions, to:

- the manufacture of a product
- a manufacturing or commercial process
- technology or commercial know-how
- a trade mark
- a patent
- a copyright
- a business format

Where licensing inputs are being provided in several of the categories, the licence would have greater potential value and the licensor would have greater potential protection of the intellectual property. Providing significant initial inputs supported by ongoing value-adding inputs to a licensee's business in the form of technology, know-how, and training will give the licensor greater control. The format and structure of the licensing agreement will need to be more complex to provide the necessary degree of protection to the licensor for their continuous input.

Much of the commercial value in a licence often derives from the know-how element, where manufacturers, in the course of their everyday operations, acquire a considerable degree of experience and expertise, which are essential to supplement a production process, product formulation or design, or business format.

Exclusivity of content of licence

The subject of the licence does need to be in some way **unique** or **exclusive** to the licensor if they are to be able to grant a licence. Therefore you should seek the maximum legal protection of your intellectual property consistent with maintaining its exclusivity and technological advantage.

A potential licensee will have no reason to pay a fee or royalty if the trade mark is not registered locally, because they could just go and apply for it themselves. The same applies if the patent is not protected, or the potential licensee finds that they could design round your patent.

Occasionally developers of a production process will prefer not to patent it, in the belief that this actually gives more security. A published patent could act as an indicator to other parties of alternative research directions that could lead to circumvention of the patent. Also, if the process is expected to have a limited exclusive life before obsolescence, the developer may prefer not to stimulate competitive research by publishing patents.

Whilst the subject of a licence may need to be exclusive to have value, the licence need not be granted exclusively to one licensee. The degree of exclusivity will depend on the nature of the product and its end uses, alternative uses of the product or know-how, and the terms the parties negotiate. A licence might be granted exclusively for one industrial application or industry in a territory, and be offered for other non-competing industrial uses in the same territory, or simply be on a non-exclusive basis even within an industry (e.g. Dolby sound system). The licence might offer a degree of territorial exclusivity.

If the product being licensed requires a particular formulation, such as a food item or perfume, then the licensing manufacturer can further protect the formula by agreeing to supply only part of it in published format within the agreement, and by providing the 'secret' part through direct sale to the licensee of the base mix ingredient (sometimes referred to as the 'heart' mix or ingredient). In this type of situation, the licensor could choose to recover their royalty fees not by a charge on finished product output sold, but by incorporation within the sale price of the base mix.

Benefits of licensing and franchising

For a licensing or franchising arrangement to be successful both the parties must see clear benefits, some tangible and some intangible, from the arrangement that will outweigh any of the disadvantages that might be identified or expected.

Benefits and disadvantages to the licensor/franchisor

The export marketer who considers licensing or franchising as a development route would be looking for the licence (or franchise) to give a reward for the time, effort and financial and physical resources invested in developing the intellectual property to the point where it has a licensable market value.

In addition to blocking competitive activity in a foreign market and expanding global market shares in product sectors there are a number of benefits of licensing or franchising to the licensor or franchisor including those listed in the following box.

As illustrated in this list, some of the returns, particularly when licensing technology, may be in a non-monetary form, such as opportunities for reciprocal grant backs

---

Benefits and disadvantages to licensor/franchisor

Benefits	**Disadvantages to licensor**
● Initial fees.	● Limited returns.
● Boosting ongoing earnings.	● Limited management control.
● Improved return on capital.	● Exposing technology.
● Recovery of research and development costs.	● Risks to confidentiality.
● Increased protection of intellectual property.	● Conflict of interest.
● Improved ongoing research programmes.	● Disputes result in misallocating management resources.
● Opportunities for research collaboration agreements.	
● Opening up foreign investment opportunities.	
● Creating new export opportunities.	
● Local knowledge and expertise.	

---

of technology from the licensee, and the research inputs that will help keep the licensor at the forefront of technology in its field.

Expansion through franchising has an added benefit of continuity in personnel in the business, as each franchisor is normally a self employed, committed and well-motivated individual, managing his franchise unit to the best of his ability to maximize his returns.

Franchising can have its own set of potential problems. The franchise network is only as strong as the weaker members of the network. Typical key **disadvantages in franchising** are listed in the following box.

Franchisors are often looking to the long term to build sales, market share and profits, but the franchisees need profit in a very short time from start-up (often by the second year) if they are to remain committed and loyal. This puts great pressure on a franchisor (or a master franchisee for a foreign market) to invest in local and national sales promotion.

All in all, however, the advantages of growth through licensing generally outweigh the disadvantages.

Disadvantages in franchising to the franchisor

● Lack of direct control over franchisees (self-employed owner-managers).
● Differing goals of the franchisor and franchisee.
● Resentment at restrictions imposed by the franchisor.
● Poor quality franchisees.
● Negative publicity or perceptions from a franchise.
● The high level of commitment to ongoing support for franchisees.

Benefits to the licensee or franchisee

For a licensee to take a licence, they need to see clear commercial benefit to their own organization, particularly if they are going to be committed to initial fees and investment. Benefits of **licensing**, which might be both tangible and intangible, could include those listed in the following box.

> ### Benefits to the licensee from taking a licence
>
> - Goodwill attached to an internationally established brand name.
> - Reduced research and development costs.
> - Access to technological advances.
> - Technical assistance.
> - Savings in research and development lead time.
> - Access to an international company's skills.
> - Measurable cost savings.
> - Complementary products.
> - New investment opportunities.

A number of these benefits also apply in **franchising**, where the franchisee is often a highly motivated independent business person with limited skills and financial resources. Key benefits to the franchisee include the following.

> ### Benefits to the franchisee from taking a franchise
>
> - Established products.
> - Supplier's goodwill.
> - Access to finance for investment in the business.
> - Lower start-up costs.
> - Training by the franchisor.
> - Operational systems suited to the business.
> - Marketing support.
> - Reduced risks in the business.

National benefits

The nation importing technology, know-how or other intellectual property is likely to benefit socially and economically from:

- increased industrial employment opportunities

- increased levels of industrial and commercial skills
- import substitution by locally produced goods and services
- conservation of scarce foreign exchange resources
- export opportunities (if not restricted under the terms of the licence)
- increased industrial activity from industries and companies providing inputs to the licensed venture.

So, all in all the benefits of licensing or franchising can be quite significant to all parties, and often outweigh the disadvantages providing the parties are well matched and conflicts are minimal.

Considerations in finding market opportunities

The international marketer who wants to expand his markets through licensing or franchising must first develop an approach to identifying and prioritizing the market opportunities, and then seek out prospective licensees or franchisees.

Prioritizing markets for licensing

If licensing or franchising seems an appropriate marketing route for your international development, then start by prioritizing target markets according to criteria such as:

- existing or potential user demand for the products or for similar or substitute products
- suitability or adaptability of the products or other intellectual property (as with a business format franchise) to specific market needs
- sales volume/value potential and related royalty/fee-earning potential
- competition (products, production facilities, marketing programmes, technology, patents)

- existence of foreign market manufacturers with compatible production facilities/products
- distribution infrastructure suited to product needs
- stage of market economic development (are they ready for your products, services, or franchised business format?)
- availability of all necessary raw materials and other inputs
- local protection rights for intellectual property
- potential import protection for locally produced goods
- industrial skill levels of the local work force
- suitable local entrepreneurs or enterprises with necessary capital
- availability of local investment grants
- availability of aid from international agencies
- foreign government attitudes and rules and regulations relating to foreign investment and/or inward licensing
- ease of repatriation of earnings
- local levels of taxation of fees, royalties and dividends
- any existing market research on markets or products
- local business culture and practices
- company resources likely to be required to implement a licensing/franchising programme.

Whilst most of these criteria may be relevant to licensing, the marketer considering franchising as a route to market development will need to prioritize the potential markets according to those criteria relevant to his type of franchise. Franchisors typically are concerned that there be sufficient sales volumes to ensure franchises are viable, and that suitable franchisees can be found in the local market. They will also want to ensure that the franchise network in the foreign market can be controlled to similar standards as are adhered to in the home market.

Identifying potential licensees

The international marketer needs to give considerable time and effort to finding suitable licensees or head franchisees for foreign markets. An agreement is for quite a number of years, usually at least five, and even at the end of an initial agreement period it can often be extremely difficult to change a licensee or head franchisee.

If the marketer is looking to grant foreign licences to intellectual property (patents, trade marks, etc.) then in many instances a little desk research will highlight potential licensees, as the starting point should always be to search out parties who have something to gain from taking a licence to the product, process or other intellectual property. In theory, any company in the target market might be selected, but in practice a licensor's choice will be narrowed to companies that fall into one of the categories of:

- producers or users of essential raw materials or other inputs required in the processing or production of the licensed product
- monopoly suppliers of raw materials or essential inputs
- producers of complementary items
- companies that would use the licensed product as a component or accessory in another product
- companies controlling access to end users, such as through distribution channels or perhaps through contract supply relationships or other reciprocal arrangements including cross shareholdings
- companies with specific expertise in the marketing and distribution of the products.

Once you have drawn up a list of prospective licensees you can progress by considering each prospect in relation to the following questions:

- Which companies in the target market/industry could have an interest in

the licence because of synergy or compatibility of products and/or markets?
- Who would see the investment in the licensed project as providing an interesting return?
- Which of the essential input contributions can each prospective licensee bring to the venture?
- What are the relative strengths and weaknesses of each prospective licensee?
- How have they performed historically in respect of sales, marketing, product development and financial achievements?

Where a head franchisee is being sought for a business format franchise in a foreign market the basic principles are similar. The starting point is usually to look for companies already having some expertise in the market sector (e.g. a fast food franchisor might look for head franchisees with experience in some form of catering to the public), and that have capital to invest in a new venture, along with proven management skills. But it is also important that a prospective head franchisee be willing to adhere to the franchisor's marketing and operational format, rather than trying to make changes that would make the franchise unrecognizable to the franchisor or customers.

The key questions licensors should seek to answer in the search for a suitable prospective licensee are:

- Who will benefit economically by taking a licence?
- Which of the parties identified in response to the above question has positive contributions to bring to the licensing venture?

Evaluating potential licensees _____

Potential licensees (or head franchisees) for foreign markets should be researched as carefully as potential distributors. Some of the main areas of information where a

licensor should be seeking information include:

- size of the organization
- access to necessary levels of capital resources for investment
- financial performance history
- corporate history (how long established, company and product development, etc.)
- ownership and corporate structure
- compatibility of existing production and distribution facilities
- marketing performance history
- market sector shares and trends
- current product range compatibility
- management skills and experience
- management training and succession
- licensee management style
- market outlet coverage (of users/consumers)
- shareholder management involvement (of key individual or corporate shareholders who particularly influence policy and programmes)
- details of key officers and managers
- after-sales service capabilities.

Once you have built up company profiles on the basis of relevant and comparable information, you will be in a good position to start making direct contacts with the appropriate level of company operatives to establish whether there is any degree of interest in your licensing proposal.

It is fundamental to the success of any licensing arrangement that the licensee is committed to using the process, product or brand name for active marketing, sales and distribution, and any agreement should ensure that there is a time limit for the commencement of production or marketing, possibly with some form of penalty clause.

The licensee must clearly have the financial standing and capital to make any necessary level of investments in plant, equipment and inventory, and in any special or supplementary distribution facilities. The licensor must be confident of the licensee's ability and willingness to honour all agreements, duties and obligations, both financially to the licensee and in respect to product quality and marketing.

It is essential that both parties take sufficient time getting to know each other to ensure that they can work together harmoniously for mutual long-term benefit.

As an aside at this point it is worth mentioning the need to sign non-disclosure or secrecy agreements at a very early stage in licensing negotiations to protect the release of any data transmitted to the potential licensee.

Who to franchise ■■■■■■■■■

A franchise arrangement should be seen as for the long term, and care must be taken in selecting early franchises, that they are judged capable of growing with the business. The availability of funds to buy a franchise should be just one criterion in selecting franchisees, not the only criteria. Where a head franchisee is appointed to a market he will have responsibility for building a network of local franchisees, working to criteria established from the franchisor's experience in other markets. Typically franchisee selection should consider:

- franchisee's personal financial resources
- franchisee's access to external financial resources
- franchisee management skills and work experience
- willingness of the franchisee to comply with tight franchisor controls over the format and operations
- franchisee's likely response to training
- commitment of the franchisee's family to supporting a self-employed 'bread winner'
- ability of the franchisee to commit full time to management of the franchise
- temperament of the franchisee considered suitable to self-employment and the franchisor's active involvement in operational matters and market development.

The key to building a successful franchise network is to find team players – who recognize their success is interdependent with the success of the overall franchise business, including all the other franchisees.

The partnership of licensing and franchising ■■■■■■■■■

A franchising or licensing arrangement is a partnership where each party to the agreement has something of value to offer the other (see Figure 26.2). Both the licensor and the licensee (or franchisor or franchisee) have valuable inputs to contribute. The inputs each party brings to the negotiating table should be complementary.

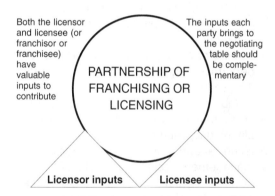

Figure 26.2 The partnership of licensing

Licensor inputs _____

The licensor (or franchisor) is likely to bring a mixture of inputs to the licensing arrangement, which could include any or all of the following:

- patented products or other exclusive intellectual property
- access to product, process or business format improvements
- goodwill in the licensor's name and products

- trade marks, brand names and/or copyright materials
- technical and commercial know-how relating to the licensed products
- plant engineering designs, plans, specifications*
- site selection for production and distribution (or retailing) facilities*
- construction planning and supervision*
- plant commissioning*
- pre- and post-launch technical and managerial assistance*
- essential input supplies (possibly including plant)*
- sourcing, purchasing and quality control of inputs*
- product designs, specifications, formulations*
- quality control of finished goods or services*
- operational manuals (possibly covering manufacturing, quality control, input purchasing, administrative systems, marketing)*
- training of managers and technicians to perform all requisite functions to operate the production/processing and distribution facilities to agreed standards*
- active marketing support and programme planning assistance*
- technical and promotional literature*
- management systems and relevant business format know-how, including the preparation of computer or manual programmes and the designing of any necessary administrative systems*
- proven product markets and established sales potential
- any signage for display of the licensor's trade names at licensed locations.*

Those items marked with an asterisk are often easier to put a tangible cost or value to when trying to value the licence or franchise. Each individual marketer should identify for his own products and markets what inputs he brings (or should bring, to ensure its success) to his licensing or franchising project.

Licensee inputs

The licensee's inputs might include:

- capital to invest in production and distribution facilities, plant and equipment (or access to the capital through local institutions or through grants, etc.)
- local market knowledge and expertise
- local management skilled in running industrial or trading operations in the local business environment
- compatible production plants or business premises
- distribution facilities to handle, store and physically distribute the finished products safely and efficiently
- access to essential inputs of raw materials, components, skilled labour, energy supplies, etc.
- complementary products (and technology) that dovetail with the licensed products for complementary distribution/production (including where the licensed products might form a component or accessory to another product)
- contacts with local government, industrial and financial institutions and key persons of influence
- after-sales service capabilities to support any needs of the licensed products
- compatible management who can work without friction with the management of the licensor and respond to training.

In some developing countries, the licensor's expectations of inputs might be limited to simply capital and contacts, particularly if the licensor is able to negotiate turnkey projects and management service agreements. As has been mentioned previously, if a business format is being franchised to a local head franchisee, then some points on the above list will also apply as franchisee inputs, including capital, local market and product sector expertise, management skills and resources, suitable business and distribution premises, and a management style compatible with that of the franchisor.

Government involvement in licensing

Three main areas can be considered in the involvement of governments in licensing:

- outward transfer
- inward licensing
- European Union considerations.

The first two will be commented on here, and I will return later in the chapter to touch on some matters concerning licensing and franchising in the European Union, a large and complex subject in itself.

Outward transfer

Outward licensing authorities are normally less concerned with the transfer of commercial intellectual property such as trade marks than they are with the transfer of technology. Areas where they show particular concern, illustrated in Figure 24.3, often include the following:

- **Nature of the technology**. Technology transfer from industries considered sensitive (e.g. defence related) may require prior approval to ensure that:
  - ◆ its export does not compromise defence of the nation
  - ◆ it is not exported to unfriendly nations
  - ◆ sale does not breach any political sanctions.

- **Returns to the licensor.** The outward controlling authority may seek to satisfy itself that commercial returns are realistic, and have particular interest in ensuring that the licensing arrangement is not just a means of reducing taxable income in the home country. In particular authorities may check that:
  - ◆ a fair price is charged for the technology and support (i.e., it is not 'under-sold' to foreign enterprises or subsidiaries of the home corporation, but is priced as an arm's length transaction)
  - ◆ returns from licensing intellectual property to foreign ventures (royalties, initial fees, management fees, etc.) are remitted to the home company initiating the export of the technology, and are not 'banked' to offshore subsidiaries to avoid tax.

Inward licensing

The inward licensing authorities usually have concerns as illustrated in Figure 26.4.

These broad concerns may extend as far as regulations or simply a requirement for approvals from regulatory agencies prior to

Figure 26.4 *Inward licensing concerns*

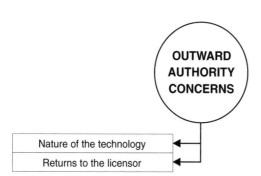

Figure 26.3 *Outward licensing concerns*

enacting a licensing agreement. At the outset of any licensing discussion the export marketer charged with the licensing responsibilities should establish any local rules or regulations that will require the involvement of local authorities in approving any content of the licence, including the areas of:

- anti-monopoly/anti-trust considerations
- the source of the licence
- the nature of the technology
- the selected licensee (that the licensee can develop the technology satisfactorily)
- terms of the licence (including duration and levels of fees and/or royalties, management control)
- import of essential inputs (initial plant and equipment and ongoing supplies)
- training provided by the licensor
- plant design
- export rights or restrictions
- pricing of supplies from the licensor
- technology improvements (that licensor improvements are passed on and that licensee improvements remain the property of the licensee)
- timing of transfer of payments due
- use of licences with subsidiaries/joint ventures to increase repatriation of earnings to overseas corporations
- taxation before repatriation of fees/royalties
- disclosures of secret formulations (i.e. where a consumer product uses a secret ingredient)
- termination clauses and rights thereafter to the intellectual property (it is often difficult to separate the licensor's know-how from that of the licensee at the end of a licence)
- which nation's laws of contract apply to the agreement
- turnkey projects (some nations prefer these, and authorities may want to approve all plans and proposals)
- quality control (to ensure production output meets acceptable international standards)

- countertrade (where a nation is short of foreign exchange, the authorities may seek to have fees and royalties paid in whole or in part with goods)
- performance bonds (possibly required to ensure that all plant and product perform satisfactorily or that requisite training is provided)
- compliance with all local industrial regulations
- avoidance of onerous price-fixing agreements (which might make the licensee uncompetitive in export markets or limit local prices)
- authorizing work permits for the licensor's personnel
- management participation by the licensor in the licensee operations
- rights of the licensor to supply exclusively any inputs
- monitoring or restricting any clauses obligating a licensee to take unrelated products from the licensor
- restrictions on sale of product from the licensed venture
- limitations on the uses of patents or know-how in other industrial applications in the licensee's operations
- obligatory combinations of patent and trade mark licences forcing the licensee to use the licensor's trade marks on output
- warranties provided by the licensor concerning the performance of plant and finished product
- restrictions within the terms of the agreement that prevent the licensee seeking other (competing or complementary) technology from other sources.

Some nations have formalized regulations covering a number of these points (the European Union has much regulatory control designed to promote competition and avoid its restriction); others will negotiate the deal on an individual basis depending on how important the subject of the licence is to their economy and development plans.

Financial aspects of licensing ▬

Your objective as licensor is normally to make a profit from your licensing activities, or at least to make a contribution towards the recovery of research and development costs incurred in developing the licensable intellectual property. It is not easy to place a value on most intellectual property. Some directly incurred costs in transferring the technology or know-how through a licence can be assessed and/or measured; but the value placed on intellectual property in any market might not relate to its development costs or the price obtainable for it. So we should consider some of the inputs to a licence or franchise arrangement, and see where these lead in assessing a value and pricing a licence.

The value in a licence _____

The licensor (or franchisor) is always most concerned to place a price on his licence, but the price he can obtain will relate to the value a licensee puts on acquiring the licence (or franchise). Estimating a value for the licensee, and pricing a licence, is not an exact science. It means identifying each of the inputs the licensor provides at start up of a project or in providing ongoing support, and estimating a value for them. Typically the licensor or franchisor would consider each of the following factors in trying to arrive at a value when negotiating with prospective licensees:

- potential earnings from the project to the licensee
- potential sales volumes/revenues
- degree of exclusivity the licence will provide (e.g. patents)
- brand name strength (goodwill) internationally or in the market
- marketing support for the product
- alternative products or processes
- alternative sources of technology (comparable or substitute technology)

- development costs to reach the present stage of technological development (i.e. costs that will be saved by a licensee)
- development lead times (a licensee will be able to enter a new market with shorter development lead times)
- licensee training needed or to be provided
- plant and engineering design inputs
- management systems and procedures
- operational manuals
- research and development and quality control inputs
- technical assistance required
- potential cost savings to the licensee/franchisee from taking a licence/franchise
- balance of patent life
- product/technology improvements (i.e. access to ongoing improvements saving on licensee research costs)
- licensor experience/reputation
- security in an investment that has a track record elsewhere.

Pricing the licence _____

Fundamentally price is governed by what the licensee or franchisee is willing to pay for the technology or other commercially valuable know-how provided through the licence.

The main factors contributing to the international marketer's thoughts in the pricing exercise include:

- the value of the licensor's inputs (covered in the previous section)
- the desirability of the licence to the licensee
- the potential returns to the licensee or franchisee
- the compatibility of licensed operations with the licensee's current business activities
- the present state of market development for the licensed products or services
- the competitive activity and market research (including ease of market entry by competitors)

- the availability of similar alternative technology
- the regulation of levels of fees and royalties in the licensee's market
- the taxation levels of fees and royalties.

Obviously, the more information the licensor has on the markets and competition, the more satisfactorily will negotiations progress.

Returns from licensing

As a licensor or franchisor you would normally expect to receive your returns from licensing by any one or a combination of:

- initial fees, usually aimed at recovering at least all start-up costs
- ongoing royalties, providing an income that relates to the volume or value of business in the market
- management service or technical assistance fees
- once-only fees for certain inputs
- profits from the sale of supplies (ingredients, other inputs or goods for resale)
- profit share.

Local contract laws and taxation considerations may have a bearing on how you would prefer to designate the components of income, but often it is preferable to break a licence agreement into the component parts for which a financial reward is due, and then to structure the agreement so that a separate income element is payable for each component part.

One reason for this approach is that the different input elements may have different balances of life: e.g. a patent may expire before the end of the management service or know-how element of the agreement, or know-how might become redundant should it enter the public domain. The **primary components** to the agreement might be the specifically protectable patents, trade marks (if any) and copyright elements. The **sec-**ondary elements** might be the intellectual know-how/show-how, supporting technical assistance and training, all of which ensure that the licensee can exploit the primary inputs. The **tertiary inputs** might include initial or ongoing supplies of plant and equipment, components, etc.

The timing of payments from the licensee to the licensor or receipt of other income, commissions or fees will normally vary according to the timing of the provision of the inputs of that component element of the licensing arrangement.

Other potential sources of income from licensing

There are a number of potential supplementary sources of income from licensing, including:

- dividends on equity stakes in the licensee
- capital appreciation of equity stakes in the licensee
- the right to convert royalties to or take equity in the licensee
- additional export opportunities for inputs and related goods to the licensee, or where the licensee might act as distributor for unrelated (unlicensed) goods
- plant and equipment supplies, including spare parts
- provision of buying services to the licensee
- acting as an international sales agent for the licensee
- leasing plant and equipment
- purchases of the output of the licensee, either licensed goods or unrelated goods produced by the licensee
- reciprocal licensing arrangements
- grant-backs of patent or process improvements
- consultancy services.

Whilst these may not provide the primary reason for licensing, they do provide scope to boost earnings opportunistically.

Returns from franchising

In general we have treated franchising as a special case of licensing within this chapter. In some situations franchising can be more demanding of the franchisor than many licences in terms of the ongoing support and management required. In other cases franchising can be more simplistic, such as in the ways the franchisor typically earns income. In **franchising** the earnings normally come from a combination of:

- initial fees (this will primarily cover start-up costs and initial training)
- ongoing royalties on sales turnover, usually a percentage of sales values
- profits or commissions on the supply of essential inputs used in the franchise. (Where franchisors do not produce some inputs themselves, they may specify particular sources, arrange pricing, and receive a margin for this service.)

Occasional income might be generated from subsequent training, but many franchisors that make a charge for training expect only to recover costs.

Using market data in the negotiating process

When it comes to negotiating a licensing or franchising deal too many licensors enter negotiations with little data on the target market. If the prospective licensee has done his homework, then he will have the edge during negotiations, obviously taking the position of down-valuing the licence and hence the price he will be asked to pay. To strengthen your negotiating position, and to have a meaningful dialogue with prospective licensees on market potential and how to develop the market, the prospective licensor should at least obtain pre-negotiation data on:

- size of potential market for product
- end users/consumers
- potential product price

- present demand for similar or substitute products
- existing market research on markets or products
- market distribution infrastructure
- local intellectual property laws
- local inward licensing regulations
- raw materials and inputs availability
- local business culture and practices
- competition:
  - competitive products
  - competitive production facilities
  - competitive marketing programmes
  - competitive technology
  - competitive patents.
- research into prospective licensees, including:
  - companies with interest in the licence because of compatibility of products
  - companies seeking investment opportunities
  - strengths, weaknesses, input contributions from prospective licensee
  - analysing historical sales, marketing, product development and financial performance.

The more you, the licensor or franchisor, know about your target markets and prospective licensees or franchisees (normally head franchisees in international markets), the better placed you will be to obtain the best price for your intellectual property and to negotiate a fair and thorough agreement, where all issues are identified in advance and a proper framework is developed for the operation and management of the licence or franchise.

Protecting intellectual property ■

Much of the value in a franchise or licence is in the invaluable intellectual property provided within the franchising or licensing package. It is important that you, the marketer:

- identify what intellectual property you have within your franchising or licensing package

- decide how you can best protect that intellectual property, either by a formal registration where that is possible, or through closely guarding the intellectual property (such as a manufacturing process) as a company secret
- develop a strategy as to which countries or markets you need to have a formal protection policy, including major export markets, those with licensing potential, or those where competitors might seek to abuse your intellectual property rights.

Copyright in operations manuals

From the perspective of many a licensor or franchisor, copyright protection could offer an essential protection, and certain practical steps might be taken prior to granting licences, such as those listed below:

- Comprehensive operating manuals should be prepared including coverage of all aspects of the production and operation of the end product, all administrative controls, procedures, specifications, designs, systems, etc.
- All designs, specifications, formulations, etc. relating to production and processing plant and products should be included either in the operational manuals or separately within the contractual documents.
- All of the above and any other communications that impart knowledge or information, systems or procedures should be identified as the copyright of the licensor, with a note that no unauthorized copying is permitted.
- Records should be kept of all copyrighted material supplied to licensees or franchisees.
- All persons who see confidential data should be aware of their individual obligations binding them to non-disclosure clauses of agreements.

Know-how

This element of intellectual property is normally the result of technical and

---

Summary of intellectual property protection guidelines

- Exchange secrecy agreements early.
- Register intellectual property in the parent company name.
- Bind prospective licensees not to pre-empt or contest registrations.
- Patents should avoid openings for designing round patents.
- Mark exchanges of communication as confidential where this will add to protection of confidential data.
- Include all proprietary data in operational manuals on loan and copyrighted.
- Record which licensee employees have access to confidential data.

---

commercial experience and expertise, and is not protectable by registration, yet it often forms the core valuable input to a licensing or franchising agreement.

The extent to which any of this know-how is marketable and has value as a part of a licensing agreement depends on the extent to which it is exclusive to the licensor or their products, and is successfully kept secret, or provides an advantage in successful production, distribution and marketing. Process know-how is easier to guard than a product, which is a physical item that can be broken down and analysed, and whose structure and design can be studied.

Valuable **know-how** could include:

- plant and engineering design
- building plans, specifications and construction
- industrial site selection
- preparing applications for planning permissions
- plant commissioning
- equipment specification and sourcing
- raw material specification and sourcing
- quality control systems and procedures
- regulatory compliance

- management control systems and procedures
- product development activities
- technical assistance and troubleshooting
- industrial engineering and work study
- preparation of operational manuals
- market research
- product sales and marketing
- staff selection, training, development
- after-sales servicing/product support.

Strategic considerations in licensing

When considering licensing or franchising as routes to market entry or development there are several strategic considerations. First the marketer should be clear on his strategic reasons to grant a licence, e.g.:

- securing market entry
- blocking competitive activity
- maintaining/increasing market share.

Once the licensing decision is taken, then several strategic and tactical factors come to the fore (see Figure 26.5). The licensor needs to consider the following points:

- **Management control aspects:** the extent to which it is necessary or desirable for the licensor to exercise operational management control over the licensee (including in such areas as quality control, production, audit controls, marketing).
- **Fulfilling licensing obligations:** the ability of the licensor to fulfil their licensing agreement obligations and provide the necessary inputs (including under separate management service agreements).
- **Maximizing returns from licensing:** the structuring of the licensing arrangement to maximize the returns repatriated to the licensor.
- **Developing an appropriate corporate structure:** the optimum corporate structure (possibly including branches or subsidiaries) to implement the licensing programme and to maximize returns to the licensor
- **Security of intellectual property:** minimizing the risks of misappropriation or infringement of the intellectual property and know-how.

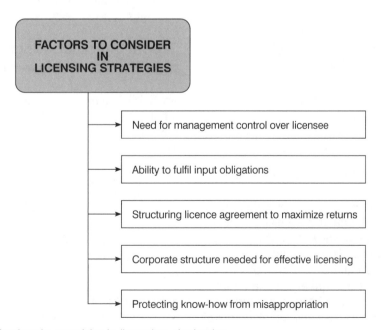

Figure 26.5 Factors to consider in licensing strategies

Corporate structural considerations

Prior to entering a licensing arrangement for any particular market the international marketer should consider how their own corporate structure may need change or modification (e.g. through a branch, subsidiary, or joint venture) to support the licensee or to form a vehicle to take the licence. Factors that influence how you organize your corporate structure include:

- the duties, obligations and rights resulting from any particular market entry scheme
- the need for local management operational control by the licensor's representative over a number of licensees or sub-licensees (see Figure 26.5)
- the need to provide local technical and other assistance to honour obligations under a management service agreement
- greater management participation in the development, planning and implementation of marketing and other programmes specific to the foreign market
- increasing the eligible level of fees and royalties which might be repatriated
- accumulating foreign earnings that exceed any repatriatable level
- regulations in the foreign market that either restrict non-national investment and equity participation in general or specific industries, or limit the management control that may be exercised by non-nationals.

Joint ventures with a foreign party, established specifically for the promotion and development of licensed or franchised products or services, in certain cases could:

- increase the total profit accruing to the licensor
- enable the licensor to accept and comply with any local regulations limiting royalties for the transfer of know-how, yet give the licensor a second opportunity to be eligible for repatriation of earnings
- give the licensor board and management participation in the joint venture, and a greater say in the use and development of their know-how.

Other licensing considerations

The licensor will also need to give consideration to the points listed opposite, when considering granting a licence.

To minimize the risk of any subsequent claim the licensor should ensure that they are responsible for developing the goodwill attached to the product and brand names. The licensor specifically should ensure that:

- they control the quality of both inputs and outputs, exercising any rights negotiated to inspect plant and product
- they enforce the operation of manufacturing facilities to their methods and standards of operation and processes
- they are seen as the main instigator of marketing and promotional programmes to promote their name and products, monitoring their implementation and results. This may be facilitated for consumer and some industrial mass market products by levying an advertising/marketing allowance spent under the control of the licensor
- they provide ongoing technical support, management and staff training, etc., to increase skills and expertise.

Structuring a licensing agreement

As with agency and distribution agreements, it is important that a good and thorough agreement is drafted at the outset, as this will minimize disputes or provide a framework for resolving them. Ideally the marketer should go to negotiations with a commercial draft model agreement, as this strengthens his negotiating position. An agreement to license a product, process or trade mark will, of course, vary greatly in length and complexity, depending on factors such as:

- the nature of the products
- the controls and restrictions on licensees the licensor feels appropriate

Legal considerations	• which country's laws can be applied to the agreement and its subsequent interpretation and enforcement
	• whether disputes can be resolved by local arbitration or should be the subject of international arbitration in the licensor's country or a neutral third nation (e.g. Switzerland).
Repatriation of earnings	• establish if there are any exchange controls or other restrictions limiting your ability to repatriate your earnings from a licence to the parent company.
Taxation	• investigate foreign market differential tax treatment of management fees, royalties, dividends, etc.
	• establish if there are local withholding taxes
	• check double taxation treaties concerning potential earnings.
Retention of rights on termination of a licence	• investigate the rights of the licensee to retain any benefits upon termination of an agreement or non-renewal at the end of a licensing period, including:
	– goodwill vested in the brand name to be vested in the licensor.
	– retention of rights to commercial know-how and any improvements made by the licensee
	– post-agreement retention and use of technology
	– post-agreement manufacture by the licensee in competition with the licensor.
Compliance with foreign market rules and regulations	• establish all the rules applicable to a target market and ensure compliance as any negative publicity may damage sales or goodwill attached to the licensor, licensee or brand names, possibly reducing the value in the licence as well as licensor earnings.
Insurance of plant, profits, royalties, etc.	• bind the licensee contractually to carry the fullest insurance on all plant and facilities at replacement values (insurances to be approved by the licensor), and to insure the interests of the licensor (profits, costs to re-establish plants and other facilities to full operational standards).
Control over sourcing and quality of inputs	• the licensor may want to retain the right to approve all input supplies for quality.
Equipment	• the licensor may also want to retain the right to specify and/or approve all operating plant and equipment for manufacturing establishments.

- the market development activities of both parties
- the processes or know-how being transferred
- the rights, duties, responsibilities and obligations of the two parties
- the legal requirements of the foreign market
- home market regulatory control relating to the transfer of the know-how.

International marketing or commercial managers of a company who are in contact with foreign potential licensees are best placed to develop the early drafts of any licensing agreement as they should have full knowledge of the range of commercial terms likely to be acceptable to both parties. Final drafts should, of course, be reviewed with the company lawyers (domestic and foreign) as well as with the licensee's lawyers. The comment in Chapter 8 covering 'Agency and distributor agreements', in the section on 'Style of agreement' apply equally to licensing agreements.

The final agreement must be very specific, because many disputes arise over what a contracting party's intentions may have been rather than what was incorporated in the licensing agreement, and courts normally can only take decisions on the basis of the contract.

Major issues covered in a licensing agreement

There are probably as many potential clauses as there are licensing agreements, or so it may seem to the lay person. Generally the key clauses and factors that are likely to be covered in a licensing or franchising agreement are as illustrated in Checklist 26.9.

Licensing in the European Union

European Commission regulations are complex and are more stringent than in most other markets. Whilst this text cannot attempt a detailed legalistic study, it would equally be wrong to ignore the subject.

The primary concern of European regulatory control is to encourage and promote the free flow of goods within the Union, minimizing barriers to trade. The key guidelines are those contained in Articles 85 and 86 of The Treaty of Rome, 1957.

Article 85 sets out to prohibit agreements that:

- directly or indirectly fix prices (purchase or selling) or trading conditions
- limit or control production, markets, investment or technical development
- share markets or supply sources between parties to an agreement
- give unequal terms and conditions to other parties in similar agreements operating within the European Union
- put unrelated conditions into an agreement that have no real relationship to the core of the agreement (e.g. the obligatory purchase of non-related inputs).

These conditions could be declared as non-applicable and exemptions granted where an agreement was acting to contribute to improving production and distribution of goods or promote technical and economic progress providing that the agreement did not:

- impose on the licensee restrictions not indispensable to achieving the above objectives
- give the parties the opportunity to eliminate competition in respect of the products being licensed.

A number of interpretative and block exemption regulations operate, covering patent and know-how licensing and commercial franchising, and specialist legal advice should be sought on these.

European Union regulations have paid particular attention to the following areas of general concern to licensors:

- **Price fixing agreements** that serve to fix product prices within the European Union would not be acceptable.

- **Quantity control** limiting maximum output would not seem acceptable.
- **Limiting exploitation rights** to one or more applications of the patent may be acceptable.
- **Reversal of new patents** developed by the licensee to the licensor would seem unacceptable. An alternative that might find acceptability would be to have a clause that the licensor had non-exclusive rights to a licence to use all such patents developed by a licensee either with or without a royalty relating to the value of the patent. Technological know-how that was not patentable could be shared similarly.
- **Royalties after expiry of patents** are not generally acceptable. An agreement could possibly be extended by mutual agreement if the licensee wished to use improvement patents after the term of the original patent or licence expired. Similarly, in agreements for know-how, once the know-how came into the public domain it would be expected that royalty payments ceased.
- **Territorial restrictions** within the European Union are not generally acceptable, but regulations recognize the need to manage marketing through some control over distribution of goods. Where an obligation is imposed on the licensee not to pursue active marketing of licensed product in another territory reserved for other licensees, this may be permissible if there are parallel patents in those other territories. Similarly, exports to other licensees' territories within the Union may be restricted for up to five years.
- **Shared markets**, whereby the European Union was divided into clearly defined sales zones would be unlikely to be sanctioned as that would in effect create territorial monopolies.
- **Dissimilar conditions** applying unequal terms to different licensees within the European Union, thereby distorting competition or the ability to compete, would only be sanctioned where this was not restrictive of competition.

- **Supplementary obligations** imposed on a licensee that were not directly related to the main licence would not be sanctioned, i.e. where they might be forced to buy inputs through the licensor that were freely (and more cheaply) available elsewhere. A stipulation that goods or services must be procured from the licensor may be acceptable where that was necessary for the proper technical exploitation of a patent.
- Clause that the licensee will not **challenge the right of ownership of intellectual property,** such as patents and trade marks, are not considered acceptable in the European Union.
- **Recognition of the patentee's ownership of rights**, indicated by a mark on products made under licence, may be an acceptable condition in the agreement.
- **Sub-licensing and assignment** of licences may be restricted.
- **Mixed patent and know-how agreements** must be checked to ensure they comply with current regulations, as in some instances they may not.

Whilst many of the typical clauses outlined in Checklist 26.9 are permissible, specialist legal advice will be needed on potentially unacceptable clauses.

Further reading

Understanding Commercial and Industrial Licensing. Brendan Fowlston (Waterlow's Business Library, 1984)

The Business of Industrial Licensing. Patrick Hearn (Gower, 2nd edition 1986)

Licensing. Michael Z. Brooke and John M. Skilbeck (Gower, 1994)

How to Find and License New Products. Kieran Comerford (Gower, 1990)

International Marketing. Stanley J. Paliwoda and Michael J. Thomas (Butterworth-Heinemann, 3rd edition 1998). Chapter 6: Market entry strategy decisions 1: direct vs indirect investment

Checklist 26.1
Licensing opportunities

Action points

In which of the following aspects of intellectual property do we have licensable opportunities:

- patents (e.g., for manufacture of a product)?
- trade marks or service marks?
- copyrights?
- designs?
- confidential technical know-how (e.g., for a manufacturing or commercial process)?
- commercial business format know-how?

Which is the most appropriate form of a licence arrangement:

- technical licence?
- artistic licence?
- commercial licence?
- business format franchise?

Which of the following reasons prompt consideration of *licensing* as an alternative market development strategy:

- short shelf life product?
- delicate product?
- product life cycle limitations (need to capitalize on value before obsolescence occurs)?
- freight costs?
- product modifications needed for local markets?
- restrictions on foreign investment in markets?
- restrictions on repatriation of profits from direct ventures foreign markets?
- restrictions on exercise of management control direct ventures in markets?
- import restrictions in foreign markets?
- local business practices that make direct investment less acceptable or more risky?
- limited number of customers for the product?
- product serves as a component in a process or another product?
- need to form a local distribution link?

Checklist 26.1 *(Continued)*

	Action points
• access to raw materials or other inputs in the market? • lower cost of inputs and production through in-market manufacture? • linking licensed products with local product? • economic pressures to manufacture locally? • need for local entrepreneurial involvement? • limited company capital resources for expansion? • early recovery of product-related research and development costs? • restrictions on direct exports? • need to combat competitive market development? • need to benefit from reciprocal licensing opportunities? • need to exploit unused intellectual property in markets where it has applications? • time constraints limiting direct market development activity by the company?	

Which of the following reasons prompt consideration of *franchising* as a market development strategy:

• branded product range or service capable of market expansion through independent franchised distributors? • company has strong brand franchise to build on internationally? • insufficient capital to expand? • identifiable (unique) business format? • distribution outlets benefit from entrepreneurial management? • franchisor can maintain quality control at all distribution points? • business format and operating systems can be standardized and communicated through training? • company has resources to provide all necessary support to franchisees?	

Checklist 26.2
Who will benefit from licensing, and how?

	Action points
How will the company benefit from licensing:	

How will the company benefit from licensing:

- initial fees?
- additional ongoing earnings?
- improved return on capital invested in the business?
- recovery of research and development costs?
- increased international protection of intellectual property?
- improved ongoing research and innovation programmes keeping company competitive?
- opportunities for research collaboration agreements?
- foreign investment opportunities?
- new investment opportunities?
- inputs of local knowledge and expertise?

Will any of the following disadvantages outweigh benefits from licensing/franchising:

- limited returns versus direct investment by the company in the market
- limited opportunities for management control over market development?
- exposing the company's technology, commercial know-how or intellectual property?
- risks of breaches of confidentiality?
- conflict of interest with other aspects of licensee's business?
  - differing goals of the partners?
- disputes occupying scarce management resources?
  - e.g. resentment at restrictions
- licensees or franchisees who prove to be of unsuitable quality
- risks to licensor's/franchisor's reputation or goodwill through activities of licensee/franchisee?

How will your licensees/franchisees benefit from a licence/franchise with you:

- opportunity to market an established product with reduced risk?
- goodwill associated with the company, product or brand?
- reduced research and development costs?

Action points

Checklist 26.2 *(Continued)*

	Action points
- access to technology protected by registrations? - early access to technological advances not developed internally? - ongoing technical assistance? - access to an international company's skills? - measurable cost savings resulting from a licence? - acquiring a licensed product to complement a licensee's range? - new investment opportunities at lower risk? - easier access to finance for a licensed/franchised project? - lower start start-up costs? - training? - operation support systems? - marketing support?	

Checklist 26.3
Prioritizing for licensing opportunities

Action points

Identify and list all those markets where you believe you may have licensing/franchising opportunities

- usually it is easiest to prepare a summary matrix, with markets listed down one axis, and criteria for prioritization (see below) listed on the other axis

Factors to consider in prioritizing markets for licensing opportunities:

- existing or potential levels of consumer/user demand
- suitability/adaptability of product to local market needs
- royalty or fee earning potential
- competition (technical, commercial)
- existence of foreign market manufacturers with compatible products or distribution to act as licensee/franchisee
- suitable distribution infrastructure in the foreign markets
- stage of market economic development (which markets are ready for the product?)
- local availability of raw materials and other inputs
- local protection rights for intellectual property
- potential import protection for locally produced goods
- availability of local entrepreneurs with capital
- availability of local (or international) investment grants or aid
- foreign government attitudes and regulations relating to inward licensing/franchising
- ease of repatriation of fee/royalty earnings
- local levels of taxation of fees/royalties
- market research surveys supporting assessment of demand potential
- local business culture and practices
- sufficient company resources to implement licensing/franchising strategy programmes.

Checklist 26.4
Identifying and evaluating potential licensees

	Action points

Can potential licensees be identified amongst companies in any of the following categories:

- producers or users of essential raw materials or other inputs associated with the licence
- monopoly suppliers of raw materials or inputs
- producers of complementary items
- companies that would use the licensed product as a component or accessory
- companies controlling access to end users (through distribution channels)
- companies with expertise in the marketing and distribution of the products in the markets
- companies who would look at the licensed venture as a good investment

Evaluate potential licensees or master franchisees on criteria such as:

- size of organization
- access to capital needed
- financial performance history
- corporate history
- ownership and corporate structure
- compatibility of existing production and distribution facilities
- marketing performance history
- market sector shares and trends
- current product range compatibility
- management skills and experience
- management training and succession
- licensee management style
- market outlet or user coverage
- management involvement of main shareholders (if a private company)
- skills and experience of key officers and managers
- after-sales service capabilities
- willingness to comply with terms of an agreement and licensor/franchisor controls
- willingness to co-operate on training and market development planning

Action points

Which of the following inputs to the licensing arrangement should, or can, the company provide:

- patented products or other exclusive intellectual property?
- access to product, process or business format improvements?
- goodwill in the licensor's name and products
- trade marks, brand names and/or copyright materials?
- technical and commercial know-how relating to the licensed products?
- plant engineering designs, plans, specifications?
- site selection for production and distribution (or retailing) facilities?
- construction planning and supervision?
- plant commissioning?
- pre- and post-launch technical and managerial assistance?
- essential input supplies (possibly including plant)?
- sourcing, purchasing and quality control of inputs?
- product designs, specifications, formulations?
- quality control of finished goods or services?
- operational manuals (e.g. manufacturing, quality control, input purchasing, administrative systems, marketing)?
- training of managers and technicians to agreed standards?
- active marketing support and programme planning assistance?
- technical and promotional literature?
- management systems and relevant business format know-how, including the preparation of computer or manual programmes and the designing of any necessary administrative systems?
- proven product markets and established sales potential?
- any signage for display of the licensor's trade names at licensed locations?

Checklist 26.6
Government involvement in inward licensing

Action points

Do the government authorities of the inward licensing market have any regulations or restrictions covering the following:

- anti-monopoly/anti-trust considerations
- the source of the licence
- the nature of the technology
- the selected licensee (that the licensee can develop the technology satisfactorily)
- terms of the licence (including duration and levels of fees and/or royalties, management control)
- import of essential inputs (initial plant and equipment and ongoing supplies)
- training provided by the licensor
- plant design
- export rights or restrictions
- pricing of supplies from the licensor
- technology improvements (that licensor improvements are passed on and that licensee improvements remain the property of the licensee)
- timing of transfer of payments due
- use of licences with subsidiaries/joint ventures to increase repatriation of earnings to overseas corporations
- taxation before repatriation of fees/royalties
- disclosures of secret formulations (i.e. where a consumer product uses a secret ingredient)
- termination clauses and rights thereafter to the intellectual property
- which nation's laws of contract apply to the agreement
- turnkey projects
- quality control (to ensure production output meets acceptable international standards)
- countertrade
- performance bonds
- compliance with all local industrial regulations
- avoidance of onerous price-fixing agreements
- authorizing work permits for the licensor's personnel
- management participation by the licensor in the licensee operations

Checklist 26.6 (*Continued*)

	Action points

- rights of the licensor to supply exclusively any inputs
- monitoring or restricting any clauses obligating a licensee to take unrelated products from the licensor
- restrictions on sale of product from the licensed venture
- limitations on the uses of patents or know-how in other industrial applications in the licensee's operations
- obligatory combinations of patent and trade mark licences forcing the licensee to use the licensor's trade marks on output
- warranties provided by the licensor concerning the performance of plant and finished product
- restrictions within the terms of the agreement that prevent the licensee seeking other (competing or complementary) technology from other sources.

Checklist 26.7
Financial aspects of licensing

Action points

When seeking to value a licence consider each of the following factors, and how they might affect the value in the licence:

- potential earnings from the project to the licensee
- potential sales volumes/revenues
- degree of exclusivity the licence will provide (e.g. patents)
- brand name strength (goodwill) internationally or in the market
- marketing support for the product
- alternative products or processes
- alternative sources of technology (comparable or substitute)
- savings to licensee in development costs to reach the present stage of technological development
- saving in development lead times for a licensee
- licensee training needed or to be provided
- plant and engineering design inputs
- management systems and procedures
- operational manuals
- research and development and quality control inputs
- technical assistance required
- potential cost savings from taking a licence/franchise
- balance of patent life
- product/technology improvements (i.e. access to ongoing improvements saving on licensee research costs)
- licensor experience/reputation
- security in an investment that has a track record elsewhere.

When attempting to negotiate a price for the licence consider each of the following:

- the value of the licensor's inputs (see above)
- the desirability of the licence to the licensee
- the potential returns to the licensee or franchisee
- the compatibility of licensed operations with the licensee's current business activities
- the present state of market development
- the competitive activity and market research (including ease of market entry by competitors)
- the availability of similar alternative technology
- the regulation of fees and royalties in the licensee's market
- the taxation levels of fees and royalties.

Checklist 26.7 (*Continued*)

	Action points

Which is the most appropriate way for the company to earn its returns from licensing or franchising:

- initial fees?
- ongoing royalties (related to sales volumes or values)?
- management service or technical assistance fees?
- once-only fees in exchange for providing certain inputs?
- profits from the sale of input supplies?
- profit share?

Have you costed all of the following to see if initial fees can be set at a level to provide recovery of these cost factors:

- market visits to evaluate prospective licensees?
- pre-market entry research?
- engineering design work, building plans and specifications?
- site selection and construction planning?
- assistance in obtaining local planning permissions?
- costs of specifying and sourcing equipment?
- plant commissioning?
- initial training of the licensee?
- special research and development costs?
- quality control procedures, specifications, training?
- developing supporting management systems and procedures?
- preparation of operational manuals?
- preparation of launch marketing programmes?
- travel and subsistence costs related to the foregoing?
- any other start-up costs related to your venture?

Are there any other potential income sources from granting a licence:

- dividends or equity stakes in the licensee (or franchisee)?
- capital appreciation of equity stakes in the licensee?
- rights to convert royalties to, or to take, equity stakes (sometimes a useful approach in markets where it is difficult to repatriate royalty earnings, or where royalties are capped?
- additional export opportunities for inputs to the licensee?
- plant and equipment supplies?
- provision of buying services to the licensee (e.g. for materials)?
- acting as an international sales agent or distributor?
- leasing plant and equipment?
- purchases of licensee's output for distribution elsewhere?
- reciprocal licensing arrangement?
- grant-backs of patent, process, business format improvements?
- provision of consultancy services?
- others specific to your venture?

Checklist 26.8
Protecting intellectual property for licensing

	Action points
Is your intellectual property suitably protected through registrations or secrecy agreements:	

- patents?
- trade marks or service marks?
- copyrights?
- designs?
- valuable know-how, including:
  - plant and engineering design?
  - building plans, specifications and construction?
  - industrial site selection expertise?
  - preparing applications for planning permissions?
  - plant commissioning?
  - equipment specification and sourcing?
  - raw material and input specification and sourcing?
  - quality control systems and procedures?
  - regulatory compliance (to meet all local market regulations)?
  - management control systems and procedures?
  - product development activities?
  - technical assistance and trouble-shooting?
  - industrial engineering and work study?
  - preparation of operational manuals?
  - market research?
  - product sales and marketing planning?
  - staff selection, training and development?
  - customer care and servicing?
  - after-sales servicing and product support?

Have you entered an agreement with your prospective licensee/ franchisee that:

- acknowledges and recognizes your ownership of all the intellectual property that forms part of the licence?
- binds the prospective licensee to keep all such information confidential and secret both before a final agreement it entered, during the agreement period, and for a reasonable period thereafter?

Checklist 26.8 *(Continued)*

	Action points

<ul><li>binds the prospective licensee (or actual licensee) not to attempt pre-emptive intellectual property registrations, not to contest your ownership or rights to any of the intellectual property before, during or after the agreement?</li><li>set up a system that identifies all communications and materials that form part of intellectual property and:
  – marks them accordingly?
  – identifies or restricts who has copies of them or access to them?</li></ul>	

Checklist 26.9
Typical clauses in a licensing/franchising agreement

Action points

A typical licensing or franchising agreement will contain coverage of many or all of the following clauses.

- Identification of the contracting parties
- Introductory recitals
- Definitions of terms used in the agreement
- Specific grants, rights and exclusivities included with the licence/franchise, e.g.:
  - to manufacture, distribute, market products
  - to use intellectual property, such as patents, trade marks, copyrights, designs, technical and/or commercial know-how, etc.
- Territorial and other limitations to the licence:
  - territory or market sectors covered by licence
  - any restrictions on exports
- Period of validity of the licence or franchise
- Location of the licensed/franchised business:
  - any restrictions on location of the licensee's/franchisee's premises or operations
- Commitment to the starting dates or other time spans:
  - key dates concerned with the licence and transfer of rights and intellectual property
- Guidelines on extensions or renewals:
  - some licence/franchise agreements address the matter of future renewal or extension and outline key terms, i.e. that the licensee shall not breach any of his obligations in the initial agreement
  - the agreement may state that renewals or extensions be on the same terms, or that a completely new agreement will be negotiated
- Assignability of the licence:
  - limitations on the licensee's rights to sell, mortgage or otherwise deal with the licence/franchise
- Product, process or business format improvements:
  - licensor's obligations to provide improvement updates to licensee/franchisee
    - grant-back rights to licensor of improvements made by licensee

Checklist 26.9 (*Continued*)

- Intellectual property registration and protection:
  - recognition by licensee of licensor's ownership of intellectual property
  - agreement by licensee not to contest licensor's ownership of intellectual property
  - co-operation of parties in effecting user agreements
  - co-operation in defending against infringements
- Sub-licensing or sub-franchising:
  - Licensee's rights to grant sub-licenses or sub-franchises, or restrictions on such rights
- Competition clauses:
  - restrictions on the licensee not to compete with similar products during the licence period
  - restrictions on the licensee not to compete after termination of the agreement
- Performance clauses:
  - minimum sales performance requirements
  - minimum fee or royalty stipulations
  - any maximum sales or production limitations (where permissible)
- Reserved rights of licensor:
  - rights of licensor to supply market or customers where the licensee fails to meet demand
- Payment clauses:
  - initial fees
  - ongoing fees and royalties (any minimums specified)
  - the timing of payments
  - penalties for late payment
  - the manner of payment
  - circumstances under which relief from royalties will be sanctioned (infringements, invalid or disputed intellectual property rights, etc.)
  - audit and control clauses
- Quality control clauses:
  - input quality control
  - output (or service) quality control
- Supply sourcing:
  - licensor's right to supply key inputs
  - licensor's right to approve source/quality of key inputs
- Technical assistance:
  - licensor's commitment to provide initial and ongoing technical assistance
  - structure of any charges to be made by licensor for technical assistance
- Management and operational support:
  - licensor's commitment to supply management and operational support

Checklist 26.9 *(Continued)*

- – (any rights the franchisor may reserve to assume operational management in the event a franchisee cannot manage the business effectively and to a required standard)
  - – any charge structures for providing management and operational support
- Warranties:
  - – details of product or process warranties provided by the licensor
  - – restrictions the licensor imposes on the licensee in respect of warranties the licensee can offer with the outputs of the licence
- Product pricing policies:
  - – any controls (where legal) the licensor wishes to impose on the licensee's product pricing in the market
- Product marketing:
  - – agreement by the parties to co-operate as appropriate in marketing planning
  - – use best endeavours to build the market
  - – any support from the licensor/franchisor with product marketing
- Reporting requirements:
  - – agreement on the regular reporting requirements the licensor/franchisor requires from the licensee/franchisee (financial, sales, marketing, etc.)
  - – data that the licensor/franchisor will feed back to the licensee/franchisee
- Training of licensee/franchisee:
  - – obligations of the licensor/franchisor to provide initial and ongoing training
  - – obligations of the licensee/franchisee to co-operate with licensor's training programmes, and to provide appropriate internal training
- Rights to visit licensee business premises:
  - – licensor's rights to visit licensee at all reasonable times to monitor the business
- Confidentiality clauses:
  - – specific restrictions on the licensee to keep secret the licensee's intellectual property, and control the dissemination of confidential information
  - – where breaches of confidentiality occur, due to licensee negligence, licensor may require an indemnity to cover potential costs or losses
- Compliance with local regulations:
  - – licensee's obligation to comply with all local regulations concerned with running the business, including with all accounting and taxation requirements

Checklist 26.9 *(Continued)*

<table>
<tr><td></td><td>**Action points**</td></tr>
</table>

- Investment:
  - licensee responsibilities for investment in plant, equipment, marketing, etc.
- Insurance:
  - product liability
  - premises, profits (fees and royalties)
- Compensation limits:
  - any agreed limit to exposure for compensation claims upon termination of a licence
- Indemnities:
  - indemnities from the licensee to cover the risk the licensor will be sued or suffer as a consequence of activities of the licensee.
- Variations to the agreement:
  - any subsequent variations to the agreement should be in writing and agreed by both parties
- Disputes and arbitration:
  - a process of handling disputes through arbitration is customarily included in an agreement
- Termination:
  - causes of premature termination
  - periods of notice
  - compensation upon termination
  - the disposal of stock
  - non-disruption of the licensor's/franchisor's markets
- Applicable laws:
  - which nation's laws apply?
  - treatment of unenforceable clauses?
- Non-waiver clause:
  - indicating that where a licensor does not enforce any rights under the agreement for a period of time those rights are not waived (i.e. the right to audit the licensee's sales performance)
- Full agreement clause:
  - all matters considered part of the agreement are contained within it, and no reliance is made on discussion or letters, etc., not included
- No agency rights:
  - the licence agreement does not convey any rights to the licensee to represent himself as agent of the licensor
- Force majeure clause:
  - default on certain obligations might be permitted without penalty where the cause of default was outside the control of the defaulting party

Glossary

Standard export terms and abbreviations

aar against all risks

ad val. (ad valorem) freight or customs duty set at a percentage of value

agent party who represents the principal (exporter) in negotiations with buyers, usually rewarded with a commission

air waybill air freight consignment note

arbitration means of resolving disputes which can be binding on the parties but save costs over legal actions

ATA carnet document covering temporary export of goods (e.g. samples and exhibition goods)

ayor at your own risk

B/E bill of exchange – a written request addressed from the exporter to the buyer ordering the buyer to pay a specified sum to a particular person or party on the set date

B/L or **B of L** bill of lading – contract between shipper and carrier generally giving ownership title or right to take possession. *Clean bill of lading* refers to receipt for goods received by the carrier in apparent good condition

bonded warehouse government-licensed warehouse where goods may be stored without duty being paid until goods are withdrawn and cleared through customs

BOTB British Overseas Trade Board

BTN Brussels tariff nomenclature

CAD cash against documents (terms of payment)

certificate of analysis required by buyers of certain products, such as food ingredients; usually certifies that product meets standards according to accepted test methods, and stating analytical composition

certificate of free sale required by some markets as evidence that the goods are normally sold on the open market and approved by regulatory authorities in the country of origin.

certificate of origin a certificate showing the country of original production of an export product. Frequently used by customs in ascertaining duties under preferential tariff programmes, or in connection with regulating imports from specific nations

certificate of quality a document intended to demonstrate to a buyer that goods meet a recognized and measurable international standard

CFR cost and freight, with the seller owning the goods and paying all freight related charges to the point of ownership transfer, usually a foreign port (insurance and clearing charges are the buyer's responsibility)

CIF cost, insurance and freight to an agreed destination

CL car load

CIP freight, carriage and insurance paid: used instead of CIF for road or multi-modal transport

commercial invoice document showing commercial values of the transaction between the buyer and the seller.

confirming house a company which acts for the buyer by placing an order with the exporter and being responsible for payment of the goods, selling the goods on to the foreign buyer often on a credit arrangement

consular invoice an invoice covering shipment of the goods certified by a consular representative of the destination country, and used normally by customs officials concerned with foreign exchange availability to ascertain the correctness of commercial invoice values

CPT carriage paid, used instead of CFR where road or multi-modal transport is used, with seller paying all transport costs to the specified destination, with the seller retaining the risk until the goods are handed over to the first carrier

customs broker person licensed to conduct business at a customs house on behalf of others

cwt hundredweight: 100 lb in USA, 112 lb in UK

DA documents against acceptance – instructions from an exporter to a bank that documents attached to a draft for collection are to be delivered against acceptance of the draft

DAF delivered at frontier: a term normally used with road or multi-modal transport where seller's responsibility transfers at the border of the destination country

DDP delivered duty paid: a term which can be used irrespective of the transport mode used, with the seller bearing risks and costs getting the goods to the buyer's specified delivery point

DDU delivered duty unpaid: goods delivered to the specified destination but without payment of taxes, duties, etc. relating to import

dead freight freight charge paid by charterer for unused space

deferred rebates rebates applied retrospectively to shippers for consistent use of certain shipping lines

del credere guarantee by an agent or representative to accept the credit risk for parties introduced as customers to the exporter

demurrage a penalty levied for exceeding free time allowed for loading or unloading at a dock or freight terminal; charges may also be levied by a container company for delays in loading, unloading or returning a container

DEQ delivered ex-quay: shipping term used for goods delivered at seller's cost on to the quay

DES delivered ex-ship: seller bearing responsibility for goods until they are ready for unloading from the ship at the destination port

distributor a party who represents the exporter in the foreign market by taking possession and ownership of the goods and redistributing them in the market to their own customers

D/P documents against payment: instructions given by an exporter to a bank that the drawee can collect documents attached to a draft only upon actual payment of the draft

DR dock receipt – normally issued by a shipping line acknowledging that goods were received for shipment; the bill of lading is issued only after goods are loaded

drawback repayment of any part of customs duty or excise duties previously collected on merchandise when those goods are exported

ECGD Export Credit Guarantee Department: a British agency providing government-sponsored insurance for exports and related activities.

E&OE errors and omissions excepted.

exchange rate units of one currency exchangeable for a certain number of units of another currency

EXW ex-works: a term of sale whereby goods are sold at the factory excluding any freight and insurance, and the buyer being responsible for collecting and loading goods onto transport

FAS free alongside ship: price quotation term where goods are delivered alongside the vessel, when ownership transfers, the buyer being responsible for getting goods onto the dockside and the vessel

FCA free carrier: a term more commonly used where road transport is used or multi-modal door-to-door operations are employed, with risk remaining with the seller until goods are handed to the carrier

FOB free on board: Incoterm price quotation term that, internationally, refers to free on board the vessel, with the seller responsible for packing and delivering the goods onto the vessel

force majeure contract clause exempting parties from performance for reasons or events beyond their control

fpa free from particular average: 'particular average' means damage caused by marine perils to the particular vessel insured

freight forwarder person licensed to engage in the business of dispatching clients' goods internationally, normally by ocean vessel, but most now include air and overland operations

FTZ free trade zone

fuel surcharge a surcharge levied on freight to cover (upward) movements in fuel costs

G/A general average: a general loss voluntarily incurred to save all interests involved in a common maritime venture from impending peril; the principle of general average applies in adjustment of all common loss, damage and expenses

GATT General Agreement on Tariffs and Trade: major international agreement between many of the world's nations

IATA International Air Transport Association

Incoterms *International Rules for the Interpretation of Trade Terms*: an International Chamber of Commerce publication (1990 latest edition)

inherent vice inherent defect in goods which can contribute to their deterioration over time or in transit

LC (L/C) letter of credit: document issued by a bank on behalf of a buyer in favour of an exporter, with the bank lending its name and support to honour the exporter's draft

lcl less than carload, or less than container load: term used in reference to freight matters when shipment volume is insufficient to fill a railcar or container

ltl less than truckload: term used when the quantity or volume does not fill a standard truck

marine extension clause clause extending insurance cover during transit delays until goods reach the final destination

marine insurance policy contract between the insurance company and the person having an insurable interest in merchandise

mate's receipt issued by the mate of the vessel acknowledging cargo receipt, particularly in the charter trade; not a negotiable document

metric tonne European measure of 2,204 lb weight, or 1,000 kg

P/L partial loss (an insurance term)

pro forma invoice draft invoice sent to an importer by an exporter prior to order confirmation and shipment to assist in matters relating to obtaining import licences, foreign exchange allocations, or simply to advise the value of the consignment so that letters of credit can be opened

Ro/Ro roll-on/roll-off ferry services

SAD Single Administrative Document: (used with the European Union for cross-border transactions)

SED Shipper's Export Declaration: a US customs document to be completed for all exports to assist the government in compiling export statistics

shipping conference organization of several ship owners operating a route whereby they contract their services to shippers on pre-agreed terms and conditions

SIC Standard Industrial Classification (of goods)

sight draft draft payable on first presentation through a bank

SITPRO Simplification of International Trade Procedures Board

SL&C shipper's load and count

TIR Transport International Routiers: bond arrangement whereby sealed (vehicular) containers are conveyed internationally

transhipment the transfer of goods from one carrier to another

TT telegraphic transfer of funds

UNCITRAL United Nations Committee of International Trade Law

VAT value added tax

WA with average: an insurance term meaning that the shipment is protected against partial damage whenever the damage exceeds a stated percentage

warranty express or implied conditions acting as a guarantee (of quality or performance)

war risk normally used in relation to insurance cover concerning action against a vessel or goods by a hostile government

warehouse receipt receipt for goods deposited at a warehouse; a non-negotiable document if delivery is specified to only one party

weight: gross weight of goods including all packaging

net weight of goods excluding packaging

tare weight of packaging or container

Useful contacts in the United Kingdom ___

The following useful contacts are sources of information and advice concerned with exporting from the United Kingdom or research information.

Arab-British Chamber of Commerce
6 Belgrave Square
London SW1X 8PH
Tel: 0171–235 4363

British Chambers of Commerce
Manning House
22 Carlisle Place
London SW1P 1JA
Tel: 0171–565 2000

British Exporters Association
16 Dartmouth Street
London SW1H 9BL
Tel: 0171–222 5419
(Membership consists of many export agents, confirming houses and export intermediaries)

British Institute of Management
Management House
Cottingham Road
Corby
Northants. NN17 1TT
Tel: 01536 204222

The British International Freight
Association
Redfern House
Browells lane
Feltham
Middlesex TW13 7EP
Tel: 0181–844 2266
Fax: 0181–890 5546

The British Library Business Information
and Research Service
96 Euston Road
London NW1 2DB
Tel: 0171-412 7457
Fax: 0171-412 7453

The British Standards Institute
389 Chiswick High Road
London W4 4AL
Tel: 0181–996 9000
Fax: 0181–240 7400
Technical Help For Exporters
Tel: 0181–996 7111
(Publishes a monthly journal)

Business Link
Central contact to identify local contact:
0345 567765

The Chartered Institute of Marketing
Moor Hall
Cookham
Berks SL4 9QH
Tel: 016285–524922

Chartered Institute of Patent Agents
Staple Inn Buildings
London WC1V 7PZ
Tel: 0171–405 9450

City Business Library
1 Brewers' Hall Gardens
London EC2 5BX
Tel: 0171–638 8215

CJN Management Consultancy
49 Pennard Road
London W12 8DW
Tel/fax: 0181-749 1210
e-mail: *noonan@cjn.co.uk*
Strategy development, management development in international marketing, marketing, sales management.

Commission of the European Communities
8 Storey's Gate
London SW1P 3AT
Tel: 0171–973 1992
Fax: 0171–973 1900

Commonwealth Secretariat
Marlborough House
Pall Mall
London SW1Y 5HX
Tel: 0171–839 3411

Confederation of British Industry
Centre Point
103 New Oxford Street
London WC1A 1DU
Tel: 0171–379 7400
Fax: 0171–240 1578/2651

Corporate Intelligence Research
Publications Ltd.
51 Doughty Street
London WC1N 2LS
Tel: 0171–696 9006
Fax: 0171–696–9004
(Market research on international retail markets)

Croner Publications Ltd
Croner House
London Road
Kingston upon Thames
Surrey KT2 6SR
Tel: 0181–547 3333
Fax: 0181–547 2637
(Croner's Reference Book for Exporters, Export Digest – two very useful guides updated periodically by Croner)

Department of Trade and Industry
Business in Europe Branch
Kingsgate House
66–74 Victoria Street
London SW1E 6SW
Tel: 0171–215 8529
(or main enquiry centre –
Tel: 0171–215 5000)

Department of Trade and Industry
Export Control and Non-Proliferation
Division (*export licensing matters*)
Kingsgate House
66–74 Victoria Street
London SW1E 6SW
Tel: 0171–215 8070/8593/8059
(or main enquiry centre – Tel: 0171–215 5000)

Department of Trade and Industry
Export Market Information Centre
Kingsgate House
66–74 Victoria Street
London SW1E 6SW
Tel: 0171–215 5444/5 (DTI main switchboard 0171–215 5000)
Fax: 0171–215 4231
Website: www.dti.gov.uk/ots/emic

Department of Trade and Industry
Single Market Compliance Unit
Kingsgate House
66–74 Victoria Street
London SW1E 6SW
Tel: 0171–215 4212
(DTI main switchboard 0171–215 5000)
Fax: 0171–215 4489

Department of Trade and Industry
Export Publications
Admail 528
London SW1 8YT
Tel: 0870 1502 500
Fax: 0870 1502 333
Website: www.dti.gov.uk/ots/publications

The Economists Intelligence Unit
40 Duke Street
London W1A 3DW
Tel: 0171–830 1000
(Market research reports)

Euromonitor Plc.
60–61 Britton Street
London EC1M 5NA
Tel: 0171–251 8024
Fax: 0171–608 3149
(Market research reports)

The Export Association
42 Broad Street
Welshpool
Powys SY21 7RR
Wales
Tel: 01938–555000
Fax: 01938–555200

Export Credits Guarantee Department
(ECGD)
2 Exchange Tower
Harbour Exchange Square
London E14 9GS
Tel: 0171–512 7000
Fax: 0171–512 7649

Institute of Export
Export House
64 Clifton Street
London EC2A 4HB
Tel: 0171–247 9812
Fax: 0171–377 5343
Website: www.export.co.uk
*(Export advice, accredited trainers in export
subjects, register of approved consultants)*

The Institute of Linguists
24a Highbury Grove
London N5 2EA
Tel: 0171–359 7445
Fax: 0171–940 3101/3112

The Institute of Management Consultants
32 Hatton Garden
London EC1N 8DL
Tel: 0171–242 2140
Fax: 0171–831 4597
Website: www.imc.co.uk

The Institute of Translating and
Interpreting
377 City Road
London EC1V 1NA
Tel: 0171–713 7600
Fax: 0171–713 7650

The International Chambers of Commerce
(ICC-UK)
British Affiliate
14 Belgrave Square
London SW1X 8PX
Tel: 0171–823 2811

Keynote Publications
Field House
Oldfield Road
Hampton
Middlesex
TW12 2HQ
Tel: 0181–481 8750
Fax: 0181–783 0049
(Market research and export reports)

London Business School Information Service
Sussex Place
Regent's Park
London NW1 4SA
Tel: 0171–723 3404/262 5050 *(information)*
Fax: 0171–706 1897
e-mail: infoserve@lbs.ac.uk

London Chamber of Commerce and
Industry
33 Queen Street
London EC4R 1BX
Tel: 0171–248 4444
(Useful library)

Mintel International Market Research
18 Long Lane
London EC1A 9HE
Tel: 0171–606 6000 (sales)
Tel: 0171–606 4533

A. C. Nielsen
Nielsen House
Headington
Oxford OX3 9RX
Tel: 01865–742742
Fax: 01865–742222
*(Market research, covering UK and many
international markets)*

Overseas Trade Services
To find closest office call:
England – Business Link
Tel: 0345–567765
(website: *www.businesslink.co.uk*)
Scotland – Scottish Trade International
Tel: 0141–228 2812/2808
Fax: 0141–221 3712
(website: *www.sti.org.uk*)
Wales – Welsh Office Overseas Trade
Services
Tel: 01222–825097
Fax: 01222–823964
(website: *www.wales.gov.uk*)
Northern Ireland – Industrial
Development Board for Northern Ireland
Tel: 01232–233233
Fax: 01232–54500
(website: *www.idbni.co.uk*)

Oxford Institute of Retail Management
Templeton College
Kennington
Oxford OX1 5NY
01865–735422

The Patent Office
45 Southampton Buildings
London WC2A 1AY
General enquiries:
Tel: 0645–500505
Copyright enquiries:
Tel: 0171–438 4766
Fax: 0171–438 4780

Patent Office (Head Office)
Concept House
Cardiff Road
Newport
Gwent NP9 1RH
Tel: 01633–814000
Fax: 01633–813600

Royal Mail International Headquarters
49 Featherstone Street
London EC1Y 8RT
Tel: 0171–320 4000
*(Useful to make contact for international
mailshots and mail order advice)*

SITPRO (The Simpler Trade Procedures
Board)
Bridge Place
88 Eccleston Square
London SW1 9SS
Tel: 0171–215 0800 or 0171–215 0825
Fax: 0171–215 0824

Technical Help For Exporters (The British
Standards Institute)
389 Chiswick High Road
London W4 4AL
Tel: 0181–996 7111
Or telephone BSI on 0181–996 9000

Index _____